MOON HANDBOOKS®

TAHITI

© M.E. DEVOS

racing canoes, Arue

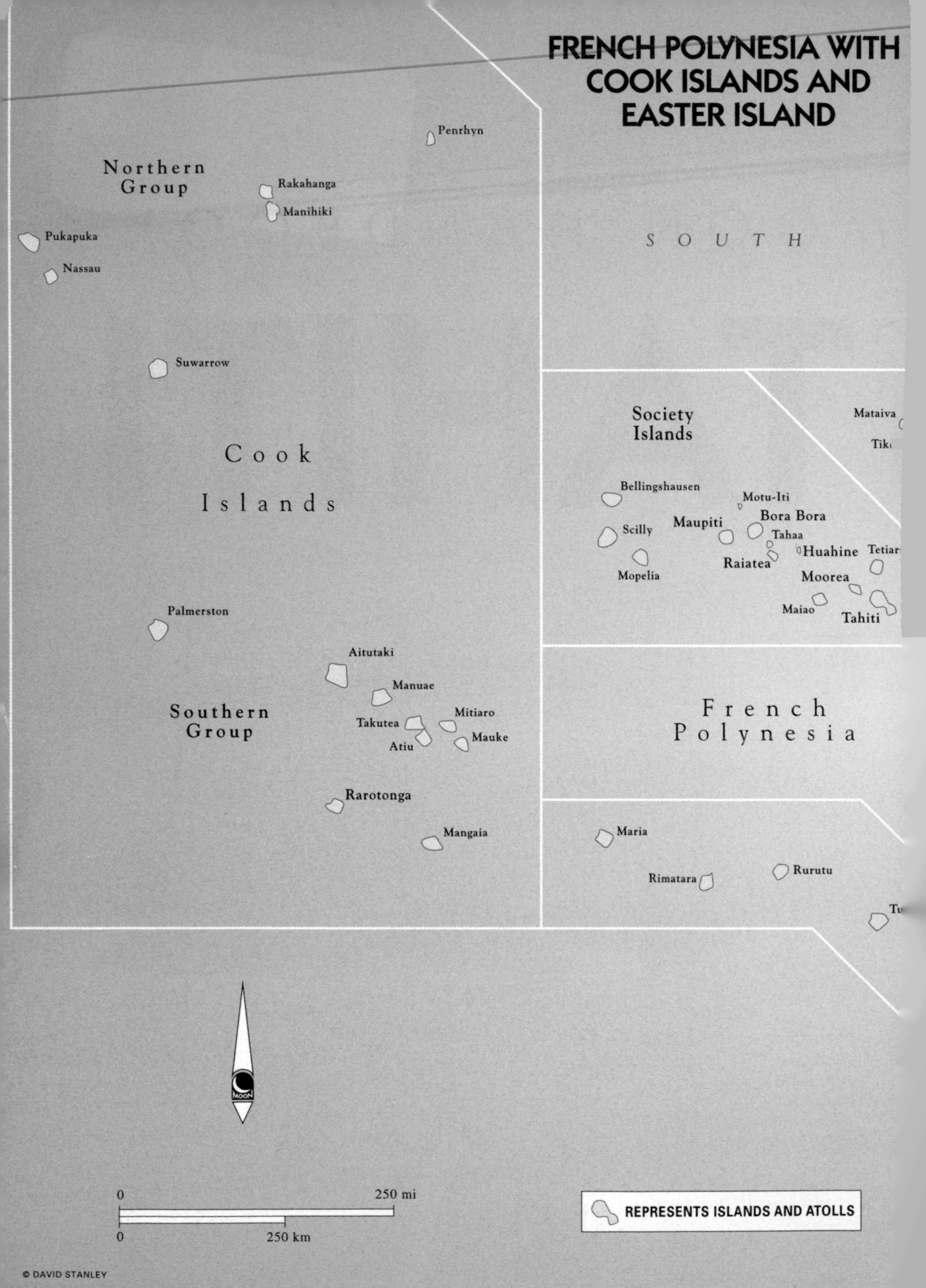

FRENCH POLYNESIA WITH COOK ISLANDS AND EASTER ISLAND

Penrhyn

Northern Group

Rakahanga

Manihiki

Pukapuka

Nassau

S O U T H

Suwarrow

C o o k

I s l a n d s

Society Islands

Mataiva

Tiko

Bellingshausen

Motu-Iti

Bora Bora

Scilly

Maupiti

Tahaa

Mopelia

Raiatea

Huahine Tetiar

Moorea

Palmerston

Maiao

Tahiti

Aitutaki

Manuae

F r e n c h

Southern Group

Takutea

Mitiaro

P o l y n e s i a

Atiu

Mauke

Rarotonga

Mangaia

Maria

Rimatara

Rurutu

Tu

MOON

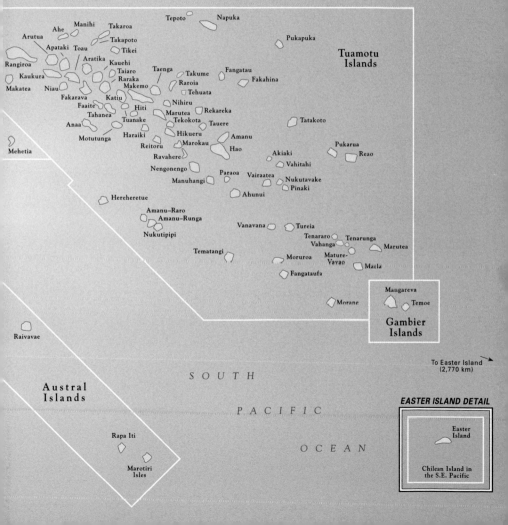

Coral Is.

Hatutu

Eiao

Motu Iti
Nuku Hiva   Ua Huka
Ua Pou   Fatu Huku
                      Hiva Oa
         Tahuata   Motane
Marquesas   Fatu Hiva
Islands

P A C I F I C

O C E A N

Tepoto   Napuka

Ahe   Manihi   Takaroa
Arutua   Pukapuka
   Apataki Toau   Takapoto
Rangiroa   Aratika Tikei   **Tuamotu**
                     Kauehi   **Islands**
Kaukura   Taiaro
              Niau   Raraka   Taenga   Fangatau
Makatea   Takume   Fakahina
         Fakarava   Katiu   Raroia
      Faaite   Tehuata
         Tahanea Hiti   Nihiru
      Anaa   Tuanake Marutea Rekareka
              Tekokota   Tatakoto
Motutunga   Haraiki   Tauere
         Reitoru   Hikueru   Amanu
Mehetia   Ravahere Marokau Hao   Pukarua
                                         Reao
              Nengonengo   Akiaki
                         Paraoa   Vahitahi
              Manuhangi   Vairaatea Nukutavake
                    Ahunui   Pinaki

         Hereheretue

         Amanu–Raro
         Amanu–Runga
      Nukutipipi   Vanavana   Tureia
                              Tenararo   Tenarunga
         Tematangi   Vahanga   Marutea
                         Moruroa   Mature-
                                   Vavao   Matia
                    Fangataufa
                                         Mangareva
                         Morane   Temoe
Raivavae   **Gambier**
                                  Islands

                    S O U T H
                                   To Easter Island →
                                   (2,770 km)

Austral
Islands   P A C I F I C

         Rapa Iti   O C E A N

    Marotiri
    Isles

EASTER ISLAND DETAIL

                         Easter
                         Island

                    Chilean Island in
                    the S.E. Pacific

Moai at Ahu Tongariki

MOON HANDBOOKS®

TAHITI

INCLUDING THE COOK ISLANDS
FIFTH EDITION

DAVID STANLEY

AVALON
TRAVEL

MAPS

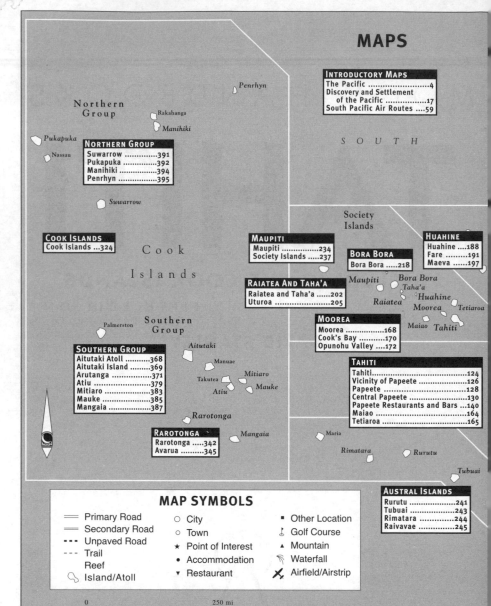

Penrhyn

Northern
Group

Rakahanga

Manihiki

Pukapuka

Nassau

S O U T H

Suwarrow

Society
Islands

C o o k

I s l a n d s

Maupiti   Bora Bora
              Taha'a
         Raiatea   Huahine
              Moorea   Tetiaroa

Palmerston

Southern
Group

Aitutaki

Maiao   Tahiti

Manuae

Mitiaro

Takutea   Mauke
     Atiu

Rarotonga

Mangaia   Maria

Rimatara   Rurutu

Tubuai

MAP SYMBOLS

=== Primary Road	○ City	▪ Other Location
=== Secondary Road	○ Town	⌨ Golf Course
--- Unpaved Road	★ Point of Interest	▲ Mountain
--- Trail	● Accommodation	☂ Waterfall
Reef	▼ Restaurant	✗ Airfield/Airstrip
⌓ Island/Atoll		

0   250 mi

0   250 km

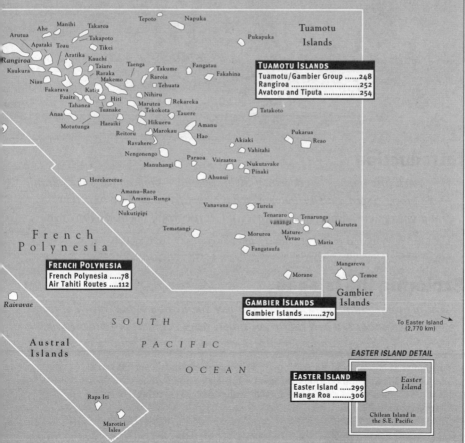

Coral Is.

Hatutu

Eiao

Motu Iti

Nuku Hiva

Ua Huka

Ua Pou

Fatu Huku

Tahuata

Hiva Oa

Motane

Marquesas
Islands

Fatu Hiva

P A C I F I C

O C E A N

Tepoto   Napuka

Manihi   Takaroa

Ahe

Arutua

Apataki   Toau   Takapoto

Rangiroa   Aratika   Tikei

Kaukura   Kauchi

Niau   Taiaro

Raraka

Fakarava   Makemo

Faaite   Katiu

Tahanea   Hiti

Anaa   Tuanake

Motutunga   Haraiki

Reitoru

Ravahere

Nengonengo

Manuhangi

Hereheretue

Amanu–Raro
Amanu–Runga

Nukutipipi

Taenga   Takume   Fangatau

Raroia   Fakahina

Tehuata

Nihiru

Marutea   Rekareka

Tekokota   Tauere

Hikueru   Amanu

Marokau   Hao

Akiaki

Vahitahi

Paraoa   Vairaatea   Nukutavake

Pinaki

Ahunui

Vanavana   Tureia

Tenararo   Tenarunga
vananga   Marutea

Tematangi   Mature-
Vavao

Moruroa   Maria

Fangataufa

Tatakoto

Pukarua   Reao

Pukapuka

Tuamotu
Islands

F r e n c h
P o l y n e s i a

Raivavae

Austral
Islands

S O U T H

P A C I F I C

O C E A N

Mangareva

Morane   Temoe

Gambier
Islands

Rapa Iti

Marotiri
Isles

To Easter Island
(2,770 km)

EASTER ISLAND DETAIL

Easter
Island

Chilean Island in
the S.E. Pacific

© DAVID STANLEY

Contents

© M.G.L. DOMENY DE RIENZI

French Polynesia/Te Ao Maohi

Tahiti 123

Lush with aquamarine lagoons and verdant valleys, rugged reefs and coconut groves, Tahiti is a study in contrasts. Cosmopolitan Papeete, the gateway to French Polynesia, entices with modern luxuries and a bustling downtown. Meanwhile, the gentle south coast offers tranquility and the ancient Marae Arahurahu temple, sheltered by high cliffs.

Moorea 166

This heart-shaped island may be Polynesia's most enticing retreat. Thatched bungalows pepper the coast, the scents from nearby coconut and pineapple plantations fill the air . . . and relaxation is inevitable.

Northeast Moorea; Maharepa; Cook's Bay; Paopao; Opunohu Bay; Opunohu Valley; Le Belvédère; Papetoai; Tiahura; Southern Moorea

Huahine 187

Huahine's fertile coast is more than a surfing haven. Schools of dolphins may greet your approaching vessel, seaside temples wait to be explored, and pétanque games begin on the waterfront at sunset. You can enjoy all of these activities and more—but with fewer crowds than on Bora Bora.

Raiatea and Taha'a 201

On the sacred isle of Raiatea, transportation is purposely scarce, so life moves at a slower pace. Enjoy its meandering paths, green meadows, and steel-blue waters. Close by, Taha'a offers organized picnics on flat, sandy reefs and tours of vanilla plantations.

Bora Bora 217

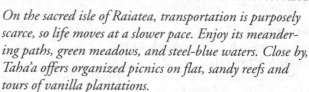

On this jewel of the South Pacific, spend your days exploring some of the most perfect beaches in the world and your nights dancing under the stars at Polynesia's trendiest resorts.

Gambier Islands 269

Enjoy the cooler climate of the Gambiers, where tall aeho
grasses blanket the hilltops and local seabirds, called
karako, *crow at dawn. A visit to the Cathedral of St.*
Michael, built atop a Polynesian temple, offers insight
into the legacy of French colonialism.

Mangareva; Aukena; Akamaru; Makaroa; Taravai; Agakautai

Marquesas Islands 273

Up until the 19th century, Marquesan artists created the
most refined and powerful art of the Pacific. You can see
examples of their intricate stone and wood carvings in
museums—or you can search for them among the water-
falls and dense, verdant foliage of these unspoiled isles.

Easter Island/Rapa Nui

The mysteries of the largest collection of prehistoric monuments in the Pacific intrigue both curious travelers and serious archaeologists, all considering the same unanswerable question: How were a thousand giant statues erected so far from their quarries?

Cook Islands

On the youngest and most populated of the Cooks, twisting valleys lead to steep ridges and towering mountains crowned in clouds. In the midst of primitive natural beauty, Rarotonga offers resort hotels, fine restaurants . . . all of the indulgences of modern life.

Whether it's a midnight party on Aitutaki or a day trip exploring remote caves, these islands guarantee an unforgettable time. Race along red-brown roads on a motor scooter, chat with mynah birds . . . or just laze on white-sand beaches—it's up to you.

Northern Group 390

These low-lying coral rings are the very image of the romantic South Seas, where friendliness seems contagious. Here you can snorkel among tropical fish or dive for mother-of-pearl oysters. Back on land, you might catch a glimpse of the endangered coconut crab, if you're lucky.

Suwarrow; Nassau; Pukapuka; Manihiki; Rakahanga; Penrhyn

Resources 397

ABOUT THE AUTHOR
David Stanley

David Stanley has spent much of the past three decades on the road. He has crossed six continents overland and visited 177 of the planet's 245 countries and territories. His travel guidebooks to the South Pacific, Micronesia, Alaska, Eastern Europe, and Cuba opened those areas to budget travelers for the first time.

For his first trip across the Pacific in 1978, Stanley bought the longest ticket ever issued in Canada by Pan American Airways. Since then he has returned many times, visiting and revisiting the islands. His career as a travel writer began with the letters he wrote to Bill Dalton and Tony Wheeler, the pioneers of budget travel to Asia in the 1970s. That feedback soon led to guides of his own, published by Avalon Travel Publishing and Lonely Planet. With over a million copies sold, he's still on the road writing guidebooks.

Though Stanley has traveled widely and become a specialist on many parts of the world, he always keeps returning to his favorite area, the South Pacific. One of the biggest treats for a guidebook writer is meeting people who are using a handbook. David researches his books incognito and the "mystery shopper" approach means he can't always admit who he is, but it's still fun hearing what unsuspecting readers think of the book. The author of *Moon Handbooks Fiji, Moon Handbooks South Pacific,* and *Moon Handbooks Tonga-Samoa,* Stanley enjoys receiving mail from those who have used his guides. His website www.southpacific.org provides contact details.

Foreword

By Rob Kay, Honolulu

No destination on earth conjures the image of paradise more vividly than Tahiti. Since the earliest days of European exploration Tahiti has been synonymous with the modern world's romantic vision of the South Seas. It's said that upon his arrival in Tahiti in 1768, the French voyager Louis Antoine de Bougainville thought he was transported into the Garden of Eden.

Through the centuries, adventurers, artists, writers and filmmakers reinforced the myth of paradise. In the late 19th century Paul Gauguin, who lived in his own self-imposed exile from Western society, forever immortalized the languid grace of Tahiti's inhabitants in his paintings. In the modern era the romantic notion of French Polynesia was further fueled by writers such as Charles Nordoff and James Hall, whose novel *Mutiny on the Bounty* rapidly became a cultural icon. Hollywood contributed to the cause with three versions of the Bounty story, which undoubtedly encouraged tourism to Tahiti.

While it's true that writers from Pierre Loti to James Michener have written rhapsodically of Tahiti's swaying palms and emerald shores, there is much more to French Polynesia than meets the eye. This is where *Moon Handbooks Tahiti* brings us down to earth by providing a richly comprehensive and entirely practical guide to Tahiti and its sister islands.

It's not that David Stanley is an iconoclast without a romantic streak. I can assure you that no one would ever spend the kind of time it takes to write about the realities of the world's most famous islands without being at least a closet romantic. In fact, I would venture to guess that no one enjoys the pleasures of travel in the South Pacific more than David, but fortunately for the reader, he is unwilling to paint only the sort of meaninglessly rosy pictures depicted in travel brochures. Rather, he tells it as it is, and in doing so, helps readers get the most out of their sojourn.

As a writer who has covered French Polynesia for more than 20 years, Stanley's knowledge of this period is extensive and even intimate. For example, David sought input for a previous edition from the legendary Bengt Danielsson, one of the foremost authorities on French Polynesia and the French nuclear testing program. Knowledge gleaned from Danielsson and other seminal writers has found its way into *Moon Handbooks Tahiti's* extensive section on modern history.

In addition to his unique historical perspective, David's understanding of French Polynesia's culture is profound. Not only does he document elements of language, custom, and society, but he provides practical advice and tips on visiting out-of-the-way places to see. If you want to get to a remote tiki on Hiva Oa or find the WWII battery tucked away on Bora Bora, David will take you there.

Then there's the prosaic matter of where to stay and where to eat, primary concerns for any visitor. Indeed a travel guide is only as good as the data on accommodations and restaurants that it holds. Here David provides a great service to the reader. Rather than merely listing a litany of hotels, guesthouses, and restaurants on every island, he often offers opinionated commentary and selective recommendations, which are immensely helpful. Likewise there are a plethora of well-drawn maps and minutiae about how to get around on and in copra boats, ferries, buses, planes, and rental cars.

The trick to a good travel guide is to make a place accessible to any traveler, from the backpacker to the rich and famous. If this is the benchmark to strive for, David Stanley has done his homework. There's an incredible array of information in this guide and I believe it will lead you to the Tahiti of your dreams.

*As this appalling ocean surrounds the verdant land,
so in the soul of man there lies one insular Tahiti,
full of peace and joy, but encompassed by all the hor-
rors of the half-known life.*

*God help thee! Push not off from that isle, thou
canst never return.*

Herman Melville

Introduction:
French Polynesia, Easter Island, Cook Islands

King Pomare II

Introduction

The Polynesian triangle between Hawaii, New Zealand, and Easter Island stretches across 8,000 km of the central Pacific Ocean—a fifth of the earth's surface. Since the late 18th century, when Captain Cook first revealed Polynesia to European eyes, artists and writers have sung the praises of the graceful golden-skinned peoples of the "many islands."

This vast region is divided into two cultural areas, Western Polynesia (Tonga, Niue, and Samoa) and Eastern Polynesia (French Polynesia, Easter Island, Cook Islands, Hawaii, and New Zealand). While the three Eastern Polynesian territories covered in this book display some ho-

mogeneity, there are also striking contrasts resulting from a history of French, Chilean, and New Zealand colonial rule.

Polynesia consists of boundless ocean and little land. Together French Polynesia, Easter Island, and the Cook Islands control 7,215,000 square kilometers of the South Pacific Ocean, an area only slightly smaller than the 48 contiguous states of the continental United States. From Rarotonga to Easter Island is about as far as from Denver to Boston. Yet in land area, the three together total just a bit more than Rhode Island. Fewer than a quarter of a million people are fortunate enough to live on these sunny tropical isles.

© M.G.L. DOMENY DE RIENZI

The striking scenic beauty of French Polynesia combines well with the archaeological mysteries of Easter Island and the easygoing island life in the Cook Islands. These three territories are closely linked by air with good connections to both Americas, Europe, and Australasia. It's a fascinating area to explore, abounding in man-made attractions, exotic legends, and stunning scenes. You'll find that travel is easy with good facilities all along the way. Through this book we've tried to show you the best of the region without ignoring the worst. Paradise it may not be, but it's still a remarkable part of our planet.

The Land

Darwin's Theory of Atoll Formation

The famous formulator of the theory of natural selection surmised that atolls form as high volcanic islands subside. The original island's fringing reef grows up into a barrier reef as the volcanic part sinks. When the last volcanic material finally disappears below sea level, the coral rim of the reef/atoll remains to indicate how big the island once was.

Of course, all of this takes place over millions of years, but deep below every atoll is the old volcanic core. Darwin's theory is well illustrated at Bora Bora, where a high volcanic island remains inside the rim of Bora Bora's barrier reef; this island's volcanic core is sinking imperceptibly at the rate of one centimeter a century. Return to Bora Bora in 25 million years and all you'll find will be a coral atoll like Rangiroa or Palmerston.

Hot Spots

High or low, most of the islands have a volcanic origin best explained by the "Conveyor Belt Theory." A crack opens in the earth's crust and volcanic magma escapes upward. A submarine volcano builds up slowly until the lava finally breaks the surface, becoming a volcanic island. The Pacific Plate moves northwest approximately 11 centimeters a year; thus, over geologic eons the volcano disconnects from the hot spot or crack from which it emerged. As the old volcanoes detach from the crack, new ones develop over the hot spot, and the older islands are carried away from the cleft in the earth's crust from which they were born.

The island then begins to sink as it's carried into deeper water and erosion also cuts into the now-extinct volcano. In the warm, clear waters a living coral reef begins to grow along the shore. As the island subsides, the reef continues to grow upward. In this way a lagoon forms between the reef and shoreline of the slowly sinking island. This barrier reef marks the old margin of the original island.

As the plate moves northwest in an opposite direction from the sliding Pacific Plate, the process is repeated, time and again, until whole chains of islands ride the blue Pacific. Weathering is most advanced on the composite islands and atolls at the northwest ends of the Society, Austral, Tuamotu, Marquesas, and Cooks chains. Maupiti and Bora Bora, with their exposed volcanic cores, are the oldest of the larger Society Islands. The Tuamotus have eroded almost to sea level; the Gambier Islands originated out of the same hot spot and their volcanic peaks remain inside a giant atoll reef. The same progression of youth, maturity, and old age can be followed in Rarotonga, Aitutaki, and Manihiki. In every case, the islands at the southeast end of the chains are the youngest.

By drilling into the Tuamotu atolls, scientists have proven their point conclusively: the coral formations are about 350 meters thick at the southeast end of the chain, 600 meters thick at Hao near the center, and 1,000 meters thick at Rangiroa near the northwest end of the Tuamotu Group. Clearly, Rangiroa, where the volcanic rock is now a kilometer below the surface, is many millions of years older than the Gambiers, where a volcanic peak still stands 482 meters above sea level. Geologists estimate that Tahiti is two to three million years old, Bora Bora seven million years old, and the Tuamotus 10 to 40 million years old.

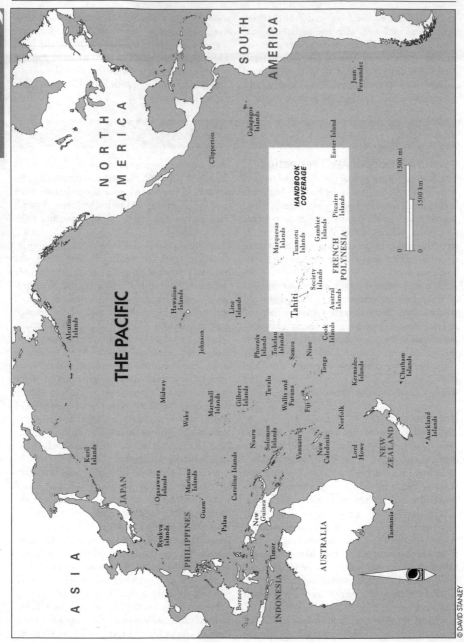

© DAVID STANLEY

Equally fascinating is the way ancient atolls have been uplifted by adjacent volcanoes. The outer crust of earth is elastic, and when this envelope is stretched taut, the tremendous weight of a volcano is spread over a great area, deforming the seabed. In the Cook Islands, for example, Atiu, Mauke, Mitiaro, and Mangaia were uplifted by the weight of Rarotonga.

Island-building continues at an active undersea volcano called MacDonald, 50 meters below sea level at the southeast end of the Australs. The crack spews forth about a cubic mile of lava every century and someday MacDonald too will poke its smoky head above the waves. The theory of plate tectonics, or the sliding crust of the earth, seems proven in the Pacific.

Life of an Atoll

A circular or horseshoe-shaped coral reef bearing a necklace of sandy, slender islets (*motu*) of debris thrown up by storms, surf, and wind is known as an atoll. Atolls can be up to 100 km across, but the width of dry land is usually only 200–400 meters from inner to outer beach. The central lagoon can measure anywhere from one km to 50 km in diameter; huge Rangiroa Atoll is 77 km long. Entirely landlocked lagoons are rare; passages through the barrier reef are usually found on the leeward side. Most atolls are no higher than four to six meters.

A raised or elevated atoll is one that has been pushed up by some trauma of nature to become a platform of coral rock rising to 70 meters above sea level. Raised atolls are often known for their huge sea caves and steep oceanside cliffs. The only raised atoll in French Polynesia is crescent-shaped Makatea in the northwestern corner of the Tuamotu group. It is 100 meters high, seven km long, and 4.5 km wide. In the Cook Islands, Atiu, Mitiaro, Mauke, and Mangaia are raised atolls.

Where the volcanic island remains there's often a deep passage between the barrier reef and shore; the reef forms a natural breakwater, which shelters good anchorages. Australia's Great Barrier Reef is 1,600 km long and 25 to 44 km offshore. Soil derived from coral is extremely poor in nutrients, while volcanic soil is known for its fertility. Dark-colored beaches are formed from volcanic material; the white beaches of travel brochures are entirely calcareous. The black beaches are cooler and easier on the eyes, and the plantlife grows closer and provides patches of shade; the white beaches are generally safer for swimming, as visibility is better.

CORAL REEFS

To understand how a basalt volcano becomes a limestone atoll, it's necessary to know a little about the growth of coral. Coral reefs are the world's oldest ecological system, covering about 200,000 square km worldwide between 35 degrees north and 32 degrees south latitude. A reef is created by the accumulation of millions of calcareous skeletons left by myriad generations of tiny coral polyps, some no bigger than a pinhead. Though the skeleton is usually white, the living polyps are of many different colors. The individual polyps on the surface often live a long time, continuously secreting layers to the skeletal mass beneath the tiny layer of flesh.

Coral polyps thrive in clear salty water where the temperature never drops below 18°C. They must have a base not more than 50 meters below the water's surface on which to form. The coral colony grows slowly upward on the consolidated skeletons of its ancestors until it reaches the low-tide mark, after which development extends outward on the edges of the reef. Sunlight is critical for coral growth. Colonies grow quickly on the windward sides of reefs because of clearer water and a greater abundance of food. A strong, healthy reef can grow four to five centimeters a year. Fresh or cloudy water inhibits coral growth, which is why villages and ports all across the Pacific are located at the reef-free mouths of rivers. Hurricanes can kill coral by covering the reef with sand, preventing light and nutrients from getting through. Erosion caused by agriculture or urban development can have the same effect.

Polyps extract calcium carbonate from the water and deposit it in their skeletons. All limy reef-building corals also contain microscopic algae within their cells. The algae, like all green plants, obtain energy from the sun and contribute this energy to the growth of the reef's

INTRODUCTION

CORALS OF THE PACIFIC

acropora

staghorn fire coral
(Millepora accicornis)

table coral

mushroom coral
(Fungia fungites)

elkhorn fire coral
(Millepora platyphylla)

brain coral
(Meandrina)

honeycomb coral (Favia matthaii)

DIANA LASICH HARPER

skeleton. As a result, corals behave (and look) more like plants than animals, competing for sunlight just as terrestrial plants do. Many polyps are also carnivorous; with minute stinging tentacles they supplement their energy by capturing tiny planktonic animals and organic particles at night. A small piece of coral is a colony composed of large numbers of polyps.

Coral Types

Corals belong to a broad group of stinging creatures, which includes polyps, soft corals, stony corals, sea anemones, sea fans, and jellyfish. Only those types with hard skeletons and a single hollow cavity within the body are considered true corals. Stony corals such as brain, table, staghorn, and mushroom corals have external skeletons and are important reef builders. Soft corals, black corals, and sea fans have internal skeletons. The fire corals are recognized by their smooth, velvety surface and yellowish brown color. The stinging toxins of this last group can easily penetrate human skin and cause swelling and painful burning that can last up to an hour. The many varieties of soft, colorful anemones gently waving in the current might seem inviting to touch, but beware: many are also poisonous.

The corals, like most other forms of life in the Pacific, colonized the ocean from the fertile seas of Southeast Asia. Thus the number of species declines as you move east. More than 600 species of coral make their home in the Pacific, compared to only 48 in the Caribbean. The diversity of coral colors and forms is endlessly amazing. This is our most unspoiled environment, a world of almost indescribable beauty.

Exploring a Reef

Until you've explored a good coral reef, you haven't experienced one of the greatest joys of nature. While one cannot walk through pristine forests because of a lack of paths, it's quite possible to swim over untouched reefs. Coral reefs are the most densely populated living space on earth—the rainforests of the sea! It's wise to bring along a high-quality mask that you've checked thoroughly beforehand as there's nothing more disheartening than a leaky, ill-fitting mask. Oth-

erwise dive shops throughout the region rent or sell snorkeling gear, so do get into the clear, warm water around you.

Conservation

Coral reefs are one of the most fragile and complex ecosystems on earth, providing food and shelter for countless species of fish, crustaceans (shrimps, crabs, and lobsters), mollusks (shells), and other animals. The coral reefs of the South Pacific protect shorelines during storms, supply sand to maintain the islands, furnish food for the local population, form a living laboratory for science, and serve as major tourist attractions. Reefs worldwide host more than two million species of life. Without coral, the South Pacific would be immeasurably poorer.

Hard corals grow only about 10 to 25 millimeters a year and it can take 7,000–10,000 years for a coral reef to form. Though corals look solid they're easily broken; by standing on them, breaking off pieces, or carelessly dropping anchor you can destroy in a few minutes what took so long to form. Once a piece of coral breaks off it dies, and it may be years before the coral reestablishes itself and even longer before the broken piece is replaced. The "wound" may become infected by algae, which can multiply and kill the entire coral colony. When this happens over a wide area, the diversity of marinelife declines dramatically.

Swim beside or well above the coral. Avoid bumping the coral with your fins, gauges, or other equipment and don't dive during rough sea conditions. Proper buoyancy control is preferable to excessive weight belts. Snorkelers should check into taking along a float-coat, which will allow equipment adjustments without standing on coral.

Do not remove seashells, coral, plantlife, or marine animals from the sea under any circumstances. Doing so upsets the delicate balance of nature, and coral is much more beautiful underwater anyway! This is a particular problem along shorelines frequented by large numbers of tourists, who can completely strip a reef in very little time. If you'd like a souvenir, content yourself with what you find on the beach

CLIMATE CHANGE

The gravest danger facing the atolls of Oceania is the greenhouse effect, a gradual warming of the earth's environment due to fossil fuel combustion and the widespread clearing of forests. By the year 2030 the concentration of carbon dioxide in the atmosphere will have doubled from preindustrial levels, and as infrared radiation from the sun is absorbed by the gas, the trapped heat melts mountain glaciers and the polar ice caps. In addition, seawater expands as it warms up, so water levels could rise almost a meter by the year 2100, destroying shorelines created 5,000 years ago.

A 1982 study demonstrated that sea levels had already risen 12 centimeters in the previous century, and in 1995, 2,500 scientists from 70 countries involved in the Intergovernmental Panel on Climate Change commissioned by the United Nations completed a two-year study with the warning that over the next century air temperatures may rise as much as 5°C and sea levels could go up 95 centimeters by 2100. Not only will this reduce the growing area for food crops, but rising sea levels will mean salt water intrusion into groundwater supplies— a troubling prospect if accompanied by the increased frequency droughts that have been predicted. Coastal erosion will force governments to spend vast sums on road repairs and coastline stabilization.

Increasing temperatures may already be contributing to the dramatic jump in the number of hurricanes in the South Pacific. In 1997 and 1998 the El Niño phenomenon brought with it a round of devastating hurricanes, many hitting the Cook Islands and French Polynesia, which are usually missed by such storms.

Coral bleaching occurs when an organism's symbiotic algae are expelled in response to environmental stresses, such as when water temperatures rise as little as 1°C above the local maximum for a week or longer. Bleaching is also caused by increased radiation due to ozone degradation, and widespread instances of bleaching and reefs being killed by rising sea temperatures have been confirmed in French Polynesia and the Cook Islands. The earth's surface has warmed 1°C over the past century and by 2080 water temperatures may have increased 5°C, effectively bleaching and killing all of the region's reefs. Reef destruction will reduce coastal fish stocks and affect tourism.

As storm waves wash across the low-lying atolls, eating away the precious land, the entire populations of archipelagos such as the Tuamotus and Northern Cooks may be forced to gradually evacuate long before they're actually flooded. The construction of seawalls to keep out the rising seas would be prohibitively expensive and may even do more harm than good by interfering with natural water flows and sand movement.

Unfortunately, those most responsible for the problem, the industrialized countries led by the United States (and including Australia), have strongly resisted taking any action to significantly cut greenhouse gas emissions, and new industrial polluters such as India and China are making matters much worse. And as if that weren't bad enough, the hydrofluorocarbons (HFCs) being developed by corporate giants such as Du Pont to replace the ozone-destructive chlorofluorocarbons (CFCs) used in cooling systems are far more potent greenhouse gases than carbon dioxide. This is only one of many similar consumption-related problems, and it seems as if one section of humanity is hurtling down a suicidal slope, unable to resist the momentum, as the rest of our race watches the catastrophe approach in helpless horror. It will cost a lot to rewrite our collective ticket but there may not be any choice.

(although even a seemingly empty shell may be inhabited by a hermit crab). Also think twice about buying jewelry or souvenirs made from coral or seashells. Genuine traditional handicrafts that incorporate shells are one thing, but by buying unmounted seashells or mass-produced coral curios you are contributing to the destruction of the marine environment. The triton shell, for example, keeps in check the reef-destroying crown-of-thorns starfish.

The anchors and anchor chains of private yachts can do serious damage to coral reefs. Pronged anchors are more environmentally friendly than larger, heavier anchors, and plastic tubing over the end of the anchor chain helps minimize damage. If at all possible, anchor in sand. A longer anchor chain makes this easier, and a good windlass is essential for larger boats. A recording depth sounder will help you find sandy areas when none are available in shallow water. If you don't have a depth sounder and can't see the bottom, lower the anchor until it just touches the bottom and feel the anchor line as the boat drifts. If it "grumbles" lift it up, drift a little, and try again. Later, if you notice your chain grumbling, motor over the anchor, lift it out of the coral and move. Not only do sand and mud hold better, but your anchor will be less likely to become fouled. Try to arrive before 1500 to be able to see clearly where you're anchoring—Polaroid sunglasses make it easier to distinguish corals. If you scuba dive with an operator who anchors incorrectly, let your concerns be known.

There's an urgent need for stricter government regulation of the marine environment, and in some places coral reefs are already protected. Appeals such as the one above have only limited impact—legislators must write stricter laws and impose fines. If you witness dumping or any other marine-related activity you think might be illegal, don't become directly involved but take a few notes and calmly report the incident to the local authorities or police at the first opportunity. You'll learn something about their approach to these matters and make them aware of your concerns.

Resort developers can minimize damage to their valuable reefs by providing public mooring buoys so yachts don't have to drop anchor and pontoons so snorkelers aren't tempted to stand on coral. Licensing authorities can make such amenities mandatory whenever appropriate, and in extreme cases, endangered coral gardens should be declared off-limits to private boats. As consumerism spreads, once-remote areas become subject to the problems of pollution and overexploitation: the garbage is visibly piling up on many shores. As a visitor, don't hesitate to practice your conservationist attitudes, and leave a clean wake.

CLIMATE

The Pacific Ocean has a greater impact on the world's climate than any other geographical feature on earth. By taking heat away from the equator and toward the poles, it stretches the bounds of the area in which life can exist. Broad circular ocean currents flow from east to west across the tropical Pacific, clockwise in the North Pacific, counterclockwise in the South Pacific. North and south of the "horse latitudes" just outside the tropics the currents cool and swing east. The prevailing winds move the same way: the southeast trade winds south of the equator, the northeast trade winds north of the equator, and the low-pressure "doldrums" in between. Westerlies blow east above the cool currents north and south of the tropics. This natural air-conditioning system brings warm water to Australia and Japan, cooler water to Peru and California.

The climate of the high islands is closely related to these winds. As air is heated near the equator it rises and flows at high altitudes toward the poles. By the time it reaches about 30 degrees south latitude it will have cooled enough to cause it to fall and flow back toward the equator near sea level. In the southern hemisphere the rotation of the earth deflects the winds to the left to become the southeast trades. When these cool moist trade winds hit a high island, they are warmed by the sun and forced up. Above 500 meters' elevation they begin to cool again and their moisture condenses into clouds. At night the winds do not capture much warmth and are more likely to discharge their moisture as rain. The windward slopes of the high islands catch the trades head-on

INTRODUCTION

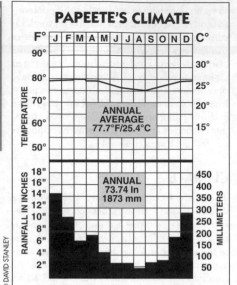

© DAVID STANLEY

Temperatures range from warm to hot year-round; however, the ever-present sea moderates the humidity by bringing continual cooling breezes. Areas nearer the equator (the Marquesas and Northern Cooks) are hotter than those farther south (the Australs and Southern Cooks). There's almost no twilight in the tropics, which makes Pacific sunsets brief. When the sun begins to go down, you have less than half an hour before darkness.

When to Go

Compared to parts of North America and Europe, the seasonal climatic variations in Polynesia are not extreme. There is a hotter, more humid season from November to April and a cooler, drier time from May to October. These contrasts are more pronounced in areas closer to the equator such as the Marquesas and less noticeable in the Cook Islands. Hurricanes can also come during the "rainy" season but they only last a few days a year. The sun sets around 1800 year-round and there aren't periods when the days are shorter or longer.

Seasonal differences in airfares are covered

and are usually wet, while those on the leeward side may be dry.

Rain falls abundantly and frequently in the islands during the southern summer months (Nov.–April). This is also the hurricane season south of the equator, a dangerous time for cruising yachts. However, New Zealand and southern Australia, outside the tropics, get their finest weather at this time; many boats head south to sit it out. The southeast trade winds or *alizés* sweep the South Pacific from May to October, the cruising season. Cooler and drier, these are the ideal months for travel in insular Oceania, though the rainy season is only a slight inconvenience and the season shouldn't be a pivotal factor in deciding when to go.

Over the past few years climatic changes have turned weather patterns upside down, so don't be surprised if you get prolonged periods of rain and wind during the official "dry season" and drought when there should be rain. A recent analysis of data shows that in 1977 the belt of storms and winds shifted abruptly eastward, making Tonga and Melanesia drier and French Polynesia wetter. Hurricanes are also striking farther east and El Niño is expected to recur more frequently.

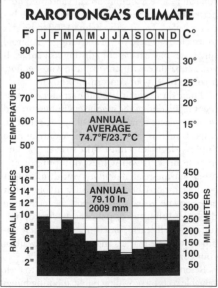

© DAVID STANLEY

INTRODUCTION

TROPICAL HURRICANES

The official hurricane (or tropical cyclone) season south of the equator is November–April, although hurricanes have also occurred in May and October. Since the ocean provides the energy, these low pressure systems can form only over water with a surface temperature above 27°C; during years when water temperatures are high (such as during the recent El Niño) their frequency increases. The rotation of the earth must give the storm its initial spin, and this occurs mostly between latitudes 5 and 20 on either side of the equator.

As rainfall increases and the seas rise, the winds are drawn into a spiral that reaches its maximum speed in a ring around the center. In the South Pacific a cyclone develops as these circular winds, rotating clockwise, increase in velocity:

force 8 to 9 winds blowing at 34 to 47 knots are called a gale, force 10 to 11 at 48 to 63 knots are a storm, force 12 winds revolving at 64 knots or more are a hurricane. Wind speeds can go as high as 100 knots with gusts to 140 on the left side of the storm's path in the direction it's moving.

The eye of the hurricane can be 10 to 30 kilometers wide and surprisingly clear and calm, although at sea, contradictory wave patterns continue to wreak havoc. In the South Pacific most hurricanes move south at speeds of 5 to 20 knots. As water is sucked into the low-pressure eye of the hurricane and waves reach 14 meters in height, coastlines can receive a surge of up to four meters of water, especially if the storm enters a narrowing bay or occurs at high tide.

in the Getting There section that follows and these should be more influential in deciding when to go. On Air New Zealand flights from North America to the Cook Islands the low season is mid-April to August, the prime time to be there. To Tahiti, on the other hand, June to August is the high tourist season for airfares, festivals, and tourism in general. French tourists are notorious for scheduling

their trips in August, and New Zealanders crowd into Rarotonga in July and August to escape the winter weather back home. Christmas is also busy with islanders returning home.

In short, there isn't really any one season that is the "best" time to come. Go whenever you can, but book your airline seat well in advance as many flights from the United States run 90 percent full.

Flora and Fauna

FLORA

The variety of floral species encountered in the Pacific islands declines as you move away from the Asian mainland. Although some species may have spread across the islands by means of floating seeds or fruit, wind and birds were probably more effective. The microscopic spores of ferns, for example, can be carried vast distances by the wind.

The high islands of Polynesia support a great variety of plantlife, while the low islands are restricted to a few hardy, drought-resistant species such as coconuts and pandanus. Rainforests fill the valleys and damp windward slopes of the high islands, while brush and thickets grow in more exposed locations. Hillsides in the drier areas are covered with coarse grasses. The absence of leaf-eating animals has allowed the vegetation to develop largely without the protective spines and thorns found elsewhere.

Distance, drought, and poor soil have made atoll vegetation among the most unvaried on earth. Though a tropical atoll might seem "lush," no more than 15 native species may be present! On the atolls, taro, a root vegetable with broad heart-shaped leaves, must be cultivated in deep organic pits. The vegetation of a raised atoll is apt to be far denser, with many more species, yet it's also likely that fewer than half will be native.

Here in Polynesia the air is sweet with the bouquet of tropical blossoms such as bursting bougainvillea, camellia, frangipani, ginger, orchids, poinsettia, and pitate jasmine. The fragrant flowers of the Polynesian hibiscus *(purau)* are yellow, not red or pink as on the Chinese hibiscus. A useful tree, the hibiscus has a soft wood used for house and canoe construction, and bast fiber used to make cordage and mats.

Mangroves are commonly found along some high island coastal lagoons. The cable roots of the saltwater-tolerant red mangrove anchor in the shallow upper layer of oxygenated mud, avoiding the layers of hydrogen sulfide below. The tree provides shade for tiny organisms dwelling in the tidal mudflats—a place for birds to nest and for fish or shellfish to feed and spawn. The mangroves also perform the same task as land-building coral colonies along the reefs. As sediments are trapped between the roots, the trees extend farther into the lagoon, creating a unique natural environment. The past two decades have seen widespread destruction of the mangroves.

> *Here in Polynesia the air is sweet with the bouquet of tropical blossoms such as bursting bougainvillea, camellia, frangipani, ginger, orchids, poinsettia, and pitate jasmine.*

FAUNA

Few land animals reached the eastern Pacific without the help of man. Ancient Polynesian navigators introduced pigs, dogs, and chickens; they also deliberately brought along rats both for their delicate bones used in tattooing and for food. Captain Cook contributed cattle, horses, and goats; Captain Wallis left behind cats. More goats were dropped off by whalers in the Marquesas. Giant African snails *(Achatina fulica)* were brought to Tahiti from Hawaii in the 1960s by a local policeman fond of fancy French food. He tried to set up a snail farm with the result that some escaped, multiplied, and now crawl wild, destroying the vegetation.

Bird-watching is a highly recommended pursuit for the serious Pacific traveler; you'll find it opens unexpected doors. Good field guides are few (ask at local bookstores, museums, and cultural centers), but a determined interest will bring you into contact with fascinating people and lead to great adventures. The best time to observe forest birds is in the very early morning—they move around a lot less in the heat of the day.

Fish

The South Pacific's richest store of life is found in the silent underwater world of the pelagic and la-

THE MIRACULOUS NONI FRUIT

In 1996 an American company began promoting the therapeutic proprieties of the knobby green fruit of the endemic *nono* or *noni* tree *(Morinda citrifolia)*, an ingredient in traditional Polynesian medicine. *Noni* pulp has become French Polynesia's largest agricultural export and the tree is now widely cultivated. The ripe fruit has an unpleasant taste and smell that once made it fit only for pig feed, but mixed with other juices it's quite palatable.

Among the claims made for *noni* juice are that it increases mental clarity and energy levels, supports proper digestion, carries beneficial substances to the skin, enhances the immune system, relieves pain, fights bacteria, retards tumor growth, and promotes longevity.

Miracle cure or spurious elixir, the *noni* juice fad has created a miniboom in producing areas such as the Marquesas. The trees blossom year-round and a yellow dye is made from the roots. Apart from the juice, *noni* extract is used as an ingredient in many personal hygiene products such as soaps, creams, and shampoos. In the United States, the Morinda company has exclusive rights.

goon fishes. Fishes are the most diverse group of vertebrates, accounting for 20,000 of 30,000 existing species, and it's estimated that half the fish remaining on our globe are swimming in this great ocean. Coral pinnacles on the lagoon floor provide a safe haven for angelfish, butterfly fish, damselfish, groupers, soldierfish, surgeonfish, triggerfish, trumpet fish, and countless more. These fish seldom venture more than a few meters away from the protective coral, but larger fish such as barracuda, jackfish, parrot fish, pike, stingrays, and small sharks range across lagoon waters that are seldom deeper than 30 meters. The external side of the reef is also home to many of the above, but the open ocean is reserved for bonito, mahimahi, swordfish, tuna, wrasses, and the larger sharks. Passes between ocean and lagoon can be crowded with fish in transit, offering a favorite hunting ground for predators.

In the open sea the food chain begins with phytoplankton, which flourish wherever ocean upswellings bring nutrients such as nitrates and phosphates to the surface. In the western Pacific this occurs near the equator, where massive currents draw water away toward Japan and Australia. Large schools of fast-moving tuna ply these waters feeding on smaller fish, which consume tiny phytoplankton drifting near the sunlit surface. The phytoplankton also exist in tropical lagoons where mangrove leaves, sea grasses, and other plant material are consumed by far more varied populations of reef fish, mollusks, and crustaceans.

It's believed that most Pacific marine organisms evolved in the triangular area bounded by New Guinea, the Philippines, and the Malay Peninsula. This "Cradle of Indo-Pacific Marinelife" includes a wide variety of habitats and has remained stable through several geological ages. From this cradle the rest of the Pacific was colonized.

Marine Mammals

Porpoises don't exist in French Polynesia but dolphins come in a variety of species. Spinner dolphins leap from the water and spin like ballerinas. Many legends tell of dolphins saving humans, especially children, from drowning (the most famous concerns Telemachus, son of Odysseus). Dolphins often try to race in front of ferries and large ships. The commercialization of dolphins in enclosures, such as the one on Moorea, is a questionable activity.

Whales generally visit the tropical South Pacific between July and October. Humpbacks arrive about this time to give birth in the warm waters. As the weather grows warmer they return to the summer feeding areas around Antarctica. Sadly, Japanese whalers continue to hunt the animals in Antarctica for "scientific purposes," and endangered fin and humpback whales are usually hidden among the 400 minke whale kills reported each year. Thanks to the efforts of Dr. Michael Poole and others, the large exclusive economic zones of both French Polynesia and the Cook Islands have been declared marine mammal sanctuaries in recent years. Whale-watching trips are offered in season at Moorea and Rurutu.

Sharks

The danger from sharks (*mao* in Tahitian, *requin* in French) has been greatly exaggerated. Of about 300 different species, only 28 are known to have attacked humans. Most dangerous are the white, tiger, and bull sharks. Fortunately, all of these usually frequent deep water far from the coasts. An average of under 100 shark attacks a year occur worldwide, so considering the number of people who swim in the sea, your chances of being involved are about one in 10 million. In the South Pacific, shark attacks on snorkelers or scuba divers are extremely rare and the tiny mosquito is a far more dangerous predator.

You're always safer if you keep your head underwater (with a mask and snorkel), and don't panic if you see a shark—you might attract it. Even if you do, they're usually only curious, so keep your eye on the shark and slowly back off. The swimming techniques of humans must seem very clumsy to fish, so it's not surprising they want a closer look. Sharks are attracted by shiny objects (a knife or jewelry), bright colors (especially yellow and red), urine, blood, spearfishing, and splashing.

Sharks normally stay outside the reef, but get local advice. White beaches are safer than dark, and clear water safer than murky. Avoid swimming in locations where sewage or edible wastes enter the water, or where fish have just been cleaned. You should also exercise care in places where local residents have been fishing with spears or even a hook and line that day.

Never swim alone if you suspect the presence of sharks. If you see one, even a supposedly harmless nurse shark lying on the bottom, get out of the water calmly and quickly, and go elsewhere. Studies indicate that sharks, like most other creatures, have a "personal space" around them that they will defend. Thus an attack could be a shark's way of warning someone to keep his distance, and it's a fact that more than half of the victims of these incidents are not eaten but merely bitten. Sharks are much less of a problem in the South Pacific than in colder waters, where small marine mammals are commonly hunted by sharks. You won't be mistaken for a seal or an otter here.

Let common sense be your guide, not irrational fear or carelessness. Many scuba divers actually come *looking* for sharks, and local divemasters seem able to hand-feed chunks of tuna to them with impunity. If you're in the market for some shark action, dive shops at Bora Bora, Moorea, and Rangiroa can provide it. Just be aware that getting into the water with feeding sharks always entails some danger. Never snorkel on your own (without the services of an experienced guide) near a spot where shark feeding is practiced as you never know how the sharks will react to a surface swimmer without any food for them. Like all wild animals, the shark deserves to be approached with respect.

Sea Urchins

Sea urchins (living pincushions) are common in tropical waters. The black variety is the most dangerous: its long, sharp quills can go right through a snorkeler's fins. Even the small ones, which you can easily pick up in your hand, can pinch you if you're careless. They're found on rocky shores and reefs, never on clear, sandy beaches where the surf rolls in.

Most sea urchins are not poisonous, though quill punctures are painful and can become infected if not treated. The pain is caused by an injected protein, which you can eliminate by holding the injured area in a pail of very hot water for about 15 minutes. This will coagulate the protein, eliminating the pain for good. If you can't heat water, soak the area in vinegar or urine for a quarter hour. Remove the quills if possible, but being made of calcium, they'll decompose in a couple of weeks anyway—not much of a consolation as you limp along in the meantime. In some places sea urchins are considered a delicacy: the orange or yellow urchin gonads are delicious with lemon and salt.

Other Hazardous Creatures

Although jellyfish, stonefish, crown-of-thorns starfish, cone shells, eels, and poisonous sea snakes are dangerous, injuries resulting from any of these are rare. Gently apply methylated spirit, alcohol, or urine (but not water, kerosene, or gasoline) to areas stung by jellyfish. Inoffensive sea cucumbers (bêche-de-mer) punctuate the lagoon shallows, but stonefish also rest on the bottom and are hard to see because of camouflaging; if you happen to step on one, its dorsal fins inject a painful poison, which burns like fire in the blood. Avoid them by dragging your feet. Fortunately, stonefish are not common.

It's worth knowing that the venom produced by most marine animals is destroyed by heat, so your first move should be to soak the injured part in very hot water for 30 minutes. (Also hold an opposite foot or hand in the same water to prevent scalding due to numbness.) Other authorities claim the best first aid is to squeeze blood from a sea cucumber scraped raw on coral directly onto the stonefish wound. If a hospital or clinic is nearby, go there immediately.

Never pick up a live cone shell; some varieties have a deadly stinger dart coming out from the pointed end. The tiny blue-ring octopus is only five centimeters long but packs a poison that can kill a human. Eels hide in reef crevices by day; most are harmful only if you inadvertently poke your hand or foot in at them. Of course, never tempt fate by approaching them (fun-loving divemasters sometimes feed the big ones by hand and stroke their backs).

Reptiles

Land snakes don't exist in eastern Polynesia and the sea snakes are shy and inoffensive. This, and the relative absence of leeches, poisonous plants, thorns, and dangerous wild animals, makes the South Pacific a paradise for hikers. One creature to watch out for is the centipede, which often hides under stones or anything else lying around. It's a long, flat, fast-moving insect not to be confused with the round, slow, and harmless millipede. The centipede's bite, though painful, is not lethal to a normal adult.

Geckos and skinks are small lizards often seen on the islands. The skink hunts insects by day; its tail breaks off if you catch it, but a new one quickly grows. The gecko is nocturnal and has no eyelids. Adhesive toe pads enable it to pass along vertical surfaces, and it changes color to avoid detection. Unlike the skink, which avoids humans, geckos often live in people's homes, where they eat insects attracted by electric lights. Its loud clicking call may be a territorial warning to other geckos. Two species of geckos are asexual: in these, males do not exist and the unfertilized eggs hatch into females identical to the mother. Geckos are the highest members of the animal world where this phenomenon takes place. During the 1970s a sexual species of house gecko was introduced to Samoa and Vanuatu, and in 1988 it arrived on Tahiti. These larger, more aggressive geckos have drastically reduced the population of the endemic asexual species.

Five of the seven species of sea turtles are present in Polynesia (the green, hawksbill, leatherback, loggerhead, and olive ridley turtles). These magnificent creatures are sometimes erroneously referred to as "tortoises," which are land turtles. All species of sea turtles now face extinction through ruthless hunting, egg harvesting, and beach destruction. Sea turtles come ashore from November to February to lay their eggs on the beach from which they themselves originally hatched, but the female turtles don't commence this activity until they are 20 years old. Thus a drop in numbers today has irreversible consequences a generation later, and it's estimated that breeding females already number in the hundreds or low thousands. Turtles are often choke on floating plastic bags they mistake for food, or they drown in fishing nets.

History and Government

THE ERA OF DISCOVERY AND SETTLEMENT

Prehistory

Oceania is the site of many "lasts." It was the last area on earth to be settled by humans, the last to be discovered by Europeans, and the last to be both colonized and decolonized. Sometime after 2000 B.C., broad-nosed, light-skinned Austronesian peoples entered the Pacific from Indonesia or the Philippines. The Austronesians had pottery and advanced outrigger canoes. Their distinctive *lapita* pottery, decorated in horizontal geometric bands and dated from 1500 to 500 B.C., has been found at sites ranging from New Britain to New Caledonia, Tonga, and Samoa. *Lapita* pottery has allowed archaeologists to trace the migrations of an Austronesian-speaking race, the Polynesians, with some precision, and recent comparisons of DNA samples have confirmed that they traveled from the south China coast to Taiwan, the Philippines, Indonesia, New Guinea, Santa Cruz, Fiji, and Samoa.

The colorful theory that Oceania was colonized from the Americas is no longer entertained. The Austronesian languages are today spoken from Madagascar through Indonesia all the way to Easter Island and Hawaii, half the circumference of the world! All of the introduced plants of old Polynesia, except the sweet potato, originated in Southeast Asia. The endemic diseases of Oceania, leprosy and the filaria parasite (which causes elephantiasis), were unknown in the Americas. The amazing continuity of Polynesian culture is illustrated by motifs in contemporary tattooing and tapa, which are very similar to those on ancient *lapita* pottery.

The Colonization of Polynesia

The early Polynesians set out from Southeast Asia 3,500 years ago on a migratory trek that would lead them to make the "many islands" of Polynesia their home. Great voyagers, they sailed their huge double-hulled canoes far and wide, steering with huge paddles and pandanus sails. To navigate they read the sun, stars, currents, swells, winds, clouds, and birds. For instance, the brown noddy returns to roost on an island at night and a sighting at sea would be a sure sign of land nearby.

Sailing purposefully, against the prevailing winds and currents, the *Lapita* peoples reached the Bismarck Archipelago by 1500 B.C., Tonga (via Fiji) by 1300 B.C., and Samoa by 1000 B.C. Around the time of Christ they pushed out from this primeval area, remembered as Havaiki, into the eastern half of the Pacific.

Perhaps because of overpopulation in Samoa, by 300 B.C. groups of Polynesians had pressed on to the Marquesas. Hawai'i (A.D. 200) and Easter Island (A.D. 300) were both discovered by Polynesians from the Marquesas. The Society Islands were reached by the Marquesans around A.D. 600, and from there or from the Marquesas the migrants continued to the Cook Islands (A.D. 800), the Tuamotus (A.D. 900), and New Zealand (before A.D. 1100). The stone food pounders, carved figures, and tanged adzes of Eastern Polynesia are not found in Samoa and Tonga (Western Polynesia), indicating that they were later, local developments of Polynesian culture.

These were not chance landfalls but planned voyages of colonization: the Polynesians could (and often did) return the way they came. That one could deliberately sail such distances against the trade winds and currents without the help of modern navigational equipment was proved in 1976 when the *Hokule'a*, a reconstructed ocean-going canoe, sailed 5,000 km south from Hawaii to Tahiti. The expedition's Micronesian navigator, Mau Piailug, succeeded in setting a course by the ocean swells and relative positions of the stars alone, which guided the group very precisely along its way. Other signs used to find an island were clouds (which hang over peaks and remain stationary), seabirds (boobies fly up to 50 km offshore, frigate birds up to 80 km), and mysterious *te lapa* (underwater streaks of light radiating 120–150 km from an island, disappearing closer in).

Since 1976 the *Hokule'a* has made several

DISCOVERY AND SETTLEMENT OF THE PACIFIC

EQUATOR

1800 mi

1800 km

0

0

CHINA

TAIWAN

PHILIPPINES

INDONESIA

AUSTRALIA

Tasmania

New Guinea

MICRONESIA

Marcus

Wake

Marshall Is.

Marianas

Saipan

Guam

Yap

Caroline Is.

Gilbert Is.

Nukuoro

Ontong Java

Solomons

Tuvalu

Vanuatu

New Caledonia

MELANESIA

Fiji Is.

Norfolk

Lord Howe

Kermadec

NEW ZEALAND

Midway

Johnston

Hawaii

Palmyra

Washington

Fanning

Howland

Christmas

Phoenix Is.

Tokelau

Samoa

Tonga

POLYNESIA

Marquesas Is.

Tuamotu Archipelago

Society Is.

Austral Is.

Cook Is.

Gambier Is.

Pitcairn Is.

Easter Is.

Chatham

© DAVID STANLEY

DATELINE: EASTERN POLYNESIA

300 B.C.: Polynesians reach the Marquesas
A.D. 300: Polynesians reach Easter Island
A.D. 600: Polynesians reach the Society Islands
1521: Magellan sights Pukapuka in the Tuamotus
1595: Mendaña contacts the Marquesas
1606: Quirós passes through the Tuamotus
1722: Roggeveen sights Easter Island and Bora Bora
1767: Englishman Samuel Wallis contacts Tahiti
1768: Frenchman Bougainville visits Tahiti
1769: Captain Cook observes transit of Venus at Tahiti
1773: Captain Cook contacts five of the Cook Islands
1774: Spanish priests spend one year on Tahiti
1777: last of Captain Cook's four visits to Tahiti
1788: Bligh's HMS *Bounty* at Tahiti
1789: Captain Bligh sights Aitutaki
1793: founding of the Pomare dynasty
1797: arrival on Tahiti of first Protestant missionaries
1803: Pomare II flees to Moorea
1812: Pomare's subjects convert to Protestantism
1815: Pomare II reconquers Tahiti
1818: foundation of Papeete by Reverend Crook
1823: missionary John Williams arrives at Rarotonga
1827: 50-year reign of Queen Pomare IV begins
1834: French Catholic missionaries arrive at Mangareva
1836: French Catholic priests are expelled from Tahiti
1838: French gunboat demands compensation
1839: Britain rejects Tahitian request for a protectorate
1842: French protectorate is declared over Tahiti and the Marquesas
1842: Herman Melville visits French Polynesia
1844: Mormon missionaries arrive on Tubuai, Austral Islands
1844–1847: Tahitian War of Independence
1847: Queen Pomare accepts French protectorate
1854: one-seventh of Tahitians die during smallpox epidemic
1862: Easter Islanders kidnapped by Peruvian slavers
1865–1866: 1,010 Chinese laborers arrive on Tahiti
1877: death of Queen Pomare IV
1880: French protectorate changes into a colony
1884: a fire destroys much of Papeete

1887: France annexes the Leeward Islands
1888: British protectorate declared in Southern Cooks
1888: Chile annexes Easter Island
1889: British protectorate declared in Northern Cooks
1889: French protectorate declared over Australs
1890: British missionaries depart Leeward Islands
1891: Paul Gauguin arrives at Tahiti
1900: Austral Islands annexed by France
1901: the Cook Islands transferred to New Zealand
1903: Paul Gauguin dies on Hiva Oa
1908: phosphate mining begins at Makatea
1914: German cruisers shell Papeete
1916: 1,000 Polynesians join Bataillon du Pacifique
1918: influenza epidemic kills 20 percent of population of Tahiti
1942: American military bases on Bora Bora and Aitutaki
1945: Tahitians become French citizens
1946: French Polynesia becomes an overseas territory
1946: territorial assembly created
1953: Chilean Navy takes over Easter Island
1958: Pouvanaa a Oopa is arrested
1961: opening of Faa'a Airport on Tahiti
1962: French halt nuclear testing in Algeria
1963: French nuclear testing moves to Polynesia
1965: Cook Islands becomes self-governing
1965: phosphate mine closes on Makatea
1966: first atmospheric nuclear explosion in the Tuamotus
1973: Rarotonga International Airport opens
1974: French nuclear testing moves underground
1977: French Polynesia is granted partial internal autonomy
1984: internal autonomy increases slightly in Polynesia
1985: South Pacific Nuclear-Free Zone Treaty signed
1987: Université française du Pacifique is established
1992: President Mitterrand suspends nuclear testing
1994: income tax introduced in French Polynesia
1995: Cook Islands dollar withdrawn from circulation
1995: President Chirac restarts nuclear testing
1996: nuclear testing ends and site is dismantled
1998: Value-Added Tax inflicted on French Polynesia
2002: whale and dolphin sanctuary declared

additional return trips to Tahiti; during 1985–1987 Hawaiian navigator Nainoa Thompson used traditional methods to guide the *Hokule'a* on a 27-month "Voyage of Rediscovery" that included a return west-east journey between Samoa and Tahiti. To date the vessel has logged well over 100,000 km using traditional methods, introducing Polynesian voyaging to countless thousands. In 1992 the canoe *Te Aurere* sailed from New Zealand to Rarotonga for the Festival of Pacific Arts—the first such voyage in a thousand years—where it joined the *Hokule'a* and a fleet of other canoes in a dramatic demonstration of the current revival of traditional Polynesian navigation. In 1995 the *Hokule'a* led a three-canoe flotilla from Hawaii to Tahiti, returning in May with another three double-hulled canoes, which joined them in the Marquesas. In 1999 the vessel reached Easter Island. (For more information on the *Hokule'a,* click on http://leahi.kcc.hawaii.edu/org/pvs.)

The Polynesians were the real discoverers of the Pacific, completing all their major voyages long before Europeans even dreamed this ocean existed. In double canoes lashed together to form rafts, carrying their plants and animals with them, they penetrated as close to Antarctica as the South Island of New Zealand, as far north as Hawaii, and as far east as Easter Island—a full 13,000 km from where it's presumed they first entered the Pacific!

Neolithic Society

The Polynesians kept gardens and a few domestic animals. Taro was cultivated in organic pits; breadfruit was preserved by fermentation through burial (still a rare delicacy). Stone fishponds and fish traps were built in the lagoons. Pandanus and coconut fronds were woven into handicrafts. On the larger islands these practices produced a surplus, which allowed the emergence of a powerful ruling class. The common people lived in fear of their gods and chiefs.

The Polynesians were cannibals, although the intensity of the practice varied from group to group: cannibalism was rife in the Marquesas but relatively rare on Tahiti. It was believed that the mana or spiritual power of an enemy would be transferred to the consumer; to eat the body of one who was greatly despised was the ultimate revenge.

Jean-Jacques Rousseau and the 18th-century French rationalists created the romantic image of the "noble savage." Their vision of an ideal state of existence in harmony with nature disregarded the inequalities, cannibalism, and warfare that were a central part of island life, just as much of today's travel literature ignores the poverty and political/economic exploitation many Pacific peoples now face. Still, the legend of the South Pacific maintains its magic hold.

EUROPEAN CONTACT

European Exploration

The first Europeans on the scene were the Spaniards. In 1595, on his second trip from Peru to the Solomon Islands, Álvaro de Mendaña sighted the southern Marquesas Islands. Eleven years later another Spanish expedition led by Pedro Fernandez de Quirós found a few of the Tuamotu atolls, but these visitors stayed only a few days and their discoveries were deliberately concealed by the Spanish authorities to avoid attracting rival powers to the area.

The systematic European exploration of the Pacific in the 18th century was actually a search for *terra australis incognita,* a great southern continent believed to balance the continents of the north. Dutchman Jacob Roggeveen's 1722 voyage failed to discover the unknown continent, but he did find Easter Island and narrowed the area of conjecture considerably.

In 1745, the British Parliament passed an act promising £20,000 to the first British subject who could, in a British ship, discover and sail through a strait between Hudson's Bay and the South Seas. Thus many explorers were spurred to investigate the region. This route would have proven infinitely shorter than the one around Cape Horn, where the weather was often foul and the ships in perpetual danger; on Samuel Wallis's voyage of 1766–1767, his two ships took four months to round the chaotic Straits of Magellan. In June 1767 Wallis "discovered" Tahiti (which was already well populated at the time).

MUTINY ON THE BOUNTY

In 1788 the HMS *Bounty* sailed from England for the Pacific to collect breadfruit plants to supplement the diet of slaves in the West Indies. Because the *Bounty* arrived at Tahiti at the wrong time of year, it was necessary to spend a long five months there collecting samples, and during this time, part of the crew became overly attached to that isle of pleasure. On April 28, 1789, in Tongan waters, they mutinied against Lieutenant William Bligh under 24-year-old Master's Mate Fletcher Christian. Bligh was set adrift in an open boat with the 18 men who chose to go with him. He then performed the amazing feat of sailing 6,500 km in 41 days, reaching Dutch Timor to give the story to the world.

After the mutiny, the *Bounty* sailed back to Tahiti. Fletcher Christian set out with eight muti-neers, 18 Polynesian men and women, and one small girl, to find a new home where they would be safe from capture. In 1791 the crew members who elected to remain on Tahiti were picked up by the HMS *Pandora* and returned to England for trial. Three were executed. An attempt to colonize Tubuai in the Austral Islands failed, and the *Bounty* sailed through the Cook Islands, Tonga, and Fiji, until Christian remembered the discovery of tiny Pitcairn Island by Captain Carteret of the *Swallow* in 1767. They changed course for Pitcairn and arrived on January 15, 1790. After removing everything of value, the mutineers burned the *Bounty* to avoid detection. For 18 years after the mutiny, the world knew nothing of the fate of the *Bounty* until the American sealer *Topaz* called at Pitcairn for water in 1808 and solved the mystery.

Captain Cook

The extraordinary achievements of James Cook (1728–1779) on his three voyages in the ships *Endeavor, Resolution, Adventure,* and *Discovery* left his successors with little to do but marvel over them. A product of the Age of Enlightenment, Cook was a mathematician, astronomer, practical physician, and master navigator. Son of a Yorkshire laborer, he learned seamanship on small coastal traders plying England's east coast. He joined the British Navy in 1755 and soon made a name for himself in Canada, where he surveyed the St. Lawrence River, greatly contributing to the capture of Quebec City in 1759. Later he charted the coast of Newfoundland. Chosen to command the *Endeavor* in 1768 though only a warrant officer, Cook was the first captain to eliminate scurvy from his crew (with sauerkraut).

The scientists of his time needed accurate observations of the transit of Venus, for if the passage of Venus across the face of the sun were measured from points on opposite sides of the earth, then the size of the solar system could be determined for the first time. In turn, this would make possible accurate predictions of the movements of the planets, vital for navigation at sea. Thus Cook was dispatched to Tahiti, and Father Hell (a Viennese astronomer of Hungarian origin) to Vardo, Norway.

So as not to alarm the French and Spanish, the British admiralty claimed Cook's first voyage (1768–1771) was primarily to take these measurements. His real purpose, however, was to further explore the region, in particular to find *terra australis incognita.* After three months on Tahiti, he sailed west and spent six months exploring and mapping New Zealand and the whole east coast of Australia, nearly tearing the bottom off his ship, the *Endeavor,* on the Great Barrier Reef in the process. Nine months after returning to England, Cook embarked on his second expedition (1772–1775), resolving to settle the matter of *terra australis incognita* conclusively. In the *Resolution* and *Adventure,* he sailed entirely around the bottom of the world, becoming the first to cross the Antarctic Circle and return to tell about it.

In 1773 John Harrison won the greater part of a £20,000 reward offered by Queen Anne in 1714 "for such Person or Persons as shall discover the Longitude at Sea." Harrison won it with the first marine chronometer (1759), which accompanied Cook on his second and third voyages. Also on these voyages was Omai, a native of Tahiti who sailed to England with Cook in 1774. Omai immediately became the talk of London, the epitome of the "noble savage," but to those who knew him he was simply a sophisticated man with a culture of his own.

In 1776 Cook set forth from England for a third voyage, supposedly to repatriate Omai but really to find a Northwest Passage from the Pacific to the Atlantic. He rounded Cape Horn and headed due north, encountering Kaua'i in the Hawaiian Islands on January 18, 1778. After two weeks on Hawai'i, Cook continued north via the west coast of North America but was forced back by ice in the Bering Strait. With winter coming, he returned to Hawaiian waters and found the two biggest islands of the group, Maui and Hawai'i. On February 14, 1779, in a short, unexpected, petty skirmish with the Hawaiians, Cook was killed. Today he remains the giant of Pacific exploration.

The Fatal Impact

Most early contacts with Europeans had a hugely disintegrating effect on native cultures. When introduced into the South Pacific, European sicknesses—mere discomforts to them—devastated whole populations. Measles, influenza, tuberculosis, dysentery, smallpox, typhus, typhoid, and whooping cough were deadly because the islanders had never developed resistance to them. The Europeans' alcohol, weapons, and venereal disease further accelerated the process.

CONVERSION, COLONIALISM, AND NUCLEAR TESTING

Conversion

The systematic explorations of the 18th century were stimulated by the need for raw materials and markets as the Industrial Revolution took hold in Europe. After the American Revolution, much of Britain's colonizing energy was deflected toward Africa, India, and the Pacific. This gave them an early lead, but France wasn't far behind. As trade developed in the late 18th and early 19th centuries, ruffian whalers, sealers, and individual beachcombers flooded in. Most were unsavory characters who acted as mercenaries or advisers to local chiefs, but one, Herman Melville, left a valuable account of early Polynesia.

After the easily exploited resources were depleted, white traders and planters arrived to establish posts and to create copra and cotton plantations on the finest land. Missionaries came to "civilize" the natives by teaching that all their customs—cannibalism, warring with their neighbors, having more than one wife, wearing leaves instead of clothes, dancing, drinking kava, chewing betel nut, etc.—were wrong. They taught hard work, shame, thrift, abstention, and obedience. Tribes now had to wear sweaty, rain-soaked, germ-carrying garments of European design. Men dressed in singlets and trousers, and the women in Mother Hubbards, one-piece smocks trailing along the ground. To clothe themselves and build churches required money, obtained only by working as laborers on European plantations or producing a surplus of goods to sell to European traders. In many instances this austere, harsh Christianity was grafted onto the numerous taboo systems of the Pacific.

Members of the London Missionary Society arrived at Tahiti in 1797, though it was not until 1815 that they succeeded in converting the Tahitians. One famous LMS missionary, the Reverend John Williams, spread Protestantism to the Cook Islands (1823) and Samoa (1830). The children of some of the European missionaries who "came to do good, stayed to do well" as merchants. Later, many islanders themselves became missionaries: about 1,200 of them left their homes to carry the word of God to other islands. The first Catholic priests arrived in Polynesia in 1834. They competed with the Protestants for influence and divided islands on religious grounds.

After the 1840s, islanders were kidnapped by "blackbirders," who sold them as slaves. Peruvians took 3,634 islanders to Peru in 1862 and 1863, of whom only 148 were returned. The populations of Easter Island and some of the northern Cooks were devastated.

Colonialism

The first European colonies in Oceania were Australia (1788) and New Zealand (1840). Soon after, the French seized French Polynesia (1842) and New Caledonia (1853). A canal across Central America had already been proposed and

WHAT'S IN A NAME?

Over the years that part of Eastern Polynesia controlled by France has been called many things. After 1880 it was the Etablissements français de l'Oceánie, becoming Polynésie française or French Polynesia in 1957, the designation still officially recognized by the authorities. French-occupied Polynesia better reflects the political reality, but variations such as (french) Polynesia, "French" Polynesia and Tahiti-Polynesia are also seen. Recently the pro-French faction in the Territorial Assembly has adopted Tahiti Nui or "Greater Tahiti" to give the impression that it enjoys more autonomy than is actually the case, whereas the pro-independence camp calls its country Te Ao Maohi, which translates to Land of the Maohi. Maohinui is also heard. Tourism officials on Tahiti often use Tahiti and Its Islands. When in doubt, "Tahiti" will get you by, although there's a lot more to this colorful region than just its largest and best-known island.

Tahiti was seen as a potential port of call on the sea routes to Australia and New Zealand. The French annexed several other island groups near Tahiti in the 1880s. Missionary pressure led Britain to declare a protectorate over the Cook Islands in 1888, the same year Chile annexed Easter Island, forestalling further French advances in those directions. In 1901 Britain transferred responsibility for the Cook Islands to New Zealand.

By the late 19th century, the colonies' tropical produce (copra, sugar, vanilla, cacao, and fruits) had become more valuable and accessible; minerals, such as phosphates and guano, were also exploited. Total control of these resources passed to large European trading companies, which owned the plantations, ships, and retail stores. This colonial economy led to a drop in the indigenous populations in general by a third, not to mention the destruction of their cultures.

There were fundamental differences in approach between the British and French colonial administrations in the South Pacific. While the French system installed "direct rule" by French officials appointed by the French government, the British practiced "indirect rule" with the *ariki*

(chiefs) retaining most of their traditional powers. Not only was this form of government cheaper, but it fostered stability. British colonial officials had more decision-making authority than their French counterparts, who had to adhere to instructions received from Paris. And while the French sought to undermine local traditions in the name of assimilation, the British (and later New Zealanders) defended the native land tenure on which traditional life was based.

During World War II, large American staging and supply bases were created on Bora Bora, Aitutaki, and Penrhyn to support the southern supply routes to Australia and New Zealand. The airfields built on those islands during the war are still in use today.

In 1960 the United Nations issued a Declaration of Granting of Independence to Colonial Countries and Peoples, which encouraged the trend toward self-government, and in 1965 the Cook Islands achieved de facto independence in association with New Zealand. As a French colony, French Polynesia has a degree of internal autonomy, although great power continues to be wielded by appointed French officials who are not responsible to the local assembly. Decolonization is a hot issue on Tahiti, where one of the South Pacific's only active independence movements is found. Easter Island also remains a colony of Chile.

French Power

New Caledonia, French Polynesia, and Wallis and Futuna are part of a worldwide chain of French colonies also including Kerguelen, Guiana, Martinique, Guadeloupe, Mayotte, Reunion, and St. Pierre and Miquelon, under the DOM-TOM (Ministry of Overseas Departments and Territories). It costs France billions of Euros a year to maintain this system, a clear indicator that it's something totally different from colonial empires of the past, which were based on economic exploitation, not subsidies. A closer analogy is the American network of military bases around the world, which serves a similar purpose—projecting power. For more than 40 years France has been willing to spend vast sums to perpetuate its status as a medium-sized world power.

These conditions contradict what has happened elsewhere in the South Pacific. During the 1960s and 1970s, as Britain, Australia, and New Zealand voluntarily withdrew from their Pacific colonies, French pretensions to global status grew stronger. This digging-in created the anachronism of a few highly visible bastions of white colonialism in the midst of a sea of English-speaking self-governing nations. When French officials summarily rejected all protests against their nuclear testing and suppression of independence movements, most Pacific islanders were outraged.

The final round of nuclear testing in the Tuamotu Islands in 1995 was a watershed as French national prestige had seldom sunk as low, both in the Pacific and around the world. Since that debacle, France has tried to mend fences by supplying economic aid to the independent states and granting enhanced autonomy to its colonies. In recent years France has come to realize that its interests in the Pacific are as well served by emphasizing social, cultural, and economic matters as by outright political and military domination. French universities have been established on Tahiti and New Caledonia. As France becomes fully integrated into the new Europe, it's quite likely its ability and desire to maintain remote colonies will decline, and the decolonization process will finally be concluded.

Nuclear Testing

No other area on earth was more directly affected by the nuclear arms race than the Pacific. From August 6, 1945, until January 27, 1996, scarcely a year passed without one nuclear power or another testing its weapons of mass destruction here. The United States, Britain, and France exploded more than 250 nuclear bombs at Bikini, Enewetak, Christmas Island, Moruroa, and Fangataufa, an average of more than six a year for more than 40 years, more than half of them by France. The U.S. and British testing was halted only by the 1963 Partial Nuclear Test Ban Treaty with the Soviets, while the French tests continued until unprecedented worldwide protests made it clear that the Cold War was really over (as usual, France was a slow learner).

The end result of the French nuclear testing is still ticking away in the genes of the thousands of servicemen and workers present during the tests. And far away in the Tuamotus at the abandoned tests sites at Moruroa and Fangataufa, deadly radioactive materials are already seeping into the Pacific through cracks created by the underground tests. (For more information, turn to The Nuclear Test Zone in this book's Tuamotu Islands section.)

The fact that the nuclear age began in their backyard at Hiroshima and Nagasaki has not been lost on the islanders. They have always seen few benefits coming from nuclear power, only deadly dangers. On August 6, 1985, eight member states of the South Pacific Forum signed the South Pacific Nuclear-Free Zone Treaty, also known as the Treaty of Rarotonga, which bans nuclear testing, land-based nuclear weapon storage, and nuclear waste dumping on their territories. Each country may decide for itself if nuclear-armed warships and aircraft are to be allowed entry. Of the five nuclear powers, China and the USSR promptly signed the treaty, while the United States, France, and Britain signed only in March 1996,when it became obvious they could no longer use the region as a nuclear playground.

Economy

The greatest source of income for all three territories included herein is budgetary aid from the mother country. France and Chile each spend millions of dollars a year subsidizing the public services of their dependencies, and New Zealand provides aid more indirectly. Tourism comes second, and in recent years cultured black pearls have become the leading export of French Polynesia and the Cook Islands.

One of the few potential sources of real wealth are the undersea mineral nodules within the huge exclusive economic zones (EEZ) of French Polynesia and the Cook Islands. The potato-sized nodules contain manganese, cobalt, nickel, and copper; total deposits are valued at US$3 trillion, enough to supply the world for thousands of years. In the past two decades Japan has spent US$100 million on seabed surveys in preparation for eventual mining, although that's still decades away.

In 1976 the French government passed legislation that gave it control of this zone, not only along France's coastal waters but also around all her overseas territories and departments. The National Marine Research Center and private firms have already drawn up plans to recover nickel, cobalt, manganese, and copper nodules from depths of more than 4,000 meters. The French government has adamantly refused to give the Territorial Assembly any jurisdiction over this tremendous resource, an important indicator as to why it is determined to hold onto its colony at any price.

TOURISM

Tourism is the world's largest and fastest-growing industry, increasing 260 percent between 1970 and 1990. About 593 million people traveled abroad in 1996 compared to only 25 million in 1950, and each year more than 25 million first-world tourists visit third-world countries, transferring an estimated US$25 billion from North to South. Tourism is the only industry that allows a net flow of wealth from richer to poorer countries, and in the islands it's one of the few avenues open for economic development, providing much-needed foreign exchange required to pay for imports. Those who buy tourism products pay their own transportation costs to the market, unlike the case with every other export.

New Zealand is the main source of visitors to the Cook Islands, while most of Easter Island's arrivals are from Europe and Chile. Americans and French are the largest single groups of travelers to French Polynesia. On a per-capita basis, the Cook Islands gets more tourists than any other South Pacific country, and it's the number one industry throughout this part of the world. Yet the "tyranny of distance" has thus far prevented the islands from being spoiled.

Arrival levels from New Zealand are expected to remain stable in coming years, and Japan, Europe, and North America are seen as the main growth markets for South Pacific tourism. Japanese interest in the region increased dramatically in the late 1980s but dropped off during the nuclear testing in 1995. Increasing numbers of European and North American visitors can be expected if airfares remain low and the region's many advantages over competing Mediterranean and Caribbean destinations can be effectively marketed.

Only about 40 percent of the net earnings from tourism actually stays in the host country. The rest is "leaked" in repatriated profits, salaries for expatriates, commissions, imported goods, food, fuel, etc. Top management positions usually go to foreigners, with local residents offered low-paying service jobs. To encourage hotel construction, local governments must commit themselves to crippling tax concessions and large infrastructure investments for the benefit of hotel companies. The cost of airports, roads, communications networks, power lines, sewers, and waste disposal can exceed the profits from tourism.

Tourism-related construction can cause unsightly beach erosion through the clearing of vegetation and the extraction of sand. Resort sewage causes lagoon pollution, while the reefs are blasted to provide passes for tourist craft and stripped of corals or shells by visitors. Locally scarce water supplies are diverted to hotels, and foods such as fruit and fish can be priced beyond the reach of local residents. Access to the ocean can be blocked by wall-to-wall resorts. "Ecotourism" can lead to the destruction of natural areas if not conducted with sensitivity.

Although tourism is often seen as a way of experiencing other cultures, it can undermine those same cultures. Traditional dances and ceremonies are shortened or changed to fit into tourist schedules, and mock celebrations are held out of season and context, and their significance is lost. Cheap mass-produced handicrafts are made to satisfy the expectations of visitors; thus the Balinese carvings sold on Bora Bora. Authenticity is sacrificed for immediate

profits. While travel cannot help but improve international understanding, the aura of glamour and prosperity surrounding tourist resorts can present a totally false image of a country's social and economic realities.

To date, most attention has focused on luxury resorts and all-inclusive tours—the exotic rather than the authentic. Packaged holidays create the illusion of adventure while avoiding all risks and individualized variables, and on many tours the only islanders seen are maids and bartenders. This elitist tourism perpetuates the colonial master-servant relationship as condescending foreigners instill a feeling of inferiority in local residents and workers. Fortunately, in all three territories included in this book, an excellent alternative exists in the form of local guesthouse tourism.

The People

The aquatic continent of Oceania is divided into three great cultural areas: Polynesia and Melanesia lie mostly below the equator while Micronesia is above it. The name Polynesia comes from the Greek words *poly* (many) and *nesos* (islands). The Polynesian Triangle has Hawaii at its north apex, New Zealand 8,000 km to the southwest, and Easter Island an equal distance to the southeast. Melanesia gets its name from the Greek word *melas* (black), probably for the dark appearance of its inhabitants as seen by the early European navigators. Micronesia comes from the Greek word *mikros* (small), thus, the "small islands."

The term Polynesia was coined by Charles de Brosses in 1756 and applied to all the Pacific islands. The present restricted use was proposed by Dumont d'Urville during a famous lecture at the Geographical Society in Paris in 1831. At the same time he also proposed the terms Melanesia and Micronesia for the regions that still bear those names. The terms are not particularly good, considering that all three regions have "many islands" and "small islands"; in Melanesia it is not the islands, but the people, that are black.

French Polynesia and the Cook Islands are

highly urbanized, and the rapid growth of Papeete has led to unemployment and social problems such as alcoholism, petty crime, and domestic violence. Cook Islanders migrate to New Zealand, people from the Australs, Tuamotus, and Marquesas to Tahiti, and Tahitians to New Caledonia, creating the problem of idled land and abandoned homes. In the Cook Islands far more islanders now live off their home islands than on them. Yet the region's charming, gentle, graceful peoples remain high among its attractions.

THE POLYNESIANS

The Polynesians, whom Robert Louis Stevenson called "God's best, at least God's sweetest work," are a tall, golden-skinned people with straight or wavy, but rarely fuzzy, hair. They have fine features, almost intimidating physiques, and a soft, flowing language. One theory holds that the Polynesians evolved their great bodily stature through a selective process on their long ocean voyages, as the larger individuals with more body fat were better able to resist the chill of evaporating sea spray on their bodies (polar animals are generally larger than equatorial animals of the same species for the same reason).

Other authorities ascribe their huge body size to a high-carbohydrate vegetable diet.

The ancient Polynesians developed a rigid social system with hereditary chiefs; descent was usually through the father. In most of Polynesia there were only two classes, chiefs and commoners, but in the Hawaiian islands, Tahiti, and Tonga an intermediate class existed. Slaves were outside the class system entirely, but slavery was practiced only in New Zealand, the Cook Islands, and Mangareva. People lived in scattered dwellings rather than villages, although there were groupings around the major temples and chiefs' residences. Their economy centered on fishing and agriculture. Land was collectively owned by families and tribes. Though the land was worked collectively by commoners, the chiefly families controlled and distributed its produce by well-defined customs. Large numbers of people could be mobilized for public works or war.

Two related forces governed Polynesian life: mana and *tapu*. Our word "taboo" originated from the Polynesian *tapu*. Numerous taboos regulated Polynesian life, such as prohibitions against taking certain plants or fish that were intended for chiefly use. Mana was a spiritual power—gods and high chiefs had the most and commoners had the least. Early missionaries would often publicly violate the taboos and smash the images of the gods to show that their mana had vanished.

Gods

The Polynesians worshiped a pantheon of gods, who had more mana than any human. The most important were Tangaroa (the creator and god of the oceans), and Oro, or Tu (the god of war), who demanded human sacrifices. The most fascinating figure in Polynesian mythology was Maui, a Krishna- or Prometheus-like figure who caught the sun with a cord to give its fire to the world. He lifted the firmament to prevent it from crushing mankind, fished the islands out of the ocean with a hook, and was killed trying to gain the prize of immortality for humanity. Also worth noting is Hina, the heroine who fled to the moon to avoid incest with her brother and so that the sound of her tapa beater wouldn't bother anyone. Tane (the god of light) and Rongo (the god of agriculture and peace) were other important gods. This polytheism, which may have disseminated from Raiatea in the Society Islands, was most important in Eastern Polynesia. The *Arioi* confraternity, centered in Raiatea and thought to be possessed by the gods, traveled about putting on dramatic representations of the myths.

The Eastern Polynesians were enthusiastic temple builders, evidenced today by widespread ruins. Known by the Polynesian names *marae, me'ae*, or *ahu*, these platform and courtyard structures of coral and basalt blocks often had low surrounding walls and internal arrangements of upright wooden slabs. Once temples for religious cults, they were used for seating the gods and for presenting fruits and other foods to them at ritual feasts. Sometimes, but rarely, human sacrifices took place on the *marae*. Religion in Western Polynesia was very low-key, with few priests or cult images. No temples have been found in Tonga and very few in Samoa. The gods of Eastern Polynesia were represented in human form. The ancestors were more important as a source of descent for social ranking, and genealogies were carefully preserved. Surviving elements of the old religion are the still-widespread belief in spirits *(aitu)*, the continuing use of traditional medicine, and the influence of myth. More than 150 years after conversion by early missionaries, most Polynesians maintain their early Christian piety and fervid devotion.

Art

The Polynesians used no masks and few colors, usually leaving their works unpainted. Art forms were very traditional, and there was a defined class of artists producing works of remarkable delicacy and deftness. Three of the five great archaeological sites of Oceania are in Polynesia: Easter Island, Huahine, and Tongatapu (the other two are Pohnpei and Kosrae in Micronesia).

RELIGION

Religion plays an important role in the lives of the Pacific islanders, holding communities together

TAHITI IN LITERATURE

Through the years European writers have traveled to Polynesia in search of Bougainville's Nouvelle Cythère or Rousseau's noble savage. Brought to the stage and silver screen, their stories entered the popular imagination alongside Gauguin's rich images, creating the romantic myth of the South Seas paradise now cultivated by the travel industry. An enjoyable way to get a feel for the region is to read a couple of the books mentioned below before you come.

Herman Melville, author of the whaling classic *Moby Dick* (1851), deserted his New Bedford whaler at Nuku Hiva in 1842 and *Typee* (1846) describes his experiences there. An Australian whaling ship carried Melville on to Tahiti, but he joined a mutiny on board, which landed him in the Papeete *calabooza* (prison). His second Polynesian book, *Omoo* (1847), was a result. In both, Melville decries the ruin of Polynesian culture by Western influence.

Pierre Loti's *The Marriage of Loti* (1880) is a sentimental tale of the love of a young French midshipman for a Polynesian girl named Rarahu. Loti's naiveté is rather absurd, but his friendship with Queen Pomare IV and his fine imagery make the book worth reading. Loti's writings moved Paul Gauguin to come to Tahiti.

In 1888–1890 Robert Louis Stevenson, famous author of *Treasure Island* and *Kidnapped*, cruised the Pacific in his schooner, the *Casco*. His book *In the South Seas* describes his visits to the Marquesas and Tuamotus. Stevenson settled at Tautira on Tahiti-iti for a time, but he eventually retired at Apia in Samoa, which offered the author better mail service. In 1890 Stevenson and his family bought a large tract of land just outside Apia and built a large, framed house he called Vailima. In 1894 he was buried on Mt. Vaea, just above his home.

Jack London and his wife Charmian cruised the Pacific aboard their yacht, the *Snark*, in 1907–1909. A longtime admirer of Melville, London found only a wretched swamp at Taipivai in the Marquesas. His *South Sea Tales* (1911) was the first of the 10 books that he wrote on the Pacific. London's story "The House of Mapuhi," about a Jewish pearl buyer, earned him a costly lawsuit. London was a

product of his time, and the modern reader is often shocked by his insensitive portrayal of the islanders.

In 1913–1914 the youthful poet Rupert Brooke visited Tahiti, where he fell in love with Mamua, a girl from Mataiea whom he immortalized in his poem *Tiare Tahiti*. Later Brooke fought in World War I and wrote five famous war sonnets. He died of blood poisoning on a French hospital ship in the Mediterranean in 1915.

W. Somerset Maugham toured Polynesia in 1916–1917 to research his novel, *The Moon and Sixpence* (1919), a fictional life of Paul Gauguin. Maugham's *A Writer's Notebook*, published in 1984, 19 years after his death, describes his travels in the Pacific. On Tahiti Maugham discovered not only material for his books but by chance found a glass door pane with a female figure painted by Gauguin himself, which he bought for 200 francs. In 1962 it sold at Sotheby's in London for $37,400.

American writers Charles Nordhoff and James Norman Hall came to Tahiti after World War I, married Tahitian women, and collaborated on 11 books. Their most famous was the *Bounty Trilogy* (1934), which tells of Fletcher Christian's *Mutiny on the Bounty*, the escape to Dutch Timor of Captain Bligh and his crew in *Men against the Sea*, and the mutineer's fate in *Pitcairn's Island*. Three generations of filmmakers have selected this saga as their way of presenting paradise.

Hall remained on Tahiti until his death in 1951 and he was buried on the hill behind his home at Arue. His last book, *The Forgotten One*, is a collection of true stories about expatriate intellectuals and writers lost in the South Seas. Hall's account of the 28-year correspondence with his American friend Robert Dean Frisbie, who settled on Pukapuka in the Cook Islands during the 1920s, is touching.

James A. Michener joined the U.S. Navy in 1942 and ended up visiting around 50 South Sea islands, among them Bora Bora. His *Tales of the South Pacific* (1947) tells of the impact of World War II on the South Pacific and the Pacific's impact on those who served. It was later made into the long-running Broadway musical, *South Pacific*. Michener's *Return to Paradise* (1951) is a readable collection of essays and short stories.

INTRODUCTION

and defending moral values. No other non-European region of the world is as solidly Christian as the South Pacific, and the South Pacific is one of the few areas of the world with a large surplus of ministers of religion. The first missionaries to arrive were Protestants, and the Catholic fathers who landed almost 40 years later had to rely on French military backing to establish missions in Tahiti and the Marquesas. Thus the established Protestant denominations are progeny of the London Missionary Society, the Evangelicals of French Polynesia, and the Cook Islands Christian Church. On Easter Island, Catholicism predominates.

Since the 1960s, the old rivalry between Protestant and Catholic has been largely replaced by an avalanche of well-financed American fundamentalist missionary groups that divide families and spread confusion in an area already strongly Christian. While the indigenous churches have long been localized, the new evangelical sects are dominated by foreign personnel, ideas, and money. The ultraconservative outlook of the new religious imperialists continues the tradition of allying Christianity with colonialism or neocolonialism.

Of course, the optimum way to experience religion in the South Pacific is to go to church on Sunday. Just be aware that the services can last 1.5 hours and will usually be in the Polynesian tongue, French, or Spanish. If you decide to go, don't get up and walk out in the middle—see it through. You'll be rewarded by the joyous singing and fellowship, and you'll encounter the islanders on a different level. After church, people gather for a family meal or picnic and spend the rest of the day relaxing and socializing. If you're a guest in an island home you'll be invited to accompany them to church.

The Mormons

Mormon missionaries arrived on Tubuai in the Austral Islands as early as 1844, and today "Mormonia" covers much of the South Pacific. According to the Book of Mormon, American Indians are descendants of the 10 lost tribes of Israel and to hasten the second coming of Christ, they must be reconverted. Like Thor Heyerdahl, Mormons believe American Indians settled Polynesia, so the present church is willing to spend a

lot of time and money spreading the word. The pairs of clean-cut young Mormon "elders" seen on the outliers, each in shirt and tie, riding a bicycle or driving a minibus, are sent down from the States for two-year stays.

You don't have to travel far in the South Pacific to find the assembly-line Mormon chapels, schools, and sporting facilities, paid for by church members who are expected to contribute 10 percent of their incomes. The Mormon church spends more than US$500 million a year on foreign missions and sends out almost 50,000 missionaries, more than any other American church by far. Mormon fascination with genealogy parallels the importance of descent in Polynesian society, where it often determines land rights. There's a strong link to Hawaii's Brigham Young University, and many island students help pay for their schooling by representing their home country at the Mormon-owned Polynesian Cultural Center on O'ahu. In Melanesia, Mormon missionary activity is a recent phenomenon, as before a "revelation" in 1978, blacks were barred from the Mormon priesthood.

Other Religious Groups

More numerous than the Mormons are adherents of the Seventh-Day Adventist Church, a politically ultraconservative group that grew out of the 19th-century American Baptist movement. This is the largest nonhistorical religious group in the South Pacific, with a large following in French Polynesia. The SDA Church teaches the imminent return of Christ, and Saturday (rather than Sunday) is observed as the Sabbath. SDAs regard the human body as the temple of the Holy Spirit, thus much attention is paid to health matters. Members are forbidden to partake of certain foods, alcohol, drugs, and tobacco, and the church expends considerable energy on the provision of medical and dental services. They're also active in education and local economic development. Like many of the fundamentalist sects, the SDAs tend to completely obliterate traditional cultures.

The Assemblies of God (AOG) is a Pentecostal sect founded in Arkansas in 1914 and at present headquartered in Springfield, Missouri. Although the AOG carries out some relief work, it opposes social reform in the belief that only God can solve humanity's problems. Disgraced American televangelists Jimmy Swaggart and Jim Bakker were both former AOG ministers.

The Jehovah's Witnesses originated in 19th-century America and since 1909 their headquarters has been in Brooklyn, from whence their worldwide operations are financed. Jehovah's Witnesses' teachings against military service and blood transfusions have often brought them into conflict with governments, and they in turn regard other churches, especially the Catholic Church, as instruments of the Devil. Members must spread the word by canvassing their neighborhoods door-to-door, or by standing on street corners offering copies of *The Watchtower.* This group focuses mostly on Christ's return, and since "the end of time" is fast approaching, it has little interest in relief work. They're numerous in French Polynesia.

> *If things work differently than they do back home, give thanks—that's why you've come. Take an interest in local customs, values, languages, challenges, and successes.*

LANGUAGE

About 1,200 languages, a third of the world's total, are spoken in the Pacific islands, though most have very few speakers. The Austronesian language family includes more than 900 distinct languages spoken in an area stretching from Madagascar to Easter Island. The Polynesians speak about 21 closely related languages with local variations and consonantal changes. They're mutually unintelligible to those who haven't learned them, although they have many words in common. For instance, the word for land varies between *whenua, fenua, fanua, fonua, honua, vanua,* and *henua.* In the Polynesian languages the words are softened by the removal of certain consonants. Thus the Tagalog word for coconut, *niog,* became *niu, ni,* or *nu.* They're musical languages whose accent lies mostly on the vowels. Polynesian is rhetorical and poetical but not scientific, and to adapt to modern life many words have been borrowed from European languages; these too are infused with vowels to make them more melodious to the Polynesian ear. Thus in Tahitian governor becomes *tavana* and frying pan *faraipani.* Special vocabularies used to refer to or address royalty or the aristocracy also exist.

Conduct and Customs

Foreign travel is an exceptional experience enjoyed by a privileged few. Too often, tourists try to transfer their lifestyles to tropical islands, thereby missing out on what is unique to the region. Travel can be a learning experience if approached openly and with a positive attitude, so read up on the local culture before you arrive and become aware of the social and environmental problems of the area. A wise traveler soon graduates from hearing and seeing to listening and observing. Speaking is good for the ego and listening is good for the soul.

The path is primed with packaged pleasures, but pierce the bubble of tourism and you'll encounter something far from the schedules and organized efficiency: a time to learn how other people live. Walk gently, for human qualities are as fragile and responsive to abuse as the brilliant reefs. The islanders are by nature soft-spoken and reserved. Often they won't show open disapproval if their social codes are broken, but don't underestimate them: they understand far more than you think. Consider that you're only one of thousands of visitors to their islands, so don't expect to be treated better than anyone else. Respect is one of the most important things in life and humility is also greatly appreciated.

Don't try for a bargain if it means someone will be exploited. What enriches you may violate others. Be sensitive to the feelings of those you wish to "shoot" with your camera and ask their permission first. Don't promise things you can't or won't deliver. Keep your time values to yourself; the islanders lead an unstressful lifestyle and assume you are there to share it.

If you're alone you're lucky, for the single traveler is everyone's friend. Get away from other tourists and meet the people. There aren't many places on earth where you can still do this meaningfully, but the South Pacific is one. If you do meet people with similar interests, keep in touch by writing. This is no tourist's paradise, though, and local residents are not exhibits or paid performers. They have just as many problems as you, and if you see them as real people you're less likely to be viewed as a stereotypical tourist. You may have come to escape civilization, but keep in mind that you're just a guest.

Most important of all, try to see things their way. Take an interest in local customs, values, languages, challenges, and successes. If things work differently than they do back home, give thanks—that's why you've come. Reflect on what you've experienced and you'll return home with a better understanding of how much we all have in common, outwardly different as we may seem. Do that and your trip won't have been wasted.

Women

In many traditional island cultures a woman seen wandering aimlessly along a remote beach was thought to be in search of male companionship, and "no" meant "yes." Single women hiking, camping, sunbathing, and simply traveling alone may be seen in the same light, an impression strongly reinforced by the type of videos available in the islands. In some cultures local women rarely travel without men, and some day hikes, excursions, and interisland ship journeys men-

tioned in this book may be uncomfortable or even dangerous for women who are unprepared. Two women together will have less to worry about in most cases, especially if they're well covered and look purposeful.

Women traveling alone should avoid staying in isolated tourist bungalows by themselves—it's wise to team up with other travelers before heading to the outer islands. In many Polynesian cultures there's a custom known as "sleep crawling," in which a boy silently enters a girl's home at night and lies beside her to prove his bravery. Visiting women sometimes become objects of this type of unwanted attention, even in well-known resorts such as Bora Bora and Moorea.

Children

Karen Addison of Sussex, England, sent me the following:

Traveling with children can have its ups and downs, but in the Pacific it's definitely an up. Pacific islanders are warm, friendly people, but with children you see them at their best. Your children are automatically accepted, and you, as an extension of them, are as well. As the majority of the islands are free of any deadly bugs or diseases, acclimatizing to the water, food, and climate would be your paramount concern. Self-contained units, where you can do your own cooking, are easy to find and cheap; having set meals every day gives children a sense of security. Not having television as a distraction, I've attempted to teach my son the rudiments of reading and writing. As a single mother with a little boy, traveling with him opened my eyes to things I'd normally overlook and has been an education to us both.

Exploring the Islands

Eastern Polynesia embraces a vast ocean area strewn with islands. Largest of the lot is **Tahiti,** anchor of the **Society Islands** chain and starting point for most visits to French Polynesia. A ride around Tahiti is recommended for its diverse scenery and historical mementos. Conveniently nearby is **Moorea,** a favorite of beach people, aquatic enthusiasts, and hikers. Moorea offers the best selection of accommodations of any island in the territory. More of the same is found on **Huahine,** where one of Polynesia's largest archaeological areas beckons. Huahine is Moorea without the crowds; neighboring Raiatea and Taha'a are where the locals live. Just northwest is legendary **Bora Bora,** a chic resort with a sheer volcanic plug surrounded by a brilliant lagoon. In the past decade tourism has proliferated on Bora Bora. To see a comparable isle still untouched by high-power developments one must travel farther west to **Maupiti.**

The second-most visited island chain of French Polynesia is the **Tuamotu Islands,** where Rangiroa, Tikehau, Manihi, and Fakarava all bear shiny new resorts. The other 74 Tuamotu atolls are largely undeveloped, although many have regular air service and family-operated pensions. **Rangiroa** is world-renowned for the tidal-drift diving through its passes. The marinelife here is spectacular, though arguably that at unfamed **Fakarava** is even better. The Tuamotus are mostly for the scuba diver or ardent beachcomber and sight-seeing possibilities above the waterline are limited.

© M.G.L.DOMENY DE RIENZI

The remote **Marquesas Islands** group has much to offer but high travel costs discourage most potential visitors. The freighter *Aranui* cruises the Marquesas 16 times a year, the easiest way to go. Islands such as **Nuku Hiva** and **Hiva Oa** harbor many archaeological and scenic wonders, plus a reasonable choice of accommodations. The path of packaged tourism still hasn't crossed Ua Pou, Ua Huka, Tahuata, and Fatu Hiva, true islands of adventure. The same applies to the unvisited **Austral Islands,** where whale-watching has recently been promoted at **Rurutu.**

Far to the southeast lies lonely **Easter Island,** one of the world's top sights. It's difficult to overstate the allure of this mysterious island with its hundreds of striking archaeological remains, wild nature, and fascinating culture. The coastal hiking here is among the best in the South Pacific. Easter Island can be included in round-the-world tickets via South America or visited as a side trip from Tahiti. It's an unforgettable experience.

If the high prices of French Polynesia are a deterrent, the **Cook Islands** offer a similar environment at half the price. **Rarotonga** resembles Moorea on a smaller scale, with more budget places to stay and fewer flashy resorts. "Raro" abounds in entertainment possibilities and things

> *Far to the southeast lies lonely Easter Island, one of the world's top sights. It's difficult to overstate the allure of this mysterious island with its hundreds of striking archaeological remains, wild nature, and fascinating culture.*

to do—a great choice for the active traveler. The second-most visited of the Cooks is **Aitutaki,** where the accommodations and snorkeling are quite good. Outer islands such as Atiu, Mauke, and Mangaia receive far fewer visitors but they do have tolerable facilities and are ideal for the intrepid.

Suggested Itineraries

Easter Island and the Cook Islands are fairly straightforward as far as itineraries go. A week is enough time to see all the main sights of Easter Island. Five busy days would also suffice, but three days are not enough. Almost all visitors to the Cook Islands arrive on Rarotonga and a week is adequate there. Another two or three days could be spent on Aitutaki or on any of the other islands of the Southern Group.

French Polynesia offers greater choice. If you have only **one week** or less, Tahiti and Moorea will keep you busy. Throw in Bora Bora if your budget is rather generous. Those with **two weeks** could include Huahine, Raiatea, and Bora Bora in their trips. Visitors with **three weeks** can do all of the above, plus the Tuamotus or Marquesas. Those with **one month** in French Polynesia could visit all five archipelagoes with the help of an Air Tahiti air pass.

Sports and Recreation

Scuba Diving

Scuba diving is offered in resort areas throughout Polynesia. Commercial scuba operators know their waters and will be able to show you the most amazing things in perfect safety. Dive centers on Aitutaki, Bora Bora, Easter Island, Fakarava, Huahine, Manihi, Moorea, Nuku Hiva, Raiatea, Rangiroa, Rarotonga, Tahiti, and Tikehau operate year-round, with marinelife most profuse July to November. Before strapping on a tank and fins you'll have to show your scuba certification card, and occasionally divers are also

asked to present a medical report from their doctors indicating that they are in good physical condition. The waters are warm, varying less than 1°C between the surface and 100 meters, so a wetsuit is not essential (although it will protect you from coral cuts). Some dive shops tack on an extra US$10 or more for "equipment rental" (regulator, buoyancy compensator, and gauges) and serious divers will want to bring their own gear.

Many of the scuba operators listed in this book offer introductory "resort courses" to those

10 SAFETY RULES OF DIVING

1. The most important rule in scuba diving is to BREATHE CONTINUOUSLY. If you establish this rule, you won't forget and hold your breath, and overexpansion will never occur.

2. COME UP AT A RATE OF 18 METERS PER MINUTE OR LESS. This allows the gas dissolved in your body under pressure to come out of solution safely and also prevents vertigo from fast ascents. Always make a precautionary decompression stop at a depth of five meters.

3. NEVER ESCAPE TO THE SURFACE. Panic is the diver's worst enemy.

4. STOP, THINK, THEN ACT. Always maintain control.

5. PACE YOURSELF. KNOW YOUR LIMITATIONS. A DIVER SHOULD ALWAYS BE ABLE TO REST AND RELAX IN THE WATER. Proper use of the buoyancy vest will allow you to rest on the surface and maintain control under water. A diver who becomes fatigued in the water is a danger to oneself and one's buddy.

6. NEVER DIVE WITH A COLD. Avoid alcoholic beverages but drink plenty of water. Get a good night's sleep and refrain from strenuous physical activities on the day you dive. Dive conservatively if you are overweight or more than 45 years of age. Make fewer dives the last two days before flying and no dives at all during the final 24 hours.

7. PLAN YOUR DIVE. Know your starting point, your diving area, and your exit areas. DIVE YOUR PLAN.

8. NEVER EXCEED THE SAFE SPORT-DIVING LIMIT OF 30 METERS. Make your first dive the deepest of the day.

9. All equipment must be equipped with QUICK RELEASES.

10. WEAR ADEQUATE PROTECTIVE CLOTHING AGAINST SUN AND CORAL.

who want only a taste of scuba diving, and most also give full CMAS, NAUI, or PADI open-water certification courses to those intending to dive more than once or twice. Scuba training will enhance your understanding and enjoyment of the sea. Lagoon diving is recommended for beginners; those with some experience will find that the reef drop-offs and passes into the lagoons nurture the most marinelife. Precise information on scuba diving is provided throughout this handbook, immediately after the sight-seeing sections.

It should be noted here that the feeding of sharks, rays, eels, and other fish as widely practiced in French Polynesia is a highly controversial activity. Supplying food to wild creatures of any kind destroys their natural feeding habits and makes them vulnerable to human predators, and handling marinelife can have unpredictable consequences. More study is required to determine whether shark feeding by tourism operators tends to attract sharks to lagoons and beaches used for public recreation. Some scuba operators forgo the easy profits to be made through shark or ray feeding and take their clients to places where things are still entirely natural. If this issue concerns you, avoid dive shops that promote fish feeding and direct your business to those whose first priority is protecting the natural environment.

Snorkeling

Even if you aren't willing to put the necessary money and effort into scuba diving, you should investigate the many snorkeling possibilities. Snorkeling is free—all you need is a mask and pipe. A few scuba operators will take snorkelers out on their regular trips for a third to a quarter of the cost of diving. This is an easy way to reach some good snorkeling spots; just don't expect to be chaperoned for that price.

Take care when snorkeling and know the dangers. Practice on a shallow sandy bottom and don't head into deep water or swim over coral until you're sure you've got the hang of it. Breathe easily; don't hyperventilate. When snorkeling on a fringing reef, beware of deadly currents and undertows in channels that drain tidal flows. Observe the direction the water is flowing before you swim into it. If you feel yourself being dragged out to sea through a reef passage, try swimming across the current rather than against it. If you can't resist the pull at all, it may be better to let yourself be carried out. Wait till the current diminishes, then swim along the outer reef face until you find somewhere to come back in. Or use your energy to attract the attention of someone onshore.

Snorkeling on the outer edge or drop-off of a reef is thrilling for the variety of fish and corals, but attempt it only on a very calm day. Even then it's wise to have someone standing onshore or paddling behind you in a canoe to watch for occasional big waves, which can take you by surprise and smash you into the rocks. Also, beware of unperceived currents outside the reef—you may not get a second chance.

A far better idea is to limit your snorkeling to the protected inner reef and leave the open waters to the scuba diver. You'll encounter the brightest colors in shallow waters anyway, as beneath six meters the colors blue out as short wavelengths are lost. Scuba divers using tanks trade off the chance to observe shallow-water species to gain access to the often larger deep-water species. The best solution is to do a bit of both. In any case, avoid touching the reef or any of its creatures as the contact can be very harmful to both you and the reef. Take only pictures and leave only bubbles.

Surfing

Polynesia's greatest gift to the world of sport is surfing. In 1771, Captain Cook saw Tahitians surfing in a canoe; board surfing was first observed off Hawai'i in 1779. Surfing was revived at Waikiki, Hawai'i, at the beginning of the 20th century and it's now the most popular sport among young Tahitians.

Famous surfing spots include Tahiti's Papara Beach and Teahupoo, Huahine's Fare Reef, and Easter Island. The top surfing season is generally July to September, when the trade winds push the Antarctic swells north. During the hurricane season from January to March tropical storms can generate some spectacular waves. Prime locales for windsurfing include Rarotonga's Muri Lagoon and many others.

Hiking

This is an excellent, inexpensive way to see the islands. A few of the outstanding treks covered in this handbook are Mt. Aorai on Tahiti, Vaiare to Paopao on Moorea, and the Cross-island Track on Rarotonga. There are many others. Easter Island and the Marquesas have excellent hiking.

Ocean Kayaking

This sport is best practiced in sheltered lagoons, such as those of Raiatea/Taha'a, Bora Bora, and Aitutaki. You can rent kayaks in some places, but it's better to bring your own folding kayak. (See Getting Around, later in this chapter, for more information on kayaking.)

Yachting

Cruising the South Pacific by yacht is covered in Getting There, and for those with less time there are several established yacht charter operations based at Raiatea. (See Yacht Tours and Charters in Getting There for more information.)

Fishing

Sportfishing is a questionable activity—especially spearfishing, which is sort of like shooting a cow with a handgun. An islander who spearfishes to feed his family is one thing, but the tourist who does it for fun is perhaps worthy of the attention of sharks. Deep-sea game fishing from gas-guzzling powerboats isn't much better, and it's painful to see a noble fish slaughtered and strung up just to inflate someone's ego. That said, one has to admit that taking fish from the sea one by one for sport is never going to endanger the stocks the way net fishing by huge trawlers does. On most big-game boats, the captain keeps the catch. Sportfishing is covered throughout this handbook.

Golf

The former New Zealand administrators left behind several golf courses in the Cook Islands, and major international competitions are held at Tahiti's Olivier Breaud Golf Course. Greens fees vary considerably, from US$45 at the Olivier Breaud to US$8 at the Rarotonga Golf Club. Club and cart rentals are usually available for a bit less than the greens fees and all of the courses have clubhouses with pleasant colonial-style bars.

More Information

Package tours incorporating the activities just mentioned are described under Getting There in this chapter. Turn to Getting Around for information on bicycling.

Entertainment and Events

Many big hotels run "island nights," or feasts where you get to taste the local food and see traditional dancing. If you don't wish to splurge on the meal it's sometimes possible to witness the spectacle from the bar for the price of a drink or a cover charge. These events are held weekly on certain days, so ask. On most islands Friday night is the time to let it all hang out; on Saturday many people are preparing for a family get-together or church on Sunday.

Music and Dance

Traditional music and dance is alive and well in the South Pacific, especially the exciting *tamure* dancing of French Polynesia and the Cook Islands. The slit-log gong beaten with a wooden stick is now a common instrument throughout Polynesia, even though the Eastern Polynesians originally had skin drums. The *to'ere* slit drum was introduced to Tahiti from Western Polynesia only after 1915, and it's marvelous the way the Tahitians have made it their own.

In the early 19th century, missionaries replaced the old chants of Polynesia with the harmonious gospel singing heard in the islands today, yet even the hymns were transformed into an original Oceanic medium. Contemporary Pacific music includes bamboo bands, brass bands, and localized Anglo-American pop. String bands have made European instruments such as the guitar and ukulele an integral part of Pacific music.

Holidays and Festivals

The special events of French Polynesia, Easter Island, and the Cook Islands are described in the respective chapters. Their dates often vary from year to year, so it's good to contact the local tourist information office soon after your arrival to learn just what will be happening during your stay.

The most important annual festivals are the Tapati Rapa Nui festival on Easter Island (late January or early February), the Heiva i Tahiti at Papeete and Bora Bora (first two weeks of July), and the Te Maeva Celebrations on Rarotonga (late July and early August). Since 1987 a Marquesas Islands Festival has been held about every four years. Catch as many as of these you can and try to participate in what's happening, rather than merely watching like a tourist.

INTRODUCTION

TAHITIAN DANCE MOVEMENTS

anuanua
rainbow

ao
day

here
to love

maeva
welcome

mana'o
to think

marama
moon

ori
to walk

LOUISE FOOTE

INTRODUCTION

Arts and Crafts

Some of the finest wood carving is from the Marquesas and Easter Island. However, the traditional handicrafts that have survived best are the practical arts done by women (weaving, basket-making, pareu painting). In cases where the items still perform their original function, they remain as vital as ever. Contemporary Tahitian pareu designs reflect the esthetic judgments of the lost art of tapa making. Among the European-derived items are the patchwork quilts *(tifaifai)* of Tahiti and the Cooks.

Whenever possible buy handicrafts from local women's committee shops, church groups, local markets, or from the craftspeople themselves, but avoid objects made from turtle shell/leather, clam shell, or marine mammal ivory, which are prohibited entry into many countries under endangered species acts. Failure to declare such items to customs officers can lead to heavy fines.

Also resist the temptation to buy jewelry or other items made from seashells and coral, the collection of which damages the reefs. Souvenirs made from straw or seeds may be held for fumigation or confiscated upon arrival.

Weaving

Woven articles are the most widespread handicrafts. Pandanus fiber is the most common, but coconut leaf and husk, vine tendril, banana stem, tree and shrub bark, and the stems and leaves of water weeds are all used. On some islands the fibers are passed through a fire, boiled, then bleached in the sun. Vegetable dyes of very lovely mellow tones are sometimes used, but gaudier store dyes are much more prevalent. Shells are occasionally used to cut, curl, or make the fibers pliable. Polynesian woven arts are characterized by colorful, skillful patterns.

Accommodations

Hotels

With *Moon Handbooks Tahiti* in hand you're guaranteed a good, inexpensive place to stay on each island. Every hotel in the region is included herein, not just a selection. We consistently do this to give you a solid second reference in case your travel agent or someone else recommends a certain place. To allow you the widest possible choice, all price categories are included, and throughout we've tried to indicate which properties offer value for money. If you think we're wrong or you were badly treated, be sure to send us a report. Equally important, let us know when you agree with what's here or if you think a place deserves a better rave. Your letter will have an impact!

We don't solicit freebies from the hotel chains; our only income derives from the price you paid for this book. So we don't mind telling you that, as usual, most of the luxury hotels are just not worth the exorbitant prices they charge. Many simply recreate Hawaii at sev-

eral times the cost, offering far more luxury than you need. Even worse, they tend to isolate you in a French/American/Kiwi environment, away from the South Pacific you came to experience. The flashy resorts are worth visiting as sight-seeing attractions, watering holes, or sources of entertainment, but unless you're a millionaire sleep elsewhere. There are always middle-level hotels that charge half what the top-end places want while providing adequate comfort. And if you really *can* afford US$600 a night and up, you might do better chartering a skippered or bareboat yacht!

In French Polynesia there's a **bed-and-breakfast** *(logement chez l'habitant)* **program** in which you pay a set fee to stay in the home of a local family or in a separate bungalow in the yard. Meals may not be included in the price, but they're often available, tending toward your host family's fare of seafood and native vegetables. In the Cook Islands, family-operated motels abound.

Dormitory or backpacker accommodations

ACCOMMODATIONS PRICE RANGES

Throughout this handbook, accommodations are generally grouped in the price categories that follow, based on room prices only and excluding tax. In French Polynesia many pensions have compulsory meal plans, and at these the food portion has been valued at CFP 5,000/7,000 for half/full board in a double.

Under US$25
US$25–50
US$50–100
US$100–150
US$150–250
US$250 and up

arc available on all of the main islands, with communal cooking facilities usually provided. If you're traveling alone these are excellent since they're just the place to meet other travelers. Couples can usually get a double room for a price only slightly above two dorm beds. For the most part, the dormitories are safe and congenial for those who don't mind sacrificing their privacy to save money.

There are organized **campgrounds** in French Polynesia and on Easter Island, but camping is forbidden in the Cook Islands. Make sure your tent is water- and mosquito-proof, and try to find a spot swept by the trades. Never camp under a coconut tree, as falling coconuts hurt (actually, coconuts have two eyes so they strike onlythe wicked). If you hear a hurricane warning, roll up your tent and take immediate cover with the locals.

Be aware that some of the low-budget places included in this book are a lot more basic than what is sometimes referred to as "budget" accommodations in the States. The standards of cleanliness in the common bathrooms may be lower than you expected, the furnishings "early attic," the beds uncomfortable, linens and towels skimpy, housekeeping nonexistent, and window screens lacking. Don't expect Sheraton service at motel prices.

A room with cooking facilities can save you a

lot on restaurant meals, and some moderately priced establishments have weekly rates. If you have to choose a meal plan, take only breakfast and dinner (Modified American Plan or *demi-pension*) and have fruit for lunch. As you check into your room, note the nearest fire exits. And don't automatically take the first room offered; if you're paying good money look at several, then choose. Single women intending to stay in isolated tourist bungalows should try to find someone with whom to share.

When choosing a hotel, bear in mind that although a thatched bungalow may be cooler and infinitely more attractive than a concrete box, it's also more likely to have insect problems. If in doubt check the window screens and carry mosquito coils and/or repellent. If you're lucky there'll be a resident lizard or two to eat the bugs. Always turn on a light before getting out of bed to use the facilities at night, as even the finest hotels in the tropics have cockroaches.

Needless to say, always ask the price of your accommodations before accepting them. In cases where there's a local and a tourist price, you'll pay the higher tariff if you don't check beforehand. Hotel prices are usually fixed and bargaining isn't the normal way to go in this part of the world.

Reserving Rooms

Booking accommodations from abroad often works to your disadvantage as full-service travel agents will begin by trying to sell you their most expensive properties (which pay them the highest commissions) and work down from there. The quite adequate middle and budget places included in this handbook often aren't on their screens or are sold at highly inflated prices. Herein we provide the rates for direct local bookings, and if you book through a travel agent abroad you could end up paying considerably more as multiple commissions are tacked on. Nowadays the Internet has made booking direct infinitely easier. Many hotels now accept Web and email bookings at normal or even reduced rates.

Although it's usually not to your advantage to reserve rooms in the medium to lower price range, you can sometimes obtain substantial discounts at the luxury hotels by including them as part of a package tour. If you intend to spend most of your time at a specific first-class hotel, you'll benefit from bulk rates by taking a package tour instead of paying the higher "rack rate" the hotels charge to individuals who just walk in off the street. Check the Getting There section of this book for agents specializing in package tours.

Food

The traditional diet of the Pacific islanders consists of root crops and fruit, plus lagoon fish and the occasional pig. The vegetables include taro, yams, cassava (manioc), breadfruit, and sweet potatoes. The sweet potato is something of an anomaly—it's the only Pacific food plant with a South American origin. How it got to the islands is not known.

Taro is an elephant-eared plant cultivated in freshwater swamps. Papaya (pawpaw) is nourishing: a third of a cup contains as much vitamin C as 18 apples. To ripen a green papaya overnight, puncture it a few times with a knife. Don't overeat papaya—unless you *need* an effective laxative.

Raw fish (*poisson cru* or *sashimi*) is an appetizing dish enjoyed in many Pacific countries. To prepare it, clean and skin the fish, then dice the fillet. Squeeze lemon or lime juice over it, and store in a cool place about 10 hours. When it's ready to serve, add chopped onions, garlic, green peppers, tomatoes, and coconut cream to taste. Local fishmongers know which species make the best raw fish, but know what you're doing before you join them—island stomachs are probably stronger than yours. Cautious health experts recommend eating only well-cooked foods and peeling your own fruit, but the islanders swear by raw fish.

Cooking

The ancient Polynesians lost the art of pottery making more than a millennium ago and in-

THE COCONUT PALM

Human life would not be possible on most of the Pacific's far-flung atolls without this all-purpose tree. It reaches maturity in eight years, and then produces about 50 nuts a year for 60 years (the 29-cm-wide metal bands around the trunk are for protection against rats). Aside from the tree's esthetic value and usefulness in providing shade, the water of the green coconut provides a refreshing drink, and the white meat of the young nut is a delicious food. The harder meat of more mature nuts is grated and squeezed, which creates a coconut cream that is used as a sauce in cooking.

The oldest nuts are cracked open and the hard meat removed and then dried to be sold as copra. It takes about 6,000 coconuts to make a ton of copra. Schooners collect bags of copra, which they carry to a mill beside the interisland wharf at Papeete. Here the copra is pressed into the coconut oil used in making vegetable oil, margarine, candles, soap, cosmetics, etc. Scented with flowers, the oil nurtures the skin. The world price for copra has been de-

pressed for years, so the government wisely pays a subsidy (more than twice the actual price) to producers to keep them gainfully employed on their home islands.

The juice or sap from the cut flower spathes of the palm provides toddy, a popular drink; the toddy is distilled into a spirit called arrack, the whiskey of the Pacific. Otherwise the sap can be boiled to make candy. Millionaire's salad is made by shredding the growth cut from the heart of the tree. For each salad, a fully mature tree must be sacrificed.

The nut's hard inner shell can be used as a cup and makes excellent firewood. Rope, cordage, brushes, and heavy matting are produced from the coir fiber of the husk. The smoke from burning husks is a most effective mosquito repellent. The leaves of the coconut tree are used to thatch the roofs of the islanders' cottages or are woven into baskets, mats, and fans. The trunk provides timber for building and furniture. Actually, these are only the common uses: there are many others as well.

stead developed an ingenious way of cooking in an underground earth oven known as an *ahimaa*. First a stack of dry coconut husks is burned in a pit. Once the fire is going well, coral stones are heaped on top, and when most of the husks have burnt away the food is wrapped in banana leaves and placed on the hot stones—fish and meat below, vegetables above. A whole pig may

be cleaned, then stuffed with banana leaves and hot stones. This cooks the beast from inside out as well as outside in, and the leaves create steam. The food is then covered with more leaves and stones, and after about 2.5 hours everything is cooked. Many resorts stage an island night when this fare is served to the accompaniment of Polynesian dancing.

Information and Services

Information Offices

Official tourist information offices are found in the towns. Their main branches open during normal business hours but the information desks at the airports open only for the arrival of international flights, if then. Always visit the local tourist office to pick up brochures and ask questions. Their overseas offices, listed in this handbook's Resources section, often mail out useful information on their countries and most have Internet websites.

VISAS AND OFFICIALDOM

If you're from an English-speaking country or Western Europe you won't need a visa to visit these territories. Otherwise check the latest requirements with your airline well ahead, as consulates are few and far between.

Everyone must have a passport, sufficient funds, and a ticket to leave. Your passport should be valid six months beyond your departure date. Some officials object to tourists who intend to camp or stay with friends, so write the name of a likely hotel on your arrival card (don't leave that space blank). To avoid another problem, make sure the name on your passport is the same as the name on your plane ticket (no nicknames or married names).

Both French Polynesia and the Cook Islands require an onward ticket as a condition for entry. Although the immigration officials don't always check it, the airlines usually do. If you're planning a long trip including locally arranged yacht travel between countries, this can be a nuisance. One way to satisfy the ticket-to-leave requirement is to buy a full-fare one-way economy ticket out of the

area from Air New Zealand (valid one year). As you're about to depart for the next country on your route, have the airline reissue the ticket so it's a ticket to leave from there. Otherwise buy a full-fare ticket across the Pacific with stops in all of the countries you'll visit, then use it *only* to satisfy check-in staff and immigration. When you finally complete your trip return the ticket to the issuing office for a full refund. Remember that airline tickets are often refundable only in the place of purchase and that the sort of deals and discount airfares offered elsewhere are not available in the South Pacific. Have your *real* means of departure planned.

Customs

Agricultural regulations in the islands prohibit the import of fresh fruit, flowers, meat (including sausage), live animals and plants, as well as any old artifacts that might harbor pests. If in doubt, ask about having your souvenirs fumigated by the local agricultural authorities and a certificate issued before departure. Canned food, biscuits, confectionery, dried flowers, mounted insects, mats, and baskets are usually okay. If you've been on a farm, wash your clothes and shoes before going to the airport, and if you've been camping, make sure your tent is clean.

MONEY

All prices herein are quoted in Pacific francs (CFP), U.S. dollars, or New Zealand dollars unless otherwise stated. If you have access to the Internet you'll find the rates for most currencies at www.xe.net/ucc/full.shtml.

Both Tahiti and Rarotonga airports have banks

UNINHABITED ISLANDS

Although virtually every island and reef in the Pacific Ocean is claimed by one jurisdiction or another, many islands lack water and other resources needed for permanent inhabitation. Such places are sanctuaries for seabirds, turtles, and other species that coexist poorly with humanity. Aspiring Robinson Crusoes are seldom welcomed by traditional landowners or governments—beachcombers take note.

In the Society Islands, Mehetia east of Tahiti and Tupai north of Bora Bora are visited only occasionally. Numerous atolls in the Tuamotus have no permanent residents, although anglers and copra collectors arrive several times a year. Among these are Ahunui, Akiaki, Anuanuraro, Anuanurunga, Fangataufa, Haraiki, Hiti, Manuhangi, Maria East, Marutea North, Matureivavao, Morane, Motutunga, Paraoa, Pinaki, Ravahere, Reitoru, Rekareka, Tahanea, Tauere, Tekokota, Tenararo, Tenarunga, Tepoto South, Tikei, Tuanake, Vahanga, and Vanavana.

Maria and Marotiri in the Austral Islands are tiny, barren islands. Most of the Gambier Islands surrounding Mangareva are uninhabited, including Agakauitai, Akamaru, Kamaka, Makaroa, Manui, and Temoe. Among the desert islands of the Marquesas are Eiao, Fatu Huku, Hatutaa, Mohotani, Motu Iti, Motu One, and Thomasset Rock. In the southern Cook Islands, Manuae and Takutea are uninhabited.

If you want to use a credit card, always ask beforehand, even if a business has a sign or brochure that says it's possible. Visa and MasterCard can be used to obtain cash advances at most banks, but remember that cash advances accrue interest from the moment you receive the money—ask your bank if it has a debit card that allows charges to be deducted from your checking account automatically.

Many banks now have automated teller machines (ATMs) outside their offices and these provide local currency against checking account Visa and MasterCard at good rates without commission. Occasionally the machines don't work because of problems with the software, in which case you'll almost always be able to get a cash advance at the counter inside. To avoid emergencies, it's wise not to be 100 percent dependent on ATMs. Ask your bank what fee it'll charge if you use an ATM abroad and find out if you need a special personal identification number (PIN).

Upon departure, avoid getting stuck with leftover local banknotes, as currencies such as the Pacific franc and Chilean peso are difficult to change and heavily discounted even in neighboring countries. Change whatever you have left over into the currency of the next country on your itinerary, but don't wait to do it at the airport.

Costwise, you'll find the Cook Islands and Easter Island a lot less expensive than French Polynesia. Thus it's smart to spend those extra days of relaxation on Rarotonga rather than on Moorea or Bora Bora. Bargaining is not common: the first price you're quoted is usually it. Tipping is *not* customary in the South Pacific and can generate more embarrassment than gratitude.

COMMUNICATIONS
Postal Services
Always use airmail when posting letters from the islands. Airmail takes two weeks to reach North America and Europe; surface mail takes up to six months. Postage rates to the United States are medium-priced from the Cook Islands and very expensive from French Polynesia. Plan your postcard-writing accordingly. Sending a picture

that change money at normal rates (check the Airport listings at the end of the introduction chapters to French Polynesia and Cook Islands). The Euro is the best currency to carry to French Polynesia as it's exchanged at a fixed rate. However, if you don't already have Euros, just go with whatever currency you have.

The bulk of your travel funds should be in traveler's checks, preferably American Express as it has travel service offices in Papeete and Rarotonga. To claim a refund for lost or stolen American Express traveler's checks call the local office (listed in the respective chapters) or its Sydney office collect (tel. 61-2/9271-8689). It'll also cancel lost credit cards, so long as you know the numbers.

postcard to an islander is a very nice way of saying thank you.

When collecting mail at poste restante (general delivery), be sure to check under the initials of your first and second names, plus any initial that is similar. Have your correspondents print and underline your last name.

Telephone Services

French Polynesia and the Cook Islands have card telephones and these are very handy. If you'll be staying in the islands more than a few days and intend to make your own arrangements, it's wise to buy a local telephone card at a post office right away. In this handbook we provide all the numbers you'll need to make hotel reservations, check restaurant hours, find out about cultural shows, and compare car rental rates, saving you a lot of time and inconvenience.

By using a telephone card to call long distance you limit the amount the call can possibly cost and won't end up overspending should you forget to keep track of the time. On short calls you avoid three-minute minimum charges. International telephone calls placed from hotel rooms are always much more expensive than the same calls made from public phones using telephone cards. What you sacrifice is your privacy as anyone can stand around and listen to your call. Card phones are usually found outside post offices or telephone centers. Check that the phone actually works before bothering to arrange your numbers and notes.

With a card, a three-minute station-to-station call to the United States will cost under US$3 from French Polynesia or US$6 from the Cook Islands. Calling from the United States to the islands is cheaper than going in the other direction, so if you want to talk to someone periodically, leave a list of your travel dates and hotel telephone numbers (provided in this book) where friends and relatives can try to get hold of you. All the main islands have direct dialing via satellite.

To place a call to a Pacific island from outside the region, first dial the international access code (check your phone book), then the country code, then the number. The country codes are 56-32 on Easter Island, 682 in the Cook Islands, and 689 in French Polynesia. There are no area codes. Local telephone numbers have five digits in the Cook Islands and six digits in French Polynesia and Easter Island.

Electronic Mail

An increasing number of tourism-related businesses in the islands have email addresses, which makes communicating with them from abroad a lot faster and cheaper.

When sending email to the islands never include a large attached file (such as photos) with your message unless it has been specifically requested, as the recipient may have to pay US$1 a minute in long-distance telephone charges to download it. It's probably better not to email any attached files to the islands at all as the recipient may not have the latest virus scanning program and your message may be deleted unread.

Internet cafés on many islands now allow you to check your web-based email at around CFP 250 per 15 minutes. In French Polynesia the computers usually have French keyboards, which vary slightly from English keyboards, leading to annoying typing problems. Ask the operator if he or she has a machine with an English keyboard or to explain the quirks of the French keyboard.

Of course, to receive email online, you'll need a web-based electronic mailbox. Many servers now provide these to their clients; otherwise you should open a Yahoo or Hotmail account before leaving home. To do so, simply click "E-mail" at www.yahoo.com or "Sign Up" at www.hotmail.com. You must check your mail at least once a month; otherwise your free account will be canceled. Communicating has never been so easy!

MEDIA

Daily newspapers are published in French Polynesia (*La Dépêche de Tahiti* and *Les Nouvelles de Tahiti*) and the Cook Islands (*Cook Islands News*). Weekly papers of note include the *Tahiti Beach Press* and the *Cook Islands Herald*. (Turn to Resources at the end of this book for more Pacific-oriented publications.)

Radio

A great way to keep in touch with world and local affairs is to take along a small AM/FM shortwave portable radio. Your only expense will be the radio itself and batteries. In this handbook we've provided the names and frequencies of a few local stations, so set your tuning buttons to these as soon as you arrive.

You can also try picking up the BBC World Service and Radio Australia. Their frequencies vary according to the time of day and work best at night.

Health

For a tropical area, the South Pacific's a healthy place. The sea and air are clear and usually pollution-free. The humidity nourishes the skin and the local fruit is brimming with vitamins. If you take a few precautions, you'll never have a sick day. Malaria and cholera don't exist here. The information provided below is intended to make you knowledgeable, not fearful. If you have access to the Internet, check www.cdc.gov/travel/austspac.htm for up-to-the-minute information.

The government-run medical facilities mentioned in this book typically provide free medical treatment to local residents but have special rates for foreigners. It's usually no more expensive to visit a private doctor or clinic, and often it's actually cheaper. Private doctors can afford to provide faster service because everyone is paying, and we've tried to list local doctors and dentists throughout the handbook. In emergencies and outside clinic hours, you can always turn to the government-run facilities. Unfortunately, very few facilities are provided for travelers with disabilities.

American-made medications may by unobtainable in the islands, so bring along a supply of whatever you think you'll need. If you have to replace anything, quote the generic name at the pharmacy rather than the brand name. Otherwise go to any Chinese general store (in French Polynesia) and ask the owner to recommend a good Chinese patent medicine for what ails you. The cost will be a third of what European medicines or herbs cost, and the Chinese medicine is often as effective or more so. Antibiotics should be used only to treat serious wounds, and only after medical advice.

Travel Insurance

The sale of travel insurance is big business but the value of the policies themselves is often ques-

tionable. If your regular group health insurance also covers you while you're traveling abroad it's probably enough (although medical costs in French Polynesia are high). Most travel policies pay only the amount above and beyond what your national or group health insurance will pay and are invalid if you don't have any health insurance at all. You may also be covered by your credit card company if you paid for your plane ticket with the card. Buying extra travel insurance is about the same as buying a lottery ticket: there's always the chance it will pay off, but it's usually money down the drain.

If you do opt for the security of travel insurance, make sure emergency medical evacuations are covered. Some policies are invalid if you engage in any "dangerous activities," such as scuba diving, parasailing, surfing, or even riding a motor scooter, so be sure to read the fine print. Scuba divers should know that there's a recompression chamber at Papeete but an emergency medical evacuation will still be costly and there isn't any point buying a policy that doesn't cover it. Medical insurance especially designed for scuba divers is available from **Divers Alert Network** (6 W. Colony Pl., Durham, NC 27705, U.S.A.; tel. 800/446-2671 or 919/684-2948, www.divers-alertnetwork.org).

Some companies will pay your bills directly while others require you to pay and collect receipts that may be reimbursed later. Ask if travel delays, lost baggage, and theft are included. In practice, your airline probably already covers the first two adequately and claiming something extra from your insurance company could be more trouble than it's worth. Theft insurance never covers items left on the beach while you're swimming. All this said, you should weigh the advantages and decide for yourself if you want a policy. Just don't be influenced by what your travel agent says as he or she will want to sell you coverage in order to earn another commission.

Acclimatizing

Don't go from winter weather into the steaming tropics without a rest before and after. Minimize jet lag by setting your watch to local time at your destination as soon as you board the aircraft. Westbound flights into the South Pacific from North America or Europe are less jolting since you follow the sun and your body gets a few hours of extra sleep. On the way home you're moving against the sun and the hours of sleep your body loses cause jet lag. Airplane cabins have low humidity, so drink lots of juice or water instead of carbonated drinks, and don't overeat inflight. It's also wise to forgo coffee, as it will only keep you awake, and alcohol, which will dehydrate you.

Scuba diving on departure day can give you a severe case of the bends. Before flying there should be a minimum of 12 hours' surface interval after a nondecompression dive and a minimum of 24 hours after a decompression dive. Factors contributing to decompression sickness include a lack of sleep and/or the excessive consumption of alcohol before diving.

If you start feeling seasick onboard a ship, stare at the horizon, which is always steady, and stop thinking about it. Anti-motion-sickness pills are useful to have along; otherwise, ginger helps alleviate seasickness. Travel stores sell acubands that find a pressure point on the wrist and create a stable flow of blood to the head, thus miraculously preventing seasickness!

Frequently the feeling of thirst is false and due only to mucous membrane dryness. Gargling or taking two or three gulps of warm water should be enough. Keep moisture in your body by having a hot drink such as tea or black coffee, or any kind of slightly salted or sour drink in small quantities. Salt in fresh lime juice is remarkably refreshing.

The tap water is safe to drink in the main towns, but ask first elsewhere. If in doubt, boil it or use purification pills. Tap water that is uncomfortably hot to touch is usually safe. Allow it to cool in a clean container. Don't forget that if the tap water is contaminated, the local ice will be too. Avoid brushing your teeth with water unfit to drink, and wash or peel fruit and vegetables if you can. Cooked food is less subject to contamination than raw.

Sunburn

Though you may think a tan will make you look healthier and more attractive, it's actually very damaging to the skin, which becomes dry, rigid, and prematurely old and wrinkled, especially on the face. Begin with short exposures to the sun, perhaps half an hour at a time, followed by an equal time in the shade. Avoid the sun 1000–1500, the most dangerous time. Clouds and beach umbrellas will not protect you fully. Wear a T-shirt while snorkeling to protect your back. Drink plenty of liquids to keep your pores open. Sunbathing is the main cause of cataracts to the eyes, so wear sunglasses and a wide-brimmed hat, and beware of reflected sunlight.

Use a sunscreen lotion containing PABA rather than oil, and don't forget to apply it to your nose, lips, forehead, neck, hands, and feet. Sunscreens protect you from ultraviolet rays (a leading cause of cancer), while oils magnify the sun's effect. A 15-factor sunscreen provides 93 percent protection (a more expensive 30-factor sunscreen is only slightly better at 97 percent protection). Apply the lotion *before* going to the beach to avoid being burned on the way, and reapply every couple of hours to replace sunscreen washed away by perspiration. Swimming also washes away your protection. After sunbathing take a tepid shower rather than a hot one, which would wash away your natural skin oils. Stay moist and use a vitamin E evening cream to preserve the youth of your skin. Calamine ointment soothes skin already burned, as does coconut oil. Pharmacists recommend Solarcaine to soothe burned skin. Rinsing off with a vinegar solution reduces peeling, and aspirin relieves some of the pain and irritation. Vitamin A and calcium counteract overdoses of vitamin D received from the sun. The fairer your skin, the more essential it is to take care.

As Earth's ozone layer is depleted through the commercial use of chlorofluorocarbons (CFCs) and other factors, the need to protect oneself from ultraviolet radiation is becoming more urgent. Deaths from skin cancer are on the increase. Previously the cancers didn't develop until age 50 or 60, but now much younger people are affected.

Ailments

Cuts and scratches infect easily in the tropics and take a long time to heal. Prevent infection from coral cuts by immediately washing wounds with soap and fresh water, then rubbing in vinegar, lemon juice, or alcohol (whiskey will do)—painful but effective. Use an antiseptic such as hydrogen peroxide and an antibacterial ointment such as neosporin, if you have them. Islanders usually dab coral cuts with lime juice. All cuts turn septic quickly in the tropics, so try to keep them clean and covered.

For bites, burns, and cuts, an antiseptic such as Solarcaine speeds healing and helps prevent infection. Pure aloe vera is good for sunburn, scratches, and even coral cuts. Bites by *no-no* sandflies itch for days and can become infected. Not everyone is affected by insect bites in the same way. Some people are practically immune to insects, while traveling companions experiencing exactly the same conditions are soon covered with bites. You'll soon know which type you are.

Prickly heat, an intensely irritating rash, is caused by wearing heavy clothing that is inappropriate for the climate. When sweat glands are blocked and the sweat is unable to evaporate, the skin becomes soggy and small red blisters appear. Synthetic fabrics such as nylon are especially bad in this regard. Take a cold shower, apply calamine lotion, dust with talcum powder, and take off those clothes! Until things improve, avoid alcohol, tea, coffee, and any physical activity that makes you sweat. If you're sweating profusely, increase your intake of salt slightly to avoid fatigue, but not without concurrently drinking more water.

Use antidiarrheal medications such as Lomotil or Imodium sparingly. Rather than take drugs to plug yourself up, drink plenty of unsweetened liquids such as green coconut or fresh fruit juice to help flush yourself out. Egg yolk mixed with nut-meg helps diarrhea, or have a rice and tea day. Avoid dairy products. Most cases of diarrhea are self-limiting and require only simple replacement of the fluids and salts lost in diarrheal stools. If the diarrhea is persistent or you experience high fever, drowsiness, or blood in the stool, stop traveling, rest, and consider seeing a doctor. For constipation eat pineapple or any peeled fruit.

Toxic Fish

More than 400 species of tropical reef fish, including wrasses, snappers, groupers, jacks, moray eels, surgeonfish, shellfish, and especially barracudas are known to cause seafood poisoning (ciguatera). There's no way of telling whether a fish will cause ciguatera: a species can be poisonous on one side of an island, but not on the other.

In 1976 French and Japanese scientists working in the Gambier Islands determined that a one-celled dinoflagellate or plankton called *Gambierdiscus toxicus* was the cause. Normally these microalgae are found only in the ocean depths, but when a reef ecosystem is disturbed by natural or human causes they can multiply dramatically in a lagoon. The dinoflagellates are consumed by tiny herbivorous fish and the toxin passes up through the food chain to larger fish, where it becomes concentrated in the head and guts. The toxins have no effect on the fish that feed on them.

French Polynesia's 700–800 cases of ciguatera a year are more than in the rest of the South Pacific combined, leading to suspicions that the former French nuclear testing program is responsible. Ciguatera didn't exist on Hao atoll in the Tuamotus until military dredging for a 3,380-meter runway began in 1965. By mid-1968, 43 percent of the population had been affected. Between 1971 and 1980 more than 30 percent of the population of Mangareva near the Moruroa nuclear test site suffered from seafood poisoning. The symptoms (numbness and tingling around the mouth and extremities, reversal of hot/cold sensations, prickling, itching, nausea, vomiting, erratic heartbeat, joint and muscle pains) usually subside in a few days. Induce vomiting, take castor oil as a laxative, and avoid alcohol if you're unlucky. Symptoms can recur for

A TRAVELER'S NOTES ON AIDS AND HIV

In 1981 scientists in the United States and France first recognized the Acquired Immune Deficiency Syndrome (AIDS), which was later discovered to be caused by a virus called the Human Immuno-deficiency Virus (HIV). HIV breaks down the body's immunity to infections, leading to AIDS. The virus can lie hidden in the body for up to 10 years without producing any obvious symptoms or before developing into the AIDS disease and in the meantime the person can unknowingly infect others.

HIV lives in white blood cells and is present in the sexual fluids of humans. It's difficult to catch and is spread mostly through sexual intercourse, by needle or syringe sharing among intravenous drug users, in blood transfusions, and during pregnancy and birth (if the mother is infected). Using another person's razor blade or having your body pierced or tattooed are also risky, but the HIV virus cannot be transmitted by shaking hands, kissing, cuddling, fondling, sneezing, cooking food, or sharing eating or drinking utensils. One cannot be infected by saliva, sweat, tears, urine, or feces; toilet seats, telephones, swimming pools, or mosquito bites do not cause AIDS. Ostracizing a known AIDS victim is not only immoral but also absurd.

Most blood banks now screen their products for HIV, and you can protect yourself against dirty needles by allowing an injection only if you see the syringe taken out of a fresh unopened pack. The simplest safeguard during sex is the proper use of a latex condom. Unroll the condom onto the erect penis; while withdrawing after ejaculation, hold onto the condom. Never try to recycle a condom, and pack a supply with you as it's a nuisance trying to buy them locally.

HIV is spread more often through anal than vaginal sex because the lining of the rectum is much weaker than that of the vagina, and ordinary condoms sometimes tear when used in anal sex. If you have anal sex, only use extra-strong condoms and special water-based lubricants since oil, Vaseline, and cream weaken the latex. During oral sex you must make sure you don't get any semen or menstrual blood in your mouth. A woman runs 10 times the risk of contracting AIDS from a man than the other way around, and the threat is always greater when another sexually transmitted disease (STD) is present.

The very existence of AIDS calls for a basic change in human behavior. No vaccine or drug exists that can prevent or cure AIDS, and because the virus mutates frequently, no remedy may ever be totally effective. Other STDs such as syphilis, gonorrhea, chlamydia, hepatitis B, and herpes are far more common than AIDS and can lead to serious complications such as infertility, but at least they can usually be cured.

The euphoria of travel can make it easier to fall in love or have sex with a stranger, so travelers must be informed of these dangers. As a tourist you should always practice safe sex to prevent AIDS and other STDs. You never know who is infected or even if you yourself have become infected. It's important to bring the subject up *before* you start to make love. Make a joke out of it by pulling out a condom and asking your new partner, "Say, do you know what this is?" Or perhaps, "Your condom or mine?" Far from being unromantic or embarrassing, you'll both feel more relaxed with the subject off your minds and it's much better than worrying afterward if you might have been infected. The golden rule is safe sex or no sex.

By 2002 an estimated 40 million people worldwide were HIV carriers, and millions had already died of AIDS. The 80 cases in French Polynesia is still extremely small compared to the million-plus confirmed HIV infections in North America. However, it's worth noting that other STDs are far more common, demonstrating that the type of behavior leading to the rapid spread of AIDS is present.

An HIV infection can be detected through a blood test because the antibodies created by the body to fight off the virus can be seen under a microscope. It takes at least three weeks for the antibodies to be produced and in some cases as long as six months before they can be picked up during a screening test. If you think you may have run a risk, you should discuss the appropriateness of a test with your doctor. It's always better to know if you are infected so as to be able to avoid infecting others, to obtain early treatment of symptoms, and to make realistic plans.

If you know someone with AIDS you should give him or her all the support you can (there's no danger in such contact unless blood is present).

up to a year, and victims may become allergic to all seafoods.

Avoid biointoxication by cleaning fish as soon as they're caught, discarding the head and organs, and taking special care with oversized fish caught in shallow water. Small fish are generally safer. Whether the fish is consumed cooked or raw has no bearing on this problem. Local residents often know from experience which species may be eaten.

Dengue Fever

Dengue fever is a mosquito-transmitted disease endemic in Polynesia. Signs are headaches, sore throat, pain in the joints, fever, chills, nausea, and rash. This painful illness, also known as "breakbone fever," can last anywhere from five to 15 days. Although you can relieve the symptoms somewhat, the only real cure is to stay in bed, drink lots of water, and wait it out. Avoid aspirin as this can lead to complications. No vaccine exists, so just try to avoid getting bitten (the *Aedes aegypti* mosquito bites only during the day). Dengue fever can kill children under 13, so extra care must be taken to protect them if an outbreak is in progress.

During the 2001 dengue fever epidemic in French Polynesia—the worst in the territory's history—there were an estimated 30,000 cases with 10,000 requiring some form of hospital treatment. Of these, 4,000 cases were considered severe, and six deaths occurred among children aged six to 12. Cook Islands and Easter Island also experienced dengue outbreaks about the same time. Fumigations and a clean-up campaign eventually overcame the disease.

Vaccinations

Most visitors are not required to get any vaccinations at all before coming to the South Pacific. Tetanus, diphtheria, and typhoid fever shots are not required, but they're worth considering if you're going off the beaten track. Tetanus and diphtheria shots are given together, and a booster is required every 10 years. The typhoid fever shot is every three years. Polio is believed to have been eradicated from the region.

A yellow-fever vaccination is required if you've been in an infected area within six days before arrival. Yellow fever is a mosquito-borne disease that occurs only in Central Africa and northern South America (excluding Chile), places you're not likely to have been just before arriving in the South Pacific. Since the vaccination is valid 10 years, get one if you're an inveterate globe-trotter.

Immune globulin (IG) and the Havrix vaccine aren't 100 percent effective against hepatitis A, but they do increase your general resistance to infections. IG prophylaxis must be repeated every five months. Hepatitis B vaccination involves three doses in a six-month period (duration of protection unknown) and is recommended mostly for people planning extended stays in the region.

What to Take

Packing

Assemble everything you simply must take and cannot live without—then cut the pile in half. If you're still left with more than will fit into a medium-sized suitcase or backpack, continue eliminating. You have to be tough on yourself and just limit what you take. Now put it all into your bag. If the total (bag and contents) weighs more than 16 kg, you'll sacrifice much of your mobility. If you can keep it down to 10 kg, you're traveling *light*. Categorize, separate, and pack all your things into clear plastic bags or stuff sacks for convenience and protection from moisture. Items that might leak should be in resealable bags. In addition to your principal bag, you'll want a day pack or flight bag. When checking in for flights, carry anything that cannot be replaced in your hand luggage.

Your Luggage

Veteran travelers often recommend a small suitcase with wheels and a retractable handle that you can sometimes take aboard flights as carry-on luggage. Officially, economy passengers are allowed only one item of cabin baggage with overall dimensions no greater than 115 centimeters.

The bag must be able to fit under the seat in front of you, and it must not weigh more than five kg. In first and business classes you may carry two bags aboard, which when added together do not exceed 115 cm or seven kg in weight. Larger bags must usually be checked in at the airline counter.

Also ideal is a soft medium-sized backpack with a lightweight internal frame. Big external-frame packs are fine for mountain climbing but get caught in airport conveyor belts and are very inconvenient on public transport. The best packs have a zippered compartment in back where you can tuck in the hip belt and straps before turning your pack over to an airline or bus. This type of pack has the flexibility of allowing you to simply walk when motorized transport is unavailable or unacceptable; and with the straps zipped in it looks like a regular suitcase, should you wish to go upmarket for a while.

Make sure your pack allows you to carry the weight on your hips, has a cushion for spine support, and doesn't pull backward. The pack should strap snugly to your body but also allow ventilation to your back. It should be made of a water-resistant material such as nylon and have a Fastex buckle.

Look for a pack with double, two-way zipper compartments and pockets you can lock with miniature padlocks. They might not *stop* a thief, but they will deter the casual pilferer. A 60-cm length of lightweight chain and another padlock will allow you to fasten your pack to something. Keep valuables locked in your bag, out of sight, as even upmarket hotel rooms aren't 100 percent safe.

Clothing and Camping Equipment

For clothes take loose-fitting cotton washables, light in color and weight. Synthetic fabrics are hot and sticky, and most of the things you wear at home are too heavy for the tropics—be prepared for the humidity. Dress is casual, with slacks and a sports shirt okay for men even at dinner parties. Local women often wear long colorful dresses in the evening, but respectable shorts are okay in daytime. The pareu (par-RAY-o) is a bright two-meter piece of cloth both men and women wrap about themselves as an all-purpose garment. Any

islander can show you how to wear it. If in doubt, bring the minimum with you and buy tropical garb upon arrival. Stick to clothes you can rinse in your room sink. In midwinter (July and August) it can be cool at night in the Cooks and even Moorea, so a light sweater or windbreaker may come in handy.

Take comfortable shoes that have been broken in. Running shoes and rubber thongs (flip-flops) are handy for day use but will bar you from nightspots with strict dress codes. Scuba divers' wetsuit booties are lightweight and perfect for both crossing rivers and lagoon walking, though an old pair of sneakers may be just as good (never use the booties to walk on breakable coral).

A small nylon tent guarantees backpackers a place to sleep every night (except in the Cook Islands), but it *must* be mosquito and water proof. Get one with a tent fly, then waterproof both tent and fly with a can of waterproofing spray. You'll seldom need a sleeping bag in the tropics, so that's one item you can easily cut. A youth hostel sleeping sheet is ideal—all HI handbooks give instructions on how to make your own or buy one at your local hostel. You don't really need to carry a bulky foam pad, as the ground is seldom cold.

Below we've provided a few checklists to help you assemble your gear. The listed items combined weigh well over 16 kg, so eliminate what doesn't suit you:

- pack with internal frame
- day pack or airline bag
- sun hat or visor
- essential clothing
- bathing suit
- sturdy walking shoes
- rubber thongs (flip-flops)
- rubber booties
- sleeping sheet

Accessories

Bring some reading material, as good books can be hard to find in the islands and any books at all in English are rare in French Polynesia.

A mask and snorkel are essential equipment—you'll be missing half of the Pacific's beauty without them. Scuba divers should bring their own regulator, buoyancy compensator, and gauges to avoid rental fees and to eliminate the possibility of catching a transmissible disease from rental equipment. A lightweight three-mm Lycra wetsuit will provide protection against marine stings and coral.

Neutral gray eyeglasses protect your eyes from the sun and give the least color distortion. Take an extra pair (if you wear them).

A flashlight is essential if you'll be walking from your resort to nearby restaurants or bars after dark. There's no street lighting away from the main towns, and it can be slightly unnerving walking along a road in the pitch dark on a moonless night. Local bicycle and scooter riders often travel without lights and the sudden appearance of a barking dog can give you a fright.

Many pensions and hostels do not provide bath towels and even the deluxe resorts rarely supply face cloths. Beach towels may also be unavailable. A small travel towel will be required unless you're staying only at very upscale places.

Also take along postcards of your hometown and snapshots of your house, family, workplace, etc; islanders love to see these. Always keep a promise to mail islanders the photos you take of them.

- portable shortwave radio
- camera and 10 rolls of film
- compass
- pocket flashlight
- extra batteries
- candle
- pocket alarm calculator
- extra pair of eyeglasses
- sunglasses
- mask and snorkel
- padlock and lightweight chain
- collapsible umbrella
- string for a clothesline
- powdered laundry soap (inside several plastic bags)
- universal sink plug
- minitowel
- silicon glue
- sewing kit
- miniscissors
- nail clippers
- fishing line for sewing gear

- plastic cup and plate
- can and bottle opener
- corkscrew
- penknife
- spoon
- water bottle
- matches
- tea bags

Toiletries and Medical Kit

Since everyone has his/her own medical requirements and brand names vary from country to country, there's no point going into detail here. Note, however, that even the basics (such as aspirin) are unavailable on some outer islands, so be prepared. Bring medicated powder for prickly heat rash. Charcoal tablets are useful for diarrhea and poisoning (they absorb the irritants). Bring an adequate supply of any personal medications, plus your prescriptions (in generic terminology).

High humidity causes curly hair to swell and bush, straight hair to droop. If it's curly have it cut short or keep it long in a ponytail or bun. A good cut is essential with straight hair. Water-based makeup is preferable, as the heat and humidity cause oil glands to work overtime. High-quality locally made shampoo, body oils, and insect repellent are sold on all the islands, and the bottles are conveniently smaller than those sold in Western countries. (See Health, earlier in this chapter, for more ideas.)

- wax earplugs
- soap in plastic container
- soft toothbrush
- toothpaste
- roll-on deodorant
- shampoo
- comb and brush
- skin creams
- makeup
- tampons or napkins
- white toilet paper
- vitamin/mineral supplement
- insect repellent
- PABA sunscreen
- lip balm
- a motion-sickness remedy
- contraceptives

- iodine
- water-purification pills
- a diarrhea remedy
- Tiger Balm
- a cold remedy
- Alka-Seltzer
- aspirin
- antihistamine
- antifungal ointment
- Calmitol ointment
- antibacterial ointment
- antiseptic cream
- disinfectant
- simple dressings
- adhesive bandages (such as Band-Aids)
- painkiller
- prescription medicines

Money and Documents

All post offices have passport applications. If you lose your passport you should report the matter to the local police at once, obtain a certificate or receipt, and then proceed to your consulate (if any!) for a replacement. If you have your birth certificate with you it expedites things considerably. Don't bother getting an international driver's license as your regular license is all you need to drive here (except in the Cook Islands, where you'll be required to buy a local license).

Traveler's checks in U.S. dollars are recommended, and in the South Pacific, American Express is the most efficient company when it comes to providing refunds for lost checks. Bring along a small supply of US$1 and US$5 bills to use if you don't manage to change money immediately upon arrival or if you run out of local currency and can't get to a bank. In French Polynesia, Euros are the best currency to have as they're exchanged at a fixed rate.

Carry your valuables in a money belt worn around your waist or neck under your clothing; most camping stores have these. Make several photocopies of the information page of your passport, personal identification, driver's license, scuba certification card, credit cards, airline tickets, receipts for purchase of traveler's checks, etc.—you should be able to get them all on one page. On the side, write the phone numbers you'd need to call to report lost documents. A brief medical history with your blood type, allergies, chronic or special health problems, eyeglass and medical prescriptions, etc., might also come in handy. Put these inside plastic bags to protect them from moisture, then carry the lists in different places, and leave one at home.

How much money you'll need depends on your lifestyle, but time is also a factor. The longer you stay, the cheaper it gets. Suppose you have to lay out US$1,200 on airfare and have (for example) US$60 a day left over for expenses. If you stay 15 days, you'll average US$140 a day ($60 times 15 plus $1,200, divided by 15). If you stay 30 days, you'll average US$100 a day. If you stay 90 days, the per-day cost drops to US$74. If you stay a year it'll cost only US$64 a day.

- passport
- airline tickets
- scuba certification card
- driver's license
- traveler's checks
- some U.S. cash
- credit card
- photocopies of documents
- money belt
- address book
- notebook
- envelopes
- extra ballpoints

M

FILM AND PHOTOGRAPHY

Scan the ads in photographic magazines or on the Internet for deals on mail-order cameras and film, or buy at a discount shop in any large city. Run a roll of film through your camera to be sure it's in good working order; clean the lens with lens-cleaning tissue and check the batteries. Remove the batteries from your camera when storing it at home for long periods. Register valuable cameras or computers with customs before you leave home so there won't be any argument over where you bought the items when you return, or at least carry a copy of the original bill of sale.

The type of camera you choose could depend on the way you travel. If you'll be staying mostly in one place, a heavy single-lens reflex (SLR) camera with spare lenses and other equipment won't trouble you. If you'll be moving around a lot for a considerable length of time, a 35-mm automatic compact camera will be better. The compacts are mostly useful for close-up shots; landscapes will seem spread out and far away. If you decide on a digital camera, make sure the resolution of your photos will suffice for your needs. A wide-angle lens gives excellent depth of field, but hold the camera upright to avoid converging verticals. A polarizing filter prevents reflections from glass windows and water, and it makes the sky bluer.

Take double the amount of film you think you'll need: film is expensive in the islands, and even then you never know if it's been spoiled by an airport X-ray on the way there. Choose 36-exposure film over 24-exposure to save on the number of rolls you have to carry. In French Polynesia camera film costs more than double what you'd pay in the United States, but you can import 10 rolls duty-free. When buying film in the islands take care to check the expiration date.

Films are rated by their speed and sensitivity to light, using ISO numbers from 25 to 1600. The higher the number, the greater the film's sensitivity to light. Slower films with lower ISOs (100–200) produce sharp images in bright sunlight. Faster films with higher ISOs (400) stop action and work well in low-light situations, such as in dark rainforests or at sunset. If you have a manual SLR you can avoid overexposure at midday by reducing the exposure half a stop, but *do* overexpose when photographing dark-skinned islanders. From 1000 to 1600 the light is often too bright to take good photos, and panoramas usually come out best early or late in the day.

Keep your photos simple with one main subject and an uncomplicated background. Get as close to your subjects as you can and lower or raise the camera to their level. Include people in the foreground of scenic shots to add interest and perspective. Outdoors a flash can fill in unflattering facial shadows caused by high sun or backlit conditions. Most of all, be creative. Look for interesting details and compose the photo before you push the trigger. Instead of taking a head-on photo of a group of people, step to one side and ask them to face you. The angle improves the photo. Photograph subjects coming toward you rather than passing by. Ask permission before photographing people. If you're asked for money (rare) you can always walk away—give your subjects the same choice.

When packing, protect your camera against vibration. Checked baggage is scanned by powerful airport X-ray monitors, so carry both camera and film aboard the plane in a clear plastic bag and ask security for a visual inspection. Some airports will refuse to do this, however. A good alternative is to use a lead-laminated pouch. The old high-dose X-ray units are seldom seen these days but even low-dose inspection units can ruin fast film (400 ISO and above). Beware of the cumulative effect of X-ray machines.

Store your camera in a plastic bag during rain and while traveling in motorized canoes, etc. In the tropics the humidity can cause film to stick to itself; silica-gel crystals in the bag will protect film from humidity and mold growth. Protect camera and film from direct sunlight and load the film in the shade. When loading, check that the takeup spool revolves. Never leave camera or film in a hot place such as a car floor, glove compartment, or trunk.

Time and Measurements

The Cook Islands and most of French Polynesia are 10 hours behind Greenwich Mean Time (GMT), but the Marquesas are 9.5 hours behind GMT and the Gambiers are nine hours behind GMT. Tahiti and Rarotonga share a time zone with Hawaii, two hours behind California. Easter Island is four hours ahead of Tahiti and two hours behind Santiago, Chile. From mid-October–mid-March clocks on Easter Island and in the Cook Islands are turned an hour ahead; standard time is used year-round in French Polynesia.

You're better calling from North America to the South Pacific in the evening as it will be midafternoon in the islands (plus you'll probably benefit from off-peak telephone rates). From Europe, call very late at night. In the other direction, if you're calling from the islands to North America or Europe, do so in the early morning as it will already be afternoon in North America and evening in Europe.

The international date line generally follows 180 degrees longitude and creates a difference of 24 hours in time between the two sides. Everything in the Eastern Hemisphere west of the date line (including Fiji and New Zealand) is a day later; everything in the Western Hemisphere east of the line (including the areas covered in this book and North America) is a day earlier (or behind). Air travelers lose a day when they fly west across the date line and gain it back when they return. Keep track of things by repeating to yourself, "If it's Sunday in Seattle, it's Monday in Manila."

In this book all clock times are rendered according to the 24-hour airline timetable system, i.e. 0100 is 1 A.M., 1300 is 1 P.M., 2330 is 11:30 P.M. The islanders operate on "coconut time"—the nut will fall when it is ripe. In the languid air of the South Seas punctuality takes on a new meaning. Appointments are approximate and service relaxed. Even the

The islanders operate on "coconut time"—the nut will fall when it is ripe. In the languid air of the South Seas punctuality takes on a new meaning.

seasons are fuzzy: sometimes wetter, sometimes drier, but almost always hot. Slow down to the island pace and get in step with where you are. You may not get as much done, but you'll enjoy life a lot more. Daylight hours in the tropics run 0600–1800 with few seasonal variations.

WEIGHTS AND MEASURES

The metric system is used throughout the region. Study the conversion table in the back of this handbook if you're not used to thinking metric. Most distances herein are quoted in kilometers—they become easy to comprehend when you know than one km is the distance a normal person walks in 10 minutes. A meter is slightly more than a yard and a liter is just over a quart. Unless otherwise indicated, north is at the top of all maps in this handbook.

Electric Currents

If you're taking along a plug-in razor, radio, computer, electric immersion coil, or other electrical appliance, be aware that 220 volts AC is commonly used in the islands. Take care, however, as some luxury hotel rooms provide 110-volt outlets as a convenience to North American visitors. A 220-volt appliance will run too slowly in a 110-volt outlet, but a 110-volt appliance will quickly burn out and be destroyed in a 220-volt outlet.

Most appliances require a converter to change from one voltage to another. You'll also need an adapter to cope with different socket types, which vary between round two-pronged plugs in the French territories and three-pronged plugs with the two on top at angles in the Cooks. Pick up both items before you leave home, as they're hard to find in the islands. Some sockets have a switch that must be turned on. Remember voltages if you buy duty-free appliances: dual voltage (110/220 V) items are best.

Videos

Commercial travel videotapes make nice souvenirs, but always keep in mind that there are three incompatible video formats loose in the world: NTSC (used in North America), PAL (used in Britain, Germany, Japan, Australia, New Zealand, and the Cook Islands), and SECAM (used in France, French Polynesia, and Russia). Don't buy prerecorded tapes abroad unless they're of the system used in your country.

Getting There

Preparations

First decide where and when you're going and how long you wish to stay. Some routes are more available or practical than others. Most North Americans and Europeans will pass through Los Angeles International Airport (code-named LAX) on their way to Tahiti, although it's also possible to arrive via Honolulu. Many people think of Tahiti as somewhere far away on the other side of the globe, but it's only 7.5 hours from Los Angeles; since it takes about five hours to fly from Los Angeles to Hawaii, the flight to Tahiti is only 2.5 hours longer.

Your plane ticket will be your biggest single expense, so spend some time considering the possibilities. Read this entire chapter right through before going any further, and check the transportation sections in the French Polynesia, Easter Island, and Cook Islands introductions. If you're online peruse the Internet sites of the airlines that interest you, then call them up directly over their toll-free 800 numbers to get current information on fares. The following airlines have flights from the United States:

Air France: tel. 800/237-2747, www.airfrance.com/us, flies from Los Angeles and Paris to Tahiti

Air New Zealand: tel. 800/262-1234, www.airnewzealand.com, flies from Auckland, Los Angeles, and Nadi to Rarotonga and Tahiti

Air Tahiti Nui: tel. 877/824-4846, www.air-tahitinui-usa.com, flies from Auckland, Los Angeles, Osaka, Paris, and Tokyo to Tahiti

Aloha Airlines: tel. 800/367-5250, www.aloha-airlines.com, flies from Honolulu to Rarotonga

Hawaiian Airlines: tel. 800/367-5320, www.hawaiianair.com, flies from Honolulu to Tahiti

Qantas Airways: tel. 800/227-4500, www.qantas.com.au, flies from Auckland, Los Angeles, and Sydney to Tahiti

Sometimes Canada and parts of the United States have different toll-free numbers, so if the number given above doesn't work, dial 800 information at 800/555-1212 (all 800, 866, and 888 numbers are free). In Canada, Air New Zealand's toll-free number is tel. 800/663-5494.

Call all of these carriers and say you want the *lowest possible fare.* Cheapest are the excursion fares but these often have limitations and restrictions, so be sure to ask. Some have an advance-purchase deadline, which means it's wise to begin shopping early. Also check the fare seasons.

If you're not happy with the answers you get, call the number back later and try again. Many different agents take calls on these lines, and some are more knowledgeable than others. The numbers are often busy during peak business hours, so call first thing in the morning, after dinner, or on the weekend. *Be persistent.*

Other Airlines

The international airlines listed below don't fly directly between North America and the South Pacific, but they do serve Tahiti:

Aircalin: tel. 800/237-2747, www.aircalin.nc, flies from Nouméa and Wallis to Tahiti

LanChile Airlines: tel. 800/735-5526, www.lanchile.com, flies from Santiago to Easter Island and Tahiti

Polynesian Airlines: tel. 800/264-0823, www .polynesianairlines.com, flies from Auckland and Sydney to Tahiti

Virtually every airline flying to or around the region is listed on www.southpacific.org/air.html.

Cheaper Fares
In recent years South Pacific airfares have been deregulated and companies such as Air New Zealand no longer publish fare price lists. Their Internet websites are also evasive, usually with tariff information undisclosed (they might have prices for their all-inclusive package tours on the web but not air prices alone). Finding your way through this minefield can be the least enjoyable part of your pretrip planning, but you'll definitely pay a premium if you take the easy route and accept the first or second fare you're offered.

With fares in flux, the airline employees you'll get at the numbers listed above aren't likely to quote you the lowest fare on the market, but at least you'll have their official prices to use as a benchmark. After you've heard what they have to say, turn to a "consolidator," specialist travel agencies that deal in bulk and sell seats and rooms at wholesale prices. Many airlines have more seats than they can market through normal channels, so they sell their unused long-haul capacity to "discounters" or "bucket shops" at discounts of 40–50 percent off the official tariffs. The discounters buy tickets on this gray market and pass the savings along to you. Many such companies run ads in the Sunday travel sections of newspapers such as the *San Francisco Chronicle, New York Times,* and *Toronto Star,* or in major entertainment weeklies. If you ask, operators at the airlines' 800 numbers will often give you the names of consolidators who deal in their tickets.

Despite their occasionally shady appearance, most discounters and consolidators are perfectly legitimate, and your ticket will probably be issued by the airline itself. Most discounted tickets look and are exactly the same as regular full-fare tickets but they're usually nonrefundable. There may also be other restrictions not associated with the more expensive tickets and penalties if you wish to change your routing or reservations. Rates are competitive, so allow yourself time to shop around. A few hours spent on the phone, asking questions and doing time on hold, could save you hundreds of dollars.

Seasons
The month of outbound travel from the United States usually determines which seasonal fare you'll pay, and inquiring far in advance could allow you to reschedule your vacation slightly to take advantage of a lower fare. On flights to Tahiti, the French carriers have timed their high seasons to correspond to holiday time in Europe: June to September and December. This also applies on Air New Zealand if you're going only as far as Tahiti.

The seasons are quite different on flights to the Cook Islands, and if you're continuing from Tahiti to Rarotonga, normal Air New Zealand fare seasons apply to the whole ticket. The following is Air New Zealand's fare season schedule for flights from North America to the Cook Islands:

Jan. 1–Feb. 25—high season
Feb. 26–April 30—shoulder season
May 1–June 21—low season
June 22–July 22—shoulder season
July 23–Sept. 2—low season
Sept. 3–Dec. 7—shoulder season
Dec. 8–Dec. 16—high season
Dec.17–Dec. 31—peak season

Air New Zealand has made March to November—the top months in the Cook Islands—its off-season because that's winter in Australia and New Zealand. If you're going only to Rarotonga and can make it at that time, it certainly works to your advantage.

For travel to Tahiti originating in New Zealand, the fare seasons are as follows:

Jan. 17–Jan. 30—shoulder season
Jan. 31–March 23—low season
March 24–June 15—shoulder season
June 16–July 23—high season
July 24–Sept. 7—shoulder season
Sept. 8–Oct. 10—high season
Oct. 11–Nov. 11—low season

Nov. 12–Dec. 2—shoulder season
Dec. 3–Jan. 16—high season

From New Zealand to the Cook Islands, the seasons are very similar, except that the high season begins on August 8 instead of September 8.

Travel Agents

Pick your agent carefully as many don't want to hear about discounts, cheap flights, or complicated routes, and will give wrong or misleading information in an offhand manner. They may try to sell you hotel rooms you could get locally for a fraction of the cost. An unethical agent might also tell you that you're free to change your return dates when in fact you're not or fudge some of the other restrictions. If you can find a local travel agent or "packager" who resells discounted tickets from major flight consolidators, you've done well. Considerable consumer protection is obtained by paying by credit card.

Discover Wholesale Travel (949 S. Coast Dr., Suite 450, Costa Mesa, CA 92626, U.S.A.; tel. 888/768-8472 or 866/215-4625, www.discoverwholesaletravel.com) sells discounted air tickets and offers rock-bottom rates on rooms at the top hotels of French Polynesia. It sometimes has significantly lower fares for passengers booking within two weeks of departure ("distressed seats"). All of Discover's staff have been selling the South Pacific for at least 10 years.

Some of the cheapest round-trip tickets to Tahiti and Rarotonga are sold by **Fiji Travel** (8885 Venice Blvd., Suite 202, Los Angeles, CA 90034, U.S.A.: tel. 800/500-3454 or 310/202-4220, www.fijitravel.com). It makes its money through high volume, and to attract customers it keeps its profit margins as low as possible. Thus you should absorb the airline's time with all your questions about fare seasons, schedules, etc., and call companies such as Fiji Travel and Discover Wholesale Travel only after you know exactly what you want and how much everyone else is charging.

For circle-Pacific or round-the-world fares try **Airtreks** (tel. 877/247-8735, www.airtreks.com) and **Air Brokers International** (tel. 800/883-3273 or 415/397-1383, www.airbrokers.com), both based in San Francisco.

Goway Travel (86751 Lincoln Blvd., Los Angeles, CA 90045, U.S.A.; tel. 800/387-8850, www.goway.com) with offices in Sydney, Toronto, and Vancouver offers competitive fares to the South Pacific. Another Canadian travel agent to try is the **Adventure Centre** (25 Bellair St., Toronto, Ontario M5R 3L3, Canada; tel. 800/267-3347 or 416/922-7584, www.theadventurecentre.com) with branches in Calgary, Edmonton, and Vancouver. Similar tickets are available in the United States from the **Adventure Center** (1311 63rd St., Suite 200, Emeryville, CA 94608, U.S.A.; tel. 800/228-8747 or 510/654-1879, www.adventurecenter.com).

Internet Bookings

For an exact fare quote you can book instantly online, simply visit an online travel agency. You type in your destination and travel dates, then watch as the site's system searches its database for the lowest fare. You may be offered complicated routings at odd hours, but you'll certainly get useful information. You can also sign up to be notified by email when a special deal to your destination becomes available.

Try a couple of sites for comparison, such as **Farebase.com** (www.farebase.com), **Lowestfare.com** (www.lowestfare.com), **Microsoft Expedia** (www.expedia.com), **OneTravel.com** (http://air.onetravel.com), **Orbitz** (www.orbitz.com), **Sabre Travelocity** (www.travelocity.com), and **Trip.com** (www.trip.com). **Priceline.com** (www.priceline.com) is unique in that it allows you to name your own price for your ticket! If your bid is accepted by an airline, your credit card will be charged immediately and the ticket cannot be changed, transferred, or canceled. Priceline promises an answer within 15 minutes.

All these companies are aimed at the U.S. market and a credit card with a billing address outside the United States may not be accepted. For the South Pacific, you'll need a paper ticket, and it's unlikely the agency will agree to send it to an address different from the one on your card. So despite the global reach of the Internet, you'll probably have to use a site based in your own country.

If you live in Europe, turn to **Flightbookers** (www.ebookers.com) in the United Kingdom and nine other European countries. **Flights.com** (www.flights.com) is in Frankfurt, Germany. **Sabre Travelocity.ca** (www.travelocity.ca) is based in Canada and there are branches in Germany and the United Kingdom. **Expedia.ca** (www.expedia.ca) is in Canada and **Expedia.co.uk** (www.expedia.co.uk) is in the United Kingdom. In Australia it's **Travel.com.au** (www.travel.com.au) and **Flightcentre.com** (www.flightcentre.com.au). Flightcentre.com links to similar sites in Canada, New Zealand, and the United Kingdom, while Travel.com.au has partners in New Zealand, Japan, and South Africa.

Many more online agencies are listed on www.etn.nl. When comparing prices, note whether taxes, processing fees, airline surcharges, and shipping are charged extra. Check beforehand if you're allowed to change your reservations or refund the ticket. After booking, print out your confirmation. If you're reluctant to place an order on unfamiliar sites, look for the contact telephone numbers and give them a call to hear how they sound. At all of these sites, you'll be asked to pay by credit card over a secure server. If that idea worries you, look for a local packager willing to order online on your behalf. Since you'll have already checked the price yourself, you'll know if you're getting a good deal. Let your agent surprise you by finding an even lower online fare. After all, he or she should know this business better than you.

Student Fares

If you're a student, recent graduate, or teacher, you can sometimes benefit from lower student fares by booking through a student travel office. There are two rival organizations of this kind: Council Travel Services, with offices in college towns across the United States and a sister organization in Canada known as Travel Cuts; and STA Travel (Student Travel Australia) with a wholesale division known as the Student Travel Network. Both organizations require you to pay a nominal fee for an official student card, and to get the cheapest fares you have to prove you're really a student. Slightly higher fares on the same

routes are available to nonstudents, so they're always worth checking.

STA Travel (www.sta-travel.com) offers special airfares for students and young people under 26 years of age with minimal restrictions. Its prices on round-trip fares to single destinations are competitive but it doesn't sell more complicated tickets (standard routings such as Los Angeles-Tahiti-Auckland-Sydney-Bangkok-London-Los Angeles are its style). Call the toll-free number (tel. 800/781-4040) for the latest information.

Different student fares are available from **Council Travel Services** (tel. 800/226-8624, www.counciltravel.com), a division of the non-profit Council on International Educational Exchange (CIEE). Both this and **Travel Cuts** (www.travelcuts.com) in Canada are stricter about making sure you're a "real" student: you must first obtain the widely recognized International Student Identity Card (US$22) to get a ticket at the student rate. Some fares are limited to students and youths under 26 years of age, but part-time students and teachers also qualify. There are special connecting flights to Los Angeles from other U.S. points.

Current Trends

High operating costs have caused the larger airlines to switch to wide-bodied aircraft and long-haul routes with less frequent service and fewer stops In the South Pacific this works to your disadvantage, as even major destinations such as Tahiti get bypassed. Most airlines now charge extra for stopovers that once were free, or simply refuse to grant any stopovers at all on the cheapest fares.

Increasingly airlines are combining in global alliances to compete internationally. Thus Qantas is part of the "Oneworld" family (www.oneworld-alliance.com) comprising Aer Lingus, American Airlines, British Airways, Cathay Pacific, Finnair, Iberia, and LanChile, while Air New Zealand is a member of the "Star Alliance" (www.star-alliance.com) of United Airlines, Air Canada, Lufthansa, SAS, Singapore Airlines, Thai, All Nippon, and others. This is to your advantage as frequent-flier programs are usually interchangeable within the blocks, booking becomes easier, flight schedules are coordinated, and through fares exist.

It's now possible to design some extremely wide-ranging trips by combining the networks of the two competing groups. For example, Oneworld's **Oneworld Explorer** allows six stops selected from more than 570 destinations worldwide. Both Easter Island and Tahiti can be included in this pass.

Similar is the Star Alliance's **Round-the-World Ticket,** valid on flights operated by the 14 members of the Star Alliance. You're allowed 29,000, 34,000, or 39,000 miles with a minimum of three and maximum of 15 stops. One transatlantic and one transpacific journey must be included, but the ticket is valid one year and backtracking is allowed. Tahiti and Rarotonga can be visited on this fare. Air New Zealand offices in North America sell these round-the-world tickets starting at US$3,360. In Britain you can buy the same thing for about half what it costs in North America.

Air New Zealand's **Circle-Pacific Fare** provides a trip around the Pacific (including Asia) on Air New Zealand and other Star Alliance carriers. With this one you get 22,000 or 26,000 miles starting at US$2,688 with all the stops you want (minimum of three). Travel must begin in either Los Angeles or Vancouver (no add-ons). It's valid six months but you must travel in a continuous circle without any backtracking. No date changes are allowed for the outbound sector but subsequent changes are free. To reissue the ticket (for example, to add additional stops after departure) costs US$75, so plan your trip carefully.

Northwest Airlines offers a Circle-Pacific Fare of US$3,154 from Los Angeles with add-on airfares available from other North American cities. This ticket allows four free stopovers in Asia and the South Pacific, additional stops US$75 each. Qantas also has a Circle-Pacific fare, so compare.

Regional Air Passes

The **Visit South Pacific Pass** allows travelers to include the services of nine regional carriers in a single ticket valid six months. You have to buy the initial two-leg air pass in conjunction with an international ticket into the region, but you can buy additional legs up to a maximum of eight after arrival. Only the first sector has to be booked

ahead. The pass doesn't include Rarotonga and the only airline serving Tahiti that accepts this ticket is the New Caledonian carrier Aircalin, which flies Tahiti-Nouméa at US$340 each way. That makes the Visit South Pacific Pass interesting only as part of a much larger trip.

Polynesian Airlines offers a **Polypass** valid for 45 days of unlimited travel between Fiji, Samoa, and Tonga, plus one round-trip from Sydney, Melbourne, Auckland, or Wellington for US$1,099. From Honolulu the pass costs US$1,349, from any one of six U.S. west coast airports US$1,699. To extend the pass from Auckland to Tahiti is US$350 extra round-trip. Restrictions are that your itinerary must be worked out in advance and can be changed only once for free (subsequent changes US$50 each). Thus it's important to book all flights well ahead. A 20 percent penalty is charged to refund an unused ticket (no refund after one year). The Polypass is not available in December and January.

Air New Zealand's **South Pacific Airpass** is valid on its flights between Tahiti, Rarotonga, and Fiji at US$210 a hop. It can also be used to travel to/from Australia and New Zealand. You can buy the Airpass together with an international ticket to the region or within 30 days of arrival in the South Pacific. There are two fare options, standard and supersaver, based on availability. It's not available to residents of Australasia and at least two flights must be booked. It's an inexpensive way of extending your trip.

For more information on any of these, click "Air Passes" on www.southpacific.org/air.html and follow the links.

AIR SERVICES
From North America

Air France, Air New Zealand, Air Tahiti Nui, and Qantas are the major carriers serving Tahiti out of Los Angeles. The Qantas flights are actually code shares with Air Tahiti Nui. Air New Zealand flies to both Tahiti and Rarotonga year-round. Passengers originating in Canada must change planes in Los Angeles and go through U.S. security and immigration controls.

Air New Zealand's schedules are built around

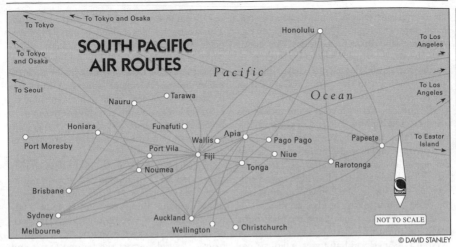

SOUTH PACIFIC
AIR ROUTES

Pacific

Ocean

To Tokyo and Osaka
To Tokyo
Honolulu
To Los Angeles
To Tokyo and Osaka
To Los Angeles
To Seoul
Nauru
Tarawa
Honiara
Funafuti
Apia
Papeete
To Easter Island
Port Moresby
Wallis
Pago Pago
Port Vila
Fiji
Niue
Rarotonga
Noumea
Tonga
Brisbane
Sydney
Auckland
Melbourne
Wellington
Christchurch

NOT TO SCALE

© DAVID STANLEY

Auckland and Los Angeles with Papeete a mere stopover, and flight times are planned so its aircraft arrive in Auckland in the morning. This means you'll land on Tahiti in the middle of the night, which isn't entirely bad. Papeete International Airport is well equipped and you'll have a few hours before dawn to change money at the airport bank, freshen up in the convenient washrooms, have a drink at the 24-hour cafeteria, and get accustomed to the humidity. As soon as the sun comes up, you'll be able to catch *le truck* into town. Air France also arrives in Papeete in the early morning. In contrast, Air Tahiti Nui flies southbound from Los Angeles during the day so you arrive in the early evening, too late to connect to Moorea or Bora Bora, forcing you to spend the night at a Papeete hotel. Air Tahiti Nui's early departure from Los Angeles may also mean that you'll need to spend the previous night in Los Angeles if you're connecting from the U.S. east coast or Canada, further inflating your costs. Northbound, both Air Tahiti Nui and Air New Zealand leave Papeete late at night, allowing you to make connections in Los Angeles the next day. Air France flies north during the day, increasing both comfort levels and your costs.

The only U.S. airline serving Tahiti is **Hawaiian Airlines,** which offers flights to Papeete via its base in Honolulu with connections to/from Las Vegas, Los Angeles, San Francisco, Portland, San

Diego, and Seattle. From the West Coast to Tahiti a nonrefundable, 14-day advance-purchase round-trip is US$735/835/935 low/shoulder/high season plus US$50 tax. From Honolulu, it's US$60 less. Fare seasons to Tahiti are complicated, so call well ahead. Date changes after ticketing are US$75. A free stop in Honolulu is available on this fare.

In early 2003 **Aloha Airlines** began flying from Honolulu to Rarotonga, with same-carrier connections from Burbank, Las Vegas, Oakland, Orange County, and Vancouver. Aloha's flights operate twice weekly October–April, weekly May–September.

Air New Zealand

Air New Zealand offers more direct flights to the South Pacific than any other airline. It's the only airline with flights to both French Polynesia and the Cook Islands, and round-trip tickets from North America to Rarotonga usually allow a stopover on Tahiti. This is the way to go if you want to take full advantage of the travel options outlined in this book. In the 1950s Air New Zealand pioneered its "Coral Route" using Solent flying boats, and the carrier still dominates long-haul air routes into the region.

Air New Zealand's first priority is to fly people to Auckland, and it's sometimes cheaper to buy a return ticket to Auckland with a couple of free stops in the islands than a round-trip ticket from

Los Angeles only as far as Tahiti–Rarotonga–Fiji. If you don't wish to visit New Zealand, you can transit Auckland airport the same day. Despite Air New Zealand's frequent services, travelers in North America and Europe often have difficulty booking flights with the carrier and it's advisable to reserve seats well ahead.

The cheapest tickets involve a number of restrictions. On Air New Zealand, if you're flying only to Tahiti the high season runs from June to September and in mid-December; the rest of the year is low season. The cheapest fare is the "APEX" at US$916/1,024 low/high round-trip between Los Angeles and Tahiti. You must buy this ticket at least 14 days in advance, there's a 35 percent cancellation penalty, and the maximum stay is one month.

From Los Angeles to Rarotonga, a return "No Stop Apex" ticket is US$1,028/1,258/1,528 low/shoulder/high at the beginning of the week. To set out on Thursday, Friday, Saturday, or Sunday is US$60 more. The maximum stay is one month and you must pay at least 21 days before departure (50 percent cancellation penalty). If you book on shorter notice the fare is almost 50 percent higher.

It's not that much more expensive to add a couple of other islands. Air New Zealand allows one stop plus your destination with additional stops available at US$150 each. Thus you can fly Los Angeles–Tahiti–Rarotonga–Fiji–Los Angeles for US$1,178/1,408/1,678/1,758 low/shoulder/high/peak season if you leave at the beginning of the week for a trip of three months maximum. Add US$150 if wish to extend your period of stay to six months, plus another US$70 if you'd like to set out on Thursday, Friday, Saturday, or Sunday. Drop either Tahiti, Rarotonga, or Fiji from your itinerary and you'll save US$150. Trips originating in Honolulu are US$200 cheaper in all cases. Remember that you must buy this fare 14 days in advance and there's a US$125 penalty to change your flight dates. A 35 percent cancellation fee also applies after the 14-day ticket deadline.

For a more wide-ranging trip with fewer restrictions, ask for Air New Zealand's "12-month Excursion Pass," which costs US$2,008/2,288/2,558/2,638 low/shoulder/high/peak season. This worthwhile ticket allows you to fly Los Angeles–Tahiti–Rarotonga–Fiji–Auckland–Tongatapu–Apia–Honolulu–Los Angeles or vice versa. Extend the ticket to Australia for US$100 more; eliminate Auckland–Tongatapu–Apia and it's about US$100 less. Begin in Honolulu and it's US$200 less again. You can stay up to one year but rerouting costs US$125 (date changes are free). There's no advance purchase requirement and you can go any day.

In Canada, Air New Zealand offers similar fares called the "Explorer fare, 12 months multistop," the "Stopover fare one month with no stops," and the "Bungy one and 12-month fare with one free stop." On most tickets special "add-on" fares to Los Angeles or Vancouver are available from cities right across the United States and Canada—be sure to ask about them. Air New Zealand's direct connections to/from Air Canada work better for Canadian passengers than the connections offered by Air Tahiti Nui and Qantas.

Air New Zealand's cabin service is professional, and you'll like the champagne breakfasts and outstanding food with free beer and wine. Another plus are the relaxing seats with adjustable head rests and lots of leg room. The *Life in Pacifica* videos about the destinations are entertaining the first time you see them, but after a while you get bored. The only reading material provided is the *Panorama* inflight magazine, the *Skyshop* duty free catalog, and the *Primetime* entertainment magazine. These are unlikely to hold your attention for long, so bring along a book or magazine of your own (the daily newspaper is provided only to passengers in first class). The service on Air Tahiti Nui is just as good.

From Australia

Qantas and Polynesian Airlines have flights to Tahiti from Auckland and Sydney, with Qantas offering connections to/from Brisbane, Cairns, and Melbourne. Qantas aircraft don't actually operate to Tahiti and all of its services are code shares with Air Tahiti Nui or Polynesian Airlines. Air New Zealand is competing fiercely in the Australian market, and it offers competitive fares to Rarotonga and Tahiti via Auckland.

INTRODUCTION

You can usually get a better price by working through an agent specializing in bargain airfares rather than buying at the airline office itself. The airlines sometimes offer specials during the off months, so check the travel sections in the weekend papers and call Flight Centres International.

Apex (advance purchase excursion) tickets must be bought 14 days in advance and heavy cancellation penalties apply. Shop around as you can often find much better deals than the published Apex fares, especially during off months.

From New Zealand

Air New Zealand, Polynesian Airlines, and Qantas all fly from Auckland to Tahiti, with Air New Zealand also serving Rarotonga. Air New Zealand fares to Tahiti often allow a stop in the Cook Islands, but it can be hard to get a seat on these fully booked planes. Ask at a number of different travel agencies for special unadvertised or under-the-counter fares. Agents to call include STA Travel and Flight Centres International. Some tickets have advance purchase requirements, so start shopping well ahead.

The excursion fare from Auckland to Tahiti on Air New Zealand is NZ$1,310/1,399/1,533 low/shoulder/high season. Twenty-one-day advance purchase fares from Auckland to Rarotonga cost NZ$1,099/1,220/1,350. Seasonal specials are regularly available. It's sometimes cheaper to buy a package tour to the islands with airfare, accommodations, and transfers included, but these are usually limited to seven nights on one island and you're stuck in a boring touristic environment. Ask if you can extend your return date and still get the tour price.

From Other Pacific Islands

French Polynesia is very poorly connected to its South Pacific neighbors. LanChile connects Tahiti to Easter Island twice a week, and Air New Zealand links Tahiti to Rarotonga and Fiji weekly. Flights on Aircalin to Nouméa, New Caledonia, are twice a week, to Wallis Island weekly. To make matters worse, these flights cannot be combined in a round-the-world ticket because LanChile belongs to the Oneworld group, while Air New Zealand (which serves Rarotonga) is part of the Star Alliance and Aircalin doesn't belong to either. Air New Zealand's weekly Tahiti–Rarotonga–Fiji "Coral Route" is the only island hopping you can do without incurring major additional expense, but it's often fully booked. There's no way to go from Tahiti or Rarotonga to Tonga or Samoa without passing through Auckland.

From South America

LanChile Airlines flies from Santiago, Chile, to Tahiti via Easter Island twice a week, with additional flights during the high southern summer season December–March. The regular one-way fare Santiago–Tahiti is US$961 economy class, plus US$50 for a stop on Easter Island. Santiago–Easter Island–Santiago is US$580 return low season. On all flights to Easter Island, low season fares are available March–November.

LanChile's round-trip fare between Tahiti and Easter Island costs US$435–727, depending on the season, how long you wish to stay, and who takes your booking. (See Tours to Easter Island in the Papeete section and Easter Island under Organized Tours in this introduction.)

LanChile's Tahiti service is heavily booked between Easter Island and Santiago but seldom full between Easter Island and Tahiti. That makes it easier to travel westbound on a round-the-world trip.

From Europe

From Paris, Air France and Air Tahiti Nui direct to Tahiti via Los Angeles. Otherwise, you may have to use a gateway city such as Singapore, Sydney, Honolulu, or Los Angeles. Air New Zealand offers daily nonstop flights London–Los Angeles with connections in Los Angeles to its Coral Route. Similarly, Lufthansa's daily Frankfurt–Los Angeles and Munich–Los Angeles flights code share with Air New Zealand's South Pacific flights. This means that European passengers can fly to Tahiti from London or Germany with only one change of aircraft (at Los Angeles).

Air New Zealand reservations numbers around Europe are tel. 03/202-1355 (Belgium), tel. 0800/907-712 (France), tel. 0180/549-4366 (Germany), tel. 800/876 126 (Italy), tel. 0800-2527 (Luxembourg), tel. 0800/022-1016 (Netherlands), tel. 900/993241 (Spain), tel. 020/792-939 (Sweden), tel. 0800/557-778 (Switzerland), and tel. 020/8741-2299 (United Kingdom). Call and ask about the Coral Route fares. Be aware that Air New Zealand flights from Europe are heavily booked and reservations should be made far in advance.

Also call your local British Airways or Qantas office and ask what connections they are offering to Tahiti. On Qantas you may transit Sydney on your way to Tahiti, a roundabout route that could be compensated for by a lower fare.

The British specialist in South Pacific itineraries is **Trailfinders** (1 Threadneedle St., London EC2R 8JX, United Kingdom; tel. 020/7628-7628, www.trailfinder.com), in business since 1970. Its 10 offices around the United Kingdom and Ireland offer a variety of discounted round-the-world tickets through the South Pacific that are often much cheaper than the published fares. It's easy to order a free copy of its magazine *Trailfinder* and brochures online.

Bridge the World (45-47 Chalk Farm Rd., Camden Town, London NW1 8AJ, United Kingdom; tel. 0870/444-7474, www.bridgetheworld.com) sells discounted tickets that include Fiji, Rarotonga, Tahiti, and a variety of stops in Asia. Also worth a try is **Tailor Made Travel** (18 Port St., Evesham, Worchestershire, WR11 6AN, United Kingdom; tel. 44-1386/712-005, www.tailor-made.co.uk). Check the ads in the London entertainment magazines for other such companies.

In Holland **Pacific Island Travel** (Herengracht 495, 1017 BT Amsterdam, the Netherlands; tel. 31-20/626-1325, www.pacificislandtravel.com) sells most of the tickets mentioned in this section, plus package tours. Its website is immense. **Barron and De Keijzer Travel** (Noordermarkt 16, 1015 MX Amsterdam, the Netherlands; tel. 31-20/625-8600, www.barron.nl) with additional offices in Antwerp, Deventer, and Rotterdam, also specializes in the Pacific islands and its website quotes exact flight prices! Also in Amsterdam, **Reisbureau Amber** (Da Costastraat 77, 1053 ZG Amsterdam, the Netherlands; tel. 31-20/685-1155) is one of the best places in Europe to pick up books on the South Pacific.

In Switzerland try **Globetrotter Travel Service** (Rennweg 35, CH-8023 Zürich, Switzerland; tel. 41-1/213-8080, www.globetrotter.ch), with offices in Baden, Basel, Bern, Biel, Fribourg, Luzern, Olten, St. Gallen, Thun, Winterthur, Zug, and Zürich. You can order a free copy of its magazine, *Globetrotter*, through the website.

Bucket shops in Germany sell a "Pacific Airpass" on Air New Zealand from Frankfurt to the South Pacific that allows all the usual Coral Route stops and is valid six months. All flights must be booked before leaving Europe, and there's a charge to change the dates once the ticket has been issued. One of the most efficient agencies selling such tickets is **Jet-Travel e.K.** (Buchholzstr. 35, D-53127 Bonn, Germany; tel. 0228/284315, www.jet-travel.de). Also check the website of **Travel Overland** (Barerstr. 73, D-80799 Munich, Germany; tel. 49-89/2727-6300, website: www.travel-overland.de) for round-the-world tickets via Tahiti.

Important Note

Airfares, rules, and regulations tend to fluctuate a lot, so some of the information above may have changed. This is only a guide; we've included a few fares to give you a rough idea how much things might cost. Your travel agent will know what's available at the time you're ready to travel, but if you're not satisfied with his/her advice, keep shopping around. Remember, however, that a mention here is not necessarily an endorsement: caveat emptor (let the buyer beware). The biggest step is deciding to go—once you're over that, the rest is easy!

PROBLEMS

When planning your trip allow a minimum two-hour stopover between connecting flights at U.S. airports, although with airport delays on the increase even this may not be enough. In the islands allow at least a day between flights. Try to avoid flying on weekends and holidays when the congestion is at its worst. In some airports flights are not called over the public address system, so keep your eyes open. Whenever traveling, always have a paperback or two, some toiletries, and a change of underwear in your hand luggage.

If your flight is canceled because of a mechanical problem with the aircraft, the airline will cover your hotel bill and meals. If it reschedules the flight on short notice for reasons of its own or you're bumped off an overbooked flight, it should also pay. The airline may not feel obligated to pay, however, if the delay is due to weather conditions, a strike by another company, national emergencies, etc., although the best airlines still pick up the tab in these cases.

It's an established practice among airlines to provide light refreshments to passengers delayed two hours after the scheduled departure time and a meal after four hours. Don't expect to get this from Air Tahiti or Air Rarotonga on an outer island, but politely request it if you're at a gateway airport. If you are unexpectedly forced to spend the night somewhere, an airline employee may hand you a form on which the airline offers to telephone a friend or relative about the delay. Don't trust the airline to do this, however. Call your party yourself if you want to be sure he or she gets the message.

Overbooking

To compensate for no-shows, most airlines overbook their flights. To avoid being bumped, ask for your seat assignment when booking, check in early, and go to the departure area well before flight time. Of course, if you *are* bumped by a reputable international airline at a major airport you'll be regaled with free meals and lodging, and sometimes even free flight vouchers (don't expect anything like this from Air Tahiti or Air Rarotonga).

Whenever you break your journey for more than 72 hours, always reconfirm your onward reservations and check your seat assignment at the same time. Get the name of the person who takes your reconfirmation so he or she cannot later deny it. Failure to reconfirm could result in the cancellation of your complete remaining itinerary. This could also happen if you miss a flight for any reason. If you want vegetarian food in-flight, request it when buying your ticket, booking, and reconfirming.

When you try to reconfirm your Air New Zealand flight the agent will tell you that this formality is no longer required. Theoretically this is true, but unless you request your seat assignment in advance, either at an Air New Zealand office or over the phone, you could be "bumped" from a full flight, reservation or no reservation. Air New Zealand's ticket cover bears this surprising message:

> *. . . no guarantee of a seat is indicated by the terms "reservation," "booking," "O.K." status, or the times associated therewith.*

It does admit in the same notice that confirmed passengers denied seats may be eligible for compensation, so if you're not in a hurry, a night or two at an upmarket hotel with all meals courtesy of Air New Zealand may not be a hardship. Your best bet if you don't want to get "bumped" is to request seat assignments for your entire itinerary before you leave home. Any good travel agent selling tickets on Air New Zealand should know enough to automatically request your seat assignments while making your bookings. In the islands Air New Zealand offices will still accept a local contact telephone number from you, thereby confirming that your booking is in its system. Check Air New Zealand's reconfirmation policy at one of its offices as it could change

Baggage

International airlines generally allow economy-class passengers 20 kilos of baggage. However, if any United States or Canadian airport is included in your ticket, the allowance is two pieces not over 32 kilos each for all your flights on that carrier. Under the piece system, neither bag must have a combined length, width, and height of more than 158 centimeters (62 inches), and the two pieces together must not exceed 272 centimeters (107 inches). On most long-haul tickets to/from North America or Europe, the piece system should apply to all sectors, but check this with the airline and look on your ticket. The frequent flier programs of some airlines allow participants to carry up to 10 kilos of excess baggage free of charge. On Air Tahiti flights within French Polynesia you may be restricted to as little as 10 kilos total, so it's better to pack according to the lowest common denominator.

Bicycles, folding kayaks, and surfboards can usually be checked as baggage (sometimes for an additional US$60 "oversize" charge), but sailboards may have to be shipped airfreight. If you do travel with a sailboard, be sure to call it a surfboard at check-in.

Tag your bag with name, address, and phone number inside and out. Stow anything that could conceivably be considered a weapon (scissors, sewing needles, razor blades, nail clippers, etc.) in your checked luggage. Metal objects such as flashlights and umbrellas that might require a security inspection should also be packed away. One reason for lost baggage is that some people fail to remove used baggage tags after they claim their luggage. Get into the habit of tearing off old baggage tags, unless you want your luggage to travel in the opposite direction! As you're checking in, look to see if the three-letter city codes on your baggage tag receipt and boarding pass are the same. If you're headed to Papeete, the tag should read PPT (Rarotonga is RAR).

Check your bag straight through to your final destination, otherwise the airline staff may disclaim responsibility if it's lost or delayed at an intermediate stop. If your baggage is damaged or doesn't arrive at your destination, inform the airline officials *immediately* and have them fill out a written report; otherwise future claims for compensation will be compromised. Keep receipts for any money you're forced to spend to replace missing items. If you notice that a bag has been mysteriously patched up with tape since you last saw it, carefully examine the contents right away. This could be a sign that baggage handlers have pilfered items from inside, and you must report the theft before leaving the customs hall to be eligible for compensation.

Claims for lost luggage can take weeks to process. Keep in touch with the airline to show your concern and hang onto your baggage tag until the matter is resolved. If you feel you did not receive the attention you deserved, write the airline an objective letter outlining the case. Get the names of the employees you're dealing with so you can mention them in the letter. Of course, don't expect any pocket money or compensation on a remote outer island. Report the loss, then wait till you get back to the main office.

BY BOAT

Even as much Pacific shipping was being sunk during World War II, airstrips were springing up

© M.E. DE VOS

ferry to Moorea

on all the main islands. This hastened the inevitable replacement of the old steamships with modern aircraft, and it's now extremely rare to arrive in the South Pacific by boat (private yachts excepted). Most islands export similar products and there's little interregional trade; large container ships headed for Australia, New Zealand, and the United States don't usually accept passengers.

Those bitten by nostalgia for the slower prewar ways may like to know that a couple of passenger-carrying freighters do still call at the islands, though their fares are much higher than those charged by the airlines. A specialized agency booking such passages is **TravLtips** (P.O. Box 580188, Flushing, NY 11358, U.S.A.; tel. 800/872-8584 or 718/224-0435, www.travltips.com). Also try **Freighter World Cruises** (180 S. Lake Ave., Suite 335, Pasadena, CA 91101, U.S.A.; tel. 800/531-7774 or 626/449-3106, www.freighterworld.com).

These companies can place you aboard a British-registered **Bank Line** container ship on its way around the world from Europe via the Panama Canal, Papeete, Nouméa, Suva, Lautoka, Port Vila, Santo, Honiara, and Papua New Guinea. A round-the-world ticket for the four-month journey is US$12,725, but segments are sold if space is available 30 days before sailing. These ships can accommodate only about a dozen passengers, so inquire well in advance.

ORGANIZED TOURS
Packaged Holidays
Most travel agents would prefer to sell you a package tour rather than only a plane ticket, and it's a fact that some vacation packages actually cost less than regular round-trip airfare! While packaged travel certainly isn't for everyone, reduced group airfares and discounted hotel rates make some tours an excellent value. For two people with limited time and a desire to stay in first-class hotels, this is the cheapest way to go by far.

The "wholesalers" who put these packages together get their rooms at rates far lower than what individuals pay, and the airlines also give

them deals. If they'll let you extend your return date to give you some time to yourself, this can be a great deal, especially with the hotel thrown in for "free." Special-interest tours are very popular among sportspeople who want to be sure they'll get to participate in the various activities they enjoy.

The main drawback to the tours is that you're on a fixed itinerary in a tourist-oriented environment, out of touch with local life. You may not like the hotel or meals you get, and singles pay a healthy supplement. You'll probably get prepaid vouchers to turn in as you go along and won't be escorted by a tour conductor. Some tour companies (including Brendan Tours, GoGo Worldwide Vacations, Happy Vacations, and Runaway Tours) do not accept consumer inquiries and require you to work through a travel agent. Do check all the restrictions.

The following companies based in Canada or the United States make individualized travel arrangements and offer package tours to both French Polynesia and the Cook Islands:

Destination World, P.O. Box 1077, Santa Barbara, CA 93102, U.S.A.; tel. 800/707-3454, www.southpacificgateway.com

Discover Wholesale Travel, 949 S. Coast Dr., Suite 450, Costa Mesa, CA 92626, U.S.A.; tel 866/215-4625, www.discoverwholesaletravel.com

Fiji Travel, 8885 Venice Blvd., Suite 202, Los Angeles, CA 90034, U.S.A.: tel. 800/500-3454 or 310/202-4220, www.fijitravel.com

Goway Travel, 86751 Lincoln Blvd., Los Angeles, CA 90045, U.S.A.; tel. 800/387-8850, www.goway.com; 3284 Yonge St., Suite 300, Toronto, Ontario M4N 3M7, Canada; tel. 800/387-8850, www.goway.com; 1200 W. 73rd Ave., Suite 1050, Vancouver, BC V6P 6G5, Canada; tel. 604/267-2111 or 800/665-4432, www.goway.com

Inta-Aussie Tours, 9841 Airport Blvd., Suite 1402, Los Angeles, CA 90045, U.S.A.; tel. 800/531-9222, www.inta-aussie.com

Islands in the Sun, 2381 Rosecrans Ave., Suite 325, El Segundo, CA 90245, U.S.A.; tel. 800/828-6877 or 310/536-0051, www.islands-inthesun.com

Newmans South Pacific Vacations, 6033 W. Century Blvd., Suite 970, Los Angeles CA 90045, U.S.A.; tel. 800/421-3326, www.new-mansvacations.com

Pacific Destination Center, 18685-A Main St., Suite 622, Huntington Beach, CA 92648 U.S.A.; tel. 800/227-5317 or 714/960-4011, www.pa-cific-destinations.com

Pacific Escapes, 1605 N.W. Sammamish Rd., Suite 310, Issaquah, WA 98027, U.S.A.; tel. 800/777-7992 or 425/657-1900, www.paci-ficescapes.com

Pacific for Less, 1993 S. Kihei Rd., Suite 21-130, Kihei, HI 96753, U.S.A.; tel. 800/915-2776 or 808/249-6490, www.pacificforless.com

Solace Destinations, 10625 N. 25th Ave., Suite 200, Phoenix, AZ 85029, U.S.A.; tel. 800/548-5331 or 602/944-8080, www.solace1.com

South Pacific Getaways, 4885 Mt. Elbrus Dr., San Diego, CA 92117, U.S.A.; tel. 800/458-2499 or 858/560-6154, www.southpacificgetaways.com

Sunspots International, 1918 N.E. 181st, Portland, OR 97230, U.S.A.; tel. 800/334-5623 or 503/666-3893, www.sunspotsintl.com

Tahiti Vacations, 9841 Airport Blvd., Suite 1124, Los Angeles, CA 90045, U.S.A.; tel. 800/553-3477 or 310/337-1040, www.tahiti-vacations.net

Wilcox Travel Cruise and Company, 615 Holly St., Junction City, OR 97448, U.S.A.; tel. 800/234-1605 or 541/998-1605, www.wilcox-travel-cruise.com

Tahiti Vacations (owned by Air Tahiti) offers packages to all parts of French Polynesia—not just Tahiti, Moorea, and Bora Bora. Trips to the Marquesas, cruises, and yacht charters are arranged, and it also has budget packages to Moorea.

The following companies offer tours to French Polynesia only:

eTravelBound, 2312 Ryan Way, Bullhead City, AZ 86442, U.S.A.; tel. 888/540-8445 or 928/763-8255, www.etravelbound.com

Griffin and Co. Travel, 406 W. Main St., Flushing, MI 48433, U.S.A.; tel 888/292-4484 or 810/659-5584, www.griffin-travel.com

Island Destinations, 1875 Palmer Ave., Suite 209, Larchmont, NY 10538, U.S.A.; tel. 888/454-4422 or 914/833-3300, www.island-destinations.com

Inta-Tahiti Tours, 9841 Airport Blvd., Suite 1402, Los Angeles, CA 90045, U.S.A.; tel. 800/531-9222 or 310/568-2060, www.inta-tahiti.com

Manuia Tours, 59 New Montgomery St., San Francisco, CA 94105, U.S.A.; tel. 866/682-4484 or 415/495-4500, www.tahitispecialist.com

Pleasant Holidays, 2404 Townsgate Rd., Westlake Village, CA 91361, U.S.A.; tel. 800/742-9244, www.2tahiti.com

Runaway Tours, 120 Montgomery St., Suite 800, San Francisco, CA 94104, U.S.A.; tel. 800/622-0733, www.runawaytours.com

Tahiti Honeymoons, 202 N. Curry St., Suite 100, Carson City, NV 89703, U.S.A.; tel. 888/226-2142 or 480/984-5245, www.come2tahiti.com

Tahiti Legends, 19891 Beach Blvd., Suite 107, Huntington Beach, CA 92648, U.S.A.; tel. 800/200-1213 or 714/374-5656, www.tahiti-legends.com

Tahiti TravelNet, 6516 W. 6th St., Los Angeles, CA 90048, U.S.A.; tel. 800/781-9356 or 323/655-2181, www.tahititravel.com

Tahiti Romance Holidays, 355 Hukilike St., Suite 207, Kahului, Maui, HI 96732, U.S.A.; tel. 888/982-4484 or 808/873-7278, www.visit-tahiti.com

Tahiti Travel Planners, New Millennium Travel, 461 Durand NE, Suite 100, Atlanta, GA 30307, U.S.A.; tel. 800/772-9231 or 404/378-4983, www.gotahiti.com

Rob Jenneve of Island Adventures (225-C N. Fairway, Goleta, CA 93117, U.S.A.; tel. 800/289-4957 or 805/685-9230, www.islandadventures.com) puts together customized flight and accommodation packages, which are only slightly more expensive than regular round-trip airfare. Rob can steer you toward deluxe resorts, which offer value for money, and he's willing to spend the time to help you find what you really want in planning your trip. According to him: "It's no problem to vary your nights, extend your return, or leave some free time in the middle for spontaneous adventure."

Rascals in Paradise (Theresa Detchemendy and Deborah Baratta, 1 Daniel Burnham Ct., Suite 105-C, San Francisco, CA 94109, U.S.A.; tel. 800/872-7225, 415/921-7000, www.rascalsinparadise.com) has been organizing personalized tours to French Polynesia and the Cook Islands for families since 1987. Since then, the company has been instrumental in initiating numerous children's programs.

Easter Island
Tahiti Vacations (9841 Airport Blvd., Suite 1124, Los Angeles, CA 90045, U.S.A.; tel. 800/553-3477 or 310/337-1040, www.tahiti-vacations.net) includes Easter Island in some of its French Polynesia packages, with tours beginning at US$1,999 including eight nights' accommodations, sight-seeing tours, and return airfare from Los Angeles to Tahiti and Easter Island.

Nature Expeditions International (7860 Peters Rd., Suite F-103, Plantation, FL 33324, U.S.A.; tel. 800/869-0639 or 954/693-8852, www.naturexp.com) runs a weekly archaeology tour of Easter Island at US$2,150 double occu-

pancy, airfare extra. The groups spend four of the tour's nine days exploring Easter Island under the guidance of local archaeologists.

Far Horizons Trips (P.O. Box 91900, Albuquerque, NM 87199, U.S.A.; 800/552-4575 or 505/343-9400, www.farhorizon.com) organizes a 10-day tour to coincide with the Tapati Rapa Nui festival in early February (US$4,495 pp double occupancy, airfare to Chile extra). A noted archaeologist or scholar escorts the group.

Most travel agencies in Papeete offer cheap package tours from Tahiti to Easter Island. For example, Tahiti Nui Travel (www.tahiti-nui.com) has three-night packages starting at US$580 inclusive of airfare from Tahiti. Off-season March–November, Vahine Tahiti Travel (www.vahine-tahiti.com) sells Papeete–Easter Island plane tickets alone at US$435 round-trip with a maximum stay of one week. To get these low prices, you must book in person in Papeete, as websites and overseas travel agents usually quote higher prices. (Turn to Tours to Easter Island in the Papeete listings in this book for more information.)

From Australia
Hideaway Holidays (Val Gavriloff, P.O. Box 121, West Ryde, NSW 2114, Australia; tel. 61 2/9743 0253, www.hideawayholidays.com.au) specializes in packages to every part of the South Pacific. It's been in the business for many years.

Talpacific Holidays (Level 1, 91 York St., Sydney, NSW 2000, Australia; tel. 61-2/9244-1850, www.talpacific.com), with a branch office in Brisbane, arranges packages to French Polynesia and the Cook Islands.

Also check Adventure World (3rd Floor, 73 Walker St., North Sydney, NSW 2060, Australia; tel. 61-2/8913-0755, www.adventureworld.com.au), and Goway Travel (350 Kent St., 8th Floor, Sydney, NSW 2000, Australia; tel. 61-2/9262-4755, www.goway.com).

For discounted airfares, try Trailfinders (8 Spring St., Sydney, NSW 2000, Australia; tel. 61-2/9247-7666, www.trailfinder.com), with additional offices in Brisbane, Cairns, Melbourne, and Perth.

From New Zealand

Ginz Travel (183 Victoria St., Christchurch, New Zealand; tel. 64-3/366-4486, www.ginz.com) arranges flights, accommodations, rental cars, and package deals to French Polynesia and the Cook Islands.

ASPAC Vacations Ltd. (151 Victoria St. W, Level 4, Auckland, New Zealand; tel. 64-9/916-9910, www.aspacvacations.co.nz) has packaged tours and cruises to most of the areas covered in this book.

Talpacific Holidays (P.O. Box 297, Auckland, New Zealand; tel. 64-9/914-8728, www.talpacific.com) also offers package tours throughout the region.

Ray Aucott's **Fathom South Pacific Travel** (P.O. Box 2557, Shortland St., Auckland, New Zealand; www.fathomtravel.com) is an adventure travel-oriented packager. Ray books rooms at all the top resorts, but he also has numerous options for scuba diving and fishing. Ninety-five percent of Ray's bookings are via the Internet.

From Europe

Austravel (17 Blomfield St., London EC2M 7AJ, United Kingdom; tel. 0870/055-0213, www.austravel.com), with nine locations in the United Kingdom, is a South Pacific-oriented tour company owned by the Thomson Travel Group.

All Ways Pacific Travel (7 Whielden St., Old Amersham, Bucks HP7 0HT, United Kingdom; tel. 01494/432747, www.all-ways.co.uk) sells packages to French Polynesia and the Cook Islands for senior or retired travelers.

Pacific Island Travel (Herengracht 495, 1017 BT Amsterdam, the Netherlands; tel. 31-20/626-1325, www.pacificislandtravel.com) has package tours from Amsterdam.

The **Pacific Travel House** (Bayerstr. 95, D-80335 Munich; tel. 49-89/530-9293, www.pacific-travel-house.com) and **Polynesia Tours** (Benekendorffstr. 87b, 13469 Berlin, Germany; tel. 49-30/4030-3085, www.polynesia-tours.de) offer a variety of package tours.

In Austria the South Pacific specialist is **Coco Weltweit Reisen** (Eduard-Bodem-Gasse 8, A-6020 Innsbruck; tel. 43-512/365-791, www.coco-tours.at).

Elsewhere in Europe, inclusive tours to French Polynesia are most easily booked through Nouvelles Frontières (www.nouvelles-frontieres.fr) offices.

Scuba Tours

The South Pacific is one of the world's prime scuba locales, and most of the islands have excellent facilities for divers. Although it's not that difficult to make your own arrangements as you go, you should consider joining an organized scuba tour if you want to cram in as much diving as possible. To stay in business, the dive travel specialists mentioned below are forced to charge prices similar to what you'd pay on the beach, and the convenience of having everything prearranged is often worth it. Before booking, find out exactly where you'll be staying and ask if daily transfers and meals are provided. Of course, diver certification is mandatory.

Before deciding, carefully consider booking a cabin on a "live-aboard" dive boat. (The catamarans and minicruise ships of this kind operated in the Tuamotu Islands by Archipels Croisieres and the Aggressor Fleet are discussed under Smaller Vessels in the introduction to French Polynesia.) They're a bit more expensive than hotel-based diving, but you're offered up to five dives a day and a total experience. Some repeat divers won't go any other way. **Live/Dive Pacific** (74-5588 Pawai Pl., Building F, Kailua-Kona, HI 96740, U.S.A.; tel. 800/344-5662 or 808/329-8182, www.livedivepacific.com) specializes in live-aboards, especially the *Tahiti Aggressor* based at Rangiroa.

Companies specializing in dive tours to French Polynesia include:

South Pacific Island Travel, 537 N. 137th St., Seattle, WA 98133, U.S.A.; tel. 877/773-4846 or 206/367-0956, www.spislandtravel.com

Sportours, 2335 Honolulu Ave., Montrose, CA 91020, U.S.A.; tel 800/774-0295 or 818/553-3333, www.sportours.com

Trip-N-Tour, 131 E. Fig St., Suite 4, Fallbrook, CA 92028, U.S.A.; tel. 800/348-0842 or 760/451-1001, www.trip-n-tour.com

World of Diving, 301 Main St., El Segundo, CA 90245, U.S.A.; tel. 800-900-7657 or 310-322-8100, www.worldofdiving.com

Dive Discovery (77 Mark Dr., Suite 18, San Rafael, CA, 94903, U.S.A.; tel. 800/886-7321 or 415/444-5100, www.divediscovery.com) caters to upscale divers who want only the best accommodations. This company also books the live-aboards in French Polynesia, and its website explains it all.

In Australia, try **Allways Dive Expeditions** (168 High St., Ashburton, Melbourne, Victoria 3147, Australia; tel. 61-3/9885-8863, www.allwaysdive.com.au).

In Europe, **Schöner Tauchen** (Hastedter Heerstr. 211, D-28207 Bremen, Germany; tel. 49-421/450-010, www.schoener-tauchen.com) sells dive trips aboard the *Tahiti Aggressor.*

Alternatively, you can make your own arrangements directly with island dive shops. (Information about these operators is included under the heading Sports and Recreation in the respective destination chapters of this book.)

Tours for Naturalists

About the only inbound tour operator dedicated to adventure/ecotourism in French Polynesia is **Tahiti Outfitters** (Frank Murphy, tel. 689/48-31-69, www.tahitioutfitters.com) in Papeete. Its main business is organizing expeditions for major U.S. adventure travel companies, but it can also put together custom trips for preformed groups, families, and even couples. These range from bird-watching groups to university field courses and active travelers who want to get out and do some hiking or sea kayaking. All of Tahiti Outfitter's trips have major natural and cultural history components, so the participants learn quite a lot about the place.

The following companies market trips of this kind a couple of times a year:

Cox and Kings, 25 Davis Blvd., Tampa, FL 33606-3499, U.S.A.; tel. 800/999-1758 or 813/258-3323, www.coxandkingsusa.com

Explorers Corner, 1201 Monterey Ave., Berkeley, CA 94707, U.S.A.; tel. 510/559-8099, www.explorerscorner.com

Geographic Expeditions, 2627 Lombard St., San Francisco, CA 94123 U.S.A.; tel. 800/777-8183 or 415/922-0448, www.geoex.com

Mountain Travel Sobek, 6420 Fairmount Ave., El Cerrito, CA 94530-3606, U.S.A.; tel. 888/687-6235 or 510/527-8100, www.mtsobek.com

Wilderness Travel, 1102 9th St., Berkeley, CA 94710, U.S.A.; tel. 800/368-2794 or 510/558-2488, www.wildernesstravel.com/pacific.html

Surfing Tours

Tahitian Blue Water Dream (www.tahitianbluewaterdream.com) offers 10-day surfing and fishing cruises aboard the 19.5 live-aboard motor launch *Runaway.* The tour cost from Papeete without flights is US$2,250 and you can book online. **Vaimiti Tours** (www.vaimititours.com) also handles the *Runaway.*

Waterways Surf Adventures, 21625 Prairie St., Chatsworth, CA 91311, U.S.A.; tel. 800/928-3757 or 818/376-0341, www.waterwaystravel.com) books surfing tours with Moana David on Tahiti, plus the boat-based surfing just mentioned.

Global Surf Trips (2033-B San Elijo Ave., Suite 322, Cardiff by the Sea, CA 92007, U.S.A.; www.globalsurftravel.com) can provide information about surfing in French Polynesia.

Tours for Seniors

Since 1989 the **Pacific Islands Institute** (354 Uluniu St., Suite 408, Kailua, HI 96734, U.S.A.; tel. 808/262-8942, www.pac-island.com) has operated educational tours to most of the South Pacific countries in cooperation with Hawaii Pacific University. Its **Elderhostel** people-to-people study programs designed for those aged 55 or over (younger spouses welcome) are offered between four and six times a year. A 19-day tour to French Polynesia and Rarotonga is US$4,985 from Los Angeles, otherwise it's US$7,797 for 28 days to Easter Island and the Marquesas.

Cruises

Several large cruise ships based at Papeete offer regular one-week cruises in the Society Islands. These include the *Paul Gauguin* of **Radisson**

Seven Seas Cruises, the *Wind Star* of **Wind Star Cruises,** and the *Tahitian Princess* of **Princess Cruises.** Princess also sells cruises between Tahiti and Rarotonga. Companies such as **Bora Bora Cruises** and **Archipels Croisieres** operate much smaller minicruise ships in the same area. Also well worth considering are the adventure cruises to the Marquesas Islands aboard the passenger-carrying freighter *Aranui.* (Turn to Transportation in the French Polynesia introduction for detailed information on all these cruises.)

Because of the inadequate harbor facilities, cruise ships are not based at either Easter Island or Rarotonga, although these islands are on the cruise ship itineraries. Several times a year **Society Expeditions** (tel. 800/548-8669, www.societyexpeditions.com) offers cruises to remote islands on the 85-stateroom expedition ship *World Discoverer.* Passengers land from Zodiacs and there are on-board lectures by leading authorities. The 21-day cruise "in the wake of the *Bounty*" includes the Society, Tuamotu, and Marquesas Islands, Pitcairn, and Easter Island, starting at US$8,989 pp double occupancy. There's also an 18-day "pearls of the South Pacific" cruise from Tahiti to Fiji starting at US$7,585 pp.

On all the cruises, check whether gratuities, port taxes, transfers, shore excursions, alcoholic drinks, and airfare are included when evaluating costs.

Yacht Tours and Charters

If you were planning to spend a substantial amount to stay at a luxury resort, consider chartering a yacht instead! Divided among the members of your party the per-person charter price will be about the same, but you'll experience much more of the Pacific's beauty on a boat than you would staying in a hotel room. All charterers visit isolated lagoons and thus receive insights into island life unspoiled by normal tourist trappings. Of course, activities such as sailing, snorkeling, and general exploring by sea and land are included in the price.

Yacht charters are available either "bareboat" (for those with the skill to sail on their own) or "crewed" (in which case charterers pay a daily fee for a skipper). (For specific information about

yacht charters at Tahiti or Raiatea with Tahiti Yacht Charter, or at Raiatea with The Moorings and Stardust/Sunsail, turn to Transportation in the introduction to French Polynesia. Also check Local Tours in the Huahine chapter for independent yacht charters.)

A few private brokers arranging bareboat or crewed yacht charters are listed below. As they don't own their own boats, they'll be more inclined to fit you to the particular yacht that suits your individual needs.

Charter World Pty. Ltd., 23 Passchendaele St., Hampton, Melbourne 3188, Australia; tel. 61-3/9521-0033 or 800/335-039, www.charterworld.com.au

Crestar Yachts Ltd., 125 Sloane St., London SW1X 9AU, United Kingdom; tel. 44-20/7730-2299, www.crestar.co.uk

Paradise Adventures and Cruises, Heidi Gavriloff, P.O. Box 121, West Ryde, NSW 2114, Australia; tel. 61-2/9743-0253, www.paradiseadventures.com.au

Sail Connections Ltd., P.O. Box 90961, 8 Madden St., Auckland 1, New Zealand; tel. 64-9/358-0556, www.sailconnections.co.nz

The Windward Islands Cruising Company, 2672 N.W. 112th Ave., Miami, FL 33172, U.S.A.; tel. 305/593-8687, www.pacific-adventure.com

Yachting Partners International, 28-29 Richmond Pl., Brighton, East Sussex, BN2 9NA, United Kingdom; tel. 800/626-0019 or 44-1273/571-722, www.ypi.co.uk

One of the most experienced brokers arranging such charters is **Ocean Voyages** (1709 Bridgeway, Sausalito, CA 94965, U.S.A.; tel. 800/299-4444 or 415/332-4681, www.oceanvoyages.com). For groups of four or six people, Ocean Voyages books charter vessels such as the catamaran *Fai Manu* based at Taha'a or the sloop *Coup de Coeur.* The Taha'a-based sloop *Bisou Futé* accommodates eight, while two couples are as many as can be accommodated on the cabin cruiser *Danae II* at Raiatea. Ocean Voyages also organizes an annual yacht trip from Mangareva to Pitcairn, about the only practicable way of actually spending a few days there.

BY SAILING YACHT

Getting Aboard

It's possible to hitch rides into the Pacific on yachts from California, Panama, New Zealand, and Australia, or around the yachting triangle Papeete–Suva–Honolulu. If you've never crewed before, consider looking for a yacht already in the islands. In Tahiti, for example, after a month on the open sea, some of the original crew may have flown home or onward, opening a place for you. Cruising yachts are recognizable by their foreign flags, wind-vane steering gear, sturdy appearance, and laundry hung out to dry. Good captains evaluate crew on personality, attitude, and a willingness to learn more than experience, so don't lie. Be honest and open when interviewing with a skipper—a deception will soon become apparent.

It's also good to know what a captain's *really* like before you commit yourself to an isolated month with her/him. To determine what might happen should the electronic gadgetry break down, find out if there's a sextant aboard and whether he/she knows how to use it. A boat that looks run-down may often be mechanically unsound too. Also be concerned about a skipper who doesn't do a careful safety briefing early on, or who seems to have a hard time hanging onto crew. If the previous crew have left the boat at an unlikely place such as the Marquesas, there must have been a reason. Once you're on a boat and part of the yachtie community, things are easy. (P.S. from veteran yachtie Peter Moree: "We do need more ladies out here—adventurous types naturally.")

Time of Year

The weather and seasons play a deciding role in any South Pacific trip by sailboat and you'll have to pull out of many beautiful places, or be unable to stop there, because of bad weather. The prime season for rides in the South Pacific is

May–October; sometimes you'll even have to turn one down. Be aware of the hurricane season (November–March in the South Pacific) as few yachts will be cruising at that time.

Also, know which way the winds are blowing; the prevailing trade winds in the tropics south of the equator are from the southeast. South of the tropic of Capricorn the winds are out of the west. Because of the action of prevailing southeast trade winds, boat trips are smoother from east to west than west to east throughout the South Pacific, so that's the way to go.

Yachting Routes

The common yachting route or "Coconut Milk Run" across the South Pacific uses the northeast and southeast trades: from California to Tahiti via the Marquesas or Hawaii, then Rarotonga, Niue, Vava'u, Suva, and New Zealand. Some yachts continue west from Fiji to Port Vila. In the other direction, you'll sail on the westerlies from New Zealand to a point south of the Australs, then north on the trades to Tahiti.

About 300 yachts leave the U.S. west coast for Tahiti every year, almost always crewed by couples or men only. Most stay in the South Seas about a year before returning to North America, while a few continue around the world. Cruising yachts average about 150 km a day, so it takes about a month to get from the U.S. west coast to Hawaii, then another month from Hawaii to Tahiti.

To enjoy the finest weather conditions many yachts clear the Panama Canal or depart California in February to arrive in the Marquesas in March. From Hawaii, yachts often leave for Tahiti in April or May. Many stay on for the *Heiva i Tahiti* festival, which ends on July 14, at which time they sail west to Tonga or Fiji, where you'll find them in July and August. By late October the bulk of the yachting community is sailing south via New Caledonia to New Zealand or Australia to spend the southern summer there. Jimmy Cornell's www.noonsite.com provides lots of valuable information for cruising yachties.

Life Aboard

To crew on a yacht you must be willing to wash and iron clothes, cook, steer, keep watch at night,

INTRODUCTION

and help with engine work. Other jobs might include changing and resetting sails, cleaning the boat, scraping the bottom, pulling up the anchor, and climbing the main mast to watch for reefs. Do more than is expected of you. A safety harness must be worn in rough weather. As a guest in someone else's home you'll want to wash your dishes promptly after use and put them, and all other gear, back where you found it. Tampons must not be thrown in the toilet bowl. Smoking is usually prohibited as a safety hazard.

Anybody who wants to get on well under sail must be flexible and tolerant, both physically and emotionally. Expense-sharing crew members pay US$50 a week or more per person. After 30 days you'll be happy to hit land for a freshwater shower. Give adequate notice when you're ready to leave the boat, but *do* disembark when your journey's up. Boat people have few enough opportunities for privacy as it is. If you've had a good trip, ask the captain to write you a letter of recommendation; it'll help you hitch another ride.

Food for Thought

When you consider the big investment, depreciation, cost of maintenance, operating expenses, and considerable risk (most cruising yachts are not insured), travel by sailing yacht is quite a luxury. The huge cost can be surmised from charter fees (US$600 a day and up for a 10-meter yacht). International law makes a clear distinction between passengers and crew. Crew members paying only for their own food, cooking gas, and part of the diesel are very different from charterers who do nothing and pay full costs. The crew is there to help operate the boat, adding safety, but like passengers, they're very much under the control of the captain. Crew has no say in where the yacht will go.

The skipper is personally responsible for crew coming into foreign ports: he's entitled to hold their passports and to see that they have onward tickets and sufficient funds for further traveling. Otherwise the skipper might have to pay their hotel bills and even return airfares to the crew's country of origin. Crew may be asked to pay a share of third-party liability insurance. Possession of drugs would probably result in seizure of the yacht. Because of such considerations, skippers often hesitate to accept crew. Crew members should remember that at no cost to themselves they can learn a bit of sailing and visit places nearly inaccessible by other means. Although not for everyone, it's *the* way to see the real South Pacific, and folks who arrive by *vaa* or *vaka* (sailing canoe) are treated differently from other tourists.

Getting Around

Both French Polynesia and the Cook Islands have domestic airlines serving the outer islands. Air Tahiti and Air Rarotonga fly small aircraft, so only 10–16 kilograms free baggage may be allowed. A typical interisland flight will cost around US$75 in the Cook Islands or US$100 in French Polynesia. Most runways are unlighted so few flights operate at night. (These services are described in the respective chapters of this guide.)

Most international travel around the South Pacific is by air but you can still get to outer islands within a single country by boat. Among the local trips you can easily do by regularly scheduled passenger boat are Tahiti–Moorea and Tahiti–Huahine/Raiatea. (Details of these and other shipping possibilities are provided in the French Polynesia and Cook Islands introductions.)

By Car

A rental car with unlimited mileage will generally cost around US$35 a day in the Cook Islands or US$70 in French Polynesia. The price of a liter of gasoline also varies considerably: Easter Island US$.60, the Cook Islands US$.79, and French Polynesia US$1. To determine the price of an American gallon, multiply any of these by 3.7854.

Because of the alternative means of travel available, you need to consider renting a car only in French Polynesia. In the Cook Islands one must buy a local driver's license (international driver's license not accepted) and it's better to tour the Cook Islands by rented bicycle anyway. Bicycle is also the way to see Bora Bora. Get around Easter Island on foot.

The car rental business in the Society Islands is competitive. Although the locally operated companies may offer cheaper rates than the franchises, it's also true that Avis, Budget, and Hertz are required to meet international standards of service and they have head offices where you can complain if anything goes seriously wrong. Always find out if insurance, mileage, and tax are included, and check for restrictions on where you'll be allowed to take the car. If in doubt, ask to see a copy of the standard rental contract before making reservations.

Driving is on the right (as in continental Europe and North America) in French Polynesia and Easter Island, and on the left (as in Britain, New Zealand, and Japan) in the Cook Islands. If you do rent a car, remember those sudden tropical downpours and don't leave the windows open. Also avoid parking under coconut trees (a falling nut might break the window), and never go off and leave the keys in the ignition. Lock the doors as you would at home.

By Bicycle

Bicycling in the South Pacific? Sure, why not? It's cheap, convenient, healthy, quick, environmentally sound, safe, and above all, *fun.* You'll be able to go where and when you please, stop easily and often to meet people and take photos, save money on taxi fares—really *see* the countries. Most roads are flat along the coast, but be careful on coral roads, especially inclines: if you slip and fall you could hurt yourself badly. On the high islands interior roads tend to be very steep. Never ride your bike through mud.

You can rent bicycles almost anywhere except on Tahiti. If you bring your own, a sturdy, single-speed mountain bike with wide wheels, safety chain, and good brakes will be ideal. Thick tires and a plastic liner between tube and tire will re-

duce punctures. Know how to fix your own bike. Take along a good repair kit (pump, puncture kit, freewheel tool, spare spokes, cables, chain links, assorted nuts and bolts, etc.) and a repair manual. A couple of good bicycle shops do exist in Papeete, but that's it. Don't try riding with a backpack: sturdy, waterproof panniers (bike bags) are required; you'll also want a good lock. Refuse to lend your bike to *anyone.*

Most international airlines will carry a bicycle as checked luggage, usually free but sometimes at the standard overweight charge or for a flat US$50 fee. Verify the airline's policy before booking. Take off the pedals and panniers, turn the handlebars sideways and tie them down, deflate the tires, and clean off the dirt before checking in (or use a special bike-carrying bag) and arrive at the airport early. The commuter airlines don't usually accept bicycles on their small planes. Interisland boats sometimes charge a token amount to carry a bike; other times it's free.

By Ocean Kayak and Canoe

Ocean kayaking is finally beginning to catch on in the South Pacific, and you can now rent kayaks on Tahiti, Moorea, Huahine, Bora Bora, Rarotonga, and Aitutaki. Almost every island has a sheltered lagoon ready-made for the excitement of kayak touring, so you can be a real independent 21st-century explorer! Many international airlines accept folding kayaks as checked baggage at no charge.

For a better introduction to ocean kayaking than is possible here, visit your local public library for sea kayaking manuals. Noted author Paul Theroux toured the entire South Pacific by kayak, and his experiences are recounted in *The Happy Isles of Oceania: Paddling the Pacific.*

If you get off the beaten track, you might have a chance to borrow an outrigger canoe. Never attempt to take a dugout canoe through even light surf: you'll be swamped. Don't try to pull or lift a canoe by its outrigger: it will break. Drag the canoe by holding the solid main body. A bailer is *essential* equipment.

French Polynesia/ Te Ao Maohi

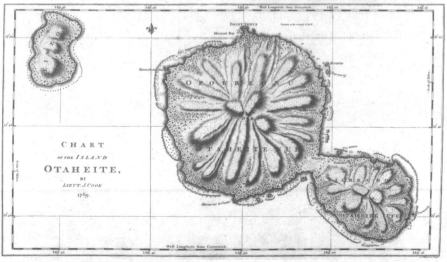

Captain Cook's 1769 map of Tahiti and Moorea

Introduction

Legendary Tahiti, isle of love, has long been the vision of "la Nouvelle Cythère," the earthly paradise. Explorers Wallis, Bougainville, and Cook all told of a land of spellbinding beauty and enchantment, where the climate was delightful, hazardous insects and diseases unknown, and the islanders, especially the women, among the handsomest ever seen. Rousseau's "noble savage" had been found! A few years later, Fletcher Christian and Captain Bligh acted out their drama of sin and retribution here.

The list of famous authors who came and wrote about these islands reads like a high-school literature course: Herman Melville, Robert Louis Stevenson, Pierre Loti, Rupert Brooke, Jack London, W. Somerset Maugham, Charles Nordhoff and James Norman Hall (the Americans who wrote *Mutiny on the Bounty*), among others. Exotic images of uninhibited dancers, fragrant flowers, and pagan gods fill the pages. Here, at least, life was meant to be enjoyed.

The most unlikely PR man of them all was a once-obscure French painter named Paul Gauguin, who transformed the primitive color of Tahiti and the Marquesas into powerful visual images seen around the world. When World War II shook the Pacific from Pearl Harbor to Guadalcanal, rather than bloodcurdling banzais and saturation bombings, Polynesia got a U.S. serviceman named James A. Michener, who added Bora Bora to the legend. Marlon Brando arrived in 1961 on one of the first jets to land in Polynesia and, along with thousands of tourists and adventurers, has been coming back ever since.

© M.G.L. DOMENY DE RIENZI

The friendly, easygoing manner of the people of French Polynesia isn't only a cliché! Tahiti gets just over 225,000 tourists a year (compared to the seven million that visit Hawaii) and many are French nationals visiting friends, so you won't be facing a tourist glut! Despite more than a century and a half of French colonialism, the Tahitians retain many of their old ways, be it in personal dress, Polynesian dancing, or outrigger canoe racing. Relax, smile, and say *bonjour* to strangers—you'll almost always get a warm response. Welcome to paradise!

The Land

French Polynesia (or Te Ao Maohi as it is known to the Polynesians themselves) consists of five great archipelagos, the Society, Austral, Tuamotu, Gambier, and Marquesas Islands, arrayed in chains running from southeast to northwest. The Society Islands are subdivided into the Windwards, or *Îles du Vent* (Tahiti, Moorea, Maiao, Tetiaroa, and Mehetia), and the Leewards, or *Îles Sous-le-Vent* (Huahine, Raiatea, Taha'a, Bora Bora, Maupiti, Tupai, Maupihaa/Mopelia, Manuae/Scilly, and Motu One/Bellingshausen).

Together the 35 islands and 83 atolls of French Polynesia total only 3,543 square km in land area, yet they're scattered over a vast area of the southeastern Pacific Ocean, between 7 degrees and 28 degrees south latitude and 131 degrees and 156 degrees west longitude. Papeete (149 degrees west longitude) is actually eight degrees *east* of Honolulu (157 degrees west longitude). Though French Polynesia is only half the size of Corsica in land area, if Papeete were Paris then the Gambiers would be in Romania and the Marquesas near Stockholm. At 5,030,000 square km the territory's 200-nautical-mile exclusive economic zone is by far the largest in the Pacific islands.

There's a wonderful geological diversity to these islands midway between Australia and South America—from the dramatic, jagged volcanic outlines of the Society and Marquesas Islands, to the 400-meter-high hills of the Australs and Gambiers, to the low coral atolls of the Tuamotu. All of the Marquesas are volcanic islands, while the Tuamotus are all coral islands or atolls. The Societies and Gambiers include both volcanic and coral types.

Tahiti, around 4,000 km from both Auckland and Honolulu or 6,000 km from Los Angeles and Sydney, is not only the best known and most populous of the islands, but also the largest (1,045 square km) and highest (2,241 meters). Bora Bora and Maupiti are noted for their combination of high volcanic peaks framed by low coral rings. Rangiroa is one of the world's largest coral atolls while Makatea is an uplifted atoll. In the Marquesas, precipitous and sharply crenelated mountains rise hundreds of meters, with craggy peaks, razorback ridges, plummeting waterfalls, deep, fertile valleys, and dark broken coastlines pounded by surf. Compare them to the pencil-thin strips of yellow reefs, green vegetation, and white beaches enclosing the transparent Tuamotu lagoons. In all, French Polynesia offers some of the most varied and spectacular scenery in the entire South Pacific.

In the evening the heat of the Tahiti afternoons is replaced by soft, fragrant mountain breezes called hupe, *which drift down to the sea. French Polynesia enjoys some of the cleanest air on earth—air that hasn't blown over a continent for weeks.*

Climate

The hot and humid summer season runs November–April. The rest of the year the climate is somewhat cooler and drier. The refreshing southeast trade winds blow consistently May–August, varying to easterlies September–December. The northeast trades Jan.–April coincide with the hurricane season. The trade winds cool the islands and offer clear sailing for mariners, making May–October the most favorable season to visit. (In fact, there can be long periods of fine,

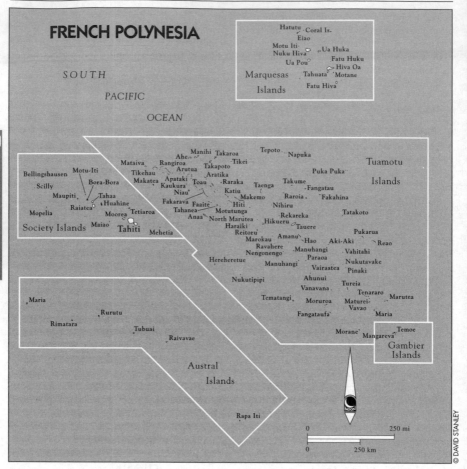

FRENCH POLYNESIA

SOUTH

PACIFIC

OCEAN

Marquesas
Islands

Hatutu Coral Is.
Eiao
Motu Iti
Nuku Hiva   Ua Huka
Ua Pou   Fatu Huku
Hiva Oa
Tahuata Motane
Fatu Hiva

Tuamotu

Islands

Manihi Takaroa
Mataiva Rangiroa Takapoto Tepoto Napuka
Ahe Tikei
Tikehau Arutua Aratika
Bellingshausen Motu-Iti Makatea Apataki Toau Raraka Puka Puka
Scilly Bora-Bora Kaukura Niau Takume
Maupiti Tahaa Fakarava Faaite Katiu Taenga Fangatau
Mopelia Raiatea Huahine Tahanea Hiti Makemo Raroia Fakahina
Moorea Tetiaroa Anaa Motutunga Nihiru
Society Islands Maiao Tahiti North Marutea Rekareka Tatakoto
Mehetia Haraiki Hikueru Tauere
Reitoru Amanu Pukarua
Marokau Hao Aki-Aki Reao
Ravahere Manuhangi Vahitahi
Nengonengo Paraoa Nukutavake
Hereheretue Manuhangi Vairaatea Pinaki
Nukutipipi Ahunui Tureia
Vanavana Tenararo
Maria Tematangi Moruroa Maturei- Marutea
Vavao
Rurutu Fangataufa Maria
Rimatara Tubuai
Raivavae Morane Temoe
Mangareva Gambier
Islands

Austral
Islands

Rapa Iti

0   250 mi
0   250 km

© DAVID STANLEY

sunny weather anytime of year and these seasonal variations should not be a pivotal factor in deciding when to come.)

Hurricanes are relatively rare, although they do hit the Tuamotus and occasionally Tahiti (but almost never the Marquesas). From November 1980 to May 1983 an unusual wave of eight hurricanes and two tropical storms battered the islands because of the El Niño phenomenon. The next hurricane occurred in December 1991. In November 1997 two hurricanes struck Maupiti and neighboring isles, one passed over the Tuamotus in February 1998,

and another hit Huahine in April 1998, again the fault of El Niño. A hurricane would merely inconvenience a visitor staying at a hotel, though campers and yachties might get blown into oblivion. The days immediately following a hurricane are clear and dry.

Rainfall is greatest in the mountains and along the windward shores of the high islands. The Societies are far damper than the Marquesas. In fact, the climate of the Marquesas is erratic: some years the group experiences serious drought, other years it could rain the whole time you're there. The low-lying Tuamotus get the least rain-

FRENCH POLYNESIA AT A GLANCE

	POPULATION (2002)	AREA (hectares)
Windward Islands	**184,224**	**118,580**
Tahiti	169,674	104,510
Moorea	14,226	12,520
Leeward Islands	**30,221**	**38,750**
Huahine	5,757	7,480
Raiatea	11,133	17,140
Taha'a	4,845	9,020
Bora Bora	7,295	2,930
Maupiti	1,191	1,140
Austral Islands	**6,386**	**14,784**
Rurutu	2,104	3,235
Tubuai	1,979	4,500
Tuamotu Islands	**14,765**	**72,646**
Rangiroa	2,334	7,900
Manihi	789	1,300
Gambier Islands	**1,097**	**4,597**
Marquesas Islands	**8,712**	**104,930**
Nuku Hiva	2,652	33,950
Hiva Oa	2,015	31,550
French Polynesia	**245,405**	**354,287**

fall of all. French Polynesia encompasses such a vast area that latitude is an important factor: at 27 degrees south latitude Rapa is far cooler than Nuku Hiva (9 degrees south).

Winds from the southeast *(maraamu)* are generally drier than those from the northeast or north. The northeast winds often bring rain: Papenoo on the northeast side of Tahiti is twice as wet as rain-shadowed Punaauia. The annual rainfall is extremely variable, but the humidity is generally high, reaching 98 percent. In the evening the heat of the Tahiti afternoons is replaced by soft, fragrant mountain breezes called *hupe,* which drift down to the sea. French Polynesia enjoys some of the cleanest air on earth—air that hasn't blown over a continent for weeks.

Tahiti and Moorea have a solar (rather than a lunar) tide, which means that the low tides are at sunrise and sunset, high tides at noon and midnight. Because of this, snorkeling in or near a reef passage will be safest in the morning as the water flows in. Shallow waters are best traversed by yachts around noon when the water is high and slack, and visibility is at its peak.

FRENCH POLYNESIA

Flora and Fauna

The national flower, the delicate, heavily scented *tiare Tahiti (Gardenia tahitiensis),* can have anywhere from six to nine white petals. It blooms year-round, but especially from September to April. In his *Plants and Flowers of Tahiti* Jean-Claude Belhay writes:

> *The tiare is to Polynesia what the lotus is to India: a veritable symbol.*

Follow local custom by wearing this blossom or a hibiscus behind your left ear if you're happily taken, behind your right ear if you're still available.

In the coastal areas of Tahiti most of the plants now seen have been introduced by humans. Avocado, banana, custard apple, guava, grapefruit, lime, lychee, mango, orange, papaya, pineapple, watermelon, and a hundred more are cultivated. Mountain bananas *(fei)* grow wild in the high country. Mape (Tahitian chestnut) grows along the streams, and other trees you'll encounter include almond, candlenut, casuarina (ironwood), flamboyant, barringtonia, purau (wild hibiscus), pistachio, and rosewood. A South American tree, Miconia calvescens, was planted at the botanical garden next to the Gauguin Museum in 1937, from which it spread across much of central Tahiti, supplanting the native vegetation.

Of the 104 species of birds in French Polynesia, half of the 30 species of native land birds are found only here. Among the 48 species of seabirds are the white-tailed tropic birds, brown and black noddies, white and crested terns, petrels, and boobies. The itatae (white tern), often seen flying about with its mate far from land, lays a single egg in the fork of a tree without any nest. The baby terns can fly soon after hatching. Its call is a sharp ke-ke-yek-yek. The oio (black noddy) nests in colonies, preferably in palm trees, building a flat nest of dead leaves, sticks, and stems. It calls a deep cra-cra-cra. Thirteen species of North American or Siberian land birds visit occasionally and another 13 species of introduced birds are always here. The most notorious among them is the hopping common mynah bird (Acridotheres tristis) with yellow beak and feet, which was introduced from Indonesia at the turn of the last century to control insects. Today these noisy, aggressive birds are ubiquitous—feeding on fruit trees and forcing the native finches and blue-tinged doves out of their habitat.

History and Government

Polynesian Culture

The eastern Polynesian islands, including those of French Polynesia, were colonized at uncertain dates around the start of the 1st millennium A.D. It's thought that about 300 B.C. the Polynesians reached the Marquesas from Samoa, and sometime before A.D. 300 they sailed on from the Marquesas to Hawai'i and Easter Island. They were on the Society Islands by 600 and sailed from there to the Cooks and New Zealand before 1100, completing the occupation of the Polynesian triangle. On these planned voyages of colonization they carried all the plants and animals needed to continue their way of life.

The Polynesians lived from fishing and agriculture, using tools made from stone, bone, shell, and wood. The men were responsible for planting, harvesting, fishing, cooking, and house and canoe building; the women tended the fields and animals, gathered food and fuel, prepared food, and made tapa clothes and household items. Both men and women worked together in family or community groups, not as individuals.

The Polynesians lost the art of pottery-making during their long stay in Havaiki (possibly Samoa) and had to cook their food in underground ovens *(umu)*. It was sometimes *tapu*

ARCHAEOLOGY

The first archaeological survey of French Polynesia was undertaken in 1925 by Professor Kenneth P. Emory of Honolulu's Bernice P. Bishop Museum. Emory's successor, Professor Yoshiko Sinoto of the same museum, has carried out extensive excavations and restorations in the area since 1960. In 1962, at a 9th-century graveyard on Maupiti's Motu Paeao, Emory and Sinoto uncovered artifacts perfectly matching those of the first New Zealand Maoris. A few years later, at Ua Huka in the Marquesas, Sinoto discovered a coastal village site dating from A.D. 300, the oldest yet found in Eastern Polynesia. Sinoto was responsible for the restoration of the Maeva *marae* on Huahine and many historical *marae* on Tahiti, Moorea, Raiatea, and Bora Bora. During construction of the Bali Hai Hôtel on Huahine in 1973–1977 Sinoto's student diggers found 10 flat hand clubs of the *patu* model, previously thought to exist only in New Zealand, plus some planks of a 1,000-year-old sewn double canoe.

(taboo) for men and women to eat together. Breadfruit, taro, yams, sweet potatoes, bananas, and coconuts were cultivated (the Polynesians had no cereals). Pigs, chickens, and dogs were also kept for food, but the surrounding sea yielded the most important source of protein.

Canoes were made of planks stitched together with sennit and caulked with gum from breadfruit trees. Clothing consisted of tapa (bark cloth). Both men and women wore belts of pandanus leaves or tapa when at work, and during leisure, a skirt that reached to their knees. Ornaments were of feathers, whale or dolphin teeth, and flowers. Both sexes were artfully tattooed using candlenut oil and soot.

For weapons there were clubs, spears, and slings. Archery was practiced only as a game to determine who could shoot farthest. Spear throwing, wrestling, boxing, kite flying, surfing, and canoe racing were popular sports. Polynesian music was made with nasal flutes and cylindrical sharkskin or hollow slit drums. Their dancing is still appreciated today.

The museums of the world possess many fine stone and wood tikis in human form from the Marquesas Islands, where the decorative sense was highly developed. Sculpture in the Australs was more naturalistic, and only here were female tikis common. The Tahitians showed less interest in the plastic arts but excelled in the social arts of poetry, oratory, theater, music, song, and dance. Life on the Tuamotus was a struggle for existence, and objects had utilitarian functions. Countless Polynesian cult objects were destroyed in the early 19th century by overzealous missionaries.

Before European contact three hereditary classes structured the Society Islands: high chiefs *(ari'i)*, lesser chiefs *(raatira)*, and commoners *(manahune)*. A small slave class *(titi)* also existed. The various *ari'i* tribes controlled wedge-shaped valleys, and their authority was balanced. None managed to gain permanent supremacy over the rest. In this rigid hierarchical system, where high chiefs had more mana than commoners, marriage or even physical contact between people of unequal mana was forbidden. Children resulting from sexual relations between the classes were killed.

Religion centered around an open-air temple, called a *marae,* with a stone altar. Here priests prayed to the ancestors or gods and conducted all the significant ceremonies of Polynesian life. An individual's social position was determined by his or her family connections, and the recitation of one's genealogy confirmed it. Human sacrifices took place on important occasions on a high chief's *marae.* Cannibalism was rife in the Marquesas and was also practiced in the Tuamotus.

Members of the Raiatea-based Arioi Society traveled through the islands performing ritual copulation and religious rites. The fertility god Oro had descended on a rainbow to Bora Bora's Mt. Pahia, where he found a beautiful *vahine.* Their child was the first Arioi. In their pursuit of absolute *free* love, the Arioi shared spouses and killed their own children.

But the Arioi were not the only practitioners of infanticide in French Polynesia. The whole social structure could be threatened by a surplus of children among the chiefly class. Such children might demand arable land from commoners who supplied the chiefs with food. And a struggle between too many potential heirs could create strife. Thus the *ari'i* often did away with unwanted infants after birth (rather than before birth as is the accepted practice today). The Arioi Society itself may have been a partial solution, as unwanted *ari'i* children were assigned a benign role as Arioi with the assurance that they themselves would never produce any offspring.

European Exploration

While the Polynesian history of the islands goes back two millennia, the European period began only in the 16th century when the Magellan expedition sailed past the Tuamotus and Mendaña visited the Marquesas. The Spaniard Quirós saw the Tuamotus in 1606, as did the Dutchmen Le Maire and Schouten in 1616, the Dutchman Roggeveen in 1722, and the Englishman Byron in 1765. But it was not until June 18,1767, that Captain Samuel Wallis on the HMS *Dolphin* happened upon Tahiti. He and most of his contemporary explorers were in search of *terra australis incognita,* a mythical southern landmass thought to balance the Northern Hemisphere.

At first the Tahitians attacked the ship, but after experiencing European gunfire they decided to be friendly. Eager to trade, they loaded

THE FIRST WOMAN TO CIRCUMNAVIGATE THE GLOBE

In late 1766, Louis-Antoine Bougainville set sail from France aboard the frigate *Boudeuse* on a voyage of discovery that would last 28 months. The expedition's second vessel, the *Etoile,* carried the king's botanist, Philibert Commerson. The ships spent longer than a year off the east coast of South America on various missions. In Brazil Commerson collected a violet flowering climber that he named *bougainvillea* for his captain.

After rounding Cape Horn, Bougainville and crew reached Tahiti in April 1768. Commerson's passion for native plants was shared by his hard-working assistant, Bonnefoy. There had been speculation aboard the *Etoile* that the fresh-faced boy dressed in baggy clothes might be a female, and all doubt was removed when "Bonnefoy" stepped ashore at Hitiaa. Tahitians immediately surrounded the youth, crying *vahine, vahine* (woman, woman) and offering to do her *les honneurs de l'isle* (the honors of the island). Jeanne Baret had to beat a hasty retreat to the ship.

Years later Bougainville described the situation in his *Journal:*

> With tears in her eyes Baret acknowledged that she was a girl, that she had misled her master (Commerson) by dressing in men's clothes, that she was an orphan from Burgundy, that a lawsuit had reduced her to poverty, and that news of a

voyage around the world had piqued her interest. I considered her case unique and admired her courage and wisdom. I took measures to ensure that nothing unpleasant happened to her. The royal court, I believe, will forgive this infringement of the rules. She was neither plain nor pretty and hardly 25 years old.

When the expedition reached the French colony of Mauritius in the Indian Ocean, Commerson and Baret disembarked. There Commerson named the *baretia,* a plant species of dubious sex, for this "valiant young woman who, adopting the dress and temperament of a man, had the curiosity and audacity to traverse the whole world, by land and sea, accompanying us without ourselves knowing anything."

Through the centuries Commerson has been largely forgotten because of his decision not to return directly to Europe with Bougainville. Though his work at Mauritius, Madagascar, and Reunion was important, many of his specimens and reports have been lost. After Commerson's death at Reunion in 1773, it became apparent that the only way Jeanne could return to France was by marrying a soldier, which she did. In 1785 Jeanne Baret, now Madame Dubernat, a widow living in Burgundy, was granted a naval pension at Bougainville's request. She died quietly in 1807.

the Englishmen down with pigs, fowl, and fruit. Iron was in the highest demand, and Tahitian women lured the sailors to exchange nails for love. Consequently, to prevent the ship's timbers from being torn asunder for the nails, no man was allowed onshore except in parties strictly for food and water. Wallis sent ashore a landing party, which named Tahiti "King George III Island," turned some sod, and hoisted the Union Jack. A year later the French explorer Louis-Antoine de Bougainville arrived on the east coast, unaware of Wallis's discovery, and claimed Tahiti for the king of France.

Wallis and Bougainville visited only briefly, leaving it to Captain James Cook to really describe Polynesia to Europeans. Cook visited "Otaheite" four times, in 1769, 1773, 1774, and 1777. His first three-month visit was to observe the transit of the planet Venus across the face of the sun. The second and third were in search of the southern continent, while the fourth was to find a northwest passage between the Pacific and Atlantic Oceans. Some of the finest artists and scientists of the day accompanied Captain Cook. Their explorations added the Leeward Islands, two Austral islands, and a dozen Tuamotu islands to European knowledge. On Tahiti Cook met a high priest from Raiatea named Tupaia, who had an astonishing knowledge of the Pacific and could name dozens of islands. He drew Cook a map that included the Cook Islands, the Marquesas, and perhaps also some Samoan islands!

In 1788 Tahiti was visited for five months by HMS *Bounty*, commanded by Lieutenant William Bligh with orders to collect young breadfruit plants for transportation to the West Indies. However, the famous mutiny did not take place at Tahiti but in Tongan waters, and from there Bligh and loyal members of his crew managed to escape by navigating an open boat 6,500 km to Dutch Timor. In 1791, the HMS *Pandora* came to Tahiti in search of the *Bounty* mutineers, intending to take them to England for trial. They captured 14 survivors of the 16 who had elected to stay on Tahiti when Fletcher Christian and eight others left for Pitcairn. Although glamorized by Hollywood, the mutineers helped destroy traditional Tahitian society by acting as

mercenaries for rival chiefs. In 1792 Bligh returned to Tahiti in another ship and completed his original mission.

By the early 19th century, ruffian British and American whalers were fanning out over the Pacific. Other ships traded with the islanders for sandalwood, bêche-de-mer, and mother-of-pearl, as well as the usual supplies. They brought with them smallpox, measles, influenza, tuberculosis, scarlet fever, and venereal diseases, which devastated the unprepared Polynesians. Slave raids, alcohol, and European firearms did the rest.

Kings and Missionaries

In March 1797 the ship *Duff* dropped off on Tahiti 18 Protestant missionaries and their wives after a 207-day journey from England. By this time Pomare, chief of the area adjoining Matavai Bay, had become powerful through the use of European tools, firearms, and mercenaries. He welcomed the missionaries but would not be converted; infanticide, sexual freedom, and human sacrifices continued. By 1800 all but five of the original 18 had left Tahiti disappointed.

In 1803 Pomare I died and his despotic son, Pomare II, attempted to conquer the entire island. After initial success he was forced to flee to Moorea in 1808. Missionary Henry Nott went with him, and in 1812 Pomare II turned to him for help in regaining his lost power. Though the missionaries refused to baptize Pomare II himself because of his heathen and drunken habits, his subjects on Moorea became nominal Christians. In 1815 this "Christian king" managed to regain Tahiti and overthrow paganism. Instead of being punished, the defeated clans were forgiven and allowed to become Christians. The persistent missionaries then enforced the 10 Commandments and dressed the Tahitian women in "Mother Hubbard" costumes—dresses that covered their bodies from head to toe. Henceforth singing anything but hymns was banned, dancing proscribed, and all customs that offended puritanical sensibilities wiped away. Morality police terrorized the confused Tahitians in an eternal crusade against sin. Even the wearing of flowers in the hair was prohibited.

In *Omoo* (1847) Herman Melville comments:

Doubtless, in thus denationalizing the Tahitians, as it were, the missionaries were prompted by a sincere desire for good; but the effect has been lamentable. Supplied with no amusements, in place of those forbidden, the Tahitians, who require more recreation than other people, have sunk into a listlessness, or indulge in sensualities, a hundred times more pernicious than all the games ever celebrated in the Temple of Tanee.

The Rape of Polynesia

Upon Pomare II's death from drink at age 40 in 1821, the crown passed to his infant son, Pomare III, but he passed away in 1827. At this juncture the most remarkable Tahitian of the 19th century, Aimata, half-sister of Pomare II, be-

came Queen Pomare Vahine IV. She was to rule Tahiti, Moorea, and part of the Austral and Tuamotu groups for half a century until her death in 1877, a barefoot Tahitian Queen Victoria. She allied herself closely with the London Missionary Society (LMS), and when two fanatical French-Catholic priests, Honoré Laval and François Caret, arrived on Tahiti in 1836 from their stronghold at Mangareva (Gambier Islands), she expelled them promptly. (Turn to The Gambier Islands for more information on Père Laval.)

This affront brought a French frigate to Papeete in 1838, demanding $2,000 compensation and a salute to the French flag. Although the conditions were met, the queen and her chiefs wrote to England appealing for help, but none came. A Belgian named Moerenhout who had formerly served as the U.S. consul was appointed

Pomare V's mother died in 1877 after reigning for 50 troubled years during which she was exhorted to accept a French protectorate over her Polynesian kingdom. A less heroic figure than his mother, King Pomare V (above left), the fifth and last of his name to hold the throne, took over a luckless dynasty and also took to drink. He was particularly fond of Benedictine and although the distinctive symbol enshrined forever atop his pylon-shaped mausoleum (above right) at Arue appears to be a massive Benedictine bottle, it is actually a Grecian vase. He died in 1891 an unhappy man.

French consul to Queen Pomare in 1838, and in 1839 a second French gunboat arrived and threatened to bombard Tahiti unless 2,000 Spanish dollars were paid and Catholic missionaries given free entry. Back in Mangareva, Laval pushed forward a grandiose building program, which wiped out 80 percent of the population of the Gambiers from overwork.

In September 1842, while the queen and George Pritchard, the English consul, were away, Moerenhout tricked four local chiefs into signing a petition asking to be brought under French "protection." This demand was immediately accepted by French Admiral Abel Dupetit-Thouars, who was in league with Moerenhout, and on September 9, 1842, they forced Queen Pomare to accept a French protectorate. When the queen tried to maintain her power and keep her red-and-white royal flag, Dupetit-Thouars deposed the queen on November 8, 1843, and occupied her kingdom, an arbitrary act that was rejected by the French king, who reestablished the protectorate in 1844. Queen Pomare fled to Raiatea and Pritchard was deported to England in March 1844, bringing Britain and France to the brink of war. The Tahitians resisted for three years: old French forts and war memorials recall the struggle.

The name "Pomare" means "night cough," from po, *night, plus* mare, *cough, because Pomare I's infant daughter died of tuberculosis in 1792.*

A French Protectorate

At the beginning of 1847, when Queen Pomare realized that no British assistance was forthcoming, she and her people reluctantly accepted the French protectorate. As a compromise, the British elicited a promise from the French not to annex the Leeward Islands, so Huahine, Raiatea, and Bora Bora remained independent until 1887. The French had taken possession of the Marquesas in 1842, even before imposing a protectorate on Tahiti. The Austral Islands were added in 1900 and only prior British action prevented the annexation of the Cook Islands. French missionaries attempted to convert the Tahitians to Catholicism, but only in the Marquesas were they fully successful.

Queen Pomare tried to defend the interests of her people as best she could, but much of her nation was dying: between the 18th century and 1926 the population of the Marquesas fell from 80,000 to only 2,000. In April 1774 Captain Cook had tried to estimate the population of Tahiti by counting the number of men he saw in a fleet of war canoes and ascribing three members to each one's family. Cook's figure was 204,000, but according to anthropologist Bengt Danielsson, the correct number at the time of discovery was about 150,000. By 1829 it had dropped to 8,568, and a low of 7,169 was reached in 1865.

Pomare V, the final, degenerate member of the line, was more interested in earthly pleasures than the traditions upheld by his mother. In 1880, with French interests at work on the Panama Canal, a smart colonial administrator convinced him to sign away his kingdom for a 5,000-franc-a-month pension. Thus, on June 29, 1880, the protectorate became the full French colony it is today, the Etablissements français de l'Oceánie. In 1957 the name was changed to Polynésie française. Right up until the 1970s the colony was run by governors appointed in Paris who implemented the policies of the French government. There was no system of indirect rule through local chiefs as was the case in the British colonies: here French officials decided everything and their authority could not be questioned. Even the 18-member Conseil Générale created in 1885 to oversee certain financial matters had its powers reduced in 1899 and was replaced in 1903 by an impotent advisory council composed of French civil servants. The only elected official with any authority (and a budget) was the mayor of Papeete.

The most earthshaking event between 1880 and 1960 was a visit by two German cruisers, the *Scharnhorst* and *Gneisenau,* which shelled Papeete, destroying the marketplace on September 22, 1914. (Two months later both were sunk by the British at the Battle of the Falkland Islands.) A thousand Tahitian volunteers subsequently served in Europe, 300 of them becoming casualties. On September 2, 1940, the colony declared its support for the Free French, and soon after Pearl Harbor the Americans arrived to establish a base on Bora Bora. Polynesia remained cut off from occupied metropolitan France until the end of the war, although several hundred Tahitians served with the Pacific battalion in North Africa and Italy. In 1946 the colony was made an overseas territory or *territoire d'outre-mer* (TOM) endowed with an elected territorial assembly. Representation in the French parliament was also granted.

The economy of the early colonial period had been based on cotton growing (1865–1900), vanilla cultivation (1870–1960), pearl shell collecting (1870–1960), copra making, and phosphate mining (1908–1966). These were to be replaced by nuclear testing (1963–1996), tourism (1961–present), and cultured pearls (1968–present).

The Nuclear Era

The early 1960s were momentous times for Polynesia. Within a few years, an international airport opened on Tahiti, MGM filmed *Mutiny on the Bounty,* and the French began testing their atomic bombs. After Algeria became independent in July 1962 the French decided to move their Sahara nuclear testing facilities to Moruroa Atoll in the Tuamotu Islands, 1,200 km southeast of Tahiti. In 1963, when all local political parties protested the invasion of Polynesia by thousands of French troops and technicians sent to establish a nuclear testing center, President Charles de Gaulle simply outlawed political parties. The French set off their first atmospheric nuclear explosion at Moruroa on July 2,1966, spreading contamination as far as Peru and New Zealand. In 1974 international protests forced the French to switch to the underground tests that continued until 1996. During those three decades of infamy 181 nuclear explosions, 41 of them in the atmosphere, rocked the Tuamotus.

In the 1960s–1970s, as independence blossomed across the South Pacific, France tightened its strategic grip on French Polynesia. The spirit of the time is best summed up in the life of one man, Pouvanaa a Oopa, an outspoken WWI hero from Huahine. In 1949 he became the first Polynesian to occupy a seat in the French Chamber of Deputies. His party gained control of the territorial assembly in 1953 and in 1957 he was elected vice president of the newly formed Government Council. In 1958 Pouvanaa campaigned for independence in a referendum vote, but when this failed because of a controversy over the imposition of an income tax, the French government reestablished central control and had Pouvanaa arrested on trumped-up charges of arson. He was eventually sentenced to an eight-year prison term and exiled to France for 15 years. De Gaulle wanted Pouvanaa out of the way until French nuclear testing facilities could be established in Polynesia, and he was not freed until 1968. In 1971 he won the French Polynesian seat in the French Senate, a post he held until his death in early 1977. Tahitians refer to the man as *metua* (father), and his statue stands in front of Papeete's Territorial Assembly.

Pouvanaa's successors, John Teariki and Francis Sanford, were also defenders of Polynesian autonomy and opponents of nuclear testing. Their combined efforts convinced the French government to grant Polynesia a new statute with a slightly increased autonomy in 1977. A year later Faa'a mayor Oscar Temaru formed Tavini Huiraatira, the Polynesian Liberation Front, the leading antinuclear, pro-independence party in the territory. The 1982 territorial elections were won by the neo-Gaullist Tahoeraa Huiraatira (Popular Union), led by the pronuclear, anti-independence mayor of Pirae, Gaston Flosse, who still heads the local government today. To stem growing support for independence, Flosse negotiated enhanced autonomy for the territory in 1984 and 1996.

Flosse's reputation for fixing government contracts earned him the title "Mr. Ten Percent" from the Paris newspaper *Libération*. There have been numerous allegations of corruption in his administration, and in early 2000 Flosse was convicted of abuse of public funds and given an eight-month suspended sentence. Flosse and Tahoeraa Huiraatira remain in office thanks to the massive subsidies French Polynesia receives. The political reality here is that a majority of voters are unwilling to jeopardize their standard of living by electing to break French Polynesia's ties with France.

The independence cause was given impetus by France's last fling at nuclear testing. In April 1992,

President Mitterrand halted the testing program at Moruroa, but in June 1995, newly elected President Jacques Chirac ordered a resumption of underground nuclear testing in the Tuamotus, and despite worldwide protests the first test was carried out on September 5, 1995. Early the next morning nonviolent demonstrators blocked the runway of Faa'a Airport after it was reported that Gaston Flosse was attempting to escape to France. When police charged the protesters to clear the runway, the demonstration turned into an ugly riot in which the airport and Papeete were ransacked.

Meanwhile, at the Moruroa test site, two large Greenpeace protest vessels had been boarded by tear gas–firing French commandos and impounded (the ships were not released until six months later). Worldwide condemnation of the test series reached unprecedented levels, and in January 1996 the French announced that the testing had been completed. The facilities on Moruroa have since been decommissioned and it's highly unlikely the testing will ever resume, yet deadly radiation may already be leaking into the sea through cracks in the atoll's porous coral cap. A mantle of secrecy hangs over France's former nuclear playground in the South Pacific and many of the 15,000 workers exposed to contamination during the 30 years of testing are now demanding an independent medical inquiry and compensation from France. (For more information, turn to The Nuclear Test Zone in the Tuamotu Islands section.)

Since 1996 Flosse and party have attempted to enhance the illusion of autonomy by developing the concept of Tahiti Nui or "Greater Tahiti." Tens of millions of Euros have been spent to build a new waterfront promenade and presidential palace (occupied by Flosse) in Papeete and an immense town hall and six-story general hospital at Pirae (Flosse's hometown). Raiatea has been given a new cruise ship terminal and five-star resorts have been erected on half a dozen islands. The government-sponsored airline, Air Tahiti Nui, has been granted landing rights in Paris, thereby forcing two French airlines (Air Lib and Corsair) to drop the route, and a territorial TV station, Tahiti Nui TV or "Télé Gaston," has been launched. Flosse has also created a red-shirted militia, the Groupement d'Intervention de la Polynésie (GIP), to carry out public works and enforce "security" in Papeete. However, a Flosse-backed constitutional amendment to have French Polynesia declared a *pays d'outre-mer* (overseas country) has been stalled in the French parliament and rumblings of discontent are being heard in France about all those Euros being used to finance grandiose projects on Tahiti. Real independence seems as remote as ever.

GOVERNMENT

In 1885 an organic decree created the colonial system of government, which remained in effect until the proclamation of a new statute in 1958. In 1977 the French granted the territory partial internal self-government, and Francis Sanford was elected premier of "autonomous" Polynesia. A new local-government statute, passed by the French parliament and promulgated on September 6, 1984, gave slightly more powers to the Polynesians, and in 1996 additional powers were transferred to the territory to slow the momentum toward full independence. Yet the constitution of the Republic of France remains the supreme law of the land and local laws can be overturned by a Constitutional Council comprising French judges.

A Territorial Assembly elects the president of the government, who chooses 15 cabinet ministers (before 1984 the French high commissioner was the chief executive). The 49 assembly members are elected every five years from separate districts. In the May 2001 elections, Flosse's Tahoeraa Huiraatira won 28 seats, the pro-independence Tavini Huiraatira 13 seats, the autonomist Fetia Api seven seats, and independents one seat. The territory is represented in Paris by two elected deputies, a senator, and a social and economic counselor. The French government, through its high commissioner (called governor until 1977), retains control over foreign relations, immigration, defense, justice, the police, the municipalities, higher education, radio and TV, property rights, and the currency.

French Polynesia is divided into 48 communes, each with an elected Municipal Council, which

FRENCH POLYNESIA

chooses a mayor from its ranks. Every main town on an island will have its *mairie* or **hôtel de ville** (town hall). These elected municipal bodies, however, are controlled by appointed French civil servants, who run the five administrative subdivisions. The administrators of the Windward, Tuamotu-Gambier, and Austral subdivisions are based at Papeete, while the headquarters of the Leeward Islands administration is at Uturoa (Raiatea), and that of the Marquesas Islands is at Taiohae (Nuku Hiva).

The territorial flag consists of three horizontal bands—red, white, and red with a double-hulled Polynesian sailing canoe superimposed on the white band. On the canoe are five figures representing the five archipelagos.

Economy

The inflow of people and money since the early 1960s has stimulated consumerism, and except for tourism and cultured pearls, the economy of French Polynesia is now dominated by French government spending. The nuclear testing program provoked an influx of 30,000 French settlers, plus a massive infusion of capital, which distorted the formerly self-supporting economy into one totally dependent on France.

French Polynesia has the highest per capita gross domestic product (GDP) in the South Pacific, about CFP 1,910,000 pp in the year 2001 or nearly seven times as much as Fiji. Paris contributes little to the territorial budget, but it finances the many departments and services under the direct control of the high commissioner, spending an average of 1,000 million Euros a year in the territory or nearly a third of the GDP. Most of it goes to the military and to the 2,200 expatriate French civil servants who earn salaries 84 percent higher than those doing the same work in France. Of the total workforce of 58,000, about 40 percent work for some level of government while the other 60 percent are privately employed. Four out of every five jobs are in services. Unemployment is 13 percent.

In 1994 the territorial government introduced an income tax of 2 percent on earnings over CFP 150,000 a month, plus new taxes on gasoline, wine, telecommunications, and unearned income. Indirect taxes, such as licensing fees and customs duties, long accounted for more than half of territorial government revenue. In 1998 it was announced that customs duties would be reduced and the lost revenue replaced by a *taxe sur la valeur ajoutée* (TVA) or value-added tax (VAT) added to the price of most goods and services. In January 2002, the TVA was increased to 6 percent on groceries and hotel rooms, 10 percent on services, and 16 percent on goods. For decades the price of imported goods has been doubled by taxation and this new consumption tax has further increased the cost of living. Imports are now taxed at the rate of 15 percent (compared to 30 percent in 1999).

The conclusion of nuclear testing in 1996 meant that 1,000 local workers had to be laid off and tax revenues on military imports suddenly dropped. To compensate for this and to shore up the fortunes of their local political allies, the French government agreed to a "Pacte de Progrès," which provides the territory with an additional subsidy of CFP 18,000 million a year. Initially these payments were to have ended in 2006 but in mid-2002 they were extended infinitely.

Trade

Before the start of nuclear testing, trade was balanced. Only 35 years later, 2001 imports stood at CFP 140,948 million while exports amounted to just CFP 18,701 million, one of the highest disparities in the world. Much of the imbalance is consumed by the French administration itself. Foreign currency spent by tourists on imported goods and services also helps steady the situation.

Nearly 45 percent of the imports come from France, which has imposed a series of self-favoring restrictions. Imports include food, fuel, building material, consumer goods, and automobiles. The main agricultural export from the outer islands is copra; copra production has been heavily subsidized by the government since 1967 to discourage migration to Tahiti. The copra is crushed into coconut oil and animal feed at the Papeete mill. Cultured pearls from farms in the Tuamotus are the biggest export by far, accounting for 75 percent of the total.

Agriculture and Fishing
Labor recruiting for the nuclear testing program caused local agriculture to collapse in the mid-'60s. Between 1962 and 1988 the percentage of the workforce employed in agriculture dropped from 46 percent to 10 percent, and today agriculture accounts for just under 5 percent of salaried employment. Vanilla and coconut oil combined now comprise only 3 percent of exports and the export of *noni* pulp to the United States for the making of juice is more important.

About 80 percent of all food consumed locally is imported. Bread and rice are heavily subsidized by the government. Local vegetables supply half of local needs, while Tahitian coffee covers 20 percent of consumption. French Polynesia does manage, however, to cover three-quarters of its own fruit requirements, and the local pineapple and grapefruit crop goes to the fruit-juice factory on Moorea. Most industry is related to food processing (fruit-juice factory, brewery, soft drinks, etc.) or coconut products. It's rumored that marijuana *(pakalolo)* is now the leading cash crop, although you won't be aware of it. Large areas have been planted in Caribbean pine to provide for future timber needs. Considerable livestock is kept in the Marquesas.

Aquaculture is being developed, with tanks for freshwater shrimp, prawns, live bait, and green mussels. Until now most deep-water fishing within the territory's huge exclusive economic zone has been done by foreign fleets, but their licenses are no longer being automatically renewed. Instead the territorial government has begun using some of the French structural adjustment money to build a tuna fishing fleet run by a territorial government-controlled company, Tahiti Rava'ai. The hope is to augment the tonnage of tuna landed locally tenfold by increasing the number of local boats from 30 to 150.

Cultured Pearls
French Polynesia's cultured pearl industry, now second only to tourism as a money earner, origi-

nated in 1963 when an experimental farm was established on Hikueru atoll in the Tuamotus. The first commercial farm opened on Manihi in 1968, but the real boom began only in the late 1980s and today hundreds of cooperative and private pearl farms operate on 26 atolls, employing thousands of people. Although small companies and family operations are still able to participate in the industry, pearl production is becoming increasingly concentrated in a few hands because of the vertical integration of farming, wholesaling, and retailing. Robert Wan's

BUYING A BLACK PEARL

The relative newness of this gemstone is reflected in varying prices. A radiant, perfectly round, smooth, and flawless pearl with a good depth of metallic green/blue can sell for many times more than a similar pearl with only one or two defects. The luster is more important than the color. Size can vary from eight millimeters to 20 millimeters with the larger pearls that much more expensive. Black pearls are now in fashion in Paris, so don't expect any bargains. A first-class necklace can cost as much as US$50,000 and individual pearls of high quality cost US$1,000 and up, but slightly flawed pearls are much cheaper (beginning at US$100). The "baroque" pearls still make exquisite jewelry when mounted in gold and platinum.

Consider buying a loose pearl and having it mounted back home. If you think you might do this, check with your local jeweler before leaving for Tahiti. Half the fun is in the shopping, so be in no hurry to decide and don't let yourself be influenced by a driver or guide who may only be after a commission. If no guide is involved the shop should pay the commission to you in the form of a discount (ask). It's preferable to buy pearls at a specialized shop rather than somewhere that also sells pareus and souvenirs (and never buy a pearl from a person on the street). A reputable dealer will always give you an invoice or certificate verifying the authenticity of your pearl. If you've made an expensive choice ask the dealer to make a fresh X-ray right in front of you in order to be sure of the quality.

Tahiti Perles now controls more than half the industry and the next four companies account for another quarter of production.

Pearl farming is drawing many people back to ancestral islands they abandoned after devastating hurricanes in 1983. Pearl farming relieves pressure on natural stocks and creates an incentive to protect marine environments. Pollution from fertilizer runoff or sewage can make a lagoon unsuitable for pearl farming, which is why the farms are concentrated on lightly populated atolls where other forms of agriculture are scarcely practiced. On the down side, the pearl farm workers often feed themselves with fish they catch in the lagoons, leading to a big decline in marinelife.

Unlike the Japanese cultured white pearl, the Polynesian black pearl is created only by the giant blacklipped oyster *(Pinctada margaritifera),* which thrives in the Tuamotu lagoons. Beginning in the 19th century the oysters were collected by Polynesian divers who could dive up to 40 meters. The shell was made into mother-of-pearl buttons; finding a pearl this way was pure chance. By the middle of the 20th century overharvesting had depleted the slow-growing oyster beds and today live oysters are collected only to supply cultured-pearl farms. The shell is now a mere by-product, made into decorative items or exported. The strings of oysters must be monitored constantly and lowered or raised if there are variations in water temperature.

It takes around three years for a pearl to form in a seeded oyster. A spherical pearl is formed when a Mississippi River mussel graft from Tennessee is introduced inside the coat; the oyster creates only a hemispherical half pearl if the graft goes between the coat and the shell. Half pearls are much cheaper than real pearls and make outstanding rings and pendants. Some of the grafts used are surprisingly large and the layer of nacre around such pearls may be relatively thin, but only an X-ray can tell. Thin coating on a pearl greatly reduces its value.

The cooperatives sell their production at Papeete auctions held twice a year. Local jewelers vie with Japanese buyers at these events, with 60,000 black pearls in 180 lots changing hands for about CFP 750 million. Private producers sell their pearls through independent dealers or plush retail outlets in Papeete. Every year about a million black pearls worth CFP 15,000 million are exported to Japan, Hong Kong, the United States, France, and Switzerland, making the territory the world's second-largest source of loose pearls (after Australia, which produces the smaller yellow pearls). To control quality and pricing, the export of loose reject pearls is prohibited, although finished jewelry is exempt.

Tourism

French Polynesia is second only to Fiji as a South Pacific destination, with 227,658 visitors in 2001, a quarter of them from France and another quarter from the United States. Japan, New Zealand, Germany, Italy, Britain, Canada, and New Caledonia also account for significant numbers. Yet tourism is far less developed here than it is in Hawaii. A single Waikiki hotel could have more rooms than the entire island of Tahiti; Hawaii gets more visitors in 10 days than French Polynesia gets in a year.

Tourism by high-budget Japanese (especially honeymooners) is being vigorously promoted and the number of European visitors is growing. The CFP 47,000 million a year generated by tourism covers a third of French Polynesia's import bill and provides thousands of jobs, but 80 percent of the things tourists buy are also imported. Many of the luxury resorts are foreign-owned and operated, and in some cases resort development has been at the expense of the environment. Lagoons have been pillaged to provide sand for artificial beaches. I've received complaints from readers about improper waste disposal on Tahiti, Huahine, and Bora Bora.

The People

The 2002 population of 245,405 is around 63 percent Polynesian, 12 percent European, 17 percent Polynesian/European, 5 percent Chinese, and 3 percent Polynesian/Chinese. All are French citizens. About 69 percent of the total population lives on Tahiti (compared to only 25 percent before the nuclear-testing boom began in the 1960s), but a total of 65 far-flung islands are inhabited.

The indigenous people of French Polynesia are the Maohi or Eastern Polynesians (as opposed to the Western Polynesians in Samoa and Tonga), and some local nationalists refer to their country as Te Ao Maohi. The word *colon* formerly applied to Frenchmen who arrived long before the bomb and made a living as planters or traders, and practically all of them married Polynesian women. Most of these *colons* have already passed away. Their descendants are termed *demis* or *afa* and they now dominate politics and the local bureaucracy. The present Europeans (*popa'a*) are mostly recently arrived metropolitan French (*faranis*). Their numbers increased dramatically in the 1960s and 1970s, and most live in urban areas where they're involved in the administration, military, or professions. In contrast, very few Polynesians have migrated to France, although 7,000 live in New Caledonia.

Local Chinese (*tinito*) dominate business throughout the territory. In Papeete and Uturoa entire streets are lined with Chinese stores, and individual Chinese merchants are found on almost every island. They're also prominent in pearl farming and tourism. During the American Civil War, when the supply of cotton to Europe was disrupted, Scotsman William Stewart decided to set up a cotton plantation on the south side of Tahiti. Unable to convince Tahitians to do the heavy work, Stewart brought in a contingent of 1,010 Chinese laborers from Canton in 1865–1866. When the war ended the enterprise went bankrupt, but many of the Chinese managed to stay on as market gardeners, hawkers, and opium dealers. Things began changing in 1964 when France recognized mainland China and granted French citizenship to the territory's Chinese (most

other Tahitians had become French citizens right after World War II). The French government tried to assimilate the Chinese by requiring that they adopt French-sounding names and by closing all Chinese schools. Despite this, the Chinese community has remained distinct.

From 1976 to 1983 about 18,000 people migrated to the territory, 77 percent of them from France and another 13 percent from New Caledonia. Nearly 1,000 new settlers a year continue to arrive. About 40,000 Europeans are now present in the territory, plus 8,000 soldiers, policemen, and transient officials. Most Tahitians would like to see this immigration restricted, as it is in virtually every other Pacific state. French citizens even have a tax incentive to come since they become legal residents after six months and one day in the territory and are thus exempt from French income tax (in French Polynesia the tax rate is only 2 percent). There's an undercurrent of anti-French sentiment; English speakers are better liked by the Tahitians.

Tahitian Life

For the French, lunch is the main meal of the day, followed by a siesta. Dinner may consist of leftovers from lunch. Tahitians traditionally eat their main meal of fish and native vegetables in the evening, when the day's work is over. People at home often take a shower before or after a meal and put flowers in their hair. Traditionally a flower behind the left ear means a person has a partner while a blossom behind the right ear means one is still looking.

Tahitians often observe with amusement or disdain the efforts of individuals to rise above the group. In a society where sharing and reciprocal generosity have traditionally been important qualities, the deliberate accumulation of personal wealth has always been viewed as a vice. Now with the influx of government and tourist money, Tahitian life is changing, quickly in Papeete, more slowly in the outer islands. To prevent the Polynesians from being made paupers in their own country, foreigners other than French are

FRENCH POLYNESIA

FRENCH POLYNESIA ON THE SILVER SCREEN

Since the days of silent movies, Hollywood has shared the fascination with Polynesia felt by poets and novelists. In fact, many of the best films about the region are based on books by Charles Nordhoff, James Norman Hall, Somerset Maugham, and James A. Michener. And like the printed works, most of the films are about Europeans in the islands rather than the islanders themselves. The clash between the simplicity of paradise and the complexity of civilization is a recurrent theme.

In 1932 Robert Flaherty teamed up with F. W. Murnau to create one of the classics of the silent movie era, *Tabu,* the story of two lovers who flee to a tiny island on Bora Bora's barrier reef. Also in 1932, Douglas Fairbanks Sr. and Maria Alba traveled to the Society Islands by private yacht for the filming of *Mr. Robinson Crusoe.*

Three generations of filmmakers have used the *Bounty* saga popularized by American novelists Charles Nordhoff and James Norman Hall as their way of presenting paradise. In 1935 Frank Lloyd's *Mutiny on the Bounty* won the Oscar for Best Picture, with Charles Laughton starring as the cruel Captain Bligh and Clark Gable as gallant Fletcher Christian. Lloyd portrayed the affair as a simplistic struggle between good and evil, and the two subsequent remakes were more historically accurate.

The extravagant MGM production of *Mutiny on the Bounty* (1962) starring Trevor Howard as Captain Bligh and Marlon Brando as Fletcher Christian is well remembered in Tahiti because of Brando's

ongoing ownership of Tetiaroa atoll. Unlike the 1935 *Bounty* movie filmed on Catalina Island, California, MGM captured the glorious color of Tahiti and Bora Bora in what may be the most spectacular movie ever made in the South Pacific. The salaries paid to the 6,000 extras used in the film had a real economic impact on Tahiti at the time.

The Bounty (1984), with Sir Anthony Hopkins as a purposeful Bligh and Mel Gibson portraying an ambiguous Christian, comes closer to reality than the other two *Bounty* films and the views of Moorea are stunning.

The theme of the despot is picked up by director John Ford, who adapted Nordhoff and Hall's story of a young couple fleeing the haughty governor of tropical Manikoora in *The Hurricane* (1937). Surprisingly, this black-and-white movie remains an audiovisual feast, and the climactic storm is not soon to be forgotten. Dorothy Lamour stars in Ford's film. In 1978 Dino de Laurentiis remade *Hurricane* on Bora Bora with Mia Farrow and Trevor Howard in the starring roles.

The Moon and Sixpence, Albert Lewin's 1943 film version of Somerset Maugham's novel about the life of Paul Gauguin in Polynesia, appeals to the mind as much as to the senses. It's the dissonance between the main character's private mission and his social obligations that gives this movie depth.

Videos and DVDs of all of the films just mentioned can be ordered through www.southpacific.org/films.html.

not usually permitted to buy land here and 85 percent of the land is still owned by Polynesians.

The educational curriculum is entirely French. Children enter school at age three and for 12 years study the French language, literature, culture, history, and geography, but not much about Polynesia. About 80 percent of the population speaks Tahitian at home but there is little formal training in it (teaching in Tahitian has been allowed only since 1984). The failure rate ranges 40–60 percent, and most of the rest of the children are behind schedule. The brightest students are given scholarships to continue studying, while many of the dropouts become delinquents. About

a quarter of the schools are privately run by the churches, but these must teach exactly the same curriculum or lose their subsidies. The whole aim is to transform the Polynesians into Pacific French. In 1989 the Université française du Pacifique opened on Tahiti, specializing in law, humanities, social sciences, languages, and science. Yet few doctors and lawyers are Polynesian and most professionals practicing in the territory are expatriate French.

Most Tahitians live along the coast because the interior is too rugged. A traditional Tahitian residence consists of several separate buildings: the *fare tutu* (kitchen), the *fare tamaa* (dining area), the *fare taoto* (bedrooms), plus bathing and sanitary outhouses. Often several generations live together, and young children are sent to live with their grandparents. Adoption is commonplace and family relationships complex. Young Tahitians generally go out as groups, rather than on individual "dates."

The lifestyle may be summed up in the words *aita e peapea* (no problem) and *fiu* (fed up, bored). About the only time the normally languid Tahitians go really wild is when they're dancing or behind the wheel of a car.

Sex

Since the days of Wallis and Bougainville, Tahitian women have had a reputation for promiscuity. Well, for better or worse, this is largely a thing of the past, if it ever existed at all. As a short-term visitor your liaisons with Tahitians are likely to remain polite. Westerners' obsession with the sexuality of Polynesians usually reflects their own frustrations, and the view that Tahitian morality is loose is rather ironic considering that Polynesians have always shared whatever they have, cared for their old and young, and refrained from ostracizing unwed mothers or attaching shame to their offspring. The Christian Tahitians of today are highly moral and compassionate.

Polynesia's *mahu* or "third sex" bear little of the stigma attached to female impersonators in the West. A young boy may adopt the female role by his own choice or that of his parents, performing female tasks at home and eventually finding a job usually performed by women, such as serving in a restaurant or hotel. Generally only one *mahu* exists in each village or community, proof that this type of individual serves a certain sociological function. George Mortimer of the British ship *Mercury* recorded an encounter with a *mahu* in 1789. Though Tahitians may poke fun at a *mahu*, they're fully accepted in society, seen teaching Sunday school, etc. Many, but not all, *mahus* are also homosexuals. Today, with money all-important, some transvestites have involved themselves in male prostitution and the term *raerae* has been coined for this category. Now there are even Miss Tane (Miss Male) beauty contests! All of this may be

seen as the degradation of a phenomenon that has always been a part of Polynesian life.

Religion

Though the old Polynesian religion died out in the early 19th century, the Tahitians are still a strongly religious people. Protestant missionaries arrived on Tahiti 39 years before the Catholics and 47 years before the Mormons, so 45 percent of the people now belong to the Evangelical Church, which is strongest in the Austral and Leeward Islands. Until the middle of the 20th century this church was one of the only democratic institutions in the colony and it continues to exert strong influence on social matters (for example, it resolutely opposed nuclear testing).

Of the 34 percent of the total population who are Catholic, half are Polynesians from the Tuamotus and Marquesas, and the other half are French. Another 5 percent are Seventh-Day Adventists and 10 percent are Mormons. A Mormon group called Sanitos, which rejects Brigham Young as a second prophet, has had a strong following in the Tuamotus since the 19th century. Several other Christian sects are also represented, and some Chinese are Buddhists. It's not unusual to see two or three different churches in a village of 100 people. All the main denominations operate their own schools. Local ministers and priests are powerful figures in the outer-island communities. One vestige of the pre-Christian religion is a widespread belief in ghosts (*tupapau*).

Protestant church services are conducted mostly in Tahitian, Catholic services are in French. Sitting through a service (one to two hours) is often worthwhile just to hear the singing and to observe the women's hats. Never wear a pareu to church—you'll be asked to leave. Young missionaries from the Church of Latter-day Saints (Mormons) continue to flock to Polynesia from the United States for two-year stays. They wear short-sleeved white shirts with ties and travel in pairs—you may spot a couple.

Language

French is spoken throughout the territory, and visitors will sometimes have difficulty making themselves understood in English, although most of those involved in the tourist industry speak some English. Large Chinese stores often have someone who speaks English. Young Polynesians often become curious and friendly when they hear you speaking English. Still, unless you're on a package tour, everything will be a lot easier if you know at least a little French. Check out some French language recordings from your local public library to brush up your high school French before you arrive. (The Basic French Glossary in Resources may also help you get by.)

Contemporary Tahitian is the chiefly or royal dialect used in the translation of the Bible by early Protestant missionaries, and today, as communications improve, the outer-island dialects are becoming mingled with the predominant Tahitian. Tahitian or Maohi is one of a family of Austronesian languages spoken from Madagascar through Indonesia, all the way to Easter Island and Hawaii. The related languages of Eastern Polynesia (Hawaiian, Tahitian, Tuamotuan, Mangarevan, Marquesan, Rarotongan, Maori) are quite different from those of Western Polynesia (Samoan, Tongan). Among the Polynesian languages the consonants did the changing rather than the vowels. The *k* and *l* in Hawaiian are generally rendered as a *t* and *r* in Tahitian.

Instead of attempting to speak French to the Tahitians, turn to the Tahitian vocabulary at the end of this book and give it a try. Remember to pronounce each vowel separately, *a* as the *ah* in "far," *e* as the *ai* in "day," *i* as the *ee* in "see," *o* as the *oh* in "go," and *u* as the *oo* in "lulu"—similar to Latin or Spanish. Written Tahitian has only eight consonants: *f, h, m, n, p, r, t, v.* Two consonants never follow one another, and all words end in a vowel. No silent letters exist in Tahitian, but there is a glottal stop, often marked with an apostrophe. A slight variation in pronunciation or vowel length can change the meaning of a word completely, so don't be surprised if your efforts produce some unexpected results!

Some of the many English words that have entered Tahitian through contact with early seamen include: *faraipani* (frying pan), *manua* (man of war), *matete* (market), *mati* (match), *moni* (money), *oniani* (onion), *painapo* (pineapple), *pani* (pan), *pata* (butter), *pipi* (peas), *poti* (boat),

taiete (society), *tapitana* (captain), *tauera* (towel), and *tavana* (governor).

Writer Pierre Loti was impressed by the mystical vocabulary of Tahitian:

> *The sad, weird, mysterious utterances of nature: the scarcely articulate stirrings of fancy. . . .* **Faa-fano:** *the departure of the soul at death.* **Aa:** *happiness, earth, sky, paradise.* **Mahoi:** *essence or soul of God.* **Tapetape:** *the line where the sea grows deep.* **Tutai:** *red clouds on the horizon.* **Ari:** *depth, emptiness, a wave of the sea.* **Po:** *night, unknown dark world, Hell.*

CONDUCT AND CUSTOMS

The dress code in French Polynesia is very casual—you can even go around barefoot. Cleanliness *is* important, however. Formal wear or jacket and tie are unnecessary (unless you're to be received by the high commissioner!). One exception is downtown Papeete, where scanty dress would be out of place. (For clothing tips, see What to Take in the main introduction.)

People usually shake hands when meeting; visitors are expected to shake hands with everyone present. If a Polynesian man's hand is dirty he'll extend his wrist or elbow. Women kiss each other on the cheeks. When entering a private residence it's polite to remove your shoes.

All the beaches of French Polynesia are public to one meter above the high-tide mark, although some watchdogs don't recognize this. Topless sunbathing is completely legal in French Polynesia and commonly practiced at resorts by European tourists, though total nudity is permissible only on offshore *motu* and floating pontoons.

Women

Despite the apparent laissez-faire attitude promoted in the travel brochures and this book, female travelers should take care: there have been sexual assaults by Polynesian men on foreign women. Peeping toms can be a nuisance in both budget accommodations and on beaches away from the main resorts, and women should avoid staying alone in isolated tourist bungalows or camping outside organized campgrounds. A California reader sent us this:

> My friend and I must have been unusual looking travelers. Though we dressed in pants and baggy clothes when we had to go to town, our age (we're both 26) and not unattractive appearance drew some very undesirable attention. Video rental stores are a common sight here and the local men seem to have developed ideas about what white women are after from watching blue movies. So we found ourselves being threatened time and again by aggressive local men.
>
> On Bora Bora we took an all-day outrigger trip and found ourselves left alone with two male guides in the afternoon. We didn't know how to cancel at that point. We were taken to a **motu** for lunch. The guides extended our time on the **motu** so long that we missed the afternoon activities we had paid for. At 1530 we had to insist they bring us back to shore. We didn't panic on the **motu** and escaped unhurt, but I think it is essential that you include a caution for all single women traveling in Tahiti to make sure there are other guests, including couples or men, on these day trips before putting themselves in the hands of strangers.
>
> Based on our experience I would say that for women, even in pairs, things like hiking, hitchhiking, or walking along the road should not be taken lightly. The harassment continued even in very rural parts of the islands and we had to learn to be very unfriendly, even rude, to keep men from aggressively entering our space/lives. Even at the main resorts we had problems with the entertainment staff hitting on us every time we went to a show. On Moorea we'd booked a charming beach **fare** and spent a positively terrible first night there. The locks on our unit were unreliable and we were soon discovered by several local men who began to slink around behind our bungalow or watch us from the corner of the beach. As it got dark, we kept hearing people standing directly outside our bungalow or darting past our windows. It was terrifying. I think women visitors are best not even saying hello to men who approach them here—rudeness seems to be the only reaction that does not signal the wrong thing. Don't think we didn't see the humor in some of this and make the most of our stay—but it would have been helpful if we'd known about it beforehand from your book.

Safety is commonly the one thing you hope to not have to think about when you arrive at your destination, and certainly in French Polynesia it is easy to become more lax about your surroundings. But with any situation—here or back at home—use common sense. Speak up when you feel uncomfortable, ignore unwanted advances, and report problems to management. If you are making reservations for a tour, whether of a lagoon by outrigger or the lush jungle on foot, it is always wise to ask a few questions: What time do we depart? What time do we return? How many stops are there along the way? How many other people have made reservations? What is the minimum amount of people you are willing to take? The tour companies offered in this book are all reputable, but it doesn't hurt to take precautions when making reservations.

Sports and Recreation

As elsewhere in the South Pacific, **scuba diving** is the most popular sport among visitors, and well-established dive shops exist on Tahiti, Moorea, Huahine, Raiatea, Taha'a, Bora Bora, Rangiroa, Manihi, Tikehau, Fakarava, Ahe, and Nuku Hiva. Drift dives and swimming with sharks, rays, eels, dolphins, and even whales are all offered. In the warm waters of Polynesia wetsuits are not required. If you take a scuba certification course make sure it's PADI accredited as the French CMAS certification may not be recognized elsewhere. **Snorkeling** is possible at many of the same places and it has the big advantage of being free.

There's good **surfing** around Tahiti, Moorea, Huahine, and Raiatea, usually hurricane swells on the north shores October–March (summer) and Antarctic swells on the south shores April–September (winter). The summer swells are the same ones that hit Hawaii three or four days ear-lier. The reef breaks off the north shore of Moorea work better than Tahiti's beach breaks. The most powerful, hollow waves are in winter. The reef breaks in the passes are a lot longer paddle than those off the beaches (where you can expect lots of company). To avoid bad vibes, make a serious effort to introduce yourself to the local surfers.

Excellent, easily accessible **hiking** areas exist on Tahiti, Moorea, and Nuku Hiva. **Horseback riding** is readily available on Moorea, Huahine, Raiatea, and in the Marquesas with the Huahine and Raiatea operations especially recommended. **Golfers** will certainly want to complete all 18 holes at the International Golf Course Olivier Breaud on Tahiti. The Leeward Islands are a sailor's paradise with numerous protected anchorages and excellent **sailing** weather, which is why most of French Polynesia's charter yacht operations are concentrated on Raiatea.

Entertainment and Events

ENTERTAINMENT

The big hotels on Tahiti, Moorea, Huahine, and Bora Bora offer exciting dance shows several nights a week. They're generally accompanied by a barbecue or traditional feast, but if the price asked for the meal is too steep, settle for a drink at the bar and enjoy the show (usually no cover charge). Many of the regular performances are listed in this book, but be sure to confirm the times and dates as these do change to accommodate tour groups.

On Friday and Saturday nights discos crank up in most towns and these are good places to meet the locals. The nonhotel bar scene is limited mostly to Papeete and Uturoa. The drinking age in French Polynesia is officially 18, but it's not strictly enforced. Consuming alcohol on the street is not allowed.

Music and Dance

Protestant missionaries banned dancing in the 1820s and the 19th-century French colonial administration forbade performances that disturbed Victorian decorum. Dancing began to reappear as early as 1853, but only after 1908 were the restrictions fully removed. Traditional Tahitian dancing experienced a revival in the 1950s with the formation of Madeleine Moua's Pupu Heiva dance troupe, followed in the 1960s by Coco Hotahota's Temaeva and Gilles Hollande's Ora Tahiti. Yves Roche founded the Takiti ma ensemble in 1962. These groups rediscovered the near-forgotten myths of old Polynesia and popularized them with exciting music, dance, song, and costumes. During major festivals several dozen troupes consisting of 20–50 dancers and 6–10 musicians participate in thrilling competitions.

The Tahitian *tamure* or *'ori Tahiti* is a fast, provocative, erotic dance done by rapidly shifting the weight from one foot to the other. The rubber-legged men are almost acrobatic, though their movements tend to follow those of the women closely. The tossing, shell-decorated fiber

EXPLORING FRENCH POLYNESIA

French Polynesia abounds in things to see and do, including many in the "not to be missed" category. Papeete's colorful morning market and captivating waterfront welcome you to Polynesia. Travelers should not pass up the opportunity to take the ferry ride to **Moorea** and see the island's stunning Opunohu Valley, replete with splendid scenery, lush vegetation, and fascinating archaeological sites. Farther afield, an even greater concentration of old Polynesian marae (temples) awaits visitors to Maeva on the enchanting island of **Huahine.** The natural wonders of **Bora Bora** have been applauded many times, and neighboring Maupiti offers more of the same, though its pleasures are less well known. Polynesia's most spectacular atoll may be **Rangiroa,** where the Avatoru and Tiputa passes offer exciting snorkel rides on the tide flows. Mysterious **Nuku Hiva** and **Hiva Oa** in the Marquesas are seldom forgotten by those who get that far. The manta ray and shark viewing on Moorea, Raiatea, and Bora Bora, and dolphin or whale encounters at Moorea and Rurutu, are memorable experiences.

skirts (mores), the hand-held pandanus wands, and the tall headdresses add to the drama.

Dances such as the aparima, 'ote'a, and hivinau reenact Polynesian legends, and each movement tells part of a story. The aparima or "kiss of the hands" is a slow dance resembling the Hawaiian hula or Samoan siva executed mainly with the hands in a standing or sitting position. The hand movements repeat the story told in the accompanying song. The 'ote'a is a theme dance executed to the accompaniment of drums with great precision and admirable timing by a group of men wearing tall headdresses and/or women with wide belts arrayed in two lines. The ute is a restrained dance based on ancient refrains.

Listen to the staccato beat of the to'ere, a slit rosewood drum, each slightly different in size and pitch, hit with a stick. A split-bamboo drum (ofe) hit against the ground often provides a contrasting sound. The pahu is a more conventional bass drum made from a hollowed coconut tree trunk with a

sharkskin cover. Its sound resembles the human heartbeat. The smallest pahu is the fa'atete, which is hit with sticks. Another traditional Polynesian musical instrument is the bamboo nose flute (vivo), which sounds rather like the call of a bird, though today guitars and ukuleles are more often seen. The ukulele was originally the braguinha, brought to Hawai'i by Portuguese immigrants a century ago. Homemade ukuleles with the half-shells of coconuts as sound boxes emit pleasant tones, while those sporting empty tins give a more metallic sound. The hollow, piercing note produced by the conch shell or pu once accompanied pagan ceremonies on the marae.

Traditional Tahitian vocal music was limited to polyphonic chants conveying oral history and customs, and the contrapuntal himene or "hymn" sung by large choirs today is based on those ancient chants. As the singers sway to the tempo, the spiritual quality of the himene can be electrifying, so for the musical experience of a lifetime attend church any Sunday.

EVENTS
Public Holidays and Festivals

Public holidays in French Polynesia include New Year's Day (January 1), Gospel Day (March 5), Good Friday and Easter Monday (March/April), Labor Day (May 1), Victory Day (May 8), Ascension Day (May), Pentecost or Whitmonday (May/June), Internal Autonomy Day (June 29), Bastille Day (July 14), Assumption Day (August 15), All Saints' Day (November 1), Armistice Day (November 11), and Christmas Day (December 25). Ironically, Internal Autonomy Day really commemorates June 29, 1880, when King Pomare V was deposed and French Polynesia became a full French colony, not September 6, 1984, when the territory achieved a degree of internal autonomy. Everything will be closed on these holidays (and maybe also the days before and after—ask).

The big event of the year is the two-week-long **Heiva i Tahiti,** which runs from the end of June to Bastille Day (July 14). Formerly known as La Fête du Juillet or the Tiurai Festival (the Tahitian word tiurai comes from the English July), the Heiva originated way back in 1882. Long before that, a pagan festival was held around this time to mark the Southern Hemisphere solstice. Today it brings contestants and participants to Tahiti from all over the territory to take part in elaborate processions, competitive dancing and singing, feasting, and partying. There are bicycle, car, horse, and outrigger-canoe races, *pétanque*, archery, and javelin-throwing contests, fire walking, sidewalk bazaars, arts and crafts exhibitions, tattooing, games, and joyous carnivals. **Bastille Day** itself, which marks the fall of the Bastille in Paris on July 14, 1789, at the height of the French Revolution, features a military parade in the capital. Ask at the Visitors Bureau in Papeete about when to see the historical reenactments at Marae Arahurahu, the canoe race along Papeete waterfront, horse racing at the Pirae track, and the Taupiti nui dance competitions at the Tahua To'ata next to the Cultural Center. Tickets to most Heiva events are sold at the Cultural Center in Papeete or at the gate. As happens during carnival in Rio de Janeiro, you must pay to sit in the stands to watch the best performances (CFP 1,500–2,500), but you get four hours or more of unforgettable nonstop entertainment.

The July celebrations on Bora Bora are as good as those on Tahiti, and festivals are also held on Raiatea and Taha'a at that time. Note that all ships, planes, and hotels are fully booked around July 14, so be in the right place beforehand or get firm reservations, especially if you want to be on Bora Bora that day. At this time of year, races, games, and dance competitions take place on many different islands, and the older women often prove themselves graceful dancers and excellent singers. On Moorea, there's a canoe race around the island during the Heiva.

Chinese New Year in January or February is celebrated with dances and fireworks. **World Environment Day** (June 5) is marked by guided excursions to Tahiti's interior and on the following weekend special activities are arranged at tourist sites around the island. The **Agricultural Fair** on Tahiti in mid-August involves the construction of a Tahitian village. Papeete's **Carnaval de Tahiti** at the end of October features dancing contests (waltz, foxtrot, rock), nightly parades along boulevard Pomare, and several gala evenings. On **All Saints' Day** (November 1) the locals illuminate the cemeteries at Papeete, Arue, Punaauia, and elsewhere with candles. On **New Year's Eve** the Papeete waterfront is beautifully illuminated and there's a seven-km foot race.

Major Sporting Events

The 42-km **Tahiti Nui Marathon** has been held on northern Moorea every February since 1988. In 1997 Patrick Muturi of Kenya set the record time for men of two hours, 21 minutes, and 31 seconds. The women's record is held by Gitte Karlshoj of Denmark, who logged two hours, 50 minutes, and 23 seconds in 1999. In May there's the **Gotcha Tahiti Pro** surfing competition off Tahiti-iti. The **Tahiti Open** at the Atimaono golf course on Tahiti is in July.

The **Te Aito** individual outrigger canoe race is held on Tahiti around the end of July. The **Hawaiki Nui Va'a** outrigger canoe race in October is a stirring three-day event with almost 100 canoe teams crossing from Huahine to Raiatea (44.5 km) the first day, Raiatea to Taha'a (26 km) the second, and Taha'a to Bora Bora (58 km) the third. The **Va'a Hine,** a women-only canoe race from Raiatea to Taha'a and back (40 km), occurs a day or two before the men's race. Also in October is **L'Aitoman de Moorea** or "Iron Man" triathlon with swimming (3.8 km), bicycle riding (180 km), and running (41 km).

Stone Fishing

This traditional method of fishing is now practiced only on very special occasions in the Leeward Islands. Coconut fronds are tied end to end until a line a half-km long is ready. Several dozen outrigger canoes form a semicircle. Advancing slowly together, men in the canoes beat the water with stones tied to ropes. The frightened fish are thus driven toward a beach. When the water is shallow enough, the men leap from their canoes, push the leaf line before them, yell, and beat the water with their hands. In this way the fish are literally forced ashore into an open bamboo fence, where they are caught. A famous scene in the Marlon Brando version of *Mutiny on the Bounty* depicts stone fishing at Bora Bora.

SHOPPING

Most local souvenir shops sell Marquesas-style wooden "tikis" carved from wood or stone. The original Tiki was a god of fertility, and really old tikis are still shrouded in superstition. Today they're viewed mainly as good-luck charms and often come decorated with mother-of-pearl. Other items carved from wood include mallets (to beat tapa cloth), *umete* bowls, and slit *to'ere* drums. Carefully woven pandanus hats and mats come from the Australs. Other curios to buy include hand-carved mother-of-pearl shell, sharks'-tooth pendants, hematite (black stone) carvings, and bamboo fishhooks.

Black-pearl jewelry is widely available throughout French Polynesia. The color, shape, weight, and size of the pearl are important. The darkest pearls are the most valuable. Prices vary considerably, so shop around before buying pearls. Be aware that the export of large numbers of unset pearls is prohibited without a license and that the folks operating the X-ray machines at the airport are on the lookout. Black pearl prices have fallen considerably since 2001 because of oversupply and poor quality control.

As this is a French colony, it's not surprising that many of the best buys are related to fashion. A tropical shirt, sundress, or T-shirt is a purchase of immediate usefulness. The pareu is a typically Tahitian leisure garment consisting of a brightly colored hand-blocked or painted local fabric about two meters long and a meter wide. There are dozens of ways both men and women can wear a pareu and it's the most common apparel for local women throughout the territory, including Papeete, so pick one up! Local cosmetics such as Monoï Tiare Tahiti, a fragrant coconut-oil skin moisturizer, and coconut-oil soap will put you in form. Jasmine shampoo, cologne, and perfume are also made locally from the tiare Tahiti flower. Vanilla is used to flavor coffee.

Early missionaries introduced the Tahitians to quilting, and two-layer patchwork *tifaifai* have now taken the place of tapa (bark cloth). Used as bed covers and pillows by tourists, *tifaifai* is still used by Tahitians to cloak newlyweds and to cover coffins. To be wrapped in a *tifaifai* is the highest honor. Each woman has individual quilt patterns that are her trademarks and bold floral designs are popular, with contrasting colors drawn from nature. A complicated *tifaifai* can take up to six months to complete and cost US$1,000. The French artist Henri Matisse, who in 1930 spent several weeks at the former Hôtel Stuart on Papeete's boulevard Pomare, was so impressed by the Tahitian *tifaifai* that he applied the same technique and adopted many designs for his *"gouaches découpees."*

Those who have been thrilled by hypnotic Tahitian music and dance will want to take some Polynesian music home with them on cassette (CFP 2,000) or compact disc (CFP 3,200), available at hotels and souvenir shops throughout the islands. The largest local company producing these CDs is Editions Manuiti or Tamure Records. Among the well-known local singers and musicians appearing on Manuiti are Bimbo, Charley Manu, Guy Roche, Yves Roche, Emma Terangi, Andy Tupaia, and Henriette Winkler. Small Tahitian groups such as the Moorea Lagon Kaina Boys, the Barefoot Boys, and Tamarii Punaruu, and large folkloric ensembles such as Maeva Tahiti, Tiare Tahiti, and Coco's Temaeva (often recorded at major festivals) are also well represented. The Tahitian recordings of the Hawaiian artist Bobby Holcomb are highly recommended. Visit www.southpacific.org/music .html for specific CD listings.

Hustling and bargaining are not practiced in French Polynesia: it's expensive for everyone. Haggling may even be considered insulting, so just pay the price asked or keep looking. Black pearl jewelry is an exception: because the markups are so high, discounts are often available.

FRENCH POLYNESIA

Accommodations

Hotel prices range from CFP 1,000 for a dormitory bed all the way up to CFP 245,000 double without meals plus tax for an overwater suite at the Bora Bora Sheraton! Price wars sometimes erupt between rival resorts, and at times you'll be charged less than the prices quoted herein! When things are really slow even the luxury hotels sometimes discount their rooms. If your hotel can't provide running water, electricity, air-conditioning, or something similar because of a hurricane or otherwise, ask for a price reduction. You might get 10 percent off.

The 11 percent hotel tax consists of a 5 percent room tax used to finance "tourism promotions" and the 6 percent value added tax (VAT). This 11 percent tax is on top of the rack room rates at the 44 "classified hotels" (seldom included in the quoted price). The 5 percent tourist development tax doesn't apply to pensions and small family-operated accommodations, but they must still collect the 6 percent VAT (often included in the basic rate). Many islands add a *taxe de séjour* (sojourn tax) to accommodation bills to cover municipal services. This varies from CFP 150 pp per day at the large hotels to CFP 50 at the pensions and it's almost always charged extra.

Be aware that the large hotels frequently tack a CFP 1,000 or 10 percent commission onto any rental cars, lagoon excursions, and scuba diving booked through their front desks. Many small hotels add a surcharge to your bill if you stay only one night and some charge a supplement during the high seasons (July, August, and mid-December–mid-January). Discounts may be offered during the low months of February, March, September, and October.

A wise government regulation prohibiting buildings higher than a coconut tree outside Papeete means that most of the hotels are low-rise affairs or consist of small Tahitian *fare*. The small hotels and bungalows often provide cooking facilities and this allows you to save a lot on food.

French Polynesia is one of the few South Pacific destinations where camping is a practical option and a tent can prove very convenient.

Regular campgrounds exist on Moorea, Huahine, Raiatea, and Bora Bora. On Rangiroa it's possible to camp at certain small hotels (listed herein). On the outer islands camping should be no problem, but ask permission of the landowner, or pitch your tent well out of sight of the road. Ensure this hospitality for the next traveler by not leaving a mess. Make sure your tent is water- and mosquito-proof, and never pitch a tent directly below coconuts hanging from a tree or a precariously leaning trunk.

There are no official youth hostels but all of the campgrounds and many of the guesthouses offer dormitory beds for only slightly more than you'd pay to pitch a tent. Communal cooking facilities are usually provided and it's a good way to meet other budget travelers. Separate dormitories for men and women are rare.

Hotel Chains

Of the large hotels, those belonging to the Sofitel/Accor/Coralia group are the oldest and most poorly maintained (Bora Bora's Sofitel Motu is an exception). Beachcomber Inter-Continental and Le Méridien are somewhere in the middle, and Sheraton has some of the newest but not necessarily best-value properties. Amanresorts and Orient Express each have one upscale property on Bora Bora, and Club Med is also at Bora Bora.

French Polynesia's homegrown hotel chain, Pearl Resorts, offers an increasing number of tasteful hotels in both the middle and top-end price range. Most of the Pearl Resorts properties are owned by Air Tahiti, Banque Socredo, and other investors. Five hotels owned by the French travel company Nouvelles Frontires are being redeveloped by the Paladien hotel chain and will serve the middle market when ready. The Maitai chain has two medium-priced resorts, which are managed by the owner of the Beachcomber chain.

Overwater Bungalows

The overwater bungalow was invented in French Polynesia in the 1960s and you'll now find them on Tahiti, Moorea, Huahine, Raiatea, Taha'a, Bora Bora, Rangiroa, and Manihi. They range in price from CFP 25,000 double plus tax at Club Bali Hai on Moorea to CFP 245,000 at the Bora Bora Sheraton.

There's no doubt that this type of accommodation is environmentally harmful. The coral formations are inevitably affected during construction and unconcerned guests do further damage by touching the living corals while snorkeling around their rooms. Much of the coral near the existing bungalows is dead and fish are present only because they are fed. We've heard reports of improper waste disposal at overwater bungalows.

The lagoons of French Polynesia are in the public domain and the resort owners are clearly profiting by using them as building sites. To boot, some resorts have employed huge dredges to suck sand from the lagoon floors for the construction of artificial beaches, thereby destroying the spawning areas of fishes and further damaging the coral.

> *There are lots of nice places to picnic, and at CFP 44 a loaf, that crisp French white bread is incredibly cheap and good. French baguettes are subsidized by the government, unlike that awful sliced white bread in a plastic package, which is CFP 250 a loaf!*

Paying Guests

A unique accommodations option is the well-established network of homestays, in which you get a private room or bungalow provided by a local family. *Logement chez l'habitant* is available on all the outer islands, and even in Papeete itself; the Visitors Bureau does a good job of providing printed lists of these places. Most travel agents abroad won't book the pensions or lodgings with the inhabitants because no commissions are paid, but you can make reservations directly with the owners themselves either by email or phone. Calling ahead from Papeete works well.

One Papeete travel agency specializing in such bookings is **Tekura Tahiti Travel** (tel. 43-12-00, fax 42-84-60), in the Vaima Center near Hawaiian Airlines, although it tends to work with the more upmarket places. Air Tahiti's "Séejours dans les îles" packages are built largely around pensions. Most pensions don't accept credit cards, and English may not be spoken. Many have a two-night minimum stay or charge extra if you leave after one night. These private guesthouses can be hard to find. There's usually no sign outside, and some don't cater to walk-in clients who show up unexpectedly. Also, the limited number of beds in each may all be taken (most pensions have under 10 rooms). Sometimes you'll get airport transfers at no additional charge if you book ahead. Don't expect hot water in the shower or a lot of privacy. Blankets and especially towels may not be provided and the room won't be cleaned every day. Often meals are included (typically seafood), which can make these places quite expensive. If you're on a budget, ask for a place with cooking facilities and prepare your own food. The family may lend you a bicycle and can be generally helpful in arranging tours, etc. It's a great way to meet the people while finding a place to stay.

FRENCH POLYNESIA

Food

The restaurants are often exorbitant, but you can bring the price down by ordering only a single main dish. Fresh bread and cold water should come with the meal. Avoid appetizers, alcohol, and desserts. No service charges are tacked on, and tipping is unnecessary, so it's not as expensive as it looks! US$15 will usually see you through an excellent no-frills lunch of fried fish at a small French restaurant. The same thing in a deluxe hotel dining room will be about 50 percent more. Even the finest places are affordable if you order this way.

Most restaurants post the menu in the window. If not, have a look at it before sitting down. Check the main plates, as that's all you'll need to take. If the price is right, the ambience congenial, and local French are at the tables, sit right down. Sure, food at a snack bar would be half as much, but your Coke will be extra, and in the end it's smart to pay a little more to enjoy excellent cuisine once in a while. A large plastic bottle of Eau Royale mineral water will add a couple of hundred francs to your bill, but you can always ask for free *eau ordinaire* (tap water). Also beware of set meals designed for tourists, as these usually cost double the average entrée. If you can't order à la carte walk back out the door.

Local restaurants offer French, Chinese, Vietnamese, Italian, and, of course, Tahitian dishes. The *nouvelle cuisine Tahitienne* is a combination of European and Asian recipes, with local seafoods and vegetables, plus the classic *maa Tahiti* (Tahitian food). The French are famous for their sauces, so try something exotic. Lunch is the main meal of the day in French Polynesia, and many restaurants offer a plat du jour designed for regular customers. This is often displayed on a blackboard near the entrance and is usually good value. Most restaurants serve lunch 1130–1400 and dinner 1800–2100. Don't expect snappy service: what's the rush, anyway?

If it's all too expensive, groceries are a good alternative. There are lots of nice places to picnic, and at CFP 44 a loaf, that crisp French white bread is incredibly cheap and good. French *baguettes* are subsidized by the government, unlike that awful sliced white bread in a plastic package, which is CFP 250 a loaf! Cheap red wines such as Selection Faragui are imported from France in bulk and bottled locally in plastic bottles. Add a nice piece of French cheese to the above and you're ready for a budget traveler's banquet. *Casse-croûtes* are big healthy sandwiches made with those long French baguettes at about CFP 250—a bargain.

There's also Martinique rum and Hinano beer (CFP 165 in grocery stores), brewed locally by the Brasserie de Tahiti. Founded in 1914, this company's first beer was called Aorai and today it produces Heineken as well as Hinano. Remember the deposit on Hinano beer bottles (CFP 60 on large bottles), which makes beer cheap to buy cold and carry out. Supermarkets aren't allowed to sell alcohol on Sundays or holidays (stock your fridge on Saturday).

The *maitai* is a cocktail made with rum, liqueur, and fruit juice. Moorea's famous Rotui fruit drinks

HINANO BEER

The Brasserie de Tahiti was launched in 1914 and for the next 39 years the denizens of Polynesia were able to quench their thirst with a brew known as Aorai. The operation underwent a major modernization in 1955, and the hearty Hinano of today was born to the delight of beer drinkers. Since 1976 the Tahiti brewery has received technical support from the Dutch brewer Heineken, whose beer is bottled in Papeete under license. A nonalcoholic beer called Vaitia was first produced in 1982, and in 1992 the Hei-Lager light beer was added to the line. Hei-Lager Gold followed in 1994. The computer-controlled cannery that opened on Tahiti in 1989 has made it possible to export canned Hinano to beer connoisseurs around the world. At present the company produces more than 30 million liters of Hinano a year and can fill 32,000 bottles and 22,000 cans an hour. It's one of the world's great beers.

BREADFRUIT

The breadfruit *(uru)* is the plant most often associated with the South Pacific. The theme of a man turning himself into such a tree to save his family during famine often recurs in Polynesian legends. Ancient voyagers brought breadfruit shoots or seeds from Southeast Asia. When baked in an underground oven or roasted over flames, the fruit of the now-seedless Polynesian variety resembles bread. Joseph Banks, botanist on Captain Cook's first voyage, wrote:

> If a man should in the course of his life-time plant 10 trees, which if well done might take the labor of an hour or thereabouts, he would completely fulfill his duty to his own as well as future generations.

The French naturalist Sonnerat transplanted breadfruit to Reunion in the Indian Ocean as early as 1772, but it's Captain William Bligh who shall always be remembered when the plant is mentioned. In 1787 Bligh set out to collect young shoots in Tahiti for transfer to the West Indies, where they were to be planted to feed slaves. On the way back, his crew mutinied in Tongan waters and cast off both breadfruit and Bligh. The indomitable captain managed to reach Dutch Timor in a rowboat and in 1792 returned to Tahiti with another ship to complete his task.

© M.E. DE VOS

The breadfruit *(Artocarpus altilis)*, a tall tree with broad green leaves, provides shade as well as food. A well-watered tree can produce as many as 1,000 pale green breadfruits a year. Robert Lee Eskridge described a breadfruit thus:

> Its outer rind or skin, very hard, is covered with a golf-ball-like surface of small irregular pits or tiny hollows. An inner rind about a half-inch thick surrounds the fruit itself, which when baked tastes not unlike a doughy potato. Perhaps fresh bread, rolled up until it becomes a semi-firm mass, best describes the breadfruit when cooked.

The starchy, easily digested fruit is rich in vitamin B. When consumed with a protein such as fish or meat it serves as an energy food. The Polynesians learned to preserve breadfruit by pounding it into a paste, which was kept in leaf-lined pits to ferment into *mahi*. Like the coconut, the breadfruit tree itself had many uses, including the provision of wood for outrigger canoes.

are sold in tall liter containers in a variety of types. The tastiest is perhaps *pamplemousse* (grape-fruit), produced from local Moorea fruit, but the pineapple juice is also outstanding. At about CFP 262 a carton, they're excellent value. At CFP 100 in supermarkets, bottled Eau Royale mineral water is also quite cheap.

If you're going to the outer islands, take as many edibles with you as possible; it's always more expensive there. Keep in mind that virtually every food plant you see growing on the islands is cultivated by someone. Even fishing floats or seashells washed up on a beach, or fish in the lagoon near someone's home, may be considered private property.

Tahitian Food

If you can spare the cash, attend a Tahitian *tamaaraa* (feast) at a big hotel and try some Polynesian specialties roasted in an *ahimaa* (underground oven). Basalt stones are preheated with a wood fire in a meter-deep pit, then covered with leaves. Each type of food is wrapped separately in banana leaves to retain its own flavor and lowered in. The oven is then covered with more banana leaves, wet sacking, and sand, and left one to three hours to bake: suckling pig, mahimahi, taro, *umara* (sweet potato), *uru* (breadfruit), and *fafa* (a spinachlike cooked vegetable made from taro tops).

Also sample the gamy flavor of *fei*, the red

cooking banana that flourishes in Tahiti's uninhabited interior. The Tahitian chestnut tree (*mape*) grows near streams and you can often buy the delicious cooked nuts at markets. *Miti hue* is a coconut-milk sauce fermented with the juice of river shrimp. Traditionally *ma'a Tahiti* is eaten with the fingers.

Poisson cru (ia ota), small pieces of raw bonito (skipjack) or yellowfin tuna marinated with lime juice and soaked in coconut milk, is enjoyable, as is *fafaru* ("smelly fish"), prepared by marinating pieces of fish in seawater in an airtight coconut-shell container. As with the durian, although the smell is repugnant, the first bite can be addicting. Other typical Tahitian plates are chicken and pork casserole with *fafa*, pork and cabbage casserole (*pua'a chou*), and goat cooked in ginger.

Po'e is a sticky sweet pudding made of starchy banana, papaya, taro, or pumpkin flour, flavored with vanilla, and topped with coconut-milk sauce. Many varieties of this treat are made throughout Polynesia. *Faraoa ipo* is Tuamotu coconut bread. The local coffee is flavored with vanilla bean and served with sugar and coconut cream.

Information and Services

INFORMATION

French Polynesia has one of the best-equipped tourist offices in the South Pacific, Tahiti Tourisme (tel. 50-57-00, fax 43-66-19, www.tahiti-tourisme .com; for a list of its overseas offices, turn to Resources at the back of this book.) Within French Polynesia the same organization calls itself the Tahiti Manava Visitors Bureau and operates tourist information offices on Tahiti, Moorea, Huahine, Raiatea, and Bora Bora. These offices can provide free brochures and answer questions, but they're not travel agencies, so you must make your own hotel and transportation bookings (they won't make phone calls for you). Ask for their current information sheets on the islands you intend to visit.

Visas and Officialdom

Everyone other than French citizens needs a passport valid six months beyond the departure date. French are admitted freely for an unlimited stay, and citizens of the European Union countries, Australia, Norway, and Switzerland, get three months without a visa. Citizens of the United States, Canada, New Zealand, Japan, and 13 other countries are granted a one-month stay free upon arrival at Papeete. If you need a visa for France, you'll also need one for French Polynesia. Call your airline beforehand to verify visa requirements, if in doubt. If you do require a visa, make sure the words *valable pour la Polynésie Française* are endorsed on the visa as visas for France are not accepted. Transit passengers only changing planes in Papeete also require a visa unless they fall into one of the categories above (this applies especially to South American passengers arriving from Chile in transit to New Zealand).

Extensions of stay are possible after you arrive, but they cost CFP 3,000 and you'll have to go to the post office to buy a stamp. You'll also need to show "sufficient funds" and your ticket to leave French Polynesia and provide one photo. The two immigration offices are listed in this book's Papeete section. People from countries outside the European Union are limited to three months total; if you know you'll be staying longer than a month, it's much better to get a three-month visa at a French consulate before arrival, making this formality unnecessary. To be married in French Polynesia involves a minimum of one month of residence and considerable red tape (most of the marriage ceremonies performed at the resorts are not legally binding).

French Polynesia requires an onward or return ticket of everyone (including nonresident French citizens). If you arrive without one, you'll be refused entry or required to post a cash bond equivalent to the value of a full-fare ticket back to your home country. If you're on an open-ended holiday, you can easily get around this requirement by buying a refundable Air New Zealand ticket back to the United States or wherever before leaving home. If you later board a yacht

FRENCH CONSULATES GENERAL

Australia: St. Martin's Tower, 31 Market St., Sydney, NSW 2000 (tel. 61-2/9261-5779); 6 Perth Ave., Yarralumla, Canberra, ACT 2600 (tel. 61-2/6216-0100)

Canada: French consulates general are found in Moncton, Montreal, Ottawa, Quebec, Toronto, and Vancouver.

Chile: Ave. Condell 65, Providencia, Santiago de Chile (tel. 56-2/470-8000)

Fiji: Dominion House, 7th floor, Scott St., Suva (tel. 679/331 2233)

Japan: 11-44, 4 Chome, Minami Azabu, Minato-Ku, Tokyo 106 (tel. 81-3/5420-8800); Crystal Tower, 10th floor, 1-2-27 Shiromi, Cho Ku, Osaka 540 (tel. 81-6/4790-1500)

Hong Kong: Admiralty Center Tower 2, 26th floor, 18 Harcourt Rd., Hong Kong (tel. 852/3196-6100)

New Zealand: Rural Bank Bldg., 13th floor, 34/42 Manners St., Wellington (tel. 64-4/384-2555)

Singapore: 101/103 Cluny Park Rd., Singapore 259595 (tel. 65/6880-7800)

United States: French consulates general exist in Atlanta, Boston, Chicago, Houston, Los Angeles, Miami, New Orleans, New York, San Francisco, and Washington. To get the address of the one nearest you, visit www.info-france-usa.org.

headed to Fiji, for example, simply have the airline reissue the ticket so it's a ticket to leave from your next destination—and on you go.

Yacht Entry

The main port of entry for cruising yachts is Papeete. Upon application to the local gendarmerie, entry may also be allowed at Bora Bora, Hiva Oa, Huahine, Mangareva, Moorea, Nuku Hiva, Raiatea, Raivavae, Rangiroa, Rurutu, Tubuai, and Ua Pou. Have an accurate inventory list for your vessel ready. It's also best to have a French courtesy flag with you as they're not always available in places such as the Marquesas. Even after clearance, you must continue to report your arrival at each respective office every time you visit any of those islands (locations and phone numbers are provided throughout this book). The gendarmes are usually friendly and courteous, if you are. Boats arriving from Tonga, Fiji, and the Samoas must be fumigated (also those which have called at ports in Central or South America during the previous 21 days).

Anyone arriving by yacht without an onward ticket must post a bond or *caution* at a local bank equivalent to the airfare back to his or her country of origin. In Taiohae the bond is US$565 for New Zealanders, US$635 for Americans, and US$800 for Europeans. This is refundable upon departure at any Banque Socredo branch, less a 3 percent administrative fee. Make sure the receipt shows the currency in which the original deposit was made and get an assurance that it will be refunded in kind. To reclaim the bond you'll also need a letter from Immigration verifying that you've been officially checked out. If any individual on the yacht doesn't have the bond money, the captain is responsible. The bond can be charged to a credit card.

Once the bond is posted, a "temporary" three-month visa (CFP 3,000) is issued. Recently, the French authorities have been refusing extensions beyond the initial three months, so ask about this while checking in. Boats can be left at Raiatea Carenage if you have to leave temporarily, but yachts staying in French Polynesia longer than a total of one year in any two-year period are charged full customs duty on the vessel. Failure to comply can result in confiscation of the boat until any outstanding fees are paid. Actually, the rules are not hard-and-fast, and everyone has a different experience. Crew changes should be made at Papeete. Visiting yachts cannot be chartered to third parties without permission.

After clearing customs in Papeete, outbound

yachts may spend the duration of their period of stay cruising the outer islands. Make sure every island where you *might* stop is listed on your clearance. You may buy duty-free fuel immediately after clearance. The officials want all transient boats out of the country by October 31, the onset of the hurricane season.

Money

The French Pacific franc or CFP (for *cour de franc Pacifique)* is legal tender in French Polynesia, Wallis and Futuna, and New Caledonia (there is no difference between the banknotes circulating in those territories). There are beautifully colored big banknotes of CFP 500, 1,000, 5,000, and 10,000, and coins of CFP 1, 2, 5, 10, 20, 50, and 100. The 10,000 note is confusingly similar in color and design to CFP 1,000, so when changing money, ask the clerk to give you CFP 5,000 notes instead.

The value of the CFP is pegged at exactly CFP 119.331 to the Euro buying or selling, so you can easily determine how many CFP you'll get for your dollar or pound by finding out how many Euros it's worth, then multiplying by 119.331. At last report US$1 = CFP 120, but a very rough way to convert CFP into U.S. dollars would be simply to divide by 100, so CFP 1,000 is US$10, etc.

All banks levy a stiff commission on foreign currency transactions. The Banque de Polynésie deducts CFP 411 commission, the Banque Socredo CFP 514, and the Banque de Tahiti CFP 566. Traveler's checks attract a rate of exchange about 1.5 percent higher than cash, but a passport is required for identification (photocopy sometimes accepted). The easiest way to avoid the high commissions and long bank lines is to change infrequently. When changing a large amount, it might be worth comparing the rates at all three banks as they do differ slightly.

The number-one currency to have with you is Euros as these are converted back and forth at a fixed rate. Traveler's checks in Euros are recommended, although U.S. dollar checks also work perfectly well. If you're from the States, you might also bring a few U.S. dollars in small bills to cover emergency expenses. Otherwise it's not a good idea to use cash U.S. dollars to cover expenses as these are usually converted at the unfavorable US$1 = CFP 100 rate.

Credit cards are accepted in many places on the main islands, but Pacific francs in cash are easier to use at restaurants, shops, etc. If you wish to use a credit card at a restaurant, ask first. Visa and MasterCard are universally accepted in the Society Islands, but American Express and Diner's Club are not. The American Express representative on Tahiti is Tahiti Tours (tel. 54-02-50) at 15 rue Jeanne d'Arc near the Vaima Center in Papeete. Most banks will give cash advances on credit cards, but it's still wise to bring enough traveler's checks to cover all your out-of-pocket expenses, and then some.

An alternative are the ATMs (automatic teller machines) outside Banque Socredo offices throughout the territory (including at Faa'a airport). These give a rate slightly better than traveler's checks without commission; however, checking account ATM cards may not work despite advertised links to international services such as Cirrus and Maestro. Several readers have reported problems with ATMs that produced "amount too high" messages instead of banknotes. Other times, only French Cirrus was accepted. If the machine doesn't work the first time, don't try again as you could be charged for each attempt without receiving any cash! Go inside the bank and complain. This situation should improve as the banks upgrade their computer systems, but meanwhile don't be too dependent on the ATMs. The weekly limit on ATM withdrawals is CFP 35,000 every seven days—if you'll need more, have several different cards.

EXCHANGE RATES

(approximate figures for orientation only)

One Euro = 119.331 Pacific Francs
One U.S. Dollar = 112 Pacific Francs
One Canadian Dollar = 76 Pacific Francs
One Australian Dollar = 67 Pacific Francs
One New Zealand Dollar = 62 Pacific Francs
One Pound Sterling = 175 Pacific Francs
One Swiss Franc = 81 Pacific Francs
100 Japanese Yen = 95 Pacific Francs

THE FRENCH PACIFIC FRANC

The *cour de franc Pacifique* or CFP grew out of the dark days of World War II when France was under German occupation. During this period, the French franc (FF) lost two-thirds of its prewar value while prices remained stable in the Pacific. When the French colonies reestablished contact with metropolitan France after the war, a new currency was needed to avoid economic chaos. Thus the French Pacific franc was created in 1945 at the rate of 2.4 FF to one CFP. Over the next few years the French franc was devalued three times and each time the CFP was devalued against it, lowering the rate to 5.5 FF to one CFP by 1949. That year, 100 old FF became one new FF, thus 5.5 new FF equaled 100 old CFP, a relationship that remained in place for more than half a century. In 2002 France adopted the Euro but the CFP remained legal tender in France's three Pacific territories at the fixed rate of one Euro to CFP 119.331. Until 1967 the Banque de l'Indochine was responsible for issuing the Pacific franc, a function now carried out by the French government.

On many outer islands credit cards, traveler's checks, and foreign banknotes won't be accepted, so it's essential to change enough money before leaving Papeete. Apart from Tahiti, there are banks on Bora Bora, Huahine, Hiva Oa, Moorea, Nuku Hiva, Raiatea, Rangiroa, Rurutu, Taha'a, Tubuai, and Ua Pou. All of these islands have Banque Socredo branches, and the Banque de Tahiti is represented on eight of them, the Banque de Polynésie on four. Bora Bora, Moorea, and Raiatea each have three different banks. If you're headed for any island other than these, take along enough CFP in cash to see you through.

Costs

Although Tahiti is easily the most expensive corner of the South Pacific, it also has the lowest inflation rate in the region. During the entire period from 1994 to 2001, there was only 8 percent inflation, or just over 1 percent a year, compared to 10 percent a year and up in many other South Pacific countries. The high price structure is directly related to the extremely high salaries paid to government employees. The minimum wage here is CFP 591 an hour.

Fortunately, facilities for budget travelers are now highly developed throughout the Society Islands, often with cooking facilities that allow you to save on meals. Bread (and indirectly the ubiquitous baguette sandwiches) are heavily subsidized and a real bargain. Beer, fruit juice, and mineral water from grocery stores are reasonable. Cheap transportation is available by interisland boat, and on Tahiti there's *le truck*. Bicycles can be hired in many places.

In 1998 a value-added tax (VAT) or *taxe sur la valeur ajoutée* (TVA) came into effect on many items. In 2002 the TVA was increased to 6 percent on groceries, rooms, and prepaid meals, 10 percent on services (including restaurants, bars, car rentals, and excursions), and 16 percent on store purchases. Large "classified hotels" are taxed 11 percent, whereas small hotels and pensions charge 6 percent. Free of tax are *le truck* and public ferry fares. The TVA is usually hidden in the basic price but the hotel taxes are charged extra.

Time is what you need the most of to see French Polynesia inexpensively, and the wisdom to avoid trying to see and do too much. There are countless organized tours and activities designed to separate you and your money, but none are really essential and the beautiful scenery, spectacular beaches, challenging hikes, and exotic atmosphere are free. Bargaining is not common in French Polynesia, and no one will try to cheat you (with the exception of the odd taxi driver). There's *no tipping*.

SERVICES

Post

The 34 regular post offices and 58 authorized agencies throughout French Polynesia are open weekdays 0700–1500. Main branches sell readymade padded envelopes and boxes. Parcels with an aggregate length, width, and height of over 90 cm or weighing more than 20 kg cannot be mailed. Rolls (posters, calendars, etc.) longer than 90 cm are also not accepted. Letters cannot weigh over two kg, and when mailing parcels it's much cheaper to keep the weight under two kilograms. Registration *(recommandation)* is CFP 500 extra and insurance *(envois avec valeur déclarée)* is also possible. Always use airmail *(poste aérienne)* when posting a letter; surface mail takes months to arrive. Postcards can still take up to two weeks to reach the United States. Though twice as expensive as in Cook Islands or Fiji, the service is quite reliable.

To pick up poste restante (general delivery) mail, you must show your passport and pay CFP 55 per piece (or CFP 28 for newspapers or magazines). If you're going to an outer island and are worried about your letters being returned to sender after 15 days, pay CFP 2,000 per month for a *garde de courrier,* which obliges the post office to hold all letters for at least two months. If one of your letters has "please hold" marked on it, the local postmaster may decide to hold all your mail for two months, but you'll have to pay the CFP 2,000 to collect it. Packages may be returned after one month in any case. For a flat fee of CFP 2,000 you can have your mail forwarded for three months. Ask for an *"Ordre de Réexpédition Temporaire."*

There's no residential mail delivery in French Polynesia and what appear to be mail boxes along rural roads are actually bread delivery boxes! Since there are usually no street addresses, almost everyone has a post office box or B.P. *(Boîte Postale).* French Polynesia issues its own colorful postage stamps—available at local post offices. They make excellent souvenirs.

Telecommunications

Public telephones are found almost everywhere in the territory but they accept local telephone cards only (no coins). Thus anyone planning on using the phone will have to pick up a telephone card *(télécarte),* sold at all post offices. They're valid for both local and international calls, and are available in denominations of 30 units (CFP 1,000), 60 units (CFP 2,000), and 150 units (CFP 5,000). Within French Polynesia, you're charged about one unit every four minutes within a single island, one unit every 2.5 minutes within an island group, and one unit every minute between island groups. From 2200–0600 it's half price.

Throughout this book we've tried to supply the local telephone numbers you'll need. Many tourist-oriented businesses will have someone handy who speaks English, so don't hesitate to call ahead. You'll get current information, be able to check prices and perhaps make a reservation, and often save yourself a lot of time and worry. If you need to consult the French Polynesia phone book, ask to see the *annuaire* at any post office. Online you can also search for numbers at www.annuaire.opt.pf.

For long-distance calls. using a card is cheaper than paying cash and you don't get hit with stiff three-minute minimum charges for operator-assisted calls (CFP 1,023 to the United States). With a card the cost of international calls per minute is CFP 100 to Australia, New Zealand, Japan, and North America, or CFP 166 to Britain and Germany. Calls to Germany and the UK are also CFP 100 a minute from midnight to 0600.

To dial overseas direct from Tahiti, listen for the dial tone, then push 00 (Tahiti's international access code). When you hear another dial tone, press the country code of your party (Canada and the United States are both 1), the city or area code, and the number. For information (in French), dial 3612 (a paid call); to get the operator, dial 19.

Operator-assisted long-distance calls are best placed at post offices, which also handle fax *(télécopier)* services. Calls made from hotel rooms are charged double or triple—you could be presented a truly astronomical bill. Collect calls overseas are possible to Australia, Canada, France, New Zealand, Vanuatu, and the United States (but not to the United Kingdom): dial 19 and say you want a *conversation payable à l'arrivée.* North American AT&T telephone cards can be used in French Polynesia.

If calling from abroad, French Polynesia's telephone code is **689.** To call direct from the United States or Canada, one must dial 011-689 and the six-digit telephone number (there are no area codes). International access codes do vary, so always check in the front of your local telephone book.

Email and the Internet were introduced to French Polynesia in 1995 and they've really caught on in recent years. We've included a directory of

Tahiti-related websites and email addresses in this book's Resources section and throughout the book in sidebar form. Internet cafés are found on all the main islands.

Media

Two morning papers appear daily except Sunday. *Les Nouvelles de Tahiti* (tel. 47-52-00, fax 47-52-09) was founded in 1961 and has a circulation of 6,700 copies. In 1964 *La Dépêche de Tahiti* (tel. 46-43-01, fax 41-25-68) merged with an existing paper and 14,000 copies a day are sold at present. Both are part of the Hersant publishing empire.

The free monthly *Tahiti Beach Press* (tel. 42-68-50, fax 42-33-56), edited by Jan Prince, includes tourist information and is well worth perusing to find out which local companies are interested in your business.

If you read French, the monthly magazine *Tahiti Pacifique* (www.tahiti-pacifique.com) is a lively observer of political and economic affairs (single copies CFP 600, airmail subscription US$85).

Television was introduced to Tahiti in 1965 and state-owned Réseau France Outre-Mer (RFO) broadcasts on two channels in French and (occasionally) Tahitian. A territorial station (Tahiti Nui TV), and three cable companies (Téléfenua, Canal +, and Tahiti Nui Satellite) also operate.

There are 10 FM radio stations around Papeete. **Radio Polynésie** (RFO) is a government-run station which presents the main news of the day (in French) at 0630. **Radio 1** also gives a news report at 0630 and plays mostly French and Anglo-American music. Radio 1's sister station, **Tiare FM,** plays more Tahitian music. Both these and **Star FM** (Anglo-American pop and reggae) are owned by the powerful Groupe Aline, which backs the political party of Gaston Flosse. Star FM's competitor, **NRJ,** owned by the newspaper *La Dépêche*, offers French and Anglo-American music. **Radio Maohi** based at Pirae is controlled by Gaston Flosse's political party. It plays Tahitian music during the day but at night it competes with NRJ and Star FM for listeners. **Pacific FM** based at Arue features Tahitian, French, and international music. It rebroadcasts

the Radio France International news (in French) at 0530, 0630, 0730, 1200, 1300, 1700, and 1800. **Radio Bleue** based in Mahina presents a mix of Tahitian and Anglo-American music. **Radio Te Reo o Tefana** is a pro-independence Tahitian-language station based at Faa'a, which features Tahitian music. In Papeete, you'll find these stations at the following frequencies:

87.8 MHz—Pacific FM
88.2 MHz—Radio Maohi
88.6 MHz—NRJ
89.0 MHz—Radio Polynésie
91.4 MHz—Radio Despoire
91.8 MHz—Radio Polynésie
92.3 MHz—Radio Maohi
92.8 MHz—Radio Te Reo o Tefana
95.2 MHz—Radio Polynésie
96.0 MHz—Radio Bleue
96.4 MHz—Star FM
97.4 MHz—Radio Te Reo o Tefana
97.8 MHz—Star FM
98.7 MHz—Radio 1
100.0 MHz—Radio 1
101.1 MHz—Radio Bleue
103.0 MHz—NRJ
103.8 MHz—Radio 1
104.2 MHz—Tiare FM
105.5 MHz—Tiare FM
105.9 MHz—Star FM
106.4 MHz—Pacific FM

Outside Papeete the frequencies used by these stations vary. At Taravao, look for Radio Polynésie at 89.0 MHz, Radio 1 at 90.9 MHz, Radio Maohi at 94.8 MHz, Tiare FM at 98.3 MHz, and Star FM at 100.8 MHz. Radio Marquises uses 101.3 MHz at Nuku Hiva and 95 MHz at Hiva Oa. Radio Polynésie broadcasts throughout the territory over **738 kHz AM.** None of the local AM/FM stations broadcasts in English.

Health

Public hospitals are found in Papeete (Tahiti), Taravao (Tahiti), Afareaitu (Moorea), Uturoa (Raiatea), Mataura (Tubuai), Taiohae (Nuku Hiva), and Atuona (Hiva Oa). Other islands have only infirmaries or dispensaries. Medical treatment is not free and in nonlife-threatening situations it's better to see a private doctor or dentist. Their attention will cost you no more than you'd pay at a hospital but their services are generally more convenient. Private clinics are found throughout the Society Islands, but there are none in the eastern outer islands (over there, ask for the *infirmerie*). Papeete's Mamao Hospital (tel. 46-62-62) has one of only two recompression chambers in the South Pacific.˙

Business Hours and Time

The sun rises and sets early in French Polynesia. Businesses also open early, often closing for a two-hour siesta at midday. Normal office hours are weekdays 0730–1130/1330–1630. Many shops keep the same schedule but remain open until 1730 and Saturday 0730–1200. A few shops remain open at lunchtime and small convenience stores are often open Saturday afternoon until 1800 and Sunday 0600–0800. Banking hours are variable, either 0800–1530 or 0800–1100/1400–1700 weekdays. A few banks in Papeete open Saturday morning (check the sign on the door). Most businesses are closed on Sunday.

French Polynesia operates on the same time as Hawaii, 10 hours behind Greenwich mean time or two hours behind California (except May–October, when it's three hours). The Marquesas are 30 minutes ahead of Tahiti and the Gambier Islands are an hour ahead of Tahiti. French Polynesia is east of the international date line, so the day is the same as that of the Cook Islands, Hawaii, and the United States, but a day behind Fiji, New Zealand, and Australia.

Transportation

GETTING THERE

Aircalin, Air France, Air New Zealand, Air Tahiti Nui, Hawaiian Airlines, LanChile Airlines, Polynesian Airlines, and Qantas Airways all have flights to Papeete. (For more information on these, turn to the main Introduction.) The local offices you may need to visit to reconfirm your flight are listed in the Papeete section.

Air Tahiti Nui began service from Papeete only in 1998, and it now flies to Los Angeles daily, to Paris three times a week, and to Auckland, Osaka, and Tokyo weekly. The airline's political clout has allowed it to muscle in on routes previously served by other French carriers. In 2002 the French Polynesian government, which owns 66 percent of the airline's shares, paid 40 percent of the cost of Air Tahiti Nui's second A340 Airbus.

France's state-owned national airline, **Air France,** flies from Paris to Papeete via Los Angeles three times a week.

Air New Zealand has flights from Los Angeles to Papeete four times a week, with connections to/from many points in North America and Western Europe. These flights continue southwest to Auckland with one calling at Rarotonga and Fiji. **Polynesian Airlines** has two flights a week direct from Auckland (not via Apia).

Qantas flies from Melbourne to Papeete via Auckland with connections from four other Australian cities. **Hawaiian Airlines** offers weekly service from Honolulu to Papeete with connections from Los Angeles, Las Vegas, San Francisco, Portland, San Diego, and Seattle.

Aircalin has flights from Nouméa to Papeete via Wallis Island. **LanChile Airlines** operates a Boeing 767 service from Santiago to Papeete via Easter Island twice a week.

By Boat

The only scheduled international passenger-carrying freighter service to Tahiti is the monthly Bank Line ship from Le Havre (France) to Auckland via the Panama Canal. Europe to Tahiti takes just under a month. The local agent is **Agence Maritime de Fare Ute** (tel. 42-55-61, fax 42-86-08).

GETTING AROUND

The domestic carrier, **Air Tahiti** (www.airtahiti-vt.com), flies to 42 airstrips in every corner of

French Polynesia, with important hubs at Papeete (Windward Islands), Bora Bora (Leeward Islands), Rangiroa (northern Tuamotus), Hao (eastern Tuamotus), and Nuku Hiva (Marquesas). Its fleet consists of four 66-seat ATR 72s, four 48-seat ATR 42s, and two 19-seat Dornier 228s. The Italian-made ATRs (Avions de Transport Regional) are economical in fuel consumption and maintenance requirements, and they perform well under island conditions. The high-winged design makes them perfect for aerial sight-seeing along the way.

Round-trip tickets are about 15 percent cheaper than two one-ways. Air Tahiti doesn't allow stopovers on its tickets, so if you're flying round-trip from Tahiti to Bora Bora and want to stop at Raiatea on the way out and Huahine on the way back, you'll have to buy four separate tickets (total CFP 31,800). Ask about the "Pass Bleu," which allows you to visit these islands plus Moorea for CFP 20,000 (certain restrictions apply).

No student discounts are available, but people under 25 and over 60 can get discounts of up to 50 percent on certain flights by paying CFP 1,000 for a discount card (carte de réduction). Family reduction cards (CFP 2,000) provide a potential 50 percent reduction for the parents and 75 percent off for children under 12. Identification and one photo are required, and application must be made at least three working days before you wish to travel. The full discount is given only on off-peak flights and bookings can be made only from within French Polynesia.

Better than point-to-point fares are the six Air Tahiti **Air Passes.** These are valid 28 days, but only one stopover can be made on each island included in the package. For example, you can go Papeete–Moorea–Huahine–Raiatea–Maupiti–Bora Bora–Papeete for CFP 30,500. Otherwise pay CFP 45,500 for Papeete–Moorea–Huahine–Raiatea–Maupiti–Bora Bora–Rangiroa–Tikehau–Manihi–Fakarava–Papeete. This compares with an individual ticket price of CFP 43,000 to do the first circuit or CFP 90,000 for the second, which makes the air passes good value. The four Society Islands Air Passes can be extended to include the Austral Islands for another CFP

20,000. To add Nuku Huva and Hiva Oa to a pass is CFP 45,000 extra. All flights must be booked in advance but date changes are possible (reroutings are not). Air Tahiti's agent in North America, Tahiti Vacations (tel. 800/553-3477), will have current information. The passes are nonrefundable once travel has begun.

Air Tahiti also offers packages (séjours) to almost all its destinations, including airfare, transfers, hotel rooms (double occupancy), and the occasional breakfast or excursion. Of course, it uses only the more upmarket hotels, but if you were planning to stay in one of them anyway, Air Tahiti's packages are cheaper than what you'd pay directly. Cruise packages are also offered. All the possibilities are clearly outlined (in French) with exact prices quoted in Air Tahiti's well-designed timetable.

Air Tahiti tickets are refundable at the place of purchase, but you must cancel your reservations at least two hours before flight time to avoid a penalty. Do this in person and have your flight coupon amended as no-shows are charged 25 percent of the value of the ticket to make a new reservation (all existing reservations will be automatically canceled). Standby passengers are given any unclaimed seats 20 minutes before each flight.

If you're told a flight you want is full, keep checking back as local passengers often change their minds and seats may become available (except around major public holidays). It's not necessary to reconfirm reservations for flights between Tahiti, Moorea, Huahine, Raiatea, Bora Bora, Rangiroa, and Manihi, but elsewhere it's essential to reconfirm. (If your bookings were made from abroad do reconfirm *everything* upon arrival in Papeete as mix-ups in communications between foreign travel agencies and Air Tahiti are routine.) Beware of planes leaving 20 minutes early.

If you buy your ticket locally, the baggage allowance on domestic flights is 10 kg, but if your Air Tahiti flight tickets were purchased seven days before your arrival in French Polynesia, the allowance is 20 kg. All baggage above those limits is charged at the rate of the full fare for that sector divided by 80 per kilogram (surfboards over 1.8 meters long or items weighing over 32 kg

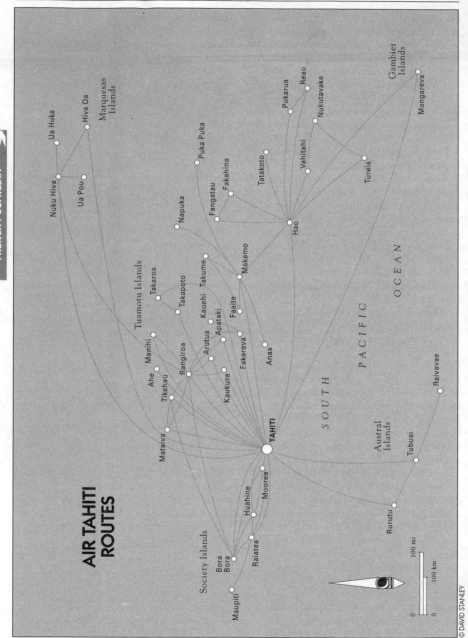

AIR TAHITI ROUTES

© DAVID STANLEY

are not accepted). Hand luggage is limited to three kilos. Fresh fruit and vegetables cannot be carried from Tahiti to the Austral, Tuamotu, Gambier, or Marquesas Islands.

On Bora Bora, Maupiti, and Mangareva passengers are transferred from the airport to town by boat. This ride is included in the airfare at Bora Bora but costs extra at Maupiti (CFP 500) and Mangareva (CFP 600). Smoking aboard the aircraft is prohibited and all flights are free seating.

The main Air Tahiti office (tel. 86-42-42, fax 86-40-69) in Papeete is at the corner of rue Maréchal Foch and rue Edouard Ahnne. It's closed on weekends. Check carefully to make sure all the flights listed in the published timetable are actually operating! Any travel agency in Papeete can book Air Tahiti flights for the same price as the Air Tahiti office, and the service tends to be better.

An Air Tahiti subsidiary, **Air Moorea** (tel. 86-41-41, fax 86-42-99), has flights between Tahiti and Moorea (CFP 3,000 one-way) leaving Papeete hourly 0600–1800. The Air Moorea terminal is in a separate building at the east end of Faa'a Airport. However, flying between Tahiti and Moorea is not recommended because going over by ferry is a big part of the experience and the transfer service to/from Moorea Airport is for travelers on prebooked tours only. People traveling individually must take a taxi from Moorea airport to their hotel and they're very expensive. A cramped, stuffy plane ride at three times the cost of the relaxing 30-minute ferry is to be avoided.

Air Tahiti Services

Air Tahiti flies from Papeete to Huahine (CFP 9,200), Raiatea (CFP 10,500), and Bora Bora (CFP 12,900) four to eight times a day. Every day there's an expensive direct connection from Moorea to Huahine (CFP 11,500); Raiatea to Maupiti (CFP 5,900) is three times a week. The five weekly transversal flights from Bora Bora to Rangiroa, Tikehau, and Manihi (CFP 21,500) eliminate the need to backtrack to Papeete.

Flights between Papeete and Rangiroa (CFP 14,200) operate one to five times a day, continuing from Rangiroa to Tikehau (CFP 4,600)

and Manihi (CFP 9,200) four times a week. Rangiroa-Fakarava (CFP 4,600) is only weekly. Air Tahiti also has flights to the East Tuamotu atolls and Mangareva. Many flights between outer islands of the Tuamotus operate in one direction only.

Flights bound for the Marquesas are the longest and most expensive of Air Tahiti's services. The ATR service from Papeete to Nuku Hiva (CFP 25,500) is daily. Once or twice a week these flights call at Hiva Oa on their way to or from Nuku Hiva, and one weekly ATR flight calls at Rangiroa. At Nuku Hiva the Papeete flights connect for Ua Pou (CFP 5,300), Hiva Oa (CFP 9,200), and Ua Huka (CFP 5,300). If you know you'll be going on to Hiva Oa, Ua Huka, or Ua Pou, get a through ticket from Papeete; the fare is only CFP 3,100 more than a ticket as far as Nuku Hiva.

The Austral group is well connected to Papeete, with flights to Rurutu (CFP 17,200) and Tubuai (CFP 19,300) four or five times a week with alternating Papeete–Rurutu–Tubuai–Papeete or Papeete–Tubuai–Rurutu–Papeete routings. The twice weekly Tubuai-Rurutu leg costs CFP 8,700.

During July and August, the peak holiday season, extra flights are scheduled. Air Tahiti is fairly reliable; still, you should avoid scheduling a flight back to Papeete on the same day that your international flight leaves Tahiti. It's always wise to allow some leeway in case there's a problem with the air service. Save your ride around Tahiti until the end.

By Sea

To save money, many budget travelers tour French Polynesia by boat. There's a certain romance and adventure to taking an interisland freighter, and you can go anywhere by copra boat, including islands without airstrips and resorts. Ships leave Papeete regularly for the different island groups. You'll meet local people and fellow travelers and receive a gentle introduction to the island of your choice. Problems about overweight baggage, tight reservations, and airport transport are eliminated, and thanks to government subsidies travel by ferry or passenger-carrying freighter is four times cheaper than the plane. Seasickness, cockroaches, diesel fumes, and the heavy scent of copra are all part of the experience.

Below you'll find specific information on the main interisland boats; the Visitors Bureau in Papeete also has lists. Prices and schedules have been fairly stable over the past few years, and new services are being added all the time. Lots of visitors travel this way to Moorea and Huahine, so don't feel intimidated if you've never done it before.

For the cheapest ride and the most local color, travel deck class. There's usually an awning in case of rain, and you'll be surrounded by Tahitians, but don't count on getting a lot of sleep if you go this way—probably no problem for one night, right? Lay your mat pointed to one side of the boat because if you lie parallel to the length of the boat you'll roll from side to side. Don't step over other peoples' mats, but if you must, first remove your shoes and excuse yourself. Otherwise take a cabin, which you'll share with three or four other passengers, still cheaper than an airplane seat. Food is included only on really long trips (ask), but snacks may be sold on board. On a long trip

LEEWARD ISLANDS FERRY SCHEDULES

MV *Aremiti III* (350 passengers)
MV *Vaeanu* (120 passengers)
MV *Hawaiki-Nui* (12 passengers)

| Northbound | | | | | | Ports of Call | | Southbound | | | | |
A	C	E	G	I				B	D	F	H	J
0800	1700	1700	1600	1600	dep	Papeete	arr	1930	0430	0130	0400	0400
1215	0130	0130	0200		arr	Huahine	dep	1500	1830	1600		1800
1230	0230	0230	0300		dep	Huahine	arr	1445	1800	1500		1700
1345	0430	0430	0530		arr	Raiatea	dep	1400	1600	1300		1400
	0630	0630	0800		dep	Raiatea	arr		1530	1230		1230
		0730			arr	Taha'a	dep		1430	1130	1600	1130
		0830			dep	Taha'a	arr		1400	1100	1530	1100
	0930	1100	1100	0645	arr	Bora Bora	dep		1130	0830	1300	0800

A—*Aremiti III* departs Papeete Monday and Friday
B—*Aremiti III* departs Raiatea Monday and Friday
C—*Vaeanu* departs Papeete Monday and Wednesday (1)
D—*Vaeanu* departs Bora Bora Tuesday and Thursday
E—*Vaeanu* departs Papeete Friday
F—*Vaeanu* departs Bora Bora Sunday
G—*Hawaiki-Nui* departs Papeete Tuesday
H—*Hawaiki-Nui* departs Bora Bora Wednesday
I—*Hawaiki-Nui* departs Papeete Thursday
J—*Hawaiki-Nui* departs Bora Bora Friday

(1) Only cabin passengers on northbound Wednesday departure.

Schedules may be modified during holidays or otherwise.

you're better off taking all your own food rather than buying a meal plan.

For any boat trip farther than Moorea check the schedule and pick up tickets the day before at the company office listed below. If you're headed for a remote island outside the Societies or want cabin class, visit the office as far in advance as possible. Take along your passport as the staff may insist on checking the expiration date of your visa before selling you a ticket to a point outside the Society Islands. Except on the tourist-class *Aranui,* it's not possible (nor recommended) to book your passage before arriving on Tahiti. If you really want to go, there'll be something leaving around the date you want. On an outer island, be wary when someone, even a member of the crew, tells you the departure time of a ship: they're as apt to leave early as late.

Boat trips are always smoother northwest-bound than southeast-bound because you go with the prevailing winds. The ferry schedules are also more convenient northbound. Take this into consideration if you plan to fly one way, in which case it would be better to come back by air. *Bon voyage.*

Ferries to Moorea

The Moorea ferries carry more than a million passengers a year, making Papeete the third-largest port under the French flag (after Calais and Cherbourg) as far as passenger movements go. Two types of ferries do this trip: fast catamarans carrying walk-on commuters only (30 minutes), and large car ferries with a capacity for 400 foot-passengers and 80 vehicles (one hour). Departure times are posted at the ferry landing on the Papeete waterfront (punctual) and reservations are not required: you just buy your ticket before you board.

Most of the ferries mentioned below go to Vaiare Wharf on the east side of Moorea. Local buses meet the ferries at Vaiare and carry passengers to any part of Moorea for a flat CFP 300 fare (the bright yellow tourist buses charge CFP 500). Don't be too slow boarding as the buses do fill up at times.

The high-speed catamarans *Aremiti IV* (tel. 42-88-88) and *Moorea Jet* (tel. 42-37-42) make four to six trips a day between Tahiti and Vaiare

at CFP 1,050 pp (bicycles CFP 210). On the Moorea cats you're allowed to sit or stand outside on the roof and get an all-round view, which makes them fun.

The large car ferries *Moorea Ferry* (tel. 45-00-30) and *Aremiti Ferry* shuttle four or five times a day between Papeete and Vaiare (CFP 850 one-way, students and children under 13 CFP 425, cars CFP 2,600, scooters CFP 725, bicycles CFP 210).

Unlike all the others, the high-speed monohull *Ono-Ono* (tel. 45-35-35) goes to a landing next to Paopao Fish Market at the head of Cook's Bay, Moorea. It runs three to five times a day and charges CFP 1,100. It's a wonderful introduction to Moorea to sail right into Cook's Bay, but unfortunately no buses meet the *Ono-Ono.*

Ferry to Huahine and Raiatea

The highspeed catamaran *Aremiti III* (tel. 74-39-40, fax 42-83-83) departs Papeete for Huahine (CFP 4,600) and Raiatea (CFP 5,200) every Monday and Friday morning at 0800. The return journey from Raiatea begins at 1400 those same days. The interisland fare between Huahine and Raiatea is CFP 1,700. You must be at the wharf an hour before departure. It's an excellent alternative to the slow, uncomfortable cargo ships and expensive flights. In windy weather, however, be prepared for a rough trip.

Cargo Ships to the Leeward Islands

All of the cargo ships depart Papeete's Motu Uta wharf, a 20-minute walk from town. Northbound the MV *Vaeanu* leaves Papeete Monday, Wednesday, and Friday at 1700; southbound it leaves Bora Bora Tuesday and Thursday at 1130, and Sunday at 0830. The MV *Hawaiki-Nui* (tel. 45-23-24, fax 45-24-44) departs Papeete for Huahine, Raiatea, and Bora Bora on Tuesday and Thursday at 1600. Beware of voyages marked "carburant" on the schedules because when fuel *(combustible)* is being carried, only cabin passengers are allowed aboard (this usually happens on the *Vaeanu's* Wednesday departures from Papeete). The cargo boat *Taporo VII* to Bora Bora no longer accepts passengers at all.

The timings are more civilized if you stay on the boat right through to Bora Bora northbound:

you get to see the sunset over Moorea, go to bed, and when you awake you'll be treated to a scenic cruise past Taha'a and into the Bora Bora lagoon. Getting off at Huahine at 0130 is no fun (although there is a shelter on the wharf where you can spend the rest of the night for free). Southbound between Bora Bora, Raiatea, and Huahine you travel during daylight hours, which makes it easy to island-hop back. Southbound you board at Huahine at dusk and there will be no disturbances before Tahiti (where you'll be asked to disembark in the middle of the night).

Although the ships do make an effort to stick to their timetables, the times are approximate—ask at the company offices. They're more likely to be running late on the return trip from Bora Bora to Tahiti. Expect variations if there's a public holiday that week. In Papeete, board the ship at least an hour before departure to be sure of a reasonable place to sleep (mark your place with a beach mat). If you've got some time to kill before your ship leaves Papeete, have a look around the coconut-oil mill next to the wharf.

You can usually buy a deck ticket at the *Vaeanu* office (tel. 41-25-35, fax 41-24-34) facing the wharf at Motu Uta a few hours before departure (except on holidays). Cabin space should be booked at least a day in advance. The *Hawaiki-Nui* accepts only 12 passengers, so the 120-passenger *Vaeanu* is a safer bet. Be sure to buy your ticket before boarding as there can be problems for anyone trying to pay once the ship is under way. In the Leeward Islands buy a ticket from the agent on the wharf as soon as the boat arrives. One-way fares from Papeete to any of the islands are CFP 1,786 deck (shared cabins begin at CFP 4,317 pp). The *Vaeanu* is the original *Aranui,* which served the Marquesas Islands 1981–1990. It offers mats in the spacious hold down below or floor space on the enclosed upper rear deck (with the lights on all night). The passengers and crew are mostly Tahitian, and the *Vaeanu* is an excellent option for the adventurous traveler. Just don't expect a tourist cruise at those prices.

Barges to Maupiti

The government supply barges *Meherio* or *Maupiti to'u Aia* leave Papeete for Maupiti

Wednesday afternoons (20 hours) calling at Raiatea on the way. Information is available from the **Groupement d'Intervention de la Polynésie** (tel. 50-66-88; weekdays 0730–1500) at Motu Uta. These ships don't carry foreign passengers very often, but they may make an exception in your case. If not, the fast ferry *Maupiti Express* (tel./fax 67-66-69) shuttles between Bora Bora and Maupiti three times a week.

Ships to the Austral Islands

The **Service de Navigation des Australes** (tel. 50-96-09, fax 42-06-09), in the building marked "Entrepot Tuhaa Pae" at the Tuamotu wharf, runs the *Tuhaa Pae III* to the Austral Islands. One-way deck/couchette/cabin fares from Papeete are CFP 3,969/5,556/7,641 to Rurutu, Rimatara, or Tubuai, CFP 5,722/8,010/11,017 to Raivavae, or CFP 7,823/10,953/15,060 to Rapa. Between Rurutu and Tubuai it's CFP 1,868/2,615/3,598. Otherwise it's CFP 30,120 cabin class for the entire 10-day round-trip. Three meals a day cost CFP 3,000/5,000 pp a day extra at the cafeteria/officer's table (or take your own food).

The *Tuhaa Pae III* has nine four-bed, two two-bed, and two one-bed cabins. Some are below the waterline and are very hot with no portholes. The rear deck has a diesely romantic feel, for a day or two. For sanitary reasons the seats have been removed from the ship's toilets (you squat). The ship calls at Rimatara, Rurutu, Tubuai, Raivavae three or four times a month. Rapa Iti is visited about once a month, Maria Atoll annually. The schedule changes at a moment's notice, so actually sailing on the *Tuhaa Pae III* requires persistence. Consider going out by boat and returning by plane.

Ships to the Tuamotus and Gambiers

The motor vessel *Dory II* leaves from Motu Uta every Monday at 1600 for Tikehau (Tuesday 1100), Rangiroa (Tuesday 1800), Ahe (Wednesday 0700), Manihi (Wednesday 1400), Arutua (Thursday 0600), and Kaukura (Thursday 1100), arriving back in Papeete Friday at 0800. This routing means it takes only 26 hours to go from Papeete to Rangiroa but 56 hours to return.

There are five double and two triple cabins, and deck/cabin fares are CFP 3,640/5,200 each way. Soft foam mattresses are provided on deck but meals are not included. This small vessel visits the islands to deliver frozen bread, chicken, and ice cream and pick up fish. Its Papeete office (tel./fax 42-30-55) is across the hall from the *Aranui* office at Motu Uta. Foreign visitors use this boat regularly, so it's a good bet.

The *Cobia II* also runs to the Tuamotus, departing Monday at 1200 for Kaukura (Tuesday 0800), Arutua (Tuesday 1300), Apataki (d 1630), Aratika (Wednesday 0700), and Toau (Wednesday 1330), returning to Papeete Friday at 1000 (CFP 3,120 one-way). No cabins are available and you must take all your own food. The office (tel. 43-36-43) is in the same building as the *Aranui* office at Motu Uta.

The *Vai-Aito* (tel. 43-99-96, fax 43-53-04) departs Motu Uta every 10 days for Tikehau (CFP 5,050 deck from Papeete), Rangiroa (CFP 5,050), Ahe (CFP 9,470), Manihi (CFP 10,100), Aratika (CFP 11,990), Kauehi (CFP 14,500), Raraka (CFP 15,150), and Fakarava (CFP 17,675). A complete round-trip costs CFP 26,512, meals included.

Many smaller copra boats, such as the *Hotu Maru, Kura Ora III, Mareva Nui, Rairoa Nui,* and *Saint Xavier Maris Stella* also service the Tuamotus. The *Nuku Hau* and *Taporo V* go as far as the Gambier Islands. Ask about ships of this kind at the large warehouses west of Papeete's Motu Uta interisland wharf.

Cargo Ship to the Marquesas

Every other Thursday at 1700 the 75-meter cargo ship *Taporo VI* departs Papeete for Takapoto, Fatu Hiva, Tahuata, Hiva Oa, Ua Huka, Nuku Hiva, and Ua Pou. Passengers pay CFP 22,000/32,000 deck/cabin one-way from Papeete to any port in the Marquesas. Otherwise you can do the whole 12-day round-trip for CFP 44,000/64,000 deck/cabin. To bring a bicycle is CFP 3,000. Only two to six hours are spent at each port, so you should plan on getting off somewhere and flying back. From Papeete, it takes three days on the open sea to reach the first Marquesan island.

The *Taporo VI* has two four-berth cabins and 12 seats on deck. Food is included but it's mar-

ginal, so take extras and bring your own bowl. Meals are served at 0600, 1030, and 1730. No pillows or towels are supplied in the cabins and the shower is open only three hours a day. Moving cargo is the ship's main business and the company is sometimes selective about who it accepts as a passenger. The agent is **Compagnie Française Maritime de Tahiti** (tel. 42-63-93, fax 42-06-17; weekdays 0730–1100/1330–1700, Saturday 0730–1100) at Fare Ute. At island stops *Taporo VI* lowers a container onto the wharfs which it uses as an office. (The CFMT itself has a place in local history, having been founded in 1890 by Sir James Donald, who had the contract to supply limes to the British Pacific fleet. At the turn of the previous century Donald's schooner, the *Tiare Taporo,* was the fastest in Polynesia, and the CFMT is still the Lloyd's of London agent.)

The Aranui

The passenger-carrying freighter *Aranui* cruises 16 times a year between Papeete and the Marquesas. It calls at all of the inhabited Marquesas Islands, plus a couple of the Tuamotus. The routing might be Papeete–Takapoto–Ua Pou–Nuku Hiva–Hiva Oa–Fatu Hiva–Hiva Oa–Ua Huka–Nuku Hiva–Ua Pou–Rangiroa–Papeete. A vigorous daily program with fairly strenuous but optional hikes is included in the tour price. The only docks in the Marquesas are at Taiohae, Hakahau, and Atuona; elsewhere everyone goes ashore in whale boats, a potential problem for passengers with mobility limitations. Still, the *Aranui* is fine for the adventuresome visitor who wants to see a lot in a short time.

This 115-meter freighter had its inaugural sailing in 2002, replacing a smaller German-built boat that had served the Marquesas since 1990. It's clean and pleasant compared to the *Taporo VI,* but more expensive. The 150 passengers are accommodated in three classes of accommodations for the 16-day, eight-island cruise. The cheapest cabin with shared bath is US$3,023 pp round-trip (double occupancy), all meals included. Cabins with private bath start at US$3,500 pp. Single occupancy costs 50 percent more. There's also an air-conditioned dormitory with upper and lower berths that costs US$1,980 pp and, of course, doesn't involve a

FRENCH POLYNESIA INTERNET RESOURCES

General Interest

Dream Islands Travel Guide
www.dream-islands.com

French Polynesia
www.polynesianislands.com/fp

Philatelic Bureau
www.tahitiphilatelie.pf

Tahiti1.com
www.tahiti1.com

Tahiti Pacifique **Magazine**
www.tahiti-pacifique.com

Tahiti Presse
www.tahitipress.com

Tahiti Tourisme, Papeete
www.tahiti-tourisme.com

Tahiti Tourisme, USA
www.gototahiti.com

Government

Institut Territorial de la Statistique
www.ispf.pf

Présidence du Gouvernement
www.presidence.pf

Université de la Polynésie française
www.upf.pf

Sports and Recreation

Tahitian Blue Water Dream
www.tahitianbluewaterdream.com

Tahiti Diving Guide
www.diving-tahiti.com

Tahiti Nui Marathon
www.tahitimarathon.com

---

single supplement. A US$75 port tax, US$105 cruise tax, and 6 percent value-added tax are extra. Deck passage is intended for local residents only, but it's sometimes possible for tourists to travel interisland within the Marquesas on deck (about CFP 3,000–8,000 a hop). The meals are good but with little choice. The roster of American/French/German passengers is congenial.

The *Aranui*'s Papeete office (**Compagnie Polynésienne de Transport Maritime,** tel. 42-62-40, fax 43-48-89) is at the interisland wharf at Motu Uta. The CPTM's U.S. office is at 2028 El Camino Real S, Suite B, San Mateo, CA 94403, U.S.A. (tel. 800/972-7268 or 650/574-2575, www.aranui.com). In the United States bookings can be made through **TravLtips** (www.travltips .com). One Australian reader wrote: "The trip is fantastic and I hope to do it again soon."

Tourist Cruises

In addition to the *Aranui,* several conventional cruise ships ply the Society Islands from Tahiti to Bora Bora on one-week trips. The operators change regularly as such vessels enjoy a five-year tax holiday in French Polynesia and they tend to leave as soon as the incentives are used up. The main market is the U.S. west coast, which is almost as close to Tahiti as it is to the better-known cruising grounds in the Caribbean.

The best established vessel at the moment is the 320-passenger *Paul Gauguin,* built at St. Nazaire, France, in 1997 and operated by *Radisson Seven Seas Cruises* (tel. 800/525-5350, www.rssc.com). This ship does seven-night cruises from Papeete to Taha'a, Bora Bora, Raiatea, and Moorea year-round, beginning at US$2,599 pp a week double-occupancy for one of the 14 cabins on the bottom deck and including airfare from Los Angeles (US$300 surcharge April–Dec., plus US$195 pp port tax). Shore excursions and shipboard gambling cost extra. You can book through www.tahitivacations.net.

In 2002 **Wind Star Cruises** (www.windstar-cruises.com) returned to Tahiti after an absence

Music and Festivals

Carnaval de Tahiti
www.carnavaldetahiti.pf

Heiva i Tahiti
www.tahiti-heiva.org

Manuiti Productions
www.manuiti.pf

Accommodations

Fédération Haere Mai des Pensions
www.haere-mai.pf

Pearl Resorts
www.pearlresorts.com

Transportation and Tours

Air Tahiti
www.airtahiti.pf

Air Tahiti Nui
www.airtahitinui-usa.com

Aranui Cruises
www.aranui.com

Archipels Croisieres
www.archipels.com

Bora Bora Cruises
www.boraborapearlcruises.com

Faa'a International Airport, Papeete
www.tahiti-aeroport.pf

Manureva Tours
www.manureva-tours.com

Tahiti Nui Travel
www.tahitinuitravel.com

Tahiti Tours
www.tahiti-tours.com

Tahiti Vacations
www.tahitivacations.net

Tekura Tahiti Travel
www.tahiti-tekuratravel.com

---

of four years. Every Friday the 134-meter four-masted tall ship *Wind Star* takes 148 passengers from Papeete to Raiatea, Taha'a, Bora Bora and Moorea. Packages from Los Angeles begin around US$3,335 pp double occupancy, plus US$195 pp port tax. In 2004 this vessel may be replaced by the 308-passenger *Wind Surf,* the former *Club Med I.*

P&O Princess Cruises (www.princess.com) operates the much larger 688-passenger *Pacific Princess* and *Tahitian Princess* on 10-day cruises out of Papeete. Three different itineraries are available on these huge love boats formerly operated by Renaissance Cruises, including Papeete to Bora Bora, Papeete to Rarotonga, and Papeete to the Marquesas. Shore excursions and alcoholic drinks are generally not included on this type of ship.

Smaller Vessels

Since 1998 the 34-meter mini-cruise ship *Haumana* has done trips around Huahine, Raiatea, Taha'a, and Bora Bora. The 19 cabins are CFP 123,800/165,200/255,300 pp double occupancy for a three/four/seven-day cruise including excursions (single occupancy about 15 percent more). It's run by **Bora Bora Cruises** (tel. 43 43-03, fax 45-10-65, www.boraborapearlcruises .com), and is less luxurious and more personal than the megaships. Two new 67-meter, 38-cabin mini-cruise ships, the *Tu Moana* and *Tia Moana,* operated by the same company, were expected to begin seven-day cruises in the same area in mid-2003 at CFP 336,000 pp. In 2004 the *Haumana* will switch to cruising the Tuamotu Islands.

If scuba's your thing, the live-aboard *Tahiti Aggressor,* part of the **Aggressor Fleet** (tel. 800/348-2628, www.pac-aggressor.com), should be your choice. Based at Rangiroa, this 32-meter vessel does one-week cruises to remote Tuamotu atolls such as Kaukura, Fakarava, Toau, and Apataki. The 16 divers each pay about US$2,395 double occupancy, plus US$50 tax, for 5.5 days of extraordinary drift diving (airfare not included). Nondivers get a US$200 discount.

Archipels Croisieres (tel. 56-36-39, fax 56-35-87, www.archipels.com) operates all-inclusive cruises on its five 17-meter, eight-passenger catamarans. It offers a six-night tour of the Leeward Islands at US$1,975 pp or two/three nights cruising the Rangiroa lagoon at US$830/1,080 pp (both double occupancy). Shore excursions and almost everything other than interisland airfare and alcohol is included. For couples it's much cheaper than chartering a yacht and your crew does all the work. Just don't expect a luxury trip with gourmet cuisine, even though the brochure may suggest it. Hope your fellow passengers will be amenable.

Also consider yacht cruises in the same areas on lesser-known vessels, such as *Danae IV* (www.danaecruise-tahiti.com) at US$230 pp a day or the *Eden Martin* (www.sailing-huahine.com) based at Huahine. **The Moorings** (www.moorings.com) offers six-night cruises of the Leeward Islands on a shared five-cabin yacht at US$3,276/4,368 single/double per cabin including meals and taxes (but not a suggested 15 percent gratuity). These happen four times a year between June and November.

Yacht Charters

Tahiti Yacht Charter (tel. 45-04-00, fax 42-76-00, www.vpm.fr), part of the Groupe Nouvelles Frontières, has 14 charter yachts available at Tahiti and Raiatea. Its Tahiti office is in the same Papeete complex as the Tahiti Manava Visitors Bureau. On Raiatea, it's based at the Marina Apooiti (tel. 66-28-86, fax 66-28-85), one km west of Raiatea Airport. Prices begin at CFP 272,720 a week for a three-cabin yacht and increase to CFP 629,090 for a large catamaran. There's a supplement in July and August and a discount from November to March. A skipper will be CFP 15,450 a day, a cook CFP 14,000. This may seem like a lot, but split among a nautical-minded group it's comparable to a deluxe hotel room.

The South Pacific's largest bareboat yacht charter operation is **The Moorings Ltd.** (tel. 66-27-13, fax 66-20-94), a Florida company with 25 yachts based at Raiatea's Marina Apooiti. Bareboat prices begin at US$3,990 a week for a yacht accommodating six and go up to US$6,090 for an eight-person catamaran. Prices are steeper during the April–September high season. Provisioning is US$32 pp a day (plus US$152 a day for a cook, if required). If you're new to sailing, a skipper must be hired at US$172 a day. Local tax is 6–16 percent, security insurance US$29 a day, and the starter kit US$87 and up. Charterers are given a complete briefing on channels and anchorages, and provided with a detailed set of charts. All boats are radio-equipped, and a voice from The Moorings is available to talk nervous skippers in and out. Travel by night is forbidden, but by day it's easy sailing. All charters are from noon to noon. Book through The Moorings Ltd., 19345 U.S. 19 N, Suite 402, Clearwater, FL 33764-3147, U.S.A. (tel. 888/952-8420, www.moorings.com). Ask about "specials" when calling.

A third yacht charter operation, **Stardust/Sunsail Yacht Charters** (tel. 60-04-85, fax 66-23-19, www.stardustyc.com), is based at Raiatea's Faaroa Bay. In the United States, it's known as Sunsail (www.sunsail.com). A four-person bareboat yacht will cost US$345/440/490 a day in the low/intermediate/high season with substantial reductions for periods longer than eight or 15 days. The top-of-the-line eight-passenger deluxe catamaran is US$1,390/1,600/1,820 a day, including two crew, full board, and water sports such as windsurfing and water-skiing. There are eight other categories in between. The high season is July and August, intermediate April–June and September–November. If you can schedule a 15-day trip between January and March you can have a bareboat yacht for as little as US$242 a day! Those without the required sailing skills will have to hire a skipper at US$140 a day.

Le Truck

Polynesia's folkloric *le truck* provides an entertaining unscheduled passenger service on Tahiti, Huahine, and Raiatea. Passengers sit on long wooden benches in back and there's no problem with luggage. Fares are fairly low and usually posted on the side of the vehicle. You pay through the window on the right side of the cab. The drivers are generally friendly and will stop to pick you up anywhere if you wave—they're all self-employed, so there's no way they'd miss a fare! Unfortunately, moves are under way to replace these colorful vehicles with air-conditioned Korean buses that stop only at official stops and require printed tickets.

On Tahiti the larger *trucks* and buses leave Papeete for the outlying districts periodically throughout the day until 1700; they continue running to Faa'a Airport and the Sofitel Maeva Beach until late. On Huahine and Raiatea service is usually limited to a trip into the main town in the morning and a return to the villages in the afternoon. On Moorea and Bora Bora buses or *trucks* meet the boats from Papeete. No public transportation is available on the roads of the Austral, Tuamotu, Gambier, or Marquesas Islands.

Car Rentals

Car rentals are available at most of the airports served by Air Tahiti. On Tahiti there's sometimes a mileage charge, whereas on Moorea, Huahine, Raiatea, and Bora Bora all rentals come with unlimited mileage. Public liability insurance is included by law, but collision damage waiver (CDW) insurance is extra. The insurance policies don't cover a flat tire, stolen radios or accessories, broken keys, or towing charges if the renter is found to be responsible. If you can get a small group together, consider renting a minibus for a do-it-yourself island tour.

Unless you have a major credit card you'll have to put a large cash deposit down on the car. Your home driver's license will be accepted, although you must have had your driver's license for at least a year. Some companies rent to people aged 18–24, but those under 25 must show a major credit card and the deductible amount not covered by the CDW insurance will be much higher.

Except on Tahiti, rental scooters are usually available and a strictly enforced local regulation requires you to wear a helmet *(casque)* at all times (CFP 5,000 fine for failure to comply). On some outer islands you can rent an open two-seater "fun car" slightly bigger than a golf cart and no helmet or driver's license is required for these. These and bicycles carry no insurance.

One major hassle with renting cars on the outer islands is that the agency usually gives you a car with the fuel tank only a quarter full, so im-

mediately after renting you must go to a gas station and tank up. Try to avoid putting in more gas than you can use by calculating how many km you might drive, then dividing that by 10 for the number of liters of gasoline you might use. Don't put in over CFP 2,500 (about 20 liters) in any case or you'll be giving a nice gift to the rental agency (which, of course, is its hope in giving you a car that's not full). Gas stations are usually only in the main towns and open only on weekdays during business hours, plus perhaps a couple of hours on weekend mornings. Expect to pay around CFP 130 a liter for gas, which works out to just under US$4 per American gallon—the South Pacific's highest-priced gasoline to drive the most region's expensive rental cars.

As in continental Europe and North America, driving is on the right-hand side of the road. Two traffic signs to know: a white line across a red background indicates a one-way street, while a slanting blue line on a white background means no parking. At unmarked intersections in Papeete, the driver on the right has priority. At traffic circles, the car already in the circle has priority over those entering. The seldom-observed speed limit is 40 kph in Papeete, 60 kph around the island, and 90 kph on the RDO expressway.

French Polynesia contains 70,000 registered vehicles and around 8,000 new cars are sold each year. Forget trying to park on the street in downtown Papeete on a weekday. Drive with extreme care in congested areas—traffic accidents are frequent (43 percent of fatal accidents involve alcohol and another 26 percent speeding). People aged 18–25 account for 57 percent of the dead and injured in accidents here.

A good alternative to renting a car are the 4WD jeep safaris offered on Tahiti, Moorea, Huahine, Raiatea, Tahaa, and Bora Bora. These take you along rough interior roads inaccessible to most rental vehicles and the guides know all the superlative spots. Prices vary CFP 3,500–8,000 pp depending on how far you go.

Others

French Polynesia has some of the most expensive taxis in the world and they're best avoided. If you must take one, always verify the fare before getting

FRENCH POLYNESIA

in. The hitching is still fairly good in Polynesia, although local residents along the north side of Moorea are fed up with it and may not stop. Hitching around Tahiti is only a matter of time.

Bicycling on the island of Tahiti is risky because of wild devil-may-care motorists, but most of the outer islands (Moorea included) have excellent, uncrowded roads. It's wiser to use *le truck* on Tahiti, though a bike would come in handy on the other islands where *le truck* is rare. The distances are just made for cycling!

International Airport

Faa'a Airport (PPT) is conveniently situated 5.5 km southwest of Papeete. The runway was created in 1959–1961, using material dredged from the lagoon or trucked in from the Punaruu Valley. A taxi into town is CFP 1,500, or CFP 2,500 after 2000, plus CFP 100 per piece of luggage. (The driver will *always* want CFP 2,500 if you don't verify the price beforehand. Some drivers even try to get CFP 2,500 per person!) *Le truck* up on the main highway will take you to the same place for only CFP 120 (CFP 200 after 1800) and starts running around 0530. Some le truck drivers ask CFP 100 for luggage, others don't. The tour buses at the airport are strictly for people on prepaid packages. Lobbying by the taxi drivers prevents the hotels from providing airport shuttles.

Many flights to Tahiti arrive in the middle of the night, but you can stretch out on the plastic benches inside the terminal (open 24 hours a day). Be aware that the people who seem to be staffing the tourist information counter at the airport during the night may in fact be taxi drivers who will say anything to get a fare. We've received complaints from readers who were driven all over town from one closed hostel to another, only to be presented with a tremendous bill (you have been warned!). Unless you're willing to spend a lot of money for the possibility of a few hours of sleep, it's better to wait in the terminal until dawn.

The **Banque de Polynésie** (tel. 86-60-56), to the left as you come out of customs, opens Monday–Thursday 0800–1200/1300–1600, Friday 0800–1200/1300–1500, and one hour before and after the arrival and departure of all international flights (ATM accessible 24 hours). It charges a commission of CFP 411 on all traveler's checks. Euros are changed at a standard rate, but for other currencies the rate is 1 percent better for traveler's checks than it is for cash. There's also a **Banque Socredo** branch (tel. 83-86-95) next to the Air Tahiti ticket office facing the parking lot at the far right (west) end of the airport. This office is not easily visible from inside the terminal, so search. It's open weekdays 0800–1145/1400–1700 (no exchanges after 1630) and an adjacent ATM is accessible 24 hours.

The airport luggage-storage office *(consigne a bagages)* is open weekdays 0600–1900, weekends 1200–1400, and two hours before international departures. It charges CFP 395 per day for a handbag, CFP 620 for a suitcase, backpack, or golf bags, CFP 730 for a bicycle, and CFP 1,040–2,500 for surfboards. This left-luggage office is poorly marked; it's behind the Fare Hei flower market in the middle of the parking lot.

Air Tahiti has a ticket office in the terminal open daily 0530–1730. These car rental companies have counters at the airport: Avis, Daniel, Europcar, Hertz, and Pierrot et Jacqueline. The airport post office is open weekdays 0600–1030/1200–1600, weekends 0600–0930. The post office sells cards for the public phones at the airport. The snack bar is open 24 hours and is surprisingly reasonable (draft beer CFP 315, baguette sandwich CFP 385). Public toilets are near the snack bar. The airport information number is tel. 86-60-61.

There's no bank in the departure lounge but you can spend your leftover Pacific francs at the duty-free shops in the departure lounge. Don't expect any bargains. The Fare Hei, just outside the terminal, sells inexpensive shell and flower leis, which the locals give to arriving and departing friends.

All passengers arriving from Samoa or Fiji must have their baggage fumigated upon arrival, a process that takes about two hours (don't laugh if you're told this is to prevent the introduction of the "rhinoceros" into Polynesia—they mean the rhinoceros *beetle*). Fresh fruits, vegetables, and flowers are prohibited entry. There's no airport tax.

Tahiti

Tahiti, largest of the Societies, is an island of legend and song lying in the eye of Polynesia. Though only one of 118, this lush island of around 160,000 inhabitants is paradise itself to most people. Here you'll find an exciting city, big hotels, restaurants, nightclubs, things to see and do, valleys, mountains, reefs, trails, and history, plus transportation to everywhere. Since the days of Wallis, Bougainville, Cook, and Bligh, Tahiti has been the eastern gateway to the South Pacific.

In 1891 Paul Gauguin arrived at Papeete after a 63-day sea voyage from France. He immediately felt that Papeete:

was Europe—the Europe which I had thought to shake off . . . it was the Tahiti of former times which I loved. That of the present filled me with horror.

So Gauguin left the town and rented a native-style bamboo hut in Mataiea on the south coast, where he found happiness in the company of a 14-year-old Tahitian *vahine* whose

face flooded the interior of our hut and the landscape round about with joy and light.

Somerset Maugham's *The Moon and Sixpence* is a fictional tale of Gauguin's life on the island.

©M.G.I. DOMENY DE RIENZI

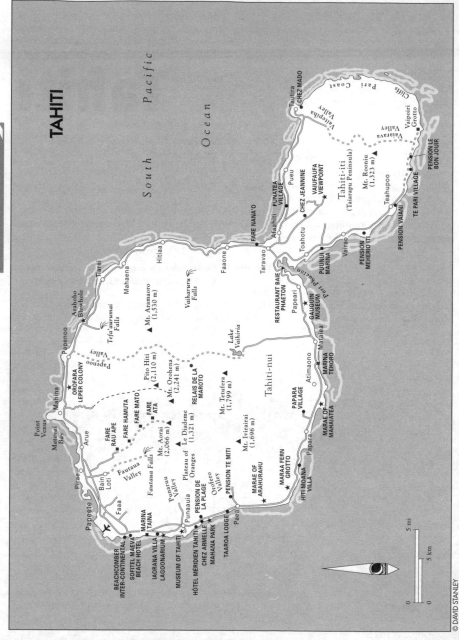

TAHITI

South Pacific Ocean

Pari Coast

Vaitepiha Valley

Vaiarava Valley

Tautira

CHEZ MADO

Vaipoiri Grotto

PENSION LE BON JOUR

TE PARI VILLAGE

Teahupoo

Mt. Rooniu (1,323 m) ▲

Tahiti-iti (Taiarapu Peninsula)

Pueu

VAUFAUFA VIEWPOINT

CHEZ JEANNINE

PUNATEA VILLAGE

Afaahiti

FARE NANA'O

Toahotu

PENSION VAIANI

PENSION MEHERIO ITI

Vairao

PUNUI MARINA

Taravao

Port Phaeton

GAUGUIN MUSEUM

Papeari

RESTAURANT BAIE PHAETON

Faaone

Vaihiria

Lake Vaihiria

Mataiea

MARINA TEHORO

Atimaono

PAPARA VILLAGE

Tahiti-nui

Point Venus

Matavai Bay

Araho'o Blowhole

Tiarei

Papenoo

Mahaena

Hitiaa

Tefaarumai Falls

Vaihururu Falls

▲ Mt. Aramaoro (1,530 m)

Papenoo Valley

Pito Hiti (2,110 m) ▲

▲ Mt. Orohena (2,241 m)

RELAIS DE LA MAROTO

Mt. Tetufera (1,799 m) ▲

OROFARA LEPER COLONY

Matina

Arue

Faaa

FARE RAU APE

FARE HAMUTA

FARE ATA

FARE MATO

Mt. Aorai (2,066 m) ▲

Le Diademe (1,321 m) ▲

Plateau of Oranges

Fautaua Falls

Punaruu Valley

Fautaua Valley

Punaauia

Orofero Valley

▲ Mt. Ivirairai (1,696 m)

PENSION DE LA PLAGE

PENSION TE MITI

MARAE OF ARAHURAHU

HITI MOANA VILLA

MARAE FERN GROTTO

MARAE OF MAHAIATEA

Papara

Pirae

Bain Loti

Papeete

BEACHCOMBER INTER-CONTINENTAL

SOFITEL MAEVA BEACH HOTEL

IAORANA VILLA

LAGOONARIUM

MUSEUM OF TAHITI

HÔTEL MÉRIDIEN TAHITI

CHEZ ARMELLE

MAHANA PARK

TAAROA LODGE

MARINA TAINA

Paea

5 mi

5 km

0

0

Legends created by the early explorers, amplified in Jean-Jacques Rousseau's "noble savage" and taken up by the travel industry, make it difficult to write objectively about Tahiti. Though the Lafayette Nightclub is gone from Arue and Quinn's Tahitian Hut no longer graces Papeete's waterfront, Tahiti remains a delightful, enchanting place. In the late afternoon, as Tahitian crews practice canoe racing in the lagoon and Moorea gains a pink hue, the romance resurfaces.

Papeete is for France what Honolulu is for the United States, a forward base projecting political and military power. Yet if you steer clear of the traffic jams and congestion in commercial Papeete and avoid the tourist ghettos west of the city, you'll get a taste of the magic Gauguin experienced. Whether you love or hate the capital, keep in mind that it's only on the outer islands, away from the motorists and military complexes, that the full flavor of old Polynesia endures.

The Land

The island of Tahiti (1,045 square km) accounts for almost a third of the land area of French Polynesia. Like Hawaii's Maui, Tahiti was formed more than a million years ago by two or three shield volcanoes joined at the isthmus of Taravao. These peaks once stood 3,000 meters above the sea, or 12,700 meters high counting from the seabed. Today the rounded, verdant summits of Orohena (2,241 meters) and Aorai (2,066 meters) rise in the center of Tahiti-nui and deep valleys radiate in all directions from these central peaks. Steep slopes drop abruptly from the high plateaus to coastal plains. The northeast coast is rugged and rocky, without a barrier reef, and thus exposed to intense, pounding surf; villages lie on a narrow strip between mountains and ocean. The south coast is broad and gentle with large gardens and coconut groves; a barrier reef shields it from the sea's fury.

Tahiti-iti (also called the Taiarapu Peninsula) is a peninsula with no road around it. It's a few hundred thousand years younger than Tahiti-nui and Mt. Rooniu (1,323 meters) forms its heart. The populations of big *(nui)* and small *(iti)* Tahiti are concentrated along the coast; the interior of both Tahitis is almost uninhabited. Contrary to the popular stereotype, mostly brown/black beaches of volcanic sand fringe this turtle-shaped island. To find the white/golden sands of the travel brochures, you must cross over to Moorea.

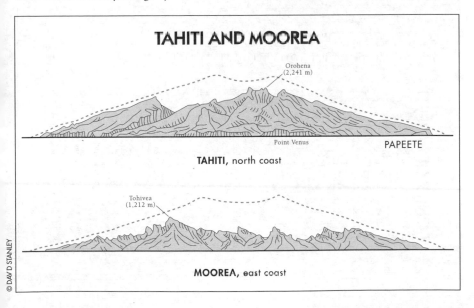

TAHITI AND MOOREA

Orohena (2,241 m)

Point Venus · PAPEETE

TAHITI, north coast

Tohivea (1,212 m)

MOOREA, east coast

© DAVID STANLEY

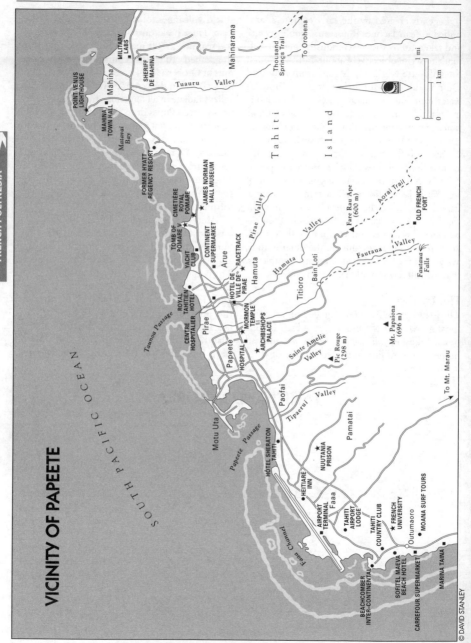

VICINITY OF PAPEETE

© DAVID STANLEY

TAHITI HIGHLIGHTS

Papeete market: shopping, food, local color
Tahua Vaiete: night food market, music, people
Point Venus: monuments, swimming, scenery
Museum of Tahiti: four exhibition halls, surfing
Marae of Arahurahu: history, nature, festivals

Orientation

Almost everyone arrives at Faa'a International Airport five km west of Papeete, the capital and main tourist center of French Polynesia. East of Papeete are Pirae, Arue, and Mahina, with a smattering of hotels and things to see, while south of Faa'a lie the commuter communities Punaauia, Paea, and Papara. On the narrow neck of Tahiti is Taravao, a refueling stop on your 117-km way around Tahiti-nui. Tahiti-iti is a backwater, with dead-end roads on both sides. Boulevard Pomare curves around Papeete's harbor to the Visitors Bureau near the market—that's where to begin. Moorea is clearly visible to the northwest.

FRENCH POLYNESIA

Papeete

Papeete (pa-pay-EH-tay) means "Water Basket." The most likely explanation for this name is that islanders originally used calabashes enclosed in baskets to fetch water at a spring behind the present Territorial Assembly. It was founded as a mission station by the Reverend William Crook in 1818, and whalers began frequenting Papeete's port in the 1820s as it offered better shelter than Matavai Bay. It became the seat of government when young Queen Pomare IV settled here in 1827. The French governors who "protected" the island from 1842 also used Papeete as their headquarters.

Today Papeete is the political, cultural, economic, and communications hub of French Polynesia. More than 100,000 people live in this cosmopolitan city, crowded between the mountains and the sea, and its satellite towns, Faa'a, Pirae, and Arue—more than half the people on the island. "Greater Papeete" extends for 32 km from Paea to Mahina. The French Naval facilities in the harbor area were constructed in the 1960s to support nuclear testing in the Tuamotus.

Since the opening of Faa'a International Airport in 1961 Papeete has blossomed with large hotels, expensive restaurants, bars with wild dancing, radio towers, skyscrapers, and rock bands pulsing their jet-age beat. Where a nail or red feather may once have satisfied a Tahitian, VCRs and Renaults are now in demand. More than 35,000 registered vehicles jam Tahiti's 200 km of roads. Noisy automobiles, motorcycles, and mopeds clog Papeete's downtown and roar along boulevards Pomare and Prince Hinoï buffeting pedestrians with pollution and noise.

Yet along the waterfront the yachts of many countries rock luxuriously in their Mediterranean moorings (anchor out and stern lines ashore). Many of the boats are permanent homes for expatriate French working in the city. "Bonitiers" moored here fish for *auhopu* (bonito) for the local market. There's no need to "tour" Papeete—instead, simply wander about without any set goal. Visit the highly specialized French boutiques, the Chinese stores trying to sell everything, and the Tahitians clustered in the market. Avoid the capital on weekends when life washes out into the countryside; on Sunday afternoons it's a ghost town. Explore Papeete, but make it your starting point—not a final destination.

> *There's no need to "tour" Papeete—instead, simply wander about without any set goal. Visit the highly specialized French boutiques, the Chinese stores trying to sell everything, and the Tahitians clustered in the market.*

Orientation

Thanks to airline schedules you'll probably arrive at the crack of dawn. Change money at the airport bank or use a couple of US$1 bills to take *le*

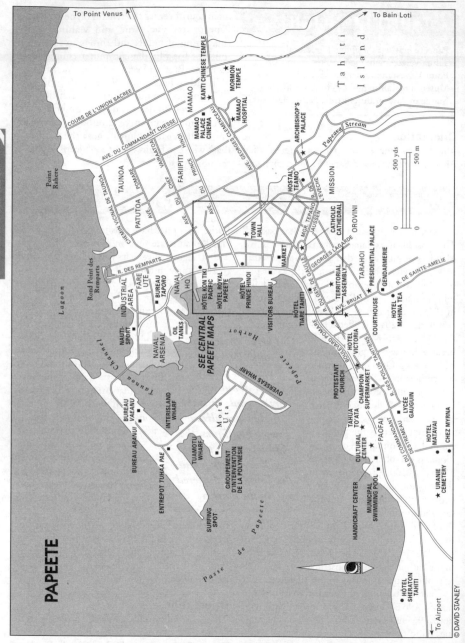

PAPEETE

To Point Venus

To Bain Loti

Tahiti Island

KANTI CHINESE TEMPLE

MORMON TEMPLE

MAMAO PALACE CINEMA

MAMAO HOSPITAL

ARCHBISHOP'S PALACE

Papeava Stream

COURS DE L'UNION SACREE

AVE. DU COMMANDANT CHESSE

AVE. GEORGES CLEMENCEAU

TAUNOA

MAMAO

HOSTAL TEAMO

MISSION

CHEMIN VICINAL DE TAUNOA

PATUTOA

AVE. DU PRINCE HINOI

FARIIPITI

VARRAATOA

AVE. DU CHEF POMARE

AVE. DU PRINCE HINOI

Point Rahere

TOWN HALL

CATHOLIC CATHEDRAL

OROVINI

MGR. TEPANO JAUSSEN

R. DE L'EVECHE

MARKET

R. DES REMPARTS

Rond Point des Remparts

INDUSTRIAL AREA

FARE UTE

BUREAU TAPORO

NAVAL HQ

HOTEL KON TIKI PACIFIC

HOTEL ROYAL PAPEETE

HOTEL PRINCE HINOI

R. DU GEN. DE GAULLE

R. GEORGES LAGARDE

TERRITORIAL ASSEMBLY

TARAHOI

PRESIDENTIAL PALACE

GENDARMERIE

R. DE SAINTE-AMELIE

Lagoon

VISITORS BUREAU

HOTEL TIARE TAHITI

AVE. BRUAT

COURTHOUSE

HOTEL MAHINA TEA

NAUTI-SPORT

OIL TANKS

NAVAL ARSENAL

SEE CENTRAL PAPEETE MAPS

Harbor

Passe de Papeete

HOTEL VICTORIA

BOULEVARD POMARE

R. DES POILUS TAHITIENS

Channel

Taunoa

Motu Uta

BUREAU VAEANU

BUREAU ARANUI

ENTREPOT TUHAA PAE

INTERISLAND WHARF

TUAMOTU WHARF

OVERSEAS WHARF

PROTESTANT CHURCH

CHAMPION SUPERMARKET

LYCEE GAUGUIN

GROUPEMENT D'INTERVENTION DE LA POLYNESIE

CULTURAL CENTER

TAHUA TO'ATA

PAOFAI

R. DU COMMANDANT DESTREMEAU

HOTEL MATAVAI

CHEZ MYRNA

SURFING SPOT

HANDICRAFT CENTER

MUNICIPAL SWIMMING POOL

URANIE CEMETERY

HOTEL SHERATON TAHITI

To Airport

500 yds

500 m

© DAVID STANLEY

truck to Papeete market. The helpful Visitors Bureau on the waterfront opens early, as do the banks nearby. You may want a hotel in town for the first couple of nights to attend to "business": reconfirm your flights, check out the boats or planes, then take off for the outer islands.

A trip around the island will fill a day if you're waiting for connections, and Papeete itself can be fun. Fare Ute, north of French naval headquarters, was reclaimed with material dredged from the harbor in 1963. West across a bridge, past more military muscle, is Motu Uta, where you can jump aboard a passenger-carrying freighter. The Moorea ferries leave from the landing behind the Visitors Bureau downtown. For a day at the beach take *le truck* to Point Venus or Punaauia.

SIGHTS

Papeete

Begin your visit at teeming **Papeete market** (rebuilt 1987) where you'll see Tahitians selling fish, fruit, root crops, and breadfruit; Chinese gardeners with their tomatoes, lettuce, and other vegetables; and French or Chinese offering meat and bakery products. The colorful throng is especially picturesque

1600–1700 when the fishmongers spring to life. Fish and vegetables are sold downstairs on the main floor, handicrafts, pareus, and snacks upstairs on the balcony. The flower displays outside make great photos and the vendors are quite friendly. The biggest market of the week begins around 0500 Sunday morning and is over by 0800.

The streets to the north of the market are lined with two-story Chinese stores built after the great fire of 1884. The US$14.5-million **Hôtel de Ville** (city hall) on rue Paul Gauguin was inaugurated in 1990 on the site of a smaller colonial building demolished to make way. The architect designed the three-story building to resemble the palace of Queen Pomare that once stood on Place Tarahoi near the present post office. A contemporary Marquesan stone tiki stands beside a pond in front of the building.

Notre Dame Catholic Cathedral (1875) is on rue du Général de Gaulle, a block and a half southeast of the market. Inside notice the Polynesian faces and the melange of Tahitian and Roman dress on the striking series of Gauguin-influenced paintings of the crucifixion.

Diagonally across the street from the cathedral is the **Vaima Center,** Papeete's finest

© M.E. DE VOS

Papeete waterfront with the steeple of Notre Dame Cathedral pointing toward Mt. Aorai

FRENCH POLYNESIA

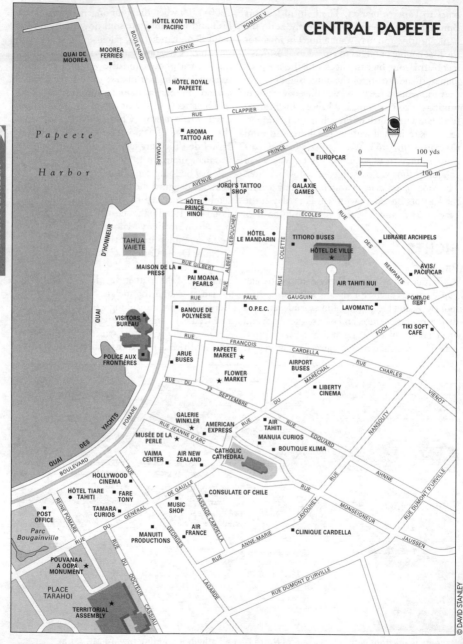

CENTRAL PAPEETE

Papeete Harbor

QUAI DE MOOREA

MOOREA FERRIES

HÔTEL KON TIKI PACIFIC

POMARE V

BOULEVARD

AVENUE

HÔTEL ROYAL PAPEETE

RUE CLAPPIER

AROMA TATTOO ART

HINOI

DU PRINCE

EUROPCAR

MOON

0   100 yds
0   100 m

AVENUE POMARE

JORDI'S TATTOO SHOP

GALAXIE GAMES

HÔTEL PRINCE HINOI

RUE DES ÉCOLES

LIBRAIRE ARCHIPELS

QUAI D'HONNEUR

TAHUA VAIETE

HÔTEL LE MANDARIN

TITIORO BUSES

HÔTEL DE VILLE

RUE DES REMPARTS

AVIS/ PACIFICAR

RUE GILBERT

MAISON DE LA PRESS

PAI MOANA PEARLS

RUE ALBERT

RUE LEBOUCHER

RUE COLETTE

AIR TAHITI NUI

PONT DE L'EST

QUAI

VISITORS BUREAU

RUE PAUL GAUGUIN

BANQUE DE POLYNÉSIE

O.P.E.C.

LAVOMATIC

POLICE AUX FRONTIÈRES

RUE FRANÇOIS

FOCH

TIKI SOFT CAFE

ARUE BUSES

PAPEETE MARKET

CARDELLA

RUE CHARLES

AIRPORT BUSES

FLOWER MARKET

RUE DU 22 SEPTEMBRE

DU MARECHAL

LIBERTY CINEMA

VIENOT

QUAI DES YACHTS

GALERIE WINKLER

RUE JEANNE D'ARC

AMERICAN EXPRESS

AIR TAHITI

RUE EDOUARD

NANSOUTY

MUSÉE DE LA PERLE

MANUIA CURIOS

BOUTIQUE KLIMA

BOULEVARD POMARE

VAIMA CENTER

AIR NEW ZEALAND

CATHOLIC CATHEDRAL

RUE

AHNNE

RUE DUMONT D'URVILLE

HOLLYWOOD CINEMA

HÔTEL TIARE TAHITI

FARE TONY

DE GAULLE

CONSULATE OF CHILE

MONSEIGNEUR

POST OFFICE

REINE POMARE

TAMARA CURIOS

GÉNÉRAL

MUSIC SHOP

PASSAGE CARDELLA

JAVOUHEY

Parc Bougainville

RUE DU

MANUITI PRODUCTIONS

RUE GEORGES

AIR FRANCE

ANNE-MARIE

CLINIQUE CARDELLA

JAUSSEN

POUVANAA A OOPA MONUMENT

RUE DU DOCTEUR CASSIAU

RUE LAGARDE

RUE DUMONT D'URVILLE

PLACE TARAHOI

TERRITORIAL ASSEMBLY

© DAVID STANLEY

window-shopping venue, erected in 1977. The **Musée de la Perle** (tel. 45-21-22; Mon.–Sat. 0830–1830, Sun. 1100–1900; admission CFP 600, children under 15 CFP 300), on rue Jeanne d'Arc on the east side of the center, introduces Polynesia's famous black pearls. A 20-minute video presentation shown on request explains how cultured pearls are "farmed" in the Gambier Islands. The center is owned by a pioneer of the black pearl industry, Robert Wan, who operates nine farms in the Gambier and Tuamotu groups.

A few blocks west along rue du Général de Gaulle is Place Tarahoi. The **Territorial Assembly** on the left occupies the site of the former royal palace, demolished in 1966. The adjacent residence of the French high commissioner is private, but the assembly building and its lovely gardens are worth a brief visit. In front of the entrance gate is a monument erected in 1982 to **Pouvanaa a Oopa** (1895–1977), a Tahitian WW I hero who struggled all his life for the independence of his country. The plaque on the monument says nothing about Pouvanaa's fight for independence and

THE STREETS OF PAPEETE

Papeete's streets bear the names of an odd assortment of French politicians, officials, military leaders, missionaries, and explorers, many of them unfamiliar to English speakers. The city's principal coastal boulevard is named for the Pomare dynasty, which ruled during the implantation of French colonialism. Similarly, Prince Hinoï (1869–1916), who succeeded the puppet king Pomare V, lent his name to the main avenue leading east from the harbor. Papeete's most prominent park bears the name of French explorer Louis-Antoine de Bougainville (1729–1811), whereas Captain Samuel Wallis, who arrived a year earlier, is not remembered and Captain Cook merits only a small side street west of the center. In contrast, an important bypass behind downtown celebrates Dumont d'Urville (1790–1842), a French explorer who visited Tahiti 55 years after Wallis.

Admiral Abel Dupetit-Thouars, who declared a French protectorate over Tahiti in 1842, and Admiral Armand Bruat, the first French governor, are acclaimed by streets near the residence of the present French High Commissioner. A busy east-west thoroughfare passing here bears the names of four prominent Frenchmen: Commandant Destremeau, who defended Papeete against German cruisers in 1914, General De Gaulle (1890–1970), who initiated nuclear testing in Polynesia in 1966, Maréchal Foch (1851–1929), the Allied military commander during the closing months of World War I, and Georges Clémenceau (1841–1929), the French premier during and after World War I. Less known are the church leaders whose names have been attached to streets around Papeete's

Catholic cathedral. Rue Monseigneur Tepano Jaussen, the road leading to the bishop's palace, recalls Florentin Étienne Jaussen (1815–1891), who was appointed vicar apostolic in 1851. This road crosses a street that commemorates Venerable Anne-Marie Javouhey (1779–1851), who founded the Sisters of St. Joseph of Cluny, which did Catholic missionary work in the French colonies. A road between Papeete's city hall and the market honors Gilles Colette, the free-thinking parish priest of Papeete in the late 19th century. Protestants have been awarded a nearby backstreet named for Huguenot missionary Charles Viénot, who promoted Protestant education on Tahiti around the beginning of the previous century. The street between rues Viénot and Jaussen recalls Edouard Ahnne, the director of Catholic boys schools on Tahiti in the early 20th century and leader of the campaign to recognize the Free French forces at the beginning of World War II.

The street in front of the Catholic cathedral recognizes Jeanne d'Arc (1412–1431), the national hero of France who was burned at the stake for heresy after helping to save France from the wicked English. Rue des Poilus Tahitiens, in front of the war memorial on avenue Bruat, memorializes the Tahitian volunteers who fought for France in World War I. Rue de la Canonnière Zélée nearby salutes the French warship sunk at Papeete by German cruisers in 1914. And last but not least, rue Paul Gauguin passes in front of Papeete city hall, a bastion of minor officialdom, the very class so despised by the painter during his lifetime.

POUVANAA A OOPA

Pouvanaa a Oopa was born at Maeva on Huahine in 1895 and during World War I he served in France. In 1942 he denounced war profiteers and was placed under arrest on Huahine. A year later he managed to escape with another man by canoe to Bora Bora in the hope of obtaining American help, but he was arrested and returned to Huahine three days later. After the war Pouvanaa continued to oppose the colonial administration and to advocate a freer political alliance with France. He was elected a deputy to the French parliament in 1949, 1952, and 1956 on an autonomy program. In 1957 he became vice president of the local administration and campaigned for independence in the 1958 referendum, but the No side got only 35 percent of the vote throughout the territory. Later that year he was falsely accused of trying to set Papeete aflame and was sentenced to 15 years' imprisonment. Finally pardoned in 1968, Pouvanaa was elected a senator in the French parliament two years later, a post he held until his death in 1977. Known to the Tahitians as *metua* (spiritual father), Pouvanaa a Oopa remains a symbol of the Polynesian struggle for independence.

against the bomb! In July 1995 nearly a third of the adult population of Tahiti gathered here to protest French nuclear testing in the Tuamotus.

Across the busy avenue from Place Tarahoi, beside the post office on the waterfront, is **Parc Bougainville.** A monument to Bougainville himself, who sailed around the world in 1766–1769, is flanked by two old naval guns. One, stamped "Fried Krupp 1899," is from Count Felix von Luckner's famous raider *Seeadler,* which ended up on the Maupihaa reef in 1917; the other is off the French gunboat *Zélée,* sunk in Papeete harbor by German cruisers in 1914.

Much of the bureaucracy works along avenue Bruat just west, a gracious tree-lined French provincial avenue. The protectorate's first governor, Admiral Armand Bruat, set up a military camp here in 1843. You may observe French justice in action at the **Palais de Justice** (weekdays 0830–1200). The public gallery is up the stairway

and straight ahead. Opposite the police station farther up avenue Bruat is the War Memorial.

In 1999 the Caserne Brioche, a military barracks dating to 1886, was demolished to make way for the **Palais Présidentiel de Papeete,** official residence of the president of French Polynesia. This elegant neocolonial structure near the gendarmerie at the top of avenue Bruat was built for Gaston Flosse, who has ruled the territory almost continuously since 1982. It's intentionally more impressive than the nearby French high commissioner's residence—a proud symbol of Tahiti Nui. You're allowed to enter the first courtyard and stroll around the fountain.

Facing the waterfront a few blocks west of avenue Bruat is the headquarters of the **Evangelical Church** in French Polynesia, with a church dating from 1875 but rebuilt in 1981. It was here that the London Missionary Society established Paofai Mission in 1818. From 1837 to 1958 the British consulate occupied the site of the six-story Paofai girl's hostel opposite the church, and George Pritchard, an early British consul, had his office here.

Continue west along the bay past the outrigger racing canoes to the **Tahua To'ata,** a striking open-air venue created in 2000 for the annual Heiva i Tahiti festival held in July. Adjacent is the neo-Polynesian **Cultural Center** (1973) or Te Fare Tauhiti Nui, which houses a public library, notice boards, and auditoriums set among pleasant grounds. This complex is run by the Office Territorial d'Action Culturelle (OTAC), which organizes the annual Heiva Festival and many other events. The **municipal swimming pool** is on the coast beyond (go upstairs to the restaurant for a view). Return to the center of town along the waterfront.

Another walk takes you east from downtown to the Catholic **Archbishop's Palace** (1869), a lonely remnant of the Papeete that Gauguin saw. To get there, take rue Jaussen behind the Catholic cathedral, keep straight, and ask for the *archevêché catholique.* Without doubt, this is the finest extant piece of colonial architecture in a territory of fast-disappearing historic buildings. The park grounds planted in citrus and the modern open-air church nearby (to the right) also merit a look. The huge mango trees here were planted in 1855 by Tahiti's first bishop, Monseigneur Tepano Jaussen.

Fautaua Valley

If you'd like to make a short trip out of the city, go to the Hôtel de Ville and take a Mamao-Titioro *truck* to the **Bain Loti,** three km up the Fautaua Valley from the Mormon Temple. A bust of writer Pierre Loti marks the spot where he had a love affair he later described in *The Marriage of Loti.* Today the local kids swim in a pool in the river here.

A dirt road continues three km farther up the Fautaua Valley but because it's part of a water catchment, private cars are prohibited, so you must walk. From the end of the road, a trail straight ahead leads directly to **Fautaua Falls** (30 minutes) with several river crossings. Back a bit on the left, just before the end of the road, is a wooden footbridge across the river. Here begins a steep one-hour trail up to a 19th-century French fort at the top of the falls. The fort controlled the main trail into Tahiti's interior, and it's still an excellent hiking area. It's open only on weekdays and you should be back before 1530 when the gate is often closed.

Back on avenue Georges Clemenceau near the Mormon Temple is the impressive **Kanti Chinese Temple,** built in 1987, which is usually open mornings until noon.

Arue

Another easy side trip is east to Arue (a-roo-AY). Begin by taking an Arue or Mahina *truck* from near the Visitors Bureau to the colonial-style **Mairie de Arue** (1892) at PK 5.6. There has always been a degree of rivalry between Arue, heartland of the old Tahitian royal family, and neighboring Pirae, power base of pro-French politician Gaston Flosse.

From Arue town hall walk back a few minutes in the direction of Papeete to the **James Norman Hall Museum** (tel. 50-01-60; Mon.–Sat. 0900–1600, admission CFP 600) on the inland side of the road. Hall achieved fame during the 1930s as coauthor of the **Bounty Trilogy** with Charles Nordhoff. He moved to Tahiti in 1920 and had this building erected in 1925. After his death in 1951, the house deteriorated to the point where it had to be completely rebuilt in 1991. The museum opened in 2002 and all captions on the exhibits are in English, French, and Tahitian. About 3,000 books from Hall's personal library are on display and there's a comfortable lounge where you can sit and read excerpts from Hall's works.

Cross the highway from the museum and walk another 200 meters west toward Papeete to the École Maternelle Ahutoru at PK 5.4, Arue. Adjacent to this school is the little-known **Cimetière Royal Pomare** with the tombs of Pomare I, II, III, and IV. A map next to the cemetery clearly identifies the many Pomare graves, including that of Pomare V's successor Prince Hinoï. The most elevated tomb here belongs to Princess Elvina Pomare Buillard, who died in 1999. The Reverend Henry Nott (1774–1884), who translated the Bible into Tahitian, is buried directly behind the school (go around behind the building to see the ornate tomb). Nott arrived on the ship *Duff* in 1796 and served with the London Missionary Society for 18 years.

At PK 4.7, Arue, less than 10 minutes west of the Pomare cemetery on foot, is the **tomb of King Pomare V,** down a side road to a point of land on the lagoon. The mausoleum surmounted by a Grecian urn was built in 1879 for Queen Pomare IV, but her remains were subsequently removed to make room for her son, Pomare V, who died of drink in 1891 at the age of 52 (Paul Gauguin witnessed the funeral). A century earlier, on February 13, 1791, his grandfather, Pomare II, then nine, was made first king of Tahiti on the great *marae* that once stood on this spot. Pomare II became the first Christian convert and built a 215-meter-long version of King Solomon's Temple here, but nothing remains of either temple.

There's an excellent view of **Matavai Bay** from the Evangelical Church compound surrounding Pomare V's tomb. In 1767 Captain Samuel Wallis anchored in this bay after having "discovered" Tahiti, and most of the early English explorers (including Fletcher Christian and Captain Bligh) also came ashore here. The 8th Nuclear Free and

Independent Pacific Conference was held in the church compound in 1999. To return to Papeete, simply walk back to the main highway and flag down the first westbound *truck*.

MOUNTAIN CLIMBING

Aorai

Tahiti's finest climb is to the summit of Aorai (2,066 meters), second-ranking peak on the island. (Some writers claim 2,110-meter Piti Hiti is the second-highest peak on Tahiti but it's actually a shoulder of Orohena.) A beaten 10-km track all the way to the top of Aorai makes a guide unnecessary, but food, water, flashlight, and long pants *are* required, plus a sleeping bag and warm sweater if you plan to spend the night up there. At last report the refuges at Fare Mato (1,400 meters) and Fare Ata (1,800 meters) were in good shape with drinking water available and splendid sunset views. Each refuge sleeps about 10 people on the floor at no charge.

The road toward the summit begins beside the **Hôtel de Ville de Pirae,** an outlandish mock-colonial building surrounded by 66 massive Doric columns constructed in 2002 at a cost of CFP 1,120 million. It could be called "Gaston's folly" for ex-mayor Gaston Flosse, who pushed the project through. Just inland from this building, take the first turn on the right and head up the hill to the access road on the left (if in doubt, ask). The trailhead is at Fare Rau Ape (600 meters) near **Le Belvédère** (tel. 42-73-44), a fancy French restaurant seven km up the narrow paved road from Pirae. Taxis want CFP 6,000 for the trip from Papeete and few people live up there, so hitching would be a case of finding tourists headed for the restaurant, and weekends are best for this. You could rent a small car at the kilometer rate but parking near the restaurant is limited.

The restaurant does provide its clients with free *truck* transportation from most Papeete hotels and this is the easiest way to get there. You can reserve the Belvédère *truck* at the Hôtel Tiare Tahiti reception in Papeete. Of course, in order to use it you'll be required to buy a complete meal for CFP 4,950 including salad, dessert, coffee, and wine. The specialty is fondue bourguignon, a meat fon-

due, but you can substitute mahimahi, steak, or shish kebab. The *truck* departs most Papeete hotels at 1130 and 1630, leaving the restaurant for the return trip to Papeete at 1430 and 2000.

To make a day of it, catch the 1130 *truck* up to the restaurant on the understanding that you'll be eating dinner and returning to town on the 2000 *truck* (make sure all of this is clearly understood before you pay—Tina Brichet at Le Belvédère speaks good English). This would give you all afternoon to cover part of the trail, although it's unlikely you'd have time to reach the top (even if you only get as far as Fare Mato, it's still well worth the effort). Take along a sandwich for lunch. You should be able to leave some clean clothes at the restaurant to change into for dinner, and be sure to bring your bathing suit and a towel so you'll be able to take a dip in the swimming pool after the hike. If you can do all of this, the CFP 4,950 pp price becomes reasonable. Also consider the guided hikes mentioned below.

A large signboard outside the restaurant maps out the hike. Just above the restaurant is the French Army's Centre d'Instruction de Montagne, where you can sign a register. From Fare Rau Ape to the summit takes seven hours: 1.5 hours to Hamuta, another two to Fare Mato (good view of Le Diadème, not visible from Papeete), then 2.5 hours to Fare Ata, where most hikers spend the first night in order to cover the last 40 minutes to the summit the following morning. Just above Fare Mato cables have been fixed along the section of trail with the steepest drops on both sides. The hut at Fare Ata is in a low depression 100 meters beyond an open shelter.

The view from Aorai is magnificent, with Papeete and many of the empty interior valleys in full view. To the north is Tetiaroa atoll, while Moorea's jagged outline fills the west. Even on a cloudy day the massive green hulk of neighboring Orohena (2,241 meters) often towers above the clouds like Mt. Olympus. A bonus is the chance to see some of the original native vegetation of Tahiti, which survives better at high altitudes and in isolated gullies. In good weather Aorai is exhausting but superb; in the rain it's a disaster. Very few people do the climb, and if you go in the middle of the week you can expect to have the mountain to yourself.

Thousand Springs Trail

A much easier hike with better parking at the trailhead leads along the side of Aorai's neighbor Orohena. Turn off the coastal highway at the office of the Sheriff de Mahina, behind the Poissonnerie de Mahina (PK 11), and follow the paved road five km straight up through Mahinarama subdivision. At the top of the ridge at about 600 meters elevation the road ends. Park here—the trail is straight ahead. Anyone at Mahinarama will be able to direct you to the "Route des Mille Sources."

A jeep track built into the slope in 1975 follows the contour six km up the Tuauru River valley to the Thousand Springs at 900 meters elevation. The trail to the 2,241-meter summit of Orohena itself begins at the Thousand Springs and climbs steeply to Pito Iti, where hikers spend the night before ascending Orohena the following morning. The Orohena climb involves considerable risks and a guide is required, but almost anyone can do the Thousand Springs hike on his or her own, enjoying the good views of the rounded peaks of Orohena to the left and Aorai's long ridge to the right. Since your car does most of the climbing, this is certainly the easiest way to see the island's unspoiled interior. There's nothing special to see at the Thousand Springs, so turn back whenever you like.

Mt. Marau

The road inland from directly opposite Faa'a Airport goes under the RDO bypass road and up the side of the island to an excellent viewpoint over northwestern Tahiti. It's a rough 10 km drive, which should be attempted only by 4WD in dry weather. You must drive through a horrendous municipal dump on the way. From the TV tower at the end of the track it's only 30 minutes on foot to the summit of Mt. Marau (1,493 meters). From here you'll get another incredible view down into the Plateau of Oranges to the south, up the Fautaua Valley to the north, and along the ridge to Le Diadème and Aorai to the east. Several tour companies offer 4WD trips up here.

Guided Hikes

Numerous hikes around Tahiti are organized by Vincent Dubousquet of **Polynesian Adventure** (tel./fax 43-25-95). He takes visitors on an easy walk up the Fautaua Valley near Papeete at CFP 6,200 pp. A bit more challenging are his climbs of Aorai and Mt. Marau (CFP 8,100 pp). The two-day trek along the Pari Coast is CFP 15,500 pp. These are only Vincent's most popular hikes and he knows many more. Call to find out which ones are scheduled during your stay.

Tahiti Evasion (tel./fax 56-48-77) does day trips to Fautaua Falls or the Orofero Valley at CFP 8,900/6,900/5,200 pp for two/three/four people. A three-day trek along the Pari Coast is CFP 23,500/18,000/15,500 on foot or CFP 32,500/24,000/20,000 by outrigger canoe. To climb Aorai in a day, it charges CFP 7,500 pp (minimum of two) including the shuttle and a picnic lunch. Tahiti Evasion also offers several excellent hikes on Moorea.

Another professional guide, **Angélien Zéna** (tel. 57-22-67), specializes in three-day hikes around the Pari Coast at the east end of Tahiti-iti, "le Circuit Vert." Time is set aside for swimming and fishing. A boat from Vairao to Vaipoiri Grotto is used on the two-day hikes, and day trips can also be arranged. You can arrange to meet Angélien at Fare Nana'o, a pension near Taravao and easily accessible from Papeete by bus.

SPORTS AND RECREATION

Information on the **International Golf Course Olivier Breaud,** on the south coast at Atimaono, can be found later in this chapter.

The Tahiti-based scuba operators cater mostly to local residents, so a knowledge of French will be helpful. Pascal Le Cointre and Arnauld Demier of **Scuba Tek Tahiti** (tel./fax 42-23-55) at the yacht club at PK 4, Arue, organize outings to offshore *faille* (faults) at 0900 and 1400 daily except Sunday afternoon and Monday. It's CFP 5,750 for one dive or CFP 26,950 for five dives. A certification course costs about the same as five dives, plus CFP 3,500 for PADI registration—good value.

On the other side of Papeete, **Tahiti Plongée** (tel. 41-00-62, fax 42-26-06), also known as

"Club Corail-Sub," offers scuba diving several times daily from its base at the former Hôtel Te Puna Bel Air opposite the Tahiti Country Club, PK 7.5, Punaauia. The charge is CFP 5,000 per dive all-inclusive, or CFP 23,500/45,000 for a five/10-dive card. You can ocean dive Tuesday–Sunday at 0800 and on Wednesday and Saturday at 1400; lagoon diving is daily at 1000 and weekdays at 1400 (no diving on Monday). Divemaster Henri Pouliquen was one of the first to teach scuba diving to children. The youngest person Henri has dived with was aged two years, six months—the oldest was a woman of 72 on her first dive. Since 1979 Tahiti Plongée has arranged more than 10,000 dives with children, certainly a unique achievement. Another specialty is diving with people with disabilities. A fish-filled site called The Aquarium near its base is safe for all divers.

Eleuthera Plongée (Nicolas Castel and Joshua Rouger, tel. 42-49-29, fax 43-66-22), at the Marina Taina beside McDonald's at PK 9, Punaauia, charges CFP 5,700/10,500/25,000 for one/two/five dives. Exploration dives are at 0900 and 1400 daily. Their introductory dive is at 1100 daily (CFP 5,500). Eleuthera also offers dive tours to Marlon Brando's atoll, Tetiaroa, for CFP 15,500.

Iti Diving International (Gilles Jugel, tel./fax 57-77-93), at the Marina Puunui on the southeast side of the island, does scuba diving at CFP 5,300 a dive. Among the nearby dive sites are the Tetopa Pass grottoes and the Marado wall.

If you want to set out on your own, **Nauti-Sport** (tel. 50-59-59, fax 42-17-75; weekdays 0800–1145/1345–1700, Sat. 0730–1130) in Fare Ute sells every type of scuba gear and also rents tanks (CFP 2,550).

The **Ski Nautique Club de Tahiti** (tel. 77-22-62; Tues.–Fri. 1200–1800, weekends 0900–1800), on the waterfront at the former Hôtel Te Puna Bel Air opposite the Tahiti Country Club, Punaauia, offers water-skiing at CFP 260/15,000 a minute/hour. Training sessions are arranged.

Surfers often stay at Pension Te Miti or Taaroa Lodge in Paea on Tahiti-nui's west coast, with Moana David in Punaauia, or at Pension Vaiani or Pension Le Bon Jouir at Teahupoo on Tahiti-iti. A few of the surfing spots around Tahiti are mentioned in our circle-island tour.

The **École de Surf Tura'i Mataare** (Olivier Napias, tel./fax 41-91-37), at Kelly Surf Boutique in the Fare Tony Commercial Center behind Big Burger in Papeete, teaches surfing and body surfing to people aged eight and up. Courses with five three-hour lessons (CFP 19,500) or 10 lessons (CFP 26,500) are offered. Boards and transportation are supplied and a certificate is issued.

Papeete's **municipal swimming pool** (tel. 42-89-24) is open to the public Tuesday–Friday 1145-1600, weekends 0730–1700 (CFP 385). Most evenings after 1800 **soccer** is practiced in the sports field opposite the municipal swimming pool.

Practicalities

ACCOMMODATIONS

Most of the places to stay are in the congested Punaauia-to-Mahina strip engulfing Faa'a International Airport and Papeete, and they tend to offer poorer value for money than comparable accommodations on Moorea. The hotel listings that follow are arranged clockwise around Papeete and Faa'a in each category. There are no regular campgrounds on Tahiti. Recently several medium-priced places to stay have sprung up on the Tahiti-iti peninsula and south side of Tahiti, offering the chance to break your trip around the island. (These, and the many selections in Punaauia within easy commuting distance of Papeete, are covered in Around Tahiti later in this chapter.)

US$25–50

Pension Dahl Fifi (Joséphine Dahl, tel. 82-63-30) is directly across the street from the airport terminal (the fourth house on the left up the hill beside Blanchisserie Pressing Mea Ma). It offers three rooms at CFP 3,500/6,000 single/double, plus several four- and five-bed dorms at CFP 2,000 pp. Two additional rooms in a separate house behind the main building are CFP 4,000/6,000. Communal cooking facilities are available, but the location is noisy because of the nearby industrial laundry and airport.

To reach **Tahiti Airport Lodge** (tel. 82-23-68, fax 82-25-00) from Pension Dahl Fifi, continue up to the end of the street, turn right and climb up the lane to the very end, where you'll find a gate with wide green and white stripes. The six rooms here are CFP 4,500/6,000 single/double with shared bath, CFP 8,000 double with private bath, breakfast included. There's a lovely small swimming pool overlooking the airport. Someone will pick you up from the airport for free if you call (no pickups after 2200).

The **Heitiare Inn** (Raymond Tarahu, tel. 83-33-52, fax 82-77-53) at PK 4.3, Faa'a, near the Mairie de Faa'a a km east of the airport, has six air-conditioned rooms at CFP 5,000 single or double with shared bath and CFP 6,500 with private bath. Communal cooking facilities are provided. The location isn't great.

Family-style **Chez Myrna** (Myrna Dammeyer, tel. 42-64-11), 106 Chemin vicinal de Tipaerui, is .5 km up the road from the Hôtel Matavai, almost opposite Limonaderie Singapour. She offers two shared-bath rooms at CFP 4,200/5,700 single/double with breakfast (minimum stay two nights). Dinner is CFP 1,500 (if desired). Myrna's husband, Walter, is a German expat who has been on Tahiti for decades. There's no sign outside, so call ahead.

During the holiday period in July and August, women can stay at the six-story **Foyer de Jeunes Filles de Paofai** (tel. 46-06-80, fax 46-06-81) near the Protestant church on boulevard Pomare. This Evangelical Church–operated female student's residence provides 116 beds in rooms of two, three, four, or six beds at CFP 2,000 pp a day, CFP 30,000 a month, breakfast included. There's a daily 2200 curfew, except Wednesday, Friday, and Saturday, when it's midnight.

The **Hôtel Mahina Tea** (tel. 42-00-97), up rue Sainte-Amélie from avenue Bruat, is about the only regular economy-priced hotel in the city. The 16 rooms are CFP 5,000 single or double, reduced to CFP 4,200 if you stay three or more nights. A room with twin beds instead of a double bed is CFP 1,000 more. Six small studios with cooking facilities cost CFP 100,000 a month double. All rooms have private bath with hot water. No cooking facilities are provided in the daily rental rooms but you may use the shared fridge downstairs. This family-operated place has been around for many years and it's excellent value for Papeete. Dogs and roosters add to the sounds of the night.

Many backpackers head straight for **Hostel Teamo** (tel. 42-47-26, fax 43-56-95), 8 rue du Pont Neuf, Quartier Mission, a century-old house hidden behind a new four-story building near the Archbishop's Palace, just a short walk east of downtown. If the door is locked when you arrive, look for the owner at No. 3 across the street. To get

FRENCH POLYNESIA

there from the market head inland on rue François Cardella, which soon becomes rue Charles Vienot. It's a little hard to find the first time, but convenient once you know it. Dormitory-style accommodations are CFP 2,000 pp in four- to six-bed dorms. The five rooms with shared bath are CFP 4,500 double, while the two with private bath are CFP 5,000. Bring your own towel or rent one for CFP 500. The shared cooking facilities can be used only 0600–0900/1800–2100. A good grocery store is nearby and there's a nice veranda with French TV. Checkout time is 1000, at which point you must vacate the premises. The receptionist will hold your luggage at CFP 200 a day. It's all rather basic but Teamo remains the choice of those in search of the cheapest possible option.

US$50–100

The pleasant **Hôtel Tahiti Country Club** (tel. 42-60-40, fax 41-09-28) is up on the hillside at PK 7.2, Punaauia, just under two km southwest of the airport. The 40 air-conditioned rooms with TV in a neat two-story building are CFP 9,000 single or double, CFP 9,170 triple, plus 11 percent tax (children under 12 free). Ask and you may receive a discount on the room rates. The dining room and swimming pool have a view of Moorea. The hike up to this hotel from the main road is quite a workout but it's a good choice if you were planning to rent a car. (The Country Club's owners, Nouvelles Frontières, planned to close the property for renovations at some point and relaunch it as part of the Paladien chain, so verify the current status before going out of your way.)

The **Hôtel Victoria** (Bruno Gatto, tel. 43-13-93, fax 43-27-28), 10 rue du Commandant Destremeau, Papeete, has seven air-conditioned rooms with bath facing the noisy road at CFP 7,000 single or double. A dorm bed here is CFP 2,500. It's overpriced but uncrowded.

The timeworn **Hôtel Royal Papeete** (tel. 42-01-29, fax 43-79-09), 291 boulevard Pomare opposite the Quai de Moorea, has 78 large air-conditioned rooms beginning at CFP 9,000 single or double, CFP 10,500 triple, including tax. This hotel looks seedy from the outside but many tourists do stay there and it's very convenient if you happen to miss the last ferry. At last report

both nightclubs in the Royal Papeete were closed and the hotel itself looked as if it might not survive much longer.

US$100–150

The 138-room **Hôtel Matavai** (tel. 42-67-67, fax 42-36-90) is CFP 14,500/19,000/23,500 single/double/triple plus 11 percent tax with bath, TV, and two double beds. You can almost tell this four-floor edifice was once a Holiday Inn, but it has gone downhill since then. Tennis and squash courts, minigolf, a swimming pool, and other sporting facilities are on the premises. This is the only hotel that Papeete's politically connected taxi drivers allow to provide free airport transfers. We've received some negative feedback about the Matavai.

Opened in 1997, the six-story **Hôtel Tiare Tahiti** (tel. 43-68-48, fax 43-68-47), at 417 boulevard Pomare on the waterfront next to the post office, has 38 air-conditioned rooms with satellite TV beginning at CFP 13,000/15,500 double/triple, plus 11 percent tax. The rooms on the side of the hotel facing the post office are the quieter. The Tiare Tahiti should be your choice if you want quality accommodations without having to stay at the Sheraton.

The six-story **Hôtel Prince Hinoï** (tel. 42-32-77, fax 42-33-66), avenue du Prince Hinoï at boulevard Pomare, has 72 small air-conditioned rooms at CFP 12,800/13,600/14,500 single/double/triple, plus 11 percent tax. The rooms are okay but it's in a seedy area with prostitutes working the adjacent streets and heavy drinking going on in the bar downstairs.

The **Hôtel Kon Tiki Pacific** (tel. 54-16-16, fax 42-11-66), 271 boulevard Pomare opposite the Quai de Moorea, has 36 spacious air-conditioned rooms beginning at CFP 11,250/13,620 single/double including tax (CFP 1,110 extra for two beds, each additional person CFP 2,150). Don't accept one of the noisy rooms near the elevator, which are always offered first, and avoid rooms on the lower floors, which are subjected to disco noise. Instead, get one with a balcony on the upper front side of the building. You'll have an excellent view straight into the adjacent French naval base.

Hôtel Le Mandarin (tel. 50-33-50, fax 42-16-32), 51 rue Colette, is a modern six-story hotel whose 37 air-conditioned rooms are over-priced at CFP 12,500/14,500 single/double, plus 11 percent tax (children under 12 free). The levels of service and cleanliness at the Mandarin vary and the location in the heart of the market area isn't the best.

The Hôtel Le Royal Tahitien (tel. 50-40-40, fax 50-40-41), off avenue du Prince Hinoï at PK 3.5, Pirae, is a peaceful two-story building facing beautifully kept grounds on a litter-strewn black-sand beach. You're unlikely to see anyone swimming here as the water is murky with no coral, but the windsurfing is good. The 40 air-conditioned rooms are CFP 17,000 single or double, CFP 20,000 triple, plus 11 percent tax. Breakfast and dinner are served on the attractive terrace overlooking the lagoon (in general, the food prices here are exorbitant). It's a long, boring walk into town (and no public transport back after 1700)—you'll get better value on Moorea for this kind of money.

US$150–250

The French-owned Sofitel Maeva Beach (tel. 86-66-00, fax 43-84-70) at PK 7.5, Punaauia, was built by UTA French Airlines in the late 1960s. The 224 air-conditioned rooms in this pyramidal high-rise cost CFP 23,000 single or double garden view, CFP 27,700 lagoon view, CFP 30,400 panoramic view, plus 11 percent tax (children under 12 free). The seven-story Maeva Beach faces a man-made white beach, but with pollution on the increase in the adjacent Punaauia Lagoon, most swimmers stick to the hotel pool. Tennis courts are available. The entire complex could use a facelift.

US$250 and up

The Tahiti Beachcomber Inter-Continental (tel. 86-51-10, fax 86-51-30), west of the airport at PK 7, Faa'a, is a former Travelodge built in 1974. It's a smart international hotel with a Polynesian flair, and is the largest resort in French Polynesia. The 232 air-conditioned rooms in the main buildings begin at CFP 30,300 single or double plus 11 percent tax; for one of the 32 overwater bungalows

it's about double. Children under 15 sharing the room with their parents stay for free. A breakfast and dinner meal plan is CFP 7,600 pp extra. Tahitian dancing and crafts demonstrations are regular features. The beach is artificial but the swim-up bar is fun. The hotel pools are reserved for guests. Paid activities include water-skiing, snorkeling trips, and scuba diving with the Aquatica Dive Center (tel. 53-34-96, fax 53-34-74). The Automatic Currency Exchange machine in the lobby of this hotel changes the banknotes of nine countries for a CFP 500 commission.

The Hôtel Sheraton Tahiti (tel. 86-48-48, fax 86-48-40), at PK 2.6 between Papeete and the airport, reopened in 1999 after being completely redeveloped by Louis Wane, brother of pearl baron Robert Wan. This site was once the residence of Princess Pomare, daughter of the last king of Tahiti, and from 1961 to 1996 a historic colonial-style hotel stood there. Outrigger Hotels of Hawaii managed the property initially but withdrew after disagreements with Wane. The 200 air-conditioned rooms are in a series of four-story American-style buildings. Rates begin at CFP 33,000 plus 11 percent tax and increase to CFP 86,500 for the best suite. There's a large beachside freshwater swimming pool with a whirlpool tub on the knoll just above the waterfall, a spa, a 500-seat banquet hall, and an overwater restaurant with splendid sunset views of Moorea. Berhard Begliomini's TOPdive center offers scuba diving from the resort. The frequent Outumaoro *trucks* pass the Sheraton, Inter-Continental, and Maeva Beach until late at night. Europcar has desks at all three resorts.

FOOD

Food Trailers

In the evening take a stroll along the Papeete waterfront past the dozens of gaily lit vans known as *les roulottes*, which form a colorful night market at Tahua Vaiete by the Quai d'honneur. Here you'll find everything from couscous, pizza, waffles, crêpes, and *brouchettes* (shish kebab) to steak with real *pommes frites*. There's no better place to sample *poisson cru*. As the city lights wink gently across the harbor, sailors promenade with their *vahine*, adding

FRENCH POLYNESIA

PAPEETE RESTAURANTS AND BARS

QUAI DE MOOREA

BOULEVARD

POMARE V

AVENUE

LE MANHATTAN DISCOTHEQUE
PARADISE NIGHT CLUB
BAR LE CHAPLIN

RESTAURANT LE GALLIENI

CLAPPIER

RESTAURANT LA SAIGONNAISE

RUE

BAR LE TAINA KAINA

SNACK JULIENNE

HINOI

0   100 yds
0   100 m

POMARE

Papeete

Harbor

LES 3 BRASSEURS

PRINCE

DU

AVENUE

LE GRENIER DE MONTMARTE

CAFÉ DE L'AMOUR

SNACK JIMMY

BAR ROYAL KIKIRIRI

RUE

DES

ÉCOLES

RUE

DES

D'HONNEUR

MANA ROCK CAFÉ

PIANO BAR

TAHUA VAIETE

RUE GILBERT

LE DRAGON D'OR

HONG KONG PEARLS

RESTAURANT WAIKIKI

RUE ALBERT LEBOUCHER

RUE COLETTE

REMPARTS

LES ROULOTTES

CAFÉ DES NÉGOCIANTS

QUAI

RUE

PAUL

POLY-SELF RESTAURANT

LA MARQUISIENNE

CHEZ MÉMÉNE

GAUGUIN

LE GRILLARDIN

PONT DE L'EST

LA PETITE AUBERGE

FOCH

TIKI SOFT CAFÉ

RUE

FRANÇOIS

RESTAURANT L'EXCUSE

BRASSERIE DES REMPARTS

CARDELLA

RUE

CHARLES

★ PAPEETE MARKET

RUE DU 22 SEPTEMBRE

MARECHAL

DU

VIENOT

BOULANGERIE L'EPI D'OR

RUE

EDOUARD

NANSOUTY

RUE JEANNE D'ARC

MARKET COFFEE

DES

YACHTS

LE RETRO
EL LATINO

VAIMA CENTER

LE RUBIS WINE BAR

MORRISON'S CAFÉ

RUE

QUAI

POMARE

BOULEVARD

SNACK HOLLYWOOD

LE ROLLS CLUB

DE GAULLE

RUE

AHNNE

RUE DUMONT D'URVILLE

LE MOTU TAHITI

BIG BURGER

CAFÉ DE LA GARE

AUX DELICES CHEZ LOUISETTE

LA PALMERIE

PASSAGE CARDELLA

JAVOUHEY

MONSEIGNEUR

REINE POMARE

GÉNÉRAL

L'O À LA BOUCHE

GEORGES

ANNE-MARIE

JAUSSEN

Parc Bougainville

DU

RUE

PIZZERIA LOU PESCADOU

RUE

LAGARDE

RUE DUMONT D'URVILLE

RUE

RUE DU DOCTEUR CASSIAU

PLACE TARAHOI

a touch of romance and glamour. The food and atmosphere are excellent, and even if you're not dining, it's a scene not to miss. On Friday and Saturday nights a live band will be playing in the bandshell. The most crowded *roulottes* generally have the best food, but you may have to wait as lots of people bring large bowls to be filled and taken home. The biggest drawback is that beer is not available. It all happens nightly 1800–0100.

At **Tahua To'ata,** a 15-minute walk west along the waterfront, a similar atmosphere prevails. Here a row of outdoor terrace restaurants, including the Soledane Grill, Chez Jimmy, Snack Moeata, Snack Mado, and La Terrase, are always crowded with local residents. Pick the one that is most crowded. They're open daily.

Self-Service

Poly-Self Restaurant (tel. 43-75-32; weekdays 0530–1430), 8 rue Gauguin behind the Banque de Polynésie, dispenses unpretentious, filling Chinese-style plate lunches at about CFP 890. Additional seating is available upstairs.

Cafétéria La Palmerie (tel. 45-00-36; weekdays 1100–1400), upstairs off passage Cardella near the Vaima Center, offers a different main plate every day at CFP 950, or CFP 1,250 including an appetizer and dessert.

The **Foyer de Jeunes Filles de Paofai** (tel. 46-06-80), opposite the Protestant church on boulevard Pomare, has a good modern self-service cafeteria open weekdays for lunch 1130–1300. Alcohol is not available here.

Inexpensive grilled meat and fish dishes are the specialty at **Snack Paofai** (tel. 42-95-76; weekdays 0500–1430, Sat. 0500–1330) near Clinique Paofai. A complete meal chosen from among the specials listed on the blackboard and consumed on the airy terrace will run CFP 850, but arrive before 1300 or you'll find little left. On Thursday it prepares a special couscous dish—CFP 950 including a Coke.

Restaurant Oriane (tel. 42-03-06; weekdays 0630–1500), 75 avenue Georges Clemenceau halfway between Rond Point and Hospital Mamao, serves hearty meals to Tahitian workers. You can get a meat and rice lunch for only CFP 500 a plate.

Snack Bars

To sample the cuisine of the people, check out the Chinese/Tahitian eateries on rue Cardella right beside the market. Try *ma'a tinito,* a mélange of red beans, pork, macaroni, and vegetables on rice (CFP 850). A large Hinano beer at these places is around CFP 500.

Upstairs in the market under a thatched awning, **La Cafeteria de Marché** (Mon.–Sat. 0400–1500) serves a typical Tahitian breakfast of a large coffee with bread and butter for CFP 225. Have your lunch elsewhere.

Snack Julienne (tel. 42-86-49; daily 0500–1700), rues Clappier and Leboucher, is an unpretentious local place with some of the best prices in town. Its morning café au lait with bread and butter is CFP 280, while the cooked lunch plates go for CFP 650–1,050. The large baguette sandwiches *(casse-croûtes)* can't be beat at CFP 130–180.

Some of the freshest baguette sandwiches in town are sold over the counter at **Boulangerie L'Epi d'Or** (tel. 43-07-13), 26 rue du Maréchal Foch near the market.

For fruit juices, sandwiches, crêpes, waffles, and ice cream cones, search no further than **Le Motu Tahiti** (tel. 41-33-59; closed Sun.), corner of rue du Général de Gaulle and rue Georges Lagarde behind the Vaima Center. The stand up tables on the corner are very Parisian. **Vitamine Glacier Saladerie** (tel. 43-37-70; closed Sun.), just upstairs from Le Motu, has a happy combination of salads, draft beer, and tasty ice cream.

Asian

All of the best Chinese restaurants are along rue Colette east from the market. **Restaurant Snack Chez Mémène** (tel. 43-09-26; Mon.–Sat. 0530–1530), 25 rue Colette, is a nice open air locale with *poisson cru* (CFP 900), *sashimi* (CFP 1,200), shrimp (CFP 1,600), chicken (CFP 900), beef (CFP 1,260), and chow mein (CFP 900). Wash it down with draft beer.

Restaurant Hong Kong Pearls (weekdays 0800–1500/1700–2200, Sat. 0800–1500, Sun. 1700–2200), 45 rue Colette, serves ordinary Chinese market food. The menu posted in the window outside lists chow mein (CFP 750), seafood (CFP 1,000–1,600), chicken (CFP 850), and steak frites or duck (CFP 900).

Le Dragon d'Or (tel. 42-96-12; Tues.–Sun. 1130–1330/1830–2130), 49 rue Colette next to Hôtel Le Mandarin, serves more upscale Chinese food at CFP 1,500–2,000 a plate. The classic Tahitian-Chinese menu includes dishes such as pork with taro or steamed fish and you'll like the large portions and friendly, reliable service.

Snack Jimmy (tel. 43-63-32; Mon.–Sat. 1130–1400/1830–2100, Sun. 1830–2100), rue Colette at rue des Écoles near Hôtel Le Mandarin, features a clean, simple dining room with specialties such as Thai curries (CFP 1,200–2,200), Vietnamese rice (CFP 950–1,100), Chinese plates (CFP 900–1,350), Chinese seafood (CFP 1,800), and filet mignon (CFP 1,800). Lobster is available at the market price.

Restaurant Waikiki (tel. 42-95-27; daily 1100–1300/1800–2100, closed Sun. lunch and Mon. dinner), rue Leboucher 20, is old and tired, but cheaper than the rest: chop suey and chow mein CFP 750, fried fish CFP 1,100. The staff don't speak English but the menu is in three languages. You'll probably have to ask for a spoon.

Restaurant La Saigonnaise (tel. 42-05-35; closed Sun.), 67 avenue du Prince Hinoï, has moderately expensive but fresh Vietnamese food served in a quiet setting. The Saigonese soup (CFP 1,150) makes a good lunch.

Finally, Papeete has its own **Sushi Bar** (tel. 45-35-25; Mon.–Wed. 1115–1400, Thurs.–Sat. 1115–1400/1815–2200) near the Qantas office in the Vaima Center. You choose from the typical Japanese specialties floating in wooden bowls in a trough along the bar, and you're charged per dish depending on the color of the bowl (CFP 260–650 each). What better place to have *sashimi?*

Italian

For a taste of the Mediterranean, **Pizzeria Lou Pescadou** (tel. 43-74-26; Mon.–Sat. 1100–1430/1830–2300), on rue Anne-Marie Javouhey a long block back from the Vaima Center, is friendly, unpretentious, breezy, inexpensive, and fun. The pizza *pescatore* (CFP 750) makes a good lunch, and a big pitcher of ice water is included in the price. Owner Mario Vitulli may be from

Marseilles, but you won't complain about his spaghetti—a huge meal for about CFP 800. And where else will you get unpitted olives on a pizza? Nonalcoholic drinks are on the house while you stand and wait for a table. The service is lively, and Lou Pescadou is very popular among local French, a high recommendation.

L'api'zzeria (tel. 42-98-30; Mon.–Sat. 1130–2200), 44 rue de Commandant Destremeau near the Protestant church, also prepares real pizza in a brick oven. This garden restaurant is a bit more expensive than Lou Pescadou (spaghetti CFP 780–1,300, pizzas CFP 770–1,400, fish CFP 1,390–2,380) but still good value. Draft beer is available.

French

For the aspiring gourmet, Papeete has much to offer. For example, **Café des Négociants** (tel. 48-08-48; Tues.–Sat. 1200–1430/1900–2200), 10 rue Gilbert next to Pai Moana Pearls, is a Parisian bistro offering a huge selection of beers and French and Tahitian dishes. Lunch mains cost CFP 800–2,000, dinner CFP 1,000–3,700.

Le Grillardin (tel. 43-09-90; Mon. 1130–1430, Tues.–Fri. 1130–1430/1900–2200, Sat. 1900–2200), rue Paul Gauguin opposite the Air Tahiti Nui office, offers fine French cuisine in a traditional country inn. Fish dishes are CFP 1,800–2,500, meat CFP 1,550–2,300.

La Petite Auberge (tel. 42-86-13; weekdays 1200–1330/1900–2130, Sat. 1900–2130), Pont de l'Est, is a fancy French country inn with linen tablecloths. The menu lists appetizers (CFP 1,150–1,350), seafoods (CFP 1,950–2,550), grilled meats (CFP 1,500–1,750), and house specialties (CFP 2,150–3,350). Snails *(escargot)* as an appetizer is CFP 850 for a half a bowl.

Restaurant L'excuse (tel. 53-13-25; Tues.–Fri. 1200–1400/1900–2130, Sat. 1900–2130), 47 rue du Maréechal Foch, is a quality air-conditioned restaurant with meat dishes at CFP 1,950–2,800, fish at CFP 1,700–2,200.

Le Rubis Wine Bar (tel. 43-25-55; Mon. 1130–1500, Tues.–Sat. 1130–1500/1800–2100, Sunday 1800–2100), rue Jeanne d'Arc below the Vaima Center, is a good upscale French restaurant with seafoods, salads, and meats (CFP

1,500–2,900). The chef Acajou has been running celebrated Papeete restaurants for a quarter century. Le Rubis claims to offer 130 different wines by the glass.

Restaurant L'O à la bouche (tel. 45-29-76; weekdays 1130–1300/1915-2200, Sat. 1915-2230), up passage Cardella opposite Air New Zealand, is an elegant French restaurant with funky blue decor. The nouvelle cuisine includes mouth-watering mains at CFP 1,450–2,900, seafood at CFP 2,550–2,850, and meat at CFP 2,450–2,900. It's popular with trendy young French locals.

More fine French cuisine is available at **Restaurant Moana Iti** (tel. 42-65-24; closed Sun.), 483 boulevard Pomare next to Club 106 just west of avenue Bruat. The menu lists grilled meat (CFP 1,500–2,000), shellfish (CFP 1,660–1,950), and house specialties (CFP 1,950–3,520).

Pub Food

Recommended is **Les 3 Brasseurs** (tel. 50-60-25; daily 0800–0100), boulevard Pomare near avenue Prince Hinoï, with a fashionable sidewalk terrace overlooking the Moorea ferries. This northeastern French style microbrewery specializes in *flammekueche* (like a pizza made with unleavened bread and no tomato sauce). The "classique" with onions and ham is CFP 850 (or CFP 1,000 with a small beer). Otherwise a half chicken with beer is CFP 1,500, with *poisson cru* CFP 1,500. Sandwiches are also available. It's all spelled out in a menu resembling a French newspaper.

Brasserie des Remparts (tel. 42-80-00; weekdays 0630–2200, Sat. 1000–1500), rue des Remparts between La Petit Auberge and Tiki Soft Cafe, is a Belgian-style pub with draft beer at CFP 500/950 a half/full liter. The meals are CFP 1,450–1,900.

Big Burger Snack Bar (tel. 43-01-98; Mon.–Sat. 0600–2300), rue du Général de Gaulle and rue Georges Lagarde, is a world better than the McDonald's across the street. The plat du jour here is CFP 1,700, and if it's sold out you can get hamburgers (CFP 600–850), spaghetti (CFP 1,100), grilled meats (CFP 1,100–2,200). It's a good place for an afternoon beer and there's often a live Tahitian group playing.

Café de la Gare (tel. 42-75-95; weekdays 0700–midnight, Sat. 1000–midnight), on rue du Général de Gaulle opposite McDonald's, is a typical French pub with draft beer. The only meal served here is lunch (CFP 1,200–1,750).

Other Restaurants

Carnivores may want to know about **Restaurant Le Gallieni** (tel. 42-05-23), on boulevard Pomare below the Hôtel Royal Papeete. Thursday–Saturday 1145–1400/1900–2130 it serves the house specialty, prime rib, at CFP 2,090–3,770. Add CFP 240 for the sauce and CFP 240 per vegetable side dish.

Jack Lobster (tel. 42-50-58; weekdays 1130–1400/1900–2130, Sat. 1900–2230), just upstairs from the newsstand in the corner of the Vaima Center closest to the port, is an upscale steakhouse with hearty grilled meats (CFP 1,700–2,500), surf and turf combos (CFP 2,500–5,000), seafood (CFP 1,700–2,500), lobster (CFP 4,100), and Tex-Mex (CFP 1,300–2,150).

Market Coffee (tel. 45-60-70; Mon.–Thurs. 0530–1600, Fri. and Sat. 0530–0100, Sun. 0700–1100), rue Edouard Ahnne behind Air Tahiti, is a lively unpretentious place with dancing on Saturday night. A full breakfast here will cost CFP 1,000. Meat and fish mains are CFP 1,200–2,400, grilled swordfish *(meka)* CFP 1,300. Also check the salads.

The Papeete equivalent of a Hard Rock Cafe is **Morrison's Café** (tel. 42-78-61; weekdays 1100–1430/1800–0100, Sat. 1800–0100), upstairs in the Vaima Center. Use the elevator on the side of the building just outside Air New Zealand. Morrison's offers a full menu (salads CFP 1,450–2,100, grilled dishes CFP 1,550–2,350) or a plat du jour (CFP 1,450) on an breezy rooftop terrace with a view of Tahiti. Some readers have reported that the lunch is of variable quality. There's an extensive wine list and live music is sometimes performed Tuesday–Saturday from 2230.

Cafés

Le Retro (tel. 42-86-83) on the boulevard Pomare side of the Vaima Center is *the* place to sit and sip a drink while watching the passing parade. The fruit-flavored ice cream is intense and for

FRENCH POLYNESIA

yachties a banana split after a long sailing trip can be heavenly. The atmosphere here is thoroughly Côte d'Azur. A sign encourages tipping.

Cheaper meals and drinks are available at **Snack Hollywood** (tel. 54-59-51; daily 0700–2030), around the corner from Le Retro on pedestrians-only rue Georges Lagarde. The menu includes large salads (CFP 800), *poisson cru* (CFP 1,000), omelettes (CFP 250), grilled cheese (CFP 350), chicken and chips (CFP 750), and steak frites (CFP 1,000). Coffee, tea, and chocolate are CFP 200. It's a good bet on Sunday when many other places are closed.

Aux Delices Chez Louisette (tel. 45-46-46; weekdays 0600–1700, Sat. 0600–1130), on passage Cardella, the narrow street running inland almost opposite Air New Zealand, is good for ice cream, pastries, quiche, and coffee. It's clean and chic with most items displayed in the window and nothing over CFP 1,000.

When the heat gets to you, **Pâtisserie La Marquisienne** (tel. 42-83-52; closed Mon.), 29 rue Colette, offers coffee and pastries in air-conditioned comfort. It's popular among French expats.

Restaurant Le Manava (tel. 42-02-91; weekdays 0500–2000, Sat. 0500–1100), avenue Bruat at Commandant Destremeau, has a nice open air sidewalk terrace, perfect for a coffee or beer.

Groceries

Downtown there's **Champion** (tel. 54-29-29; Mon.–Sat. 0700–1930, Sun. 0630–1200), a large supermarket on rue du Commandant Destremeau. Get whole barbecued chickens and chow mein in the deli section.

At PK 8.3, Punaauia, just south of the junction of the auto route to Papeete, is **Carrefour,** Tahiti's first enclosed shopping mall, which opened in 1986. Some of the cheapest groceries on the island are available at the large adjoining Continent supermarket (tel. 46-08-08; Mon.–Sat. 0800–2000, Sun. 0800–1200). The deli section has a good selection of takeout items including barbecued chicken, and there's also a fancy snack bar on the mall. The supermarket doesn't sell only groceries but also clothing and mass-produced souvenirs at the best prices on the island. Carrefour is easily accessible from Papeete on the frequent Outumaoro *truck,* which finishes its route across the highway.

Other big supermarkets around the island include **Supermarche Venustar** (tel. 48-10-13; Mon.–Sat. 0630–1930, Sun. 0600–1130) at the turnoff to Point Venus on the circle island highway (PK 10), and **Champion** (tel. 57-16-76; Mon.–Sat. 0600–1900, Sun. 0600–1200) in Taravao. All of these are good places to pick up picnic supplies.

ENTERTAINMENT AND EVENTS

Five Papeete cinemas show B-grade films dubbed into French (admission CFP 850). The Concorde is in the Vaima Center; Hollywood I and II are on rue Georges Lagarde beside the Vaima Center; Liberty Cinema is on rue du Maréchal Foch near the market; and the Mamao Palace is near Mamao Hospital.

Nightlife

After dark local carousers and French sailors take over the little bars crowding the streets around rue des Écoles and east on boulevard Pomare. Yet for the glitzy capital of a leading French resort, the nightlife is surprisingly downmarket.

The places with live music or a show generally impose a CFP 1,000–1,500 cover charge on men, which includes one drink. Nothing much gets going before 2200, and by 0100 everything is very informal (many bars stay open until 0400). Male visitors should ensure they've got their steps right before inviting any local ladies onto the floor—or face immediate rejection.

French soldiers and sailors out of uniform patronize the bars along boulevard Pomare opposite the Quai de Moorea, including **Bar Le Chaplin** (tel. 42-73-05), next door to Paradise Night Club, and **Bar Le Taina Kaina** (tel. 42-64-40), 301 boulevard Pomare at rue Clappier.

Paradise Night Club (tel. 42-73-05; nightly 1900–0100, weekends until 0200), next to Hôtel Kon Tiki opposite the Moorea ferries, has West African and reggae music. Wednesday–Saturday after 2200 admission is CFP 2,000 pp including one drink and a dress code applies. Sunday–Tuesday nights it's karaoke. The restaurant serves meals in the CFP 1,400–2,400 range Friday and Saturday 1900–midnight.

Le Manhattan Discotheque (tel. 42-63-65; Wed.–Sat. 2200–0400, CFP 1,500 cover charge), 271 boulevard Pomare below Hôtel Kon Tiki, is similar to Paradise Night Club.

Le Grenier de Montmarte (tel. 45-47-77; Tues.–Sat. 2200–0300), 7 avenue Prince Hinoï, is a small Parisian-style nightclub with live music and no cover charge.

Mana Rock Café (tel. 48-36-36), boulevard Pomare at rue des Écoles in front of Hôtel Prince Hinoï, is a popular meeting place. There's karaoke from 2200 in the disco upstairs, dancing from 2300–0400 nightly (CFP 1,500–2,000 admission for males Friday and Saturday nights). A small beer costs CFP 1,000.

The **Piano Bar** (tel. 42-88-24), beside Hôtel Prince Hinoï on rue des Écoles, is the most notorious of Papeete's *mahu* (transvestite) discos. It's open daily 1500–0300 with a special show at 0130. Many of the people dressed in sexy miniskirts along rue des Écoles are not exactly what they appear to be! Notice the folks beckoning from upstairs windows.

Café de l'amour (tel. 42-51-33), across rue des Écoles from the Piano Bar, has beer on tap and usually no cover. A lively crowd patronizes this colorful establishment, where a seasoned Tahitian band plays on weekends. Just don't believe the low drink prices advertised outside.

Bar Royal Kikiriri (tel. 43-58-64; Wed.–Sun. 2200–0300), rue Colette at rue des Écoles, is another Tahitian disco. Entry costs CFP 1,000 Friday and Saturday including one drink.

Le Rolls Club (tel. 43-41-42; Wed.–Sun. 2100–0400, Fri. 1400–0400, admission CFP 1,000), in the Vaima Center upstairs opposite Big Burger, was once a flashy youth disco but now it plays mostly Tahitian dance music for a local crowd.

El Latino (tel. 42-40-01; weekdays 0900–0100, Sat. 1700–0300), rue Georges Lagarde behind El Retro, is an upscale pub with Mexican decor. There's disco dancing here after 2300 (no cover charge).

Club 106 (tel. 42-72-92; Thurs.–Sat. 2200–0400), 483 boulevard Pomare just west of avenue Bruat, caters to a slightly older crowd than

the other places. It has a different DJ every night and admission for men is CFP 2,000, which includes a drink.

Cultural Shows for Visitors

A Tahitian dance show takes place in the Bougainville Restaurant, downstairs at the **Sofitel Maeva Beach** (tel. 86-66-00), Friday and Saturday at 2000. If you're not interested in having dinner, a drink at the Bar Moorea by the pool will put you in position to see the action (no cover charge). Sunday this hotel presents a full Tahitian feast at 1200, complete with earth oven *(ahimaa)* and dancing at 1300.

The **Tahiti Beachcomber Inter-Continental** (tel. 86-51-10) stages one of the top Tahitian dance shows on the island; attend for the price of a drink at the bar near the pool (no cover charge). The Grand Ballet de Tahiti (Lorenzo) often performs here. The dancers' starting time is officially Wednesday, Friday, and Sunday at 2000, so arrive early and be prepared to wait. The seafood dinner show on Friday is CFP 6,950.

The **Hôtel Sheraton Tahiti** (tel. 86-48-48) has a Tahitian show in the restaurant Friday at 2030 and Sunday at 1300. **Hôtel Méridien Tahiti** (tel. 47-07-07) in Punaauia presents Tahitian dancing on Friday nights.

There's often Tahitian dancing in the **Captain Bligh Restaurant** (tel. 43-62-90) at the Punaauia Lagoonarium (PK 11.4) on Friday and Saturday nights at 2100. The buffet here is CFP 4,850 but you can also simply order a few drinks.

Be sure to check these times and days before going out of your way as things change. If you want dinner, do reserve.

SHOPPING

Normal shopping hours in Papeete are weekdays 0730–1130/1330–1730, Saturday 0730–1200. Papeete's largest shopping complex is the **Vaima Center,** where numerous shops sell black pearls, designer clothes, souvenirs, and books. It's certainly worth a look; then branch out into the surrounding streets. **Galerie Winkler** (tel. 42-81-77), 17 rue Jeanne d'Arc beside American Express, sells contemporary paintings of Polynesia.

Don't overlook the local fashions. Several shops along rue Paul Gauguin sell very chic island clothing.

If you're a surfer, check **Kelly Surf** (tel. 45-29-30), rue du 22 Septembre near the market, for boards, plus all attendant gear. **Magasin 360°** (tel. 42-98-86), 41 rue Colette, also sells trendy surfing gear.

Nauti-Sport (tel. 50-59-59) in Fare Ute carries a good selection of quality snorkeling/dive masks at reasonable prices.

The **Centre Philatelique** (tel. 41-43-35) at the main post office sells the stamps and first-day covers of all the French Pacific territories. Some are quite beautiful and inexpensive.

Photo Lux (tel. 42-84-31), 30 rue du Maréchal Foch near the market, has some of the cheapest color print film you'll find, and it repairs Minolta cameras.

Souvenirs

The best handicraft shopping is upstairs in Papeete Market. The pareus are outstanding. Surprisingly, handicrafts are often cheaper in Papeete than on their island of origin.

For Marquesan woodcarvings have a look in **Manuia Curios** (tel. 42-04-94), 7 run Jaussen on the east side of the cathedral. **Tamara Curios** (tel. 42-54-42), rue du Général de Gaulle opposite McDonald's, is another large craft shop with mass-produced objects.

Serious collectors should visit **Galerie Ganesha** (tel. 43-04-18), just down from Hawaiian Airlines in the Vaima Center. The top-quality handicrafts here include Fatu Hiva tapa, tikis, bowls, Marquesas nose flutes, and carved mother of pearl. There are also objects from other areas, such as Fiji. Prices are high but fair.

Music

The **Music Shop** (tel. 42-85-63), 13 rue du Général de Gaulle behind the Vaima Center, has a large selection of compact discs of Tahitian music. You can use headphones to listen to the music.

If you're serious about building a Polynesian music collection, visit **Manuiti Productions** (tel. 42-82-39; weekdays 0900–1100/1200–1600), above Pharmacie Fare Rau on rue du

Général de Gaulle (entry from the alley beside McDonald's, rear stairwell and up to the second floor). It has the best selection of Tahitian music CDs and cassettes anywhere, including more than 50 CDs and 100 cassettes from its own studio, founded by Yves Roche in 1962. It also sells sheet music and has manuals that teach Tahitian singing.

Pearls

Pai Moana Pearls (tel. 43-31-10), 8 rue Gilbert (down the alley between the Banque Socredo and La Maison de la Press from Tahua Vaiete), can give you a free copy of Rick Steger's excellent brochure *Pricing Pearls: The Consumer's Guide to Tahitian Black Pearls.*

O.P.E.C. (tel. 45-36-26), 20 rue Gauguin (upstairs), and **Tahiti Pearl Dream** (tel. 50-22-00), rue Leboucher 10 (upstairs), are black pearl sales rooms a block from the market. They'll show you a free video about the pearls if they think you're a potential buyer.

Several dozen other jewelers around Papeete, including **Vaima Perles** (tel. 42-55-57), **Tahiti Perles** (tel. 46-15-15), and **Sibani Perles** (tel. 54-24-24) in the Vaima Center, also sell pearls, and it's wise to visit several before making such an important purchase. Tahiti Perles specializes in classic settings using large pearls while Sibani uses slightly simpler settings. **Frédéric Misser Joaillier** (tel. 43-37-98), on boulevard Pomare just west of the Vaima Center, displays many original creations. At all the black pearl outlets, remember to ask for a discount on the sticker price.

Tattoo Shops

Many visitors leave Tahiti with a fresh Polynesian tattoo, and you can too. The shops mentioned below all have albums illustrating their designs and the proprietors usually speak English. Inquire about sanitary precautions, including clean razors and disposable needles—a listing here is no guarantee. Buy the antiseptic cream they tell you to buy, and don't expose your tattoo to salt water or the sun until it has healed.

Aroma Tattoo Art (tel. 78-06-73 or 41-29-00; Mon.–Sat. 1000–1800), 303 boulevard Pomare at rue Clappier above Bar Le Taina Kaina, uses 80 colors in a freehand style with single tattoos priced CFP 5,000–40,000 (or CFP 800,000 for a complete body tattoo). The owner, Aroma Salmon, does beautiful work.

Jordi's Tattoo Shop (tel. 42-45-00, fax 83-04-91; Tues.–Sat. 1000–1200/1300–1900), 43 rue Leboucher directly behind Hôtel Prince Hinoï, is more expensive with tattoos starting at CFP 10,000. Established in 1980, Jordi's was the first professional tattoo shop in French Polynesia and tourists are its main clientele.

Mano Tattoos (tel. 74-69-14; Mon.–Sat. 0900–1700), upstairs in the Papeete market, applies Marquesan-style designs from CFP 5,000 and up.

INFORMATION

The Tahiti Manava Visitors Bureau (tel. 50-57-12; weekdays 0730–1700, Sat. 0800–1200) is at Fare Manihini, a neo-Polynesian building between boulevard Pomare and the Quai d'honneur where the cruise ships tie up. The staff can answer questions and supply a free map of Papeete but they don't make phone calls or reservations on behalf of visitors. Pick up their lists of "small hotel" accommodations on virtually all of the islands, and inquire about special events or boats to the outer islands.

The Institut Territorial de la Statistique (tel. 54-32-32, fax 42-72-52; Mon.–Thurs. 0730–1500, Fri. 0730–1200), 1st floor, Immeuble Uupa, rue Edouard Ahnne (next to Honolulu), puts out a useful annual abstract *La Polynésie en Bref.*

Bookstores

You'll find Papeete's biggest selection of books in English at Librairie Archipels (tel. 42-47-30, fax 45-10-27), 68 rue des Remparts.

The Librairie du Vaima (tel. 45-57-44, fax 45-53-45) in the Vaima Center is Papeete's largest French bookstore. It carries antiquarian books about the South Pacific, topographical maps, and posters.

There's a news kiosk (tel. 41-02-89) with magazines in English in front of the Vaima Center by the taxi stand on boulevard Pomare.

Maps

Topographical maps (CFP 1,500 a sheet) of many islands are available from the Section Topographie of the Service de l'Urbanisme (tel. 46 82 18, fax 43-49-83), 4th floor, Administrative Building, 11 rue du Commandant Destremeau.

La Boutique Klima (tel. 42-00-63, fax 43-28-24), 13 rue Jaussen behind the cathedral, sells nautical charts (CFP 3,000) and many interesting French books on Polynesia.

Nauti-Sport (tel. 50-59-59) in Fare Ute also retails French nautical charts of Polynesia at CFP 3,100 a sheet, and Marine Corail (tel. 42-82-22), next to the Canon Center nearby, has more of the same.

Library

A public library (tel. 54-45-44, fax 42-85-69; Mon.–Thurs. 0800–1700, Fri. 0800–1600) is in the Cultural Center, 646 boulevard Pomare. Visitors cannot take books out but you're welcome to sit and read. The padded chairs in the air-conditioned reading room are great for relaxing.

Airline Offices

Reconfirm your international flight at your airline's Papeete office. Many of the airline offices are in the Vaima Center: Air New Zealand (tel. 54-07-47), Hawaiian Airlines (tel. 42-15-00), LanChile (tel. 42-64-55), and Qantas (tel. 43-88-38). Qantas represents Polynesian Airlines. Air Tahiti Nui (tel. 45-55-55) is at 61 rue Gauguin near the Hôtel de Ville. Air France (tel. 47-47-47), which also represents Aircalin, is on rue Georges Lagarde inland from the Vaima Center. If the clerk tells you it's not necessary to reconfirm, check your seat assignment and leave a local contact phone number to ensure that your booking is still in the system.

SERVICES

Money

The MG Change Office (tel. 43-22-77; weekdays 0830–1200/1300–1600, Sat. 0800–1530, Sun. 0900–1200), adjacent to the Tahiti Manava Visitors Bureau on boulevard Pomare, changes cash or traveler's checks for a standard rate without commission. It's a good deal if you're changing US$150 or less; otherwise the banks give a fractionally better rate which you must line up to receive.

The Banque de Polynésie (tel. 46-66-66; Mon.–Thurs. 0745–1530, Fri. 0745–1430), boulevard Pomare 355, directly across from the Visitors Bureau, takes CFP 411 commission. The Banque de Tahiti (tel. 50-42-42; weekdays 0800–1145/1330–1630, Sat. 0800–1130), on boulevard Pomare west of the Vaima Center, charges CFP 551 commission.

Several banks around town have automatic tellers where you can get cash if the machine's software recognizes your card. Banque Socredo (tel. 45-31-83), boulevard Pomare 411, on the waterfront just east of the post office, has an ATM accessible 24 hours a day. Adjacent is a nifty Automatic Currency Exchange machine, which changes the banknotes of nine countries for CFP 500 commission (an identical machine is at the Tahiti Beachcomber Inter-Continental). Complaints have been received about Tahiti ATMs that didn't work, so using one of these machines at a time when the bank itself is closed is not recommended.

Post and Telecommunications

The main post office (weekdays 0700–1800, Sat. 0800–1100) is on boulevard Pomare across from the yacht anchorage. Pick up poste restante (general delivery) mail downstairs (CFP 55 per piece). The public fax number at Papeete's main post office is fax 689/43-68-68 (you'll pay CFP 250 a page to pick up faxes sent to this number). The post office is also a place to make a long-distance telephone call, but there's a stiff three-minute minimum for operator-assisted calls and it's cheaper to use a telephone card for such calls.

Around Tahiti, small branch post offices with public telephones are found in Arue, Faa'a Airport, Mahina, Mataiea, Paea, Papara, Papeari, Pirae, Punaauia, and Taravao.

If you have an American Express card you can have your mail sent c/o Tahiti Tours, B.P. 627, 98713 Papeete, French Polynesia. Its office (tel. 54-02-50, fax 42-50-50) is at 15 rue Jeanne d'Arc next to the Vaima Center.

Courier Services

TTI-Tahiti (tel. 83-00-24, fax 83-76-27; Mon.–Thurs. 0730–1200/1300–1700, Fri. 0730–1200/1300–1530) is the DHL Worldwide Express agent. Its office is on the main highway in the first building toward Papeete from Faa'a Airport. Parcels to North America begin at CFP 5,650 for half a kilo (documents and shipments to California are slightly less). Specials include a 25-kg "Jumbo Box" costing CFP 26,600 and a 10-kg "Jumbo Junior" for CFP 17,000 (size limits apply). Optional insurance is 1.5 percent of value.

Cowan et Fils (tel. 82-44-25), upstairs above the Air Tahiti freight office in the airport itself, is the United Parcel Service agent. It's considerably more expensive than TTI-Tahiti.

Federal Express (tel. 45-36-45) has an office on avenue Bruat near boulevard Pomare.

Internet Access

La Maison de la Press (tel. 50-93-93; Mon.–Thurs. 0700–1900, Fri. and Sat. 0700–2200), 343 boulevard Pomare opposite Tahua Vaiete, has a very popular Internet café upstairs (CFP 250 per 15 minutes). The service is friendly but all eight computers are often occupied.

Tiki Soft Cafe (tel. 88-93-98; weekdays 0700–0100, Sat. 1400–0100), rue des Remparts at rue du Maréchal Foch, also charges CFP 250 for 15 minutes of Internet access.

Galaxie Games (tel. 42-63-63; weekdays 0800–1700, Sat. 0800–1600), 91 rue des Remparts, provides Internet access at CFP 100 per seven minutes.

Immigration Office

If you arrived by air, visa extensions are handled by the Police Aux Frontières (tel. 80-06-00; weekdays 0800–1200/1400–1700) at the airport (up the stairs beside the snack bar). Drop by at least a week before your current visa will expire. Yachties are handled by the Police Aux Frontières (tel. 42-40-74; weekdays 0730–1100/1400–1500) on the waterfront behind the Visitors Bureau in the center of town. If you wish to extend a three-month visa, ask the Visitors Bureau where you need to go to apply. Be patient and courteous with the officials if you want good service.

For those uninitiated into the French administrative system, the police station (in emergencies tel. 17) opposite the War Memorial on avenue Bruat deals with Papeete matters, while the gendarmerie (tel. 46-73-73) at the head of avenue Bruat is concerned with the rest of the island. The locally recruited Papeete police wear blue uniforms, while the paramilitary French-import gendarmes are dressed in khaki. The ubiquitous security personnel in red shirts along the Papeete waterfront belong to the Groupement d'Intervention de la Polynésie (GIP), a body used to provide employment for Flosse supporters.

Consulates

The honorary consul of New Zealand (tel. 54-07-40) is upstairs in the Air New Zealand office in the Vaima Center. The Consulate of Chile (tel. 43-89-19; Wed.–Fri. 0900–1200) is at 3 passage Cardella near the Vaima Center. Other countries with honorary consuls in Papeete are Austria (tel. 43-91-14), Belgium (tel. 80-08-08), Denmark (tel. 54-04-54), Finland (tel. 43-60-67), Germany (tel. 42-99-94), Israel (tel. 42-41-00), Italy (tel. 43-45-01), Japan (tel. 45-45-45), Netherlands (tel. 42-49-37), Norway (tel. 43-79-72), South Korea (tel. 43-64-75), Sweden (tel. 42-73-93), and the United Kingdom (tel. 41-98-41).

Australia, Canada, China, and the United States are not represented in French Polynesia. All U.S. visa applications or requests for the replacement of lost American passports must go via the U.S. Embassy (tel. 679/331-4466; www.amembassy-fiji.gov) in Suva, Fiji. TTI-Tahiti (tel. 83-00-24) near Faa'a International Airport will send passports or documents to Fiji at CFP 7,200 with the return prepaid.

Launderettes

Lavomatic du Pont de l'Est (tel. 43-71-59; Mon.–Sat. 0630–1200/1330–1730), 64 rue Gauguin, charges CFP 750 to wash six kg, another CFP 750 to dry, and CFP 100 for soap.

Laverie Automatique "Lavex ça m'plein" (tel. 41-26-65; weekdays 0700–1730, Sat. 0630–1130), 303 boulevard Pomare opposite the Quai de Moorea, asks CFP 1,650 to wash and dry up to seven kilograms.

Public Toilets

Public toilets are found on Tahua Vaiete near the Visitors Bureau, beside the Flower Market, and at the Tahua To'ata west along the waterfront. Bring your own toilet paper.

Yachting Facilities

Yachts must report their arrival to the port authorities over VHF channel 12 before entering the pass. Customs and immigration are in the building behind the Visitors Bureau. A one-time entry fee and optional daily electricity and water hookup are charged. Yachts pay a daily fee based on the length of the vessel to moor Mediterranean-style (stern-to, bow anchor out) along the quay on boulevard Pomare.

It's cheaper to anchor at the Marina Taina (tel. 41-02-25) at PK 9, Punaauia, accessible via the Faa'a Channel without exiting the lagoon. Otherwise visiting boats can use one of the anchor buoys at the Yacht Club of Tahiti (tel. 42-78-03) at PK 4, Arue, for a monthly fee. Another popular anchorage is Port Phaeton at Taravao. Tahiti's sunny west and south coasts are excellent cruising grounds, while there are few good anchorages on the windward, rainy, and often dangerous east and north coasts.

Health

Mamao Territorial Hospital (tel. 46-62-62) is always crowded with locals awaiting free treatment, so unless you've been taken to the recompression chamber there or it's an emergency, you're better off attending a private clinic. At the Clinique Paofai (tel. 46-18-18) on boulevard Pomare you can see a doctor anytime in the emergencies *(urgences)* department on the first floor (brief consultations CFP 3,300 from 0700–1900, CFP 7,300 from 1900–0700). The facilities and attention are excellent.

In case of emergencies around Papeete call S.O.S. Médecins at tel. 42-34-56. To call an ambulance dial 15.

Two dentists, Dr. Michel Ligerot and Dr. Valérie Galano-Serra (tel. 43-32-24), are on the second floor of the building next to the Hôtel Tiare Tahiti at boulevard Pomare 415.

The Pharmacie de la Cathedrale (tel. 42-02-

24), across the street from the Catholic cathedral, opens weekdays 0700–1800, Saturday 0730–1230. There are many other pharmacies around Papeete.

TRANSPORTATION

For information on air and sea services from Papeete to the other islands, see Transportation in the introduction to French Polynesia.

Le Truck

You can go almost anywhere on Tahiti by *le truck,* converted cargo vehicles with long benches in back. *Trucks* marked Outumaoro run from Papeete to Faa'a International Airport and the Sofitel Maeva Beach every few minutes throughout the day, with sporadic service after dark until midnight, then again in the morning from 0500 on. Weekdays the last trip from Papeete to Mahina, Paea, and points beyond is around 1700.

Trucks to Arue, Mahina, Papenoo, Taravao, and Tautira leave from both sides of boulevard Pomare near the Visitors Bureau. Those to the airport, Outumaoro, Punaauia, Paea, and Papara are found in front of the Banque de Tahiti on rue du Maréchal Foch. Local services to Motu Uta (infrequent), Mission, Mamao, Titioro, and Tipaeriu depart from rue Colette near the Hôtel de Ville.

Destinations and fares are posted on the side of the vehicle: CFP 120 to the airport (CFP 200 after 1800), CFP 140 to Punaauia, CFP 160 to Mahina, CFP 170 to Paea, CFP 180 to Papenoo, CFP 190 to Papara, CFP 220 to Mataiea, CFP 240 to Papeari, CFP 300 to Taravao, and CFP 350 to Teahupoo or Tautira. After dark all *truck* fares increase. Outside Papeete you don't have to be at a stop: *trucks* stop anywhere if you wave. Some drivers ask CFP 100 for luggage, others carry it free.

Sad to say, a plan is being implemented to replace *le truck* with air-conditioned Korean buses, a change that will probably raise prices and reduce frequencies. Fixed bus stops, routes, schedules, and printed tickets may also be introduced. Local politics is involved as the territorial government has granted special concessions to Maeva Transport (a company controlled by supporters of President Gaston Flosse's party), while limiting the rival Tefana Rumana Transport group (which generally backs the pro-independence party) to less profitable rural areas. Check with the Visitors Bureau for current information on the public transportation system.

Taxis

Taxis in Papeete are extremely expensive, and it's important not to get in unless there's a meter that works or you've agreed to a flat fare beforehand. The basic fare is CFP 800 during the day (0600–2000) or CFP 1,200 at night (2000–0600). Add to that the per-kilometer fee of CFP 120 by day or CFP 240 at night. The flat rate per hour is CFP 4,000 during the day or CFP 6,000 at night. Waiting time is CFP 2,000 an hour by day, CFP 3,000 at night. Baggage is CFP 50–100 per piece.

During the day expect to spend at least CFP 1,000 for a short trip within Papeete (including to the Sheraton), CFP 1,500 to the airport, or CFP 1,700 to the Beachcomber Inter-Continental or Maeva Beach. Taxi stands are found at the Vaima Center (tel. 42-33-60), Mana Rock Café (tel. 45-23-03), and airport (tel. 83-30-07). If you feel cheated by a taxi driver, take down the license number and complain to the Visitors Bureau, although what you consider a ripoff may be the correct amount. We've received numerous complaints about Papeete taxi drivers and they're best avoided if at all possible.

Car Rentals

If you want to whiz the island and pack in as many side trips as you can in a day, an unlimited-mileage car rental is for you, and with a few people sharing it's not a bad deal. Don't rent on a per-kilometer basis unless you plan to keep the car for at least three days and intend to use it only for short hops. Most agencies impose a 50-km daily minimum on their per-km rentals to prevent you from traveling *too* slowly; most rentals are for a minimum of 24 hours. Almost all the car rental companies have kiosks inside Faa'a Airport, and most offer clients a free pickup and drop-off service to the hotels and airport.

Check the car as carefully as they check you; be sure to comment on dents, scratches, flat tires, etc. All the car rental agencies include third-party public liability insurance in the basic price, but collision damage waiver (CDW) varies from CFP 900 to CFP 3,500 extra per day with CFP 20,000 and up deductible (called the *franchise* in French). Most agencies charge the client for stolen accessories and damage to the tires, insurance or no insurance, and Tahiti insurance isn't valid if you take the car to Moorea. You'll also pay for towing if you are judged responsible. On Tahiti the car comes full of gas, and you'll see Mobil and Total gas stations all around the island.

Avis/Pacificar (tel. 54-10-10, fax 42-19-11), 56 rue des Remparts at pont de l'Est, at the east end of rue Paul Gauguin, is open weekdays 0600–1900, Saturday 0700–1830, Sunday 0800–1830. It also has a kiosk facing the Quai de Moorea, opposite the Hôtel Royal Papeete, and a desk at the airport. Avis/Pacificar has unlimited-km cars from CFP 9,600/18,000/26,000 for one/two/three days, including insurance.

Europcar (tel. 45-24-24, fax 41-93-41; Mon.–Sat. 0600–1930, Sun. 0700–1930) is at the corner of avenue du Prince Hinoï and rue des Remparts, two blocks back from the Quai de Moorea. Europcar desks are also found at several hotels and the airport. Its Fiat Pandas are CFP 1,875, plus CFP 41 a km. With unlimited kms and insurance it's CFP 8,100/15,000/21,060 for one/two/three days. The minimum age is 21 but the insurance coverage is limited for those under 25.

Hertz (tel. 42-04-71, fax 43-49-03) has a main office at the Peugeot dealer on rue du Commandant Destremeau at the west entrance to Papeete and a desk at the airport (tel. 82-55-86). Its cars begin at CFP 2,080 a day, plus CFP 41 a km, plus CFP 1,400 insurance. Otherwise it's CFP 8,820/22,050/45,860 for one/three/seven days with unlimited mileage and insurance.

Robert Rent-a-Car (tel. 42-97-20, fax 42-63-00) on rue du Commandant Destremeau has cars from CFP 1,926 daily, plus CFP 43 a km, plus CFP 954 insurance. Robert's unlimited-km rentals begin at CFP 6,800, plus CFP 954 insurance.

Location de Voitures Daniel (tel. 82-30-04, fax 85-62-64) at the airport terminal begins at CFP 2,033 a day, plus CFP 37 a km, plus CFP 1,070 insurance. With unlimited mileage it's CFP 7,800/12,840/18,840 for two/three/seven days, insurance included.

The least expensive car available from **Location de Voitures Pierrot et Jacqueline** (tel. 81-94-00, fax 81-07-77), also known as Tahiti Rent a Car, is CFP 1,800 a day, plus CFP 38 a km and CFP 1,200 insurance. With unlimited kms it's CFP 7,800/14,000/17,700 for two/three/seven days, insurance included. This company will allow you to take the car to Moorea if you ask before, but the insurance won't be valid over there. In any case, drivers are responsible for the first CFP 50,000 in damages to the car. The minimum age to rent is 21. This friendly, efficient company has an office at the airport.

Parking

As yet it's still free to park on the street anywhere in Papeete, which explains the heavy traffic. Double parking and parking on the sidewalk are commonplace, and European-style parking fee machines are long overdue! You're well advised to take public transportation into town.

If you must park, there's underground parking at the Hôtel de Ville (weekdays 0600–1800, Sat. 0600–1200), accessible from rue Colette opposite Hôtel Le Mandarin, costing CFP 120 the first hour, CFP 60 subsequent hours. Otherwise, Parking du Centre Vaima (tel. 42-44-14; Mon.–Thurs. 0700–1900, Fri. 0700–2200, Sat. 0700–1700), entrance from rue Georges Lagarde off rue du Général de Gaulle in front of Hollywood Cinema, asks CFP 170 an hour.

Bicycle Rentals

Unfortunately the fast and furious traffic on Tahiti's main highways makes cycling dangerous and unpleasant, and motor scooter rentals have been discontinued after fatal accidents.

Garage Bambou (tel. 42-80-09), on avenue Georges Clemenceau near the Chinese temple, sells new Peugeot bicycles from CFP 40,000 and does repairs. **Pacific Bike Shop** (tel. 42-49-00), 33 avenue Georges Clemenceau, also does bicycle repairs.

Local Tours

Patrice Bordes of **Tahiti Safari Expédition** (tel. 42-14-15, fax 42-10-07) offers 4WD jeep tours to Mt. Marau, the Papenoo Valley, and Lake Vaihiria. The highly recommended day trip across Tahiti via the Relais de la Maroto (CFP 8,000 with lunch) not only provides a rare glimpse of the interior but a good introduction to the flora and fauna of the island. Most hotel receptions (including the Hôtel Tiare Tahiti) will book this tour. You can arrange the same thing at CFP 6,000 without lunch by calling Patrice direct (four-person minimum participation).

Natura Exploration (Arnaud Luccioni, tel. 43-03-83, fax 43-03-99) does the same trip across the island at CFP 7,500/6,500 with/without a picnic lunch. Natura does a half-day Mt. Marau 4WD trip at CFP 5,000 pp. **Patrick Adventure** (Patrick Cordier, tel. 83-29-29) also does cross-island tours.

Marama Tours (tel. 83-96-50, fax 82-16-75), at the Sheraton and Maeva Beach Hotels, does six-hour circle-island tours at CFP 4,415 (admission fees extra). It also sells the 4WD tours just mentioned at CFP 8,475 including a picnic lunch. **Tahiti Nui Travel** (tel. 54-02-00) at the Vaima Center and various hotels also offers circle-island tours.

William Leeteg of **Adventure Eagle Tours** (tel. 77-20-03) takes visitors on a full-day tour around the island at CFP 4,500 (admissions and lunch not included). William speaks good English and offers special guided tours for groups of up to seven.

Day Cruises

Many of the yachts and catamarans tied up along boulevard Pomare opposite the Vaima Center offer excursions to Tetiaroa, deep-sea fishing, scuba diving, yacht charters, etc. Departures are often announced on notice boards and a stroll along the waterfront will yield current information.

Croisieres L'Escapade (tel. 72-85-31) does Tetiaroa day trips on a 14-meter yacht at CFP 10,000 pp including breakfast, lunch, and drinks. Weekend cruises (Friday afternoon to Sunday night) are CFP 30,000 pp. **Biotherm Charters** (tel./fax 41-04-09) also does Tetiaroa day trips at

CFP 10,000 pp. **Jet France** (tel. 56-15-62), on the waterfront opposite the Hôtel Tiare Tahiti, does this trip for CFP 11,000 on Wednesday, Saturday, and Sunday 0700–2000.

Tours to Easter Island

From Tahiti it's cheaper to make a side trip to Easter Island than to go to the Marquesas! Most Papeete travel agencies sell three- and seven-night packages designed for Tahiti residents that include airfare, accommodations, transfers, and often sight-seeing tours. There's usually no single supplement. Check several agencies as prices vary considerably, and inquire about the price of a return air ticket alone at the LanChile office in the Vaima Center (low off-season fares available March–November). You'll probably need only a passport to visit Easter Island.

Vahine Tahiti Travel (tel. 50-44-20, fax 43-60-06), off boulevard Pomare below the Vaima Center, has three/seven-night packages to Easter Island costing CFP 75,500/92,100 all inclusive. It sells Papeete–Easter Island air tickets alone at US$435 round-trip with a maximum stay of one week or US$515 round-trip for longer than one week. Tahiti Nui Travel (tel. 54-02-00, fax 42-74-35), adjacent to Vahini Tahiti Travel, lists tour prices on its website.

Also check Manureva Tours (tel. 43-69-63 or 50-91-00, fax 42-48-43), on boulevard Pomare next to the Banque de Tahiti just west of the Vaima Center, Tekura Tahiti Travel (tel. 43-12-00, fax 42-84-60), in the Vaima Center near Hawaiian Airlines, Pacifica Tahiti Travel (tel. 42-93-85, fax 42-90-29), rue Georges Lagarde almost opposite Air France, and Nouvelles Frontières (tel. 53-41-64) on boulevard Pomare opposite the Quai de Moorea. Visit them all as prices do vary and check the vouchers carefully after you've booked.

Getting Away

The **Air Tahiti** booking office (tel. 47-44-00; weekdays 0800–1700, Sat. 0800–1100) is at the corner of rue du Maréchal Foch and rue Edouard Ahnne just inland from the market. **Air Moorea** (tel. 86-41-41) is at Faa'a International Airport. (Interisland services by air and sea are covered in the French Polynesia Introduction.)

The ferries to Moorea depart from the landing just behind the Visitors Bureau downtown. All other interisland ships, including the cargo vessels *Vaeanu* and *Hawaiki-Nui,* leave from the Tuamotu wharf or Quai des Caboteurs in Motu Uta, across the harbor from downtown Papeete.

You can catch *le truck* directly to Motu Uta from the Hôtel de Ville, if you're lucky (it's very infrequent). The ticket offices of some of the vessels are in Fare Ute just north of downtown, while others are at Motu Uta (addresses given in the French Polynesia Introduction).

Around Tahiti

A 117-km Route de Ceinture (Belt Road) runs right around Tahiti-nui, the larger part of this hourglass-shaped island. Construction began in the 1820s as a form of punishment. For orientation you'll see red-and-white kilometer stones, called PK *(pointe kilométrique),* along the inland side of the road. These are numbered in each direction from the Catholic cathedral in Papeete, meeting at Taravao.

Go clockwise to get over the most difficult stretch first; also, you'll be riding on the inside lane of traffic and less likely to go oover a cliff in case of an accident (an average of 55 people a year are killed and 700 injured in accidents on this island). Southern Tahiti is much quieter than the northwest, whereas from Paea to Mahina it's even hard to slow down as tailgating motorists roar behind you.

If you're adventurous, it's possible to do a circle-island tour on *le truck,* provided you get an early start and go clockwise with no stop until Taravao. *Trucks* don't run right around the island, although some go as far as Tautira and Teahupoo on Tahiti-iti. *Trucks* and buses to Taravao leave from boulevard Pomare near the Visitors Bureau regularly throughout the day. *Trucks* to Tautira go via the south coast, so if you want to do a full-circle trip, ask for one going to Taravao via Papenoo. Avoid trying this on the weekend when service is reduced.

A large bus to Taravao via Papenoo leaves Papeete from the same side of boulevard Pomare as the Visitors Bureau weekdays at 0830, 0900, 1000, 1130, and 1600 (1.5 hours, CFP 300). The departure from Taravao to return to Papeete is at 0530, 0630, 0730, 0830, 1030, 1130, and 1400. Once at Taravao, look for a *truck* coming from Tautira or Teahupoo to take you back to Pa-

peete along the south coast. The last *truck* from Taravao via Paea is around 1300, but it's not 100 percent reliable. Be aware that many of the *trucks* you see around Taravao are carrying students and they won't stop.

After Papara the *truck* frequency increases, so feel free to get out at Mara Fern Grotto or elsewhere. The Papara *trucks* stop running around 1500, but if you get stuck, it's comforting to know that hitchhiking *(l'autostop)* is fairly easy and relatively safe on Tahiti. There's abundant traffic along the south coast highway all day and it's almost certain you'll get a ride. However you travel around Tahiti, it's customary to smile and wave to the Tahitians you see (outside Papeete).

Toward Point Venus

East of Arue (covered in the Papeete section), the highway climbs sharply to the **Point de View du Tahara'a** on One Tree Hill (PK 8), where there's a splendid view across Matavai Bay to Papeete and Moorea. Adjacent to the viewpoint is the entrance to the former Hôtel Tahara'a erected by Pan American Airways in 1968. From 1988 to 1997 this was a Hyatt Regency, and then it became the Hôtel Royal Matavai Bay, run by Réginald Flosse, son of Gaston Flosse, before closing in 1998. The Tahara'a is empty at present and moves to convert the structure into a residential apartment complex have not been going well. If the main gate is open it's worth going in to get a closer look at this 190-room structure, built on a spectacular series of terraces down the hillside to conform to a local regulation that no building should be more than two-thirds the height of a coconut tree. There's another glorious view from the Governor's Bench on the knoll beyond the swimming pool above the hotel door.

Continue to Mahina (PK 10) and turn left beside Supermarche Venustar to **Point Venus.** Captain Cook camped on this point between the river and the lagoon during his visit to observe the transit of the planet Venus across the sun on June 3, 1769. Captain Bligh also occupied Point Venus for two months in 1788, while collecting breadfruit shoots for transportation to the West Indies. On March 5, 1797, the first members of the London Missionary Society landed here, as a monument recalls. From Tahiti, Protestantism spread throughout Polynesia and as far as Vanuatu.

Today there's a park on the point, with a 25-meter-high lighthouse (1867) among the palms and ironwood trees. The view of Tahiti across Matavai Bay is superb, and twin-humped Orohena, highest peak on the island, is in view (you can't see it from Papeete itself). Weekdays, Point Venus is a peaceful place, the perfect choice if you'd like to get away from the rat race in Papeete and spend some time at the beach, but on weekends it gets crowded. Any Mahina *truck* will bring you here.

The Northeast Coast

The coast is very rugged all along the northeast side of Tahiti with no barrier reef at many points between Point Venus and Mahaena. The **leper colony** at Orofara (PK 13.2) was founded in 1914. Previously the colony was on Reao atoll in the Tuamotus, but this proved too remote to service. Although leprosy is now a thing of the past, about 50 of the former patients' children who grew up there and have nowhere else to go remain at Orofara, along with a couple of older leprosy victims.

From November to March surfers ride the waves at Chinaman's Bay, Papenoo (PK 16), one of the best rivermouth beach breaks on the north side of the island. The bridge over the broad **Papenoo River** (PK 17.9) allows a view up the largest valley on Tahiti. A paved road leads a few km up the valley before becoming a rough track across the island. (See The Interior later in this chapter for a description of this route.)

At the **Arahoho Blowhole** (PK 22), jets of water shoot up through holes in the lava rock beside the highway at high tide. It's dangerous to get too close to the blowhole as a sudden surge

could toss you out to sea! A nice picnic area is provided here. Just a little beyond the blowhole, a road to the right leads 1.3 km up to the three **Tefa'aurumai Waterfalls** (admission free), also known as the Faarumai Falls. Vaimahuta Falls is accessible on foot in five minutes along the easy path to the right across the bridge. The 30-minute trail to the left leads to two more waterfalls, Haamaremare Iti and Haamaremare Rahi. The farthest falls has a pool deep enough for swimming. Bring insect repellent and carefully lock your rental car before heading off to see the falls (the same applies at the blowhole).

At **Mahaena** (PK 32.5) is the battleground where 441 well-armed French troops defeated a dug-in Tahitian force twice their size on April 17, 1844, in the last fixed confrontation of the French-Tahitian War. The Tahitians carried on a guerrilla campaign another two years until the French captured their main mountain stronghold. No monument commemorates the 100 Tahitians who died combating the foreign invaders here.

The French ships *La Boudeuse* and *L'Étoile*, carrying explorer Louis-Antoine de Bougainville, anchored by the southernmost of two islets off **Hitiaa** (PK 37.6) on April 6, 1768. Unaware that an Englishman had visited Tahiti a year before, Bougainville christened the island "New Cythera," after the Greek isle where love goddess Aphrodite rose from the sea. A plaque near the bridge recalls the event. A clever Tahitian recognized a member of Bougainville's crew as a woman disguised as a man, and an embarrassed Jeanne Baret entered history as the first woman to sail around the world. (Bougainville lost six large anchors during his nine days at this dangerous windward anchorage.)

From the bridge over the Faatautia River at PK 41.8 **Vaiharuru Falls** are visible in the distance. The American filmmaker John Huston intended to make a movie of Herman Melville's *Typee* here in 1957, but when Huston's other Melville film, *Moby Dick,* became a box-office flop, the idea was dropped.

Taravao

At Taravao (PK 53), on the strategic isthmus joining the two Tahitis where the PKs meet, is an

old fort built by the French in 1844 to cut off the Tahitians who had retreated to Tahiti-iti after the battle mentioned above. Germans were interned here during World War II, and the fort is still occupied today by the 1st Company of the Régiment d'Infanterie de Marine du Pacifique.

The assortment of supermarkets, banks, post office, gasoline stations, and restaurants at Taravao make it a good place to break your trip around the island. For lunch, consider **Restaurant L'Escale** (tel. 57-07-16; Tues.–Sat. 1000–1400/1800–2000, Sun. 1000–1400), an atmospheric old French country inn on the highway near Total gas station in Taravao. The plat du jour is indicated on a blackboard outside (CFP 1,500–1,700); otherwise order a seafood dish (CFP 1,450–2,500) from the menu. Another good choice is **Restaurant Baie Phaeton** (tel. 57-08-96; Wed.–Sat. 1000–1400/1800–2100, Sun. 1000–1400), between Taravao and the Gauguin Museum. The Chinese and French entrées are reasonably priced at CFP 900–1,100, and there's a lovely terrace overlooking the bay.

Tahiti-iti

If you have your own transportation, three roads are explorable on rugged Tahiti-iti. An excellent 18-km highway runs east from Taravao to quaint little **Tautira.** Two Spanish priests from Peru attempted to establish a Catholic mission here in 1774 but it lasted for only one year. Scottish author Robert Louis Stevenson stayed at Tautira for two months in 1888 and called it

the most beautiful spot, and its people the most amiable, I have ever found.

The road peters out a few km beyond Tautira but you can continue walking 12 km southeast to the Vaiote River, where there are petroglyphs, sacred rocks, and *marae*. These are difficult to find without a guide, and a few km beyond are the high cliffs that make it almost impractical to try hiking around the Pari Coast to Teahupoo. Intrepid sea kayakers have been known to paddle the 30 km around, although there's a wild four-km stretch not protected by reefs and most visitors go by speedboat.

Another paved nine-km road climbs straight up the Taravao Plateau from just before the hospital in Taravao, 600 meters down the Tautira road from Champion supermarket. Turn right, then left on the second road (no sign). If you have a car and time to take in only one of Tahiti-iti's three roads, this should be your choice. At the 600-meter level on top is the **Vaiufaufa Viewpoint,** with a breathtaking view of both Tahitis. You'll witness spectacular sunsets from here and the herds of cows grazing peacefully among the grassy meadows give this upland an almost Swiss air. A rough side road near the viewpoint cuts down to rejoin the Tautira road near the PK 3 marker.

The third road on Tahiti-iti runs 18 km along the south coast to Teahupoo. Seven km east of Taravao is a **marina** with an artificial beach (PK 7). American pulp Western writer Zane Grey had his fishing camp near here in the 1930s. Just east of the marina is **Toouo Beach,** a long stretch of natural white sand beside the road where you'll see fishermen spearing by torchlight on the opposite reef in the evening. In the afternoon it's a great picnic spot. The two huge moorings near the shore were used by ocean liners before Papeete harbor was developed in the 1960s, as this is the finest natural deep-water harbor on Tahiti. Some of Tahiti's best reef break surfing is possible out there in the Tapuaeraha Pass, but you'll need a boat. Yachts can tie up to a pier near the *mairie* in **Vairoa.** An oceanographic research station studying shrimp breeding is nearby.

The **Teahupoo** road ends abruptly at a river crossed by a narrow footbridge. There's an excellent mountain view from this bridge, and walk east along the beach to get a glimpse of Polynesian village life. After a couple of km the going becomes difficult because of yelping dogs, seawalls built into the lagoon, fences,

Captain Louis-Antoine de Bougainville

© M.G.L DOMENY DE RIENZI

fallen trees, and *tapu* signs. Beyond is the onetime domain of the "nature men" who tried to escape civilization by living alone with nature almost a century ago.

Three hours on foot from the end of the road is **Vaipoiri Grotto,** a large water-filled cave best reached by boat. Try hiring a motorized canoe or hitch a ride with someone at the end of the road. Beyond this the 300-meter-high cliffs of the Pari Coast terminate all foot traffic along the shore; the only way to pass is by boat. All the land east of Teahupoo is well fenced off, so finding a campsite would involve getting someone's permission. (Two pensions, Le Bon Jouir and Te Pari Village, on the Pari Coast east of Teahupoo, are listed under Accommodations Around Tahiti, later in this chapter.)

Gauguin Museum

Port Phaeton on the southwest side of the Taravao Isthmus is a natural "hurricane hole" with excellent holding for yachts in the muddy bottom and easy access to Taravao from the head of the bay. (The entire south coast of Tahiti is a paradise for yachties with many fine protected anchorages.) Timeless oral traditions relate that the first Polynesians to reach Tahiti settled at **Papeari** (PK 56—measured now from the west). In precontact times the chiefly family of this district was among the most prestigious on the island.

The Gauguin Museum (tel. 57-10-58; daily 0900–1700, CFP 600 admission) is at PK 51.7 in Papeari District, 12 km southwest of Taravao. The museum opened in 1965 thanks to a grant from the Singer Foundation (of sewing machine fame), and a couple of minor Gauguin prints, small wood carvings, and other objects associated with the painter are in the collection. These are displayed in the air-conditioned "Salle Henri Bing" to the left of the entrance, but unfortunately the captions are in French only and it's hard to distinguish the originals from the copies (most of the copies are marked "Fac-similé" in small letters). The other three exhibition rooms provide haphazard English translations. The display on the tormented life of Gauguin is well presented with numerous illustrations and explanations in English. Strangely, Gauguin's Tahitian mistresses receive little attention and his

THE PAINTER PAUL GAUGUIN

One-time Paris stockbroker Paul Gauguin arrived at Papeete in June 1891 at age 43 in search of the roots of "primitive" art. He lived at Mataiea with his 14-year-old mistress, Teha'amana, for a year and a half, joyfully painting. In August 1893 he returned to France with 66 paintings and about a dozen woodcarvings, which were to establish his reputation. Unfortunately, his exhibition flopped and in August 1895 Gauguin returned to Tahiti a second time, infected with VD and poor, settling at Punaauia. After an unsuccessful suicide attempt he recovered somewhat, and in 1901 a Paris art dealer named Vollard signed a contract with Gauguin, assuring him a monthly payment of 350 francs and a purchase price of 250 francs per picture. His financial problems alleviated, the painter left for Hiva Oa, Marquesas Islands, to find an environment uncontaminated by Western influences. During the last two years of his life at Atuona, Gauguin's eccentricities put him on the wrong side of the ecclesiastical and official hierarchies. He died in May 1903 at age 53, a near outcast among his countrymen in the islands, yet today a Papeete street and school are named after him!

clashes with the colonial authorities are swept under the carpet. A hall at the back of the museum contains a model of Gauguin's "Maison de Jouïr" in Atuona, Hiva Oa, plus bronze replicas of his wood carvings. The final room deals with Gauguin's influences and influences on Gauguin. Two huge stone tikis are in the garden outside. The one closest to the beach stands 272 cm tall, the largest ancient stone statue in Polynesia outside of Easter Island. It's said to be imbued with a sacred *tapu* spell, and Tahitians believe this tiki, carved on the island of Raivavae hundreds of years ago, still lives. The three Tahitians who moved it here from Papeete in 1965 all died mysterious deaths within a few weeks. A curse is still said to befall all who touch the tiki. A campaign is now under way to have these statues returned to Raivavae.

A **botanical garden** rich in exotic species is

part of the Gauguin Museum complex (CFP 430 additional admission). This 137-hectare garden was created in 1919–1921 by the American botanist Harrison Smith (1872–1947), who introduced more than 200 new species to the island, among them the sweet grapefruit (pomelo), mangosteen, rambutan, and durian. Two large Galapagos tortoises traipse through the east side of the gardens, the last of several such animals given to the children of writer Charles Nordhoff back in the 1930s. Yachts can enter the lagoon through Temarauri Pass and anchor just west of the point here.

The South Coast
At PK 49 is the **Jardin Public Vaipahi** with a lovely waterfall minutes from the road (admission free). It's a good substitute if you missed the botanical garden. A few hundred meters west of Vaipahi is the **Bain du Vaima,** a strong freshwater spring with several deep swimming pools. This is one of the favorite free picnic spots on the island and on weekends it's crowded with locals. Yachts can anchor offshore.

In 1891–1893 Gauguin lived near the Oriental-style church at **Mataiea** (PK 46.5).

The **International Golf Course Olivier Breaud** (tel. 57-43-41; daily 0800–1700) at PK 41, Atimaono, stretches up to the mountainside on the site of Terre Eugenie, a cotton and sugar plantation established by Scotsman William Stewart at the time of the U.S. Civil War (1863). Many of today's Tahitian Chinese are descended from Chinese laborers imported to do the work, and a novel by A. T'Serstevens, *The Great Plantation,* was set here. The present 5,405-meter, 18-hole course was laid out by Californian Bob Baldock in 1970 with a par 72 for men, par 73 for women. If you'd like to do a round, the greens fees are CFP 5,315, plus CFP 2,500 for clubs and CFP 4,200 for a cart. Since 1981 the Tahiti Open in July has attracted golf professionals from around the Pacific. The course restaurant is said to be good.

The **Marae of Mahaiatea** (PK 39) at Papara was once the most hallowed temple on Tahiti, dedicated to the sea god Ruahatu. After a visit in 1769 Captain Cook's botanist Joseph Banks wrote:

It is almost beyond belief that Indians could raise so large a structure without the assistance of iron tools.

Less than a century later planter William Stewart raided the *marae* for building materials, and storms did the rest. All that's left of the 11-story pyramid today is a rough heap of stones. Still, it's worth visiting for its aura and setting, and you can swim off the beach next to the *marae* if you pay attention to the currents. The unmarked turnoff to the *marae* is 100 meters west of Magasin Maruia Junior (large Coca-Cola sign), then straight down to the beach. From April to October surfers often take the waves at black-colored **Taharuu Beach** on nearby Popoti Bay (PK 38.5), one of the top beach break sites on southern Tahiti.

Beside Temple Zion at **Papara** (PK 36) is the grave of Dorence Atwater (1845–1910), U.S. consul to Tahiti 1871–1888. During the American Civil War, Atwater recorded the names of 13,000 dead Union prisoners at Andersonville Prison, Georgia, from lists the Confederates had been withholding. Himself a Union prisoner, Atwater escaped with his list in March 1865. His tombstone provides details.

Maraa Fern Grotto (PK 28.5) is by the road just across the Paea border. An optical illusion, the grotto at first appears small but is quite deep and some Tahitians believe *varua ino* (evil spirits) lurk in the shadowy depths. Others say that if you follow an underground river back from the grotto you'll emerge at a wonderful valley in the spirit world. Paul Gauguin wrote of a swim he took across the small lake in the cave. You're welcome to jump in the blue-gray water. Also fill your water bottle with fresh mineral water from eight spouts next to the parking lot. Maraa Pass is almost opposite the grotto and yachts can anchor in the bay.

The West Coast
Paea and Punaauia are Tahiti's sheltered "Gold Coast," with old colonial homes hidden behind trees along the lagoonside and *nouveau riche* villas dotting the hillside above. From 1896 to 1901 Gauguin had his studio at Punaauia, but nothing

remains of it; his *Two Tahitian Women* was painted there. The view of Moorea is excellent from all along here.

The **Marae Arahurahu** at PK 22.5, Paea, is easily the island's most beautiful archaeological site (open daily, admission free). It's up the road inland from Magasin Laut—take care, the sign faces Papeete, so it's not visible if you're traveling clockwise. This temple, lying in a tranquil, verdant spot under high cliffs, is perhaps Tahiti's only remaining pagan mystery. The ancient open altars built from thousands of cut stones were carefully restored in 1954, the first such restoration in French Polynesia. Historical pageants (CFP 1,500–3,000 admission) recreating pagan rites are performed here in July.

Mahana Park (admission free) at PK 18.3, Papehue, is a territorial beach park with a restaurant (tel. 48-19-99) and café. It's not as affected by pollution as the beaches closer to Papeete and is the perfect place to stop for an afternoon swim or even a sunset over Moorea.

> *The Marae Arahurahu is easily the island's most beautiful archaeological site. This temple, lying in a tranquil, verdant spot under high cliffs, is perhaps Tahiti's only remaining pagan mystery. The ancient open altars built from thousands of cut stones were carefully restored in 1954.*

At Pointe des Pêcheurs, Punaauia, is the **Museum of Tahiti and the Islands** (tel. 58-34-76; Tues.–Sun. 0930–1730; admission CFP 600, groups CFP 500, students and children free), which opened in 1977. In a large air-conditioned complex on Punaauia Bay, about 600 meters down a narrow road from PK 14.7, this worthwhile museum has four halls devoted to the natural environment and settlement, Polynesian material culture, the social and religious life, and the history of Polynesia. Outside is an anchor Captain Cook lost at Tautira in 1773. Most of the captions are in French, Tahitian, and English (nonflash, noncommercial photography allowed).

If it's too late for any more sight-seeing, don't worry as the museum makes an excellent half-day excursion from Papeete by *le truck*. Any of the Paea or Papara *trucks* on rue du Maréchal Foch near Papeete market will bring you to the turnoff in 30 minutes. The road to the museum begins beside a Total gas station, 100 meters south of the large bridge over the Punaruu River just beyond a major traffic circle (ask). Go in the morning as the last *truck* back to town is at 1600.

When the waves are right, you can sit on the seawall behind the museum and watch the Tahitian surfers bob and ride, with the outline of Moorea beyond. It's a nice picnic spot. On your way back to the main highway from the museum, look up to the top of the hill at an **old fort** used by the French to subjugate the Tahitians in the 1840s. The crown-shaped pinnacles of **Le Diadème** (1,321 meters) are also visible from this road.

At the traffic circle just north of the bridge, you have a choice of taking a fast bypass highway straight back to Papeete or continuing on the older coastal road to the Lagoonarium (the coastal road is the second, smaller exit from the circle). The **Lagoonarium** (tel. 43-62-90; closed Mon.), below the lagoon behind Captain Bligh Restaurant at PK 11.4, Punaauia, provides a vision of the underwater marinelife of Polynesia safely behind glass. The big tank full of black-tip sharks is a feature and the shark feeding takes place around noon. Entry is CFP 500 pp, open daily, free for restaurant customers, and CFP 300 for children under 12. Straight out from the Lagoonarium is the Passe de Taapuna, southern entrance to the Punaauia Lagoon and another popular surfing venue.

To continue north, you must rejoin the bypass briefly. At PK 8, Outumaoro, just past the huge Carrefour shopping center, is the turnoff for the RDO autoroute to Papeete, Tahiti's superhighway. Follow the Université signs from here up to the ultramodern campus of the **Université de la Polynésie française** (tel. 80-38-03) with its fantastic hilltop view of Moorea.

On the old airport road just north are two of Tahiti's biggest hotels, the **Sofitel Maeva Beach** (PK 7.5) and **Beachcomber Inter-Continental** (PK 7), each worth a stop—though their beaches are polluted. From the point where the Beachcomber Inter-Continental is today, the souls of deceased Tahitians once leapt on their journey to the spirit world. A sunset from either of these hotels, behind Moorea's jagged peaks across the Sea of the Moon, would be a spectacular finale to a circle-island tour. The **Mairie de Faa'a** (PK 5), just east of the airport, was erected in the traditional Maohi style in 1989 (Faa'a mayor Oscar Temaru is the territory's leading independence advocate).

The Interior

A dirt track across the center of Tahiti begins next to the bridge over the Papenoo River (PK 17.9) on the north coast. In the dry season, you could drive a rental car 15 km up the track to the suspension bridge across the Vaitamanu River and perhaps another km to the Vaituoru Dam. Beyond that, only a 4WD vehicle could proceed, as a large sign proclaims. If you wish to go farther, you'll have to park at the bridge or dam and continue on foot. In the rainy season use your own judgment as to how far you wish to drive.

From coast to coast it's a four-hour, 37-km trip by 4WD jeep, or two days on foot. The easiest (and probably best) way to do this trip is with one of the adventure tour operators that leave their brochures at the Visitors Bureau. Expect to pay CFP 8,000 pp, including a good lunch. (See Local Tours earlier in this chapter for listings.)

The Papenoo Valley is the caldera of Tahiti-nui's great extinct volcano, considered by the ancient Tahitians the realm of the gods. On the slopes of Mt. Orohena (2,241 meters), 10 km south of Papenoo, is the entrance to the **Parc naturel Te Faaiti,** Tahiti's first (and as yet undeveloped) territorial park. On the east side of the Papenoo Valley stands Mt. Aramaoro (1,530 meters). Since 1980, the rivers here have been harnessed for hydroelectricity and they now supply more than a third of Tahiti's electric requirements.

Up a steep incline two km south of the Vaituoru Dam, a side road to the right leads to **Marae Farehape** (admission CFP 200), a well-restored archaeological site with an archery platform, a *marae* with stone backrests, and the outlines of other buildings. A large dam, the Barrage Tahinu, is a couple of km west of Marae Farehape. A primitive campsite exists next to Marae Farehape, and if anyone is around, it's CFP 300 pp to pitch a tent or CFP 600 pp to sleep in an on-site hut.

The tour groups stop for lunch at the **Relais de la Maroto** (tel. 57-90-29, fax 57-90-30), at 217 meters elevation above the junction of the Vaituoru and Vainavenave Rivers. It's only a km from Marae Farehape, 18 km from Papenoo. This cluster of solid concrete buildings was built to house workers during construction of the hydroelectric installations here. The 10 rooms in a long block beside the parking lot rent for CFP 7,500 single or double, while the three bungalows on the ridge are more expensive. Add CFP 1,100/2,500/5,100 pp for breakfast/lunch/dinner. If you wish to stay, call ahead to make sure the Relais is open and has a room for you (at last report it was for sale). Tahiti Safari Expedition may agree to bring you here on one of its tours at CFP 6,000 pp each way.

South of the Relais de la Maroto, the track climbs five km to 780 meters elevation, where the 110-meter Urufau Tunnel (opened in 1989) cuts through to the south coast watershed. The track then winds down to Lake Vaihiria, Tahiti's only lake, at 473 meters elevation, 25 km south of Papenoo. Sheer cliffs and spectacular waterfalls squeeze in around this spring-fed lake. Native floppy-eared eels known as *puhi taria,* up to 1.8 meters long, live in these cold waters, as do prawns and trout. With its luxuriant vegetation, this rain-drenched spot is one of the most evocative on the island.

Just south of the lake, a concrete track with a 37-degree incline drops to a dam and upper power station. Four km beyond this is a smaller dam and lower power station, then it's seven km on a rough dirt track to PK 47.6 on the south coast highway near Mataiea.

ACCOMMODATIONS AROUND TAHITI

Taravao and Tahiti-iti

Fare Nana'o (Monique Meriaux, tel. 57-18-14, fax 57-76-10) is an unusual place to stay. It's beside the lagoon in a colorful compound overflowing with vegetation and fragments of

TAHITI INTERNET RESOURCES

Sports and Recreation

Aquatica Dive Center
www.aquatica-dive.com

École de Surf Tura'i Mataare
surfschool@mail.pf

Eleuthera Plongée
www.dive-tahiti.com

Iti Diving International
www.itidiving.pf

Moana Surf Tours
moanasurftours@mail.pf

Scuba Tek Tahiti
www.chez.com/scubatek

Accommodations

Chez Armelle
www.pension-armelle.com

Chez Myrna
dammeyer.family@mail.pf

Fare Nana'o
www.farenanao.com

Hiti Moana Villa
www.papeete.com/moanavilla

Hôtel Kon Tiki Pacific
kontiki@mail.pf

Hôtel Le Mandarin
www.hotelmandarin.com

Hôtel Le Royal Tahitien
royalres@mail.pf

Hôtel Matavai
www.hotelmatavai.pf

Hôtel Prince Hinoï
www.hotel-princehinoi.com

Hôtel Sheraton Tahiti
www.sheratonsintahiti.com

Hôtel Tahiti Country Club
trhppt@mail.pf

Hôtel Tahiti Méridien
www.lemeridien-tahiti.com

Iaorana Villa
iaoranavilla@mail.pf

Pension de la Plage
www.pensiondelaplage.com

Pension Fare Maïthé
www.chez-maithe.com

Pension Le Bon Jouir
www.bonjouir.com

Pension Te Miti
www.pensiontemiti.com

sculpture, very near the PK 52 marker, a km north of the old French fort at Taravao. The three thatched *fare* with shared bath are CFP 7,500 single or double. Another four with private bath and cooking facilities cost CFP 11,000. An additional person is CFP 1,000 extra in any of these. Although unique and wonderful, this Robinson Crusoe–style place is not for everyone: the walls are constructed of tree trunks and branches, and in the night you may be aware of the presence of crabs, lizards, and a marauding cat. You might have to wade through the lagoon or climb into a tree to get to your room. The Fare Nana'o website provides many photos.

A good sight-seeing base is **Chez Jeannine** (Jeannine Letivier, tel./fax 57-07-49), also known as "L'Eurasienne," on the Route de Plateau five km above Taravao. You'll need a rental car to stay here as it's way up on the road to the Vaiufaufa Viewpoint and *le truck* doesn't pass anywhere nearby. The four two-story bungalows with cooking facilities and wicker furniture are CFP 8,000/45,000/100,000 double a day/week/month, while the three rooms above the restaurant are CFP 5,000 double. The cool breezes and good views are complemented by a swimming pool. Jeannine's restaurant features Vietnamese dishes and seafood.

Punatea Village
punatea_village@hotmail.com

Relais de la Maroto
maroto@mail.pf

Relais Fenua
relais.familial@mail.pf

Taaroa Lodge
www.taaroalodge.com

Tahiti Beachcomber Inter-Continental
tahiti@interconti.com

Te Pari Village
www.tahiti1.com/tepari

Tiare Tahiti Hotel
hotltiaretahiti@mail.pf

Tattooing

Jordi's Tattoo Shop
www.jorditattoo.ps

Black Pearls

Perles de Tahiti
www.perlesdetahiti.net

Tahiti Perles
www.tahiti-perles.com

Vaima Perles
www.vaima-perles.com

Transportation and Tours

Avis
avis.tahiti@mail.pf

Europcar
fmeuropcar@mail.pf

Hertz
hertz@mail.pf

Location de Voitures Daniel
tahiti.safari@mail.pf

Marina Taina, Tahiti
marina@mail.pf

Natura Exploration
www.natura-exploration.com

Polynesian Adventure
www.polynesianadv.com

Tahiti Evasion
www.tahitievasion.com

Tahiti Safari Expédition
www.tahiti-safari.com

TTI-Tahiti
www.tti-tahiti.pf

FRENCH POLYNESIA

Punatea Village (tel./fax 57-71-00) is at PK 4.6, between Taravao and Pueu on the road to Tautira. The four bungalows with private bath facing a black pebble beach are CFP 11,000 double plus tax, while the five rooms with shared bath in a long thatched building cost CFP 7,000. Meals are CFP 600/2,000/2,500 for breakfast/lunch/dinner (cooking facilities not provided). There's a swimming pool.

Right adjacent to the Punatea Village is **Pension Fare Maïthé** (Maïthé Romero, tel. 57-18-24, fax 57-18-24) with two rooms with shared kitchen facilities and TV at CFP 7,000 double. It's in a quiet area near the sea with lush tropical vegetation.

The backpacker's best bet is **Chez Mado** (no phone), the snack bar on the east beach in Tautira. The friendly folks running the restaurant rent three rooms with shared bath in their own home, 500 meters down the beach beyond the end of the road. The CFP 3,500 pp charge includes all meals at the snack bar. Mado does her grocery shopping on Monday mornings, so if she's not there when you arrive, just wait around. It's a great place for lunch even if you're not staying, with dishes such as steak frites, chow mein, and *poisson cru* for CFP 850–950.

On the opposite side of the Tahiti-iti peninsula is **Pension Meherio Iti** (Marie Maitere, tel./fax

52-17-50), at PK 11.9 in Vairao district on the road to Teahupoo. There are two bungalows with cooking facilities down near the lagoon, 400 meters off the road. These cost CFP 6,000/8,000 single/double (extra person CFP 1,000). The pension also rents a small flat in a house up near the main road for the same price, but it's not at all as nice. This place is usually fully booked by local French families on weekends but it's a possibility during the week.

Pension Vaiani (tel./fax 57-96-16) at PK 16.5, Teahupoo, operates mainly as a surfing camp with 14 beds in a large attractive house, plus two beach bungalows with another three beds each. It's CFP 6,500 pp including all meals and the surf boat to the reef. Boat trips to the grotto are CFP 1,000 pp, to Pari Coast CFP 1,500 pp (minimum of four people). This place is always packed with surfers in April and May.

On the Pari Coast beyond the end of the road at Teahupoo is **Pension Le Bon Jouir** (Annick Paofai, tel. 57-02-15, fax 43-69-70). The three bungalows start at CFP 7,500 triple; otherwise camping is CFP 1,200 pp. You can cook for yourself or order breakfast and dinner at CFP 4,000 pp a day. Return boat transfers are CFP 1,400 pp and it costs CFP 500 a day for parking at the wharf in Teahupoo. Le Bon Jouir is in a verdant location backed by hills and it makes a great base for exploring this area. It's right opposite the famous Teahupoo surfing break.

On the same coast but a bit closer to Teahupoo than Le Bon Jouir is **Te Pari Village.** There is no direct phone at the guesthouse but you can call tel. 42-59-12 in Papeete for information. The three bungalows are CFP 9,500 pp double including all meals and boat transfers are free. The wharf where both these establishments pick up their guests is at PK 17.1, a km back from the end of the road.

Southwestern Tahiti

Papara Village (Thomas Chave, tel. 57-75-58, fax 57-79-00) is up on a hill a km off the south coast highway at PK 38.5, Papara. The two solid bungalows with private bath, fridge, and TV (but no cooking) are CFP 7,000/10,000 single/double. There's also a large family bungalow

with kitchen at CFP 15,000 for up to four people. A swimming pool is on the premises.

Hiti Moana Villa (Steve Brotherson, tel. 57-93-93, fax 57-94-44), at PK 32, is right on the lagoon between Papara and Paea. The four bungalows with a kitchen, living room, TV, terrace, and private bath are CFP 9,500 single or double, or CFP 13,000 for four peope. Four additional units without kitchens are CFP 9,000 (tax included but CFP 2,000 surcharge for one night). There are a swimming pool and pontoon, and the manager has a boat and motor for rent at CFP 7,000. Airport transfers are CFP 1,500 pp each way. This place is often full—especially on weekends—and advance bookings are recommended.

One of the best low-budget places on Tahiti is **Pension Te Miti** (Frédéric and Crystal Cella, tel./fax 58-48-61) at PK 18.5, Paea, in Papehue village, 450 meters up off the main road. The six rooms in two adjacent houses cost CFP 5,500–7,000 double depending on the size of the room. Backpackers and surfers often choose one of the four beds available in each of the two dorms at CFP 2,500 pp. Breakfast is included. Amenities include a communal fridge, cooking facilities, TV corner, luggage storage, bicycles, and Internet access. Use of the washing machine is CFP 500. Airport transfers are CFP 1,000 pp but it's fairly easy to get there on *le truck*. Mahana Park and various shops and restaurants are nearby.

Taaroa Lodge (Ralph Sanford, tel. 58-39-21), a large house right on a rocky beach behind Restaurant Snack PK 18 at PK 18.1, Paea, offers a 10-mattress dorm at CFP 2,300 pp, one room at CFP 5,000 single, and two bungalows at CFP 16,000/66,000/96,000 a day/week/month. There's a common kitchen. Surfers are the main clientele and several surf breaks including Sapinus Reef are nearby. The atmosphere is good.

Directly across the highway from the Taaroa Lodge access road at PK 18, Paea, is **Relais Fenua** (Laurent Lyon, tel./fax 45-01-98) with three rooms on each side of a new V-shaped building at CFP 7,000/8,400 single/double. Breakfast/dinner are CFP 1,000/2,000. Parking space is provided.

Iaorana Villa (tel./fax 54-49-11), PK 10.8, Punaauia, was a vacation center for military personnel involved in the French nuclear testing program until 2001. It's right on the coast with 24 thatched air-conditioned garden bungalows at CFP 12,000/72,000/240,000 for one/seven/30 nights (higher in July, August, and around Christmas). The 20 nonair-conditioned standard rooms are CFP 8,000/45,000/150,000. Some of the rooms are in bad repair, so you might ask to see yours before accepting it. Avoid the units across the busy highway, away from the rest of the hotel and the beach. There's a high diving platform over the lagoon.

Chez Armelle (Raimana Rivière, tel. 58-42-43, fax 58-42-81), at PK 15.5 in Punaauia (almost opposite a large Mobil service station), has eight rooms at CFP 5,500/7,000/8,000 single/double/triple. A bungalow is CFP 8,000 double. Breakfast and tax are included in all rates and dinner is available at CFP 1,500 pp. The minimum stay is two nights. There's a pleasant snack bar facing the beach but the rooms are ensconced in the complex. No parking space is provided and rental cars must be left overnight at a public beach park nearby. Snorkeling gear, canoes, kayaks, and bicycles are available. Airport transfers are CFP 500/1,000 pp day/night each way. This pension caters more to French migrants who pay by the month but it's still worth a look.

Pension de la Plage (tel. 45-56-12, fax 82-83-48), PK 15.4, Punaauia, across the highway from Chez Armelle, has two long motel-style blocks of six rooms each at CFP 6,000/7,200 single/double (CFP 7,000/9,200 with kitchenette). The rooms face a small pool and beach access is nearby.

In 1998 the **Hôtel Méridien Tahiti** (tel. 47-07-07, fax 47-07-08) opened at PK 15, Punaauia, about nine km southwest of the airport. The 138 air-conditioned rooms in the four-story main building begin at CFP 35,000 single or double, while the 12 overwater bungalows are CFP 48,000 single or double, plus 11 percent tax. There's a huge sand-bottomed swimming pool linked to the beach and a 500-seat conference center. The waters off the sandy beach are pollution-free, the Museum of Tahiti and the Islands is just a 15-minute walk away, the atmosphere is pleasingly European, and the sunsets over Moorea are superb. Considerable controversy surrounded the building of this hotel as Tahitian protesters occupied the site for nearly four years to protect an ancient Moahi burial ground. In January 1996 French gendarmes were called in to evict the demonstrators and construction went ahead under tight security.

On the mountain side of the highway at PK 8.3, Punaauia, up the hill and above Carrefour shopping center, is a five-bed dormitory and one double room provided by **Moana Surf Tours** (Moana David, tel./fax 43-70-70). There's no sign, so ask. A bed here will set you back US$110 pp a day including breakfast, dinner, and unlimited transfers to the surf breaks off Tahiti. The busy season is April–November, and most surfers stay a week. Other months you can stay in the dorm at CFP 4,000 pp including breakfast. This place is of interest only to surfers and is overpriced for other guests.

Other Windward Islands

Maiao

Maiao, or Tapuaemanu, 70 km southwest of Moorea, is a low coral island with an elongated, 180-meter-high hill at the center. On each side of this hill is a large greenish-blue lake. Around Maiao is a barrier reef with a pass on the south side accessible only to small boats. About 250 people live in a small village on the southeast side of 8.3-square-km Maiao, all of them Polynesians. Problems with an Englishman, Eric Trower, who attempted to gain control of Maiao for phosphate mining in the 1930s, have resulted in a ban on Europeans and Chinese living on the island. Most of the thatch used in touristic constructions on Moorea and Tahiti originates on Maiao.

There are no tourist accommodations on Maiao and an invitation from a resident is required to stay. Proposals to develop the island for tourism have been rejected by the inhabitants and there's no airstrip. For information on the monthly supply ship *Taporo V* from Papeete, contact the **Compagnie Française Maritime de Tahiti** (tel. 42-63-93) at Fare Ute. A round-trip voyage on this ship would at least give you a glimpse of Maiao for CFP 2,654 deck. Two nights will be spent aboard ship and it's possible to get off at Moorea on the return trip.

MAIAO

Tepuatau Point

Lake Roto Iti

▲ (154 m)

Vavatunu Point

Paparoa Point

Lake Roto Rahi

Lagoon

Auparirua Point

Apootoo Pass

0   1 mi
0   1 km

© DAVID STANLEY

Mehetia

Mehetia is an uninhabited volcanic island about 100 km east of Tahiti. Although Mehetia is less than two km across, Mt. Fareura reaches 435 meters. There's no lagoon and anchorage is untenable. Landing is possible on a black beach on the northwest side of the island but it's difficult. Anglers from the south coast of Tahiti visit occasionally.

TETIAROA

Tetiaroa, 55 km north of Tahiti, is a low coral atoll with a turquoise lagoon and 13 deep-green coconut-covered islets totaling 490 hectares. Only small boats can enter the lagoon. Tahuna Iti has been designated a seabird refuge (fenced off) and the lagoon is a marine reserve. Three-km-long Rimatuu islet served as a retreat for Tahitian royalty, and the remains of Polynesian *marae* and giant *tuu* trees may be seen.

In 1904 the Pomare family gave Tetiaroa, once a Tahitian royal retreat, to a Canadian dentist named Walter J. Williams to pay their bills. Dr. Williams, who served as British consul from 1916 until his death in 1937, had a daughter who sold Tetiaroa to actor Marlon Brando in 1966. Brando came to Tahiti in 1960 to play Fletcher Christian in the MGM film *Mutiny on the Bounty* and he ended up marrying his leading lady, Tarita Teriipaia (who played Mameetee, the chief's daughter). She and her family still run the small tourist resort on Motu Onetahi. Tarita and Marlon had two children, son Teihotu, born in 1965, and daughter Cheyenne, born in 1970.

The gunshot death of Dag Drollet, Cheyenne's ex-boyfriend and father of her son, Tuki, at the Brando residence in Los Angeles in 1990, resulted in a 10-year prison sentence for Cheyenne's half-brother, Christian Brando, on an involuntary manslaughter plea bargain. On Easter Sunday 1995 Cheyenne committed suicide and she was buried next to Dag in the Drollet family crypt at Papeete's Uranie Cemetery. These tragedies continue to haunt the Brando family, and the resort on

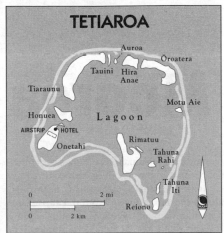

TETIAROA

Auroa

Oroatera

Tauini Hira
          Anae

Tiaraunu

Motu Aie

Honuea   L a g o o n

AIRSTRIP HOTEL

Onetahi   Rimatuu

Tahuna
Rahi

Tahuna
Iti

0   2 mi

0   2 km   Reiono

© DAVID STANLEY

Tetiaroa has been seriously neglected as a result. Brando is seldom present on Tetiaroa these days, and when he's on the atoll, it's closed to tourists.

Getting There

A reservation office (Maimiti Teriipaia, tel. 82-63-02, fax 85-00-51) in the Air Moorea terminal at Faa'a International Airport arranges flights to Tetiaroa. A seven-hour day trip, including airfare, bird island tour, and lunch is CFP 24,800 pp. If you arrange this trip through your hotel, their commission will inflate the price. To stay in one of the 14 thatched bungalows at the **Hôtel Tetiaroa Village** costs CFP 32,900/59,600/77,400 single/double/triple plus tax for a one-night package, or CFP 42,900/79,800/110,700 for a two-night package, air ticket, bungalow, meals, and excursion included. If you arrive in the morning you must also leave in the morning.

Yachts and catamarans tied up opposite the Vaima Center offer day trips to Tetiaroa and their departure times and rates are posted. Prices vary according to whether lunch is included and the quality of the boat. (See Transportation in the Papeete section for listings of day cruises to Tetiaroa.) On all of the boat trips from Papeete, be aware that up to three hours will be spent traveling each way and on a day trip you'll have only about four hours on the atoll. The boat trip tends to be rough and many people throw up their fancy lunch on the way back to Papeete. (In 1995 Marlon Brando won a lawsuit to prohibit "floating hotels" in the Tetiaroa lagoon, so overnight trips are now only possible for those staying at the Hôtel Tetiaroa Village.)

Cruising yachts with careless captains sometimes make an unscheduled stop at low-lying Tetiaroa as it's directly on the approach to Papeete from Hawaii. Several good boats have ended their days here.

FRENCH POLYNESIA

Moorea

Moorea, Tahiti's heart-shaped sister island, is clearly visible across the Sea of the Moon, just 21 km northwest of Papeete. This enticing island offers the white-sand beaches rare on Tahiti, plus long, deep bays, lush volcanic peaks, and a broad blue-green lagoon. Much more than Tahiti, Moorea is the laid-back South Sea isle of the travel brochures. And while Bora Bora has a reputation as Polynesia's most beautiful island, easily accessible Moorea seems more worthy of the distinction (and it's a lot less expensive too). When Papeete starts to get to you, Moorea is only a hop away.

With a population of just 12,000, Moorea lives a quiet, relaxed lifestyle; coconut, pineapple, and vanilla plantations alternate with pleasant resorts and the vegetation-draped dwellings of the inhabitants. Tourism is concentrated along the north coast around Paopao and Tiahura; many of the locals live in the more spacious south. Yet like Bora Bora, Moorea is in danger of becoming overdeveloped and traffic already roars along the north coastal road all day. The choicest sections of shoreline have been barricaded by luxury resorts. On the plus side, most of the hotels are clusters of thatched bungalows, and you won't find many of the monstrous steel, glass, and cement edifices that

MOOREA HIGHLIGHTS

Cook's Bay: scenery, restaurants, shopping
Marae Titiroa: archaeology, nature, spirits
Belvédère: viewpoint, hiking
Dolphin watch: whale- and dolphin-watching tour
rays and sharks: snorkeling, diving, marinelife

scream at you in Hawaii. Still, the accommodations are plentiful and good, and weekly and monthly rentals make even extended stays possible. Don't try to see Moorea as a day trip from Tahiti: this is a place to relax!

The Land

This triangular, 125-square-km island is actually the surviving southern rim of a shield volcano once 3,000 meters high. Moorea is twice as old as its Windward partner, Tahiti, and weathering is noticeably advanced. Two spectacular bays cut into the north coast on each side of Mt. Rotui (899 meters), once Moorea's core. The crescent of jagged peaks facing these long northern bays is scenically superb.

A hole right through the summit of Mt. Mouaputa (830 meters) is said to have been made by the spear of the demigod Pai, who tossed it across from Tahiti to prevent Mt. Rotui from being carried off to Raiatea by Hiro, the god of thieves.

Shark tooth shaped Mouaroa (880 meters) is a visual triumph, but Mt. Tohivea (1,207 meters) is higher. Polynesian chiefs were once buried in caves along the cliffs. Moorea's peaks protect the north and northwest coasts from the rain-bearing southeast trades; the drier climate and scenic beauty explain the profusion of hotels along this side of the island. Moorea is surrounded by a coral ring with several passes into the lagoon. Three *motu* enhance the lagoon, one off Afareaitu and two off Club Med.

Moorea's interior valley slopes are unusually rich, with large fruit and vegetable plantations and human habitation. At one time or another, coconuts, sugarcane, cotton, vanilla, coffee, rice, and pineapples have all been grown in the rich soil of Moorea's plantations. Stock farming and

fishing are other occupations. Vegetables such as taro, cucumbers, pumpkins, and lettuce, and fruit such as bananas, oranges, grapefruit, papaya, star apples, rambutans, avocados, tomatoes, mangoes, limes, tangerines, and breadfruit make Moorea a veritable Garden of Eden.

History

Legend claims that Aimeho (or "Eimeo," as Captain Cook spelled it) was formed from the second dorsal fin of the fish that became Tahiti. The present name, Moorea, means "yellow" *(rea)* "lizard" *(moo)* for a yellow lizard that appeared to a high priest in a dream. It has also been called Fe'e or "octopus" for the eight ridges that divide the island into eight segments. A hole right through the summit of Mt. Mouaputa (830 meters) is said to have been made by the spear of the demigod Pai, who tossed it across from Tahiti to prevent Mt. Rotui from being carried off to Raiatea by Hiro, the god of thieves.

Captain Samuel Wallis was the European discoverer of the Windward Islands in 1767. After leaving Tahiti, he passed along the

MONOÏ OIL

The Maohi women produce monoï by squeezing coconut pulp to liberate the oil, which is then allowed to cure for several weeks. Blossoms of the *tiare Tahiti,* a white-petaled flower often used as a symbol of Tahiti, are added to the oil to give it a special fragrance. Monoï is judged by its fluidity and purity, and it's primarily a skin conditioner used as a moisturizer after showers or in traditional Polynesian massage. On Tahiti, newborn babies are bathed in monoï rather than water during their first month of life. Monoï is also a sure remedy for dry hair. It doesn't prevent sunburn and can even magnify the sun's rays, but it does provide instant relief for sunburned skin.

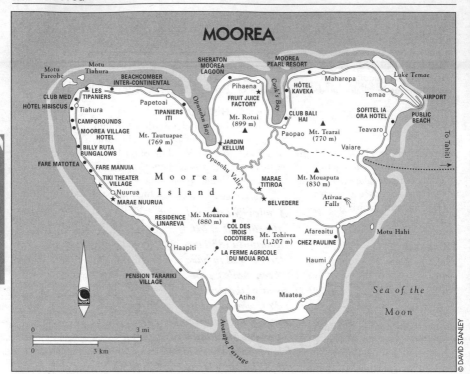

MOOREA

Motu Fareohe   Motu Tiahura

SHERATON
MOOREA
LAGOON

MOOREA
PEARL RESORT

BEACHCOMBER
INTER-CONTINENTAL

Lake Temae

CLUB MED   LES TIPANIERS

HÔTEL HIBISCUS   Tiahura

Papetoai

Pihaena

Maharepa

HÔTEL KAVEKA

Temae

AIRPORT

TIPANIERS ITI

FRUIT JUICE FACTORY

Cook's Bay

SOFITEL IA ORA HOTEL

PUBLIC BEACH

CAMPGROUNDS

MOOREA VILLAGE HOTEL

Mt. Tautuapae
(769 m)

Mt. Rotui
(899 m)

CLUB BALI HAI

Mt. Tearai
(770 m)

Teavaro

To Tahiti

JARDIN KELLUM

Paopao

BILLY RUTA BUNGALOWS

FARE MATOTEA   FARE MANUIA

Moorea Island

Opunohu Valley

Opunohu Bay

Vaiare

MARAE TITIROA

Mt. Mouaputa
(830 m)

TIKI THEATER VILLAGE

Nuurua

MARAE NUURUA

BELVEDERE

Atiraa Falls

Motu Hahi

RESIDENCE LINAREVA

Mt. Mouaroa
(880 m)

COL DES TROIS COCOTIERS

Mt. Tohivea
(1,207 m)

Afareaitu

CHEZ PAULINE

Haapiti

LA FERME AGRICOLE DU MOUA ROA

Haumi

PENSION TARARIKI VILLAGE

MOON

Atiha

Maatea

Sea of the Moon

Avarapa Passage

0   3 mi
0   3 km

© DAVID STANLEY

north coast of Moorea without landing. He named it Duke of York's Island. The first European visitors were botanist Joseph Banks, Lieutenant Gore, the surgeon William Monkhouse, and Herman Sporie. Captain Cook anchored in Opunohu Bay for one week in 1777, but he never visited the bay that today bears his name! His visit was uncharacteristically brutal, as he smashed the islanders' canoes and burned their homes when they refused to return a stolen goat.

In 1792 Pomare I conquered Moorea using arms obtained from the *Bounty* mutineers. Moorea had long been a traditional place of refuge for defeated Tahitian warriors, thus in 1808 Pomare II fled into exile here after his bid to bring all Tahiti under his control failed. A party of English missionaries established themselves at Papetoai in 1811, and Moorea soon earned a special place in the history of

Christianity: here in 1812 the missionaries finally managed to convert Pomare II after 15 years of trying. On February 14, 1815, Patii, high priest of Oro, publicly accepted Protestantism and burned the old heathen idols at Papetoai, where the octagonal church is today. Shortly afterward the whole population followed Patii's example. The *marae* of Moorea were then abandoned and the Opunohu Valley depopulated. The first Tahitian translation of part of the Bible was printed on Moorea in 1817. From this island Protestantism spread throughout the South Pacific.

After Pomare II finally managed to reconquer Tahiti in 1815 with missionary help (the main reason for his "conversion"), Moorea again became a backwater. American novelist Herman Melville visited Moorea in 1842 and worked with other beachcombers on a sweet-potato farm in Maatea. His book *Omoo* contains a marvelous description of his tour of the island. Cotton and coconut plantations were created on Moorea in the 19th century, followed by vanilla and coffee in the 20th, but only with the advent of the travel industry has Moorea become more than a beautiful backdrop for Tahiti.

Orientation

If you arrive by ferry you'll probably get off at Vaiare, four km south of Temae Airport. Your hotel may be at Maharepa (Moorea Pearl Resort), Paopao (Club Bali Hai, Motel Albert), Pihaena (Sheraton Moorea Lagoon), or Tiahura (Club Med, the campgrounds, Hôtel Moorea Village), all on the north coast. The Paopao hotels enjoy better scenery, but the beach is far superior at Tiahura. Add a CFP 150 pp per day municipal services tax to the accommodations prices quoted below.

The PKs (kilometer stones) on Moorea are measured in both directions from PK 0 at the access road to Temae Airport. They're numbered up to PK 35 along the north coast via Club Med and up to PK 24 along the south coast via Afareaitu, meeting at Haapiti halfway around the island.

Our circle-island tour and the accommodations and restaurant listings below begin at Vaiare Wharf and go counterclockwise around the island in each category.

Sights of Moorea

Northeast Moorea

You'll probably arrive on Moorea at **Vaiare Wharf,** which is officially PK 4 on the 59-km road around the island. To the north is the **Sofitel Ia Ora** (PK 1.3), built in the mid-1970s. If you have your own transport, stop for a look around the resort and a swim. It's also enjoyable to walk north along the beach from this hotel or even to go snorkeling. At PK 1 on the main road, high above the Ia Ora, is the fine **Toatea Lookout** over the deep passage, romantically named the Sea of the Moon, between Tahiti and Moorea.

One of the only public beach parks on Moorea is at **Temae,** about a km down a gravel road to the right a bit before you reach the airport access road. Watch out for black spiny sea urchins here. The Temae area is a former *motu* now linked to the main island and surfers will find an excellent long right wave around the point next to the airstrip. There's good snorkeling here.

In 2002 the territorial government approved tax exemptions for a US$75 million 18-hole golf course and 150-room five-star hotel in this area, so watch out for construction. But don't take this for granted as Moorea residents have fought long and hard against golf courses and other tourism developments that strain the island's limited resources. In 1991 Moorea voters rejected a proposal to build an Arnold Palmer golf course and Sheraton hotel in the unspoiled Opunohu Valley. Moves to sweep sand from the lagoon to create artificial beaches at resorts have also been strongly opposed.

Around Cook's Bay

At PK 5.4 just west of the Moorea Pearl Resort on the mountain side of the road is the "White House," the stately mansion of a former vanilla plantation, now used as a pareu salesroom.

At the entrance to Cook's Bay (PK 7) is the **Galerie Aad Van der Heyde** (tel. 56-14-22), as much a museum as a gallery. Aad's paintings hang outside in the flower-filled courtyard; inside are his black-pearl jewelry, a large collection of Marquesan sculpture, and more paintings. The mock-colonial **Cook's Bay Resort Hôtel** at PK 7.2 is closed at present but it belongs to the same crowd that owns French Polynesia's three Sheratons and may be redeveloped eventually.

Paopao is the capital of Moorea with the gendarmerie, mairie, and several supermarkets serving the local community. The **Fish Market** is worth a stop to admire the large wall painting of a market scene by François Ravello. The fish market itself only opens Sunday 0500–0800. The catamaran *Ono-Ono* discharges passengers from Papeete here.

A rough four-km dirt road up to the paved Belvédère viewpoint road begins just west of the

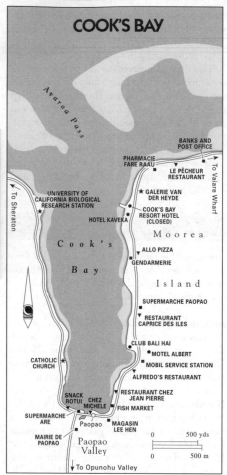

COOK'S BAY

Avaroa Pass

BANKS AND POST OFFICE
PHARMACIE FARE RAAU
LE PÊCHEUR RESTAURANT
To Vaiare Wharf
★ GALERIE VAN DER HEYDE
UNIVERSITY OF CALIFORNIA BIOLOGICAL RESEARCH STATION
COOK'S BAY RESORT HOTEL (CLOSED)
HOTEL KAVEKA
To Sheraton
Moorea
Cook's
▼ ALLO PIZZA
GENDARMERIE
Bay
Island
▼ SUPERMARCHE PAOPAO
▼ RESTAURANT CAPRICE DES ILES
★ CLUB BALI HAI
● MOTEL ALBERT
■ MOBIL SERVICE STATION
CATHOLIC CHURCH ★
ALFREDO'S RESTAURANT
RESTAURANT CHEZ JEAN PIERRE
SNACK ROTUI ▼ CHEZ MICHELE ■ FISH MARKET
SUPERMARCHE ARE
Paopao
MAGASIN LEE HEN
MAIRIE DE PAOPAO
Paopao Valley
0   500 yds
0   500 m
↓ To Opunohu Valley

© DAVID STANLEY

bridge at Paopao (PK 9), and it's nice to hike up past the pineapple plantations. This is a good shortcut to the Opunohu Valley easily covered by rental car or worth a walk.

On the west side of Cook's Bay, a km farther along the north-coast highway, is a new **Catholic church** (PK 10). In the older St. Joseph's Church next door is an interesting altar painting with Polynesian angels done by the Swedish artist Peter Heyman in 1948. Unfortunately this building is usually closed.

It's possible to visit the Distillerie de Moorea

fruit-juice factory (tel. 56-11-33, fax 56-21-52), 300 meters up off the main road at PK 12. Aside from the excellent papaya, grapefruit, and pineapple juices made from local fruits, the factory produces apple, orange, and passion fruit juices from imported concentrate, with no preservatives added. It also makes 40-proof brandies (carambola or "star fruit," ginger, grapefruit, mango, orange, and pineapple flavors) and 25-proof liqueurs (coconut, ginger, and pineapple varieties). These are for sale, and if the staff thinks you might buy a bottle, they'll invite you to sample the brews (no free samples for obvious backpackers). The sales room is open weekdays 0830–1630, but the factory 0800–1400 only.

Opunohu Bay to Le Belvédère

The Hôtel Sheraton Moorea Lagoon at PK 14 is the only large hotel between Paopao and Tiahura. A trail up **Mt. Rotui** (899 meters) begins opposite the "Faimano Village" accommodations nearby. Go up the driveway directly opposite Faimano Village and turn right before the house on the hill. A red arrow painted on a coconut tree points the way, but you may have to contend with the local dogs as you start up the hill. Once up behind the house the trail swings right and onto the ridge, which you follow to the summit. The land at the trailhead belongs to the Faimano Village's owner and he doesn't mind climbers, but you should ask permission to proceed of anyone you happen to meet near the house. From on top you'll have a sweeping view of the entire north coast. It's better not to go alone as there are vertical drops from the ridge and steep rocks in places, and after rains the trail could be dangerous. This is not a climb to be undertaken lightly.

Reader Greg Sawyer of Lafayette, Indiana, sent us this:

> *The trail up Mt. Rotui is quite strenuous but you're rewarded with billion-dollar views. It should be attempted in fair weather only, as it follows a razorback ridge quite narrow in places. In the rain it would be dangerous. Start very early and allow most of a day to really enjoy the trail and*

© M.E. DE VOS

view of Cook's Bay from Hôtel Kaveka

views (though fit people could push it through in four to five hours return). Mt. Rotui is Moorea's second-highest peak, and lies alone between the two bays on the north shore. There's little shade and no water but there are a couple of fixed ropes near the top at a couple of short steep pitches. Take care. The trail is not maintained but it's easy to follow once found. Just get to and stay on the ridgeline.

At PK 17.5 is the **Jardin Kellum Stop** (tel. 56-18-52), a tropical garden along Opunohu Bay with a colonial-style house built in 1925. Marie Kellum is an amateur archaeologist whose personal collection is full of interest and she can tell you anything you need to know about Tahitian medicinal plants. Until 1962 the Kellum family owned most of the Opunohu Valley. The garden is open Wednesday–Saturday mornings until noon. Ring the cow bell on the gate—it's CFP 500 pp admission. A famous yacht anchorage called Robinson's Cove is just offshore. Moorea residents have had to fight a running battle with developers to keep Opunohu Bay the way it is, and from the unspoiled surroundings it's easy to

understand why the 1984 remake of *The Bounty* was filmed here.

Freshwater shrimp are bred in large basins at the head of Opunohu Bay (PK 18). From here a paved five-km side road runs up the largely uninhabited **Opunohu Valley** to the Belvédère view point. After two km you reach the junction with the dirt connecting road from Cook's Bay previously mentioned, then another km up and on the right is the **Lycée Professionnel Agricole**, Moorea's agricultural high school. This worthy institution, with students from all the islands of French Polynesia, has hundreds of hectares planted in pineapples, vanilla, coffee, fruit trees, decorative flowers, and native vegetables on land seized from a German company in 1914.

Another km above this is **Marae Titiroa**, largest of a group of Polynesian temples restored in 1969 by Professor Y. H. Sinoto of Honolulu. The small platform or *ahu* at the end of this *marae* was a sacred area reserved for the gods, and stone backrests for chiefs and priests are also seen. Here the people offered gifts of tubers, fish, dogs, and pigs, and prayed to their gods, many of whom were deified ancestors. Near the water

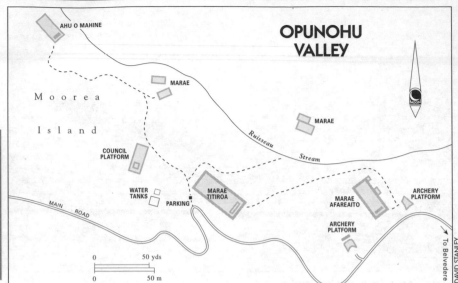

OPUNOHU VALLEY

AHU O MAHINE

MARAE

MARAE

Moorea

Island

COUNCIL PLATFORM

Ruisseau Stream

WATER TANKS

PARKING

MARAE TITIROA

MARAE AFAREAITO

ARCHERY PLATFORM

ARCHERY PLATFORM

MAIN ROAD

To Belvedere

© DAVID STANLEY

0   50 yds
0   50 m

tanks just 50 meters northwest of Marae Titiroa is a long council platform, and 50 meters farther are two smaller *marae* surrounded by towering Tahitian chestnut trees *(mape)*. The most evocative of the group is four-tiered **Marae Ahu o Mahine,** about 250 meters down the trail.

About 500 ancient structures have been identified in this area, and if you're very keen, you should be able to find a few in the forest across the stream, evidence of a large population with a highly developed social system. Following the acceptance of Christianity in the early 19th century, the Opunohu Valley's importance declined sharply. Today lots of side trails lead nowhere in particular but you'll discover many crumbling *marae* walls. Naturalists will enjoy the natural vegetation.

Continue up the main road from Marae Titiroa about 200 meters and watch for some stone **archery platforms** on the left. Here kneeling nobles once competed to see who could shoot an arrow the farthest. The bows and arrows employed in these contests were never used in warfare. Just up on the left is access to another archery platform and **Marae Afareaito.** The stone slabs you see sticking up in the middle of the *marae* were backrests for participants of honor.

From the archaeological area the winding road climbs steeply another km to the **Belvédère,** or Roto Nui, a viewpoint high up near the geographical center of the island. Much of northern Moorea is visible from here and it's easy to visualize the great volcano that once existed. Mt. Rotui (899 meters) in front of you was once the central core of an island more than three times as high as the present. The north part is now missing, but the semicircular arch of the southern half is plain to see. (An ice cream from the *roulotte* in the parking lot may be a welcome treat.)

Although most easily toured by rental car, this intriguing area can also be explored on foot. If you're staying anywhere around Cook's Bay, begin by hiking up the four-km dirt road from the bridge in Paopao. If staying at Tiahura, take the boat bus to Cook's Bay to get started. After "doing" the *marae* and Belvédère, walk down the Opunohu Valley road if you're returning to Tiahura. For experienced hikers, a trail through the bush to Paopao begins at the rear left corner of the Belvédère parking lot. (Don't take a left turn near three pine trees as this branch only returns to the *marae.*) Carry lots of water and a picnic lunch and make a day of it.

Papetoai to Club Med

Back down on the coastal highway, continue west along Opunohu Bay. **Papetoai** (PK 22) is the oldest village on Moorea, where all the early explorers and missionaries initially came. The octagonal Protestant church behind the post office was built on the site of the temple of the god Oro in 1822. Despite having been rebuilt several times, the church is known as "the oldest European building still in use in the South Pacific."

At **Tiahura** the road begins to curve around the northwest corner of Moorea, passing a number of large resorts, including the Beachcomber Inter-Continental (PK 24.5), Club Med (PK 26.5), and the Hôtel Moorea Village (PK 27.9). Unfortunately, there are no public beaches anywhere along here, so walk through the grounds of one of the hotels. The beach at Tiahura looks nice but the water is rather shallow unless you go far out. The scuba operators or recreation people at the resorts will ferry you over to much better snorkeling areas off small islands such as Tarahu and Tiahuru for a fee. For example, Scubapiti at Hôtel Les Tipaniers charges CFP 700 pp round-trip for *motu* transfers. There's excellent reef break surfing in Taotai Pass off the Inter-Continental.

Patrice Bredel's **Galerie Api** (tel. 56-13-57, fax 56-28-27; Mon.–Sat. 1000–1200/1430–1730), in a stunning location overlooking the lagoon northeast of Club Med, displays the works of the late François Ravello, who painted in a Gauguin-like style. Bredel's personal collection of old Pacific artifacts is fascinating.

In **Le Petit Village** shopping mall, across the street from Club Med, are a tourist information kiosk, bank, grocery store, snack bar, gas station, and many tourist shops. Drop into **Pai Moana Pearls** (tel. 56-25-25) between Club Med and Le Petit Village and ask for a free copy of owner Rick Steger's excellent brochure on pricing pearls. **Roonui Tattoo** (Roonui Mercer, tel. 56-37-53), opposite Club Med, does some beautiful work if you'd like a lifelong souvenir.

Southern Moorea

The south coast of Moorea is much quieter than the north. You'll drive for kilometers through the open coconut plantations past unspoiled villages and scenic vistas. At PK 31 is **Tiki Theater Village** (described in Cultural Shows for Visitors later in this chapter), the only one of its kind in the territory. Just past the Fire Department at PK 31.5 Haapiti is **Marae Nuurua,** on the beach across the soccer field. This three-tiered *marae* restored in 1991 bears a petroglyph of a turtle, and beyond is the much higher rubble heap of an unrestored *marae.*

At PK 33 you can have your photo taken in front of a huge concrete Tahitian warrior! You might also stop for an upmarket lunch or a drink at **Résidence Linareva** (PK 34). The Linareva's upscale floating seafood restaurant, the *Tamarii Moorea I,* is an old ferryboat that once plied between Moorea and Tahiti. Colorful reef fish swim around the dock, which also affords an excellent mountain view.

At PK 35/24, Haapiti, the kilometer numbering begins its descent to Temae Airport. The twin-towered **Église de la Sainte Famille** (1891) at Haapiti was once the head church of the Catholic mission on the island. There's good anchorage here for yachts entering Matauvau Pass and a tall left hander for the surfers out there.

Tiny Motu Hahi lies just off **Afareaitu** (PK 9), the administrative center of southern Moorea. After Papetoai, this was the second center of missionary activity on Moorea, and on June 30, 1817, at the printing works at Afareaitu, King Pomare II ceremonially printed the first page of the first book ever published on a South Pacific island, a Tahitian translation of the Gospel of St. Luke. Before the press was moved to Huahine a year later, more than 9,000 books totaling more than half a million pages had been printed at Afareaitu! After 1821 the London Missionary Society established its Academy of the South Seas here to instruct the children of the missionaries and the Tahitian chiefs.

From opposite the old Protestant church (1912) in Afareaitu, the road between Magasin Ah Sing and a school leads up the **Afareaitu Valley** to a high waterfall, which cascades down a sheer cliff into a pool, a one-hour walk. You can drive a car two-thirds of the way up the valley. Park at the point where a normal car would have problems and hike on up the road to the right. When this road begins to climb steeply, look for a well-beaten

174 Moorea

footpath on the right, which will take you directly to the falls. You'll need a bit of intuition to find the unmarked way on your own.

You get a good view of **Mt. Mouaputa,** the peak pierced by Pai's spear, from the hospital just north of Afareaitu. The first road inland north of the hospital leads to a different waterfall, **Atiraa Falls.** The access road is very rough, so park just before a small concrete bridge and continue the 30-minute hike on foot.

Across the Island

An excellent day hike involves taking a morning bus to Vaiare Wharf, then hiking over the mountains to Paopao. From there you can catch another bus back to your accommodations, or try hitching. The shaded three-hour trail, partly marked by red, white, and green paint dabbed on tree and rock, does demand attention and perseverance, however. There are a few steep ascents and descents, and after rains it can be muddy and slippery.

Take the road inland beside Magasin Chez Meno, about 50 meters south of the first bridge south of the Vaiare ferry wharf. As you follow the dirt road up the valley, you'll take two forks to the right. Don't cross the stream after the second fork but go left and walk past some houses, just beyond which is an old Polynesian *marae* on the left. Farther along you cross the stream and continue past a number of local gardens. The trail to Paopao leads off to the left near the last garden, and once you're on it it's fairly easy to follow if you keep your eyes open. When you see an old stone stairway on the left five minutes after leaving the gardens you'll know you're on the correct trail. All of the locals know about this trail and if you say "Paopao?" to them in a questioning way, they'll point you in the right direction.

When you reach the divide, go a short distance south along the ridge to a super viewpoint. On a clear day the rounded double peak of Orohena, Tahiti's highest, will be visible, plus the whole interior of Moorea. On the way down the other side avoid taking the wrong turn at a bamboo grove. You'll come out among the pineapple plantations of central Moorea behind Paopao. It's not possible to do this hike eastbound from Paopao to Vaiare without a guide, but westbound an experienced hiker should have no difficulty, and it's worth going simply to see a good cross section of the vegetation. Take water and wear sturdy shoes.

Transportation-wise, the easiest way to do this hike is as a day trip from Tahiti! If you take an early ferry from Papeete to Vaiare, you'll have ample time to do the hike before catching the afternoon *Ono-Ono* sailing back to Tahiti from Cook's Bay. The last departure from Paopao to Papeete is just after 1600 daily (check the exact time before leaving Papeete).

SPORTS AND RECREATION

TOPdive (Philippe Molle, tel. 56-17-32, fax 56-15-83), also known as M.U.S.T. Plongée, is centrally located near the Hôtel Kaveka on Cook's Bay. It offers diving daily at 0800, 1000, and 1400 for CFP 6,500/58,500 for one/10 dives. Guests at some hotels (such as the Kaveka and Hibiscus) are given a 15 percent discount.

Juan Pedro Duran's **Bathy's Club** (tel. 56-31-44, fax 56-38-10), at the Beachcomber Inter-Continental, offers scuba diving for CFP 5,500, plus CFP 1,500 for gear. This is the only PADI five-star facility in the territory, a classy and genuinely helpful outfit. Bathy's and TOPdive do underwater fish, eel, ray, and shark feeding. At sites such as The Tiki the swarm of fish sometimes becomes so thick the guide is lost from sight, yet as the resident shark scatters the mass of fish to steal the bait, the divemaster is seen again patting *le requin* as it passes.

Scubapiti (Daniel Cailleux, tel./fax 56-20-38), at Hôtel Les Tipaniers at Tiahura, offers scuba diving daily at 0800 and 1400 (CFP 5,000). Instead of putting on a show, Daniel keeps things natural on his cave, canyon, and drift dives. Shark feeding and other gimmicks are not offered. He also offers PADI or CMAS scuba certification courses (CFP 30,000) and free hotel transfers from anywhere in northwestern Moorea.

Moorea's only female divemaster, Pascale Souquieres, runs **Moorea Fun Dive** (tel. 56-40-38, tel./fax 56-40-74) at the Hôtel Moorea Village and the Sofitel Ia Ora. It's CFP 5,300 a dive or CFP 4,800 a dive for five dives or more including all gear (except a wetsuit). Ocean dives are at 0830 and 1400, lagoon diving at 1030, and hotel pickups are available from almost anywhere on northern Moorea. This is a professional yet laid-back operation we can recommend.

The "Activities Nautiques" kiosk on the wharf at the **Beachcomber Inter-Continental** (tel. 55-19-19) rents personal watercraft or "wave runners" at CFP 7,750 for half an hour, CFP 12,180 for one hour, or try your hand at parasailing (CFP 6,460).

Surfing is possible in most of the passes around the island or off the beach next to the airstrip, but it's not quite as good as on Tahiti or Huahine. A boat or a long paddle is required to reach the reef breaks. Surfers often stay at Pension Tarariki Village on the south side of the island.

Deep-sea fishing is offered by **Tea Nui Charters** (Chris Lilley, tel./fax 56-15-08), based at the Beachcomber Inter-Continental, at CFP 15,000 pp for a half/full day (four-person minimum).

Tiahura Ranch (tel. 56-28-55), across the highway from the Hôtel Moorea Village, offers horseback riding at 0845 and 1545 daily except Monday (CFP 5,000 for two hours). You must reserve at least an hour in advance.

Rupe-Rupe Ranch (tel. 56-26-52), at PK 2 between Vaiare Wharf and the Sofitel Ia Ora, also offers horseback riding. It's best to call ahead as often no one is there.

Practicalities

ACCOMMODATIONS

Camping

One of the South Pacific's nicest campgrounds is **Camping Chez Nelson** (Nelson and Josiane Flohr, tel. 56-15-18), near the Hôtel Hibiscus, just south of Club Med (PK 27, Tiahura). It's beautifully set in a coconut grove right on the beach. The camping charge is CFP 1,100 pp, with recently upgraded toilets, showers, refrigerator, and communal cooking facilities provided. No tents are for rent, but the 10 two-bed "dormitory" rooms go for CFP 1,300 pp (CFP 1,600 for one night). The five cabins are CFP 2,800 single or double (CFP 3,400 for one night); four larger rooms in a long building near the office are CFP 3,800 single or double (CFP 4,300 for one night). The sunset cabin near the beach is CFP 4,000 (CFP 4,500 for one night). Kayaks and bicycles are for rent. The campground office is open only Monday–Saturday 0800–1800, Sunday 0800–1130. Josiane can be rather reserved at first, but she has a heart of gold. This place is clean, quiet, breezy, spacious, and well equipped, but don't leave valuables unattended or within reach of an open window at night.

A second campground is just a little south of Chez Nelson, near the Hôtel Moorea Village. Friendly **Moorea Camping** (tel. 56-14-47, fax 56-30-22), also known as "Chez Viri et Claude," faces the same white-sand beach and has nine four-bed dorms at CFP 1,200 pp (CFP 1,800 for one night), plus another 10 double rooms in a long building at CFP 2,400 single or double (CFP 3,400 for one night). The five beachfront bungalows are CFP 4,500 single or double (CFP 5,500 for one night). Camping is CFP 1,000 pp (CFP 1,200 for one night). All rooms at both campgrounds have shared bath only and French residents of Papeete often book all of the better units on weekends. The reception is open 0800–1200/1330–1700 only (closed Sunday afternoon). Communal kitchen and washing facilities are provided but sheets are not supplied in the dormitory. For CFP 1,500 pp they'll take you to a *motu* and their shark-feeding tours are very good. One-person kayaks are for rent at CFP 500/1,000 an hour/four hours. Bicycles are CFP 1,300 for eight hours. But as at Chez Nelson, we've heard of things going missing from the dorms, so take precautions. Both campgrounds are great for young low-budget travelers and other adventurers—you'll meet some wonderful people. Two grocery stores (with cold beer) are between the two camping grounds.

FRENCH POLYNESIA

US$25–50

Motel Albert (Iris Haring, tel. 56-12-76, fax 56-58-58), on the slope opposite Club Bali Hai at Paopao (PK 8.5), catches splendid views across Cook's Bay. The four older apartments with one double bed, kitchen, and private bath are CFP 4,000 single or double, while four larger apartments with two double beds, kitchen, and private bath are CFP 5,000 double or triple (two-night minimum stay). The 10 two-bedroom bungalows with kitchen and private bath are CFP 8,000 for up to four people. The larger apartments are often taken by monthly rentals at CFP 150,000. Each unit has cooking facilities, fridge, and hot water in a garden setting on spacious grounds. Several stores are nearby and the Mobil service station next door sells bread and groceries. It's excellent value and often full (try to make reservations).

Chez Dina (Dina Dhieux, tel./fax 56-10-39) is behind Magasin Pihaena at PK 13, Pihaena, a km east of the Sheraton. The three thatched bungalows are CFP 5,500 double, CFP 6,500 for up to four (reductions on a weekly basis). Cooking facilities are provided, and the bathroom is communal.

One of the least expensive places to stay is **Te Fare Oa Oa** (tel. 56-25-17) at Pihaena, directly behind the PK 13 marker. It's down the road inland from Jean-Marc Fouchegu Avocat. Ask for Hervé. The four rooms with shared bath in a pleasant A-frame house are CFP 2,200/12,000/43,100 a day/week/month. Shared cooking facilities are provided.

Billy Ruta Bungalows (tel. 56-12-54) at PK 28.3, Tiahura, has 12 thatched A-frame bungalows lined up along the beach, beginning at CFP 5,000 double without kitchenette, CFP 6,000 double with kitchen. They're rented to French workers who pay by the month (CFP 65,000) and are often full. Another eight rooms in a long block with shared bath are CFP 3,000 single or double, but they're noisy because of permanent Tahitian residents who get up very early. On Saturday night, be prepared for disco dancing in an adjacent club until very late. Billy runs the local bus service and is a very friendly guy. You'll find him in the house on the opposite side of the disco from the bungalows.

Pension Tarariki Village (tel./fax 56-35-83) at PK 21.5, Haapiti, has four bungalows with private bath at CFP 7,520 single or double, one bungalow with shared bath at CFP 5,400, a tiny individual cabin at CFP 2,000, and a common dorm at CFP 1,600 pp. There's a nice secluded beach below the pension's large treehouse and it's only a couple of km to the pass for surfing. May–October the owner provides boat transfers to Haapiti Pass for surfers at CFP 2,000 for one or two, plus CFP 1,000 each additional person. A grocery store is nearby.

La Ferme Agricole du Moua Roa (Marie-Thérèse Buisson, tel./fax 56-58-62), off the south coast road at PK 21 between Haapiti and Maatea, is used mainly to accommodate school groups. This large colonial mansion has nine four-bed dorms at CFP 2,000 pp, plus CFP 3,000 pp for an organic breakfast and dinner. This hiking base camp is a 45-minute walk up a rough jeep track, which begins next to a Mormon church. Guests are not allowed to drive in and must arrive on foot. You can climb most of Moorea's mountains from here.

Chez Pauline (Jean-Pierre Bouvier, tel./fax 83-71-21) at PK 9, Afareaitu, is between the two stores near the church. It's a lovely old colonial house with five rooms with double beds and shared bath at CFP 4,000/5,500/7,000 single/double/triple including breakfast. One larger room sleeping five is CFP 12,000. A picturesque restaurant with tikis on display rounds out this establishment, which has great atmosphere. Dinner here is around CFP 3,800 (fish and Tahitian vegetables) and it must be ordered in advance.

US$50–100

The **Hôtel Kaveka** (tel. 56-50-50, fax 56-52-63), PK 7.4 at the east entrance to Cook's Bay, has 24 wooden bungalows with fridge from CFP 9,800–23,800 double including tax. You'll need to burn a mosquito coil at night. The breakfast and dinner plan in the thatched restaurant is CFP 3,900 pp extra. The snorkeling is fine off the small artificial beach and there's a great view of Cook's Bay.

Several small places rent bungalows near the Hôtel Sheraton Moorea Lagoon, PK 14, Pihaena.

Chez Nani (Maeva Bougues, tel./fax 56-19-99) on the west side of the resort has three thatched bungalows with kitchenettes at CFP 8,000 single or double. The signposted **Faimano Village** (Faimano and Denis Feildel, tel. 56-10-20, fax 56-36-47), next to Chez Nani, has seven lovely thatched *fare* with cooking facilities at CFP 12,500 for up to six people or CFP 8,500/10,500 double/triple plus 6 percent tax (three-night minimum stay). Faimano Village has a nice garden setting facing the beach and easygoing atmosphere, but single women should avoid it as there have been reports of prowlers. The doors and windows cannot be properly locked. **Chez Francine** (Francine Lumen, tel./fax 56-13-24), 400 meters farther west, doesn't have a sign but look for three buildings with red tile roofs between the highway and the shore. A two-room house is CFP 8,500 double with kitchenette or CFP 6,500 double without kitchenette. The beach and view are excellent.

Repeat visitors to Moorea often stay at **Hôtel Tipaniers Iti** (tel. 56-12-67) at PK 21, Papetoai, on the west side of Opunohu Bay. It's a low-key place with five tin-roofed, self-catering bungalows in a garden setting at CFP 7,900, plus 11 percent tax, for up to four people. Weekly rates are available. There's no beach but the long wooden deck offers great view of the bay. The reception is open 0900–1300 only.

Hôtel Les Tipaniers (Geneviève Lemaire, tel. 56-12-67, fax 56-29-25) at PK 25.9, Tiahura, is cramped around the reception, but spacious and attractive as you approach the beach. The 22 bungalows start at CFP 8,750/10,800 single/double, plus 11 percent tax (the 12 units with kitchen are CFP 13,500 and up). Four garden rooms are CFP 6,300 double. Les Tipaniers' well-known restaurant offers Italian and seafood dishes. The hotel will shuttle you over to a nearby *motu* for snorkeling or lend you a bicycle or outrigger canoe at no charge. This hotel has a good reputation and a resident dive master.

Moorea Fare Auti'ura (Viri Pere, tel. 56-14-47, fax 56-30-22), on the inland side of the road opposite Moorea Camping at PK 27.5, Tiahura, has six thatched bungalows on elevated concrete platforms at CFP 7,000 single or double (mini-

mum stay two nights). Cooking facilities are provided. It's run by Moorea Camping, so check there if nobody seems to be around.

The **Hôtel Moorea Village** (tel. 56-10-02, fax 56-22-11) at PK 27.9, Tiahura, is also known as "Fare Gendron." It offers 70 fan-cooled thatched bungalows beginning at CFP 9,000/10,000 single/double plus 11 percent tax, or CFP 12,500 for up to four people. To be on the beach is another CFP 2,500. The 10 new units with kitchen are double price; all units have fridges. The breakfast and dinner plan costs CFP 4,200 pp but the quality of the food is uneven. Saturday at 1900 there's fire dancing; the Tahitian feast with Polynesian dancing is Sunday at noon. The eel and shark feeding tour is CFP 2,500. This place is somewhat of a hangout for local Tahitians and it's probably your best bet if you like to party.

Fare Matotea (Iris Cabral, tel. 56-14-36, fax 56-32-54), on a spacious beach just south of Billy Ruta (PK 29, Tiahura), is CFP 8,840 for four, CFP 10,400 for six (minimum stay two nights). All nine large thatched *fare* on the spacious grounds have full cooking facilities and private bath. It's a good choice for families and small groups. Very little English is spoken.

Near the south end of the west coast strip (PK 30) is **Fare Manuia** (Jeanne Salmon, tel. 56-26-17, fax 56-10-30) with six *fare* with cooking facilities at CFP 9,500 for up to four people, CFP 12,000 for up to six people, or CFP 15,000 on the beach, plus tax. The minimum stay is two nights. Both this place and Fare Matotea are a little isolated from the restaurants and other facilities of Tiahura.

Résidence Linareva (tel./fax 56-15-35) sits amid splendid mountain scenery at PK 34 on the wild side of the island. Prices begin at CFP 8,700/10,500 single/double and increase to CFP 19,500 double, with 10 percent weekly discounts. Each of the eight units is unique, with TV, fan, and full cooking facilities. Bicycles and an outrigger canoe are loaned free. It's good value.

US$100–150

Club Bali Hai (tel. 56-13-68, fax 56-13-27) at PK 8.5, Paopao, has 20 rooms in the main two-story building starting at CFP 14,000 single or double, plus 19 beachfront or overwater bungalows at CFP 19,000–25,000. A third person pays CFP 4,000 and the 11 percent tax is extra (you may be quoted higher prices in U.S. dollars here). Most rooms have a spectacular view of Cook's Bay. This is the last survivor of the famous Bali Hai hotel chain, which once stretched clear across the Society Islands. To stay afloat, many units have been sold to Americans on a time-share basis, with each owner getting two weeks a year at the Club. There's a swimming pool by the bay. Avis has a desk here.

The **Moorea Beach Club,** next to Hôtel Les Tipaniers at Tiahura, is closed. The owners, Nouvelles Frontières, planned to reopen the property eventually as part of the Paladien chain.

In early 2002 the 350-bungalow **Club Méditerranée** at PK 26.5, Tiahura, closed for major renovations and it's possible it may never open again. Labor costs have cut into Club Med's profitability and a huge investment will be required to bring this property up to the standards of the smaller, smarter Club Med on Bora Bora. It's rumored the Club Med also had problems renewing its lease. At last report Club Med was still saying the Moorea property would reopen in early 2005, so check with its office (tel. 42-96-99, fax 42-16-83) in Papeete's Vaima Center to find out what's happening.

The **Hôtel Hibiscus** (tel. 56-12-20, fax 56-20-69), on the beach right next to Club Med (PK 27, Tiahura), offers 29 thatched bungalows beneath the coconut palms at CFP 13,200 triple in the garden or CFP 15,400 on the beach, plus 11 percent tax. A fourth person is CFP 1,500 extra. There's a 10 percent discount on a weekly basis but air-conditioned units cost more. The breakfast and dinner plan is CFP 4,770 pp, but all units have kitchenettes and fridge so this is a good choice for families. The location adjacent to Club Med has the advantage of fewer bugs due to frequent fumigations at the resort but the disadvantage of occasional noise from the disco. However, as long as Club Med remains closed, these factors don't apply.

Fare Vai Moana (tel./fax 56-17-14) is next to a large restaurant overlooking the beach adjacent to Camping Chez Nelson at PK 27.1, Tiahura.

The 12 attractive thatched bungalows are CFP 12,000 double in the garden or CFP 14,300 facing the beach, plus 11 percent tax. Half board at its seafood restaurant is CFP 3,850 pp.

US$150–250

The **Sofitel Ia Ora** (tel. 55-03-55, fax 56-12-91), at PK 1.3 between Vaiare and the airport, sits on one of the finest beaches on the island with a splendid view of Tahiti. The 110 tastefully furnished thatched bungalows begin at CFP 29,600 single or double, plus 11 percent tax. Upgrade to air-conditioned if possible as many of the older units are inadequately screened. Breakfast and dinner are CFP 6,400 pp extra together. Because the Sofitel is rather isolated some of the Paopao restaurants won't pick up diners here (Le Pêcheur will). Unfortunately, the service at the Ia Ora deteriorates fast when large groups are present. We've heard of local children with improper toilet training using the hotel pool, so keep to the beach. Scuba diving is CFP 6,000/25,000 for one/five dives. There's a Europcar desk in the lobby.

In 2002 the **Moorea Pearl Resort** (tel. 55-17-50, fax 55-17-51) at PK 5.3, Maharepa, was erected on the site of the former Hôtel Bali Hai dating to 1961. The new resort features 30 rooms and suites in a long two-story concrete block with a thatched roof starting at CFP 24,000/29,000 double/triple, 37 garden and beach bungalows from CFP 33,000/38,000, and 28 overwater bungalows on reinforced concrete piles beginning at CFP 59,000/64,000 (children under 13 sleep free). Add 11 percent tax to these rates. Breakfast and dinner are CFP 7,600 pp extra. The Polynesian and seafood buffets are CFP 5,600 pp (or CFP 2,000 if you've bought a meal plan). Many banks, shops, and restaurants are only a short walk away.

A good alternative to the large resorts is family-style **Pension Anahoa** (tel. 56-35-32), down the street beside Chez Serge at Tiahura. The large two-room bungalows here are CFP 26,500 plus 6 percent tax for up to four people including breakfast. Dinner can be ordered at CFP 2,750 pp plus 10 percent tax. Laurence and Coco are helpful in making restaurant or tour reservations, and they provide outrigger canoes, kayaks, and snorkeling gear free to guests. Ask them where to paddle out to see the manta rays.

US$250 and up

The **Hôtel Sheraton Moorea Lagoon** (tel. 55-11-11, fax 55-11-55) at PK 14, Pihaena, has 52 garden and beach bungalows from CFP 39,900 double, plus 54 overwater bungalows beginning at CFP 74,800, plus 11 percent tax. There's excellent snorkeling offshore, a swimming pool, and a spa. The air-conditioned rooms are well equipped but the entire resort is crowded for the site. The service is surly and the location poor, with no local restaurants nearby. The activities desk tacks a 10 percent surcharge onto anything booked through it. The Sheraton was originally to have been managed by Outrigger Hotels of Hawaii, but it withdrew after falling out with property owner Louis Wane. As the resort was being built in 2000, local protesters in canoes surrounded a dredge attempting to pump lagoon sand onto the resort's artificial beach. Legal action eventually forced the construction company to withdraw the environmentally unfriendly dredge. In late 2002 Sheraton unveiled plans to build another 31 overwater bungalows to make the resort more profitable and local residents mounted a fresh campaign to confront this new threat to Moorea's ecosystem.

Unlike the Sheraton, the 147-room **Moorea Beachcomber Inter-Continental** (tel. 55-19-19, fax 55-19-55) at PK 24.5, has a friendly, welcoming atmosphere. The 48 standard air-conditioned rooms in the main building erected in 1987 start at CFP 31,800 single or double plus 11 percent tax, but it's better value to pay CFP 35,700 for a garden bungalow. Beach bungalows are CFP 44,700. For one of the 50 overwater bungalows, have your CFP 58,900 ready (considerably less than you'd pay for the same thing on Bora Bora). A third person pays CFP 6,660 for an uncomfortable extra bed, but children under 15 are free (this resort has a comprehensive children's activities program at additional cost). The breakfast and dinner plan is CFP 7,740 pp (alternative eateries are quite a walk away). This spacious resort has a large swimming pool and abundant paid sporting activities are available (only tennis and snorkeling gear are free

for guests). The hotel's captive Hawaiian dolphins are a controversial attraction (admission is charged to the dolphin enclosure), but the large stingrays swimming freely just off the resort's artificial beach can easily be visited with a mask and snorkel. Europcar has a desk here.

FOOD

Maharepa

Restaurant Le Mahogany (tel. 56-39-73; Thurs.–Tues. 1100–1500/1800–2200), at PK 4, Maharepa, offers French and Chinese dishes in the CFP 1,550–2,000 range. A bit west is the popular **Restaurant Le Cocotier** (tel. 56-12-10; Wed.–Mon. 1130–1430/1830–2130) with meat dishes priced CFP 1,950–2,650 and fish at CFP 1,950–2,250. There's a menu at the entrance.

Snack Le Sylésie (tel. 56-15-88), next to the post office at PK 5.5, Maharepa, has a nice terrace and fast service—perfect for breakfast or lunch. It's also good for pastries, sandwiches, and crêpes, and try the coconut ice cream. Of course, the coffee here is *magnifique!*

Le Pêcheur Restaurant (tel. 56-36-12; closed Sun.), also at Maharepa (PK 6), near the pharmacy at the east entrance to Cook's Bay, has an excellent reputation for its seafood dishes, which begin around CFP 2,200. The service is also good. If you lack transportation, someone will come and pick you up.

The overwater **Fishermen's Wharf Restaurant** (tel. 56-50-50) at the Hôtel Kaveka (PK 7.4) serves seafood in the CFP 1,800–2,100 range. Happy hour is 1800–1900 with live music provided. The view from the terrace is superb and there's even a beach.

Allo Pizza (tel. 56-18-22; Tues. 1700–2100, Wed.–Sat. 1100–1400/1700–2100), opposite the gendarmerie at PK 7.8, bakes 38 kinds of thin-crust takeout pizzas costing CFP 900–1,900. You must consume these picnic-style elsewhere (the nearby TOPdive wharf is a good choice).

Paopao

Restaurant Caprice des Îles (tel. 56-44-24; closed Tues.), occupies a thatched pavilion next to Supermarché Paopao on the mountain side of the road, 150 meters north of Club Bali Hai. It offers Chinese dishes (CFP 1,300–1,500), fish (CFP 1,950–2,850), and meat (CFP 1,650–2,950)—more expensive than other places along this way. We've heard rave reviews of the seafood.

Restaurant Chez Jean Pierre (tel. 56-18-51; Sun. 1815–2115, Mon. 1115–1415, Tues. and Thurs.–Sat. 1115–1415/1815–2115), close to Paopao market, is one of the less expensive places. The specialty is roast suckling pig in coconut milk (CFP 2,200) served on Saturday night, but there's also chicken (CFP 1,150–1,250), duck (CFP 1,250), and seafood (CFP 1,150–1,950), plus Chinese dishes. Cheaper still is the outdoor snack bar at Paopao Market, which is only open in the evening.

Alfredo's Restaurante/Chez Jules et Claudine (tel. 56-17-71; closed Mon.), on the inland side of the road a few hundred meters south of Club Bali Hai, has pizza (CFP 1,450) and pasta (CFP 1,550–1,950), plus fish (CFP 1,900–2,450) and meat (CFP 1,950–2,750) dishes. Call for a free hotel pickup.

Also check **Chez Michèle** (tel. 56-34-80), by the river at the head of Cooks Bay, which lists its menu (CFP 1,200–1,500) on a blackboard facing the terrace.

Snack Rotui (tel. 56-18-16; Tues.–Sat. 0700–1700), just west of the bridge at Paopao, could be the cheapest place on the island with sandwiches (CFP 150–180), chicken wings, french fries, cake, egg rolls, and ice cream. Its terrace overlooks Cook's Bay, it's friendly, and English is spoken.

Tiahura

Aside from the selections that follow, remember the excellent Italian restaurant at **Hôtel Les Tipaniers** (tel. 56-12-67). The mahimahi with vanilla sauce and *tartare de thon* are excellent, and don't miss the homemade desserts, especially the crème brulée and coconut pie.

Restaurant L'Aventure (tel. 56-53-59; Tues. 1800–2130, Wed.–Sun. 1100–1400/1800–2130), next to Hôtel Hibiscus, has pastas (CFP 1,020–1,980), meat and fish dishes (CFP 1,250–,980), and vegetarian dishes (CFP 850–1,650). Specials are advertised on a blackboard menu.

Good pizza/pasta (CFP 1,100/1,200) and ocean views are available at beachfront **Le Sunset Pizzeria** (tel. 56-26-00; daily 1130–1430/1800–2130) at the Hôtel Hibiscus (but avoid the salads). **Pâtisserie Le Sylésie** (tel. 56-20-45) is nearby.

Snack Coco d'Isle (tel. 56-59-07), between the two campgrounds, has excellent lunch specials, such as swordfish or mahimahi in vanilla sauce for CFP 1,000. Its *poisson cru* is superb, and you can eat on a terrace beside the road. The fine French cuisine at **Restaurant Le Pitcairn** (tel. 56-55-46) nearby has been recommended by readers.

Rôtisserie Royal Chicken (tel. 78-53-53; Tues.–Sat. 1100–1330/1800–1930), a take-out place beside the road near Moorea Camping, sells huge thick-crust half chickens for CFP 600. It's one of the best deals in French Polynesia—arrive soon after it opens as it sells out fast.

Groceries

If you've got access to cooking facilities, shop at one of the many grocery stores spread around Moorea. The largest and cheapest is **Toa Moorea** (tel. 56-18-89; Mon.–Thurs. 0800–1900, Fri. 0800–1900, Sat. 0800–2000, Sun. 0600–1100), a km south of the Vaiare ferry wharf.

Libre Service Maharepa (tel. 56-35-90), at PK 5.5, is almost opposite the Banque de Tahiti in Maharepa. **Supermarché Pao Pao** (tel. 56-17-34), 150 meters north of Club Bali Hai, opens Monday–Saturday 0530–1200/1430–1800, Sun. 0500–0900.

At the head of Cook's Bay you have a choice of **Magasin Lee Hen** (tel. 56-15-02; Mon.–Sat. 0530–1200/1400–1830, Sun. 0500–1200) or **Supermarché Are** (tel. 56-10-28) just west of the bridge nearby. Lee Hen and some of the others sell lots of local take-out snacks.

The nearest grocery store to the Sheraton is **Magasin Pihaena** at PK 13. The supermarket in **Le Petit Village** opposite Club Med opens Monday–Saturday 0700–1930 and Sunday 0700–1300/1600–1930.

All that you're likely to find in the **municipal market** at Paopao is a limited selection of fish. Fresh produce is much harder to obtain on Moorea than it is on Tahiti, so buy things when you see them and plan your grocery shopping carefully. Ask the stores what time the bread arrives, then be there promptly. The hybrid lime-grapefruit grown on Moorea has a thick green skin and a unique taste.

ENTERTAINMENT

The **Iguana Rock Café** (tel. 56-17-16) at Le Petit Village in Tiahura has live music Saturday after 2000.

The disco at **Billy Ruta Bungalows** (tel. 56-18-12), at PK 28.3, Tiahura, is a nice, very Polynesian scene with a good music mix of Tahitian, French, American, reggae, etc. It's a fun place that gets very busy with some very talented dancers (Sat. from 2230, CFP 1,500 cover charge).

Cultural Shows for Visitors

See Tahitian dancing in the Sofitel Ia Ora's **La Pérouse Restaurant** (tel. 56-12-90) on Tuesday, Thursday, and Saturday at 2000 (buffet CFP 4,000–6,000). At **Club Bali Hai** (tel. 56-22-77) there's Polynesian dancing Wednesday at 1800. The Tahitian show at the **Moorea Beachcomber Inter-Continental** (tel. 55-19-19) is on Monday, Wednesday, and Saturday nights after 2000. The **Hôtel Moorea Village** (tel. 56-10-02) presents Polynesian dancing Friday and Saturday at 1900 and Sunday at lunchtime. These times often change, so check. The Tahitian feasts that come with the shows cost CFP 4,500 and up, but you can often observe the action from the bar for the price of a drink. It's well worth going.

Since 1986 Moorea has had its own instant culture village, the **Tiki Theater Village** (Olivier Briac, tel. 55-02-50, fax 56-10-86) at PK 31, Haapiti. The doors are open Tuesday–Saturday 1130–1500, with a charge of CFP 2,200 to visit the village and see the small dance show at 1300. The guided tour of the recreated Tahitian village is informative and the 32 dancers and other

If you've got CFP 135,000 to spare, a "royal" Tahitian wedding can be arranged at the village (bring your own partner, same-sex couples welcome). The ceremony lasts two hours, from 1600 to sunset. The bridegroom arrives by canoe and the newlyweds are carried around in procession by four "warriors."

staff members who live in the village year-round are enthusiastic, but sometimes they're a little disorganized so you might obtain some details about the show time before parting with your francs. Lunch is available in the à la carte restaurant. On Tuesday, Wednesday, Friday, and Saturday at 1800 there's a big sunset show with a *tamaaraa* buffet and open bar (CFP 7,200, reservations required). Transportation is CFP 1,000 pp round-trip, if required. If you've got CFP 135,000 to spare, a "royal" Tahitian wedding can be arranged at the village (bring your own partner, same-sex couples welcome). The ceremony lasts two hours, from 1600 to sunset. The bridegroom arrives by canoe and the newlyweds are carried around in procession by four "warriors." Otherwise there's the less extravagant "princely" wedding for CFP 110,000, photos included. Yes, it's kinda tacky, but that's show biz! (Such weddings are not legally binding.)

INFORMATION AND SERVICES

Information

The Moorea Visitors Bureau (tel. 56-29-09; closed Sun.) has a poorly marked but helpful kiosk next to the gas station in front of Le Petit Village. Activities and tours can be booked here. An unstaffed tourist information counter at Temae Airport dispenses self-service brochures.

Kina Maharepa (tel. 56-22-44), next to the post office at PK 5.5, Maharepa, sells books and magazines in French. There's also a newsstand in Le Petit Village opposite Club Med. Newspapers in English are not available at either.

Services

The Banque Socredo, Banque de Polynésie, and Banque de Tahiti are all near the Moorea Pearl Resort at Maharepa. Banque Socredo has a second office opposite Vaiare Wharf. Another Banque de Polynésie branch is in Le Petit Village

MOOREA INTERNET RESOURCES

Accommodations

Camping Chez Nelson
www.camping-nelson.pf
campingnelson@mail.pf

Club Bali Hai
www.balihaihotels.com
reservations@clubbalihai.pf

Faimano Village
www.faimanovillage.com
faimanodenis@mail.pf

Fare Matotea
www.farematotea.com
mtt@mail.pf

Fare Vai Moana
farevaimoana@mail.pf

Hôtel Hibiscus
www.hotel-hibiscus.pf
mail@hotel-hibiscus.pf

Hôtel Kaveka
www.hotelkaveka.com
kaveka@mail.pf

Hôtel Les Tipaniers
www.lestipaniers.com
tipaniersresa@mail.pf

Hôtel Moorea Village
mooreavillage@mail.pf

Moorea Beachcomber Inter-Continental
moorea@interconti.com

Pension Anahoa
www.pension-anahoa.com
pensionanahoa@yahoo.fr

Résidence Linareva
www.linareva.com
linareva@mail.pf

---

shopping mall opposite Club Med. None of these banks are open on Saturday but most have ATMs accessible 24 hours.

The main post office (tel. 56-10-12; Mon.–Thurs. 0730–1200/1330–1600, Fri. 0730–1200/1330–1500, Sat. 0730–0930) is near the banks at Maharepa. A branch post office (tel. 56-13-15) is found at Papetoai.

The gendarmerie (tel. 56-13-44) is at PK 7.8, Paopao, just south of the Hôtel Kaveka.

The Iguana Rock Café (tel. 56-17-16) at Le Petit Village in Tiahura provides Internet access at CFP 25 a minute.

Health

The island's hospital (tel. 56-23-23) is at Afareaitu, on the opposite side of the island from most of the resorts. In case of need, it's much easier to see a private doctor or dentist. Moorea doctors charge around CFP 3,300 for office visits, or CFP 5,000 plus CFP 100 a km for hotel visits.

General practitioners Dr. Christian Jonville and Dr. Jean-Pierre Senechal share the Gabinet Medical (tel. 56-32-32; weekdays 0700–1200/1400–1800), behind the Banque de Polynésie at PK 5.5, Maharepa, a short walk from the Moorea Pearl Resort. Both are fluent in English. In the same building is Dr. Frédéric Avet's Cabinet Dentaire (tel. 56-32-44; weekdays 0800–1130/1500–1800, closed Wed. afternoon).

General practitioner Dr. Hervé Paulus (tel. 56-10-09, in emergencies tel. 56-10-25; weekdays 0900–1200/1500–1800, Sat. 0900–1200) is conveniently located at Le Petit Village near Club Med. Dr. Dominique Barraille (tel. 56-27-07) has an office next to Camping Chez Nelson. Also near Camping Chez Nelson and opposite Magasin Rene Junior at PK 27, Tiahura, is the joint office of Dr. Nicolas Marchadier (tel. 56-47-51), a dentist, and Dr. Brigitte Busseuil (tel. 56-26-19, residence tel. 56-13-98), a medical doctor.

Pharmacie Tran Thai Thanh (tel. 56-10-51; weekdays 0730–1200/1400–1800, Sat.y 0800–1200/1530–1800, Sun. 0800–1100) is at PK 6.5 between Maharepa and Paopao. There's also Pharmacie de Haapito (tel. 56-38-37; weekdays

Sports and Recreation

Bathy's Club
bathys@mail.pf

Moorea Fun Dive
www.fundive.pf
fundive@mail.pf

Scubapiti
www.scubapiti.com
scubapitidaniel@mail.pf

TOPdive-MUST Dive Center
www.mooreaisland.com/mustdive
mustdive@mail.pf

Transportation and Tours

Albert Activities
alberttransport@mail.pf

Moorea Explorer
moorea.explorer@mail.pf

Tea Nui Charters
teanuiservices@mail.pf

Tropic Escape
www.mooreahiking.com

Others

Dolphin Quest
dqfp@mail.pf

Tiki Theater Village
www.tikivillage.pf
info@tikivillage.pf

0900–1200/1600–1830, Sun. 0900–1100) at PK 30.5, Haapiti, near Tiki Theater Village.

TRANSPORTATION AND TOURS

Air Moorea and **Air Tahiti** (both tel. 56-10-34) are based at Moorea Temae Airport. (For information on the planes and ferries linking Tahiti, Moorea, and Huahine, turn to Transportation in the introduction to French Polynesia.)

Buses await the ferries from Tahiti at Vaiare Wharf. Although they don't go right around the island, the northern and southern bus routes meet at Le Petit Village opposite Club Med, so you could theoretically effect a circumnavigation by changing buses there, provided you caught the last service back to Vaiare from Le Petit Village at 1530. You should have no problem catching a bus when you arrive on Moorea from Tahiti by ferry, but be quick to jump aboard.

Be aware that the bright yellow "Moorea Explorer" buses at the wharf charge CFP 500, while the older buses most of the locals use ask only

CFP 300. The fare is the same to anywhere on the island.

Buses leave Le Petit Village for the ferry weekdays at 0430, 0530, 0630, 0930, 1130, 1330, 1430, and 1530, Saturday at 0430, 0530, 0630, 0830, 0930, 1130, 1330, 1430, and 1530, and Sunday at 0430, 0630, 1230, 1330, 1430, and 1630. If you have to catch a bus somewhere along its route, add the appropriate traveling time and ask advice of anyone you can. Some of the buses run 30 minutes early.

A taxi on Moorea is actually a minibus with a white letter **T** inside a red circle. Taxis fares are exorbitant and you should consider bargaining. Hitching is wearing thin with Moorea motorists, although it's still possible. If you really need the ride, you'll probably get it; just be prepared to do some walking.

Car Rentals

Europcar (tel. 56-34-00, fax 56-35-05) has a main office opposite Club Med and branches at Vaiare Wharf, the Sofitel, Sheraton, and several other locations. Its unlimited-mileage cars begin at CFP 8,100/15,000/21,060 for one/two/three days. Scooters are CFP 4,500/5,000/5,500 four/eight/24 hours, bicycles CFP 1,000/1,500/2,000. Despite these prices many of Europcar's vehicles are in bad shape. If you don't have a credit card it'll want a cash deposit of CFP 100,000. Clients are responsible for the first CFP 100,000 in damages to the vehicle; to reduce this liability to CFP 25,000 a fee of CFP 1,400 a day must be paid.

Avis (tel. 56-32-68) at Vaiare wharf, the airport, Club Bali Hai, and opposite Club Med has cars from CFP 8,721/16,371 for one/two days including kilometers and insurance. These cheaper cars are often unavailable and you'll find yourself being quoted CFP 10,400/19,500. Though more expensive, its vehicles and service are superior to those of Europcar.

Rental cars and bicycles are also obtained at **Albert Activities Center** (tel./fax 56-10-42), with locations at the airport and opposite Club Bali Hai (tel. 56-19-28) and Club Med (tel. 56-33-75). Unlimited-mileage cars begin at CFP 7,000/8,000/14,500 for eight/24/48 hours, including insurance. Some of the vehicles are of the "rent a wreck" variety, so look the car over before signing the credit card voucher and insist on a replacement or a discount if it's a high-mileage bomb. Its scooters are CFP 4,500/5,000/9,000. Bicycles cost about CFP 1,000/1,300 for a half/full day.

If your time is limited, it's best to reserve an Avis or Europcar vehicle a day or two ahead at one of their offices in Papeete as all cars on Moorea are sometimes taken. There are five gasoline stations around Moorea: Mobil a km south of Vaiare Wharf, Shell opposite Vaiare Wharf, Total at the airport access road, another Mobil near Motel Albert at Paopao, and another Total opposite Club Med. The maximum speed limit is 60 kph.

Local Tours

Moorea Explorer (tel. 56-12-86) at the airport offers upscale bus and boat tours for people on package tours. Its bright yellow buses are newer than those of the other companies, but the tours tend to be rushed with fewer stops and little flexibility.

The tours offered by **Albert Activities** (tel. 56-13-53, fax 56-40-58), at the airport and opposite Club Bali Hai and Club Med, are much more personal than those of Moorea Explorer, and the guides are generally more receptive to individual requests. If you get one of the Haring brothers as your guide, you'll definitely enjoy it. Daily at 0900 Albert does a three-hour circle-island bus tour, including a visit to the Belvédère, at CFP 2,500 (lunch not included). Albert's five-hour 4WD jeep safari is CFP 3,500 pp (do it in the morning).

Several other companies, including **Ben Tours** (Benjamin Teraiharoa, tel. 56-26-50) at the airport, offer much the same. Whichever circle-island tour you choose, be prepared for a stop at whichever black pearl showroom is paying the guides the highest commission.

Tropic Escape (Rémy Costa, tel. 56-42-49) specializes in hiking and mountain climbing with half/full day trips at CFP 3,000/5,000.

Inner Island Safari Tours (Alexandre Haamatearii, tel. 56-20-09, fax 56-34-43), based at Maharepa, offers an exhilarating 4WD tour to various viewpoints and around Moorea for CFP 4,800 pp.

Archaeologist Mark Eddowes (tel. 56-34-20) leads a **"Path of the Ancients"** tour that visits numerous *marae* on a two-km hike through the Opunohu Valley. He does this half-day trip (CFP 5,750 pp) mostly for cruise ship passengers or when a group of at least 10 people has booked. Call him up to find out what's scheduled.

Day Cruises

Archipels Croisières (tel. 56-58-41), based at PK 17 on Opunoho Bay near the Jardin Kellum, offers a day cruise around Moorea on the *Fetia Ura,* a 34-meter classic schooner, with various snorkeling and sight-seeing stops. The cruise visits "Le Monde de Mu," an underwater sculpture garden in the lagoon off Papetoai with 10 large tikis created in 1998 by the renowned Tahitian stone carver Tihoti. These trips operate Wednesday–Sunday 0830–1630 (CFP 11,500 including a buffet lunch). There's also a 1530–1830 sunset cruise daily except Thursday and Sunday (CFP 6,000).

At 0930 and 1400 daily the **Moorea Beachcomber Inter-Continental** (tel. 55-19-19) offers a three-hour cruise on the catamaran *Manu* at CFP 6,300 pp. The 1.5-hour sunset cruise is CFP 3,200 including drinks. You can take a one-hour ride in a glass-bottom motorboat called the *Aquascope* at CFP 3,200 pp and it'll go anytime between 0900 and 1200 (both have four-person minimums).

Snorkeling Trips

Albert Activities (tel./fax 56-10-42) runs a five-hour motorized aluminum canoe ride right around Moorea with a stop for snorkeling (gear provided), departing Tuesday, Wednesday, Friday, and Sunday at 0900 (CFP 5,000 pp, minimum of four). For a free pickup, inquire at one of the three Albert Activities centers around Moorea. You could see dolphins, whales, and human surfers on this trip.

Other companies run a variety of trips, such a *motu* excursion by outrigger or a *motu* picnic party. On many of these, the canoes are without radios, life jackets, or flotation devices, and they can be frightening if you're not a good swimmer. The snorkeling itself is great. **Moorea Explorer** (tel. 56-12-86, fax 56-25-52) at the airport combines shark feeding with its island tours (CFP 6,500/7,500 pp by bus/4WD).

Moorea Camping (tel. 56-14-47) at Tiahura runs an excellent shark-feeding tour to a *motu* at 1000 and 1400 daily. This trip costs CFP 1,500/2,000 for campground residents/nonresidents, and if you're not staying at the campground, be sure to call ahead for information. Bring your own mask as ones supplied don't fit very well. The **Hôtel Moorea Village** (tel. 56-10-02) offers a similar tour for CFP 2,500.

Unfortunately, the shark-feeding event has become just a bit too popular, especially when four boats each carrying 10 tourists arrive at the same time. The guides throw a few pieces of tuna to three or four well-fed little sharks, which sniff disinterestedly at the bait. Some of the tourists who get in the water become overexcited and begin thrashing around behind the rope that separates them from the beasts, trying to be in front. It's still unknown if this activity will eventually attract larger sharks into the Moorea lagoon but to date no incidents have been reported.

The unexpected highlight of these trips is the chance to swim alongside groups of manta rays.

Dolphin-Watching

Dolphin Quest at the Moorea Beachcomber Inter-Continental (tel. 56-19-48, fax 56-16-67) gives tourists the opportunity to pay CFP 16,500 each to spend 30 minutes wading around a shallow lagoon enclosure with four captive dolphins (touching and even kissing the penned mammals is allowed). These activities begin at 0930, 1330, and 1530. At 1030 and 1530 it's possible to don a mask and snorkel and actually swim with the dolphins in a deeper part of the enclosure at CFP 18,700 (the Inter-Continental tacks on a CFP 1,000 surcharge in either case if you're not a hotel guest). You're in the water with the animals only a short time and photos are charged extra. This whole business has environmental and moral implications. Dolphin Quest's brochure claims that part of the proceeds "helps fund education, research, and conservation programs around the world" without being specific. The dolphins now held here were flown in from Hawaii after the native dolphins proved impossible to tame and kept trying to escape. It's also clear that somebody is making a lot of money by exploiting these captive animals as a tourist attraction.

A quite different type of dolphin encounter is offered by Dr. Michael Poole of **Dolphin and Whale Watching Expeditions** (tel. 56-23-22 or 56-14-70, fax 56-14-70). Dr. Poole has been on Moorea researching dolphins and whales since 1987 and he's now in charge of the Marine Mammal Research Program at CRIOBE, a French biological research station on Moorea. In May 2002 French Polynesia's government declared its entire exclusive economic zone a whale and dolphin sanctuary, protecting, forever, these animals in more than five million square kilometers of ocean. Dr. Poole was the author of this proposition, worked 10 years to bring it to fruition, and wrote the original guidelines that were used as a basis for the legislation.

On his trips, small groups are taken out in boats to see acrobatic spinner dolphins—the only dolphins to spin vertically in the air like tops or ballerinas—in the wild. A Florida reader sent us this:

We were taken to Opunohu Bay and watched 45 spinner dolphins for a long time. It was exciting as several dolphins spun in the air, did tail slaps, and swam right next to the boat. We were all taking photos like crazy. Dr. Poole is very nice and he will tell you what he has learned through his research.

You may also observe dolphins surfing (!), and from July to October humpback whales are often seen. These 3.5-hour trips go out early on Thursday and Sunday mornings, costing CFP 6,700 pp with half-price reductions for children 12 and under. Included in the price are boat pickups at all hotels between the Pearl Resort and the Moorea Village (bus transfers arranged from the Sofitel). Space is quite limited, so reserve well ahead through one of the Moorea activities offices, a hotel tour desk, or by calling the numbers above. Be sure to state clearly that you want "Dr. Poole's boat" as several unscientific imitators are trying to do the same thing with varying success. The activities desks at resorts such as the Sheraton push the captive dolphin show at the Inter-Continental for the commissions they earn and may claim not to know of Dr. Poole.

Moorea Airport

Moorea Temae Airport (MOZ) is in the northeast corner of the island. The airport transfer service is only for people on prebooked tours, so unless you rent a car, you'll be stuck with a rip-off taxi fare in addition to the airfare: CFP 1,500 to Vaiare Wharf or the Moorea Pearl Resort, CFP 3,000 to the Sheraton, CFP 3,500 to the Inter-Continental, and CFP 4,000 to Club Med.

Thanks to intimidation from the taxi drivers, none of the hotels are allowed to offer airport pickups. The bright yellow Moorea Explorer transfer buses at the airport are allowed to carry passengers with vouchers only. Try to buy one as you're checking in for your flight to Moorea in Papeete. If you ask at the Moorea Explorer counter (tel. 56-12-86) inside the terminal you'll almost certainly be told to take a taxi. Your hotel reception should be able to book your return trip to the airport on these buses for CFP 550.

Albert, Avis, and Europcar have counters at the airport, but it's essential to reserve beforehand. Otherwise they may not have a car for you and you'll be subjected to the scam just mentioned.

Considering this, you should seriously consider using the ferry to/from Moorea. At a third the price of the plane (CFP 1,000 compared to CFP 3,000), the scenic 30-minute catamaran ride to/from Tahiti may end up being one of the highlights of your visit. It's mostly tourists on prepaid packages who arrive by air—those traveling individually usually take the ferry. If you do fly, try to sit on the left side of the aircraft on the way to Moorea and on the right on the way to Papeete.

Huahine

Huahine, the first Leeward island encountered on the ferry ride from Tahiti, is a friendly, inviting island, 175 km northwest of Papeete. In many ways, lush, mountainous Huahine (74 square km) has more to offer than overcrowded Bora Bora. The variety of scenery, splendid beaches, deep bays, exuberant vegetation, archaeological remains, and charming main town all invite you to visit. Huahine is a well-known surfing locale, with consistently excellent lefts and rights in the two passes off Fare (try to befriend the local surfers before entering their space). Schools of dolphins often greet ships arriving through Avapeihi Pass. Huahine's mosquito population is also surprisingly large.

It's claimed the island got its name because, when viewed from the sea, Huahine has the shape of a reclining woman—very appropriate for such a fertile, enchanting place. *Hua* means "phallus" (from a rock on Huahine-iti) while *hine* comes from *vahine* (woman). A narrow channel crossed by a concrete bridge slices Huahine into Huahine-nui and Huahine-iti (Great and Little Huahine, respectively). The story goes that the demigod Hiro's canoe cut this strait.

The almost entirely Polynesian population numbers 5,500, yet some of the greatest leaders in the struggle for the independence of Polynesia, Pouvanaa a Oopa among them, have come from

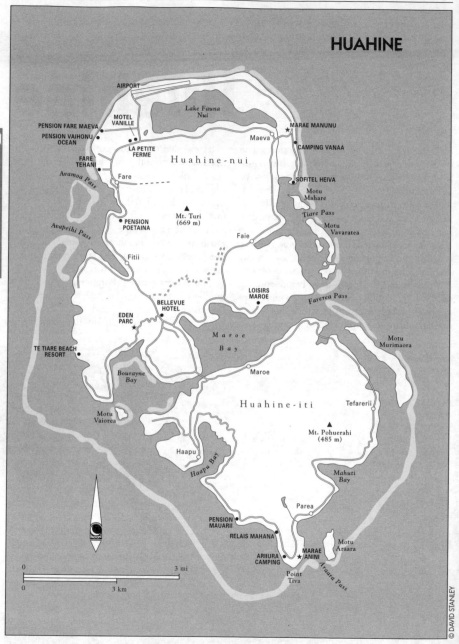

HUAHINE

AIRPORT

Lake Fauna Nui

PENSION FARE MAEVA
PENSION VAIHONU OCEAN

MOTEL VANILLE

MARAE MANUNU

Maeva

CAMPING VANAA

FARE TEHANI

LA PETITE FERME

Fare

Avamoa Pass

Huahine-nui

SOFITEL HEIVA

Motu Mahare

Tiare Pass

Avapeihi Pass

PENSION POETAINA

▲ Mt. Turi (669 m)

Faie

Motu Vavaratea

Fitii

LOISIRS MAROE

Farerea Pass

BELLEVUE HOTEL

EDEN PARC ★

Maroe Bay

Motu Murimaora

TE TIARE BEACH RESORT

Bourayne Bay

Maroe

Motu Vaiorea

Huahine-iti

Tefarerii

Haapu

▲ Mt. Pohuerahi (485 m)

Haapu Bay

Mahuti Bay

Parea

PENSION MAUARII

RELAIS MAHANA

ARIIURA CAMPING

Motu Araara

MARAE ANINI ★

Point Tiva

Araara Pass

MOON

0 ——————— 3 mi
0 ——————— 3 km

FRENCH POLYNESIA

© DAVID STANLEY

HUAHINE HIGHLIGHTS

Fare waterfront: atmosphere, restaurants, facilities
Faahia valley: hiking, nature
Maeva: archaeology, nature, hiking
Eden Parc: food, nature, botany
Avea Bay: beach, swimming, snorkeling, marinelife

this idyllic spot. The artist Bobby Holcomb and poet Henri Hiro are also well remembered.

In recent years Huahine has been discovered by international tourism, and deluxe hotels and bungalow-style developments are now found in different parts of the island. Luckily Huahine has been able to absorb this influx fairly painlessly, as it's a much larger island than Bora Bora, and the resorts are well scattered and constructed in the traditional Tahitian style. It's an oasis of peace after Papeete. The island has also become a major port of call for the yachts that anchor off Fare. Backpackers pioneered Huahine in the mid-1980s, and good facilities still exist for them too.

Archaeology

Archaeologists have found that human habitation goes back at least 1,300 years on Huahine; Maeva village was occupied as early as A.D. 850. In 1925 Dr. Kenneth P. Emory of Hawaii's Bishop Museum recorded 54 *marae* on Huahine, most of them built after the 16th century. In 1968 Professor Yosihiko H. Sinoto found another 40. Huahine-nui was divided into 10 districts, with Huahine-iti as a dependency. As a centralized government complex for a whole island, Maeva, on the south shore of Lake Fauna Nui, is unique in French Polynesia. Here all the district chiefs on Huahine-nui lived side by side and worshiped their ancestors at their respective marae, 28 of which are recorded here.

Since 1967 about 16 *marae* have been restored, and they can be easily visited today. The great communal *marae* at Maeva and Parea have two-stepped platforms *(ahu)* that served as raised seats for the gods. Like those of Raiatea and Bora Bora, the Huahine *marae* are constructed of large coral slabs, whereas comparable structures on Tahiti and Moorea are made of round basalt

stones. During construction of the defunct Hôtel Bali Hai just north of Fare in 1972, a *patu* hand club was uncovered, suggesting that New Zealand's Maoris originated in this area.

History of the Leeward Islands

Huahine was settled by Polynesians around 850. Roggeveen, coming from Makatea in the Tuamotus, sighted (but did not land on) Bora Bora and Maupiti on June 6, 1722. Captain Cook "discovered" the other Leeward Islands in July 1769, which was quite easy since the Tahitians knew them well. In fact, Cook had the Raiatean priest Tupaia on board the *Endeavour* as a pilot. Cook wrote:

> To these six islands, as they lie contiguous to each other, I gave the names of Society Islands.

Later the name was extended to the Windward Islands. In 1773 a man named Omai from Raiatea sailed to England with Cook's colleague, Captain Furneaux, aboard the *Adventure;* he returned Cook in 1777 and was dropped off on Huahine.

During the 19th century, American whalers spent their winters away from the Antarctic in places such as Huahine, refurbishing their supplies with local products such as sugar, vegetables, oranges, salted pork, and *aito*, or ironwood. These visits enriched the island economy, and the New England sailors presented the islanders with foreign plants as tokens of appreciation for the hospitality received. English missionaries arrived in 1808 and later Pomare II extended his power to Huahine, abolishing the traditional religion. In 1822 missionary law was imposed. Among the missionaries was William Ellis, whose book, *Polynesian Researches,* published in London in 1829, has left us a detailed picture of the island at that time.

Though Tahiti and Moorea fell under French control in 1842, the Leeward Islands remained a British protectorate until 1887, when these islands were traded for fishing rights off Newfoundland and a British interest in what was then New Hebrides (today Vanuatu). Marines from the French warship *Uranie* had attacked Huahine in 1846, but they were defeated at Maeva. A year later France promised Britain that

FRENCH POLYNESIA

it would not annex the Leeward Islands, yet in 1887 it proceeded to do so. The local chiefs refused to sign the annexation treaty until 1895, and resistance to France, especially on Raiatea, was overcome only by force in 1897. The French then expelled the English missionary group that had been there 88 years; nonetheless, today 80 percent of the population of the Leewards remains Protestant.

In 1918 a Spanish influenza epidemic wiped out a fifth of the population, including the last queen, Tehaapapa III. Only in 1945 was missionary law finally abolished and French citizenship extended to the inhabitants. In the 1958 referendum, 76 percent of the population of Huahine voted in favor of independence.

Tourism began in 1973 with the building of the airstrip and the Hôtel Bali Hai. In 1999, a land dispute and strike led to the closing of this hotel, which is sad as it was one of the finest of its kind in French Polynesia, tastefully placed between a lake and the beach. Several new upscale resorts have since appeared but they're much more expensive and isolated from town.

Fare

The unsophisticated little town of Fare, with its tree-lined boulevard along the quay, is joyfully peaceful after the roar of Papeete. A beach runs right along the west side of the main street and local life unfolds without being overwhelmed by tourism. Local men play *pétanque* on the Fare waterfront around sunset. From here Bora Bora is visible in the distance to the left while the small twin peaks of Taha'a are to the right. The seven other villages on Huahine are linked to Fare by winding, picturesque roads. The snorkeling offshore north of town is great, but despite the easygoing atmosphere, it's unwise to leave valuables unattended on the beach (and beware of unperceived currents).

> The unsophisticated little town of Fare, with its tree-lined boulevard along the quay, is joyfully peaceful after the roar of Papeete. A beach runs right along the west side of the main street and local life unfolds without being overwhelmed by tourism.

SIGHTS

After you've explored the Fare waterfront, visit the beautiful *mape* (chestnut) forest up the Faahia valley. Walk inland 15 minutes along the road that begins two houses south of the house marked "Oliveti" near the Total service station. This road becomes a jungle trail that you can easily follow another 15 minutes up a small stream into a tropical forest laced with vanilla vines and the sweet smell of fermenting fruit. By the stream is a long bedlike rock known as Ofaitere, or

"Traveling Rock," but you'd need to have someone point it out to you. A guide will certainly be required to continue right to the summit of Huahine's highest peak, Mt. Turi (669 meters), in about three hours, as it's rough going.

A side road from Hôtel Bellevue, six km south of Fare, leads one km west to **Eden Parc** (tel. 68-86-58; Mon.–Sat. 0900–1600, admission CFP 300), a commercial tropical garden where an organically grown lunch (from CFP 1,000) and fruit drinks (CFP 400) are served to visitors.

Sports and Recreation

Pacific Blue Adventure (Didier Forget, tel. 68-87-21, fax 68-80-71) at Fare offers scuba diving at CFP 5,500/20,000 for one/four dives. Trips to sites such as Avapeihi Pass, Fa'a Miti, Coral City, and Yellow Valley leave at 0900 and 1400, depending on demand. Pacific Blue will take snorkelers only if things are really slow, and it picks up at hotels around Fare.

La Petite Ferme (Pascale Liaudois, tel./fax 68-82-98), between Fare and the airport, offers riding with Pascale, Yvon, and their 16 small, robust Marquesan horses. A two-hour ride along the beach is CFP 4,500 pp, and they also offer a full day of riding into the mountains or along

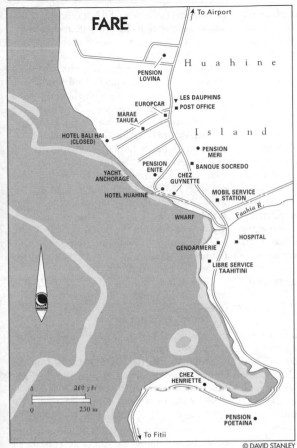

FARE

To Airport

Huahine

PENSION LOVINA

EUROPCAR
LES DAUPHINS
POST OFFICE

MARAE TAHUEA

Island

HOTEL BALI HAI (CLOSED)

PENSION MERI

PENSION ENITE
BANQUE SOCREDO

YACHT ANCHORAGE

CHEZ GUYNETTE

HOTEL HUAHINE

MOBIL SERVICE STATION

Faahia R.

WHARF

GENDARMERIE

HOSPITAL

LIBRE SERVICE TAAHITINI

CHEZ HENRIETTE

PENSION POETAINA

To Fitii

250 yds
0   250 m

© DAVID STANLEY

FRENCH POLYNESIA

percent tax with fan and private bath. The eight-bed dorm at the back of the building is CFP 1,500 pp. You can cook your own food in the communal kitchen here. It's a pleasant, clean place; no shoes are allowed in the house. Upon arrival peruse the list of rules and rates—rigorously applied (for example, it's lights out in the kitchen at 2200). On departure day the rooms must be vacated by 1000, but you can leave your bags at the reception until 1800 if catching a late ferry. Most readers say they liked the efficiency. Thankfully, the management doesn't allow overcrowding and will turn people away rather than pack them in for short-term gain.

Nearby on the waterfront is three-story **Hôtel Huahine** (tel. 68-82-69), at CFP 3,500/4,500/5,500 single/double/triple, or CFP 1,500 in a dorm. A supplement of CFP 500 is charged if you stay only one night. The 10 bare rooms are large, each with its own unreliable toilet and shower. No cooking facilities are provided. Fish dishes in the restaurant start at CFP 1,000, but you may also sit and watch TV for the price of a beer. Stalwart surfers who don't care for the house rules at Pension Guynette often stay here. Love it or leave it.

Under a km north of town is **Pension Vaihonu Ocean** (Etienne Faaeva, tel. 68-87-33, fax 68-77-57) with three *fare* at CFP 2,800/4,000 single/double and a six-bed dorm at CFP 1,500. Two self-catering duplexes with private bath are CFP 6,500 double plus 6 percent tax. Camping is CFP 1,000 pp. There's an open communal kitchen in the small compound jammed with potted flowers. Unfortunately access to the nearby beach is blocked by residential construction and you'll have to go back toward Fare to find a place to surf or swim.

the beach for CFP 9,800. Call the day before to let them know you're coming. This is the number-one horseback-riding operation in French Polynesia—recommended.

ACCOMMODATIONS

US$25–50

Pension Chez Guynette (Marty and Moe Temahahe, tel./fax 68-83-75), also known as "Club Bed," is on the waterfront to the left as you get off the ship. The seven rooms, each with the name of a different Society island, are CFP 3,900/4,700/5,700 single/double/triple plus 6

La Petite Ferme (Pascale Liaudois, tel./fax 68-82-98), between Fare and the airport, has one room with shared bath at CFP 3,250/4,400 single/double and a six-bed dorm at CFP 1,850 pp, including breakfast (CFP 500 extra for one night). In addition, there's a self-catering bungalow at CFP 5,250/7,900/9,450 single/double/triple (two-night minimum stay). All prices include tax and airport transfers. It's a great place to stay if you're at all interested in horseback riding.

Chez Henriette (tel./fax 68-83-71) is a pleasant 15-minute walk south of Fare, beside the lagoon a few hundred meters beyond Pension Poetaina. The six thatched *fare* all have basic cooking facilities. The three smaller units with double bed, mosquito net, fridge, hot plate, and shared bath are CFP 4,675 double, while the three larger *fare* with two double beds and private bath are CFP 7,675 for up to four people—okay for a family with two children. It's sort of like staying in a local village while retaining a measure of privacy.

US$50–100

Pension Enite (Enite Temaiana, tel./fax 68-82-37) is an eight-room boardinghouse at the west end of the waterfront beyond the snack bar. Rooms with shared bath are CFP 15,000 double with half board (two-night minimum stay, no room rentals without meals, no singles). The meals are served in a thatched cookhouse on the beach and the food is good. Middle-of-the-night arrivals mustn't knock on the door before 0700. French expats often stay here.

Just behind of Fare is **Pension Meri** (Milton Brotherson, tel. 68-82-44, fax 68-85-96), down the road behind Banque Socredo. The three bungalows with private bath and cooking facilities are CFP 7,500 single or double, or CFP 8,000 for up to four (minimum stay five nights).

Several good places to stay are between Fare and the airport, about 800 meters north of the wharf. Aside from Pension Vaihonu Ocean previously mentioned, **Pension Lovina** (Lovina Richmond, tel./fax 68-88-06) has five small *fare* with TV and shared bath at CFP 4,500/6,500 single/double. For families and groups, there are three oversized thatched bungalows with cooking

and bathing facilities at CFP 6,500/8,000/12,000 single/double/triple, CFP 17,000 for up to five people, CFP 24,500 for seven people. Dormitory accommodations are CFP 1,800 pp, and camping is CFP 1,250 pp. All guests have access to communal cooking facilities (and mosquitoes). The minimum stay is two nights, and discounts may be negotiable. Airport pickups cost CFP 1,200 pp return; from the harbor it's CFP 600 pp.

Fare Tehani (Frédéric Girard, tel./fax 68-71-00) is on the beach down the road from the back entrance to Pension Lovina, between Fare and the airport. The three *fare* with kitchen and fridge are CFP 12,000/14,000 double/quad or CFP 70,000 a week. Nearby an American named **Rande Vetterli** (tel. 68-86-27) has two self-catering houses right on the beach at CFP 7,200/12,000 for one/two bedrooms (three-night minimum stay). Bicycles and a rowboat are lent free. It's one heck of a deal.

Chez Ella (Ella Mervin, tel./fax 68-73-07), next to Motel Vanille at the airport turnoff, has three bungalows with kitchen, fridge, and TV at CFP 7,500 single or double, plus CFP 1,500 per additional person. You can ask to use the washing machine.

Motel Vanille (tel./fax 68-71-77) is on the corner of the airport access road and the Fare-Maeva highway. The six thatched bungalows positioned around the swimming pool are CFP 8,900 single or double with bicycles and airport transfers included (two-night minimum stay). Breakfast and dinner are CFP 2,900 pp. It's all rather informal, but a kilometer from the beach.

Pension Fare Maeva (tel. 68-75-53, fax 68-70-68) is on a rocky shore, 900 meters down an access road west from the airport road. It's a bit less than two km from the airport or three km from Fare. The 10 self-catering bungalows are CFP 9,010 single or double, while the 10 motel-style rooms go for CFP 5,770, breakfast included. When booking, ask about packages including a car. There's a restaurant, swimming pool, and garden. The pension will even do your laundry for a small fee. Airport transfers are free.

In a valley a km south of Fare (inland from the second bridge) is **Pension Poetaina** (Jean-Pierre Amo, tel./fax 68-89-49), a large two-story building with spacious balconies and lounge. The four rooms with shared bath are CFP 7,500 single or double, while two larger rooms with private bath are CFP 9,500 (two-night minimum stay). Communal cooking facilities are provided and there's a pool. Boat trips around Huahine are arranged at CFP 7,500 pp plus tax including lunch and snorkeling. It's a bit overpriced.

The **Hôtel Bellevue** (tel. 68-82-76, fax 68-85-35), six km south of Fare, offers 10 bungalows without cooking facilities at CFP 6,000/7,000 single/double, plus 11 percent tax. The poor lighting makes it hard to read in the evening. There's a figure-eight shaped swimming pool. The restaurant has a lovely view of Maroe Bay but the meals are pricey. Round-trip airport transfers are CFP 1,000 pp. Considering the expense, isolation, and absence of a beach, the Bellevue has little going for it.

US$250 and up

In 1999 the **Te Tiare Beach Resort** (tel. 60-60-50), part of the Pearl Resorts chain, opened on the west side of Huahine-nui. The 25 garden and beach bungalows start at CFP 37,000 double, while the 16 overwater bungalows with whirlpool bath are from CFP 67,600, plus 11 percent tax. Half board is CFP 7,500 pp. There's a freshwater swimming pool and overwater restaurant. To enhance the sense of isolation, this resort is accessible only by boat. Airport transfers are CFP 5,500 pp round-trip.

(Other campgrounds and hotels around Huahine are listed separately under Maeva and Huahine-iti in this chapter.)

FOOD AND ENTERTAINMENT

Food Trailers

Between 8 and 10 food trailers or *roulottes* park at Fare Wharf at different times of day selling spring rolls, pastries, and long French sandwiches. Coffee and bread is CFP 200. At night you can get steak frites, chicken and chips, or *poisson cru* for CFP 800. Look for the trailer that parks next to a row of telephone booths as it has excellent fish brochettes for CFP 150.

Restaurants

Opposite the car rental offices on the waterfront is **Restaurant Te Vaipuna** (tel. 68-70-45; Mon.–Sat. 1100–1430/1800–2130) with Chinese and French dishes. A cheaper snack bar is next door.

Pension Guynette (tel. 68-83-75) serves an inexpensive breakfast and lunch on its popular waterfront terrace bar, and this is also a good choice for only coffee and a snack. There's nowhere better to sit and watch the sunset while meeting old and new friends.

Restaurant Te Marara (tel. 68-81-70; closed weekends) at the west end of the waterfront has a nice terrace built over the lagoon, fine for a sunset beer. It's quite elegant, with fish dishes costing CFP 950–1,400, meat dishes CFP 1,100–1,400.

Restaurant Tiare Tipanier (tel. 68-80-52; Mon. 1800–2045, Tues.–Sat. 1130–1345/1800–2045), next to the *mairie* (town hall) at the north entrance to Fare, is a typical French rural restaurant without the tourist touches of some of the others. It serves meat and fish dishes in the CFP 1,300–1,800 range, while the set menu is CFP 2,200 including wine. A large Hinano is CFP 500.

Groceries

Super Fare-Nui (tel. 68-84-68; daily 0530–1900), on the Fare waterfront, sells groceries and cold beer. An alternative place to shop is **Libre Service Taahitini** (tel. 68-89-42; weekdays 0600–1200/1330–1900, Sat. 0600–1200/1600–1900, Sun. 0600–1100/1700–1900), just beyond the gendarmerie south of town. **Magasin Matehau** at Fitii also has groceries.

If you see a cruise ship tied up at Fare one morning, pop into the supermarket quickly to buy your daily bread before the ship's cook comes ashore to snap up the day's entire supply, a classic example of how tourism exploits small island communities. (Bread is heavily subsidized as an essential staple.)

The tap water on Huahine can be clouded after heavy rains.

Entertainment

There's traditional dancing at the **Sofitel Heiva Huahine** (tel. 60-61-60) at Maeva on Monday,

Thursday, and Saturday nights, but you'll need motorized transportation to get there.

Les Dauphins (tel. 68-78-54), beside the post office north of town, offers disco dancing to local Tahitian groups on Friday and Saturday nights from 2100 (admission CFP 1,000 including a drink). It's also open for lunch daily except Sunday and Monday.

INFORMATION AND SERVICES

Information

The Comité du Tourisme information office (tel. 68-78-81; weekdays 0730–1130) is below the Internet place next to Photo Jojo on the main street.

Services

ATMs are outside the Banque de Tahiti (tel. 68-82-46; weekdays 0745-1145/1330–1630), facing the Fare waterfront, and the Banque Socredo (tel. 68-82-71; weekdays 0730–1130/1330–1600), on the first street back from the waterfront.

The post office (Mon.–Thurs. 0700–1500, Fri. 0700–1400), on the road between the airport and Fare, has a convenient Coca-Cola vending machine. The gendarmerie (tel. 68-82-61) is opposite the hospital over the bridge at the south end of town.

An Internet café is next to Pension Chez Guynette and upstairs.

Huahine Matic (tel. 23-61-70; Mon.–Fri. 0800–1630, Sat. 0800–1430), next to the Mobile gas station in Fare, is a launderette charging CFP 700 a kilo to wash and dry. The price goes down as the number of kilos increases.

Public toilets and washbasins are in one of the yellow buildings on the waterfront (if open).

Health

A Gabinet Medical-Dentaire (tel. 68-82-20) is next to the Mobil service station on the next street back from the wharf. Dr. Hervé Carbonnier and Dr. Pascal Matyka, general practitioners, see patients 0730–1200/1400–1600.

La Pharmacie de Huahine (tel. 68-80-90; weekdays 0730–1130/1400–1700, Sat. 0730–1130), is across the street from the Mormon church north of town on the way to the post office.

TRANSPORTATION

Getting There

Air Tahiti (tel. 68-82-65) has an office at the airport. (For information on flights and ships to Huahine from Papeete, Moorea, Raiatea, and Bora Bora see Transportation in the introduction to French Polynesia.) Air Tahiti's direct flight between Huahine and Moorea would be great if it didn't cost CFP 11,500 when the flight to/from Papeete is only CFP 9,200.

The fast catamaran *Aremiti III* (tel. 73-52-73) departs Huahine for Raiatea (45 minutes, CFP 1,700) Monday and Friday at 1230. To Papeete (3.5 hours, CFP 4,600) it leaves Huahine the same days at 1500.

The Papeete cargo ships tie up to the wharf in the middle of town. If you arrive in the middle of the night you can sleep in the large open pavilion until dawn. Northbound, the *Vaeanu* calls at Huahine on Tuesday, Thursday, and Saturday at 0130; southbound on Tuesday and Thursday at 1830, and Sunday at 1500. Deck fares from Huahine are CFP 749 to Raiatea or CFP 1,786 to Papeete. The Thursday trip northbound may be carrying fuel, in which case only cabin passengers will be allowed. The *Hawaiki-Nui* also passes twice a week.

Tickets for *Vaeanu* go on sale at its office (tel. 68-73-73) adjoining the yellow warehouse on the wharf four hours before sailing or you can buy one as the ship is loading.

Getting Around

Getting around Huahine is not easy. A few *trucks* operate from outlying villages to Fare and back on weekday mornings—ask the drivers of any you see parked along the waterfront. Otherwise, the locals are fairly good about giving lifts. The only sure way of getting around is to rent something, although the 4WD excursions are a good alternative.

Europcar (tel. 68-82-59, fax 68-80-59) is opposite the post office with branch offices at the airport, Sofitel Heiva, Relais Mahana, and Te Tiare Beach Resort. Its smallest car is CFP 3,600 a day plus CFP 58 a kilometer, or CFP 8,400/15,100 for one/two days with unlimited kilometers. Bi-

HUAHINE INTERNET RESOURCES

Accommodations

Chez Ella
ella@iaorana-huahine.com

La Petite Ferme
www.la-petiteferme.com
lapetiteferme@mail.pf

Motel Vanille
www.motelvanille.com

Pension Chez Guynette
chezguynette@mail.pf

Pension Fare Maeva
faremaeva@mail.pf

Pension Mauarii
www.mauarii.com
vetea@mail.pf

Pension Poetaina
pensionpoetaina@mail.pf

Pension Vaihonu Ocean
vaihonu@mail.pf

Relais Mahana
www.relaismahana.com
relaismahana@mail.pf

Sofitel Heiva Huahine
www.sofitel-hciva.com

Te Tiare Beach Resort
www.tetiarebeachresort.com
welcome@tetiarebeachresort.pf

Sports and Recreation

Huahine Nautique
www.huahine-nautique.com

Pacific Blue Adventure
www.divehuahine.com
info@divehuahine.com

Sailing Huahine
www.sailing-huahine.com
eden@sailing-huahine.com

Others

Eden Parc
www.edenparc.org

Europcar
kake@mail.pf

Huahine Explorer
www.iaorana-huahine.com/en/explorer.html
h-explorer@mail.pf

Huahine Pearl Farm
www.huahinepearlfarm.com

Island Eco Tours
www.island-eco-tours.com
islandecotours@mail.pf

cycles/scooters are CFP 2,000/5,900 a day. All prices include tax.

Avis (tel. 68-73-34, fax 68-73-35) is next to Super Fare-Nui on the waterfront, at the Mobil service station a block back, and at the airport. Its cars start at CFP 8,025/14,900 for one/two days including mileage (collision insurance CFP 1,500 a day extra). It also has bicycles/scooters at CFP 1,800/5,900 a day.

Huahine has only two gas stations, both in Fare: Mobil (tel. 68-81-41) is open weekdays 0630–1745, Saturday 0700–1100, Sunday 0630–0930, while Total (tel. 68-71-25) is open weekdays 0630–1700, Saturday 0630–1100, Sunday 0630–0930.

Huahine Lagoon (tel. 68-70-00), next to Restaurant Te Marara at the north end of the Fare waterfront, rents small aluminum boats with outboard motor for CFP 3,000/5,000/8,000 for two/four/eight hours (gas not included). Masks, snorkels, life jackets, anchor, oars, and an ice chest come with the boat. Bicycles are for rent here at CFP 1,500 a day, kayaks CFP 2,000/3,000 a half/full day.

Photos Jojo (tel. 68-89-16), next to Pension Guynette, also has bicycles and represents Europcar.

Local Tours

Island Eco Tours (tel./fax 68-79-67), based at Maeva village, offers four-hour 4WD tours of Huahine twice daily at CFP 5,000. What sets these trips apart from the usual photo-op affairs is the emphasis on archaeology and natural history. It also schedules hiking tours of the Maeva ruins upon request. Owner Paul Atallah is a former student of Professor Yosihiko H. Sinoto, who restored many of the territory's ancient *marae* and he's the only guide on Huahine who has conducted scientific research on the sites he now shows his clients.

Félix Tours (tel. 68-81-69) does a three-hour morning archaeological tour at CFP 3,500 daily except Sunday.

Huahine Land (tel. 68-89-21, fax 68-86-84) offers 3.5-hour 4WD safaris at CFP 4,000 pp, which is a good alternative to renting a car.

Huahine Explorer (tel. 68-87-33, fax 68-77-57), based at Pension Vaihonu Ocean, offers a four-hour 4WD tour (CFP 4,240 pp) twice a day and a daily combined boat and 4WD tour (CFP 10,450, 7.5 hours). Experienced guides introduce the land and flora.

Sailing Huahine (Claude and Martine Bordier, tel./fax 68-72-49) offers snorkeling cruises on the 15-meter yacht *Eden Martin*. A half/full day costs CFP 6,000/12,000 pp including lunch or refreshments (minimum of four people). It's also possible to charter the yacht for one-week cruises within the Society Islands at CFP 60,000 a day, including the skipper and fuel (meals and a CFP 11,000 "boat cleaning" fee are extra). The same in the Tuamotu Islands is CFP 77,000 a day.

Huahine Nautique (tel. 68-83-15) offers a circle-island boat tour (CFP 7,500 pp) with a picnic lunch served on a *motu* and shark feeding.

Photos Jojo (tel. 68-89-16) runs a seven-hour boat trip Monday–Saturday at 1000 for CFP 7,500 pp including lunch.

Airport

The airport (HUH) is three km north of Fare. Make arrangements for the regular airport minibus (CFP 600 pp) at Pension Enite. Avis and Europcar have counters at the airport.

Maeva

At Maeva, six km east of Fare, you encounter that rare combination of an easily accessible archaeological site in a spectacular setting. Here each of the 10 district chiefs of Huahine-nui had his own *marae,* and huge stone walls were erected to defend Maeva against invaders from Bora Bora (and later France). The plentiful small fish in Lake Fauna Nui supported large chiefly and priestly classes (ancient stone fish traps can still be seen near the bridge at the east end of the village). In the 1970s Professor Y. H. Sinoto of Hawaii restored many of the structures strewn along the lakeshore and in the nearby hills. The two small stores in the village sell cold drinks.

There's an **archaeological museum** (no phone, Mon.–Sat. 0900–1600, donations appreciated) in round-ended Fare Pote'e, a replica of an old communal meeting house on the shores of the lake. **Marae Rauhuru** next to Fare Pote'e bears petroglyphs of turtles. From here, walk back along the road toward Fare about 100 meters, to a **fortification wall** on the left, built in 1846 with stones from the *marae* to defend the area against the French. Follow this inland to an ancient well at the foot of the hill, then turn right and continue around the base of the hill until you find the trail up onto Matairea Hill (opposite a stone platform). Twenty meters beyond a second, older fortification wall along the hillside is the access to **Marae Te Ana** on the right. The terraces of this residential area for chiefly families, excavated in 1986, mount the hillside.

Return to the main trail and continue up to the ruins of **Marae Tefano,** which are engulfed by an immense banyan tree. **Marae Matairea Rahi,** to the left, was the most sacred place on Huahine, dedicated to Tane, the principal god of Huahine associated with warfare and canoe building. The

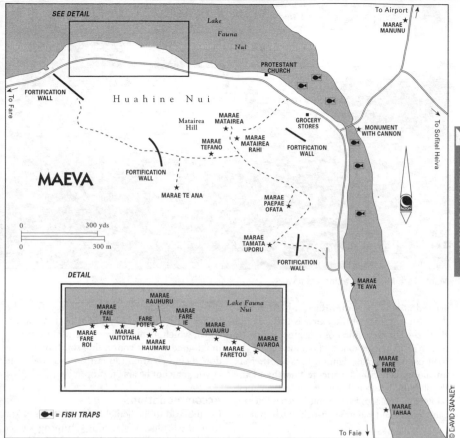

backrests of Huahine's principal chiefs are in the southernmost compound of the *marae,* where the most important religious ceremonies took place. Backtrack a bit and keep straight, then head up the fern-covered hill to the right to **Marae Paepae Ofata,** which gives a magnificent view over the whole northeast coast of Huahine.

Continue southeast on the main trail past several more *marae* and you'll eventually cross another fortification wall and meet a dirt road down to the main highway near **Marae Te Ava.** Throughout this easy two-hour hike, watch for stakes planted with vanilla by the present villagers (please don't touch).

When you get back down to the main road,

walk south a bit to see photogenic **Marae Fare Miro,** then backtrack to the bridge, across which is a **monument** guarded by seven cannon. Beneath it are buried French troops killed in the Battle of Maeva (1846), when the islanders successfully defended their independence against marauding French marines sent to annex the island. The ancient fish traps in the lagoon, recently repaired, are still being used. Fish enter the stone traps with the incoming and outgoing tides.

Seven hundred meters farther along toward the ocean and to the left is two-tiered **Marae Manunu,** the community *marae* of Huahine-nui, dedicated to the gods Oro and Tane. According to a local legend, Princess Hutuhiva

FRENCH POLYNESIA

© DAVID STANLEY

Marae Fare Miro at Huahine's Maeva

arrived at this spot from Raiatea hidden in a drum. In the base of the *marae* is the grave of Raiti, the last great priest of Huahine. When he died in 1915 a huge stone fell from the *marae*. The road passing Marae Manunu runs another six km along the elevated barrier reef north of Lake Fauna Nui directly to Huahine Airport, an alternative route back to Fare. White beaches line this cantaloupe- and watermelon-rich north shore.

Faie

Below the bridge in the center of **Faie,** five km south of Maeva, is a river populated by sacred blue-eyed eels. Legend holds that it was the eels who brought fresh water to the village. You can buy fish to feed them at the red kiosk.

Also at Faie is the **Huahine Pearl Farm** (tel. 78-30–20; daily 1000–1600), which offers a free boat tour of its operation in the hope that you'll buy a pearl.

From Faie the very steep Route Traversiere crosses the mountains to Maroe Bay (2.5 km), making a complete circuit of Huahine-nui pos-

> *Below the bridge in the center of Faie is a river populated by sacred blue-eyed eels. Legend holds that it was the eels who brought fresh water to the village.*

sible. Two hundred meters up this road from the bridge is **Faie Glace** (tel. 68-87-95; closed weekends), which manufactures ice cream from natural ingredients. If continuing south by bicycle don't begin coasting too fast on the other side as you may not be able to stop.

Accommodations

On the road to the Sofitel Heiva Huahine, a km from the bridge at Maeva, is **Camping Vanaa** (Vanaa Delord, tel. 68-89-51) with 13 small thatched *fare* on the beach at CFP 2,500/5,000 single/double including breakfast. Camping is CFP 1,000 pp. Meals in the restaurant are in the CFP 1,000–1,200 range. Your generous hosts try to make you feel at home, and it's a shady spot, conveniently located for exploring the *marae*. The huts are a bit better than those at Ariiura Camping (see Accommodations for Huahine-iti), but the beach isn't as good as the one at Parea. Bring insect repellent.

In 1989 the **Sofitel Heiva Huahine** (tel. 60-61-60, fax 68-85-25) opened in a coconut grove

BOBBY HOLCOMB

Dancer, choreographer, musician, composer, singer, and painter, Bobby Holcomb (1947–1991) personified the all-round artist. He was born in Honolulu, child of a half-Hawaiian, half-Portuguese prostitute and an American sailor. Later he traveled widely, with periods as a rock musician in France and an actor in Venice. From Salvador Dalí he absorbed surrealism. In 1976 Holcomb arrived at Huahine aboard a friend's yacht and there he established his studio at Maeva. Prints of his colorful painting of Polynesian mythology and legends are widely available in the islands, as are recordings of his joyful Tahitian music. With his dreadlocks and tattoos on arms and legs Holcomb personified living theater. He's buried near Marae Fare Miro at Maeva.

on a *motu* two km southeast of Maeva. The 24 rooms in long blocks are CFP 24,500 single or double, the 12 thatched garden bungalows CFP 34,200, and the 18 beach bungalows CFP 51,500, plus 11 percent tax. Six overwater suites

are CFP 62,700 single or double (children under 12 free). Don't drink the tap water. The breakfast and dinner plan is CFP 6,400 pp and it's prudent to be punctual at mealtimes as the staff will refuse to serve latecomers. Happy hour at the Manuia Bar is 1700–1800 (drinks two for one). One of the best Polynesian cultural shows you'll ever see usually takes place here on Monday, Thursday, and Saturday nights at 2000, complete with fire dancing, acrobatics, and coconut tree climbing.

Evocative neo-Polynesian paintings by the late artist/singer Bobby Holcomb highlight the decor in the public areas at the Heiva, and ancient *marae* are preserved in the gardens. Though picturesque, the rooms themselves are poorly constructed and rather dark. Unspoiled white beaches stretch all along this section of the lagoon and there's passable snorkeling off the oceanside beach. A swimming pool is available. The hotel tacks a hefty surcharge on any tours or activities arranged through its reception, but the Maeva archaeological area is only a 30-minute walk away. Europcar has a desk at this hotel. Airport transfers are CFP 2,100/3,400 pp round-trip by bus/limousine.

Huahine-iti

Though the concrete "July Bridge" joins the two islands, Huahine-iti is far less accessible than Huahine-nui. It's 24 km from Fare to Parea via Haapu and another 16 km from Parea back to the bridge via Maroe.

Haapu village was originally built entirely over the water, for lack of sufficient shoreline to house it. The only grocery store on Huahine-iti is at Haapu; otherwise three grocery trucks circle the island several times daily—the locals will know when to expect them. There's a wide white beach along **Avea Bay** with good swimming right beside the road as you approach the southern end of the island. Yachts can follow a protected channel inside the barrier reef down the west coast of Huahine to the wonderful (if occasionally rough) anchorage at Avea Bay but shallows at Point Tiva force sailboats to return to Fare.

On another white beach on the east side of Point Tiva, one km south of Parea, is **Marae**

Anini, the community *marae* of Huahine-iti. It was built by an ancestor of Hiro sometime between 1325 and 1400 as an offshoot of Marae Taputapuatea on Raiatea. Look for petroglyphs on this two-tiered structure, dedicated to the god of war Oro, where human sacrifices once took place. The *marae* is unmarked and hard to find. Go down the track without a bread delivery box, 900 meters north of Ariiura Camping or 500 meters south of Parea. After 200 meters this track reaches the beach, which you follow 100 meters to the right (south) to the huge stones of the *marae*. Surfing is possible in Araara Pass, beside the *motu* just off Marae Anini. If snorkeling here, beware of an outbound current in the pass.

Accommodations

Pension Hine Iti (Pablo and Repeta Serrano, tel./fax 68-74-58) at Haapu, 15 km south of

Fare, has four rooms at CFP 3,000 pp (minimum stay two nights). A common kitchen is available downstairs.

Pension Mauarii (Vetea Breysse, tel./fax 68-86-49), 20 km south of Fare, sits on Avea Bay's lovely shaded white beach. Some of the finest snorkeling in French Polynesia is available along here. Rooms in the main building are CFP 6,500/7,500 single/double, or CFP 9,000 in the mezzanine. The two new beach rooms are also CFP 9,000. The two garden bungalows are CFP 10,000 double or CFP 15,000 for four people. A beach bungalow is also CFP 15,000, all prices plus 6 percent tax. No cooking facilities are provided but a breakfast/dinner plan is available at CFP 3,000 pp. The restaurant is open 1200–1400/1800–2000. If enough guests are present, there's a Friday buffet dinner 1900–2300 with local music. Polynesian seafood is the specialty. The sports center here offers hobie sailing, windsurfing, boat rentals, and a snorkeling trip.

Relais Mahana (tel. 68-81-54, fax 68-85-08) is on the same long white beach as Pension Mauarii, a little over two km west of Parea. The 22 units with fridge are CFP 17,952 single or double, CFP 21,012 triple for a garden bungalow, CFP 2,000 more for a beach bungalow, plus 11 percent tax. For continental breakfast add another CFP 1,120 pp. Bicycles, kayaks, and snorkeling gear are lent free. Recreational activities and the pool/beach are strictly for hotel guests only but the restaurant/bar is open to all, with excellent meals in the CFP 2,000–3,000 range. The Tahitian dance show here on Saturday night is CFP 4,000 (no additional charge for guests on meal plans). Annie's scuba diving center at the resort is also open to all, with dives at 0830 and 1330. Round-trip airport transfers are CFP 2,544 pp.

Ariiura Camping (Hubert Bremond, tel./fax 68-85-20), 22 km south of Fare and 1,400 meters from Parea, shares the same lovely white beach with Relais Mahana, 800 meters northwest. There are 12 small open *fare,* each with a double bed and no lock on the door, at CFP 2,800/3,800 single/double. Camping is CFP 1,200 pp a day, and a communal kitchen and pleasant eating area overlook the turquoise lagoon. Bring food as no grocery stores are nearby, although grocery trucks pass daily, once in the morning and twice in the afternoon Monday–Saturday and twice in the morning on Sunday. Also bring insect repellent and coils. An outrigger canoe is available, and you may be able to rent bicycles at Relais Mahana. The snorkeling and surfing here are superb. The owner will pick you up at the airport or wharf at CFP 2,000 pp round-trip; watch for his pickup truck on the wharf if you arrive by ferry from Papeete.

The **Huahine Beach Club** at Parea is closed as the owners, Nouvelles Frontières, ponder what to do with the property. When it reopens, it should be part of the Paladien hotel chain.

Raiatea and Taha'a

Raiatea

At 171 square km, Raiatea is the second-largest island of French Polynesia. Its main town and port, Uturoa, is the business, educational, and administrative center of the Leeward Islands or Îles Sous-le-Vent (islands under the wind). The balance of Raiatea's population of about 12,000 lives in eight flower-filled villages around the island: Avera, Opoa, Puohine, Fetuna, Vaiaau, Tehurui, Tevaitoa, and Tuu Fenua. The west coast of Raiatea south of Tevaitoa is old Polynesia through and through.

Raiatea is traditionally the ancient Havai'i, the "sacred isle" from which all of eastern Polynesia was colonized. It may at one time have been reached by migrants from the west as the ancient name for Taha'a, Uporu, corresponds to Upolu, just as Havai'i relates to Savai'i, the largest islands of the Samoan chain. A legend tells how Raiatea's first king, Hiro, built a great canoe he

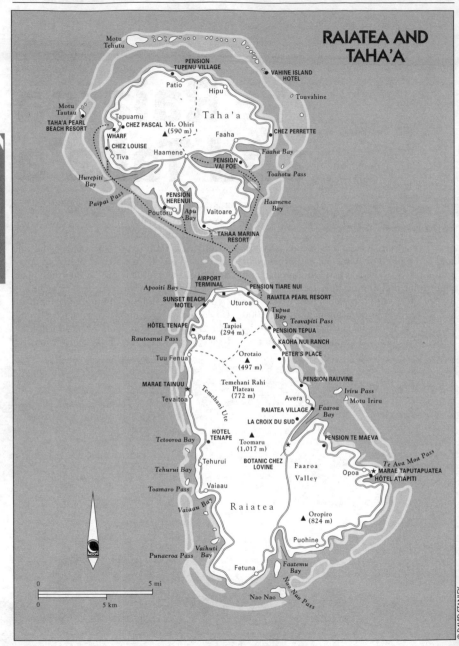

RAIATEA AND
TAHA'A

Motu
Tehutu

PENSION
TUPENU VILLAGE

VAHINE ISLAND
HOTEL

Patio   Hipu

Tuuvahine

Taha'a

Motu
Tautau

TAHA'A PEARL
BEACH RESORT

Tapuamu
CHEZ PASCAL   Mt. Ohiri
WHARF   ▲ (590 m)

CHEZ PERRETTE

CHEZ LOUISE
Tiva   Haamene   Faaha

Faaha Bay

PENSION
VAI POE   Toahotu Pass

Hurepiti
Bay

Paipai Pass

PENSION
HERENUI
Poutoru   Apu
Bay   Vaitoare

Haamene
Bay

TAHAA MARINA
RESORT

AIRPORT
TERMINAL

Apooiti Bay   PENSION TIARE NUI

SUNSET BEACH   RAIATEA PEARL RESORT
MOTEL   Uturoa
Tupua
HÔTEL TENAPE   Tapioi   Bay   Teavapiti Pass
▲ (294 m) PENSION TEPUA
Rautoanui Pass   Pufau

KAOHA NUI RANCH
Tuu Fenua   Orotaio   PETER'S PLACE
▲ (497 m)

Temehani Rahi   PENSION RAUVINE
Plateau
(772 m)   Iriru Pass
MARAE TAINUU   Motu Iriru
Avera
Tevaitoa   Faaroa
RAIATEA VILLAGE   Bay
LA CROIX DU SUD
HOTEL   ▲   PENSION TE MAEVA
TENAPE   Toomaru
Tetooroa Bay   (1,017 m)   Te Ava Moa Pass
BOTANIC CHEZ   MARAE TAPUTAPUATEA
Tehurui   LOVINE   Faaroa   Opoa   ★ HÔTEL ATIAPITI
Tehurui Bay   Valley
Vaiaau
Toamaro Pass

Raiatea

▲ Oropiro
(824 m)
Vaiaau Bay
Puohine

Vaihuti
Punaeroa Pass   Bay
Fetuna   Faatemu
Bay
Nao Nao   Nao Nao Pass

0   5 mi

0   5 km

© DAVID STANLEY

RAIATEA AND TAHA'A HIGHLIGHTS

Gare Maritime: restaurants, information
Tapioi Hill: hiking, viewpoint
Marae Taputapuatea: archaeology, spirits
Taha'a lagoon tour: swimming, snorkeling, scenery
pearl farms: shopping, educational visits

used to sail to Rarotonga. Today Raiatea and Taha'a are mostly worth visiting if you want to get off the beaten tourist track. Though public transportation is scarce, the island offers good possibilities for scuba diving, charter yachting, and hiking, and the varied scenery is worth a stop.

The Land

Raiatea, 229 km northwest of Tahiti, shares a protected lagoon with Taha'a three km away. Legends tell how the two islands were cut apart by a mythical eel. About 30 km of steel-blue sea separates Raiatea from both Huahine and Bora Bora. The highest mountain is Toomaru (1,017 meters), and some of the coastlines are rugged and narrow. All of the people live on a coastal plain planted in coconuts, where cattle also graze.

Tradition maintains that the great Polynesian voyages to Hawaii and New Zealand departed from these shores.

According to Polynesian mythology the god Oro was born from the molten rage of Mt. Temehani (772 meters), the cloud-covered plateau that dominates the northern end of the island. *Tiare apetahi*, a sacred white flower that exists nowhere else on earth and resists transplantation, grows above the 400-meter level on the slopes around the summit. The fragile one-sided blossom represents the five fingers of a beautiful Polynesian girl who fell in love with the handsome son of a high chief, but was unable to marry him because of her lowly birth. The petals pop open forcefully enough at dawn to make a sound and local residents sometimes spend the night on the mountain to be there to hear it. These flowers are protected and there's a minimum CFP 50,000 fine for picking one. Small pink orchids also grow here.

No beaches are found on big, hulking Raiatea itself. Instead, picnickers are taken to picture-postcard *motu* in the lagoon. Surfing is possible at the 10 passes that open onto the Raiatea/Taha'a lagoon, and windsurfers are active. The Leeward Islands are the most popular sailing area in French Polynesia, and most of the charter boats are based at Raiatea. Many pearl farms dot the lagoon around Raiatea and Taha'a.

History

Originally called Havai'i, legend holds that the island was rechristened by Queen Rainuiatea in honor of her parents, Rai, a warrior from Tahiti, and Atea, queen of Opoa. Before European encroachment, Raiatea was the religious, cultural, and political center of what is now French Polynesia. Tradition maintains that the great Polynesian voyages to Hawaii and New Zealand departed from these shores.

Raiatea was Captain Cook's favorite island; he visited three times. During his first voyage in 1769 he called first at Opoa July 20–24. After having surveyed Bora Bora from the sea, he anchored for a week in the Rautoanui Pass on the northwest coast of Raiatea, near the village of Tuu Fenua. During his second voyage Cook lay at anchor twice, first September 8–17, 1773, and again May 25–June 4, 1774, both times at Rautoanui. His third visit was November 3–December 7, 1777, again at Rautoanui. It can therefore be said that Rautoanui (which he calls "Haamanino Harbour" in his journals) was one of Cook's favorite anchorages.

These islands accepted Christianity soon after the Tahitians were converted. The noted Protestant missionary John Williams arrived in 1818, as recalled by a monument in the form of a black basalt pillar standing in front of the Protestant church just north of Uturoa. From Raiatea, Williams carried the gospel to Rarotonga in 1823 and Samoa in 1830. Later Queen Pomare IV spent the years 1844–1847 in exile on Raiatea. When France annexed the island in 1887, Chief Teraupoo launched a resistance campaign that lasted until 1897, when

French troops and warships conquered the island. Teraupoo was captured after six weeks of fighting and deported to New Caledonia, where he remained until 1905. The Queen of Raiatea and 136 of her followers were exiled to remote Eiao Island in the Marquesas.

Uturoa

Uturoa (pop. 4,000) is the territory's second city and the first stop on any exploration of the island. It's an easy place to find your way around with a row of Chinese stores along a main drag opening onto the new Gare Maritime. In 2001 the Uturoa waterfront was entirely redeveloped with a new cruise ship terminal, information offices, restaurants, and shops, plus a traditional-style handicraft market. All of the ferries plying between Tahiti and Bora Bora call here and there's a frequent shuttle to Taha'a. The island's airport is three km west of town with the main yacht charter base, Marina Apooiti, a km beyond that.

Large cruise ships call here several times a week, flooding the little town with visitors. If you'd like to be able to sit at a waterfront café in peace or have the undivided attention of shop clerks, try to find out when love boats such as the *Paul Gauguin, Wind Surf,* and *Tahitian Princess* will be in port and avoid Uturoa those days. Rental cars will be in high demand, so reserve well ahead. If you're a cruise ship passenger yourself, be aware that the various excursions sold on board are highly inflated by multiple commissions. You'll probably save money by dealing directly with the tour operators inside the Gare Maritime right on the wharf, although you could also miss out. The large groups on rushed tours don't have the same experience as those who take the time to spend a few days on these islands.

Hiking

For a view of four islands, climb **Tapioi Hill** (294 meters), the peak topped by a TV antenna behind Uturoa—one of the easiest and most satisfying climbs in French Polynesia. Take the road beside the gendarmerie. This is private property, and although the owners allow visitors to climb the hill on foot, they've posted a sign just before the cattle grid at the bottom of the hill asking that private cars not be used, and this request should be respected. The fastest time on record for climbing Tapioi is 17 minutes, but it's best to allow two or three hours to hike up and down.

Sports and Recreation

The coral at Raiatea is rather poor, but there's ample marinelife, including gray sharks, moray eels, barracudas, manta rays, and countless tropical fish in places such as Tevavapiti Pass. Just off the Raiatea Pearl Resort is the century-old wreck of a 50-meter Dutch coal boat, the *Nordby,* the top of which is 18 meters down.

Hémisphère Sub (Hubert Clot, tel. 66-12-49, fax 66-28-63, VHF channel 68), at the Marina Apooiti and Raiatea Pearl Resort, offers scuba diving at CFP 5,900 per dive (10 dives CFP 50,000). It goes out daily at 0830 and 1430 and offers free pickups.

Diving is also offered by **Te Mara Nui Plongée** (tel. 72-60-19, tel./fax 66-11-88) at the marina just north of Uturoa.

Nauti-Sports (tel. 66-35-83), next to the Kuomintang building at the south end of Uturoa, sells quality snorkeling gear.

There's good swimming in a large pool open to the sea at the **Centre Nautique** *("la piscine")* on the coast just north of Uturoa, beyond the new yacht harbor. The local Polynesians keep their long racing canoes here.

John's Tours (John and Ann Walker, tel./fax 66-33-44) offers fishing from an open speedboat at CFP 10,000 pp a half day (minimum of two).

The **Kaoha Nui Ranch** (Patrick Marinthe, tel./fax 66-25-46) at PK 6, Avera, a few hundred meters north of Pension Manava, charges CFP 4,000 for horseback riding (two hours). A half-day hiking tour to the waterfalls is CFP 2,500. You must reserve 24 hours in advance, and there's a two-person minimum.

(Turn to Transportation in the French Polynesia Introduction for information on yacht charters.)

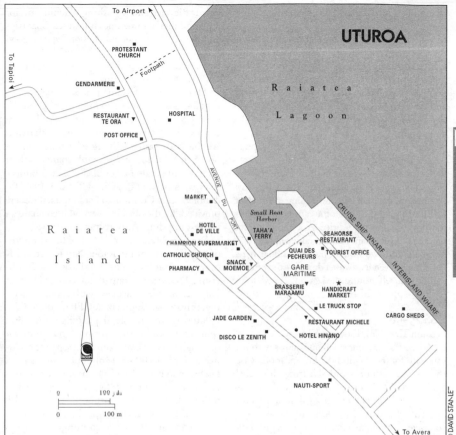

FRENCH POLYNESIA

© DAVID STANLEY

PRACTICALITIES

Most of the places to stay are on the northeast side of Raiatea and we've arranged them here from north to south in each price category. (Accommodations in southern and western Raiatea are covered later under Around Raiatea.) The proprietors often pick up guests who call ahead for reservations at the airport or harbor. The transfers are often free, but ask.

Under US$25

You can camp free on **Motu Iriru,** a tiny island on the south side of Iriru Pass off Avera. It's owned by the territory and serves as a public park with picnic tables, barbecue pits, outdoor showers, and flush toilets. A caretaker keeps the island clean. Permission to picnic or camp here is not required but take food and drinking water. To get there contact West Coast Charters (tel. 79-28-78 or 66-45-39) in the Gare Maritime d'Uturoa. Boat transfers to the *motu* are CFP 5,000 for one person, CFP 3,000 pp for two or three, CFP 2,500 pp for four or five, or CFP 2,000 pp for six or more. The owners of most of the pensions listed below will arrange transfers to Iriru at cheaper rates.

The backpacker's number-one choice on Raiatea is **Peter's Place** (Peter Brotherson, tel. 66-20-01) at Hamoa, six km south of Uturoa and just beyond Pension Manava. The eight neat double rooms in a long block are CFP 1,300 pp, or you can pitch a tent in the large grassy area facing the rooms at CFP 900 pp. A large open pavilion is used for communal cooking but there are no grocery stores nearby, so bring food. The pavilion doubles as a traveler's library with good lighting and it's very pleasant to sit there on a rainy night as torrents of water beat on the tin roof. Bicycles are for rent.

Peter is the progeny of a Danish sea captain named Brotherson who left hundreds of descendants on Raiatea. He or his son Frame sometimes take guests on a hike up the valley to a picturesque waterfall with swimming in the river, fish feeding, and a tour of a vanilla plantation for a negotiable group price. Ask about guided hikes to the Temehani Plateau, taking about three hours up and two hours down, and boat trips. Peter might even lend you a dugout canoe free to paddle yourself around the lagoon. Transfers are CFP 600 pp round-trip.

US$25–50

Pension Tiare Nui (Patrick Bardou, tel. 66-34-06, fax 66-16-06) has four small bungalows with private bath for rent behind the Europcar office between the airport and Uturoa. It's CFP 5,300/5,830/6,360 single/double/triple, or pay CFP 10,930 double for a bungalow and an unlimited mileage car. It's a deal worth checking if you were planning to rent a car anyway, but cooking facilities are not provided. In Uturoa, Techni Isles Sarl (tel. 66-37-81; weekdays 0730–1200/ 1330–1700, Sat. 0730–1200), between Champion Supermarket and Snack Moemoea, books rooms here with cars. At the airport, ask Europcar.

Pension Tepua (tel. 66-33-00, fax 66-32-00) is by the lagoon just beyond Magasin Andre Chinese store, 2.5 km south of Uturoa. The four rooms with shared bath are CFP 6,000 single or double. Five bungalows with kitchen and TV are CFP 9,000 in the garden or CFP 12,000 facing the lagoon. There are also dormitories with four beds (CFP 2,500 pp) and 12 beds (CFP 1,500). A supplement of up to CFP 1,000 is charged if you stay only one night. Common cooking facilities and a swimming pool are provided. Bicycles and a washing machine are for rent, and there's sometimes hot water. Boat trips are offered. The lagoon off Pension Tepua is good for windsurfing and there's surfing off Taoru Island in nearby Teavapiti Pass. Airport transfers are CFP 1,000 pp round-trip.

Three of the best-value places to stay on Raiatea are close together six km south of Uturoa, a CFP 1,500 taxi ride from Uturoa. Aside from Peter's Place previously mentioned, **Pension Kaoha Nui Ranch** (Patrick Marinthe, tel./fax 66-25-46) has four rooms with shared bath at CFP 3,400 single or double. The two bungalows with private bath are CFP 6,300/7,300 double/triple. Communal cooking facilities are provided. It's the obvious selection if you have an interest in riding. Airport transfers are free.

Pension Manava (tel. 66-28-26, fax 66-16-66), right next door to Kaoha Nui Ranch at PK 6, Avera, is run by Andrew and Roselyne Brotherson. This warm, sympathetic couple has four Polynesian-style bungalows with cooking facilities, private bath, and fan at CFP 6,000 or CFP 7,000 single or double, depending on the unit (plus CFP 1,000 per additional person or for one-night stays). Two rooms in a separate building are CFP 4,700 single or double with shared kitchen and bath. A half-day boat trip to southern Raiatea is CFP 3,500 pp, and they also do a full-day boat trip right around Taha'a at CFP 5,500 including lunch (six-person minimum)— these trips are also open to nonguests. *Motu* transfers are CFP 1,500 pp (four-person minimum). Bicycles are for rent. Ask Roselyne to show you how she paints Tahitian pareos. Call for a free airport and harbor pick-up.

Pension Rauvine (Josiah Bordes, tel./fax 66-25-50), at PK 8, Avera, has eight bungalows with cooking facilities at CFP 4,500 single or double, plus CFP 1,000 per extra person. Ask for Francis, who speaks good English and runs 4WD excursions at CFP 4,000. He'll take you over to Motu Iriru for picnicking free upon request. Airport transfers are free upon request.

Pension Yolande (Yolande Roopinia, tel./fax 66-35-28) is in an attractive location facing the lagoon at PK 10, Avera. The four rooms are CFP 5,000/6,000 single/double (private bath). Cooking facilities are provided, but you may be asked to take half pension (CFP 3,500 pp). You'll like the family atmosphere. Airport transfers are CFP 1,500 pp round trip.

US$50–100

The friendly **Sunset Beach Motel Apooiti** (Moana Boubée, tel. 66-33-47, fax 66-33-08) is in a coconut grove five km west of Uturoa. It's on the point across the bay from Marina Apooiti, about 2.5 km west of the airport. The 21 comfortable, well-spaced bungalows with cooking facilities and private bath (hot water) are CFP 8,000/9,000/10,000/11,000 single/double/triple /quad—good value for families (children under 13 are CFP 550 each, under three free). Camping is CFP 1,100 pp here, and there's a large communal kitchen. Discounts of 10 percent a fortnight and 20 percent a month are available, but there's a CFP 1,000 surcharge if you stay only one night. Bicycles are for rent and hitching into Uturoa is easy. It's one of the nicest places to stay in the islands and the managers speak English. Call for free airport transfers.

Bed and Breakfast Bellevue (Max Boucher, tel./fax 66-15-15) has five attractive rooms facing the swimming pool at CFP 7,000/7,900 single/double including breakfast. Each includes private bath, fridge, and TV, but no cooking facilities. It's on the north side of Uturoa, 700 meters up the hill from the Lycée des Îles Sous-le-Vent. Airport transfers are CFP 1,400 pp.

The **Hôtel Hinano** (Augustin Moulon, tel. 66-13-13, fax 66-14-14), conveniently situated on the main street in the center of Uturoa, has 10 basic rooms at CFP 6,000/7,000/8,000 single/double/triple (CFP 1,000 extra for one of the four air-conditioned rooms). Cooking facilities are not available.

The 12-unit **Raiatea Village** (Philippe Roopinia, tel. 66-31-62, fax 66-10-65) is at the mouth of Faaroa Bay (PK 10). A garden bungalow with kitchenette and terrace is CFP 7,215/8,325/ 9,435/10,545 single/double/triple/quad. Airport transfers are CFP 1,100 pp extra.

On the hillside a little beyond is **Pension La Croix du Sud** (Annette and Eric Germa, tel./fax 66-27-55). The three rooms with bath are CFP

7,200/7,700 single/double including breakfast. Cooking facilities are not provided but meals can be ordered. Facilities include a swimming pool and bicycles. Airport transfers are CFP 1,500 pp.

US$100–150

The 28-unit **Raiatea Pearl Resort** (tel. 66-20-23, fax 66-20-20), 1.5 km south of Uturoa, is Raiatea's only luxury hotel. This is the former Raiatea Bali Hai, destroyed by a kitchen fire in 1992 and completely rebuilt in 1994 as the Hôtel Hawaiki Nui. In 1998 it was purchased by Pearl Resorts and it's now at the bottom end of the chain in both services and price. The layout is attractive with a swimming pool overlooking the lagoon. There's no beach but you can snorkel off the end of the pier. The rates are CFP 15,000 double for one of the eight garden rooms, CFP 22,000 for the eight thatched garden bungalows, or CFP 42,000 for the 12 overwater bungalows, plus 11 percent tax. There's a Polynesian dance show Friday and Saturday nights at 2000. A Europcar desk is here. Airport transfers are CFP 1,500 pp each way.

Food

Unpretentious **Restaurant Michele** (tel. 66-14-66; weekdays 0500–1530/1800–2100, Sat. 0500–1430), below Hôtel Hinano (rear side of the building), is a good place for breakfast with coffee, bread, and butter at CFP 310. Chinese meals start around CFP 1,000, otherwise take one of the French dishes costing CFP 1,300–1,800 listed on the menu. The *poisson cru* is CFP 800, a small glass of beer CFP 400.

Brasserie Maraamu (tel. 66-46-64; weekdays 0600–2100, Sat. 1000–1400), is in the corner of the new Gare Maritime facing town. The lunch menu tilts toward Chinese food with main plates CFP 950–1,550. There's also excellent *poisson cru* (CFP 600/950 small/large). A large Hinano is CFP 550.

Brasserie Le Quai des Pêcheurs (tel. 66-43-19; daily 0930–2100), in the side of the Gare Maritime facing the small boat harbor, offers a nice view from its terrace and excellent food. The menu includes *poisson cru* (CFP 950), sashimi (CFP 1,150), fish (CFP 1,500–2,400),

FRENCH POLYNESIA

and meat dishes (CFP 1,600–2,200), bowls of ice cream (CFP 600–800), and draft beer (CFP 400). Ice cream cones are sold from a window facing the harbor. Le Quai des Pêcheurs presents Polynesian dancing Saturday at 2030.

The **Sea Horse Restaurant** (tel. 66-16-34; Mon.–Sat. 1000–1330/1800–2130), on the side of the Gare Maritime facing the cruise ship wharf, serves Chinese dishes CFP 900–1,800 and seafood at CFP 1,500–1,800.

A more upscale choice would be the **Restaurant Jade Garden** (tel. 66-34-40; Wed.–Sat. 1100–1300/1830–2100) on the main street, offering some of the tastiest Chinese dishes this side of Papeete.

Snack Moemoea (tel. 66-39-84; weekdays 0600–1700, Sat. 0600–1400), on the small boat harbor, serves hamburgers (CFP 500) plus a range of French and Chinese dishes on its terrace. Despite the name it's rather upscale with meat dishes at CFP 1,300–1,700, fish at CFP 1,600, and Chinese food at CFP 1,200–1,500.

The largest supermarket is **Champion** (tel. 66-45-45; Mon.–Sat. 0730–1830), facing the small boat harbor. Whole barbecued chickens are CFP 790. A bit north is the **Marché Municipal de Uturoa** (Mon. 0630–1600, Tues.–Fri. 0530–1600, Sat. 0600–1130, Sun. 0430–0730). Most of the stores in Uturoa close for lunch 1200–1330 and it's a ghost town after 1030 on Sunday.

Entertainment

Discothèque Le Zénith (tel. 66-27-49), above Super Marché Leogite opposite Banque Socredo, opens Friday and Saturday at 2200. Entry is free for men until 2230 (for women until 2300), then it begins collecting a CFP 1,000 cover charge.

Information and Services

In the Gare Maritime opposite the cruise ship wharf is a tourist office (tel. 60-07-77, fax 60-07-76; daily 0800–1600).

None of Uturoa's banks open on Saturday but ATMs accessible 24 hours are outside the Banque Socredo and Banque de Tahiti.

The large modern post office (tel. 66-35-50; Mon.–Thurs. 0730–1500, Fri. 0700–1400, Sat.

0800–1000) is opposite the new hospital just north of town, with the gendarmerie (tel. 66-31-07) about 50 meters beyond on the left.

For Internet access, there's Phenix (tel. 66-24-79) between Uturoa and the airport.

There are free public toilets (*sanitaires publics*) in the Gare Maritime facing the main wharf, not far from the tourist office. It's hard to find, so ask.

A km west of the Sunset Beach Motel is Raiatea Carenage Services (tel. 66-22-96), a repair facility often used by cruising yachts. The only easily accessible slip facilities in French Polynesia are here (maximum 22 tons).

Health

Uturoa's public hospital (tel. 60-08-00) is on the north side of town.

Dr. Patrick Lazarini (tel. 66-23-01), general practitioner, has an office above La Palme d'Or in the center of Uturoa. It's open weekdays 0700–1200/1330–1730, Saturday 0800–1200.

Several private doctors have offices above the pharmacy opposite the Catholic church in central Uturoa. Among them are Dr. Alain Repiton-Préneuf and Dr. Bruno Bataillon, general practitioners.

The Pharmacy (tel. 66-34-44), opposite the Catholic church, is open weekdays 0730–1200/1330–1730, Saturday 0730–1200, Sunday 0930–1030.

TRANSPORTATION

Getting There and Away

The **Air Tahiti** office (tel. 60-04-44) is at the airport. Flights from Raiatea to Maupiti (CFP 5,900) operate three times a week. (For information on flights and ships from Papeete, Huahine, and Bora Bora see Transportation in the introduction to French Polynesia.)

You can catch the *Vaeanu* and *Hawaiki-Nui* to Bora Bora, Huahine, and Papeete twice weekly. (Consult the schedule in the introduction to French Polynesia.) Tickets for the *Vaeanu* (tel. 66-22-22) are sold when the ship arrives. The *Hawaiki-Nui* office (tel. 66-42-10; weekdays 0800–1100) is at the south end of the main wharf.

The fast catamaran *Aremiti III* (tel. 77-90-

99) uses the same office as the *Hawaiki-Nui* but tickets are sold only when the vessel arrives. It leaves for Huahine (CFP 1,700) and Papeete (CFP 3,200) Monday and Friday at 1400.

A government supply barge, the *Meherio III,* shuttles twice a month between Raiatea and Maupiti, usually departing Raiatea on Thursday. The exact time varies, so check with the Capitainerie Port d'Uturoa (tel. 66-31-52) on the interisland wharf.

The yellow and blue *Maupiti Express* (tel. 66-37-81, tel./fax 67-66-69), a fast ferry with 62 airline-type seats, charges CFP 2,500/3,500 one-way/round-trip between Raiatea and Bora Bora, departing Uturoa for Bora Bora Monday, Wednesday, and Friday afternoons. It's not possible to go directly from Raiatea to Maupiti on this vessel—you must overnight on Bora Bora—although you can buy a through ticket for CFP 3,500.

The fast ferries *(navettes)* of **S.A.R.L. Enota** (tel./fax 65-61-33) shuttle between Raiatea and Taha'a at CFP 850 pp each way (bicycles CFP 500). The fleet consists of two 57-seat ferries painted yellow and blue. The *Uporu* serves Taha'a's west coast (Taha'a Marina, Poutoru, Patii, Tiva, Tapuamu) while the *Iripau* serves the east coast (Haamene, Faaha Quai Amaru). Both leave Uturoa at 1045 and 1645 on weekdays, but one of the *Uporu's* trips terminates at the Taha'a Marina. On Monday, Wednesday, and Friday one of the *Iripau* trips has a bus connection between Faaha Quai Amaru and Patio. On Saturday only the west coast service operates—once in the morning. There's no schedule at all on Sunday and holidays.

The 66-passenger ferry *Tamarii Taha'a* (tel. 65-65-29) also operates between Raiatea and Taha'a twice on weekdays and once on Saturday morning. Verify the schedules a day before.

Getting Around

Getting around Raiatea by *le truck* isn't easy. You should be able to use them to get into town in the morning and the people where you're staying will know at what time you have to be waiting. In Uturoa the *trucks* usually park in front of Restaurant Michele and the drivers themselves are the only reliable source of departure information.

In theory they leave Uturoa for Opoa at 1015 and 1515 and for Fetuna at 0930 and 1530 on weekdays only.

Raiatea Location Europcar (tel. 66-34-06 or 78-33-53, fax 66-16-06), between the airport and Uturoa, is the main car rental operator on Raiatea. The cars begin around CFP 9,000 a day, including mileage and insurance (minimum age 18). Ask about the package that gives you a bungalow behind the main office and a small car at CFP 10,930. Bicycles are CFP 1,700/2,200/3,300 for four/eight/24 hours (expensive). Apart from cars and bikes, Raiatea Location rents a four-meter boat with a six-horsepower motor at CFP 6,600/8,800 a four/eight hours. Scooter rentals are generally unavailable.

Avis (tel. 66-20-80) is at the airport only. Its cars start at CFP 9,000/16,371/23,754 for one/two/three days all inclusive.

Garage Motu Tapu (tel. 66-33-09), in a poorly marked building a few hundred meters east of the airport, also rents cars.

Local Tours

Many of the hotels and pensions run circle-island bus tours and boat trips to a *motu* or Taha'a. **Raiatea Discovery** (Gérard and Maria, tel./fax 66-24-16) offers 4WD excursions into the interior at CFP 4,400 (four-person minimum). The same as part of a full-day package including a boat trip, snorkeling, and picnic on a *motu* is CFP 9,000 (six-person minimum).

West Coast Charters (Anne-Marie and Tony Tucker, tel./fax 66-45-39), in the Gare Maritime, offers a full-day boat tour around Taha'a or Raiatea (CFP 6,500 pp including lunch, minimum of six) and a half-day Faaroa River tour (CFP 4,500 pp, minimum of four).

Almost Paradise Tours (tel. 66-23-64), run by Faaroa Bay resident Bill Kolans, offers a very good three-hour minibus tour in American English at US$50 pp (minimum of four).

Airport

The airport (RFP) is three km northwest of Uturoa. A taxi from the Uturoa market taxi stand (tel. 66-20-60) to the airport is CFP 1,000 (double tariff late at night). Most of the hotels pick up clients at the airport free of charge upon request. Avis and Europcar both have car rental desks inside the terminal.

The Air Tahiti reservations office is in a separate building adjacent to the main terminal. The Tourist Board information kiosk at the airport is open at flight times only. The airport restaurant offers a good plat du jour at lunchtime.

Around Raiatea

It will take the better part of a day to ride a bicycle the 150 km around Raiatea; by car you can take anywhere from a couple of hours to a leisurely day.

The road down the east coast circles fjordlike **Faaroa Bay,** associated with the legends of Polynesian migration. Stardust Marine has a yacht charter base on the north side of the bay, and from the anchorage there's a fine view of Toomaru, highest peak in the Leeward Islands. Boat trips are offered up the Apoomau River, which drains the Faaroa Valley. It's navigable for about a kilometer, and if you're on a yacht you could explore it with your dingy. Yellow hibiscus flourishes along the river's banks.

At the head of Faaroa Bay is **Botanic Chez Lovine** (tel. 66-14-45; admission CFP 200), PK 14.5, which displays a wide variety of local plant species in a lush garden.

Instead of crossing the island, keep left and follow the coast around to a point of land just beyond Opoa, 32 km from Uturoa. Here stands **Marae Taputapuatea,** one of the largest and best preserved temples in Polynesia, its mighty *ahu* measuring 43 meters long, 7.3 meters wide, and between two and three meters high. Before it is a rectangular courtyard paved with black volcanic rocks. A small platform in the middle of the *ahu* once bore the image of Oro, god of fertility and war (now represented by a reproduction); backrests still mark the seats of high chiefs on the courtyard. Marae Taputapuatea is directly opposite Te Ava Moa Pass, and fires on the *marae* may once have been beacons to ancient navigators.

Several of the temple platforms have been restored. **Hauvivi** was the welcoming *marae* where guests would have been received as they disembarked from their canoes. They would then proceed to Marae Taputapuatea, the main temple, where rituals were performed. Meals were served

on **Hiti Tai,** a temple platform on the north side of the complex. **Papa Ofeoro** was the place of sacrifice (about 5,000 skulls were discovered during excavations at the site). **Opu Teina** near the beach was the temple platform where visitors would say their farewells. Departing chiefs would often take a stone from this *marae* to be planted in new *marae* elsewhere, which would also receive the name Marae Taputapuatea.

In 1995 a fleet of traditional Polynesian voyaging canoes, including three from Hawaii and two each from Cook Islands and Tahiti, plus an Easter Island raft, gathered at Taputaputea to lift a 650-year-old curse and rededicate the *marae.* The seven canoes then left for the Marquesas, navigating by the stars and swells. Some carried on to Hawaii and the west coast of the United States in an amazing demonstration of the current revival of this aspect of traditional culture. In April 2000, a Tattoo Festival took place at Marae Taputapuatea. During important events, firewalking is practiced at a site across the road from the main temples.

The only places to buy food in the southern part of Raiatea are the two Chinese grocery stores at **Fetuna** and another at **Vaiaau,** on the west side of Raiatea. Vaiaau Bay marks the end of the protected inner channel from Uturoa around Raiatea clockwise and yachts must exit the lagoon through Toamaro Pass in order to continue northward. At Rautoanui Pass sailboats can come back in behind the barrier reef to continue the circumnavigation, with the possibility of a side trip south to Tevaitoa.

Behind Tevaitoa church is **Marae Tainuu,** dedicated to the ancient god Taaroa. Petroglyphs on a broken stone by the road at the entrance to the church show a turtle and some other indistinguishable figure. At Tevaitoa Chief Teraupo and his people fought their last battles against the French invaders in early 1897.

© M.E. DE VOS

FRENCH POLYNESIA

Marea Taputapuatea on Raiatea is among the most sacred sites in Polynesia.

The territory's largest yacht charter base is the **Marina Apooiti,** which opened in 1982 one km west of the airport. Aside from The Moorings and Tahiti Yacht Charter, there's a large restaurant/bar here and a dive shop. (For information on chartering, see Yacht Charters in the French Polynesia Introduction.)

Accommodations Around Raiatea

Pension Te Maeva (tel. 66-37-28), at PK 23.5 Est toward Opoa, has two bungalows on the hillside at CFP 6,500/7,200 single/double including breakfast. Dinner is CFP 3,000 pp. There's a swimming pool and free bicycles. Airport transfers are free if you stay two nights.

The **Hôtel Atiapiti** (Marie-Claude Rajaud, tel./fax 66-16-65), on the beach just south of Marae Taputapuatea at PK 31 Est, Opoa, has six self-catering beach bungalows and one garden bungalow from CFP 9,500 double or CFP

12,500 for up to five (children under 12 free). Half board is CFP 4,000 pp, or if you'd rather order à la carte, the restaurant has meat dishes (CFP 1,000–1,500) and fish (CFP 1,600–2,200). The managers organize excursions to a *motu* and around the island, and there's great snorkeling off their wharf. The view of Huahine from here is excellent. Bicycles are CFP 1,000 a day. The hotel's biggest drawback (or advantage!) is its isolation, but someone will pick you up at the port or airport if you call ahead (CFP 2,200 pp round-trip). It's good for a couple of days of relaxation.

In 1999 the **Hôtel Tenape** (Marie-Hélène Viot, tel. 60-01-00, fax 60-01-01) opened at PK 10, Pufau, on the west coast. The 17 air-conditioned rooms in this long two-story building start at CFP 18,500 single or double (transfers CFP 1,500 pp). The rectangular swimming pool substitutes for a beach.

Taha'a

Raiatea's 90-square-km lagoonmate Taha'a is shaped like a hibiscus flower with four long bays cutting into its rugged south side. Mount Ohiri (590 meters), highest point on the island, got its name from Hiro, god of thieves, who was born here. Taha'a is known as the "vanilla island" for its plantations that produce 70 percent of the territory's "black gold." The Taha'a Festival in late October includes stone fishing, with a line of people in canoes herding the fish into a cove by beating stones on the surface of the lagoon. In November the Hawaiki Nui Outrigger Canoe Race passes Taha'a on its way from Huahine to Bora Bora.

It's a quiet island, with little traffic and few tourists. Most families use speedboats to commute to their gardens on the reef islets or to fishing spots, or to zip over to Raiatea on shopping trips, so they don't really need cars. Beaches are scarce on the main island but the string of *motu* off the northeast side of Taha'a has fine white-sand beaches. The pension owners and tour operators arrange picnics on a few of these, and pearl farms have been established on some. This is the only Society Island you can sail a yacht or cruise ship right around inside the barrier reef, and the many anchorages and central location between Raiatea, Huahine, and Bora Bora make Taha'a a favorite of both cruisers and charterers.

There aren't many specific attractions on Taha'a, and a dearth of inexpensive places to stay and lack of public transportation has kept this island off the beaten track. The easy way to visit Taha'a is still an all-day outrigger canoe tour from Raiatea. This could change, but meanwhile the isolation has made the 4,500 Taha'a islanders rather wary of outsiders.

Orientation

The administrative center is at Patio (or Iripau) on the north coast, where the post office, *mairie,*

> *The Taha'a Festival in late October includes stone fishing, with a line of people in canoes herding the fish into a cove by beating stones on the surface of the lagoon.*

and gendarmerie (tel. 65-64-07) share one compound. A second post office is at Haamene where four roads meet. The ship from Papeete ties up to a wharf at Tapuamu, and there's a large covered area at the terminal where you could spread a sleeping bag in a pinch. The Banque Socredo branch is also at Tapuamu, while the Banque de Tahiti (tel. 65-63-14) is at Haamene.

The 67-km coral road around the main part of the island passes six of the eight villages; the other two are south of Haamene. A scenic road goes over the 141-meter Col Taira between Haamene and Tiva. There are ferries from Raiatea to Tapuamu and Haamene but no regular public transportation.

Sights

The mountain pass between Haamene and Tiva offers excellent views of Hurepiti and Haamene Bays, two of the four deep fjords cutting into the southern side of the island. You could also follow the rough track from Haamene up to the Col Vaitoetoe for an even better view. This track continues north, coming out near the hospital in Patio.

Rarahu, the girl immortalized in Pierre Loti's 1880 novel *The Marriage of Loti,* is buried near Vaitoare village at the south end of Taha'a, east of the Taha'a Marina Resort.

Activities

Shark Dive (Bertil Venzo, tel. 65-65-55, fax 65-65-60) at Hurepiti Bay visits more than 20 diving spots around Raiatea and Taha'a islands for CFP 6,000 including gear.

ACCOMMODATIONS

US$25–50

The most convenient and least expensive place is **Chez Pascal** (Pascal Tamaehu, tel./fax 65-60-42). From the Tapuamu ferry wharf you'll see a

VANILLA

Vanilla, a vine belonging to the orchid family, is grown on small family plantations. Brought to Tahiti from Manila in 1848, the *Tahitensis* type, which has a worldwide reputation, originated from a mutation of *Fragrans vanilla*. The plants must be hand-pollinated, then harvested between April and June. The pods are then put out to dry for a couple of months—an exceptionally time-consuming process. Between 1915 and 1933 Tahiti produced 50–150 tons of vanilla a year, peaking in 1949 at 200 tons. Production remained high until 1966, when a steady decline began because of the producers' leaving for paid employment in Papeete related to nuclear testing. By 1990 production had fallen to only 39 metric tons, though things have picked up since then.

small bridge at the head of the bay. Turn left as you leave the dock and head for this. Chez Pascal is the first house north of the bridge on the inland side. The rate for the four bungalows and two rooms is CFP 4,500 pp for bed, breakfast, and dinner, or CFP 3,000 pp with breakfast only. Boat trips to a *motu* and the loan of the family bicycle are possible.

Chez Louise (tel. 65-66-88) at Tiva has dormitory space for 12 people at CFP 5,000 pp including all meals. Bicycles are for rent. Yachties often stop to have a meal here.

Pension Tupenu Village (Henri and Karine Manea, tel. 65-62-01) in Patio offers three rooms downstairs and two upstairs at CFP 5,000 single or double (two-night minimum stay). The bathrooms and kitchen are shared.

US$50–100

Pension Herenui (tel./fax 65-64-17) at Poutoru has three *fare* at CFP 7,000 single or double (children under 12 free), plus CFP 3,500 pp for half board. There's a circular swimming pool. It's easily accessible weekdays by ferry to Poutoru.

Hôtel L'Hibiscus (tel. 65-61-06, fax 65-65-65) is on the northeast side of Haamene Bay. There are two plain rooms with shared bath at CFP 6,084

and three small bungalows with bath at CFP 9,260 plus tax. Meals are CFP 4,056/6,140 pp for half/full board. Cooking facilities and common drinking water are not supplied (bring bottled water). Verify all prices carefully upon arrival as misunderstandings have occurred in past.

Nearby on Haamene Bay is **Pension Vai Poe** (Patricia and Daniel Amaru, tel./fax 65-60-83) with four self-catering bungalows at CFP 8,000 double. It's better value than L'Hibiscus. Call for boat transfers from Uturoa (CFP 3,600 pp round-trip). Otherwise the ferry from Uturoa will drop you at Faaha Quai Amaru near here.

Chez Perrette (Perrette Tehuitua, tel. 65-65-78) is on a reasonable beach at Faaopore, 10 km east of Haamene. It's CFP 17,000 double with all meals in the one self-catering bungalow.

US$100–150

Pension Au Phil de Temps (tel./fax 65-64-19) at Tapuamu has two *fare* at CFP 12,000 pp plus tax (three-night minimum stay). All meals, boat trips, and 4WD land tours are included.

The **Taha'a Marina Resort** (tel. 65-61-01, fax 65-63-87, VHF channel 68), also known as the Hôtel Marina Iti, sits at the isolated south tip of Taha'a on Taha'a's only sandy beach. From here there are marvelous views of the mountains of Taha'a and across to Raiatea. The five beach bungalows are CFP 22,000 single or double, or pay CFP 15,000 for the one garden bungalow. A third person pays CFP 2,000. Cooking facilities are not provided and meals are CFP 5,200 pp extra for breakfast and dinner. Use of bicycles, canoe, and snorkeling gear is included, and scuba diving is available. As you'll have guessed, the Taha'a Marina caters to an upmarket crowd on yacht charters from Raiatea, and numerous cruising yachts anchor in the calm waters offshore. The ferry *Uporu* from Raiatea stops here.

US$250 and up

In 2002 the **Taha'a Pearl Beach Resort and Spa** (tel. 50-84-53) opened on Motu Tautau opposite the shipping wharf at Tapuamu. The 12 beach bungalows with private swimming pools start at CFP 70,000 double, while the 48 over-water bungalows are from CFP 72,000, plus 11 percent tax. Full board is another CFP 10,500 pp. Verify the price of boat transfers beforehand is it can range CFP 3,000–10,000 pp.

Hôtel Vahine Island (tel. 65-67-38, fax 65-67-70, VHF channel 68), on Motu Tuu-vahine off the northeast side of the island, has six seafront bungalows at CFP 32,000 single or double, plus three overwater units at CFP 49,000, plus 11 percent tax. For half/full board add CFP 7,000/10,300 pp, for airport transfers CFP 6,000 pp. Outrigger canoes, windsurf-ing, snorkeling, and fishing gear are free, and moorings are provided for yachts.

OTHER PRACTICALITIES

Food
Village stores are at Tapuamu, Tiva, Haamene, and Patio. Grocery trucks circle the island daily except Sunday and any resident will know when to watch for them.

Health
There's a medical center (tel. 65-63-31) at Patio. Dr. Laurent Jereczek (tel. 65-60-60) is at Haamene.

Getting There
There's no airport on Taha'a. Large ships and ferries call at Tapuamu Wharf on the west side of Taha'a just behind the Total service station. There's a telephone booth on the wharf that you could use to call your hotel to have someone pick you up.

The *Vaeanu* departs Taha'a for Raiatea, Huahine, and Papeete Tuesday and Thursday at 1500, and Sunday at 1130; it goes to Bora Bora Sunday at 0900. The *Hawaiki-Nui* visits Taha'a southbound only. The *Maupiti Express* leaves Taha'a for Bora Bora Monday, Wednesday, and Friday at 1615 (CFP 2,500).

RAIATEA AND TAHA'A INTERNET RESOURCES

Accommodations

Bed and Breakfast Bellevue, Raiatea
raiateabellevue@mail.pf

Hôtel Atiapiti, Raiatea
atiapiti@mail.pf

Hôtel L'Hibiscus, Taha'a
www.tahaa-tahiti.com
hibiscus@tahaa-tahiti.com

Hôtel Tenape, Raiatea
www.raiatea.com/tenape
hoteltenape@yahoo.fr

Hôtel Vahine Island, Taha'a
www.ila-chateau.com/vahine/index.htm
vahine.island@mail.pf

Pension Au Phil de Temps, Taha'a
moutte.junior@mail.pf

Pension Kaoha Nui Ranch, Raiatea
www.tahitidecouvrir.com
kaoha.nui@mail.pf

Pension Manava, Raiatea
www.manavapension.com
manava@free.fr

Pension Rauvine, Raiatea
www.pensionrauvine.pf
pensionrauvine@mail.pf

Pension Te Maeva, Raiatea
www.temaeva.com
temaeva@mail.pf

Pension Tepua, Raiatea
pension-tepua@mail.pf

Pension Vai Poe, Taha'a
v.p@mail.pf

Raiatea Pearl Resort, Raiatea
h.raiateapearl@mail.pf

Raiatea Village, Raiatea
raiatea.village@mail.pf

Sunset Beach Motel Apooiti, Raiatea
www.raiatea.com/sunsetbeach
sunsetbeach@mail.pf

The **Le Navette des Îles** leaves Taha'a for Raiatea at 0515 and 1210 on weekdays and only in the morning on Saturday (CFP 850 pp each way, bicycles CFP 500). Make sure to verify the routes and times, as they vary. (For more information see Raiatea, earlier in this chapter.)

Getting Around

Trucks on Taha'a are for transporting school-children only, so you may have to hitch to get around. It's not that hard to hitch a ride down the west coast from Patio to Haamene, but there's almost no traffic along the east coast.

Rental cars are available from **Europcar** (tel. 65-67-00, fax 65-68-08) at the Total station next to Tapuamu Wharf, **Taha'a Transport Services** (tel. 65-67-10) at the Taha'a Marina Resort, and **Avis** (tel. 65-66-77) at Haamene Wharf. The Taha'a Marina also rents bicycles. Avis charges CFP 7,900 a day with 100 kilo-meters (extra kms CFP 40 each); Europcar is CFP 8,200 a day with unlimited kilometers and insurance. It's smart to book ahead if you want to be sure of a car.

Local Tours

Several companies offer full-day outrigger canoe trips right around Taha'a at CFP 10,000 pp, such as **Taha'a Pearl Tour** (Bruno Fabre, tel. 66-10-90). Lunch, snorkeling, a visit to a pearl farm and vanilla plantation, and transfers on Raiatea are included. Bruno takes his guests to the best snorkeling spots around Taha'a, not just the convenient but less spectacular "coral gardens" off eastern Taha'a, which the quickie tours from Raiatea prefer to visit. He doesn't cater to large groups off cruise ships.

Land tours by 4WD are popular on Taha'a. **Vai Poe Tours** (tel./fax 65-60-83), based at Pension Vai Poe on Haamene Bay, does a half-day trip including a drive across the island at CFP

Sports and Recreation

Bisou Futé
www.multimania.com/tahiticharter

Hémisphère Sub, Raiatea
www.diveraiatea.com
hemis-subdiving@mail.pf

Shark Dive, Taha'a
www.dive.pf
shark@dive.pf

Te Mara Nui Plongée, Raiatea
www.temaranui.pf
temaranui@mail.pf

Transportation and Tours

Danae cruises
www.danaecruise-tahiti.com
claudine.danae@mail.pf

Europcar, Raiatea and Taha'a
europcar-loc@mail.pf

les Navettes des Îles
rtts@mail.pf

Raiatea Discovery, Raiatea
www.raiateadiscovery.fr.st
raidiscovery@mail.pf

Taha'a Pearl Tour, Taha'a
www.tahaa.net
tpt@mail.pf

Taha'a Transport Services, Taha'a
www.xroy.com/islv/tts.htm

Vanilla Tours, Taha'a
vanilla.tours@mail.pf

5,000, or CFP 7,000 for a full day including a canoe ride and picnic lunch. **Edwin Mama** (tel. 65-62-18) at Haamene offers about the same. **Vanilla Tours** (Alain and Cristina Plantier, tel. 65-62-46), near Sophie Boutique at Hurepiti Bay, is a half-day, ethno-botanical tour by 4WD which operates whenever four people have booked (CFP 5,000 pp without lunch). Alain is very knowledgeable about the island's botany and speaks English.

Bora Bora

Bora Bora, 260 km northwest of Papeete, is everyone's idea of a South Pacific island. Dramatic basalt peaks soar 700 meters above a gorgeous, multicolored lagoon. Slopes and valleys blossom with hibiscus. Some of the most perfect beaches you'll ever see are here, replete with topless sunbathers. Not only are the beaches good but there's plenty to see and do. The local population of 6,000 lives in three villages, Anau, Faanui, and Vaitape. Many are skilled dancers. To see them practicing in the evening, follow the beat of village drums back to their source.

The Land

Seven-million-year-old Bora Bora (29 square km) is made up of a 10-km-long main island, a few smaller high islands in the lagoon, and a long ring of *motu* on the barrier reef. Pofai Bay marks the center of the island's collapsed crater with Toopua and Toopuaiti as its eroded west wall. Mount Pahia's gray basalt mass rises 649 meters behind Vaitape, and above it soar the sheer cliffs of Otemanu's mighty volcanic plug (727 meters). The wide-angle scenery of the main island is complemented by the surrounding coral reef and numerous *motu*, one of which bears the airport. Motu Tapu of the travel brochures was featured in F. W. Murnau's classic 1931 silent movie *Tabu* about two young lovers who escape to this tiny island.

BORA BORA

Te Ava Nui Pass is the only entry through the barrier reef.

History

The letter "b" doesn't exist in Tahitian, so Bora Bora is actually Pora Pora, meaning "first born" since this was the first island created after Raiatea. The island's traditional name, Vava'u, suggests Tongan voyagers may have reached here centuries ago. It's believed Bora Bora has been inhabited since the year 900 and 42 *marae* ruins can still be found around the island. The Bora Borans

of yesteryear were indomitable warriors who often raided Maupiti, Taha'a, and Raiatea.

"Discovered" by Roggeveen in 1722, Bora Bora was visited by Captain James Cook in 1769 and 1777. The first European to live on the island was James O'Connor, a survivor of the British whaler *Matilda* wrecked at Moruroa atoll in 1793. O'Connor made his way to Tahiti where he married into the Pomare family, and eventually ended up living in a little grass shack on "Matilda Point," later corrupted to Matira Point. In 1895 the island was annexed by France.

BORA BORA HIGHLIGHTS

Mt. Otemanu: scenery, geology
Bloody Mary's: atmosphere, scenery, food
Matira Beach: swimming, snorkeling, marinelife
Fitiiu Point: war relics, scenery
lagoon tours: snorkeling, marinelife, scenery

In February 1942 the Americans hastily set up a refueling and regrouping base, code-named "Bobcat," on the island to serve shipping between the U.S. west coast or Panama Canal and Australia/New Zealand. You can still see remains from this time, including eight huge naval guns placed here to defend the island against a surprise Japanese attack that never materialized. The big lagoon with only one pass offered secure anchorage for as many as 100 U.S. Navy transports at a time. The Americans built Farepiti Wharf and a cable was stretched across Faanui Bay. Ships would hock onto the cable instead of dropping an-

The letter "b" doesn't exist in Tahitian, so Bora Bora is actually Pora Pora, meaning "first born" since this was the first island created after Raiatea.

chor. A road was built around the island and by April 1943 the present airfield on Motu Mute had been constructed. The 4,400 American army troops also left behind 130 half-caste babies, 40 percent of whom died of starvation when the base closed in June 1946 and the abandoned infants were forced to switch from their accustomed American baby formulas to island food. The survivors are now approaching ripe middle age. Novelist James A. Michener, a young naval officer at the time, left perhaps the most enduring legacy by modeling his Bali Hai on this "enchanted island," Bora Bora.

Orientation

You can arrive at Motu Mute airport and be carried to Vaitape Wharf by catamaran, or disembark from a ship at Farepiti Wharf, three km north of Vaitape. Most of the stores, banks, and offices are near Vaitape Wharf (and free public toilets are provided in the souvenir shop on the wharf itself). The finest beaches are at Matira Point at the island's southern tip.

Sights of Bora Bora

Vaitape

Behind the Banque de Tahiti at Vaitape Wharf is the **monument to Alain Gerbault,** who sailed his yacht, the *Firecrest,* solo around the world 1923–1929—the first Frenchman to do so. Gerbault's first visit to Bora Bora was in 1926. He returned to Polynesia in 1933 and stayed until 1940. A supporter of the Pétian regime in France, he left Bora Bora when the colony declared its support for General de Gaulle and died at Timor a year later while trying to return to Vichy France.

To get an idea of how the Bora Borans live, take a stroll through Vaitape village: go up the road that begins just south of the Protestant church.

Around the Island

The largely paved and level 32-km road around the island makes it easy to see Bora Bora by

rented bicycle. At the head of **Pofai Bay** notice the odd assortment of looted war wreckage across the road from Alain Linda Galerie d'Art. Surrounded by a barbed wire fence are a seven-inch American gun dragged here from Tereia Point in 1982 and two huge anchors. The locations of seven other MK II naval guns that have thus far escaped desecration are given below.

Stop at **Bloody Mary's Restaurant** to scan the goofy displays outside the gate, but more important to get the classic view of the island's soaring peaks across Pofai Bay as it appears in countless brochures. For an even better view go inland on the unmarked road that begins at a double electricity pole 100 meters north of Bloody Mary's. This leads to a jeep route with two concrete tracks up the 139-meter-high hill to a **radio tower,** a 10-minute hike. From the

© DAVID STANLEY

one of eight U.S. naval guns left behind in 1945

tower you get a superb view of the south end of the island.

The finest beach on the island stretches east from Hôtel Bora Bora to Matira Point. Some of the best **snorkeling,** with a varied multitude of colorful tropical fish, is off the small point at Hôtel Bora Bora. Enter from east of the hotel grounds (such as via the Bora Diving Center or the beach beyond) and let the current pull you toward the hotel jetty, as the hotel staff don't appreciate strangers who stroll through their lobby to get to the beach. From the way they approach you, the small fish are quite obviously accustomed to being fed here. Stay on the east side of the point, away from the overwater bungalows. For a more natural scene you could also snorkel due south to the northern edge of the barrier reef. Just beware of getting run over by a boat.

Two **naval guns** sit on the ridge above Hôtel Matira, but unfortunately residential construction has blocked the access route and it's no longer possible to visit.

Bora Bora's most popular public beach is **Matira Beach Park** in front of the huge open thatched pavilion directly across the street from the Beachcomber Inter-Continental on Matira Point. Don't leave valuables unattended here. At low tide you can wade from the end of **Matira Point** right out to the reef. These same shallows prevent yachts from sailing around the island inside the barrier reef. Northwest of the point is **Motu Piti uu Uta** with the Sofitel Motu Resort and more great snorkeling (if you swim over, don't enter the Sofitel Motu grounds as you won't be welcome).

Proceed north to the **Sofitel Marara,** a good place for a leisurely beer. Visitors are also unwelcome at Club Med, which the road climbs over a hill to avoid. The two general stores at **Anau** can supply a cold drink or a snack.

On the north side of Vairou Bay the road begins to ascend a ridge. Halfway up the slope, look down to the right and by the shore you'll see the *ahu* of **Marae Aehautai,** the most intact of the three *marae* in this area. From the *marae* there's a stupendous view of Otemanu and you should be able to pick out Te Ana Opea cave far up on the side of the mountain. To visit the two American **seven-inch guns** on Fitiiu Point, follow the rough jeep track to the right at the top of the ridge a few hundred meters east (on foot) to a huge black rock from which you can see the guns. The steep unpaved road on the other side of this ridge can be

FRENCH POLYNESIA

dangerous on a bicycle, so slow down or get off and walk. There's a municipal dump in this area and you might catch a stench of burning garbage.

Just before Taihi Point at the north end of the main island is a **Musée de la Marine** (tel. 67-75-24; donations accepted) on the right, which is usually closed. Just beyond Taihi Point you'll notice a concrete trestle running right up the side of the hill from the ruins of a group of platforms meant to be the overwater bungalows. This is all that remains an undercapitalized **Hyatt Regency hotel** project that went broke in the early 1980s. Actors Jack Nicholson and Marlon Brando are reputed to be among the owners of the overwater condominiums nearby.

One American **naval gun** remains on the hillside above the rectangular concrete water tank with a transformer pole alongside at Tereia Point. The housing of a second gun, vandalized in 1982, is nearby. The remains of several American concrete wharves can be seen along the north shore of **Faanui Bay.** Most of the American wartime occupation force was billeted around here and a few Quonset huts linger in the bush. Just beyond the small boat harbor (a former American submarine base) is **Marae Fare Opu,** notable for the petroglyphs of turtles carved into the stones of the *ahu.* Turtles, a favorite food of the gods, were often offered to them on the *marae.* (Mindless guides sometimes highlight the turtles in chalk for the benefit of tourist cameras.)

Between Faanui and Farepiti Wharf, just east of the Brasserie de Tahiti depot and the electricity-generating plant, is **Marae Taianapa;** its long *ahu,* restored in 1963, is visible on the hillside from the road. The most important *marae* on Bora Bora was **Marae Marotetini,** on the point near Farepiti Wharf—west of the wharf and accessible along the shore at low tide. The great stone *ahu,* 25 meters long and up to 1.5 meters high, was restored by Professor Sinoto in 1968 and can be seen from approaching ships.

The last two **American guns** are a 10-minute scramble up the ridge from the main road between Farepiti Wharf and Vaitape. Go straight up the concrete road a bit before you reach Otemanu Tours (where you see several *trucks* parked). At the end of the ridge there's a good view of Te Ava Nui Pass, which the guns were meant to defend, and Maupiti is farther out on the horizon. This is private property so ask permission to proceed of anyone you meet.

SPORTS AND RECREATION
Scuba Diving

The **Bora Diving Center** (Anne and Michel Condesse, tel. 67-71-84, fax 67-74-83, VHF channel 8), just east of Hôtel Bora Bora, offers scuba diving daily at 0845, 1345, and 1845. Prices are CFP 6,100/11,800 for one/two tanks, CFP 29,000 for a five-dive package, or CFP 7,100 for night dives. Snorkelers are welcome to tag along for CFP 1,800 when things are slow. Both PADI and CMAS open-water certification courses are offered at CFP 41,000 (three days). Gear is included. Ten different sites are visited (those around Toopua Island are recommended for snorkelers). It also has an activity called "Aqua Safari" (CFP 6,600) during which you walk along the lagoon floor wearing a diving helmet connected to the boat. Bookings can be made through the dive shop on Matira Beach (if you book through your hotel reception a 10 percent surcharge may be added). Hotel pickups are available to divers who have booked ahead.

Scuba diving can also be arranged through **Nemo World Diving** (tel./fax 67 77 85) by the road between the Sofitel Marara and Hôtel Paladien and at the Hôtel Méridien Bora Bora. It charges CFP 12,500 for two dives, gear included. Introductory dives (CFP 6,800) are offered in the afternoon and hotel pickups are available. Nemo's specialty is diving with huge manta rays off Fitiiu Point (worth doing to see the mantas, sharks, and turtles, though you won't see much else in that area as the coral is mostly dead and the waters fished out). Since it's a long way around to the single pass, most scuba diving at Bora Bora is within the lagoon and visibility is limited from January to April.

Bora Bora's newest scuba operator is **TOPdive** (tel. 60-50-50, fax 60-50-51), just north of Vaitape. It charges CFP 6,500/13,000/58,500 for one/two/10 tanks with free pickups. Its equipment is in good shape. It's the best-positioned operation for dives outside the reef where the

FRENCH POLYNESIA

visibility is better and the schools of fish (especially sharks) are larger.

Mountain Climbing

If you're experienced and determined, it's possible to climb **Mt. Pahia** in about four hours of rough going. Take the road inland just south of the Protestant church in Vaitape and go up the depression past a series of mango trees, veering slightly left. Circle the cliffs near the top on the left side, and come up the back of Snoopy's head and along his toes. (These directions will take on meaning when you study Pahia from the end of Vaitape's Wharf.) The trail is unmaintained and a local guide would be a big help. Avoid rainy weather, when the way will be muddy and slippery. Otemanu Tours (tel. 67-65-97) offers an all-day Mt. Pahia hiking tour in the dry season (CFP 15,000 for one or two people, bring your own lunch).

Despite what some tourist publications claim, slab-sided **Otemanu,** the high rectangular peak next to pointed Pahia, has *never* been climbed. It's possible to climb up to the shoulders of the mountain, but the sheer cliffs of the main peak are inaccessible because clamps pull right out of the vertical, crumbly cliff face. Helicopters can land on the summit, but that doesn't count. Otemanu's name means "It's a bird."

Other Activities

Sportfishing from a luxury catamaran is a Bora Bora eccentricity invented by ex-Californian Richard Postma of **Taravana Charters** (tel./fax 67-77-79). His 15-meter *Taravana* based at Hôtel Bora Bora is fitted with a flybridge and two fighting chairs, and the sails and multihull stability make for a smooth, quiet ride. Any doubts you may have about fishing from a sailboat can be laid aside as this prototype vessel ranks among the best. A half-day fishing charter is CFP 95,400 for up to four people, while up to eight can go on a full-day charter (CFP 127,200).

Parasailing at Hôtel Bora Bora begins at CFP 17,490 pp.

Horseback riding is available at **Ranch Reva Reva** (Olivier Ringeard, tel. 67-63-63) on Motu Pitiaau, the long coral island east of Matira Point. Organized riding is CFP 6,000 for 1.5 hours. Book through **Miki Miki Jet Ski** (tel. 67-76-44) at Matira, which arranges free transfers to the *motu.*

Practicalities

ACCOMMODATIONS

Be prepared for some of the highest room rates in the South Pacific: In all categories you'll pay about 50 percent more than you would for the same thing on Moorea. However, most guests at the top hotels arrive on prepaid packages and pay considerably less than the prices quoted herein. Tour operators engaged in packaging Bora Bora are listed in this book's main introduction. The places charging under US$100 seldom discount their rooms.

That said, there's a good choice of places to stay and only at holiday times—especially during the July festivities—does everything fill up. When things are slow, the budget hotel owners meet the airport ferry and interisland ships in search of guests. If someone from the hotel of your choice isn't on the dock when you arrive, get on the blue *truck* marked Vaitape-Anau and ask to be taken wherever you want to go. This should cost CFP 500 pp from Farepiti Wharf or CFP 350 pp from Vaitape Wharf, plus CFP 100 for luggage. However, if you're staying at a luxury resort you could be charged as much as CFP 4,200 pp return for airport transfers (ask).

Despite a desalination plant that opened in 2001, Bora Bora still suffers from water shortages, so use it sparingly, and protect yourself against theft by carefully locking your room when you go out. A daily CFP 50–150 pp municipal services tax is collected at all accommodations.

US$25–50

At the entrance to Pofai Bay three km south of Vaitape is **Blue Lagoon** (tel./fax 67-65-64) with five clean rooms with shared bath at CFP 2,200 pp (singles may be required to share). For another CFP 2,200 pp you get breakfast and dinner. Communal cooking facilities are not provided and there's considerable traffic noise and no beach. Their restaurant is open daily 1000–0200 with pizza on offer. Internet access is CFP 400 per 15 minutes and users are expected to order a drink. Transfers from the harbor are free.

The **Pension Lagoonarium** (tel. 67-71-34, fax 67-60-29), at Anau a km north of Club Med, has four rooms with shared bath at CFP 6,000 double, three bungalows with bath at CFP 8,000, and dorm beds at CFP 2,300 pp. Camping is CFP 1,500 pp. Communal cooking facilities are provided. It's right on the lagoon but there's no beach here.

US$50–100

Moon B&B (Muna Teriitehau, tel./fax 67-74-360, next to Galerie d'Art Alain Linda on Pofai Bay, has two well-constructed bungalows with fan and fridge at CFP 7,500/8,500 single/double plus 6 percent VAT. Camping beside the lagoon is CFP 1,000 pp and you can use the kitchen in the house. This friendly place opened in 2001.

Pension Chez Rosina (tel./fax 67-70-91), next to Perlissima Boutique a few hundred meters north of Village Pauline on Pofai Bay, has seven rooms at CFP 5,500/7,000 single/double with private bath and shared cooking facilities. Two larger bungalows are CFP 13,000 for up to four people. Add 6 percent VAT and CFP 50 pp local tax per day. Transfers are included. Rosina is friendly and her place is less crowded and less touristy than Pauline's, but there's no beach.

In 1997 **Village Pauline** (Pauline Youssef, tel. 67-72-16, fax 67-78-14) moved from the white beach where the Hôtel Le Maitai Polynesia now stands to a new inland location on Pofai Bay. Despite the downgrade, prices went up and you'll now pay CFP 2,500 pp to camp (own tent), CFP 3,070 pp in the eight-bed dormitory, or CFP 7,000 single or double for one of the seven small bungalows with shared bath. The four larger thatched bungalows are CFP 12,000 triple. Add 6 percent VAT and a CFP 50 pp tax per day (children under 10 are free). Communal cooking facilities are provided for campers. Sacha's Snack (Mon.–Sat. 1000–1300/1700–2000) at Village Pauline serves meals in the CFP 1,200–1,400 range. Bicycles and kayaks are for rent. Heavy traffic on the adjacent road makes it a rather noisy place to camp.

On the Matira Point peninsula are two excellent alternatives to the upmarket hotels. **Pension Chez Nono** (Noël Leverd, tel. 67-71-38, fax 67-74-27) faces a great beach across from the Beachcomber Inter-Continental. It has two large bungalows (CFP 12,290), two smaller bungalows with private bath (CFP 9,110), and a six-room thatched guesthouse with shared kitchen at CFP 5,880/6,990 single/double per room, plus 6 percent tax. The CFP 800 breakfast isn't worth it. Ventilation spaces between the ceilings and walls mean you hear *everything* in the other rooms, but the atmosphere is amiable and all guests soon become good friends (though a few of the staff seem rather jaded). Tahitians from other islands and local French often stay here. The garden is a pleasant place to sit, but the bungalows occasionally experience noise from beach parties. The solar hot water heating only works when the sun is shining. Bring mosquito coils and toilet paper. Its boat tour around the island 0930–1600 includes shark feeding (CFP 8,000 with lunch). Kayaks rent for CFP 2,500/3,500 a half/full day.

Also good is **Chez Robert et Tina** (tel. 67-63 55, fax 67 72 92), down the road from Chez Nono at the tip of Matira Point, with 15 rooms in three European-style houses at CFP 5,000/6,000 single/double. Shared cooking facilities are provided. Robert offers lagoon trips at CFP 7,000 pp. You'll enjoy it more if you know a little French. The location between two perfect snorkeling locales can't be beat.

In Anau village to the north of Club Med is **Pension Chez Teipo** (tel. 67-78-17, fax 67-73-24), also known as Pension Anau, with six neat little thatched bungalows by the lagoon at CFP 7,000/8,500/9,500 single/double/triple (children under 12 free). Cooking facilities are provided. Transfers and bicycles are free.

US$100–150

Bungalows Temanuata (tel. 67-75-61, fax 67-62-48), just north of the Beachcomber Inter-Continental at Matira, has two thatched beachfront bungalows at CFP 16,000 double, seven garden bungalows at CFP 12,820, and two garden bungalows with kitchen at CFP 16,000. Extra people are CFP 2,170, and tax is included.

The **Bora Bora Beach Lodge** (tel. 67-78-21, fax 67-77-57), formerly known as the Bora Bora Motel, between Hôtel Le Maitai Polynesia and the Sofitel Marara at Matira, shares a white beach with the Sofitel. Its four studios with bedroom, living room, dining room, kitchen, and fridge are CFP 13,600 double, while the three slightly larger apartments are CFP 17,800 double, extra people CFP 3,700 each. The one beachfront unit is CFP 19,800 (children under 13 years CFP 1,600, under age six free). You'll probably have an ocean view from your deck in this long thatched complex built in 1991. The cooking facilities make the lodge ideal for families and there's a supermarket across the street. Unfortunately mosquitoes can be a nuisance. Transfers from Vaitape are CFP 1,700 pp round-trip.

US$150–250

Hôtel Matira (tel. 67-70-51, fax 67-77-02), toward Matira Point, has four thatched bungalows with fridge near the restaurant at CFP 38,435 single or double. The 16 deluxe bungalows in the annex, 500 meters down the road toward the Beachcomber Inter-Continental, are CFP 21,285 to CFP 35,850, plus 11 percent tax. Prices have more than doubled here in recent years. The Matira's beachfront restaurant (0700–1000/1100–1400/1800–2100 daily) is reasonable with fish dishes around CFP 1,550, chicken at CFP 1,350, and Chinese dishes at CFP 1,050–1,550. Breakfast is rather expensive at CFP 1,335/1,890 continental/American, so visit one of the nearby cafés. The beach is excellent. Airport transfers are CFP 1,300 pp return.

Hôtel Le Maitai Polynesia (tel. 60-30-00, fax 67-66-03) at Matira is the only major resort owned by a local Bora Boran, Pauline Youssef. Until 1997 there was a campground here, but this real estate was far too valuable for backpackers and in 1998 a deluxe, two-story hotel was built. The 28 air-conditioned rooms in the main building start at CFP 25,500 single or double, CFP 30,500 triple, plus 11 percent tax. The six beach bungalows go for CFP 41,000, while the 11 overwater bungalows are CFP 53,000. Ask for a room with a good view. A hundred meters north and behind Tiare Supermarket is **Vairupe Villas,** which is under the same management. The 10 spacious thatched villas with kitchen and TV are CFP 38,040. Although the cooking facilities are useful, the villas are not on the beach and seem rather exorbitant.

In 2002 the former **Bora Bora Beach Club,** between the Bora Bora Beach Lodge and the Sofitel Marara, was being redeveloped by the Paladien hotel chain for the owners, Nouvelles Frontières. This 80-room hotel was to reopen in 2003 but room rates were unavailable at press time.

The 150-bungalow **Club Méditerranée** (tel. 60-46-04, fax 60-46-10) on the southeast side of Bora Bora is the largest resort on the island. Built in 1993 to replace an earlier Club Med north of Vaitape, the circuminsular road had to be rerouted around this US$30 million enclave just north of the Sofitel Marara. The guys at the gate are security freaks and it's not possible to stroll in and rent a room at Club Med as only prepackaged guests are allowed inside. Book ahead at the Club Med office in Papeete's Vaima Center (tel. 42-96-99) or at any travel agency (two-night minimum stay). Lavish buffet meals and a wide range of nonmotorized nautical activities are included in the basic price. The gaudy orange and yellow bungalows go for CFP 15,820–26,155 pp plus 11 percent tax in the garden or CFP 18,985–31,385 pp on the beach, double occupancy (singles can be matched with other same-sex singles). The prices vary according to season with Christmas to New Year's the most expensive period by far. Some of the "oceanview" units are far from the water. Club Med is good value for Bora Bora when you consider how much you save on food. There's a dazzling beach and a canoe shuttle out to a fabulous snorkeling spot. Plenty of regimented "animation" is laid on by the staff, and the eclectic clientele can be fun, if you're sociable. The Club's disco is the top wildest nightspot on the island. Club Med's G.O.s (*gentils organisateurs*) tend to resist the unusual or nonroutine (such as requesting a specific room or not sitting where you're told in the restaurant), so try to "go with the flow" (i.e., conform). Unfortunately, bicycles are not available.

US$250 and up

The **TOPdive Resort** (tel. 60-50-60), between Vaitape and Farepiti Wharf, has six tightly packed thatched garden bungalows at CFP 31,910 double and three overwater bungalows (which aren't really overwater) at CFP 49,200, plus 11 percent tax. It caters mostly to scuba divers but it's an excellent alternative to the luxury resorts. There are a small swimming pool and an outstanding restaurant.

Hôtel Bora Bora (tel. 60-44-60, fax 60-44-66), which opened on a spectacular point in 1961, was the island's first large hotel. At CFP 112,200 single or double for a premium overwater bungalow, it's one of the most exclusive millionaire's playgrounds in the South Pacific. Actors Pierce Brosnan and Eddy Murphy are regulars. Garden rooms in this 55-unit resort begin at CFP 66,000 single or double, plus 11 percent tax. Rather than pay CFP 105,600 for a rather poorly situated overwater bungalow, take one of the eight pool *fare*, each with its own private swimming pool, for the same price. Beware of noisy rooms near the road. Breakfast and dinner are CFP 10,000 pp extra. The hotel restaurant's cuisine is exceptional though the table service is sullen. The beach is superb. Amanresorts manages the property.

The **Hôtel Beachcomber Inter-Continental** (tel. 60-49-00, fax 60-49-99), on a superb white-sand beach at Matira Point, opened in 1987. One of the 10 beachfront bungalows here will set you back CFP 65,490 single or double plus 11 percent tax; the 41 overwater bungalows are CFP 82,140 (children under 15 free). It's CFP 8,586 pp extra for breakfast and dinner (you can ask to have breakfast delivered to your room by outrigger canoe!). There's a swimming pool. Inter-Continental had plans to build a 100-bungalow resort on one of the *motu*.

The **Hôtel Sofitel Marara** (tel. 60-55-00, fax 67-74-03), near the north end of the Matira hotel strip, was built in 1978 to house the crew filming Dino de Laurentiis's *Hurricane* with Mia Farrow and Trevor Howard. The film flopped but the hotel has been going strong ever since. The name

Marara means "Flying Fish." The 32 garden bungalows are CFP 38,500 single or double, the 11 beach bungalows CFP 51,000, and the 21 larger overwater units are CFP 58,900, plus 11 percent tax. The "overwater" units are much closer to shore than those at the other resorts. There's a swimming pool and watersports center. Guests staying at the Sofitel Marara are *not allowed* to take the free shuttle across to Sofitel Motu, but the water is shallow and you could just snorkel across. This entire property is becoming a little worn for the price but renovations are said to be in the pipeline. The food in the restaurant isn't highly rated and the service is incredibly slow. Luckily there are lots of other restaurants nearby.

Offshore Resorts

Mai Moana Island (Stan Wisnieswski, tel. 67-62-45, fax 67-62-39), on a tiny *motu* between the Pearl Beach Resort and the airport, has three thatched bungalows, at CFP 33,600/38,400 double with half/full board, plus 6 percent tax. It's possible to rent the entire island for two people at CFP 52,000 with half board—less than you'd pay for a single room at most of the other island resorts! The owner is a retired Polish filmmaker, and show business personalities often choose his place for a secluded getaway. Round-trip transfers from the airport/Vaitape are CFP 2,400/4,800 for one or two people. Island tours and scuba diving can be arranged.

The new **Bora Bora Pearl Beach Resort** (tel. 60-52-00, fax 60-52-22), on Teveiroa Island between the airport and Vaitape, has 20 garden suites with private pool at CFP 48,000 double, 10 beach bungalows with whirlpool bath at CFP 55,000, and 50 overwater bungalows starting at CFP 62,000, plus 11 percent tax. Half/full pension is an extra CFP 7,500/10,500 pp, and the meals have received good reviews. There are a swimming pool, a Blue Nui Dive Center (Gilles Petre, tel./fax 67-79-07), and a full range of activities, including a free shuttle to Farepiti wharf (airport transfers CFP 5,000 pp).

The **Bora Bora Lagoon Resort** (tel. 60-40-00, fax 60-40-01), part of the Orient Express chain, is perched on Toopua Island opposite Vaitape. Opened in 1993, this place offers wonderful views

FRENCH POLYNESIA

of Mt. Pahia, and the large swimming pool compensates for the average beach and shallow lagoon. The seven garden bungalows are CFP 59,375 double, the 21 beach bungalows CFP 70,625, the 37 overwater bungalows CFP 95,625, and the 13 pontoon bungalows CFP 106,875, plus 11 percent tax. Rates include a buffet breakfast. Other meals are extra and it's forbidden to bring your own food and drink into the resort. Free activities include tennis, sailing, windsurfing, canoeing, the fitness center, and the launch to Vaitape or the airport. Check-in time is 1500.

In 2002, the 120-unit **Sheraton Bora Bora Nui Resort and Spa** (tel. 60-33-00, fax 60-33-01) opened on the west side of Motu Toopua. This is the most expensive place to stay in French Polynesia with 16 lagoon view suites beginning at CFP 65,000 double and increasing to a whopping CFP 245,000 for the two "overwater royal horizon suite bungalows." Add CFP 8,500/12,000 pp for half/full board. Of course, few pay these outlandish prices as the vast majority of guests at all of the luxury resorts arrive on all-inclusive packages.

Under separate management from the Sofitel Marara and much more luxurious is the **Sofitel Motu** (tel. 60-56-00, fax 60-56-66), which opened on Motu Piti uu Uta off the east side of the Matira peninsula in 1999. The 30 island/overwater bungalows are CFP 60,000/75,000 double, plus 11 percent tax. There's an artificial waterfall off the lobby and the service is excellent. The views of Bora Bora are unforgettable. Romantic couples are the target market here, and unlike almost every other resort in French Polynesia, there are no special deals for families with small children.

In 2001 the **Bora Bora Eden Beach Resort** (tel. 60-57-60, fax 67-69-76) was built by the lagoon on 10-km-long Motu Piti Aau south of the Hôtel Méridien Bora Bora. The eight garden bungalows are CFP 25,000 double and the seven beach bungalows CFP 30,000, plus 11 percent tax. This is much cheaper than its sister properties in the upmarket Pearl Resorts chain. Add CFP 6,100/8,000 pp for half/full board and CFP 4,200 pp for boat transfers. The Eden Beach prides itself in being the only "green" hotel in French Polynesia with solar energy, water conservation, and recycling.

In 1998 **Hôtel Méridien Bora Bora** (tel. 60-51-51, fax 60-51-52) was built on Motu Piti Aau opposite Fitiiu Point. The 82 thatched overwater bungalows start at CFP 76,500 single or double, while the 18 beach bungalows are CFP 65,400, plus 11 percent tax (children under 12 free). Add CFP 7,800/11,500 pp for two/three meals. All the usual sporting activities are offered, including scuba diving. A day tour to Tupai Atoll is CFP 15,000 pp. The resort launch goes to Anau rather than Vaitape, a disadvantage if you want to go shopping. When the wind is blowing the wrong way you may get a whiff of the smoldering debris at the horrendous municipal dump on the north side of Fitiiu Point.

FOOD

Vaitape

Snack Bora Bora Burger (no phone; Mon.–Sat. 0800–1700), on the main road just south of the Banque de Polynésie near the wharf, serves hamburgers (CFP 660), french fries (CFP 300), baguette sandwiches (CFP 220), small/large coffees (CFP 200/300), and small beers (CFP 370).

Snack Chez Richard (tel. 67-69-09; Tues.–Sat. 1100–1300/1800–2030), near Farepiti Rent a Car opposite the Centre Artisanal, sells Chinese take-out meals in the CFP 850–1,000 range. At night only it sells waffles at CFP 250–500.

L'Appetisserie (tel. 67-78-88; Mon.–Sat. 0600–1800), at back of the Centre Commercial La Pahia opposite the Protestant church just north of the wharf, offers things such as crêpes (CFP 420–680), hot sandwiches (CFP 420–850), ice cream (CFP 150–700), cakes (CFP 300–450), coffee, and beer. At lunchtime the plat du jour will be around CFP 1,400. Internet access is available weekdays 0900–1300/1600–1800, Saturday 0900–1300, at CFP 40 a minute.

Snack Michel (tel. 67-71-43; weekdays 0600–1200), opposite the college just north of Magasin Chin Lee, serves filling meals for CFP 750 (but no alcohol). Try the *ma'a tinito*. You eat at picnic tables behind a thatched roof. This good local place is a little hard to find as the sign is not visible from the street.

Restaurant Bar Au Cocotier (tel. 67-74-18;

Mon., Wed., and Fri. 0800–2030, Tues., Thurs., and Sat. 0800–1730), between Snack Michel and Pharmacie Fare Ra'au, serves Chinese dishes (CFP 1,200–2,000), meat dishes (CFP 1,300–2,000), and fish (CFP 1,200–2,100). **Ker Yann Pizza** (tel. 67-68-00), next to Pharmacie Fare Ra'au, has take-out pizza.

Surprisingly, one of the best restaurants on the island is at the **TOPdive Resort** (tel. 60-50-60; 0700–1000/1200–1400/1900–2200), between Vaitape and Farepiti Wharf. Dinner mains average CFP 2,900–3,400, and there's a nice harbor view from most tables. If you call, it'll provide free transportation.

Cold Hinano beer is available for a reasonable price at the **Jeu Association Amical Tahitien Club** next to Farepiti Wharf. You must consume your beer at one of its picnic tables as the club doesn't want to lose any bottles. It's a good stop on your way around the island and the perfect place to sit and wait for your boat.

Pofai Bay

The **Bamboo House Restaurant** (Peter Eberhardt, tel./fax 67-76-24; daily 1130–1430/1830–2130), next to Le Jardin Gauguin on Pofai Bay, serves everything from pasta dishes (from CFP 1,500) to grilled lobster (CFP 5,500). Other specialties include mahimahi (CFP 2,800), scampi (CFP 3,000), crab (CFP 3,500), and sirloin steak (CFP 3,000). Free transportation is provided in the evening.

Bloody Mary's (tel. 67-72-86; Mon.–Sat. 1130–1500/1800–2100), on Pofai Bay a km south of Le Jardin Gauguin, is the longest established nonhotel restaurant on the island with a tradition dating to 1979. A board outside lists "famous guests," including Jane Fonda and Baron George Von Dangel. The lunch menu includes teriyaki, fish kabob, and *poisson cru* (all CFP 1,250), though when things are slow it doesn't bother dishing out lunch at all. At dinner you choose from the upscale seafood (CFP 2,500–6,000) laid out in front of you. For ambience, menu, service, and staff it's hard to beat, although the food itself is only so-so. Don't miss the zany toilets! Free hotel pickups for diners are available at 1830 if you call ahead.

Matira

Ben's Snack (tel. 67-74-54), between Hôtel Bora Bora and Hôtel Matira, turns out pizza (CFP 850–1,540), lasagna, pasta, steaks, and omelettes, but it's only open irregularly. Clients are not allowed to share meals in the evening. One reader said that her hamburger was reminiscent of a "where's the beef?" commercial. Frankly, the beachside Chinese restaurant at Hôtel Matira nearby may be better value.

Snack Matira (tel. 67-77-32; Tues.–Sun. 1000–1700), across the street and a bit east of Ben's, is the best place around for a budget lunch. The menu includes hamburgers (CFP 450), mahimahi with frites (CFP 1,000), steak frites (CFP 1,100), pizza (CFP 1,200–1,500), *poisson cru* (CFP 1,000), and big **casse-croûte** sandwiches (CFP 150–600). The food is good, but no beer is available on the nice beachfront terrace.

Snack Restaurant Moi Here (tel. 67-68-41; daily 0630–2200), right on Matira Beach between Hôtel Matira and the Beachcomber Inter-Continental, is good for the large *casse-croûte* sandwiches (CFP 200–600) and mahimahi with fries (CFP 1,300). Other meals are in the CFP 1,000–1,550 range. Its agreeable terrace overlooks the beach.

Restaurant Fare Manuia (tel. 67-68-08; Mon. 1000–2200, Tues.–Sat. 1130–1400/1800–2200), at Bungalows Temanuata near the turnoff to the Beachcomber Inter-Continental, offers excellent if rather expensive Chinese dishes and French specialties. Local seafood dishes are in the CFP 2,400–2,700 range, meat CFP 2,100–3,900. Try the prawns breaded with coconut, steak with mushrooms, or *poisson cru*. It fills up quickly in the evening.

Snack Mandarin (tel. 72-43-62), opposite Matira Pearls between the Beachcomber Inter-Continental and Hôtel Le Maitai Polynesia, has chow mein, steak frites, chicken, *poisson cru*, and mahimahi, all for around CFP 1,000.

Restaurant-Snack La Bounty (tel. 67-70-43; Tues.–Sun. 1130–1400/1830–2100), near Taire Market close to the Bora Bora Beach Lodge, has an open air terrace under a thatched roof. Its lunch plates are CFP 1,400–1,600, dinner CFP 1,400–1,700, pizzas CFP 1,250–

1,550. The largely French clientele doesn't seem to mind the slow service—reader reviews are favorable.

Snack Patoti (tel. 67-61-99; Mon.–Sat. 0800–1400/1900–2100), 300 meters north of the Sofitel Marara, serves hamburgers with fries (CFP 800), *poisson cru* (CFP 1,300), chow mein (CFP 1,300), steak frites (CFP 1,300), and beer (CFP 400).

Groceries

Bora Bora's best established supermarket is **Magasin Chin Lee** (tel. 67-63-07; Mon.–Sat. 0500–1900, Sun. 0500–1100), opposite the island's Mobil gas station north of Vaitape Wharf. Takeaway meals at the checkout counters are CFP 700. **Super To'a Amok** and the Total service station are farther north.

Tiare Market (tel. 67-61-38; Mon.–Sat. 0630–1900, Sun. 0630–1300/1500–1830), opposite the Bora Bora Beach Lodge at Matira, is very well stocked with a good wine section and even some fresh vegetables. It's always crowded with tourists from the upmarket hotels.

Other places to buy groceries are the two general stores at Anau (closed Sunday), halfway around the island, and a small grocery store at the head of Pofai Bay. A grocery truck passes Matira around noon and 1600 daily except Sunday.

ENTERTAINMENT AND EVENTS
Disco

Le Récife Bar (tel. 67-73-87), between Vaitape and Farepiti Wharf, is Bora Bora's after-hours club, open Friday and Saturday from 2230. Disco dancing continues almost until dawn, but expect loud, heavy-on-the-beat music with few patrons. Steer clear of the local drunks hanging around outside.

Otherwise, the evening activity on Bora Bora is geared toward honeymooners or couples rescuing their marriages, staring into each others eyes and trying to make this the romantic peak of their

BORA BORA INTERNET RESOURCES

Accommodations

Blue Lagoon
borabluelagoon@mail.pf

Bora Bora Lagoon Resort
www.boraboralagoonresort.orient-express.com
bblr@mail.pf

Bora Bora Beach Lodge
www.boraboramotel.pf
boraboramotel@mail.pf

Hôtel Beachcomber Inter-Continental
borabora@interconti.com

Hôtel Bora Bora
www.amanresorts.com
reservations@hotelborabora.pf

Hôtel Le Maitai Polynesia
info@bora.hotelmaitai.com

Hôtel Matira
hotel.matira@mail.pf

Hôtel Méridien Bora Bora
www.lemeridien-borabora.com

Mai Moana Island
www.mai-moana-island.com
stan@mail.pf

Moon B&B
moonbungalow@netcourrier.com

Pension Chez Rosina
adesaintpierre@mail.pf

Pension Chez Teipo
teipobora@mail.pf

Pension Lagoonarium
lagonarium@mail.pf

TOPdive Resort
www.topdive.com
info@topdive.pf

Village Pauline
vpauline@mail.pf

lives. Singles looking for some fun or an authentic island scene could leave a little disappointed.

Cultural Shows for Visitors

To see Polynesian dancing on the beach at **Hôtel Bora Bora** (tel. 60-44-60) grab a barside seat before it starts at 2030 on Friday night (buffet CFP 7,000).

Additional Tahitian dancing occurs after dinner Thursday night at 2030 at the **Beachcomber Inter-Continental** (tel. 60-49-00). You can watch it for the price of a drink.

Hôtel Le Maitai Polynesia (tel. 60-30-00) has Tahitian dancing in the restaurant Wednesday at 2000 (buffet CFP 6,000). Here too it's possible to watch the show from the bar for the price of a drink.

Another Tahitian dance show takes place at the **Sofitel Marara** (tel. 60-55-00) every Tuesday, Thursday, and Saturday night at 2000. Saturday at 1800 they open the earth oven and the feast begins. Unless you're taking the buffet (CFP 4,800, reservations required) you'll have to pay a CFP 2,000 cover charge (which includes one drink) to see the show at the Sofitel Marara.

Events

The **Fêtes de Juillet** are celebrated at Bora Bora with special fervor. The canoe and bicycle races, javelin throwing, flower cars, singing, and dancing competitions run until 0300 nightly. A public ball goes till dawn on the Saturday closest to July 14. Try to participate in the 10-km foot race to prove that all tourists aren't lazy, but don't take the prizes away from the locals. If you win, be sure to give the money back to them for partying. You'll make good friends that way and have more fun dancing in the evening. The stands are beautiful because the top decorations win prizes, too.

SHOPPING AND SERVICES
Shopping

Plenty of small boutiques around Vaitape sell black coral jewelry, pearls, pareus, T-shirts,

Sports and Recreation

Aquascope
www.boraboraisland.com/aquascope

Bora Bora Blue Nui Dive Center
boraborabluenui@mail.pf

Bora Diving Center
www.boradive.com
boradiving@mail.pf

Nemo World Diving
www.nemodivebora.com
mail@nemoworld.pf

TOPdive
www.topdive.com
info@topdive.pf

Transportation and Tours

Europcar
europcarborabox@mail.pf

Farepiti Rentacar
farepiticarhire@mail.pf

Héli-inter Polynésia
helico-tahiti@mail.pf

Moana Adventure Tours
www.moanatours.com

Taravana Charters
www.taravana.com
taravana@mail.pf

Tupuna Safaris
tupuna.bora@mail.pf

Others

Erwin Christian
www.tahitibooks.com

Garrick Yrondi
yrondi.art@mail.pf

Matira Pearls and Fashions
www.matirapearls.com

designer beachwear, etc. The **Centre Artisanal** near Vaitape Wharf is a good place to buy a shell necklace or a pareu directly from the locals.

A cluster of shops on Pofai Bay offers some of Bora Bora's best tourist shopping. **Boutique Gauguin** (tel. 67-76-67) has tropical clothing, T-shirts, souvenirs, and jewelry. Next door is an upmarket black pearl showroom called **O.P.E.C.** (tel. 67-61-62) where numbered black pearls complete with X-ray and certificate go for US$300–1,400. The pearls can be set in gold as earrings or necklaces in one day. A full pearl necklace will cost US$9,000–15,000—the gift of a lifetime.

Alongside O.P.E.C. is **Art du Pacifique** (tel. 67-63-85) with a display of woodcarvings from the Marquesas Islands. Just behind is the gallery of neoimpressionist Basque painter and sculptor **Garrick Yrondi** (tel. 67-79-66), who has spent most of his life in French Polynesia. These shops surround a small garden called *Le Jardin Gauguin* with a series of tacky plaster sculptures depicting scenes from Gauguin's paintings.

At photographer Erwin Christian's **Moana Art Boutique** (tel. 67-70-33), just north of Hôtel Bora Bora, you can buy striking postcards, photo books, and other souvenirs.

Information and Services
A Visitors Bureau (tel./fax 67-76-36; weekdays 0800–1500) is in the Centre Artisanal next to Vaitape Wharf.

The three main banks all have offices near Vaitape Wharf, but they're only open weekdays 0745–1130/1330–1600. Many yachties "check out" of French Polynesia at Bora Bora and reclaim their bond or *caution* at these banks. It's wise to check with the Banque Socredo (tel. 60-50-10) a few days ahead to make sure it'll have your cash or traveler's checks ready. At last report, such refunds were available only on Tuesday and Thursday.

The post office (tel. 67-70-74; Mon. 0800–1500, Tues.–Fri. 0730–1500, Sat. 0800–1000), gendarmerie (tel. 67-70-58), and health clinic *(Santé Publique)* are within a stone's throw of Vaitape Wharf.

In past, the Yacht Club de Bora Bora (tel. 67-70-69), near Farepiti Wharf and opposite Te Ava Nui Pass, has provided moorings, fresh water,

and showers for cruising yachties. These services were free to cruisers who splashed out in their upscale seafood restaurant; otherwise they cost CFP 2,500 per day per group, plus CFP 300 per shower (drinks at the bar were not good enough for free mooring). The Yacht Club was being rebuilt at press time and future conditions were still unknown. Beware of theft off yachts anywhere around this island.

Health
The private Cabinet Médical (tel. 67-70-62) behind Snack Bora Bora Burger is open weekdays 0700–1200/1500–1800, Saturday 0700–1200.

Dr. François Macouin's Cabinet Dentaire (tel. 67-70-55; weekdays 0730–1800, Sat. 0730–1200) is in the Centre Commercial Le Pahia opposite Magasin Chin Lee and the large Protestant church.

Dr. F. Duval (tel. 67-67-07; weekdays 0730–1130/1530–1800, Sat. 0730–1130, Sun. and holidays 0730–0830) is just north of Pharmacie Fare Ra'au. Consultations are CFP 3,000 (double price at night). Dr. Dominique Bourda (tel. 67-69-42; weekdays 0730–1200/1430–1730, Sat. 0730–1200), a dentist, is adjacent.

Pharmacie Fare Ra'au (tel. 67-70-30; weekdays 0800–1200/1530–1800, Sat. 0800–1200/1700–1800, Sun. 0900–0930) is north of the wharf.

TRANSPORTATION
Getting There
Air Tahiti (tel. 67-70-35; weekdays 0730–1130/1330–1630) is beside the Banque de Tahiti on Vaitape Wharf. It has a useful transversal flight direct from Bora Bora to Rangiroa and Tikehau (both CFP 23,400) five times a week. (For information on flights and ships to Bora Bora from Papeete, Huahine, and Raiatea, see Transportation in the introduction to French Polynesia.)

Ships from Raiatea and Papeete tie up at Farepiti Wharf, three km north of Vaitape. The shipping companies have no representatives on Bora Bora, so for departure times just keep asking. Drivers of the *trucks* are the most likely to know. You buy your ticket when the ship arrives. Officially the *Vaeanu* (tel. 67-68-68) departs

Bora Bora for Raiatea, Huahine, and Papeete Tuesday and Thursday at 1130, and Sunday at 0830 (CFP 749/1,786 deck to Raiatea/Papeete). The *Hawaiki-Nui* calls here twice a week. Beware of early departures.

A fast yellow-and-blue passenger ferry, the *Maupiti Express* (tel./fax 67-66-69), departs Vaitape Wharf for Maupiti, Taha'a, and Raiatea. It leaves for Maupiti on Tuesday, Thursday, and Saturday at 0830 (CFP 2,500), for Taha'a and Raiatea on Monday, Wednesday, and Friday at 0700 (CFP 2,500). Tickets are sold on board.

Getting Around

Getting around is a bit of a headache, as *le truck* service is irregular and at lunchtime everything stops. Public *trucks* usually meet the boats, but many of the *trucks* you see around town are for guests of the luxury hotels. If you do find one willing to take you, fares between Vaitape and Matira vary CFP 350–500, plus CFP 100 for luggage. Taxi fares are high, so check before getting in. If you rent a bicycle, keep an eye on it when you stop to visit the sights.

Farepiti Rentacar (tel. 67-65-28, fax 67-65-29l; closed Sun.), opposite the Centre Artisanal in Vaitape, at the Hôtel Le Maitai Polynesia, and opposite the Sofitel Marara, has cars from CFP 4,800/5,800/6,600/7,300 for two/four/eight/24 hours with unlimited kms. The smaller cars are usually all taken, and it's likely you'll be charged CFP 6,000/7,000/8,000/9,000 for an air-conditioned car. Insurance is included. Scooters are CFP 3,800/4,350/5,400/6,500 (motorcycle license required). Bicycles cost CFP 850/1,000/1,250/1,850. You must leave a deposit of CFP 100,000/50,000/30,000 on the cars/scooters/bicycles.

Europcar (tel. 67-70-15, fax 67-79-95; daily 0730–1800), next to the gendarmerie opposite Vaitape Wharf and with desks at the Inter-Continental, Sofitel Marara, Club Med, and Le Méridien, has Fiats from CFP 7,350/8,500 for an eight/24-hour day. The price includes insurance and unlimited km. A two-seater Mini Cabriolet is CFP 6,800/8,400 for four/eight hours. It also has bicycles for CFP 1,400/1,800/1,900 for four/eight/24 hours.

If you rent a car and drive at night, watch out for scooters and bicycles without lights. However, to better enjoy the scenery and avoid disturbing the environment, we suggest you dispense with motorized transport here. Little Bora Bora is perfect for cycling as there's an excellent paved road right around the island (with only one unpaved stretch on the incline at Fitiiu Point), almost no hills, and lots of scenic bays to shelter you from the wind. Do exercise caution with fast-moving vehicles between Vaitape and Matira Point, however.

Land Tours

Otemanu Tours (tel. 67-70-49), just north of Vaitape, offers a 2.5-hour truck tour around Bora Bora daily except Sunday at 1400 (CFP 2,750).

Tupuna Safaris (tel. 67-75-06), at Moana Art Boutique near Hôtel Bora Bora, does Land Rover tours up a steep ridge opposite Otemanu at CFP 6,500.

Héli-inter Polynésia (tel. 67-62-59), next to the Air Tahiti office at Vaitape wharf, charges CFP 14,000 for a 15-minute scenic flight (three-person minimum).

Day Cruises

Like Aitutaki in the Cook Islands, Bora Bora is famous for its lagoon trips. Prices vary depending on whether lunch is included, the length of the trip, the luxury of boat, etc., so check around. A seafood picnic lunch on a *motu*, reef walking, and snorkeling gear are usually included, and you get a chance to see giant clams, manta rays, and shark feeding. For the latter you don a mask and snorkel, jump into the shark-infested waters, and grasp a line as your guide shoves chunks of fish at a school of generally innocuous reef sharks in feeding frenzy. It's an encounter with the wild you'll never forget. (See the Pension Chez Nono and Chez Robert et Tina accommodations listings for two possibilities.) Motorized canoe trips right around Bora Bora are also offered. An excursion of this kind is an essential part of the Bora Bora experience, so splurge on this one.

Moana Adventure Tours (tel. 67-61-41, fax 67-61-26), on Pofai Bay near Village Pauline, does shark and ray feeding (CFP 6,600 pp) several times a week, departing around 1300. A half-day deep-sea fishing charter is CFP 38,500 for two people.

Ioane (John) of **Matira Tour** (tel. 67-70-97), on Matira Point near Chez Robert et Tina, does lagoon tours from 0930–1500 at CFP 6,000 including lunch (minimum of six).

Three-hour tours to the **Bora Lagoonarium** (tel. 67-71-34, fax 67-60-29) on a *motu* off the main island occur daily except Saturday at 0915 and 1300 (CFP 6,990). The price is reduced to CFP 5,500 if you book directly at the Lagoonarium office at Anau, a km north of Club Med. A slightly different tour occurs at 1400 and 1630 (CFP 6,330/4,500 hotel/direct bookings). You'll see more colorful fish than you ever thought existed. Call for a free hotel pickup.

René et Maguy Boat Rental (tel. 67-60-61, fax 67-61-01), next to Tiare Supermarket at Matira, rents small boats with motor at CFP 6,050/7,150/8,250/11,550 two hours/three hours/half day/full day (gasoline extra). *Motu* transfers are CFP 1,815 pp return.

The **Aquascope** (tel. 67-61-92) is a step above a glass-bottom boat in that you view the marinelife through large windows. It departs Vaitape Wharf five times a day, charging CFP 4,300 pp for a one-hour trip inside the lagoon or CFP 8,000 for three hours beyond the pass.

> *Motorized canoe trips right around Bora Bora are also offered. An excursion of this kind is an essential part of the Bora Bora experience, so splurge on this one.*

Airport

Bora Bora's vast airfield (BOB) on Motu Mute north of the main island was built by the Americans during World War II. The first commercial flight from Paris to French Polynesia landed here in October 1958, and until March 1961 all international flights used this airstrip; passengers were then transferred to Papeete by Catalina amphibious or Bermuda flying boat seaplanes. Today, a 25-minute catamaran ride brings arriving air passengers to Vaitape Wharf (included in the plane ticket). Make sure your luggage is loaded on/off the boat at the airport.

When the catamaran from the airport arrives at Vaitape Wharf, all of the luxury hotels will have guest transportation waiting, but the budget places don't always meet the flights (the deluxe places don't bother meeting the interisland boats). As you arrive at the wharf, shout out the name of your hotel and you'll be directed to the right *truck* (they don't have destination signs). At the airport the resorts use color-coded flower leis to sort out their guests.

If you're flying from Papeete to Bora Bora go early in the morning and sit on the left side of the aircraft for spectacular views—it's only from the air that Bora Bora is the most beautiful island in the world!

Maupiti

Majestic Maupiti (Maurua), 52 km west of Bora Bora, is the least known of the accessible Society Islands. Maupiti's mighty volcanic plug soars above a sapphire lagoon, and the vegetation-draped cliffs complement the magnificent *motu* beaches. Almost every bit of level land on the main island is taken up by fruit trees, while watermelons thrive on the surrounding *motu*. Maupiti abounds in native seabirds, including frigate birds, terns, and others. The absence of Indian mynahs allows you to see native land birds that are almost extinct elsewhere.

The 1,125 people live in the adjacent villages of Vai'ea, Farauru, and Pauma. Tourism is not promoted because there aren't any regular ho-tels, which is a big advantage! It's sort of like Bora Bora was 30 years ago, before being "dis-covered" by the world of package tourism.

Sights

It takes only three hours to walk right around this 11-square-km island. The nine-km crushed-coral road, lined with breadfruit, mango, ba-nana, and hibiscus, passes crumbling *marae*, freshwater springs, and a beach.

Marae Vaiahu, by the shore a few hundred meters beyond Hotuparaoa Massif, is the largest *marae*. Once a royal landing place opposite the pass into the lagoon, the *marae* still bears the king's throne and ancient burials. Nearby is the

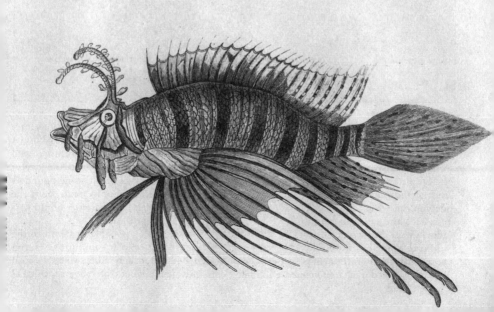

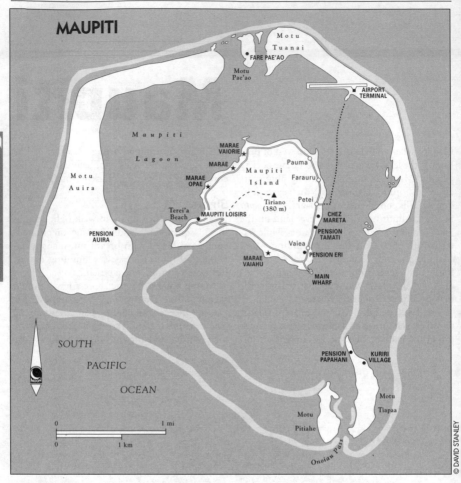

MAUPITI

Motu Tuanai

FARE PAE'AO

Motu Pae'ao

AIRPORT TERMINAL

Maupiti Lagoon

MARAE VAIORIE

MARAE

Pauma

Farauru

MARAE OPAE

Maupiti Island

Motu Auira

Petei

Tiriano (380 m)

Terei'a Beach

MAUPITI LOISIRS

CHEZ MARETA

PENSION TAMATI

Vaiea

PENSION AUIRA

PENSION ERI

MARAE VAIAHU

MAIN WHARF

SOUTH PACIFIC OCEAN

PENSION PAPAHANI

KURIRI VILLAGE

Motu Tiapaa

Motu Pitiahe

Onoiau Pass

0   1 mi

0   1 km

© DAVID STANLEY

sorcerers' rock: light a fire beside this rock and you will die. Above the road are a few smaller *marae*.

Terei'a Beach, at the west tip of Maupiti, is the only good beach on the main island. At low tide you can wade across from Terei'a's white sands to Motu Auira in waist-deep water.

Marae Vaiorie is a double *marae* with freshwater springs in between. As many as two dozen large *marae* are hidden

The nine-km crushed-coral road, lined with breadfruit, mango, banana, and hibiscus, passes crumbling **marae,** *freshwater springs, and a beach.*

in Maupiti's mountainous interior, and the island is known for its ghosts. Maupiti is well known among archaeologists for its black basalt stone pounders and fishhooks made from the seven local varieties of mother-of-pearl shell.

It's possible to climb to the 380-meter summit of Maupiti from the 42-meter-high saddle where the road cuts across Terei'a Point. You follow the ridge all

MAUPITI HIGHLIGHTS

Onoiau Pass: scenery, drama, accommodations
Motu Tuanai: airport, swimming, gardens
Marae Vaiahu: archaeology, scenery
Mt. Tiriano: hiking, scenery, viewpoint
Motu Auira: camping, swimming, scenery

the way to the top and the whole trip shouldn't take over three hours round-trip.

PRACTICALITIES

Accommodations

Several of the inhabitants take paying guests, and they usually meet the flights and boats in search of clients. The absence of a regular hotel on Maupiti throws together an odd mix of vacationing French couples, backpackers, and "adventuresome" tourists in the guesthouses (none of which have signs). Agree on the price beforehand and check your bill when you leave. You could camp on the airport *motu*, but obtaining drinking water would be a problem and there are *no-nos* (insects). Maupiti experiences serious water shortages during the dry season.

Chez Mareta (Manuela Mohi, tel. 67-80-25), in the center of Vai'ea village, is the house with the sloping blue roof a few minutes' walk from the *mairie*. It offers three rooms at CFP 2,500 pp including breakfast. You can cook your own food or pay CFP 1,500 for dinner. An agreeable sitting room faces the lagoon downstairs. Upon request, they'll drop you on a *motu* for the day (beware of sunburn). Chez Mareta is okay for a couple of days, but not an extended stay. The church choir in the next building practices its singing quite loudly each night.

Chez Floriette Tuheiava (tel./fax 67-80-85) on the north side of Chez Mareta has two pleasant bungalows at CFP 5,500 pp including breakfast, dinner, activities, and airport transfers. Floriette speaks reasonable English. South of Chez Mareta is **Pension Eri** (Emmanuel Mohi, tel. 67-81-29) with four rooms in a separate house at CFP 5,500 pp with breakfast and dinner.

Pension Tamati (Ferdinand and Etu Tapuhiro,

tel. 67-80-10), a two-story building at the south end of Vai'ea, rents nine bleak rooms at CFP 2,500 pp with breakfast or CFP 4,500 pp with half board. Unfortunately, tourists are usually given the inside rooms without proper ventilation, but communal cooking facilities are available.

Maupiti Loisirs (tel. 67-80-95), near Tereia Beach, provides camping facilities here or on Motu Auira at CFP 4,500 pp including breakfast and dinner. Bicycle rentals are CFP 1,000 a day.

Fare Pae'ao (Janine Tavaearii, tel. 67-81-01 or 67-80-08, fax 67-81-92) on Motu Pae'ao is quiet and offers a superb white beach with some of the finest snorkeling on Maupiti. The three thatched bungalows with bath are CFP 10,000 single or double, CFP 11,000 triple. Meals cost CFP 3,500/6,000 pp for two/three meals. Reservations are required to ensure an airport pickup (CFP 1,000 pp round-trip). (In 1962 Kenneth Emory and Yosihiko Sinoto excavated a prehistoric cemetery on Pae'ao and found 15 adzes of six different types, providing valuable evidence for the study of Polynesian migrations.)

Pension Auira (Edna Terai, tel. 67-80-26) on Motu Auira, the *motu* opposite Terei'a Beach, has five thatched bungalows. The garden variety are CFP 7,000 pp a day including breakfast and dinner; the better-quality beach bungalows are CFP 8,000 pp. The food is good but the beach could use a cleaning. Boat transfers from the airport are CFP 2,000 pp return.

In addition, there are three small resorts on Motu Tiapaa, one of the islands framing Onoiau Pass. **Pension Papahani** (Vilna Tuheiava, tel./fax 67-81-58) has five thatched bungalows with private bath beginning at CFP 7,500 pp, breakfast and dinner included. Return airport transfers are CFP 1,000 pp. More upscale are the five *fare* with bath at the **Kuriri Village** (tel./fax 67-82-23, kuriri@bigfoot.com) at CFP 11,200/13,200 pp with half/full board. Also on Tiapaa is **Fare Rose des Îles** (Areti and Juliette Tauaroa, fax 67-82-00) with one bungalow at CFP 6,500 pp.

Services

Banque Socredo (tel. 67-81-95) has a branch on Maupiti, but it's not always operating, so change beforehand and don't count on using your credit cards. The post office and *mairie* are nearby. The bakery is in the power plant on the edge of town. It's important to check when the baguettes come out of the oven and to be punctual, as they sell out fast. The island youths come here an hour before and hang around waiting. Not all stores sell beer and the island's supply does run out at times.

Getting There

Maupiti's airport (MAU) is on a *motu* and you must take a launch to the main island (CFP 500 pp). **Air Tahiti** has flights to Maupiti from Raiatea (CFP 5,900 one-way) and Papeete (CFP 13,200) three times a week. At last report, the flights between Bora Bora and Maupiti weren't operating—ask. Reconfirm with the Air Tahiti agent (tel. 67-80-20) near the *mairie*.

The 62-seat fast ferry *Maupiti Express* arrives from Bora Bora (CFP 2,500 each way) on Tuesday, Thursday, and Saturday mornings, returning to Bora Bora the same afternoon.

The government supply barges *Meherio III* or *Maupiti Tou Ai'a* depart Papeete for Raiatea and Maupiti Wednesday at 1900, departing Maupiti for the return Friday at 0800. (See the French Polynesia Introduction for more information.)

Ships must enter the channel during daylight, thus the compulsory morning arrival, and the boats usually depart from Maupiti on the afternoon of the same day. Onoiau Pass into Maupiti is narrow, and when there's a strong southerly wind it can be dangerous—boats have had to turn back. At low tide a strong current flows out through this pass and the optimum time for a yacht to enter is around noon.

Other Leeward Islands

Tupai

Tupai or Motu Iti (Small Island), 24 km north of Bora Bora, is a tiny coral atoll measuring 1,100 hectares. The opposing horseshoe-shaped *motu* enclose a lagoon that small boats can enter through a pass on the east side. A small airstrip is in the northwest corner of the atoll. In 1860, the king of Bora Bora gave the atoll to a planter named Stackett and for decades a few dozen people were employed to make copra from coconuts off the 155,000 trees on Tupai. In 1997, the territorial government bought Tupai from its last owner, a Mr. Lejeune, for US$8 million with an eye to resort development. Although there are no permanent inhabitants at the moment, the 1,000 traditional landowners are contesting the title. Recently members of the Groupement d'Intervention de Polynésie (GIP), a militia created by Gaston Flosse, have undergone training on Tupai by former Foreign Legionnaires and army parachutists. The scuba operators on Bora Bora often arrange trips here.

> *In 1860, the king of Bora Bora gave the atoll to a planter named Stackett and for decades a few dozen people were employed to make copra from coconuts off the 155,000 trees on Tupai.*

Maupihaa

Tiny 360-hectare Maupihaa (Mopelia), 185 km southeast of Maupiti, is the only Society Islands atoll that can be entered by yachts but to attempt to do so in stormy weather is dangerous. Narrow, unmarked Taihaaru Vahine Pass on Maupihaa's northwest side can only be found by searching for the strong outflow of lagoon water at low tide. Despite this, cruising yachts traveling between Bora Bora and Cook Islands or Samoa often anchor in the atoll's lagoon.

In July 1917 the notorious German raider *Seeadler* was wrecked at Maupihaa after capturing 15 Allied ships. The three-masted schooner was too large to enter the lagoon, and while being careened outside the pass, a freak wave picked the vessel up and threw it onto the reef. Eventually the ship's chivalrous captain, Count Felix von Luckner, was able to carry on to Fiji in a small boat, where he was captured at Wakaya Island. Count von Luckner's journal, *The Sea Devil*, became a best-seller after the war.

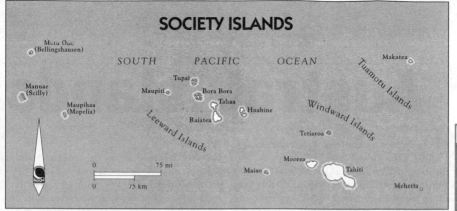

SOCIETY ISLANDS

SOUTH   PACIFIC   OCEAN

Motu One
(Bellingshausen)

Manuae
(Scilly)

Maupihaa
(Mopelia)

Tupai

Maupiti

Bora Bora

Tahaa

Raiatea

Huahine

Leeward Islands

Windward Islands

Tuamotu Islands

Makatea

Tetiaroa

Moorea

Maiao

Tahiti

Mehetia

0   75 mi

0   75 km

© DAVID STANLEY

About 50 people from Maupiti live on Maupihaa, where they run a nursery to supply oysters to black pearl farms in the Tuamotus. Sea turtles come to Maupihaa to lay their eggs only to be butchered for their flesh by poachers. Large numbers of terns, boobies, and frigate birds nest on the small *motu* and the seabird fledglings are slaughtered for their meager meat while the unhatched eggs are collected according to need. All of this is supposed to be prohibited but it's hard to control what goes on in such an isolated place.

Manuae

Manuae (Scilly), 75 km northwest of Maupihaa, is the westernmost of the Society Islands. This atoll is 15 km in diameter but totals only 400 hectares. Pearl divers once visited Manuae. In 1855 the three-masted schooner *Julia Ann* sank on the Manuae reef. It took the survivors two months to build a small boat, which carried them to safety at Raiatea.

Motu One

Motu One (Bellingshausen), 65 km north of Manuae, got its second name from the Russian explorer Thadeus von Bellingshausen, who visited Tahiti in 1820. Tiny 280-hectare Motu One is circled by a guano bearing reef, with no pass into the lagoon. Of the 10 people present on Motu One when Hurricane Martin swept through in November 1997, the sole survivor was a woman named Alice Haano who tied herself to a coconut tree.

Austral Islands

The inhabited volcanic islands of Rimatara, Rurutu, Tubuai, Raivavae, and Rapa, plus un-inhabited Maria (or Hull) atoll, make up the Austral group. This southernmost island chain in the South Pacific is a 1,280-km extension of the same submerged mountain range as the southern Cook Islands, 900 km northwest. The islands of the Australs seldom exceed 300 meters, except Rapa, which soars to 650 meters. The southerly location makes these islands notably cooler and drier than Tahiti. Collectively the Australs are known as Tuhaa Pae, the "Fifth Part" or fifth administrative subdivision of French Polynesia. It's still a world apart from tourism.

History

Excavations carried out on the northwest coast of Rurutu uncovered 60 round-ended houses arranged in parallel rows, with 14 *marae* scattered among them, demonstrating the presence of humans here as early as A.D. 900. Ruins of *marae* can also be seen on Rimatara, Tubuai, and Raivavae. Huge stone tikis once graced Raivavae, but most have since been destroyed or removed. The terraced mountain fortifications, or *pa,* on Rapa are unique.

The Australs were one of the great art areas of the Pacific, represented today in many museums. The best-known artifacts are sculpted sharkskin drums, wooden bowls, fly whisks,

and tapa cloth. Offerings that could not be touched by human hands were placed on the sacred altars with intricately incised ceremonial ladles. European contact effaced most of these traditions and the carving done today is crude by comparison.

Rurutu was spotted by Captain James Cook in 1769; he found Tubuai in 1777. In 1789 Fletcher Christian and the *Bounty* mutineers attempted to establish a settlement at the northeast corner of Tubuai. They left after only three months, after battles with the islanders in which 66 Polynesians died. The European discoverer of Rapa was Captain George Vancouver in 1791. Rimatara wasn't contacted until 1813, by the Australian captain Michael Fodger.

English missionaries converted most of the people to Protestantism in the early 19th century. Whalers and sandalwood ships introduced diseases and firearms, which decimated the Austral islanders. The French didn't complete their annexation of the group until 1901. Since then the Australs have gone their sleepy way.

The People
The 6,500 mostly Polynesian inhabitants are fishermen and farmers who live in attractive villages with homes and churches built of coral limestone. The rich soil and moderate climate stimulate agriculture with staple crops such as taro, manioc, Irish potatoes, sweet potatoes, leeks, cabbage, carrots, corn, and coffee. The coconut palm also thrives, except on Rapa. Today many Austral people live in Papeete.

Getting There
Air Tahiti has four or five flights a week to Rurutu and Tubuai. Two operate Papeete–Tubuai–Rurutu–Papeete, the other two Papeete–Rurutu–Tubuai–Papeete. One-way fares from Tahiti are CFP 17,200 to Rurutu and CFP 19,300 to Tubuai. Rurutu–Tubuai is CFP 8,700. In 2002 an airport was opened on Raivavae and another is under construction on Rimatara.

The Austral Islands are also accessible by boat. (For information on the sailings of the *Tuhaa Pae III* from Papeete, see Transportation in the introduction to French Polynesia.)

Rurutu

This island, 565 km south of Papeete, is shaped like a miniature replica of the African continent. Rurutu is estimated to be 11 million years old, and it would normally have eroded to sea level, except that four million years ago it was uplifted by the movement of tectonic plates. This history accounts for the juxtaposition of coastal coral cliffs with volcanic interior hills. For the hiker, 32-square-km Rurutu is a more varied island to visit than Tubuai. Grassy, fern-covered Taatioe (389 meters) and Manureva (384 meters) are the highest peaks, and coastal cliffs on the southeast side of the island drop 30 meters to the sea. A narrow fringing reef surrounds Rurutu, but there's no lagoon.

The climate of this northernmost Austral island is temperate and dry. The recent history of Rurutu revolves around four important dates: 1821, when the gospel arrived on the island; 1889, when France declared a protectorate over the island; 1970, when Hurricane Emma devastated the three villages; and 1975, when the airport opened.

In January and July Rurutuans practice the ancient art of stone lifting or *amoraa ofai*. Men get three tries to hoist a 150-kg boulder coated with *monoï* (coconut oil) up onto their shoulders, while women attempt a 60-kg stone. Dancing and feasting follow the event. The women of Rurutu weave fine pandanus hats, bags, baskets, fans, lamp shades, and mats. A handicraft display is laid out for departing passengers. Rurutu's famous Manureva (Soaring Bird) Dance Group has performed around the world. The main evening entertainment is watching dancers practice in the villages.

Orientation

The pleasant main village, Moerai, boasts a post office, medical center, four small stores, two bakeries, and a bank. An Italian runs a goat cheese factory in Moerai. Two other villages, Avera and Hauti, bring the total island population to about 2,000. Neat fences and flower gardens surround the coral limestone houses. This is the Polynesia of 50 years ago: though snack bars have appeared and electricity functions 24 hours a day, there's almost none of the flashy tourism development you see in the Society Islands nor the pearl farms common in the Tuamotus.

Public transportation is also lacking on the 36-km road around Rurutu, and even by bicycle it can be quite an effort to circle the island as the route climbs away from the coast on four occasions to avoid high cliffs. South of Avera the road reaches 190 meters, dropping back down to sea level at the southern tip, then rising again to 124 meters on the way up to Hauti. The direct road from Moerai to Avera also climbs to 168 meters. For hikers a three-km foot trail across the center of the island between Avera and Hauti makes a variety of itineraries possible. Beaches, waterfalls, valleys, bluffs, and limestone caves beckon the undaunted explorer.

One of the nicest spots is near **Toataratara Point** where a side road cuts back up the east coast to a *marae* and a few small beaches. It's quite easy to hike to the TV tower on the summit of **Manureva** from either the 200-meter-high Tetuanui Plateau toward the airport or the saddle of the Moerai-Avera road. Rurutu's highest peak, Taatioe, is nearby.

From July to October, the Raie Manta Club offers **humpback whale-watching** at Rurutu, costing CFP 10,000 a half day. You can even snorkel with the beasts. Scuba diving is available at different sites.

Accommodations

The **Hôtel Rurutu Village** (tel. 94-03-92, fax 94-05-01), on a beach a km southwest of the airport, is the only regular hotel in the Austral Islands. The eight tin-roofed bungalows with bath go for CFP 4,500/5,500 single/double, or CFP 8,800/14,100 with breakfast and dinner. Facilities include a restaurant, bar, and swimming pool.

Pension Ariana (tel. 94-06-69, fax 94-07-14), near the Hôtel Rurutu Village, has two rooms at CFP 7,200/11,400 single/double and three bungalows at CFP 7,700/11,900, both rates including half board.

On the beach a few km south of the Rurutu Village and six km from Moerai is **Pension Teautamatea** (tel./fax 94-02-42) with three rooms at CFP 3,800/5,600 single/double. Half board is CFP 2,500 pp extra. It rents bicycles at CFP 1,000 a day.

Pension Temarama (tel./fax 94-02-17), between the airport and Moerai, has six rooms in a two-story house at CFP 3,800/4,800. Meals are extra (no cooking facilities). It provides a good base for visiting the village.

Pension Catherine (tel. 94-02-43), in a concrete building behind Moerai's Protestant church, has 10 rooms at CFP 4,500/5,500 single/double, or CFP 7,400/11,400 including half board.

Chez Paulette (tel. 94-05-82), near the wharf in Moerai, rents three rooms but its main business is its snack bar, which serves good local meals.

Services and Transportation

Banque Socredo (tel. 94-04-75) and the post office are at Moerai. The gendarmerie (tel. 94-03-61) is at the east end of Moerai.

Unaa Airport (RUR) is at the north tip of Rurutu, four km from Moerai. All of the hotels offer free transfers to guests who have booked. **Air Tahiti** can be reached at tel. 94-03-57. The supply ship from Papeete ties up at Moerai.

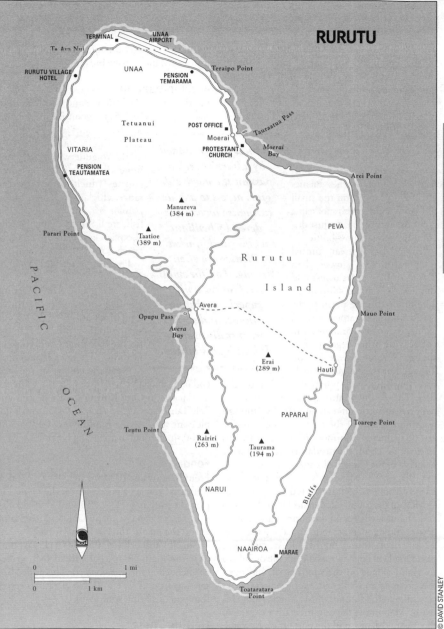

RURUTU

UNAA
AIRPORT
TERMINAL
Te Ava Nui
RURUTU VILLAGE
HOTEL
UNAA
Teraipo Point
PENSION
TEMARAMA

Tetuanui
Plateau
POST OFFICE
Moerai
Tauraatua Pass
VITARIA
PROTESTANT
CHURCH
Moerai
Bay
PENSION
TEAUTAMATEA
Arei Point

Manureva
(384 m)
PEVA
Parari Point
Taatioe
(389 m)
R u r u t u
I s l a n d
Avera
Mauo Point
Opupu Pass
Avera
Bay
Erai
(289 m)
Hauti
Teutu Point
PAPARAI
Toarepe Point
Rairiri
(263 m)
Taurama
(194 m)
P A C I F I C

O C E A N
NARUI
Bluffs

NAAIROA
MARAE
0   1 mi
0   1 km
Toataratara
Point

Tubuai

Ten-km-long by five-km-wide Tubuai, largest of the Australs, is 643 km south of Tahiti. Hills on the east and west sides of this oval 45-square-km island are joined by lowland in the middle; when seen from the sea Tubuai looks like two islands. Mount Taitaa (422 meters) is its highest point. Tubuai is surrounded by a barrier reef; a pass on the north side gives access to a wide turquoise lagoon bordered by brilliant white-sand beaches. Picnics are often arranged on the small reef *motu*, amid superb snorkeling grounds, and surfers are just discovering Tubuai's possibilities.

> *Tubuai is surrounded by a barrier reef; a pass on the north side gives access to a wide turquoise lagoon bordered by brilliant white-sand beaches. Picnics are often arranged on the small reef* motu, *amid superb snorkeling grounds, and surfers are just discovering Tubuai's possibilities.*

Tubuai has a mean annual temperature 3°C lower than Tahiti and it's at its driest and sunniest September–November. The brisk climate permits the cultivation of potatoes, carrots, cabbage, lettuce, oranges, and coffee, but other vegetation is sparse. Several *marae* are on Tubuai, but they're in extremely bad condition, with potatoes growing on the sites. The *Bounty* mutineers unsuccessfully attempted to settle on Tubuai in 1789 (though nothing remains of their Fort George, southeast of Taahuaia). Mormon missionaries arrived as early as 1844, and today there are active branches of the Church of Latter-day Saints in all the villages. The islanders weave fine pandanus hats, and some woodcarving is done at Mahu.

Most of the 2,050 inhabitants live in Mataura and Taahuaia villages on the north coast, though houses and hamlets are found all along the level 24-km road around the island. An eight-km paved road cuts right across the middle of Tubuai to Mahu village on the south coast, but even this presents no challenges for bicyclists (it's an easy hike to the summit of Mt. Taitaa from this road). Mataura is the administrative center of the Austral Islands, and the post office, hospital, dental clinic, gendarmerie (tel. 95-03-33), and the branches of two banks are here. The two stores at Mataura bake bread.

Accommodations

Pension Yolande (Yolande and Sam Tahuhuterani, tel./fax 95-05-52), lagoonside in Mataura, has five rooms at CFP 3,090/5,150 single/double. For CFP 2,500 Yolande will serve you a huge dinner of up to seven courses (duck with tamarind sauce, chicken in lemon sauce, *poisson cru*, spring rolls, baked fish, etc.). Sam is a guitarist who also plays keyboard. An excellent beach is just 50 meters away.

Pension Vaitea Nui (Mélinda Bodin, tel. 93-22-40, fax 93-22-42), inland a bit from Mataura, has five rooms with bath in a long block at CFP 3,300/5,300 single/double, plus CFP 3,400 pp for half board (no cooking facilities). There's a restaurant.

Near the college at the west end of Taahueia village, just under three km east of Mataura, is **Chez Karine et Talé** (Karine and Talé Tahuhuterani, tel./fax 95-04-52) with one pleasant self-catering bungalow at CFP 5,000/8,000 single/double including breakfast.

Food

From **Restaurant Te Motu** (tel. 95-05-27) near Taahueia, you get a good view of the *motu*. The plat du jour is CFP 1,250 and smoked fish *(tazard)*, *poisson cru*, mahimahi, and roast lamb are on the menu. You can order drinks.

Snack Vahinerii (tel. 95-03-97; closed Sun.), near the main wharf, has grilled fish, grilled chicken, chou mein, *poisson cru*, and grilled beef starting around CFP 750. No alcohol is served (but you can bring your own).

Getting There

Tubuai Airport (TUB), in the northwest cor-

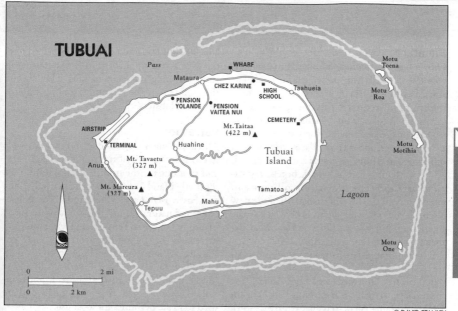

© DAVID STANLEY

ner of the island, opened in 1972. The best beach on the main island is beside the five-km road from the airport to Mataura. All the accommodations offer free transfers to guests. **Air Tahiti** (tel. 95-04-76) arrives from Rurutu and Papeete several times a week.

Ships enter the lagoon through a passage in the barrier reef on the north side and proceed to the wharf a km east of Mataura. Otherwise, the lagoon is too shallow for navigation.

Getting Around

There's no public transportation on Tubuai. You can rent a bicycle or car from **Tubuai Photo** (tel. 95-04-05) near Mataura. It's run by Donald Travers, an American from Los Angeles who has been on the island since 1974. Donald does day trips to *motu*. **Garage Le Guilloux** (tel. 95-06-01), near Tamatoa, also rents cars. The only gas station is run by a Canadian named Larry Miller near the wharf at Mataura.

ÉRIC DE BISSCHOP

At Moerai village lies the tomb of French navigator Éric de Bisschop, whose exploits equaled, but are not as well known as, those of Thor Heyerdahl. Before World War II de Bisschop sailed a catamaran, the *Kaimiloa*, from Hawaii to the Mediterranean via the Indian Ocean and the tip of Africa. His greatest voyage was aboard the *Tahiti Nui*, a series of three rafts, each of which eventually broke up and sank. In 1956 the *Tahiti Nui* set out from Tahiti to Chile to demonstrate the now-accepted theory that the Polynesians had visited South America in prehistoric times. There, two of his four crewmembers abandoned ship, but de Bisschop doggedly set out to return. After a total of 13 months at sea the expedition's final raft foundered on a reef in the Cook Islands and its courageous leader, one of the giants of Pacific exploration, was killed.

Other Austral Islands

Rimatara

Only a narrow fringing reef hugs Rimatara's lagoonless shore; arriving passengers are landed at Amaru or Mutua Ura by whaleboat and it's customary for newcomers to pass through a cloud of purifying smoke from beachside fires. The women of Rimatara make fine pandanus hats, mats, and bags, and shell necklaces. *Monoï* (skin oil) is prepared from gardenias and coconut oil. As yet without a harbor, wharf, hotels, restaurants, bars, and taxis, Rimatara is still a place to escape the world. This will change when the new airport begins receiving flights. The wreck of the interisland ship *Vaeanu II* sits on the reef at Rimatara, where it was lost in April 2002.

This smallest (nine square km) and lowest (84 meters) of the Australs is home to fewer than 1,000 people. Dirt roads lead from Amaru, the main village, to Anapoto and Mutua Ura. **Pension Umarere** (Tama Aténi Tereopa, tel. 83-25-84), at Mutua Ura, five km southwest of Amaru, has two rooms with shared bath at CFP 2,500/4,000 single/double or CFP 60,000 a month. Cooking is possible but bring food and drink to Rimatara. Water is short in the dry season.

Uninhabited Maria (or Hull) is a four-islet atoll 192 km northwest of Rimatara, visited once or twice a year by men from Rimatara or Rurutu for fishing and copra making. They stay on the atoll two or three months, among seabirds and giant lobsters.

Raivavae

This appealing, nine-km-long and two-km-wide island is just south of the tropic of Capricorn, and thus outside the tropics. It's the third most southerly island in the South Pacific (only Rapa and Easter Island are farther south). For archaeology and natural beauty, this is one of the finest islands in Polynesia. Fern-covered Mt. Hiro (437 meters) is the highest point on 18-square-km Raivavae. A barrier reef encloses an emerald lagoon, but the 20 small coral *motu* are all on the southern and eastern parts of the reef. The tropical vegetation is rich: rose and sandalwood are used to make perfumes for local use.

A few years after the arrival of Protestant missionaries in 1822, a malignant fever epidemic reduced the people of Raivavae from 3,000 to a mere 80 in 1834. The present population of around 1,050 lives in four coastal villages, Rairua, Mahanatoa, Anatonu, and Vaiuru, linked by a dirt road. A shortcut route direct from Rairua to Vaiuru crosses a 119-meter saddle, with splendid views of the island. The post office is in Rairua.

Different teams led by Frank Stimson (1917), Thor Heyerdahl (1956), and Donald Marshall (1957) have explored the ancient temples and defensive terraces of Raivavae. Many two- to three-meter-high red stone statues once stood on the island, but most have since been smashed, and two were removed to Tahiti, where they can be seen on the grounds of the Gauguin Museum. One big tiki is still standing by the road between Rairua and Mahanatoa villages. Christian converts destroyed most of Raivavae's 92 *marae*. At **Pomoavao Marae** on the south side of the island huge stone blocks tilt upward among the undergrowth.

Pension Moana (Haamoeura Teehu, tel./fax 95-42-66) at Mahanatoa has three rooms a

RIMATARA

Anapoto

Teruahu Point

Rimatara   Island

Hiava Pass

Amaru

▲
Uahu
(83 m)

Iriiriroa Point

Mutuaura

0   0.5 mi

0   0.5 km

© DAVID STANLEY

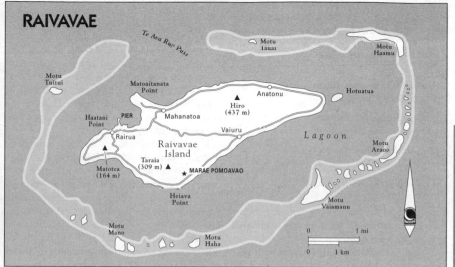

RAIVAVAE

Te Ava Rua Pass

Motu Tuitui

Motu Iauai

Motu Haamu

Matoaitanata Point

Anatonu

Hotuatau

Haatani Point

PIER

Mahanatoa

Hiro (437 m)

Raivavae Island

Rairua

Vaiuru

Lagoon

Motu Araoo

Taraia (309 m)

MARAE POMOAVAO

Matotea (164 m)

Heiava Point

Motu Vaiamanu

Motu Mano

Motu Haha

0   1 mi

0   1 km

© DAVID STANLEY

M

FRENCH POLYNESIA

CFP 2,500/4,000 single/double, plus CFP 2,500 pp for half board. **Pension Ataha** (Odile Tamaititahio, tel./fax 95-43-69) and **Pension**

The famous tiki from Raivavae is now at Tahiti's Gauguin Museum.

Rau'uru (Edmond Flores, tel. 95-42-88) at Rairua are similar.

In 2002 an airport was constructed on land reclaimed from the lagoon south of Rairua, six km from Mahanatoa, and Air Tahiti operates flights from Papeete twice a week via Tubuai. Ships enter the lagoon through a pass on the north side and tie up to the pier at Rairua. A boat calls at the island about every 10–14 days.

Rapa

At 27°38' south latitude, Rapa is the southernmost island in the South Pacific, and one of the most isolated and spectacular. Its nearest neighbor is Raivavae, 600 km away, and Tahiti is 1,244 km north. It's sometimes called Rapa Iti (Little Rapa) to distinguish it from Rapa Nui (Easter Island). Soaring peaks reaching 650 meters form a horseshoe around magnificent Haurei Bay, Rapa's crater harbor, the western section of a drowned volcano. This is only one of 12 deeply indented bays around the island; the absence of reefs allows the sea to cut into the 40-square-km island's outer basalt coasts. Offshore are several sugarloaf-shaped islets. The east slopes of the mountains are bare, while large fern forests are found on the west. Coconut trees cannot grow in

AUSTRAL ISLANDS INTERNET RESOURCES

Chez Karine et Talé, Tubuai
charles@mail.pf

Pension Teautamatea, Rurutu
pension.teautamatea@free.fr

Pension Temarama, Rurutu
pension.temarama@free.fr

Pension Vaitea Nui, Tubuai
http://chez.mana.pf/~bodinm

Pension Vaitea Nui, Tubuai
bodinm@mail.pf

the foggy, temperate climate. Instead coffee and taro are the main crops.

A timeworn **Polynesian fortress** with terraces is situated on the crest of a ridge at Morongo Uta, commanding a wide outlook over the steep, rugged hills. Morongo Uta was cleared of vegetation by a party of archaeologists led by William Mulloy in 1956 and is still easily visitable. About a dozen of these *pa* (fortresses) are found above the bay, built to defend the territories of the different tribes of overpopulated ancient Rapa. Today the young men of Rapa organize eight-day bivouacs to hunt wild goats, which range across the island.

During the two decades following the arrival of missionaries in 1826, Rapa's population dropped from 2,000 to 300 because of the introduction of European diseases. By 1851 it was down to just 70, and after smallpox and dysentery arrived on a Peruvian ship in 1863 it was a miracle that anyone survived at all. The present population of about 550 lives at Area and Haurei villages on the north and south sides of Rapa's great open bay, connected only by boat.

If you're planning to stay on Rapa, it might be useful to write Le Maire, Rapa, Îles Australes, French Polynesia, well in advance, stating your name, nationality, age, and profession. Information may also be available from the Subdivision Administrative des Îles Australes (tel. 46-86-76, fax 46-86-79), rue des Poilus Tahitiens, Papeete.

Mrs. Titaua Jean (tel. 95-72-59, fax 95-72-60) rents a house with cooking facilities in Ahurei at CFP 4,000/60,000 a day/month. A number of local residents also rent rooms in their homes. The *Tuhaa Pae III* calls at Rapa monthly, so that's how long you'll be there.

Marotiri, or the "Bass Rocks," are nine uninhabited islets totaling just four hectares, 74 km southeast of Rapa. Amazingly enough, some of these pinnacles are crowned with man-made stone platforms and round "towers." One 105-meter-high pinnacle is visible from Rapa in very clear weather. Landing is difficult.

Tuamotu Islands

Arrayed in two parallel northwest-southeast chains scattered across an area of ocean 600 km wide and 1,500 km long, the Tuamotus are the largest group of coral atolls in the world. Of the 78 atolls in the group, 21 have one entrance (pass), 10 have two passes, and 47 have no pass at all. Some have an unbroken ring of reef around the lagoon, while others appear as a necklace of islets separated by channels. Although the land area of the Tuamotus is only 726 square km, the lagoons of the atolls total some 6,000 square km of sheltered water.

Variable currents, sudden storms, and poor charts make cruising this group by yacht extremely hazardous—in fact, the Tuamotus are popularly known as the Dangerous Archipelago, or the Labyrinth. Wrecks litter the reefs of many atolls. The breakers become visible only when one is within eight km of the reef, and once in, a yacht must carry on through the group. The usual route is to sail either between Rangiroa and Arutua after a stop at Ahe, or through the Passe de Fakarava between Toau and Fakarava. Winds are generally from the east, varying to northeast November–May and southeast June–October.

The resourceful Tuamotu people have always lived off seafood, pandanus nuts, and coconuts. They once dove to depths of 30 meters and more, wearing only tiny goggles, to collect mother-of-pearl shells. This activity has largely ceased as

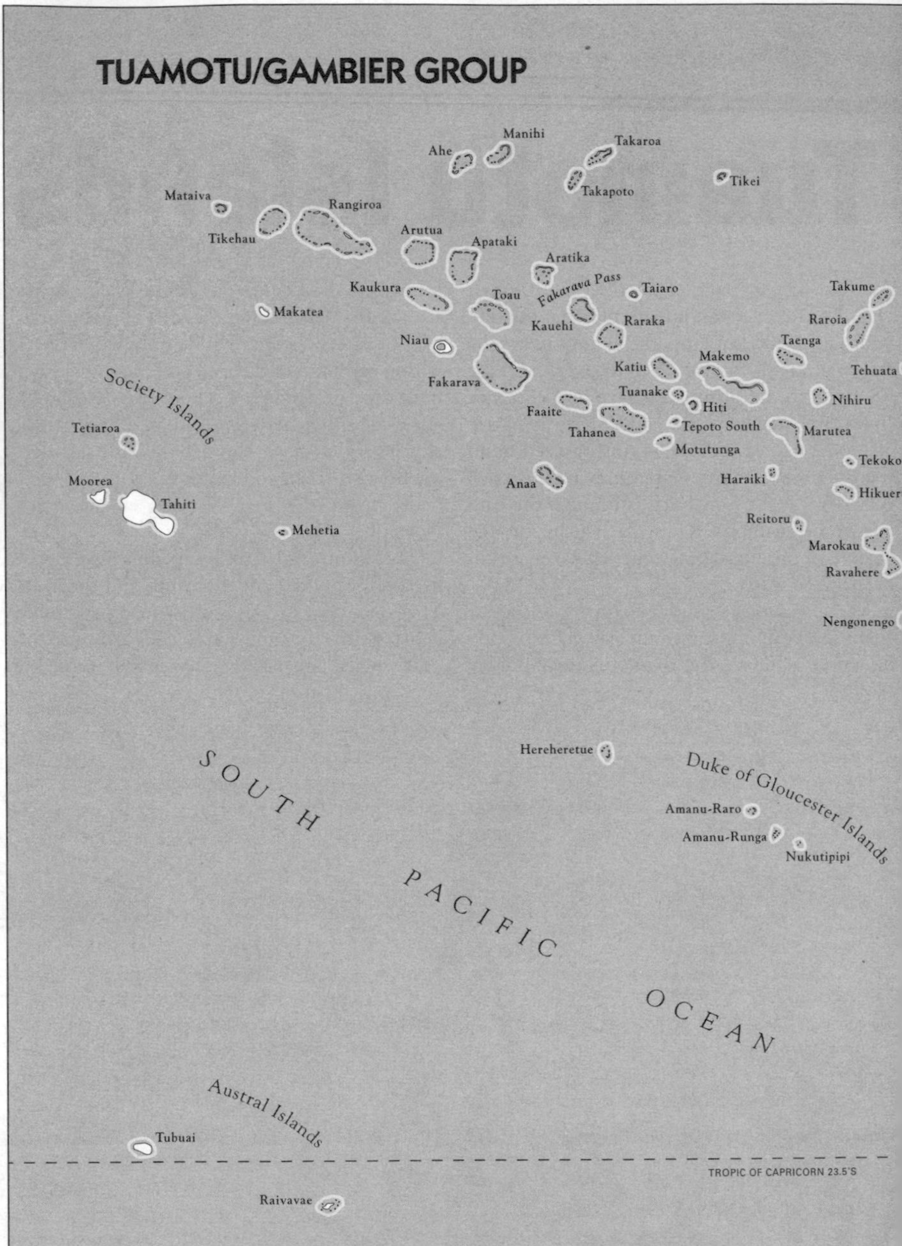
TUAMOTU/GAMBIER GROUP
Manihi
Ahe
Takaroa
Takapoto
Tikei
Mataiva
Rangiroa
Tikehau
Arutua
Apataki
Aratika
Fakarava Pass
Taiaro
Kaukura
Toau
Takume
Makatea
Kauehi
Raraka
Raroia
Niau
Taenga
Makemo
Katiu
Tehuata
Society Islands
Fakarava
Tuanake
Hiti
Nihiru
Faaite
Tepoto South
Marutea
Tetiaroa
Tahanea
Motutunga
Tekoko
Moorea
Anaa
Haraiki
Hikuer
Tahiti
Reitoru
Mehetia
Marokau
Ravahere
Nengonengo
Hereheretue
Duke of Gloucester Islands
SOUTH
Amanu-Raro
Amanu-Runga
Nukutipipi
PACIFIC
OCEAN
Austral Islands
Tubuai
TROPIC OF CAPRICORN 23.5'S
Raivavae

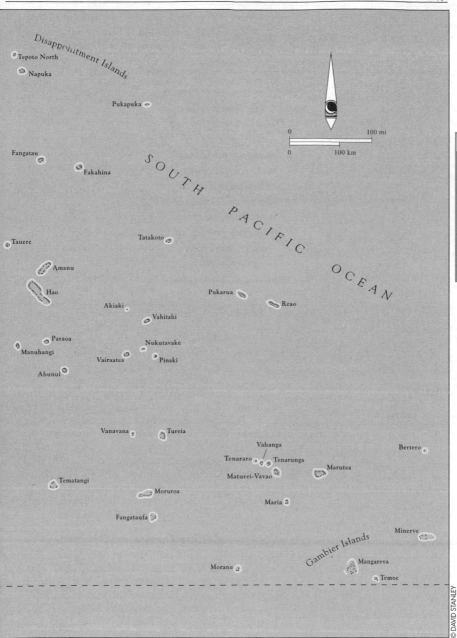

FRENCH POLYNESIA

overharvesting has made the oysters rare. Today, cultured-pearl farms operate on Ahe, Aratika, Arutua, Fakarava, Hao, Hikueru, Katiu, Kaukura, Kauehi, Makemo, Manihi, Marutea South, Nengonengo, Raroia, Takapoto, Takaroa, Takume, Taenga, and others. Cultured black pearls *(Pinctada margaritifera)* from the Tuamotus and Gambiers are world famous. The pearl industry has reversed the depopulation of the atolls and spread prosperity through this remote region.

The scarcity of land and fresh water has always been a major problem. A total of around 14,500 people live on the 48 inhabited islands. Many of these dry, coconut-covered atolls have only a few hundred inhabitants. Although airstrips exist on 26 islands, the isolation has led many Tuamotuans to migrate to Papeete. Deluxe resorts exist on Rangiroa, Tikehau, Manihi, and Fakarava, and homestay accommodations are available on most of the other atolls.

Beware of eating poisonous fish all across this archipelago.

The resourceful Tuamotu people have always lived off seafood, pandanus nuts, and coconuts. They once dove to depths of 30 meters and more, wearing only tiny goggles, to collect mother-of-pearl shells.

History

The Tuamotus were originally settled around A.D. 1000 from the Society and Marquesas Islands, perhaps by political refugees. The inhabitants of the atolls frequently warred among themselves or against those of a Society island, and even King Pomare II was unable to conquer the group despite help from the missionaries and European firearms. Ironically, the Pomare family itself originated on Fakarava.

Magellan's sighting of Pukapuka on the northeast fringe of the Tuamotus in 1521 made it the first South Pacific island ever to be seen by European eyes. Other famous explorers who passed through the Tuamotus included Quirós (1606), Schouten and Le Maire (1616), Roggeveen (1722), Byron (1765), Wallis (1767), Bougainville (1768), Cook (1769), Bligh (1792), Kotzebue (1816), and Bellingshausen (1820), yet it was not until 1835 that all of the islands had been

"discovered." Of the 14 European expeditions between 1606 and 1816, only eight bothered to go ashore. Of these, all but Quirós were involved in skirmishes with the islanders. Centuries later, a group of Scandinavians under the leadership of Thor Heyerdahl ran aground on Raroia atoll on August 7, 1947, after having sailed 7,000 km from South America in 101 days on the raft *Kon Tiki* to prove that Peruvian Indians could have done the same thing centuries before.

Pearl shells and bêche-de-mer were being collected by European trading ships as early as 1809. An American Mormon missionary arrived in 1845, followed by Catholics from Mangareva in 1851, and today two-thirds of the people are Catholic, the rest Mormon. Most of the Mormons are actually Sanitos ("saints") affiliated with the Reorganized Mormon Church of Independence, Missouri, which rejects many of the teachings of the Utah Mormons.

After Tahiti came under French "protection" in 1842 the Tuamotus were gradually brought under French rule through dealings with the local chiefs and Catholic missionary activity. For more than a century, making copra and collecting mother-of-pearl shell were about the only monetary activities. By comparison, French military activity, tourism, and cultured black pearls are recent developments. During the 19th century French naval officers were posted on Anaa and Fakarava but since 1923 the group has been administered from Papeete. Local government is split into 16 communes.

Getting There

Air Tahiti has flights to Ahe, Apataki, Arutua, Fakarava, Kauehi, Kaukura, Manihi, Mataiva, Rangiroa, Takapoto, Takaroa, and Tikehau in the northern Tuamotus, and Anaa, Faaite, Fakahina, Fangatau, Hao, Makemo, Mangareva, Napuka, Nukutavake, Pukapuka, Pukarua, Reao, Takume, Tatakoto, Tureia, and Vahitahi in the south.

Interisland boats call at most of the Tuamotu

TUAMOTU ISLANDS HIGHLIGHTS

Tiputa Pass, Rangiroa: drift diving, dolphins, sharks

Blue Lagoon, Rangiroa: swimming, snorkeling, marinelife

Garuae Pass, Fakarava: sharks, spectacular marinelife

Makatea: ruins of phospate mining

Moruroa: pollution threat from nuclear testing

Papeete is given in the French Polynesia Introduction.) However you come, be aware that it's very difficult to change foreign currency on the atolls, so bring enough cash.

All the Tuamotu atolls offer splendid snorkeling possibilities (take snorkeling gear), though scuba diving is developed only on Fakarava, Manihi, Rangiroa, and Tikehau. The advantage of atolls other than Manihi, Rangiroa, and Tikehau is that the people will be far less affected by packaged tourism. There it should be easy to hitch rides with the locals across to *le secteur* (uninhabited *motu*) as they go to cut copra or tend the pearl farms. Just don't expect many facilities on these tiny specks of sand scattered in a solitary sea.

atolls about once a week, bringing imported foods and other goods and returning to Papeete with fish. (Information on the cargo boats from

Rangiroa

Rangiroa, 300 km northeast of Papeete, is the Tuamotus' most populous atoll. Its 1,020-square-km aquamarine lagoon is 78 km long, 24 km wide (too far to see), and 225 km around—the island of Tahiti would fit inside its reef. The name Rangiroa means "extended sky." Some 240 *motu* sit on this reef. Although Rangiroa is the largest atoll in eastern Polynesia, it's not the biggest in the South Pacific as all of the brochures claim. On tong Java in the Solomon Islands encloses 1,400 square km of lagoon. The world's biggest atoll—as the brochures concede—is 2,174-square-km Kwajalein in the Marshall Islands.

Two deep passages through the north side of Rangiroa's coral ring allow a constant exchange of water between the open sea and the lagoon, creating a fertile habitat. While lagoons in the Society Islands are often murky because of runoff from the main volcanic islands and pollution from coastal communities, the waters of the Tuamotus are clean and fresh, with some of the best swimming, snorkeling, and scuba diving in the South Pacific. You've never seen so many fish! However, in May 1998 it was revealed that 80 percent of the reefs at Rangiroa had suffered bleaching because of increased water temperatures brought about by the El Niño phenomenon, completing the destruction wrought earlier

by hurricanes. What draws people to Rangi (as everyone calls it) is the marinelife in the lagoon, not the coral. This one of the prime shark-viewing locales of the world. Most tourists to Rangiroa are French or Italian. Nondivers (and especially honeymooners) may get bored here.

Orientation

Rangiroa's twin villages, each facing a passage 500 meters wide, house 2,700 people. Avatoru village on Avatoru Pass is at the west end of the airport island, about six km from the airport itself. A paved 10-km road runs east from Avatoru past the airport and the Hôtel Kia Ora Village to Tiputa Pass. Tiputa village is just across the water. The accommodations listings that follow are arranged by category from west to east along this road.

Both villages have small stores; the town hall, gendarmerie (tel. 96-03-61), and hotel school are at Tiputa, and the medical center, college, and marine research center are at Avatoru. Avatoru has better commercial facilities, but Tiputa is less touristed and offers the chance to escape by simply walking and wading southeast. **Gauguin's Pearl** (tel./fax 96-05-39; Mon.–Sat. 0830–1400), a pearl farm between Avatoru and the airport, offers a free one-hour tour weekdays at 0830 and 1400.

Most of the accommodations face the tranquil lagoon rather than the windy sea, and large ships can enter the lagoon through either pass. For yachts, the sheltered anchorage by the Hôtel Kia Ora Village near Tiputa Pass is recommended (as opposed to the Avatoru anchorage, which is exposed to swells and chop). Far less English is spoken on Rangiroa than in the Society Islands.

SPORTS AND RECREATION

The strong tidal currents (opape) through Avatoru and Tiputa passes generate flows of three to six knots. It's exciting to shoot these 30-meter-deep passes on an incoming tide, and all the dive shops offer this activity using small motorboats or Zodiacs. Some of the dives tend to be longer and deeper than the norm. The Tiputa Pass current dive begins 45 meters down and is only for advanced divers; even the Tiputa Pass Shark Cave dive to 35 meters calls for some experience. Beginners should ask for the Motu Nuhi Nuhi dive.

On all the dives, the marinelife is fantastic, and humphead wrasses, manta rays, barracudas, dolphins, and sharks are seen in abundance. Most of the time the sharks are harmless black-tip or grey reef sharks (but don't risk touching them, even if you see other divers doing so). Big hammerhead sharks frequent Tiputa Pass from December to March, while spotted eagle rays are common from July to October. The dive schedules vary according to the tides, winds, and number of tourists on the atoll, and it's wise to book ahead. All of the operators mentioned below offer free hotel pickups.

Rangiroa's original scuba operator is the friendly **Raie Manta Club** (Yves Lefèvre, tel. 96-84-80 or 72-31-45, fax 96-85-60), with branches near Rangiroa Lodge in Avatoru village and next to Pension Marie et Teina on Tiputa Pass. Diving costs CFP 5,800 pp for one tank, including a float through the pass. For the more enthusiastic, a 10-dive package is CFP 52,000 (can be shared by a couple and also used at Tikehau). Every dive is different (falling, pass, cave, undulating bottom, hollow, and night). Snorkelers can go along when practical; otherwise an introductory dive is CFP 6,500. Divers come from all parts of the world to dive with Yves and his highly professional seven-instructor team.

Rangiroa Paradive (Bernard Blanc, tel. 96-05-55, fax 96-05-50) is next to Chez Glorine at Tiputa Pass. It's CFP 6,300 per dive; the package prices are CFP 30,000/58,000 for five/10 dives. Night dives are CFP 1,000 extra (minimum of five). You can ask for a small price reduction if you haven't booked ahead. Bernard isn't as aggressive about shark feeding as Yves but he does explore the shark caves and you'll see legions of sharks on his drift dives. He's obliging, hospitable, and one of the most highly qualified instructors in Polynesia. There's no provision for snorkelers here and divers must show their cards. Without a card you could still do an introductory dive for CFP 6,500.

The **Six Passengers** (Ugo Mazzavillani, tel. 96-03-05, fax 96-02-60) is in a hut between Chez Glorine and the Kia Ora. Ugo charges about the same as Yves and Bernard. Diving from a Zodiac is CFP 6,200/12,400/56,000 for one/two/10 tanks, night dives CFP 7,700, gear and pickups included. The name refers to the number of people he can take out each time. Snorkelers are not accepted, but a four-day CMAS certification course is offered at CFP 43,680.

TOPdive (tel. 96-05-60), on the beach just west of the Kia Ora, offers scuba diving at 0800, 1000, and 1400 (one/10 dives CFP 6,500/ 58,500). You can also use its 10-dive package at TOPdive centers on Moorea and Bora Bora.

The **Blue Dolphins Diving Center** (Junko Kida and Pascal Jagut, tel./fax 96-03-01), based at the Hôtel Kia Ora Village, has Japanese-speaking monitors. Exploration/introductory dives are CFP 6,600/7,150.

Popular lagoon excursions include picnics to the **Blue Lagoon**, a fish-filled pool at Motu Taeoo, to the **Île aux Récifs**, a number of uplifted coral formations on the south side of the lagoon, to the **Sables Roses**, a stretch of pink sand at the southeast end of the lagoon, and to tiny **Motu Paio**, a midlagoon bird sanctuary. Several companies offer a snorkel through the pass at CFP 4,200. A glass-bottom boat visit to **The Aquarium** at Motu Nuhi Nuhi near the Tiputa Pass with Tepa Matahi (tel. 96-84-48) is CFP 2,200. **Sharky Club Excursions** (tel. 96-84-73), at Chez Punua et Moana in Avatoru, organizes some good value trips starting at CFP 3,500. **Oviri Excursions** (Celine and Hugo, tel. 96-05-87) does excellent full-day trips to Sables Roses at CFP 10,000 pp and to Île aux Récifs at CFP 7,500 pp (four-person minimum).

ACCOMMODATIONS

Under US$25

Chez Nanua (Nanua and Marie Tamaehu, tel./fax 96-83-88), between the airport and Avatoru village, allows budget travelers to pitch tents in a rather poor location at CFP 3,050 pp with two meals. The four simple thatched bungalows with shared/private bath are CFP 3,550/4,550 pp including two meals. You eat with the owners—a little fish and rice every meal. There's no hot water. Ask about bicycle and scooter rentals at Carole Pareo nearby.

US$25–50

Pension Henriette (Henriette Tamaehu, tel./fax 96-84-68), by the lagoon in Avatoru village, is a two-bungalow place charging CFP 5,000 pp with half pension. It can be a little noisy here but the food is excellent (especially the banana crêpes) and it's possible stop by for lunch even if you're staying elsewhere.

The son and daughter-in-law of the folks mentioned at Chez Nanua above operate **Chez Punua et Moana** (Punua and Moana Tamaehu, tel. 96-84-73) in Avatoru village. The three thatched bungalows are CFP 3,500 pp with breakfast, or CFP 4,500 pp with half board. Camping is CFP 3,000 pp with half board. It's right by the road and can be noisy from the activities of the surrounding village. Watch your gear here. For those who really want to get away, Punua can arrange overnight stays on Motu Teavahia. Otherwise all are welcome on the daily lagoon tours and "Sharky Club" excursions costing CFP 3,500 pp and up.

Rangiroa Lodge (Jacques and Rofina Ly, tel. 96-82-13) in Avatoru has four rooms at CFP 2,000/4,000 single/double with shared bath or CFP 5,000 with private bath (plus CFP 200 for a fan, if desired). A place in one of the two three-bed dorms is CFP 1,700 pp. This is one of the few places with communal cooking facilities, though the proprietors also prepare meals upon request. The snorkeling just off the lodge is outstanding and they'll loan you gear if you need it. Divers from the adjacent Raie Manta Club often stay here.

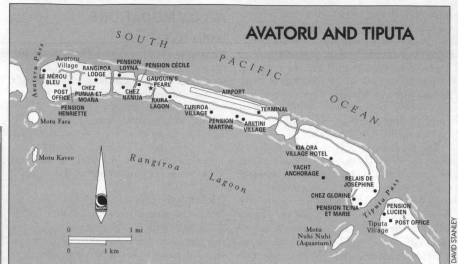

AVATORU AND TIPUTA

The **Turiroa Village** (Olga Niva, tel./fax 96-04-27), less than a km west of the airport terminal, has four bungalows at CFP 6,000/8,000 for two/four people. If required, half board is CFP 2,750 pp. No English is spoken.

US$50-100

Pension Herenui (Victorine Sanford, tel./fax 96-84-71), next to the Raie Manta Club right in Avatoru village, four km from the airport, offers three thatched bungalows with private bath and terrace (but no cooking) at CFP 4,500 pp with breakfast, plus CFP 1,000/2,000 pp for lunch/dinner.

Pension Hinanui (René and Mareta Bizien, tel. 96-84-61), on a quiet beach near Avatoru, four km from the airport, has three bungalows at CFP 4,500/8,000/9,500 single/double/triple, plus CFP 2,500/3,500 pp for half/full board.

Pension Loyna (Loyna Fareea, tel. 96-82-09), oceanside near Avatoru, has a large house with a dormitory and two rooms with shared bath on the mezzanine at CFP 5,565 pp, two rooms with shared bath downstairs at CFP 6,095 pp, and five rooms with private bath in two other buildings at CFP 6,625 pp. All prices include half board and Loyna speaks good English.

Next to Gauguin's Pearl on the lagoon between the airport and Avatoru is **Pension Cécile** (Alban and Cécile Sun, tel./fax 96-05-06) where the eight bungalows are CFP 4,500 pp, plus CFP 2,000 pp for half board (no cooking). Lobster is often on the menu. Reader Rowland Burley writes that:

this was the friendliest accommodation I found in French Polynesia. Cécile speaks excellent English, the units are spotlessly clean, and dinner is superb.

Alban does lagoon tours in his boat upon request. The beach in this vicinity is poor.

Pension Tuanake (Roger and Iris Terorotua, tel. 96-04-45, fax 96-03-29), by the lagoon next to Gauguin's Pearl two km west of the airport, has six thatched bungalows with bath (but no cooking facilities) at CFP 6,000/9,000/11,000 single/double/triple. Airport transfers are free.

Pension Martine (Martine and Corinne Tetua, tel. 96-02-51), by the lagoon near the airport terminal, has five fan-cooled bungalows with private bath and terrace (but no cooking) at CFP 6,500 pp with half board (lots of fresh fish). There's no single supplement if you're alone, and it's friendly, clean, and relaxed. Ask Corinne to show you around the family pearl farm.

A five-minute walk west of the airport terminal is the **Ariitini Village** (Félix and Judith Tetua, tel. 96-04-41), previously known as Pension Félix, with nine beach bungalows at CFP 7,500 pp including breakfast and dinner.

A sister of the Henriette mentioned previously runs the popular **Pension Glorine** (Glorine To'i, tel. 96-04-05, fax 96-03-58), next to the wharf at Tiputa Pass, four km from the airport. The seven spacious thatched bungalows with private bath are CFP 7,000 pp including two meals (specialty fresh lagoon fish). Children under 13 are half price and bicycle rentals are available. Airport transfers are CFP 800. Nonguests can order meals here (reserve ahead).

Pension Marie et Teina (Tahuhu Maraeura, tel. 96-03-94, fax 96-84-44), behind Pension Glorine at Tiputa Pass, four km east of the airport, has six duplex garden rooms at CFP 6,000 pp and five thatched beach bungalows at CFP 7,000 pp, all including breakfast and dinner. The three three-bed dorms upstairs in a concrete house are CFP 3,500 including breakfast only. When things get crowded, a lounge is converted into another six-bed dorm. Communal cooking facilities are not provided. Transfers are free. This place gets mixed reviews.

Pension Lucien (Lucien and Esther Pe'a, tel. 96-73-55), near the pass in Tiputa village, offers three beach bungalows with private bath at CFP 6,000 pp with half board. Airport transfers are CFP 1,000 pp.

The **Pension Relais Mihiroa** (Maurice and Monique Guitteny, tel. 96-72-14, fax 96-75-13), in a coconut grove on Tiputa Island four km from the village, has four cubical bungalows with bath and terrace at CFP 7,200 for up to three people, plus CFP 2,400/3,900 pp for half/full board. Boat transfers from the airport are CFP 1,500 pp.

US$100–150

The **Miki Miki Village** (tel. 96-83-83, fax 96-82-90), also known as the Rangiroa Village, is a seven-bungalow resort near Avatoru: CFP 10,000/17,000 single/double, including breakfast and dinner. It's not worth the price.

The **Raira Lagon** (Maxime and Pascale Boetsch, tel. 96-04-23, fax 96-05-86), a bit over a km west of the airport terminal, offers 10 small thatched bungalows with private bath and fridge (but no cooking facilities) at CFP 12,500/20,000 single/double with half board and airport transfers. A few well-used bicycles are lent free and it's right on the beach. The beachfront restaurant is open to the public.

The former **Rangiroa Beach Club,** next to the Raira Lagon, is closed awaiting renovations by the owners, Nouvelles Frontières. This property may eventually be operated by the Paladien hotel chain.

US$150–250

Les Relais de Joséphine (Denise Thirouard, tel./fax 96-02-00), facing directly onto Tiputa Pass, has three deluxe bungalows with four-post beds and terrace at CFP 14,000/28,000 single/double, including tax, continental breakfast, dinner, and airport transfers. A third person pays CFP 10,500. Giant trees keep the mosquito-rich compound shady all day and the tall *fare* with their dysfunctional teak furnishings are consummately romantic. Dolphins frolic just offshore and the sound of the waves at night is wonderful. Denise's husband, Guy, is the only private doctor on Rangiroa and they're quite a couple! Joséphine's website has an online booking form.

Le Mérou Bleu (Friedrich Pierre and Sonya, tel. 79-16-82), facing Avatoru Pass, has three thatched bungalows beginning at CFP 11,000/20,000 single/double with half board. For hot water add CFP 2,000. Airport transfers are included. Some of Rangiroa's best surfing is just off its beach.

Rangiroa's top resort is the **Hôtel Kia Ora Village** (tel. 96-03-84, fax 96-02-20), established in 1973 near Tiputa Pass, a bit over two km east of the airport by road. It's right on the best beach of this part of the island. The 30 beach bungalows are CFP 40,000 double, while the five larger garden bungalows are CFP 20,000, plus 11 percent tax. The 10 overwater units go for CFP 55,000. Add another CFP 7,200 pp for breakfast and dinner. Yachties anchored offshore are certainly not welcome to dingy in and use the facilities, but the pricey seafood restaurant is open to all (slow service, variable food, beautiful view). A wide range of lagoon excursions and activities are offered at higher than usual prices.

US$250 and up

In 1991 the Kia Ora Village began offering accommodation in five thatched bungalows at **Kia Ora Sauvage** on Motu Avaerahi on the far south side of the lagoon. It's CFP 34,000 single or double, plus 11 percent tax, plus a compulsory three-meal plan at CFP 7,600 pp, plus CFP 5,000 pp for return boat transfers (two-night minimum stay). The boat leaves at 0900 daily, so you'll probably have to wait one night to go. Kia Ora Sauvage is a Robinson Crusoe experience most people rave about!

FOOD AND SERVICES

Food

Restaurant Le Kai Kai (tel. 96-03-39; no lunch Sun.), opposite Ana Gandy's pearl atelier west of the airport terminal, has a varied meat and seafood menu (main plates CFP 1,500–2,400). *Poisson cru* (CFP 1,100) is a good choice for lunch, and it has great desserts, such as chocolate mousse, crème brûlée, and ice cream for around CFP 500. The espressos come with chunks of dark chocolate. You eat on an outdoor terrace and the staff will switch on a fan to keep you cool.

Pizzeria Vaimario (tel. 96-05-96; closed Sun. and Mon.), on the ocean side of the road just west of the airport, has 10 tables on a tiled outdoor terrace and a couple more inside. There are hamburgers and sandwiches for lunch, and a more extensive menu at dinner. Try one of the exotic pizzas (CFP 1,600).

A great place for lunch is the **Relais** (no phone; Mon.–Sat. 0800–1500, Sun. 0530–0930), next to the wharf at Tiputa Pass on the Avatoru side. There's a nice terrace overlooking the lagoon, good atmosphere, and pleasant music. The menu includes a plat du jour (CFP 800), fried fish (CFP

TUAMOTU ISLANDS INTERNET RESOURCES

Accommodations

Hôtel Kia Ora Village, Rangiroa
www.hotelkiaora.com
resa@hotelkiaora.pf

Hôtel Le Maitai Dream, Fakarava
maitaifa@mail.pf

Le Mérou Bleu, Rangiroa
http://le-merou-bleu.ifrance.com
merou-bleu@hotmail.com

Les Relais de Joséphine, Rangiroa
relaisjosephine@mail.pf

Manihi Pearl Beach Resort
manihi.pearl.b@mail.pf

Motu Aito Paradise, Fakarava
www.fakarava.org

Pension Lucien, Rangiroa
http://pensionlucien.free.fr

Pension Glorine, Rangiroa
pensionglorine@mail.pf

Pension Havaiki, Fakarava
http://chez.mana.pf/~havaiki
havaiki@mail.pf

Pension Loyna, Rangiroa
http://membres.lycos.fr/pensionloyna
pensionloyna@mail.pf

Pension Marie et Teina, Rangiroa
rangiroa@mail.pf

Pension Tuanake, Rangiroa
http://chez.mana.pf/~tuanake

Raira Lagon, Rangiroa
www.raira-lagon.pf
rairalag@mail.pf

Relais de Joséphine, Rangiroa
http://relaisjosephine.free.fr

Tetamanu Village, Fakarava
www.tetamanuvillage.pf
tetamanuvillage@mail.pf

1,000), *croques monsieur* grilled cheese (CFP 250), hamburgers (CFP 400), and other choices costing CFP 800–1,300. A large beer is CFP 350.

Services

The Banque de Tahiti (tel. 96-85-52) has a branch at Avatoru, while Banque Socredo (tel. 96-85-63) has branches at the *mairies* in both Avatoru and Tiputa. All branches are open limited hours according to a variable timetable (in Tiputa only on Mon., Tues., and Thurs.).

Post offices are found in Avatoru, Tiputa, and the airport. Taaroa Web (tel./fax 96-03-04; daily 0830–1900), on the east side of the Hôtel Kia Ora Village, offers Internet access at CFP 500 a half hour. It also sells black pearls.

There are a medical center (tel. 96-03-75) two km east of Avatoru and an infirmary (tel. 96-73-96) at Tiputa. Dr. Guy Thirouard (tel. 96-04-44) has a private Cabinet Médical at Avatoru. It's prudent to drink bottled water on Rangiroa.

TRANSPORTATION

Getting There

Air Tahiti (tel. 96-03-41) flies Tahiti–Rangiroa several times daily (CFP 14,200 one-way). Five times a week a flight arrives direct from Bora Bora (CFP 21,500), but from Rangiroa to Bora Bora there's only a twice-weekly flight. There's service four times a week from Rangiroa to Tikehau (CFP 4,600) and Manihi (CFP 9,200), weekly to Fakarava (CFP 4,600). A weekly flight operates from Rangiroa to Nuku Hiva and Hiva Oa in the Marquesas (CFP 25,500). Seats on flights to the Marquesas should be booked well in advance.

The motor vessel *Dory II* leaves Papeete every Monday at 1600 for Rangiroa (CFP 3,640), arriving Tuesday at 1800. It takes only 26 hours to go from Papeete to Rangiroa but 56 hours to return. Every 10 days the *Vai-Aito* departs Papeete for Rangiroa (CFP 5,050 including meals). To return to Papeete, ask about these

Tikehau Pearl Beach Resort, Tikehau
welcome@tikehaupearlbeach.pf

Turiroa Village, Rangiroa
pension.turiroa@mail.pf

Sports and Recreation

Ahe Plongée Diving Center, Ahe
http://ahe.plongee.free.fr

Blue Dolphins Diving, Rangiroa
www.bluedolphinsdiving.com
bluedolphins@mail.pf

Blue Nui Dive Center, Tikehau
www.bluenui.com
tikehaubluenui@mail.pf

Diving Center Te Ava Nui, Fakarava
http://tuamotu.plongee.free.fr

Manihi Blue Nui, Manihi
manihi.blue.nui@mail.pf

Raie Manta Club, Rangiroa
http://raiemantaclub.free.fr
raiemantaclub@mail.pf

Rangiroa Paradive, Rangiroa
www.chez.com/paradive
paradive@mail.pf

The Six Passengers, Rangiroa
www.the6passengers.com
the6passengers@mail.pf

Others

Arenahio Location, Rangiroa
carpom@mail.pf

Gauguin's Pearl, Rangiroa
phcab@mail.pf

Taaroa Web, Rangiroa
www.taaroa-web.com
taaroa-web@mail.pf

Tuamotu Islands
www.manihi.com

vessels and the copra boats *Rairoa Nui* and *Saint Xavier Maris Stella*. The *Aranui* stops at Rangiroa on the way back to Papeete from the Marquesas and you could disembark here. (For more information on boats and flights to the Tuamotus, see Transportation in the introduction to French Polynesia.)

Archipels Croisieres (tel. 56-36-39, fax 56-35-87) offers two/three-night cruises around the Rangiroa lagoon on a 17.5-meter, eight-passenger catamaran at US$830/1,080 pp double occupancy (excluding airfare). It's a great way to explore the atoll and it'll go even if only two people reserve. When you consider that all meals and activities are included, it's no more expensive than staying at the Kia Ora.

Getting Around

There's no public transportation on Rangiroa although the scuba operators offer shuttles to their clients. To reach Tiputa village across Tiputa Pass from the airport island wait for a lift on the dock next to Chez Glorine (watch for dolphins in the pass). A boat ferrying school children across the Tiputa Pass leaves the airport side weekdays at 0600, returning from Tiputa at 1130 and 1600. The usual fee to be taken across is CFP 500 pp each way.

Europcar (tel./fax 96-03-28), with an office near Avatoru and a desk at the Kia Ora Village, has cars beginning at CFP 6,500/8,000 for four/eight hours, scooters at CFP 4,000/5,500, bicycles CFP 850/1,400. Two-person "fun cars" are slightly cheaper than the regular cars.

Avis (tel. 96-04-53) at the airport has cars at CFP 7,900/14,200 for one/two days including kms (collision insurance CFP 1,500 a day extra).

Arenahio Location (Carole Plovier, tel./fax 96-82-45), at Carole Pareo between the airport and Avatoru village, rents bicycles at CFP 700/1,300 a half/full day and scooters at CFP 3,800/5,200. Cars are available at CFP 6,000/8,000 and Carole speaks good English. Many of the pensions also rent bicycles.

Airport

The airstrip (RGI) is about six km from Avatoru village by road, accessible to Tiputa village by boat. Most of the Avatoru pensions offer free airport transfers to those who have booked ahead (ask).

Tikehau

Rangiroa's smaller neighbor, Tikehau (400 inhabitants), is an almost circular atoll 26 km across with the shallow Passe de Tuheiava on its west side. Tuherahera village and the airstrip share an island in the southwest corner of the atoll. Five pearl farms operate on Tikehau and tourism is growing fast. There's a far better choice of places to stay than you'll find on Manihi, and it's less developed than Rangiroa. Tikehau's beaches are unsurpassed.

All of the pensions organize boat trips to bird islands such as Puarua, picnics on a *motu*, snorkeling in the pass, visits to Eden Point, etc., costing CFP 3,500–8,000 pp.

Scuba diving (CFP 6,500) is available with the **Raie Manta Club** (Bertrand Varichon, tel./fax 96-22-53) based at the Tikehau Village. Prices are the same as those at the Raie Manta Club on Rangiroa and the 10-dive packages can be used at both centers. They'll show you huge manta rays, sea turtles, shark-infested caves, great schools of barracuda, and fabulous red reefs.

Accommodations

Pension Panau Lagon (Arai and Lorina Natua, tel./fax 96-22-99) sits on a white beach a few minutes' walk from the airport. The four simple bungalows with bath are CFP 5,000 pp with breakfast and dinner. Camping may be possible.

Also in the direction away from the village and a few minutes beyond Pension Panau Lagon is **Chez Justine** (Justine and Laroche Tetua, tel. 96-22-87, fax 96-22-26) with two *fare* at CFP 5,000 pp with half board.

Pension Tematié (Nora Hoioré, tel./fax 96-22-65), near the airport, has three beach bungalows at CFP 6,500 pp plus 6 percent tax with half board.

The **Tikehau Village** (Caroline and Pa'ea Tefaiao, tel./fax 96-22-86), on the beach between the airstrip and the village, has nine *fare* starting at CFP 6,500 pp including two meals. Nonguests can order meals here.

Several residents of Tuherahera village provide rooms with shared bath in a family home at CFP 4,500–6,000 pp including breakfast and dinner. Among the people offering this are Isidore and Nini Hoiore (tel. 96-22-89) and Hélène Teakura (tel. 96-22-52).

The **Aito Motel Colette** (Coletter Huri, tel. 96-22-47) in Tuherahera has five rooms with a shared kitchen at CFP 3,500 pp. The three *fare* are CFP 10,200/15,600 single/double with half board.

Pension Kahaia Beach (Merline Natua, tel. 96-22-77, 96-22-81), on the pink sands of Motu Kahaia between the village and the Pearl Beach Resort, has five *fare* at CFP 5,000 pp with half board and transfers. The owner doesn't speak English but hand gestures will do! The snorkeling is good and several other deserted *motu* are nearby.

In June 2001 the upscale **Tikehau Pearl Beach Resort** (tel. 96-23-00, fax 96-23-01) opened on tiny Motu Tiano, a bit east of Motu Kahaia. There are 14 beach bungalows at CFP 38,000 single or double, plus 16 overwater bungalows starting at CFP 52,000, plus 11 percent tax. Add CFP 6,900/9,800 pp for half/full board. Boat transfers are CFP 4,000 pp round-trip. As if the excellent beach wasn't enough, there's a swimming pool. Diving is provided by the Blue Nui Dive Center (Carol Tilleffer, tel./fax 96-22-40) on the wharf at the resort.

Getting There

Air Tahiti flies to Tikehau from Papeete (CFP 14,200) once or twice a day and from Rangiroa (CFP 4,600) four times a week. The airstrip is conveniently situated a bit over a km east of Tuherahera village.

Every Monday at 1600 the motor vessel *Dory II* leaves Papeete for Tikehau, arriving the next morning at 1100. The return trip follows a roundabout route, so this service is only really practical eastbound. You can easily use it to go to Rangiroa, the next stop. You can also get to Tikehau (CFP 5,050 deck from Papeete, meals included) on the *Vai-Aito* (tel. 43-99-96, fax 43-53-04) every 10 days. These and other ships tie up to a lagoonside wharf.

Fakarava

Fakarava is the second-largest Tuamotu atoll, about 250 km southeast of Rangiroa and 435 km northeast of Tahiti. A pass gives access to each end of this rectangular 60-by-25-km lagoon, which is dotted and flanked by 80 coconut-covered *motu*. There's spectacular snorkeling and drift diving in the passes or along the vertical drop-offs. Garuae Pass in the north is almost a km wide, nine meters deep, and the haunt of countless sharks, dolphins, barracuda, and rays. Tumakohua Pass in the south is smaller and accessible to snorkelers.

The French colonial administration for the Tuamotus moved here from Anaa in 1878 and Fakarava's Catholic church is one of the oldest in the group. Robert Louis Stevenson visited Fakarava aboard the yacht *Casco* in 1888 and spent two weeks living in a house near the church in the center of the village, Rotoava. French painter Henri Matisse visited briefly in 1930 and the beauty of the atoll influenced his art for years to come. The present airstrip, four km from village, opened only in 1995. About 500 people live on the atoll and a number of pearl farms have been established around the lagoon. Fakarava is still in the early stages of being developed for tourism.

Scuba Diving

Jean-Christophe Lapeyre operates the **Diving Center Te Ava Nui** (tel. 98-42-50) at Rotoava. The spectacular Garuae Pass drift dive is for experienced divers only and shark feeding is unnecessary since the pass is already thick with sharks. Jean-Christophe's website provides details and many photos of Fakarava.

Accommodations

Pension Havaiki (Joachim and Clotilde Petit-Dariel, tel./fax 98-42-16), two km from the

FRENCH POLYNESIA

airport on a potholed road, has four nice bungalows at CFP 10,000/18,000 single/double including full board (Clotilde's meals are huge and tasty). A long pier points out into the lagoon toward Joachim's pearl farming shack and the beach is good. Kayaks and bicycles are lent free.

The **Vahitu Dream** (Jacqueline Moeroa, tel. 98-42-63), on the beach next door, offers five basic rooms with shared bath at CFP 5,700 pp including half board and taxes. Loud music is on in the snack bar all day and the folks here stay up late. It's used mostly by French scuba divers.

The least expensive place to stay is the **Relais Marama** (Marama Teanuanua, tel. 98-42-51), oceanside in Rotoava village, four km from the airstrip. The three rooms with shared bath in the main house are CFP 3,600/4,600/5,600 single/double/triple; otherwise it's CFP 4,400/5,400/6,400 for the garden bungalow. Cooking facilities are available.

The three-star **Hôtel Le Maitai Dream Fakarava** (tel. 98-43-00, fax 98-43-01), six km south of Rotoava, opened in 2003. The 30 units range in price from CFP 38,500/44,000 single/double for a garden bungalow to CFP 43,500/49,000 for a beach bungalow, plus 11 percent tax. The restaurant/bar has a deck for sunset viewing.

At the other end of the atoll is the **Tetamanu Village** (Annabelle and Sané Richmond, tel. 43-92-40, fax 42-77-70). The six waterfront *fare*

> *Robert Louis Stevenson visited Fakarava aboard the yacht* **Casco** *in 1888 and spent two weeks living in a house near the church in the center of the village, Rotoava. French painter Henri Matisse visited briefly in 1930 and the beauty of the atoll influenced his art for years to come.*

here are CFP 47,500 pp for three nights including all meals, activities, taxes, and airport transfers (1.5 hours each way by boat). A private bathing pontoon in the adjacent Tumakohua Pass facilitates snorkeling at slack tide. "Tetamanu Sauvage" on a small *motu* has another five beachfront fare at the same rates. Complete facilities are offered for scuba divers. Ask Sané to show you around his pearl farm.

Also near Tumakohua Pass, **Motu Aito Paradise** (Manihi and Tila Salmon, tel./fax 41-29-00) offers rooms in a rustic thatched complex on a tiny coral *motu* at CFP 10,000 pp, including all meals, transfers, and excursions (three-night minimum stay). Divers from Te Ava Nui often have lunch here after diving the pass. The sense of remoteness is perfect here. In Papeete, information is available from Salmon Aroma at Tattoo Tour Styles above Bar Le Taina, 303 boulevard Pomare.

Getting There

Air Tahiti flies from Papeete to Fakarava (CFP 15,300) six times a week with one flight going on to Rangiroa (CFP 4,600).

The supply boat *Vai-Aito* (tel. 43-99-96) leaves Papeete, Tikehau, Rangiroa, and Manihi for Fakarava about every 10 days. The voyage from Papeete costs CFP 17,675 deck, meals included. The ship returns directly to Papeete so you could use it to go back to Tahiti, but the eastbound trip is long and roundabout.

Manihi

Manihi, 175 km northeast of Rangiroa, is also on the package tour circuit, with visions of white-sand beaches and cultured black pearls radiating from its glossy brochures. Unless you have a keen interest in pearl farming, scuba diving is the only reason to come. The accommodations are isolated and remarkably overpriced.

You can see right around Manihi's six-by-30-km lagoon, and the 50,000 resident oysters on the 60 commercial pearl farms outnumber the 1,000 human inhabitants 50 to one. Because of the pearl industry, the people of Manihi have become more affluent than those on some of the other Tuamotu Islands.

Turipaoa (or Paeua) village and its 50 houses face Tairapa Pass at the west end of a sandy strip just over a kilometer long. The airport island and main resort are just across the pass from Turipaoa, and many of the other *motu* are also inhabited.

Scuba Diving

Manihi Blue Nui (Stéphane Hamon, tel./fax 96-42-17) at the Manihi Pearl Beach Resort offers year-round scuba diving on the outer reef walls. A one-tank dive is CFP 6,500 (or CFP 7,000 for night diving). Five/10-dive packages are CFP 30,000/60,000. Rental of a wetsuit or water-proof light is CFP 500. It'll also take snorkelers on the boat at CFP 2,000 pp, including mask and snorkel. Both PADI and CMAS certification courses are offered; otherwise a one-dive resort course is CFP 7,000.

It's exciting to shoot Tairapa Pass on the in-coming tide, and since it's shallower than the passes at Rangiroa, you see more. Reef sharks are less common here but manta and eagle rays are often seen, as are countless Moorish idols. Just inside the lagoon at the mouth of the pass is a site called "The Circus" frequented by huge, sci-ence fiction–like rays with enormous socket eyes, and it's a fantastic experience to swim near them (also possible at Rangiroa).

The ocean drop-off abounds in gray sharks, Napoleon fish, giant jack fish, and huge schools of snappers, barracudas, and tuna. Each year,

around late June or early July, thousands of mar-bled groupers gather here to breed in one of the most fascinating underwater events in the world. Among other favorite spots are "West Point" with fire, antler, and flower-petal coral in 65-meter visibility, and "The Break," where black-tip, white-tip, gray, and occasionally hammerhead sharks are seen.

Accommodations

The **Manihi Pearl Beach Resort** (tel. 96-42-73, fax 96-42-72), by the lagoon one km from the airport, was known as the Kaina Village until a hurricane blew it away in 1993. Now rebuilt, the five standard beach bungalows are CFP 28,000 single or double, the 17 superior beach bungalows CFP 34,000, the 14 deluxe overwater bungalows CFP 49,000, and the five premium overwater bungalows CFP 54,000, all plus 11 percent tax. Add CFP 9,800 pp plus 10 percent tax for full board. Round-trip airport transfers are CFP 2,200 pp (or walk it in 10 minutes). Al-most all guests arrive on prepaid packages. There's a swimming pool facing the rather poor beach.

Nine km northeast of the airport is **Chez Jeanne** (Jeanne Huerta, tel. 96-42-90, fax 96-42-91), formerly known as Le Keshi, at Motu Taugaraufara. The two self-catering beach bun-galows here are CFP 9,000 for up to three people, while the overwater unit is CFP 13,000 double (minimum stay two nights). Food, drinking water, and excursions are extra.

The **Vainui Perles Lodge** (Edmond and Vaiana Buniet, tel. 96-42-89, fax 96-43-30) is across the lagoon on Motu Marakorako. The six small du-plex rooms with shared bath and one leaky-roofed beach bungalow go for CFP 8,800 pp a day in-cluding airport transfers, activities, and meals. Bring a flashlight to be able to find the outhouse after the electricity is switched off at 2130. A free tour of the owner's pearl farm is offered.

Getting There

Manihi airport (XMH) is 2.5 km north of Turipaoa village by boat. Most Air Tahiti (tel.

96-43-34) flights to Manihi from Papeete (CFP 17,200) or Bora Bora (CFP 24,300) are via Rangiroa. Flights between Manihi and Rangiroa are CFP 9,200.

The motor vessels *Dory II* and *Vai-Aito* both travel from Papeete to Manihi (CFP 10,100 deck) regularly, a 46-hour trip. They enter the lagoon and tie up to a wharf at Turipaoa.

Other Islands and Atolls

Ahe

Ahe, 13 km west of Manihi, is often visited by cruising yachts, which are able to enter the 16-km-long lagoon through Tiarero Pass on the northwest side of the atoll. Tenukupara village is south across the lagoon. Facilities include two tiny stores, a post office, and a community center where everyone meets at night. Despite the steady stream of sailing boats, the 400 people are very friendly. All of the houses have solar generating panels supplied after a hurricane in the early 1980s. Only a handful of small children are seen in the village; most are away at school on Rangiroa or Tahiti. Many families follow their children to the main islands while they're at school, so you may even be able to rent a whole house. As well as producing pearls, Ahe supplies oysters to the pearl farms on Manihi.

The **Pension Coco Perle** (tel. 96-44-08), on Motu Maruaruki, 10 minutes by boat from the airport, has six bungalows at CFP 10,035/18,090 single/double with half board and shared bath or 12,015/22,050 with private bath. Valérie and René at Ahe Plongée offer scuba diving on Ahe (see their website for details).

In 1998 the Foreign Legion constructed an airport on Ahe and Air Tahiti now has seven flights a week from Tahiti (CFP 17,200).

Anaa

Anaa is 424 km due east of Tahiti and it receives a weekly Air Tahiti flight from Papeete (CFP 15,600) continuing to Hao (CFP 15,200). Unlike most of the other atolls covered here, Anaa is part of the southern Tuamotu group that was out-of-bounds to non-French during the nuclear testing era. Devastating hurricanes hit Anaa in 1906 and 1983.

The 450 inhabitants live in five small settlements scattered around Anaa's broken coral ring and there's no pass into the shallow elongated lagoon. Anaa's tattooed warriors were once widely feared, yet this was the first Tuamotuan atoll to accept Christianity after a local missionary returned from training on Moorea in 1817. In 1845 an American named Benjamin Grouard converted the inhabitants to Mormonism. Catholic missionaries followed in 1851, leading to a mini-religious war and the banning of Mormon missionaries from the colony by the French authorities (they were not allowed to return until 1892). From 1853 to 1878 the French colonial administration of the Tuamotus was based here.

Accommodations are available at **Te Maui Nui** (François Mo'o, tel. 98-32-75) at Tokerau village, 400 meters from the airstrip on the northeast side of Anaa. The two bungalows are CFP 6,000 pp including all meals, while a room in a three-room *fare* is CFP 4,000 pp with two meals. François used to run a snack bar in Papeete and speaks a little English.

Joël Teaku operates **Toku Kaiga** (tel. 98-32-69) in Tokerau village, 400 meters from the airport. The two bungalows here go for CFP 4,500/5,500 pp with half/full board.

Arutua

Numerous black pearl farms grace the 29-km-wide lagoon of this circular atoll between Rangiroa and Apataki. Rautini village near the only pass was rebuilt after devastating hurricanes in 1983, and among the 500 inhabitants are some locally renowned musicians and storytellers. **Pension Te Hinano** (Neri and Hinano Fau'ura, tel. 96-52-55) at Rautini has two rooms at CFP 6,000 pp, including all meals. Arutua receives Air Tahiti flights from Papeete (CFP 14,600) three times a week. The airstrip is 30 minutes by boat north from the village (transfers CFP 2,000 pp round-trip).

THE LOST TREASURE OF THE TUAMOTUS

During the War of the Pacific (1879-1883) four mercenaries stole 14 tons of gold from a church in Pisco, Peru. They buried most of the treasure on Pinaki or Raraka atolls in the Tuamotus before proceeding to Australia, where two were killed by aboriginals and the other two were sentenced to 20 years' imprisonment for murder. Just before his death the surviving mercenary told prospector Charles Edward Howe the story.

In 1913 Howe began a 13-year search, which finally found part of the treasure on an island near Raraka. He reburied the chests and returned to Australia to organize an expedition that would remove the gold in secret. Before it could set out, however, Howe disappeared. But using Howe's treasure map, diver George Hamilton took over in 1934. Hamilton thought he found the cached gold in a pool but was unable to extract it. After being attacked by a giant octopus and moray eel, Hamilton abandoned the search and the expedition dissolved.

In 1994 a descendant of Hamilton chartered a boat at Fakarava and headed for Tepoto atoll, which had been identified from an old photograph as the site of the treasure. Soon after their arrival at Tepoto, the weather turned nasty and the expeditionaries turned back after narrowly escaping death on the reef.

As far as is known, the US$1.8 million in gold has never been found, but the legend is still very much alive and traces of old diggings can be seen in a dozen places, mostly around Pinaki's only passage (which is too shallow for even dinghies to enter). Only landowners are allowed to dig for treasure, so a foreigner would have to marry a local first. At night the treasure is guarded by the spirits of two whites and a black (who were killed after burying the gold).

Some claim the islanders found the gold long ago and, believing it to be cursed, dumped it in the sea. Most scholars say the whole thing is a hoax, yet treasure hunters still dream of finding this elusive treasure!

Hao

Hao Atoll (population 1,400) was visited by the Spaniard Quirós in 1606. Kaki Pass gives access to the 50-km-long lagoon from the north. The pass has been dredged to a depth of seven meters and medium-sized ships can enter and proceed eight km to the anchorage off Otepa village on the northeast side of the atoll.

Hao is strategically situated in the heart of French Polynesia, equidistant from Tahiti, Mangareva, and the Marquesas. From 1966 to 1996 a giant French air base on Hao served as the main support base for nuclear testing on Moruroa, 500 km southeast, allowing the French military to fly materials directly into the area without passing through Papeete's Faa'a Airport. Hao's 3,380-meter airport runway is the longest in the South Pacific, long enough to be considered a potential emergency landing site for the NASA space shuttles.

Before 1996 non-French visitors were forbidden to transit the atoll, but with the windup of nuclear testing on Moruroa in 1996, the French military base here has closed. Now moves are under way to convert Hao into a tax haven for foreign corporations! Some current Air Tahiti flights to Mangareva and the southern Tuamotus are via Hao.

Kaukura

A narrow pass gives limited access to Kaukura's shallow, 40-km-long lagoon, midway between Rangiroa and Fakarava. Air Tahiti has flights twice a week from Papeete to Kaukura (CFP 14,600). Accommodations are available at **Pension Rekareka** (Mrs. Titaua Parker, tel. 96-62-40, fax 96-22-39) in Raitahiti village, a km from the airstrip at the west end of the atoll. It's CFP 5,000 pp including meals in a six-room house in the village and it also has six self-catering *fare* on a *motu* at CFP 6,000 pp including meals. Fewer than 400 people live on Kaukura.

Makatea

Unlike the low coral atolls of the Tuamotus, Makatea, 230 km northeast of Tahiti, is an uplifted limestone block eight km long and 110 meters high. Gray cliffs plunge 50 meters to the sea. Phosphate was dug up here by workers with shovels from 1908 to 1966 and exported to Japan and New Zealand by the Compagnie française des Phosphates de l'Océanie. Between the world wars, 115,000 tons of raw ore was produced each year, increasing to 300,000 tons in the 1960s. During the first half of the 20th century this operation was the main element of the French Polynesian economy.

At one time 2,000 workers were present but today just over 50 people live here, hunting coconut crabs, fishing for lobster, and making copra. Five huge concrete pylons remaining from the mining era dominate the L-shaped landing on the west side of the island, and from here, a steep concrete ramp climbs to the central plateau. Half a dozen abandoned locomotives from the phosphate railway rust along the roadsides and near the contemporary villages, Temao, Moumu, and Vaitepau. Across the island at Moumu, a couple of km beyond Viatepau, is a long white beach. On the way there you'll pass a grotto with steps leading down to a pool. There are no flights to Makatea.

Mataiva

Tiny Mataiva, westernmost of the Tuamotus and 40 km from Tikehau, receives two Air Tahiti flights a week from Papeete (CFP 14,200). The airstrip is 400 meters from Pahua village on the west side of the atoll. The village is divided into two parts by a shallow pass crossed by a wooden bridge.

Only 10 km long and five km wide, Mataiva (population 225) is worth considering as an off-beat destination. A coral road covers most of the 35 km around the atoll with narrow concrete bridges over the nine shallow channels or "eyes" that gave the island its name (*mata* means eye, *iva* is nine). Exploratory mining of a 12-million-tonne phosphate deposit under the lagoon ended in 1982 and further mining has been strongly opposed by residents aware of the environmental devastation that would be inflicted.

Mr. Aroma Huri of Pahua runs a small resort called **Super Mataiva Cool** (tel./fax 96-32-53) on a white beach south of the pass. To stay in one of the four *fare* is CFP 5,500/10,000 single/double including two meals.

Ava Hei Pension (Benjamin Mahetau Lacour,

tel. 96-32-39, fax 96-32-00), by the lagoon at Tevaihi 3.5 km south of the airport, offers three *fare* at CFP 7,000 pp plus 6 percent tax with half board. Lagoon excursions and airport transfers are included. Camping is CFP 1,500 pp.

Another place to stay is the **Mataiva Village** (Edgar Tetua, tel. 96-32-95), on a beach north of the pass, with five bungalows with bath at CFP 5,500 pp with half board. Camping is CFP 1,500 pp including breakfast. The guesthouses rent bicycles and arrange excursions.

Niau

The shark-free lagoon at Niau, 50 km southeast of Kaukura, is enclosed by an unbroken circle of land. Low-grade phosphate deposits on the island were judged too poor to mine. This lonely island of 450 souls does not receive any Air Tahiti flights.

Reao

No pass gives access to the lagoon of this easternmost inhabited Tuamotu atoll. In 1865 Catholic missionaries from Mangareva arrived on Reao and in 1901 they established a leper colony here that accepted patients from all over the Tuamotus and Marquesas until it was moved to Tahiti in 1914. About 300 people live on the atoll today. Reao receives three Air Tahiti flights a month from Papeete (CFP 28,600).

Taiaro

In 1972 the private owner of Taiaro, Mr. W. A. Robinson, declared the atoll a nature reserve and in 1977 it was accepted by the United Nations as a biosphere reserve. Scientific missions studying atoll ecology sometimes visit tiny Taiaro, the only permanent inhabitants of which are a caretaker family. There are no flights to this isolated island northeast of Kauehi and Raraka.

Takapoto

Takapoto and Takaroa atolls are separated by only eight km of open sea, and on both the airstrip is within walking distance of the village. Air Tahiti flies three or four times a week from Papeete to Takapoto (CFP 17,200) and Takaroa (CFP 18,800). The freighter *Taporo VI* carries passengers from Papeete to Takapoto (36 hours,

CFP 11,000/15,000 deck/cabin including meals) every two weeks, continuing to the Marquesas. The more upscale *Aranui* also calls at Takapoto.

There's no pass into the lagoon but landing by whaleboat at Fakatopatere at the southwest end of the atoll is easy. Jacob Roggeveen lost one of his three ships on Takapoto's reef in 1722. Today the 16-km-long lagoon is a nursery for black pearl oysters and more than 600 people live here.

The **Takapoto Village** (Pimati and Marie Toti, tel. 98-65-44, fax 98-64-81), right on the beach facing the lagoon a short walk from Fakatopatere, has two neat little bungalows with bath and fridge at CFP 6,700/12,400 single/double plus 6 percent tax including breakfast and dinner. A room with shared bath in the family home is CFP 1,000 pp cheaper.

Pension Tepuna Lagoon (tel./fax 98-64-75), on a pearl farm a 30-minute walk from the village, has one bungalow at CFP 6,500 pp plus 6 percent tax including breakfast and dinner. It's run by Miri and Tainui Ehu, who speak perfect English. Tainui makes jewelry from their pearls, while Miri creates pareus for sale to *Aranui* passengers. Airport transfers are free.

The **Faana Restaurant** (tel. 98-64-01) in Fakatopatere is a good place to have a cold beer.

Takaroa

This northeasterly atoll is 24 km long and up to eight km wide. The 30-meter-wide pass is barely three meters deep and the snorkeling here is second to none. On the outer reef near Takaroa's airstrip are two wrecks, one of a four-masted sailing ship here since 1906. Pearl farming flourishes in the Takaroa lagoon, which offers good anchorage everywhere. Since the appearance of this industry, visits by cruising yachts have been discouraged because of the danger of boats hitting poorly marked oyster platforms in the lagoon. Most of the 450 inhabitants of Teavaroa village belong to the Mormon church and their village is often called "little America." Tea, coffee, alcohol, and cigarettes are all frowned on but dog is considered a delicacy. *Marae* remains lurk in the bush.

Accommodations are available at **Chez Vahinerii** (Mrs. Vahinerii Temanaha, tel. 98-23-59), between the airport and the village, where a room with shared bath in the house is CFP 3,000 double. The one bungalow with cooking facilities is CFP 5,000/6,500 double/triple.

It's also possible to stay at a pearl farm on Motu Vaimaroro at the **Poerangi Village** (Eléonore Parker, tel. 98-23-82, fax 98-23-09). The three self-catering beach bungalows here are CFP 5,000/6,000 single/double. The food is good and the owners convivial.

Toau

Yachts can enter the lagoon at Toau, between Kaukura and Fakarava, though the pass is on the windward side. No flights land on Toau.

The Nuclear Test Zone

The former French nuclear test site operated by the Centre d'Expérimentations du Pacifique until 1996 is at the southeastern end of the Tuamotu group, 1,200 km from Tahiti. The main site was 30-km-long Moruroa atoll, but Fangataufa atoll 37 km south of Moruroa was also used. In 1962 the French nuclear testing facilities in the Algerian Sahara had to be abandoned after that country won its independence, so in 1963 French president Charles de Gaulle officially announced that France was shifting the program to Moruroa and Fangataufa. Between 1966 and 1996 a confirmed 181 nuclear bombs, reaching up to 200 kilotons, were set off in the Tuamotus at the rate of six a year. By 1974 the French had conducted 41 *atmospheric* tests, 36 over or near Moruroa and five over Fangataufa. Five of these were megaton hydrogen bombs.

Way back in 1963, the United States, Britain, and the USSR agreed in the Partial Test Ban Treaty to halt nuclear tests in the atmosphere. France chose not to sign. On June 23, 1973, the World Court urged France to discontinue the nuclear tests, which might drop radioactive material on surrounding territories. When the French government refused to recognize the court's jurisdiction in this matter, New Zealand Prime Minister Norman Kirk ordered the New Zealand frigate *Otago* to enter the danger zone off Moruroa, and on July 23, Peru broke diplomatic relations with France. On August 15, French commandos boarded the protest vessels *Fri* and *Greenpeace III*, attacking and arresting the crews.

In 1974, with opposition mounting in the Territorial Assembly and growing world indignation, French President Giscard D'Estaing ordered a switch to *underground* tests. Eighteen years and 134 tests later, as the Greenpeace *Rainbow Warrior II* confronted French commandos off Moruroa, French prime minister Pierre Bérégovoy suddenly announced on April 8, 1992, that nuclear testing was being suspended. President Boris Yeltsin had already halted Russian nuclear testing in October 1991, and in October 1992 U.S. president George Bush would follow suit by halting underground testing in Nevada. Despite the French moratorium, the testing facilities in the Tuamotus were maintained at great expense, and in June 1995 newly elected President Jacques Chirac ordered the testing to resume without bothering to consult the Polynesians.

On August 31, 1995, with the first test imminent, the Greenpeace ship *Rainbow Warrior II* reached Moruroa just over 10 years after its predecessor had been sunk by French terrorists at Auckland, New Zealand. As the ship crossed the 12-mile limit and launched six Zodiacs toward the French drilling rigs in the lagoon, the *Rainbow Warrior II* was boarded by French commandos who fired tear gas at the unresisting crew and smashed computers, generators, and the ship's engine. The MV *Greenpeace* was nearby in international waters at the time, and the French seized it too on the pretext that it had launched a helicopter that crossed the territorial limit. With the main protest vessels impounded and their crews deported, the French hoped they could carry on with the tests without further interference.

So on September 5, 1995, despite opposition from 63 percent of the French public and a large majority of Polynesians, the French military exploded the first of a planned series of eight bombs under Moruroa. This led to the worst rioting ever seen in French Polynesia as thousands of enraged Tahitians ran amok, ransacking Faa'a Airport and much of Papeete. The independence leader Oscar Temaru managed to calm the crowd, and the French brought in additional riot police to guard the capital. After a second blast on October 2 the South Pacific Forum carried out its threat to suspend France as a "dialogue partner."

In an attempt to deflect mounting worldwide condemnation, Chirac announced that the number of tests would be reduced from eight to six. Additionally, France, the United States, and Britain said they would finally sign the protocols of the 1985 South Pacific Nuclear-Free Zone Treaty. The sixth and last test was carried out below Fangataufa atoll on January 27, 1996. Since then the facilities on Moruroa have been demolished and it's unlikely there will ever be another nuclear test in this area.

Moruroa

Obviously, an atoll, with its porous coral cap sitting on a narrow basalt base, is the most dangerous place in the world to stage underground nuclear explosions. This was not the initial intention. Moruroa was chosen for its isolated location, far from major population centers that might be affected by fallout. However, by 1974, when atmospheric testing had to cease, the French military had a huge investment in the area. So rather than move to a more secure location in France or elsewhere, it decided to take a chance. Underground testing was to be carried out in Moruroa's basalt core, 500–1,200 meters below the surface of the atoll. Eventually 130 bombs were exploded below Moruroa and 10 below Fangataufa, making France the only nuclear state that has conducted tests *under* a Pacific island.

On September 10, 1966, President Charles de Gaulle was present at Moruroa to witness the atmospheric test of a bomb suspended from a balloon. Weather conditions caused the test to be postponed, and the following day conditions were still unsuitable, as the wind was blowing in the direction of inhabited islands to the west instead of toward uninhabited Antarctica to the south. De Gaulle complained that he was a busy man and could afford to wait no longer, so the test went ahead, spreading radioactive fallout

VOYAGES OF THE RAINBOW WARRIOR

Beginning in 1978 the *Rainbow Warrior* confronted whalers, sealers, and nuclear waste dumpers in the North Atlantic. In 1980 the ship was seized in international waters by the Spanish navy while interfering with the Spanish whale kill. After five months under arrest in Spain the ship made a dramatic escape. In 1981–1982 *Rainbow Warrior* led the struggle against the Canadian harp seal slaughter, bringing about a European Economic Community ban on the import of all seal products. The next year the ship battled Soviet whalers in Siberia, finally escaping to Alaska with naval units in hot pursuit. A confrontation with Peruvian whalers led to the termination of that whale hunt. In 1985, fresh from being fitted with sails in Florida, the *Rainbow Warrior* reentered the Pacific to rescue nuclear victims from Rongelap in the Marshalls. In July 1985, as the valiant little ship lay at anchor in Auckland Harbor, New Zealand, externally attached terrorist bombs tore through the hull in the dead of night to prevent a voyage to Moruroa to protest French nuclear testing in the Pacific.

across the Cook Islands, Niue, Tonga, Samoa, Fiji, and Tuvalu. Tahiti itself was the most directly affected island, but the French authorities have never acknowledged this fact.

Archive documentation published by the French weekly *Nouvel Observateur* in 1998 has confirmed that French defense officials knew very well that nearby islands such as Mangareva, Pukarua, Reao, and Tureia were receiving high doses of radiation during the 1966 texts, even as spokespeople publicly described the tests as "innocuous." France's radiological security service recommended at the time that the four islands be evacuated, but the newly discovered documents only note that "the hypothesis of an evacuation was excluded for political and psychological reasons."

A serious accident occurred on July 25, 1979, when a nuclear device became stuck halfway down an 800-meter shaft. Since army engineers were unable to move the device, they exploded it where it was, causing a massive chunk of the

outer slope of the atoll to break loose. This generated a huge tsunami, which hit Moruroa, overturning cars and injuring seven people. After the blast, a crack 40 cm wide and two km long appeared on the surface of the island. As a precaution against further tsunamis and hurricanes, refuge platforms were built at intervals around the atoll. For an hour before and after each test all personnel had to climb up on these platforms.

By 1981 Moruroa was as punctured as Swiss cheese and sinking two centimeters after every test, or a meter and a half between 1976 and 1981. In 1981, with the atoll's 60-km coral rim dangerously fractured by drilling shafts, the French switched to underwater testing in the Moruroa lagoon, in order to be closer to the center of the island's core. In 1987 the famous French underwater explorer Jacques Cousteau filmed spectacular cracks and fissures in the atoll as well as submarine slides and subsidence, and described the impact of testing on the atoll as creating "premature and accelerated aging." By 1988 even French officials were acknowledging that the 108 underground blasts had severely weakened the geological formations beneath Moruroa, and it was announced that, despite the additional cost involved, the largest underground tests would take place henceforth on nearby Fangataufa atoll. The military base remained on Moruroa, and small groups of workers and technicians were sent over to Fangataufa every time a test was made there.

The French government always claimed that it owned Moruroa and Fangataufa because in 1964 a standing committee of the Territorial Assembly voted three to two to cede the atolls to France for an indefinite period. This was never ratified by the full assembly, and French troops had occupied the islands before the vote was taken anyway. The traditional owners of Moruroa, the people of Tureia atoll, 115 km north, were not consulted and have never been compensated.

Impact

On June 21, 1987, Jacques Cousteau was present for a test at Moruroa and the next day he took water samples in the lagoon, the first time such independent tests had been allowed. Two samples collected by Cousteau nine km apart contained traces of cesium-134, an isotope with a half-life of two years. Though French officials claimed the cesium-134 remained from atmospheric testing before 1975, a 1990 study by American radiologist Norm Buske proved that this was not scientifically feasible, and that leakage from underground testing was the only possible explanation. Buske also found traces of cesium-134 in plankton collected in the open ocean, outside the 12-mile exclusion zone, indicating that the release of contamination into the Pacific from the numerous cracks and fissures had started.

A 1990 computer model of Moruroa developed by New Zealand scientists indicated that radioactive groundwater with a half-life of several thousand years may be seeping through fractures in the atoll at the rate of 100 meters a year and, according to Professor Manfred Hochstein, head of Auckland University's Geothermal Institute, "in about 30 years the disaster will hit us."

In July 1998 the International Atomic Energy Agency reported that about eight kilograms of plutonium and other dangerous elements still rest in sediments in the Moruroa and Fangataufa lagoons as a result of atmospheric testing and plutonium safety trials. With sea level rises, these sediments may eventually be swept into the ocean, but more worrisome are the tritium levels in the Moruroa lagoon, which are 10 times higher than those of the surrounding sea, a result of leakage from cavities created by the underground tests. In 1999, after years of secrecy and denials, France's Atomic Energy Commission (CEA) finally admitted that fractures exist in the coral cones of Moruroa and Fangataufa.

No one is allowed to visit Moruroa or Fangataufa without official approval and inspections by independent international observers are banned. Initially a detachment of foreign legionnaires kept watch over the abandoned wharf, airstrip, and concrete bunkers at the dismantled Moruroa test site while Fangataufa was abandoned. In January 2000 Admiral Jean Moulin, commander of the French forces in the territory, announced that the troops were being withdrawn

over fears that a tsunami could be generated if the atoll's external coral cliffs were suddenly to collapse. Such an event would likely release a torrent of radioactivity into the Pacific Ocean and the CEA has installed satellite-controlled seismic sensors at the deserted site to give early warning of a collapse.

Unlike the United States, which has paid millions of dollars in compensation money to the Marshallese victims of its nuclear testing program, France still refuses to acknowledge the obvious effects of its 41 atmospheric nuclear tests. From 1963 to 1983, no public health statistics were published in the territory, and now the rates of thyroid cancer, leukemia, brain tumors, and stillbirths are on the upswing in French Polynesia. The problem of seafood poisoning (ciguatera) in the nearby Gambier Islands is clearly related.

After the end of the testing, the Tahitian nongovernmental organization Hiti Tau surveyed 737 of the 12,000 Polynesians who worked at Moruroa between 1966 and 1996, and found that many had experienced adverse health effects. Before being employed at the base, all workers at Moruroa had to sign contracts binding them to eternal silence and waiving access to their own medical records or to any right to compensation for future health problems. Yet in July 2001 the Association Moruroa e Tatou was founded, bringing together 1,160 former test site workers, and both they and a parallel group of more than 900 French veterans are now demanding that their records be released and appropriate action taken. No official studies of this impact have been carried out as yet and no compensation has been paid. The archives are still closed. The story is far from over.

French radioactivity will remain in the Tuamotus for thousands of years and the future consequences of the tests are as uncertain as ever. The atolls remain wrapped in the same sinister mystery that has dogged them since 1966. (For more information on these matters, visit the website of the Centre de Documentation et de Recherche sur la Paix et les Conflits at www.obsarm.org.)

Gambier Islands

The Gambier (or Mangareva) Islands are just north of the tropic of Capricorn, 1,650 km southeast of Tahiti. The southerly location means a cooler climate. The archipelago, contrasting sharply with the atolls of the Tuamotus, consists of 10 rocky islands enclosed on three sides by a semicircular barrier reef 65 km long. In all, there are 46 square km of dry land. The Polynesian inhabitants named the main and largest island Mangareva, or "Floating Mountain," for 482-meter-high Mt. Duff. Unlike the Marquesas, where the mountains are entirely jungle-clad, the Gambiers have hilltops covered with tall *aeho* grass. Black pearls are cultured on numerous platforms on both sides of the Mangareva la-goon. A local seabird, the *karako,* crows at dawn like a rooster.

History

Mangareva, which was originally settled from the Marquesas Islands before A.D. 1100, was the jumping-off place for small groups that discov-ered and occupied Pitcairn and perhaps Easter Is-land. In 1797 Captain James Wilson of the London Missionary Society's ship *Duff* named the group for English Admiral James Gambier (1756–1833), a hero of the Napoleonic wars who had helped organize the expedition. France made the Gambiers a protectorate in 1871 and annexed the group in 1881.

FRENCH POLYNESIA

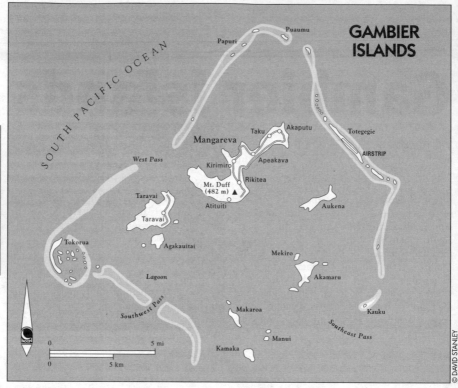

GAMBIER ISLANDS

© DAVID STANLEY

Mangareva was the area of operations for a fanatical French priest, Father Honoré Laval of the Congregation for the Sacred Hearts. Upon hearing whalers' tales of rampant cannibalism and marvelous pearls, Laval left his monastery in Chile and with another priest reached the Gambiers in 1834. An old Mangarevan prophecy had foretold the coming of two magicians whose god was all-powerful, and Laval himself toppled the dreaded stone effigy of the god Tu on the island's sacred *marae*. He then single-handedly imposed a ruthless and inflexible moral code on the islanders, recruiting them as virtual slaves to build a 1,200-seat cathedral, con-

You can still see Father Honoré Laval's 1848 architectural masterpiece—the Cathedral of St. Michael with its twin towers of white coral rock from Kamaka and altar shining with polished mother-of-pearl—a monument to horror and yet another lost culture.

vents, and triumphal arches—116 stone buildings in all—with the result that he utterly destroyed this once vigorous island culture and practically wiped out its people. During Laval's 37-year reign the population dropped from 9,000 to 500. You can still see his architectural masterpiece—the Cathedral of St. Michael with its twin towers of white coral rock from Kamaka and altar shining with polished mother-of-pearl—a monument to horror and yet another lost culture. The cathedral was built between 1839 and 1848 on the *ahu* of the island's principal *marae,* and Laval's colleague, Father François Caret, who died in 1844, lies buried in a crypt

GAMBIER ISLANDS HIGHLIGHTS

Cathedral of St. Michael: history, architecture
nuclear-fallout shelter: vestige of French nuclear testing
Mt. Duff: hiking, viewpoint
Aukena: beach, historic remains
Taravai: ruins, scenery

Orientation

Most of the current 1,100 inhabitants of the Gambiers live on eight-by-1.5-km **Mangareva,** of which Rikitea is the main village. A post office, seven small shops, a gendarmerie (tel. 97-82-68), an infirmary, schools, and a cathedral three times as big as the one in Papeete make up the infrastructure of this administrative backwater.

Sights

before the altar. In 1871 Laval was removed from Mangareva by a French warship, tried for murder on Tahiti, and declared insane.

For a glimpse of the Gambiers half a century ago and a fuller account of Père Laval, read Robert Lee Eskridge's *Manga Reva, The Forgotten Islands.*

The Nuclear Impact

A dramatic intensification of the ciguatera problem in the Gambiers since the late 1960s is believed to be linked to reef damage or pollution originating at the former nuclear-testing base on Moruroa, 400 km northwest. During the atmospheric testing series (until 1974), the Mangarevans had to take refuge in French-constructed fallout shelters whenever so advised by the military. Before each of the 41 atmospheric tests, French warships would evacuate the 3,000 people from Moruroa, usually to Mangareva, Hao, and Fakarava. Upon arrival the ships were washed down with seawater, spreading radioactive contamination into the lagoons, yet the French never made the slightest attempt to clean up after themselves.

Between 1971 and 1980 the annual incidence of ciguatera remained above 30 percent, peaking at 56 percent in 1975. Each of the inhabitants has suffered five to seven excruciating attacks of seafood poisoning and lagoon fish can no longer be eaten. Now, increases in birth defects, kidney problems, and cancer among the inhabitants are being covered up by the authorities.

It's believed that a deciding reason for the French decision to launch a terrorist attack on Greenpeace's *Rainbow Warrior* at Auckland in 1985 was an intelligence report indicating that the ship intended to proceed to Mangareva with doctors aboard to assess the radiation exposure of residents.

The tomb of Grégoire Maputeoa, the 35th and last king of Mangareva (died 1868), is in a small chapel behind the cathedral. Follow the path behind the church to the top of the hill and go through the gate on the left (close it after you as dogs dig up the graves). Among the walled ruins of Rouru convent in Rikitea one can pick out the chapel, refectory, infirmary, and a dormitory for 60 local nuns. On the opposite side of Rikitea is a huge nuclear-fallout shelter called the "Maison Nucléaire" built during the French atmospheric testing at Moruroa.

A 28-km road runs around Mangareva offering ever-changing views. At the north end of the island it passes St. Joseph's Chapel (1836) at Taku, place of worship of the Mangarevan royal family. The south coast of Mangareva is one of the most beautiful in Polynesia, with a tremendous variety of landscapes, plants, trees, smells, and colors.

The white sands of **Aukena** make a good daytrip destination by boat. The Church of St. Raphael here is the oldest in the Gambier Islands and to the south are the ruins of the Rehe Seminary (1840). The Church of Notre-Dame-de-la-Paix (1844) on abandoned **Akamaru** has twin towers added in 1862. Solitary **Makaroa** is a barren, rugged 136-meter-high island.

St. Gabriel Church (1868) on **Taravai** has a neo-Gothic facade decorated with seashells. In a cliffside cave on the uninhabited island of **Agakauitai** the mummies of 35 generations of cannibal kings are interred.

PRACTICALITIES

Accommodations

Chez Pierre et Mariette (tel. 97-82-87) near the wharf has three rooms at CFP 4,400 pp with half board.

FRENCH POLYNESIA

Pension Bianca et Benoit (tel./fax 97-83-76, biancabenoit@mail.pf) is a modern two-story house with three rooms at CFP 6,180 pp including two meals. It's just above Rikitea and the view across to Aukena is lovely.

Five km north of the village is **Chez Jojo** (Jocelyne and Joseph Mamatui, tel./fax 97-82-61) with two rooms CFP 6,000 pp including two meals. Camping is possible here.

Tara Etu Kura (tel. 97-83-25) by the lagoon charges CFP 8,500 pp including all meals, plus CFP 1,000 pp for airport transfers.

Transportation

The airstrip (GMR) is on Totegegie, a long coral island eight km northeast of Rikitea. Arriving passengers pay CFP 600 pp each way for the boat ride to the village. The weekly Air Tahiti flights from Papeete (CFP 28,600 one way) are either nonstop or via Hao. Coming/going, remember the one-hour time difference between Tahiti and Mangareva.

The supply ships *Nuku Hau* and *Taporo V* from Papeete are only monthly. Large vessels can enter the lagoon through passes on the west, southwest, and southeast. Mr. Ioane Anania (tel. 97-82-92), nicknamed "Siki," offers speedboat charters and fishing trips.

Marquesas Islands

The Marquesas Islands are the northernmost high islands of the South Pacific, on the same latitude as the Solomons. Though the group was known as Te Henua Enana (The Land of Men) by the Polynesian inhabitants, depopulation during the 19th and 20th centuries has left many of the valleys empty. The 10 main islands form a line 300 km long, roughly 1,400 km northeast of Tahiti, but only six are inhabited today: Nuku Hiva, Ua Pou, and Ua Huka in a cluster to the northwest, and Hiva Oa, Tahuata, and Fatu Hiva to the southeast. The administrative centers, Atuona (Hiva Oa), Hakahau (Ua Pou), and Taiohae (Nuku Hiva), are the only places with post offices, banks, gendarmes, etc.

The difficulty in getting there has kept many potential visitors away. Budget accommodations are scarce and public transport is nonexistent, which makes getting around a major expense unless you're prepared to rough it. Of the main islands, Hiva Oa has the most colorful recent history but Nuku Hiva is more varied. Cruising yachts from

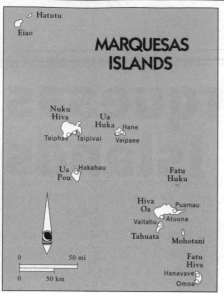

MARQUESAS ISLANDS

Hatutu
Eiao

Nuku Hiva
Ua Huka   Hane
Taiphae Taipivai   Vaipaee

Ua Pou Hakahau

Fatu Huku

Hiva Oa   Puamau
Vaitahu   Atuona
Tahuata   Mohotani

Fatu Hiva
Hanavave
Omoa

0   50 mi
0   50 km

© DAVID STANLEY

from Chile in 1856, and today they're almost a symbol of the Marquesas. The islands are abundant with lemons, tangerines, oranges, grapefruit, bananas, mangoes, and papayas. Taro and especially breadfruit are the main staples. Birdlife is rich, and the waters around the Marquesas teem with lobster, fish, and sharks.

The subtropical climate is hotter and drier than that of Tahiti. July and August are the coolest months. The deep bays on the west sides of the islands are better sheltered for shipping, and the humidity is lower there than on the east sides, which catch the trade winds. The precipitation is uneven, with drought some years, heavy rainfall the others. The southern islands of the Marquesas (Hiva Oa, Tahuata, Fatu Hiva) are green and humid; the northern islands (Nuku Hiva, Ua Huka, Ua Pou) are brown and dry.

HISTORY AND EVENTS
Pre-European Society

Marquesan houses were built on high platforms (*paepae*) scattered through the valleys (and still fairly easy to find). Every tribe had a rectangular ceremonial plaza (*tohua*) where important festivals took place. Archaeologists have been able to trace stone temples (*me'ae,* called *marae* elsewhere in French Polynesia), agricultural terraces, and earthen fortifications (*'aka'ua*) half hidden in the jungle, evocative reminders of a vanished civilization. Then as now, the valleys were isolated from one another by high ridges and turbulent seas, yet warfare was vicious and cannibalism an important incentive. An able warrior could attain

California often call at the Marquesas on their way to Papeete, and yachties should steer for Hiva Oa first to enjoy the smoothest possible sailing through the rest of the group. For hikers prepared to cope with the humidity, the Marquesas are paradise. Multitudes of waterfalls tumble down the slopes, and eerie overgrown archaeological remains tell of a golden era long gone. If you enjoy quiet, unspoiled places, you'll like the Marquesas.

The Land

These wild, rugged islands feature steep cliffs and valleys leading up to high central ridges, sectioning the islands off into a cartwheel of segments, which creates major transportation difficulties. Large reefs don't form due to the cold south equatorial current though there are isolated stretches of coral. The absence of protective reefs has prevented the creation of coastal plains, so no roads go right around any of the islands. Most of the people live in the narrow, fertile river valleys. The interiors are inhabited only by hundreds of wild horses, cattle, and goats, which have destroyed much of the original vegetation. A Catholic bishop introduced the horses

---

MARQUESAS ISLANDS HIGHLIGHTS

Hatiheu ruins, Nuku Hiva: archaeology, nature, spirits
Anaho Beach, Nuku Hiva: beach, snorkeling, hiking
Vaipaee Museum, Ua Huka: woodcarvings, shopping
Gauguin's grave, Hiva Oa: history, viewpoint
tikis of Puama'u, Hiva Oa: largest statues, spirits

great power. Local hereditary chiefs exercised authority over commoners.

The Marquesans' artistic style was one of the most powerful and refined in the Pacific. The ironwood war club was their most distinctive symbol, but there were also finely carved wooden bowls, fan handles, and tikis of stone and wood, both miniature and massive. The carvings are noted for the faces: the mouth with lips parted and the bespectacled eyes. Both men and women wore carved ivory earplugs. Men's entire bodies were covered with bold and striking tattoos, a practice banned by the Catholic missionaries. Stilts were used by men in ceremonies and by boys for racing and mock fighting. This was about the only part of Polynesia where polyandry was common. There was a strong cult of the dead: the bodies or skulls of ancestors were carefully preserved. The northern Marquesas Islands may have been inhabited as early as 300 B.C., and both Hawaii (around A.D. 200) and Easter Island (around A.D. 300) were colonized from here.

> *Both men and women wore carved ivory earplugs. Men's entire bodies were covered with bold and striking tattoos, a practice banned by the Catholic missionaries.*

European Contact

The existence of these islands was long concealed from the world by the Spanish, to prevent the English from taking possession of them. The southern group was found by Álvaro de Mendaña in July 1595 during his second voyage of exploration from Peru. He named them Las Marquesas de Mendoza after his benefactor, the Spanish viceroy. The first island sighted (Fatu Hiva) seemed uninhabited, but as Mendaña's *San Jerónimo* sailed nearer, scores of outriggers appeared, paddled by about 400 robust, light-skinned islanders. Their hair was long and loose, and they were naked and tattooed in blue patterns. The natives boarded the ship, but when they became overly curious and bold, Mendaña ordered a gun fired, and they jumped over the side.

Then began one of the most murderous and shameful of all the white explorers' entries into the South Pacific region. As a matter of caution, Mendaña's men began shooting natives on sight, in

Madisonville, Nuku Hiva: On November 19, 1813, Captain David Porter of the U.S. frigate *Essex* took possession of Nuku Hiva, Marquesas Islands, for the United States.

one instance hanging three bodies in the shore camp on Santa Cristina (Tahuata) as a warning. They left behind three large crosses, the date cut in a tree, syphilis, and more than 200 dead Polynesians. When Captain Cook arrived at Tahuata in 1774 it soon became obvious that knowledge of the earlier Spanish visit had remained alive in oral traditions, and Cook and his crew were shunned.

The northern Marquesas Islands were "discovered" by Joseph Ingraham of the American trading vessel *Hope* on April 19, 1791. After that, blackbirders, firearms, disease, and alcohol reduced the population. American whalers called frequently from 1800 onwards. Although France took possession of the group in 1842, Peruvian slavers kidnapped some Marquesans to South America in 1863 to work the plantations and mines. Those few able to return thanks to diplomatic lobbying by their French protectors brought a catastrophic smallpox epidemic. The Marquesans clung to their warlike, cannibalistic ways until 95 percent of their number had died—the remainder adopted Catholicism. (The Marquesas today is the only island group of French Polynesia with a Catholic majority.) From 80,000 at the beginning of the 19th century, the population fell to about 15,000 by 1842, when the French "protectors" arrived, and to a devastated 2,000 by 1926. Even today the total population is just 8,000.

The Marquesas Today

Slowly the Marquesas are catching up with the rest of the world—VCRs are the latest craze. Yet the islands remain very untouristy. Though there are some negative attitudes toward the French, the Marquesans realize that without French subsidies their economy would collapse. Hospitalization, drugs, and dental care are provided free by the government.

The Marquesan language, divided into north and south dialects, is only about 50 percent comprehensible to a Tahitian and is actually a bit closer to Rarotongan and Hawaiian. There's a small separatist movement here that believes the Marquesas will receive more benefits as a distinct colony of France, or failing that, as a country independent of Tahiti. And just to complicate

matters, twice as many Marquesans live in Papeete as in the Marquesas itself.

Events

The Marquesas Islands Festival or *Matava'a o te Henua Enata* is a major cultural event celebrated every four years in December with dancing, singing, drumming, and sports, plus handicraft displays and feasts. Aside from strengthening and reviving traditional knowledge and skills, numerous archaeological sites have been restored or rebuilt in preparation for these events. Previous festivals have been at Ua Pou (1987), Nuku Hiva (1989), Hiva Oa (1991), Ua Pou (1995), Nuku Hiva (1999), and Hiva Oa (2003). Future festivals will be on Ua Pou (2007) and Nuku Hiva (2011).

UNINHABITED ISLANDS

Motane (Mohotani) is an eight-km-long island rising to 520 meters, about 18 km southeast of Hiva Oa. The depredations of wild sheep on Motane turned the island into a treeless desert. When the Spaniards "discovered" it in 1595, Motane was well-wooded and populated, but today it's uninhabited.

Uninhabited Eiao and Hatutu islands, 85 km northwest of Nuku Hiva, are the remotest (and oldest) of the Marquesas. **Eiao** is a 40-square-km island, 10 km long and 576 meters high, with rather difficult landings on the northwest and west sides. The French once used Eiao as a site of deportation for criminals or "rebellious" natives. The Queen of Raiatea and 136 Raiateans who had fought against the French were interned here from 1897 to 1900. In 1972 the French Army drilled holes 1,000 meters down into Eiao to check the island's suitability for underground nuclear testing, but deemed the basalt rock too fragile for such use. Wild cattle, sheep, pigs, and donkeys forage across Eiao, ravaging the vegetation and suffering from droughts. In contrast, the profusion of fishlife off Eiao is incredible.

Hatutu, the northernmost of the Marquesas, measures 7.5 square km. Thousands of birds nest here.

TRANSPORTATION

Getting There

Direct international flights to Nuku Hiva have been discussed for years, but nothing much has been done and an expensive round-trip from Tahiti is still required. An **Air Tahiti** ATR flies from Papeete to Nuku Hiva daily (3.5 hours, CFP 25,500) with one of the flights via Rangiroa. Ask about Air Tahiti's "Extension Marquises" pass, which allows return flights from Papeete to Nuku Hiva and Hiva Oa for CFP 45,000 when purchased in combination with another Air Tahiti pass.

Dornier flights between Nuku Hiva and Ua Huka (CFP 5,300) operate weekly, connecting with one of the ATR flights from Papeete. From Nuku Hiva to Ua Pou (CFP 5,300) the flights are three times a week. To Hiva Oa (CFP 9,200) it's five times a week. No flight goes straight from Ua Pou to Ua Huka—you must backtrack to Nuku Hiva. Get a through ticket to your final destination, as flights to Hiva Oa, Ua Pou, and Ua Huka are all the same price from Papeete (Nuku Hiva is CFP 3,100 cheaper). Tahuata and Fatu Hiva are without air service. All flights are heavily booked. Coming or going, remember the 30-minute time difference between Tahiti and the Marquesas.

Two ships, the *Aranui* and *Taporo VI*, sail regularly from Papeete, calling at all six inhabited Marquesas Islands. The more convenient and comfortable of the two by far is the freighter *Aranui*, which does round-trip voyages custom designed for tourists flown in from the United States and Europe. These trips cost cruise-ship prices and the other main interisland ship, *Taporo VI*, is much cheaper at CFP 22,000/32,000 deck/cabin including food one-way from Papeete to any Marquesan island. However, it's basic and only a few hours are spent in each port. The ships tie up to the wharves at Taiohae, Atuona, Vaipae'e, and Hakahau; at Tahauta and Fatu Hiva, passengers must go ashore by whaleboat. In stormy weather, the landings can be dangerous. (For more information on boats and flights, turn to Transportation in the French Polynesia Introduction.)

Getting Around

To island hop within the Marquesas, you can fly with Air Tahiti or try using the ships mentioned above, if they happen to be going where you want to go. Ask at local town halls about the supply boat *Ka'oha Nui*, a large luxury yacht owned by the territory that often sails among the islands picking up school children on holidays, etc. Private boats run from Taiohae to Ua Pou fairly frequently, and there are municipal boats from Atuona to Tahuata and Fatu Hiva at least once a week. Chartering boats interisland is extremely expensive, and to join a regular trip you just have to be lucky, persistent, and prepared to wait. You can also islandhop by helicopter if you've got the money.

Getting around the individual islands can be a challenge as there's no organized public transportation other than expensive airport transfers, and because of the condition of the roads, rental cars are limited to a few pricey vehicles at Taiohae and Atuona. It's fairly easy to hire a chauffeur-driven vehicle on Hiva Oa, Nuku Hiva, Ua Huka, and Ua Pou, but expect to pay CFP 15,000–20,000 a day. Since this amount can be shared among as many people as can fit inside, you'll want to join or form a group. While making your inquiries, keep your ears open for any mention of boat tours as these are often no more expensive than land tours.

Hitchhiking is complicated because many of the private vehicles you see out on the roads double as taxis, and drivers who depend on tourists for a large part of their incomes are unlikely to be eager to give rides for free. An option for hardy backpackers is just to count on having to walk the whole way and accept any lifts that happen to be offered. It's too far to walk in one day from Nuku Hiva airport to Taiohae or from Atuona to Puama'u, but many other stretches can be covered on foot. If you're fit you can walk from Taiohae to Taipivai and from Taipivai to Hatiheu on Nuku Hiva, and from Atuona to Ta'aoa or the airport on Hiva Oa. Almost everywhere on Fatu Hiva, Tahuata, Ua Huka, and Ua Pou is accessible on foot, provided you've got the time and strength. If you pack a tent, food, and sufficient water, you'll be self-sufficient and able to see the islands on a shoestring budget.

FRENCH POLYNESIA

LES MARQUISES

By Jacques Brel

Ils parlent de la morte comme tu parles d'un fruit
They speak of death as you would speak of a fruit
Ils regardent la mer comme tu regardes un puits
They gaze at the sea as you look into a well
Les femmes sont lascives au soleil redouté
The women are enticing under the dreaded sun
Et s'il n'y a pas d'hiver cela n'est pas l'été
And if there's no winter, that doesn't make it summer
La pluie est traversière elle bat de grain en grain
The rain sweeps by, beating heavier and heavier,
Quelques vieux chevaux blancs qui fredonnent
    Gauguin
On old white horses that recall Gauguin
Et par manque de brise le temps s'immobilise
And, without a breeze, time seems frozen
Aux Marquises.
In the Marquesas.

Du soir montent des feux et des points de silence
From the darkness rise fires and silent places
Qui vont s'élargissant et la lune s'avance
Which widen as the moon comes up
Et la mer se déchire infiniment brisée
And the sea breaks, shattering infinitely
Par des rochers qui prirent des prénoms affolés

On rocks named with wild names
Et puis plus loin des chiens des chants de repentance
And further from the dogs and penitent songs
Et quelques pas de deux et quelques pas de danse
And some two-steps and other dance steps
Et la nuit est soumise et l'alizé se brise
And the night is subdued and the trade winds die down
Aux Marquises.

Leur rire est dans le coeur le mot dans le regard
Their laughter is from the heart and speech with the eyes
Le coeur est voyageur l'avenir est au hasard
The heart wanders, the future is left to fate
Et passent des cocotiers qui écrivent des chants
    d'amour
And then pass collectors of coconuts who write love songs
Que les soeurs d'alentours ignorent d'ignorer
Which the local nuns choose to ignore
Les pirogues s'en vont les pirogues s'en viennent
The canoes go out, the canoes come in
Et mes souvenirs deviennent ce que les vieux en font
*And my memories become whatever the elders make
    of them*
Veux-tu que je te dise gémir n'est pas de mise
May I say to you, complaining is not the way
Aux Marquises.

Nuku Hiva

Nuku Hiva is the largest (339 square km) and most populous (2,375 inhabitants) of the Marquesas. Taiohae (population 1,700) on the south coast is the administrative and economic center of the Marquesas. It's a modern little town with a post office, a hospital, a town hall, a bank, grocery stores, street lighting, and several hotels. Winding mountain roads lead northeast from Taiohae to Taipivai and Hatiheu villages or northwest toward the airport. In the center of the island Mt. Tekao (1,224 meters) rises above the vast, empty Toovii Plateau.

Taiohae Bay is a flooded volcanic crater guarded by two tiny islands called The Sentinels. Ua Pou is clearly visible across the waters. Though open to the south, Taiohae's deep harbor offers ex-

cellent anchorage. Cruising yachts toss in the hock on the east side of the bay, while the *Aranui* and *Taporo* tie up to a wharf at the southeast end of town. Take care with the drinking water at Taiohae. Unfortunately, many beaches around Nuku Hiva are infested with sandflies called *no-nos* that give nasty bites (the bugs disappear after dark). Luckily, Hiva Oa is free of these pests.

History

In 1813 Captain David Porter of the American frigate *Essex* annexed Nuku Hiva for the United States, though the act was never ratified by Congress. Britain and the United States had gone to war in 1812 and Porter's mission was to harass British shipping in the Pacific. After capturing a

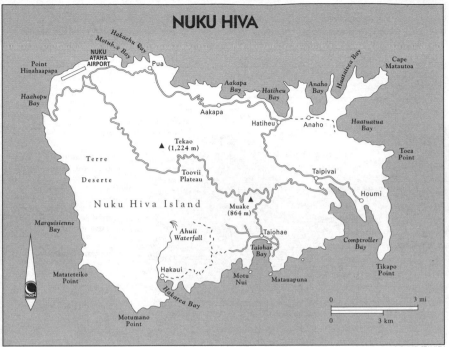

NUKU HIVA

Hakaehu Bay
Motuh...e Bay
Haatuatua Bay
NUKU ATAHA AIRPORT
Point Hinahaapapa
Pua
Cape Matautoa
Haahopu Bay
Aakapa Bay
Hatiheu Bay
Anaho Bay
Aakapa
Hatiheu
Anaho
Haatuatua Bay
Tekao (1,224 m) ▲
Terre
Toovii Plateau
Toea Point
Deserte
Nuku Hiva Island
Muake (864 m) ▲
Taipivai
Houmi
Marquisienne Bay
Ahuii Waterfall
Taiohae
Taiohae Bay
Comptroller Bay
Matateteiko Point
Hakaui
Motu Nui
Matauapuna
Tikapo Point
Hakatea Bay
Motumano Point

0 ___ 3 mi
0 ___ 3 km

© DAVID STANLEY

dozen ships off South America, Porter arrived at Nuku Hiva and built a fort at the present site of Taiohae, which he named Madisonville for the U.S. president of his day. Porter allowed himself to be drawn into local conflicts among the Polynesian tribes. A few months later he left to continue his raiding and was defeated by two British warships off Chile. In 1842 the French erected Fort Collet on the site of Porter's fort, above the marina at the east end of Taiohae.

Sandalwood traders followed Porter, then whalers. Herman Melville arrived on the American whaling ship *Acushnet* in 1842, and his book *Typee,* written after a one-month stay in the Taipi Valley, is still the classic narrative of Marquesan life during the 19th century. A half century later Scottish writer Robert Louis Stevenson visited the island. In 2002 Nuku Hiva was back in the limelight with the filming on the island of the American TV series *Survivor* at a cost of US$100 million.

SIGHTS OF TAIOHAE

Taiohae's new post office is on a slight plateau in the heart of the official quarter, with the **Residence** of the subdivisional administrator just below toward the beach and the old **Administrative Center** across the street. On a grassy knoll topped by a navigational light above these buildings is the site of **Fort Collet,** which offers a sweeping view of Taiohae Bay. Nothing remains of Porter's original fort overlooking what he called Massachusetts Bay. Just north of this hill above the old marina is the colonial jail.

The **Monument to the Dead obelisk** (1928), marked by an anchor and cannon, is west along the waterfront past the bank.

Two towers retained from an earlier church give access to the open courtyard of **Notre-Dame Cathedral** (1974) on the west side of central Taiohae. The cathedral's interior is notable for its fine woodcarvings, including a massive

TAIOHAE

To Muake, Taipivai, and Airport

ANDY'S DREAM

Nuku Hiva Island

NOTRE-DAME CATHEDRAL

HÔTEL MOANA NUI

CHEZ FETU

COLLEGE DE TAIOHAE

TEMEHEA TOHUA

RESTAURANT LE KOVIVI

MAIRIE

PENSION MAVE MAI

MONUMENT TO THE DEAD

RADIO MARQUISES

TYPEE MEMORIAL

BANQUE SOCREDO

OLD JAIL

ADMINISTRATIVE CENTER

PENSION PAAHATEA NUI

CEMETERY

OLD MARINA

GENDARMERIE

PENSION PUA

CENTRE PLONGÉE

POST OFFICE

NUKU HIVA VILLAGE

SITE OF FORT COLLET

RESIDENCE

HOSPITAL

BOUTIQUE AND MUSÉE

KEIKAHANUI PEARL LODGE

CEMETERY

SABINE TEIKITEETINI

To Haaotupa Bay

YACHT ANCHORAGE

HELICOPTER LANDING AREA

SERVICE DE L'EQUIPMENT

MAIN WHARF

Taiohae Bay

0   0.5 mi
0   0.5 km

wooden pulpit bearing the symbols of the four evangelists. The floor behind the pulpit is paved with flower stones from Ua Pou. Among the outstanding wooden Stations of the Cross carved by Damien Haturau, note especially Station No. 1 which depicts Jesus in the Garden of Breadfruit (instead of the Garden of Olives).

Across a small bridge just west of the cathedral is the **Temehea Tohua,** also known as the Tohua Piki Vehine, created for the Marquesas Islands Festival in 1989. Among the modern tikis on this platform are the figures of Temoana and Vaekehu, who were designated king and queen of the island by the French in 1842.

Next to a small cemetery 600 meters further west along the waterfront is the wooden **Typee Memorial** (1842-1992) by Séverin Kahe'e Taupotini (who also carved the cathedral's pulpit).

At the southwest end of the bay, just around corner from the Nuku Hiva Village Hôtel, is the **Boutique and Musée Hôtel Keikahanui** (tel. 92-03-82; donations) run by American art collector Rose Corser. Rose and her late husband, Frank, opened the original Keikahanui Inn in 1979, which in 1999 became the Keikahanui Pearl Lodge with Rose remaining an investor. A good part of her museum collection is on loan from Taiohae's bishop and other local residents. Her boutique displays a tasteful selection of Marquesan handicrafts, including Fatu Hiva tapa. Prices are comparable to those at other outlets around town. Many stone- and woodcarvers work on Nuku Hiva, and their wooden tikis, bowls, ukuleles, ceremonial war clubs, and paddles are keenly sought after.

The road now leaves the bay and climbs two km over the ridge to secluded **Haaotupa Bay,** also called Colette Bay, a nice picnic spot.

West of Taiohae

At Hakaui, 15 km west of Taiohae, a river runs down a narrow steep-sided valley. Fantastic 350-meter **Ahuii Waterfall,** highest in the territory, drops from the plateau at the far end of the valley, four km from the coast. It's a two-hour walk from Hakaui to the waterfall with a few thigh-high river crossings after rains (guide not required). The trail passes many crumbling platforms, indicating that the valley was once well populated. If you swim in the pool at the falls beware of falling pebbles. A boat from Taiohae to Hakaui would cost CFP 15,000 and up return, but an overgrown 12-km switchback trail also crosses the 535-meter ridge from above Haaotupa Bay to uninhabited Hakaui.

You'll need to be adventurous and good at finding your own way to follow it (allow four hours each way between Taiohae to Hakaui).

Above Taiohae

For a sweeping view of Taiohae Bay, hike up to **Muake** (864 meters) on the ridge due north of town. A steep concrete road zigzags seven km to the point where the airport and Taipivai roads divide. Turn left toward the airport, then left again into the forest. There was once a Marquesan fort near where the radio tower presently stands. This is a favorite takeoff point for paragliders and groups from the *Aranui* have a picnic lunch here. Farther west toward the airport is a market gardening area and agricultural station on the 900-meter-high **Toovii Plateau.** Herds of cattle range across the pine-covered plateau.

Sports and Recreation

Xavier Curvat's **Centre Plongée Marquises** (tel./fax 92-00-88; office hours Wed.–Fri. 1430–1700, Sat. 0900–1200), at the old marina in Taiohae, offers scuba diving daily at 0800 for CFP 5,500/10,000/45,000 for one/two/10

Hakaui on Nuku Hiva's south coast, home of the Taioa tribe

dives including gear. A maximum of eight people are taken out every day, so book the day before. It also fills tanks for yachties at CFP 1,000 each. Xavier arrived in 1979 and he has thoroughly explored the archipelago during his years here. There's not much coral to be seen around Nuku Hiva but the underwater caves and spectacular schools of hammerhead sharks and pygmy orcas compensate. Snorkelers are welcome when space is available and the orcas are easily seen this way. The dive shop sells carvings and crafts.

Horseback riding is offered by Jean Paul and Sabine Teikiteetini (tel. 92-05-68), who live near the helicopter landing area above the main wharf in Taiohae. In the local area it's CFP 5,000 a half day, and rides from Taiohae to Taipivai are possible.

PRACTICALITIES

Accommodations

Pension Mave Mai (tel. 73-76-01, tel./fax 92-08-10), up the steep road between the old jail and Radio Marquises from near the old marina, has six rooms in a two-story building at CFP 5,800/6,800 single/double. The upstairs rooms have balconies with great views of the bay. The owners, Regina and Jean-Claude, can provide meals and organize a variety of excursions at the usual rates.

The least expensive place to stay is **Chez Fetu** (Cyprien Peterano, tel. 92-03-66), just up the hill from the Monument to the Dead on the waterfront, off Taipivai Road behind Magasin Kamake, a 10-minute walk from the wharf in Taiohae. The three-bed bungalow is CFP 2,000/4,000/6,000 single/double/triple. Communal cooking facilities are available and there's a terrace facing the valley.

The friendly, two-story **Hôtel Moana Nui** (Charles Mombaerts, tel. 92-03-30, fax 92-00-02), on the waterfront in the middle of Taiohae, has seven clean rooms with private bath (hot water) above its popular restaurant/bar. Bed and breakfast is CFP 5,500/6,000 single/double, other meals CFP 2,500 each. Mosquitoes and bar noise are drawbacks, the excellent views from the terrace a definite plus. Cars are for rent at CFP 10,000 a day (often unavailable) and boat excursions can be arranged. Airport transfers are CFP 4,000.

Andy's Dream (André Teikiteetini, tel. 92-00-80) is at Hoata, about a km up from the Temehea Tohua. The small bungalow with bath is CFP 3,500 pp including breakfast or CFP 7,500 pp with all meals. The price of the bungalow is okay if you're able to cook your own food but you'll hear a lot of rooster noise at night. Andy's taxi tours are not the cheapest.

Pension Paahatea Nui (Justin and Julienne Mahiatapu, tel./fax 92-00-97), next to the Nuku Hiva Village Hôtel, has only a sign which reads "Sculpture La Maison Verte." It's up the road running inland from near the small cemetery beside the Typee Memorial. The two larger rooms with private bath are CFP 3,000 pp, while the four rooms with shared bath go for CFP 2,500 pp. The two bungalows are CFP 4,000 pp. Use of the common kitchen is CFP 500 pp. Camping in the grassy yard is CFP 1,000 pp.

The rather rundown **Nuku Hiva Village Hôtel** (Bruno and Gloria Gendron, tel. 92-01-94, fax 92-05-97), opposite the yacht anchorage on the west side of Taiohae Bay, has six thatched *fare* with private bath at CFP 6,500/7,500/8,500 single/double/triple, plus CFP 3,800 pp a day for breakfast and dinner. A local band plays in the large restaurant some Saturday nights. Excursions by 4WD, horseback riding, and scuba diving can be arranged.

In 2002 part of the Nuku Hiva Village compound came under separate management as **Pension Pua** (tel. 92-06-87). The six bungalows without kitchens are CFP 4,000/5,500 single/double, while the three with kitchens are CFP 5,500/7,500. Check the website for current prices and details of its excursions.

The **Keikahanui Pearl Lodge** (tel. 92-07-10, fax 92-07-11), just up the hill from the Nuku Hiva Village, was completely rebuilt in 1999 with a small but spectacular cliffside swimming pool. The 20 new air-conditioned bungalows start at CFP 26,000 double, plus 11 percent tax. Cooking facilities are not provided, so for breakfast and dinner add CFP 6,600 pp. Airport transfers arranged by the hotel are CFP 9,000/15,000 pp round-trip by road/helicopter. The Keikahanui is named after a tattooed chief.

Food

The **Hôtel Moana Nui** (tel. 92-03-30) on the waterfront is famous for its pizza (CFP 1,000–1,500). It's a popular place to eat and drink.

Restaurant Le Kovivi (tel. 92-00-14; closed Sun.), near Banque Socredo, has a nice porch overlooking the bay. The plat du jour is around CFP 1,500, a large beer CFP 650.

If you're lucky, you might be able to buy fresh vegetables at the Saturday morning market at the old marina in Taiohae. Be there by 0500 as not much will be left at 0600. The only fresh produce available at the various supermarkets is potatoes and garlic (fresh veggies are easier to find on Hiva Oa).

Information

Tourist information is available from Comité Tourisme Nuku Hiva (Déborah Kimitete, tel. 92-08-24), at the Subdivision du Service de l'Urbanisme in the old jail (back door) between the *mairie* and the post office. It sells good topographical maps of the Marquesas at CFP 1,500.

Radio Marquises broadcasts from Taiohae over 101.3 MHz with the Réseau France Outre-Mer (RFO) news in French at 0700 and 1230.

Services

Central Taiohae boasts a Banque Socredo branch (tel. 92-03-63; weekdays 0730–1130/1330–1600). The post office on the east side of town sells telephone cards you can use at the public phone outside and at several other locations around the island. The post office also has public computer terminals for Internet access at reasonable rates and sells the Tahiti newspapers.

Don't have your mail sent c/o poste restante at the post office as it will be returned via surface after 15 days. Instead have it addressed c/o Rose Corser, B.P. 21, 98742 Taiohae, Nuku Hiva, French Polynesia (tel. 92-03-82, fax 92-00-74). In a pinch, Rose will provide Internet access at her Boutique and Musée below the Keikahanui Pearl Lodge at CFP 500 per 15 minutes.

The gendarmerie (tel. 92-03-61) is just up the road to the left of the post office, while the public hospital (tel. 92-03-75) is to the right. The Taiohae gendarmes invariably insist on

yachties posting their arrival bonds, if they haven't already done so. A private dentist, Dr. Pierre Puech (tel. 92-00-83; weekdays 0730–1200), is next to Héli-Inter near the *mairie*.

Transportation

Air Tahiti (tel. 92-03-41) is in a poorly marked office behind Héli-Inter near the *mairie*.

Information on the *Ka'oha Nui, Meherio,* and other government boats can be obtained from the Service de l'Equipment next to the main wharf at Taiohae.

The only public transportation on Nuku Hiva is the expensive airport transfer. It's possible to walk from Taiohae to Taipivai and Hatiheu in two days if you're fit, camping or staying at local pensions along the way. A road now links Hatiheu to the airport via Aakapa and Pua.

Island tours by Land Rover are the usual way of getting around, but get ready for some astronomical charges, such as CFP 20,000 for a visit to Hatiheu. Car rentals often come with a driver and thus cost taxi prices. An example of this is **Teiki Transports** (Mr. Lucien Puhetini, tel. 92-00-90) which offers chauffeur-driven cars. To rent a car without a driver for something approaching normal rates, ask at the Hôtel Moana Nui (tel. 92-03-30), though its vehicles are often all taken.

Héli-Inter Marquises (tel. 92-02-17), next to the Mairie de Taiohae, does helicopter transfers from Taiohae to the airport or Hatiheu at CFP 7,500 pp. The helicopter will take pre-booked passengers from Hatiheu to the airport for the usual CFP 7,000, so it's not necessary to return to Taiohae. There are occasional trips from Taiohae to Ua Pou at CFP 12,500 pp, but only charters go to the other islands. In Taiohae, the helicopters use a heliport near the main wharf. The baggage allowance is 15 kg (or 20 kg with an international ticket).

Airport

Nuku Ataha Airport (NHV) is in the arid Terre Déserte at the northwest corner of Nuku Hiva, 32 km from Taiohae along a twisting dirt road over the Toovii Plateau. Upon arrival from Papeete or Rangiroa turn your watch ahead 30 minutes. A restaurant and hotel are near the terminal. The main drawback to flying into Nuku Hiva is the

MARQUESAS ISLANDS INTERNET RESOURCES

Accommodations

Chez Yvonne Katupa, Nuku Hiva
hinakonui@mail.pf

Hanakéé Pearl Lodge, Hiva Oa
hiva.oa.pearl@mail.pf

Keikahanui Pearl Lodge, Nuku Hiva
keikahanui@mail.pf

Mairie de Atuona, Hiva Oa
communehivaoa@mail.pf

Nuku Hiva Village Hôtel, Taiohae
nukuvillage@mail.pf

Pension Gauguin, Hiva Oa
pens.gauguin@mail.pf

Pension Mave Mai, Nuku Hiva
pension-mavemai@mail.pf

Pension Moehau, Hiva Oa
moehaupension@mail.pf

Pension Pua, Nuku Hiva
www.puaexcursions.pf
info@puaexcursions.pf

Pension Pukuéé, Ua Pou
http://chez.mana.pf/~pukuee
pukuee@mail.pf

Pension Temetiu Village, Hiva Oa
heitaagabyfeli@mail.pf

Others

Comité Tourisme Nuku Hiva, Taiohae
tourisme@marquises.pf

Héli-Inter Marquises, Nuku Hiva
helico-nuku@mail.pf

Robert C. Suggs
www.marquesasnow.com

Rose Corser, Nuku Hiva
rose.corser@mail.pf

---

cost of airport transfers, which run CFP 4,000 pp each way by 4WD Toyota Landcruiser for the 2.5-hour drive or CFP 7,500 pp each way by helicopter. When shopping for woodcarvings during your stay on Nuku Hiva keep in mind the problem of getting the stuff back to Papeete. While waiting for your flight it's worth examining the excellent Marquesan low-relief woodcarvings made to decorate the airport's bar and shop when the airport was built in 1979.

TAIPIVAI

Several hundred people live at Taipivai, a five-hour, 16-km walk from Taiohae over the Col Teavanui (576 meters). Vanilla grows wild throughout this valley. At Hooumi, on a fine protected bay near Taipivai, is a truly magical little church. The huge *tohua* of Vahangeku'a at Taipivai is a whopping 170 by 25 meters. Eleven great stone tikis watch over the **Pa'eke Me'ae,** a couple of km up the Taipi Valley toward Hatiheu and then up the slope to the right. Robert Suggs excavated this site in 1957. About two km farther up the road to

Hatiheu is a monument to the left of the road marking the spot where Herman Melville spent a month with his tattooed sweetheart Fayaway in 1842. In his novel, *Typee* (his spelling for Taipi), he gives a delightful account of the life of the great-grandparents of the present inhabitants.

Accommodations

By the river in Taipivai village, **Chez Martine Haiti** (tel. 92-01-19, fax 92-05-34) has two bungalows at CFP 2,000/3,500 single/double. You can cook for yourself or order dinner at CFP 2,000 pp. Call ahead as this pension was reported to have temporarily closed.

Tata Thomas at **Snack Heiau** (tel. 92-06-13), near the landing on the river in the center of Taipivai village, has one basic room for rent behind the snack bar (price negotiable).

HATIHEU AND ANAHO

From Taipivai it's another 12 km via the Col Teavaitapuhiva (443 meters) to Hatiheu on the north coast. Some spectacular falls are seen in the distance to the left of the road near the mountain pass. A statue of the Virgin Mary stands on a rocky peak high above Hatiheu Bay and its black sand beach. (Yachts are better off anchoring in protected Anaho Bay than here.) Hatiheu was destroyed by a tsunami in 1946 but 350 people live there today.

The restored **Hikoku'a Tohua** is a bit over a kilometer from Hatiheu back toward Taipivai. Several of the tikis on the structure were added during the 1989 Marquesas Islands Festival while others are old (notice the phallic fertility statue at the entrance on the left). In the jungle a kilometer farther up the road is the **Te I'ipoka Me'ae,** where many human sacrifices were made to the goddess Te Vana'uau'a. The victims were kept in a pit beneath a huge sacred banyan tree until their turn arrived to be consumed at cannibal feasts. Up the steep wooded slope from here is the overgrown **Kamui-hei Tohua** with petroglyphs. These sites are among the largest and most intriguing in the Marquesas.

Anaho is two km east of Hatiheu on horseback or foot over a 217-meter pass (no road). It's one of the most beautiful of Nuku Hiva's bays, with a powdery white beach and some of the finest snorkeling in the Marquesas (lovely coral and the possibility of seeing turtles or reef sharks).

From Anaho it's an easy 45-minute walk east along the south side of the bay and over the low Isthmus to uninhabited **Haatuatua Bay** where you could camp wild. Ancient Marquesan stone platforms are hidden in the bush here (go in-land on one of the grassy strips near the south end of the beach till you find a southbound trail). No one lives there, though wild horses are seen.

Accommodations

In Hatiheu village, **Chez Yvonne Katupa** (tel. 92-02-97, fax 92-01-28) offers five pleasant bungalows without cooking facilities or hot water at CFP 4,500/7,000 single/double, breakfast included. The bungalows are set in their own garden across a small bridge from Yvonne's restaurant, facing the beach on Hatiheu Bay. Passengers off the *Aranui* enjoy a superb fish and lobster lunch at Yvonne's. Ask to see her collection of artifacts at the *mairie.* It's possible to rent sit-on-top kayaks here at CFP 500/1,500/2,500 an hour/half day/full day or to hire horses at CFP 5,000 a day. Yvonne arrange transfers from Hatiheu to the airport (75 km) by 4WD at CFP 5,000 pp.

You can also stay at **Te Pua Hinako** (Juliette Vaianui, tel. 92-04-14), also known as Chez Juliette, at the northwest end of the beach at Anaho. The two rooms with shared bath are CFP 2,500 pp with breakfast, or CFP 5,500 pp with all meals.

Juliette's son Raymond operates **Kaoha Tiare** (Raymond Vaianui, tel. 92-00-08), next to Te Pua Hinako. The five bungalows with bath are CFP 2,500/5,000 single/double, plus CFP 3,000 pp for all meals. Juliette and Raymond hosted TV crews from *Survivor* for several months in late 2001.

Other Northern Islands

UA POU

At 105 square km, Ua Pou is the third-largest Marquesan island. This spectacular, diamond-shaped island lies about 40 km south of Nuku Hiva and it's very arid. Ua Pou is the only island in the Marquesas with the sort of towering volcanic plugs seen on Moorea and Bora Bora. One of these sugarloaf-shaped volcanic plugs inspired Jacques Brel's song "La Cathédrale" and the name Ua Pou itself means "the pillars." Mount Oave (1,203 meters), highest point on Ua Pou, is often cloud-covered.

The island's population of over 2,000 is larger than that of Hiva Oa. The main village is Haka-hau on the northeast coast, with solid concrete streets, government services, and the only port. In 1988, 500 French foreign legionnaires rebuilt the breakwater at Hakahau, and ships can now tie up to the concrete pier.

Sights

The first stone church in the Marquesas was erected at Hakahau in 1859, and the present **Church of Saint-Etienne** (1981) has a pulpit shaped like a boat carved from a single stump

UA POU

ANEOU AIRSTRIP

WHARF

Motu Mokohe

Hakahetau

Hakahau

Point Punahu

Haakuti

Oave (1,203 m)

Hakamoui Bay

Vaiehu Bay

Ua Pou Island

Paaumea Bay

Hakamaii

Hohoi

Hohoi Bay

Hakatao

Motutakaae

Motu Oa

0   2 mi

0   2 km

© DAVID STANLEY

by a group of sculptors. The wooden cross in the church is by Damien Haturau.

The **Tenai Paepae** in the center of the village was restored for the 1995 Marquesas Islands Festival, the same occasion that saw the inauguration of the small **Musée de Ua Pou** at the south end of Hakahau.

Lovely **Anahoa Beach** is a scenic 30-minute walk east of the marina, but unfortunately the beach is infested with *no-nos*. There's a superlative bird's-eye view from the cross overlooking Hakahau on the ridge halfway there.

South of Hakahau

A road leads south from Hakahau to a beach beyond Hohoi. On 88-meter-high **Motu Oa** off the south coast, millions of seabirds nest.

The road from Hohoi to **Hakatao** on the southwest coast crosses a high pass and the steep descent to Hakatao is only possible in the dry season. The track between Hakatao and **Hakamaii** can be covered only by canoe, hoof, or on foot (a four-hour walk). You can drive the rest of the way around the island.

West of Hakahau

West of Hakahau the road runs to the airport (10 km), Hakahetau (16 km), and Haakuti (22 km). Sea turtles lay their eggs on the white sands of uninhabited **Hakanahi Beach** between the airport and Hakahetau, and large sharks wait

offshore to feed on the hatchlings (swimming not advisable). You can often see the sharks from the road above the beach.

Around 200 people live in the charming small village of **Hakahetau.** Local handicrafts are made from the *kea pua* (flower stone), a black volcanic stone with yellow streaks found only on the beaches here. Ask for Jean Marc Nguyen van Chinh (tel. 92-53-93), who produces unique wooden necklaces and bracelets.

Accommodations

The best established pension in Hakahao is **Pension Pukuéé** (Hélène and Doudou Kautai, tel./fax 92-50-83), just a few minutes walk from the wharf on the road to Anahoa Beach. Set on a hill overlooking the village, the seven shared-bath rooms are CFP 3,000/5,500 single/double, plus 6 percent tax. Children under 12 are half price, under four free. Breakfast/dinner are CFP 500/2,500. Yachties often order seafood meals here. Airport transfers are CFP 2,000 per car (up to five passengers). Readers have liked it here.

Pension/Snack Vehine (Claire Teikiehuupoko, tel. 92-50-63), two blocks east of the Tenai Paepae, has two rooms for rent at CFP 3,000 pp. The restaurant (closed Sunday) serves good meals at the CFP 700–1,100 range with *poisson cru* at CFP 750. Claire also runs the island's traditional dance group (notice the photos along the bar). It's the best place to eat and drink on the island.

Pension Vaitiare (tel. 92-50-95), next to a general store at the western entrance to Hakahau from the airport, offers three rooms with bath at CFP 5,000 double including breakfast. Other meals are CFP 800–900. Make this your last choice.

Pension Chez Dora (Madame Dora Teikiehuupoko, tel./fax 92-53-69), in a quiet location south of town at the top of the hill beyond the museum, has three rooms at CFP 3,000 pp and two bungalows at CFP 4,000 pp, breakfast included. Dinner is CFP 2,000 pp. The room downstairs has a private bath, while those upstairs share a bath. Airport transfers are CFP 1,500 pp return.

In Hakahetau, ask for Étienne Hokaupoko (no phone) who lives up on the hillside, a 10-minute walk from the port. His son lives next to the Protestant church in the village and should be able to provide information. In past Étienne has accommodated visitors at the usual rates and you'll probably be welcome to stay with him and his wife. Étienne is working on an Marquesan English dictionary and he knows many stories he's only too happy to share. Yachties often drop in to sign his guest book.

Food
CETAD (tel. 92-53-83) operates a culinary school at the Collège de Ua Pou opposite the beach not far from the wharf in Hakahau. Fridays at noon the students prepare an excellent lunch (CFP 1,500–2,000), which you can enjoy if you reserve a few days ahead.

Shopping
An Artisanat shop near the wharf at Hakahau sells local carvings and shell jewelry. Several woodcarvers work in Hakahau village—just ask for *les sculpteurs*. If you're buying, shop around at the beginning of your stay, as many items are unfinished and you should allow the time to have something completed.

Information and Services
Motu Haka (Georges "Toti" Teikiehuupoko, tel. 92-53-21) is a cultural organization that promotes Marquesan language instruction, archaeological projects, and traditional arts while rejecting cultural domination by Tahiti. The Marquesas Islands Festival is one of Motu Haka's projects. You can contact Toti through Pension Chez Dora.

The Banque Socredo (tel. 92-53-63), *mairie,* and a post office are all adjacent opposite the defunct market and not far from the beach. The gendarmerie (tel. 92-53-61) is a bit south. Infirmaries are in Hakahau, Hakatao, and Hakamaii. Six or seven stores are to be found in Hakahau.

Getting There
Ua Pou's Aneou airstrip (UAP) is on the north coast, 10 km west of Hakahau via a rough road over a ridge. It's in a valley just back from a long black beach between Hakahau and Hakahetau. The pensions in Hakahau offer airport transfers for CFP 1,500–2,000 pp return. You can reach Air Tahiti in Hakahau at tel. 92-53-41.

A launch from Nuku Hiva to Hakahau (1.5 hours each way, CFP 4,000 one-way or CFP 6,000 for a round-trip the same day) operates irregularly. It's better to check on this a few days before.

UA HUKA
Ua Huka lies 35 km east of Nuku Hiva and 56 km northeast of Ua Pou. Crescent-shaped Ua Huka is the surviving northern half of an ancient volcano and its 575 inhabitants live in the truncated crater in the south. Mount Hitikau (884 meters) rises northeast of Hane village. Vaipae'e is the main village of the island, although the hospital is at Hane.

Goats and wild horses range across this arid, 83-square-km island, while the tiny islands of Teuaua and Hemeni, off the southwest tip of Ua Huka, are a breeding ground for millions of *kaveka* (sooty terns). Sadly, local residents use these flat islands surrounded by sheer cliffs as a source of eggs.

Archaeological excavations by Professor Y. H. Sinoto in 1965 dated a coastal site on Ua Huka to A.D. 300, which makes it the oldest in French Polynesia; two pottery fragments found here suggest that the island was probably a major dispersal point for the ancient Polynesians. Sinoto believes the migratory paths of Ua Huka's terns may have led the ancient Polynesians on their way to new discoveries.

Sights
Between the airport and Vaipae'e is a plantation that has been converted into a **Botanical Garden** (weekdays 0700–1430, free) complete with an aviary. Unfortunately the plants are not labeled.

Near the post office in Vaipae'e is a small but admirable **Musée Communal** (weekdays 0700–1400, free) of local artifacts and seashells, and replicas made by local artist Joseph Tehau Va'atete. Many other woodcarvers are active here. The craft shop adjacent to the museum only opens when tour groups are present.

In Hane is a **Centre Artisanal/Musée de la Mer,** by the beach just below the hospital. Three small tikis cut from red rock are in a mango

FRENCH POLYNESIA

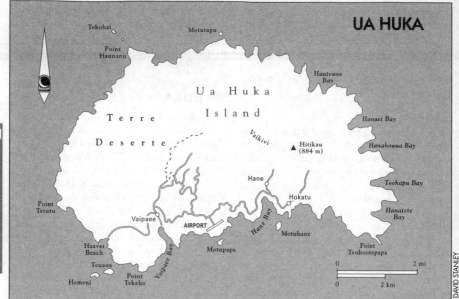

UA HUKA

Tekohai

Motutapu

Point Haunanu

Haateaoa Bay

Ua Huka Island

Terre

Hanaei Bay

Deserte

Vaikivi

Hitikau (884 m)

Hanahouua Bay

Hane

Toohapu Bay

Hokatu

Point Tetutu

Vaipaee

AIRPORT

Hane Bay

Hanatete Bay

Haavei Beach

Motupapa

Motuhane

Point Teohootepapa

Teuaua

Hemeni

Point Tekeho

0   2 mi

0   2 km

© DAVID STANLEY

forest up the valley behind Hane, a 25-minute walk from the Auberge Hitikau.

Accommodations

Chez Alexis (Alexis Scallamera, tel. 92-60-19, fax 92-60-12) in Vaipae'e village, a bit toward the wharf from the post office, is a two-room house with shared bath at CFP 4,700 pp including half board. You're also welcome to cook your own food. Alexis can arrange horseback riding (CFP 5,000) and boat excursions.

The **Mana Tupuna Village** (Teiki Taiaapu, tel. 92-60-08, fax 92-61-01) offers three bungalows on the hillside above the road on the north side of Vaipae'e at CFP 5,500/10,000 single/double including breakfast and dinner. Teiki or *le petit chef* is an affable guy.

Also in Vaipae'e is **Chez Christelle** (Christelle Fournier, tel./fax 92-60-85), a four-room house with shared bath at CFP 2,000 pp, plus CFP 1,000/2,000 for breakfast/dinner. It's run by the Air Tahiti agent and is down by the river on the north side of town.

In Hane village, the **Auberge Hitikau** (Céline and Jean Fournier, tel./fax 92-61-74) offers three rooms with shared bath next to its restaurant at CFP 2,000/3,500 single/double with breakfast. Lobster is served in the large restaurant at CFP 2,500—*Aranui* passengers often enjoy a meal here.

Also worth checking is **Chez Maurice et Delphine** (Maurice and Delphine Rootuehine, tel./fax 92-60-55) at Hokatu village, 13 km from the airport. The three rooms with shared bath in the family residence above their store in the village are CFP 2,200 pp with breakfast or CFP 5,200 pp with all meals. They also have two bungalows with private bath on a hill some distance away at CFP 2,700 pp with breakfast, or CFP 5,700 pp with all meals. Maurice can arrange a rental car.

Getting There

The airstrip (UAH) is on a hilltop between Hane and Vaipae'e, six km from the latter. The pensions generally provide free airport transfers. The Air Tahiti number is tel. 92-60-85. The *Aranui* enters the narrow fjord at Vaipae'e and anchors. It's quite a show watching the ship trying to turn around.

Hiva Oa

Measuring 40 by 19 km, 315-square-km Hiva Oa (population 1,900) is the second largest of the Marquesas and main center of the southern cluster of islands. Mount Temetiu (1,276 meters), highest peak in the Marquesas, towers above Atuona to the west. Steep ridges falling to the coast separate lush valleys on this long crescent-shaped island. Ta'aoa, or "Traitors'," Bay is a flooded crater presently missing its eastern wall, while Puama'u sits in a younger secondary crater. The administrative headquarters for the Marquesas group has switched back and forth several times: Taiohae was the center until 1904, then it was Atuona until 1944, then Taiohae took over once again.

SIGHTS OF ATUONA

The **Musée Gauguin** (admission CFP 300) in central Atuona displays 24 colorful reproductions of Gauguin's paintings created in 1997 and 1998 by Alin Marthouret (born 1945). In 1991 a replica of Gauguin's thatched "Maison du Jouïr" (House of Pleasure) was built next to the museum and a few reproductions of his prints are inside. Jacques Brel's aircraft *Jojo* is also on the grounds. Handicrafts are sold at the Fare Artisanal here. The *paepae* platforms near the museum were built for the Marquesas Islands Festival in December 1991. If the museum is closed when you arrive, ask for Jo Reus who lives nearby and has the key.

In 2003 Hiva Oa hosted its second Marquesas Islands Festival and a new **Cultural Center and Museum** was erected in the center of town to mark the centenary of Gauguin's death. The original well used by Gauguin during his stay here is on the site.

Back on the main street is **Magasin Gauguin** where Gauguin left an unpaid wine bill when he died. Go up the hill from beside the nearby gendarmerie and take the first fork in the road to the left to reach **Calvary Cemetery,** which hosts the graves of Jacques Brel (1929–1978) and Paul Gauguin (1848–1903). Gauguin's leading detractor, Monseigneur R. J. Martin (1849–1912), is buried under a large white tomb surrounded by a metal fence, higher up in the cemetery than Gauguin. The views of Atuona from here are excellent.

Other sights worth seeking out if you have the time include the **Catholic church** with its fine carved doors and interior visible through the open walls, and the Salle des Marriages at the **Mairie de Atuona** which contains another large Gauguin reproduction by Marthouret.

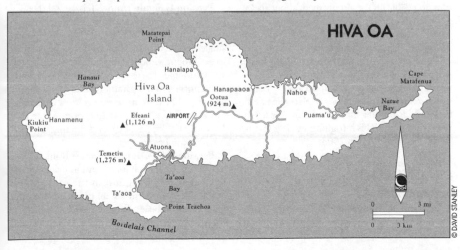

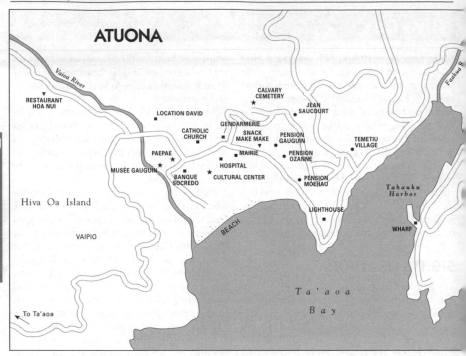

ATUONA

FRENCH POLYNESIA

Chanson singer Jacques Brel lived at Atuona 1975–1978. He intended to build his home on a ridge overlooking the entire valley, but died before the work could be done. The **Brel Belvédère** is now accessible off the airport road, about six km out of Atuona. A plaque bears the inscription *Veux-tu que je te dise, Gémir n'est pas de mise, Aux Marquises.* The view from here is superb.

The beach at Atuona is poor and for better swimming, take the road six km southwest along the bay to the black beach at **Ta'aoa.** A big restored *tohua* with several *me'ae* platforms and a basalt tiki is found a bit over a kilometer up the river from there. This intriguing site was also restored for the festival in 2003.

PRACTICALITIES

Accommodations

The **Mairie de Atuona** (tel. 92-73-32, fax 92-74-95) rents five well-equipped bungalows behind the town hall and post office at CFP 2,800/3,300

single/double. These have cooking facilities and private bath but they can only be booked directly at the *mairie* during business hours (weekdays 0730–1130/1300–1600). Ask for Claire.

Pension Gauguin (André Teissier, tel./fax 92-73-51), a bit east of Snack Make Make and up around the corner, charges CFP 6,000/11,000 single/double with half board. It may be possible to get a room without meals at CFP 3,500/6,000 single/double. There are two rooms downstairs and another four upstairs (the upstairs rooms are best). The upstairs terrace is most agreeable. Deep-sea fishing trips and excursions to the Brel Belvédère (CFP 4,000) and Puama'u (CFP 20,000) can be arranged.

Pension John Ozanne (Ozanne Rohi, tel./fax 92-73-43), up the hill from Pension Gauguin, offers a two-story bungalow in the yard at CFP 3,500. Cooking facilities are provided. Ozanne has a 12-meter boat called the *Denise II,* which he uses for excursions and trips to Tahuata (CFP 20,000) or Fatu Hiva (CFP 50,000). Ask to see

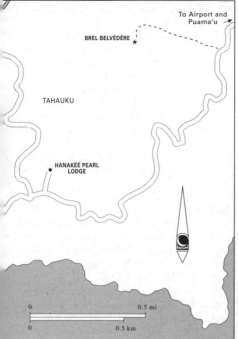

To Airport and Puama'u →

BREL BELVÉDÈRE ★

TAHAUKU

HANAKÉÉ PEARL LODGE

0   0.5 mi
0   0.5 km

MOON

© DAVID STANLEY

Ozanne's log books, which date to the 1970s and contain dozens of entries by cruisers who have passed this way over the years.

For a longer stay, **Jean Saucourt** (tel. 92-73-33) rents rooms by the week in a house above the cemetery. Ask Aline Saucourt at the handicraft shop in the Cultural Center about this.

Pension Moehau (tel./fax 92-72-69) is at the east entrance to Atuona, just up the hill from Snack Make Make on the way to the harbor. It offers eight rooms in a new two-story building on the hillside at CFP 5,000/8,000/10,000 single/double/triple.

Overlooking Tahauku Bay is the **Pension Temetiu Village** (Gabriel Heitaa, tel. 92-73-02), also known as Chez Gabi, just up the hill from SMA des Marquises a km east of Atuona on the way to the harbor. The five bungalows with bath are CFP 8,300/12,600 single/double with half pension (no cooking facilities). Nonguests are welcome at the terrace restau-

rant. Gabriel rents out his eight-passenger boat, the *Pua Ote Tai.*

Atuona's upmarket place, the **Hanakéé Pearl Lodge** (tel. 92-75-87, fax 92-75-95), is on the airport road about five km east of Atuona on the hillside overlooking Takauku Bay. There's a swimming pool with a panoramic deck. The 14 stylish bungalows and six suites start at CFP 26,000/31,000 double/triple, plus 11 percent tax. Breakfast and dinner are CFP 6,600 pp extra, airport transfers CFP 4,800 pp return. The manager sometimes allows yachties to check their email here at CFP 250 per eight minutes.

Food

Snack Make Make (tel. 92-74-26), also called Snack Atuona, 100 meters east of the post office and across the street, has juicy hamburgers (CFP 450), large *poisson cru* (CFP 950), grilled fish (CFP 1,050), and cold beer (CFP 400 a can). It's open for drinks weekdays 0730–1600 but meals served 1100–1330 only. The atmosphere is excellent.

Snack Kaupe (tel. 92-70-62; Tues.–Sun. 0900–1700, plus Fri. and Sat. nights), next to Magasin Gauguin, features specialties from Reunion Island in the Indian Ocean, including *curcuma* (chicken, CFP 1,300) and *Massalé de Thon* (spicy tuna, CFP 1,450). There's also good pizza (CFP 1,100–1,400), Chinese dishes (CFP 1,100–1,300), and fish (CFP 1,100–1,650). A large beer is CFP 500 and this is the only place with real ice cream (CFP 100 a scoop). The manager speaks some English—ask about free transportation from the wharf. The restaurant does laundry for yachties.

Restaurant Hoa Nui (tel. 92-73-63), next to a school on the road up the Vaioa Valley just west of town, serves Chinese and Marquesan dishes nightly at 1900 by reservation only (CFP 2,300). *Aranui* passengers are often served a meal here.

Information and Services

Ernest Teapuaoteani at the Mairie de Atuona (tel. 92-73-32) is a great source of information and he speaks good English.

Banque Socredo (tel. 92-73-54) is next to the Air Tahiti office. The post office, town hall, dental center, and hospital (tel. 92-73-75) are two

FRENCH POLYNESIA

FAMOUS RESIDENTS OF ATUONA

Atuona was made forever famous when Paul Gauguin came to live here in 1901. Despite the attentions of his 14-year-old mistress, Vaeoho, he died of syphilis a year later at age 55 and is buried in the cemetery above the town. When Tioka, Gauguin's neighbor, found him stretched out with one leg hanging over the side of his bed, he bit him on the head as the Marquesans do to see if he really was dead. No, there was no doubt. *"Ua mate Koke!"* he cried, and disappeared. Gauguin was constantly in conflict with the colonial authorities, who disapproved of his heavy drinking sessions with the locals. Just a week before his death, Gauguin was summarily convicted of "libel of a gendarme in the course of his official duties," fined, and sentenced to three months in prison.

The famous Belgian *chanson* singer Jacques Brel and his companion Maddly Bamy came to the Marquesas aboard his 18-meter yacht, the *Askoy II,* in 1975. Jacques decided to settle at Atuona and sold his boat to an American couple. Maddly, who had been a dancer on her native Guadeloupe, gave dancing lessons to the local girls, while Jacques ran an open-air cinema. His plane, nicknamed *Jojo,* was kept at Hiva Oa airport for trips to Papeete, 1,500 km southwest. The album *Brel 1977* on the Barclay label includes one of his last songs, "Les Marquises." In 1978, chain-smoker Brel died of lung cancer and was buried in Atuona cemetery near Gauguin.

blocks east with the gendarmerie (tel. 92-73-61) diagonally opposite.

Transportation

A lighthouse on the point between Tahauku Bay and Atuona looks south across Traitors Bay. Yachts anchor behind the breakwater in Tahauku harbor, two km east of the center of town. The *Taporo* and *Aranui* also tie up here. The gas station at the wharf has a well stocked grocery store (if you want bread, order it the day before).

In theory, the cabin cruiser *Te Pua O Mioi* leaves Atuona for Tahuata Tuesday at noon, but this boat is often laid up with mechanical problems.

The catamaran *Auona II* should leave Atuona

for Fatu Hiva Thursday at noon (CFP 4,000 pp) but it's often out of service.

Location David (Augustine Kaimuko, tel. 92-72-87), next to Magasin Chanson up from the museum, rents cars at around CFP 15,000 a day all inclusive. To hire a four-passenger Land Rover with driver from Atuona to Puama'u will run you CFP 20,000 for the vehicle.

Atuona Rent Car (tel. 92-76-07) has cars for a mere CFP 13,000 a day. You must call for a delivery.

Before renting a car, ask if the gas station at Tahauku wharf has any fuel available as it often runs out.

Airport

The airstrip (AUQ) is on a 441-meter-high plateau, eight km northeast of Atuona. In 1991 the runway was upgraded to allow it to receive direct ATR 42 flights from Papeete (via Nuku Hiva). Air Tahiti is at tel. 92-73-41.

It's a two-hour downhill walk from the airport to Atuona. The normal taxi fare from the airport to Atuona is CFP 1,800 pp each way, but the amount collected by the various hotels seems to vary, so check when booking.

Companies such as Taxi Marie-Thérèse (tel. 92-71-59) and Taxi Clark (tel. 92-71-33) should ask CFP 1,000 to Tahauku wharf, CFP 1,800 to the airport, CFP 8,000 to Taaoa, CFP 12,000 to Hanaiapa, CFP 20,000 to Puamau. In the case of the longer trips, this should be the price for the whole car round-trip.

THE NORTH COAST

A second village, **Puama'u,** is on the northeast coast of Hiva Oa, 30 km from Atuona over a winding mountain road. It's a good eight-hour walk from Atuona to Puama'u, up and down all the way. A few remote descendants of Gauguin are among the 300 people who live there today.

Aside from the village's golden beach, the main reason for coming are the five huge stone tikis to be seen on the **Me'ae Iiopona** among the breadfruit trees in the valley behind Puama'u, a 15-minute walk from the village soccer field. One named Takii stands 243 cm high—the largest old stone statue in the Marquesas. Notice the statue of the priestess who died in childbirth and the sculpted heads of victims of human sacrifice. The site was restored in 1991. You're supposed to pay the CFP 200 fee to visit the *me'ae* at Snack Aimee (tel. 92-71-53) on the waterfront.

You can stay in Puama'u at **Chez Heitaa** (Bernard and Marie-Antoinette Heitaa, tel. 92-72-27) in the upper part of the village, not far from the Me'ae Iipona. The two rooms with shared bath are CFP 5,720 pp including half board. Airport transfers are CFP 15,000 for up to four people. Horses are for hire at CFP 5,000.

The tombs of the last queen of the area and her family are behind the pension.

At **Hanaiapa** on the north coast, ask for William, who keeps a yachties' log. He's happy to have his infrequent visitors sign, and is generous with fresh fruit and vegetables. Barren **Hanamenu Bay** in the northwest corner of Hiva Oa is now uninhabited, but dozens of old stone platforms can still be seen. If you'd like to spend some time as a hermit in the desert, ask for Ozanne in Atuona, who has a house at Hanamenu he might be willing to rent. To the right of Ozanne's house is a small, crystal-clear pool. The trails into this area have become overgrown and it's now accessible only by boat.

Other Southern Islands

TAHUATA

Tahuata (population about 650) is just six km south of Hiva Oa across Bordelais Channel. Fifteen km long by nine km wide, 69-square-km Tahuata is the smallest of the six inhabited islands of the Marquesas. A 17-km track crosses the island from Motopu to Vaitahu, the main village on the west coast. The anchorage at Hana Moe Noa north of Vaitahu is protected from the ocean swells. There's a lovely white beach and the water here is clear, as no rivers run into this bay.

Archaeological sites exist in the Vaitahu Valley and there's a small collection of artifacts in the school opposite the post office in Vaitahu. Tahuata was the point of first contact between Polynesians and Europeans anywhere in the South Pacific. Mendaña anchored in Vaitahu Bay in 1595, followed by Captain Cook in 1774. Here too, Admiral Abel Dupetit-Thouars took possession of the Marquesas in 1842 and established a fort, despite strong resistance led by Chief Iotete.

Sights

The **Catholic church** at Vaitahu was completed in 1988 to mark the 150th anniversary of the arrival here of missionaries. It has the largest stained glass window in the territory. Local sculptor Damien Haturau carved the huge wooden statue of the Virgin above the church entrance from a 400-year-old *temanu* tree.

Hapatoni village, farther south, is picturesque, with a century-old *tamanu*-bordered road and petroglyphs in the Hanatahau Valley behind. Coral gardens are found offshore and white-sand beaches skirt the north side of the island.

Accommodations

Pension Fara (Marguerite Kokauani, tel. 92-92-84) in Vaitahu has five rooms with shared bath at CFP 3,500 pp with breakfast, plus CFP 2,000 for dinner.

Ask about **Chez Leonie Teraiharoa** (tel. 92-93-07 or 20-74-99) on a brownish beach a 15-minute walk west of Vaitahu. Rates for the five bungalows were unknown at press time.

Getting There

There's no airport on Tahuata. To charter a six-passenger boat to/from Atuona is CFP 20,000–25,000 (one hour). Small boats leave Hiva Oa for Tahuata almost daily, so ask around at the harbor on Takauku Bay near Atuona.

When operating, the cabin cruiser *Te Pua O Mioi*, belonging to the Commune of Tahautu (tel. 92-92-19), shuttles between Atuona and Vaitahu on Tuesday and Thursday (one hour,

CFP 1,000 pp each way). It leaves Tahuata around dawn, departing Hiva Oa for the return at noon. Southbound, take groceries with you.

FATU HIVA

Fatu Hiva (84 square km) is the southernmost and youngest of the Marquesas Islands, 56 km southeast of Tahuata. It's far wetter than the northern islands, and the vegetation is lush. Mount Tauaouoho (960 meters) is the highest point. Fatu Hiva was the first of the Marquesas to be seen by Europeans (Mendaña passed by in 1595). None landed until 1825 and Catholic missionaries couldn't convert the inhabitants until 1877. In 1937–1938 Thor Heyerdahl spent one year on this island with his young bride Liv and wrote a book called *Fatu Hiva,* describing their far from successful attempt "to return to a simple, natural life."

This is the most remote of the Marquesas, and only a few French officials are present. With 650 inhabitants, Fatu Hiva has only two villages, Omoa and Hanavave, in the former crater on the western side of the island. Surfing off the rocky beach at Omoa can be pretty exciting! Hanavave on the Bay of Virgins offers one of the most fantastic scenic spectacles in all of Polynesia, with tiki-shaped cliffs dotted with goats. Yachts usually anchor here. Horses and canoes are for hire in both villages.

Fatu Hiva is one of the last places in French Polynesia where tapa cloth is still widely made. Until the 1960s, Fatu Hiva tapa bore no designs, instead the human body was decorated with tattoos. Today a revival of the old crafts is taking place and it's again possible to buy not only wooden sculptures but painted tapa cloth. Hats and mats are woven from pandanus. *Monoï* oils are made from coconut oil, gardenia, jasmine, and sandalwood.

Fatu Hiva doesn't have any *no-nos,* but ample mosquitoes. If you plan on staying longer than four months, get some free anti-elephantiasis pills such as Notézine at any clinic.

© DAVID STANLEY

> *Hanavave on the Bay of Virgins offers one of the most fantastic scenic spectacles in all of Polynesia, with tiki-shaped cliffs dotted with goats.*

Activities

It takes about five hours to hike the 17-km dirt road linking Omoa and Hanavave, up and down over the mountains amid breathtaking scenery. It's a long gentle incline from Omoa to a 600-meter pass, followed by a very steep descent into Hanavave. **Vaiéé-Nui Falls** is a pleasant one-hour walk back into the valley from Hanavave. Unfortunately Hanavave is overrun by skinny half-starved dogs the locals use to hunt pigs.

Omoa is the main center for tapa production in all of French Polynesia. William Grelet has a small private museum with some exquisite woodcarvings behind the *mairie* and handicraft center at Omoa. A bakery and two small stores are also in Omoa.

Accommodations and Food

Several families in Omoa village take paying guests. **Chez Heimata** (Albertine Tetuanui; tel. 92-80-58) has two rooms at CFP 2,500 pp with breakfast, plus CFP 1,500 each for other meals. **Norma Ropati** (tel./fax 92-80-13) and **Cécile Gilmore** (tel. 92-80-54) rent rooms at similar rates.

Pension Chez Lionel (Lionel and Bernadette Cantois, tel./fax 92-80-80) at Omoa has one bungalow with cooking facilities at CFP 5,000 double.

Pension Manauea (Fernand Tholance, tel./fax 92-80-02), at the back of Omoa village toward the valley, has rooms at CFP 8,000/14,000 single/double including half board.

In Hanavave, **Pension Chez Noela** (Justine Pavaouau, tel./fax 92-80-60) has three rooms at CFP 3,000/4,000 single/double (meals available). Noela is a well-known Fatu Hiva woodcarver.

Getting There

There's no airstrip on Fatu Hiva but the Mairie de Fatu Hiva (tel. 92-80-23) operates the 30-passenger catamaran *Auona II* once a week between Atuona and Omoa. In past it has left Fatu Hiva on Tuesday and Thursday at 0600. From Atuona, it usually leaves Tuesday and Thursday at noon (ask), and on the return trip it may agree to drop you on Tahuata. The trip takes just over three hours and costs CFP 4,000 pp each way.

To hire a speedboat, such as the red and yellow *Rautea Nui* owned by Joel Coulon, from Omoa to Tahuata will cost around CFP 40,000 for the boat.

FRENCH POLYNESIA

Easter Island/ Rapa Nui

birdman with the first egg

Easter Island

The mystery of Easter Island (Isla de Pascua) and its indigenous inhabitants, the Rapanui, has intrigued travelers and archaeologists for many years. Where did these ancient people come from? How did they transport almost 1,000 giant statues from the quarry to their platforms? What cataclysmic event caused them to overthrow all they had erected with so much effort? And most important, what does it all mean? With the opening of Mataveri airport in 1967, Easter Island became more easily accessible, and many visitors now take the opportunity to pause and ponder the largest and most awesome collection of prehistoric monuments in the Pacific. This is one of the most evocative places you will ever visit. (Herein we follow the convention of spelling the island name Rapa Nui and its people and their language Rapanui.)

The Land

Barren and detached, Easter Island lies midway between Tahiti and Chile, 4,050 km from the former and 3,700 km from the latter. Pitcairn Island, 1,900 km west, is the nearest inhabited land. No other populated island on earth is as isolated as this. At 109°26' west longitude and 27°09' south latitude, it's the easternmost and almost the southernmost island of the South Pacific (Rapa Iti in French Polynesia is a bit farther south). Easter Island is triangular, with an extinct volcano at each corner. It measures 23 by 11 km, totaling 171 square km.

The interior consists of high plateaus and craters surrounded by coastal bluffs. Ancient lava flows from Maunga Terevaka (507 meters), the highest peak, covered the island, creating a rough, broken surface. Maunga Pukatikei and Rano Kau (to the east and south respectively) are nearly 400 meters high. Many parasitic craters exist on the southern and southeast flanks of Maunga Terevaka. Three of these, Rano Aroi,

row of massive *moai* on Ahu Tongariki

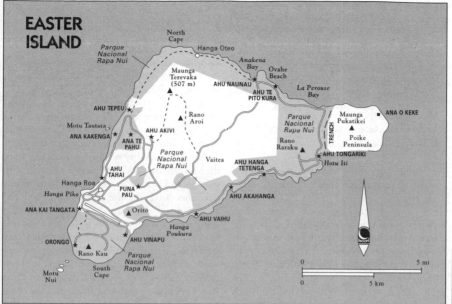

© DAVID STANLEY

Rano Raraku, and Rano Kau, contain crater lakes, with the largest (in Rano Kau) over a kilometer across. Since 1935 about 40 percent of the island, including the area around Rano Kau and much of the island's shoreline, has been set aside as **Parque Nacional Rapa Nui** administered by the Corporación Nacional Forestal (CONAF). In 1995 the park was added to UNESCO's World Heritage List, the first place in Chile to be so honored.

Small coral formations occur along the shoreline, but the lack of any continuous reef has allowed the sea to cut cliffs around much of the island. These bluffs are high where the waves encountered ashy material, low where they beat upon lava flows. Lava tubes and volcanic caves are other peculiarities of the island. The only sandy beaches are at Ovahe and Anakena, on the north coast.

Barren and detached, Easter Island lies midway between Tahiti and Chile, 4,050 km from the former and 3,700 km from the latter. Pitcairn Island, 1,900 km west, is the nearest inhabited land. No other populated island on earth is as isolated as this.

Climate

The subtropical climate is moderated by the cool Humboldt current and the annual average temperature is 20.3°C. The hottest month is February; the coolest are July and August. Winds can make it feel cooler. The climate is moist, and some rain falls 140 days a year. March to June are the rainiest months; July to October are generally the coolest. August to December are the driest months, although heavy rains are possible year-round (much of it falling at night). Drizzles and mist are common, and a heavy dew forms overnight. Snow and frost are unknown, however. The porous volcanic rock dries out quickly, so the dampness need not deter the well-prepared hiker.

Flora and Fauna

The forests of Easter Island were wiped out by the indigenous inhabitants long ago, and during

EASTER ISLAND HIGHLIGHTS

Museo Antropológico, Hanga Roa: exhibition, shopping, information
Orongo: archaeology, scenery, hiking, volcano
Rano Raraku quarry: archaeology, statues, hiking, scenery
Ahu Tongariki: statues, scenery
Anakena Beach: swimming, archaeology, hiking

the 19th century sheep finished off most of the remaining native vegetation. The last indigenous *toromiro* tree died in the 1960s and attempts to reintroduce the species from overseas botanical gardens have largely failed. Grasslands now envelop the green, windswept landscape; few endemic plants survive. Large tracts of eucalyptus were planted in the 1940s and 1950s. The crater lakes feature thick, floating bogs of peat; *nga'ata (totora)* reeds related to South American species surround and completely cover their surfaces. Pollen studies have determined that these reeds have existed here for at least 30,000 years.

Most of the native birds, even the sooty terns *(manutara)* that once nested on Motu Nui in their thousands, were wiped out by humans long ago. The brown hawks *(manu toketoke)*, small gray finches *(manu puhi)*, and tinamous *(vivi)* have all been introduced from the continent in recent years. The numerous dogs encountered in Hanga Roa are also new arrivals. Most are inoffensive and the others will soon retreat if you pretend to pick up a stone. About 4,000 horses and cattle range across the island, damaging the archaeological sites.

HISTORY

Polynesian Genesis

It's believed that Easter Island was colonized around A.D. 300 by Polynesians from the Marquesas Islands or Mangareva, as part of an eastward migratory trend that originated in Southeast Asia around 2000 B.C. Here developed one of the most remarkable cultures in all of Polynesia.

Long platforms or *ahu* bearing slender statues known as *moai* were built near the coasts, with long retaining walls facing the sea. Each *ahu* generally carried four to six *moai* towering four to eight meters high. These statues, or *aringa ora* (living faces), were portraits of known ancestors, and they looked inland towards the villages to project the mana (protective power) of the *aku-aku* (ancestral spirits) they represented. About 887 *moai* have been counted on Easter Island, of which 288 were actually erected on the *ahu*.

The vast majority of *moai* were all cut from the same quarry at Rano Raraku, the yellowish volcanic tuff shaped by stone tools. Some writers have theorized that the statues were "walked" to their platforms by a couple of dozen men using ropes to lean the upright figures from side to side while moving forward; others claim they were pulled along on a sledge or log rollers. Some statues bore a large cylindrical topknot *(pukao)* carved from the reddish stone of Puna Pau. Eyes of cut coral were fitted into the faces. South of Puna Pau, Maunga Orito contains black obsidian, which the islanders used for weapons and tools.

Other unique features of Easter Island are the strange canoe-shaped house foundations *(hare paenga)* with holes for wall supports, the so-called chicken houses *(hare moa)* thought to be tombs, and the incised wooden tablets *(rongorongo)*, the only ancient form of writing known in Oceania. Only 25 examples survive, and Dr. Steven Roger Fischer, Director of the Institute of Polynesian Languages and Literatures in Auckland, has shown how the neat rows of symbols on the boards record procreation chants. Some scholars believe that the development of *rongorongo* was prompted by early exposure to European writing.

The oldest *ahu* (Ahu Tahai) is dated 690 A.D. and the most recent (Ahu Akivi) dated to 1460, after which the focus of the culture shifted from statue carving to the "birdman" cult at Orongo. Overpopulation, depletion of resources, and famine may explain the change. In 1774 Captain Cook reported internecine fighting among the islanders, with statues toppled and their platforms damaged, and by 1840 all of the *moai* had been thrown off their *ahu,* either by earthquakes or rival tribes.

Fantasy and Fact

The first comprehensive explorations of Easter Island were carried out by Katherine Routledge in 1914–1915, Alfred Métraux in 1934, and Thor Heyerdahl in 1955–1956. Earlier, in 1947, Heyerdahl had achieved notoriety by sailing 6,500 km from South America to the Tuamotu Islands in a balsa raft, the *Kon Tiki.* His 1955 Norwegian Archaeological Expedition was intended to uncover proof that Polynesia was populated from South America, and Heyerdahl developed a romantic legend that still excites the popular imagination today.

Heyerdahl postulated that Easter Island's first inhabitants (the "long ears") arrived from South America around A.D. 380. They dug a three-km-long defensive trench isolating the Poike Peninsula and built elevated platforms of perfectly fitted basalt blocks. Heyerdahl noted a second wave of immigrants, also from South America, who destroyed the structures of the first group and replaced them with the *moai*-bearing *ahu* mentioned above. Heyerdahl saw the toppling of the *moai* as a result of the arrival of Polynesian invaders (the "short ears") who arrived from the Marquesas and conquered the original inhabitants in 1680. According to Heyerdahl, the birdman cult, centering on the sacred village of Orongo, was initiated by the victors.

Modern archaeologists discount the South American theory and see the statues as having developed from the typical backrests of Polynesian *marae.* The civil war would have resulted from overexploitation of the island's environment, leading to starvation, cannibalism, and the collapse of the old order. Previous destruction of the forests would have deprived the inhabitants of the means of building canoes to sail off in search of other islands. The Poike trench was only a series of discontinuous ditches dug to grow crops, probably taro. Despite decades of study by some of the world's top archaeologists, no South American artifacts have ever been excavated on the island.

Heyerdahl argued that the perfectly fitted,

a canoe-shaped building foundation at Ahu Tahai in Hanga Roa

polished stonework of the stone wall of Ahu Vinapu (Ahu Tahira) was analogous to pre-Incan stone structures in Cuzco and Machu Picchu, but fine stonework can be found elsewhere in Polynesia (for example, the *langi*, or stone-lined royal burial mounds, of Mu'a on Tongatapu). Easter Island's walls are a facade holding in rubble fill, while Peruvian stonework is solid block construction. Recent DNA evidence proves that the Rapanui originated in Southeast Asia. In academic circles Heyerdahl (who passed away in 2002) was always considered a maverick who started out with a conclusion to prove instead of doing his homework first. And his whole hypothesis is rather insulting to the island's present Polynesian population, as it denied them any credit for the archaeological wonders we admire today.

A sequel to this story occurred in 1999 when members of the Polynesian Voyaging Society sailed the catamaran *Hokule'a* from Hawaii to Easter Island and back using the traditional navigational techniques the ancients would have used. By crossing from Mangareva to Rapa Nui in just 17.5 days, the *Hokule'a* demonstrated vividly the mastery of the seas for which the Polynesians are renowned.

European Penetration

European impact on Easter Island was among the most dreadful in the history of the Pacific. When Jacob Roggeveen arrived on Easter Sunday 1722, there were about 4,000 Rapanui (though the population had once been as high as 20,000). Roggeveen's landing party opened fire and killed a dozen islanders; then the great white explorer sailed off. González (1770), Cook (1774), and La Pérouse (1786) were the next to call, but contacts with whalers, sealers, and slavers were sporadic until 1862 when a fleet of eight Peruvian blackbirders kidnapped some 1,400 Rapanui to work in the coastal sugar plantations of Peru and to dig guano on the offshore islands. Among those taken were the king and the entire learned class. Missionaries and diplomats in Lima protested to the Peruvian government, and eventually 15 surviving islanders made it back to their homes, where they sparked a deadly smallpox epidemic.

French Catholic missionaries took up residence on Easter Island in 1866 and succeeded in converting the survivors; businessmen from Tahiti arrived soon after and acquired property for a sheep ranch. Both groups continued the practice of removing Rapanui from the island: the former sent followers to their mission on Mangareva, the latter sent laborers to their plantations on Tahiti. Returnees from Tahiti introduced leprosy. By 1877 the total population had been reduced to 110. One of the business partners, Jean Dutrou-Bornier, had the missionaries evicted in 1871 and ran the island as he wished until his murder by a Rapanui in 1876. The estate then went into litigation, which lasted until 1893.

The Colonial Period

In 1883 Chile defeated Peru and Bolivia in the War of the Pacific. With their new imperial power, the Chileans annexed Easter Island in 1888, erroneously believing that the island would become a port of call after the opening of the Panama Canal. Their lack of knowledge is illustrated by plans to open a naval base when no potential for harbor construction existed on the island. As this became apparent, they leased most of it to a British wool operation, which ran the island as a company estate until the lease was revoked in 1953. The tens of thousands of sheep devastated the vegetation, causing soil erosion, and stones were torn from the archaeological sites to build walls and piers. During this long period, the Rapanui were forbidden to go beyond the Hanga Roa boundary wall without company permission, to deter them from stealing the sheep.

In 1953 the Chilean Navy took over and continued the same style of paternal rule. The islanders remained confined to area around Hanga Roa until 1966. After local protests, the moderate Christian Democratic government of Chile permitted the election of a local mayor and council in 1965. Elections were terminated by Pinochet's 1973 military coup, and Easter Island, along with the rest of Chile, suffered autocratic rule until the restoration of democracy in 1990. In 1984 archaeologist Sergio Rapu became the first Rapanui governor of Easter Island, and all subsequent governors have also been

Rapanui. The 1993 filming of Kevin Costner's US$20 million epic *Rapa Nui* brought the world to Easter Island in the way the 1962 filming of *Mutiny on the Bounty* transformed Tahiti.

GOVERNMENT

Easter Island is part of the Fifth Region of Chile, with Valparaíso (Chile) as capital. The president of Chile nominates the governor; the mayor and council are elected locally. Policy decisions affecting the island's development are made by officials in faraway Chile. Most Rapanui leaders want Easter Island made a separate region of Chile, a change that would greatly enhance local autonomy. This could happen when ex-dictator Pinochet finally dies and his 1980 constitution is replaced or fundamentally changed. The people of Easter Island pay no taxes and all government services on the island are underwritten by Chile. If the island were to become self-governing as a separate region, this might change.

The story is told that during the annexation ceremony in 1888, King Atamu Tekena leaned forward and pulled out a handful of grass, which he gave to Captain Policarpo Toro with the words "this is for you." Then he picked up a handful of soil and put it in his pocket saying "this is for us." The Rapanui of today are becoming more assertive in reclaiming their rights and land.

Politics

After the return to democracy in Chile an indigenous rights group, the Consejo de Ancianos (Council of Elders), was created to represent the island's 36 original families. In 1994 the Consejo split into two factions over the question of land rights: the original Consejo No. 1 headed by former mayor Alberto Hotus and a radical Consejo No. 2 led by Mario Tuki.

Most of Easter Island's land is still held by the Chilean State but any local will be able to tell you which part of the island once belonged to his/her original clan. In 1994 supporters of Consejo No. 2 set up a tent city outside the church in Hanga Roa with banners demanding the return of indigenous lands. To the embarrassment of Chile, this protest lasted five years.

In 1999 Chilean officials finally persuaded the demonstrators to take down their banners in exchange for the promise of a land redistribution. A Comisión de Desarrollo (development committee) comprised of six elected Rapanui, six members of various government agencies, the governor, and the mayor was established under Chile's Indigenous Law. In November 2001 clear title to more than 1,400 hectares of land on the slopes of Maunga Terevaka was granted to 472 Rapanui individuals or families, but the redistribution was done by lottery with no attempt to match current residents with ancestral lands. In 2003 another 2,000 hectares of land south of Vaitea was due to be handed out in the same way.

These events have not pleased everyone. Many people were given rocky, eucalyptus-covered plots unsuitable for agriculture or cattle grazing. Only about 20 percent of the island is being distributed and members of Consejo No. 2 have demanded that the government turn over most of the island, despite the very negative effect this would have on the environment and ancient sites. The rich farmlands around Vaitea, which have very little in the way of archaeological remain, are not on the table.

Hanga Roa is still the only sizable permanent settlement on Rapa Nui, but unserviced shacks are springing up all over the island. Fields are being plowed or bulldozed without any environmental impact studies being carried out and houses have been constructed on or near archaeological sites. As you travel around the island, watch for the Rapa Nui flags depicting a red *reimiro* or crescent-shaped pectoral on a white background that fly above the squatter camps.

The most provocative occupations have been inside Parque Nacional Rapa Nui itself, but the park authorities hesitate to expel anyone out of fear of provoking major unrest or losing their jobs. In 1999, the park's head, José Miguel Ramírez, was sacked for objecting to park land's being redistributed. Among the Rapanui themselves opinions on how to handle the land issue differ sharply, with many people concerned that redistributions could have a negative impact on tourism by damaging the visual esthetics of the island.

At times officials in far-off Chile have come up

EASTER ISLAND/RAPA NUI

with reckless development plans of their own, such as a proposed "monumental" lighthouse on a hill overlooking the airport flight path to proclaim Chilean sovereignty. The Sociedad Agrícola y Servicios Ltda. (SASIPA), which provides water and electricity to the island and operates a large cattle ranch, wants to exploit its valuable lands at Vaitea for a golf course, luxury resort, and botanical garden. "Progress" is catching up with this remote island and no coherent management plan exists for Easter Island as a whole, no long pants in paradise. It's just one special-interest group clawing against another, the world on a small scale.

THE PEOPLE

The original name of Easter Island was Te Pito o Te Henua, "navel of the world." The Rapanui believe they are descended from Hotu Matu'a, who arrived by canoe at Anakena Beach from Te Hiva, the ancestral homeland. The statues were raised by magic. The original inhabitants wore tapa clothing and were tattooed like Marquesans; in fact, there's little doubt that their forebears arrived from Eastern Polynesia. The language of the Rapanui is Austronesian, closely related to all the other languages of Polynesia, with no South American elements.

The Rapanui have interbred liberally with visitors for more than a century, but the Polynesian element is still strong. Three-quarters of the 3,800 people on Easter Island are Rapanui or Rapanui-related. The island receives around 20,000 tourists a year from Chile, Europe, the United States, and Japan, and many Rapanui earn a living as innkeepers, guides, drivers, and craftspeople. Others are employed by the Chilean government. About a thousand *continentales* (mainlanders) also live here, most of them government employees and small shopkeepers. Many mainlanders live in Mataveri south of the airstrip.

Since 1966 the Rapanui have been Chilean citizens, and quite a few have emigrated to the mainland. About 1,200 Rapanui live abroad, most of them in Chile with about 150 on Tahiti. People generally speak Rapanui in private, Spanish in public, French if they've been to Tahiti,

and English almost not at all. Spanish is gradually supplanting Rapanui among the young, and it's feared the language will go out of everyday use within a generation or two. Television is diluting the local culture.

Conduct

The archaeological sites on Easter Island are fragile and easily damaged by thoughtless actions, such as climbing on the fallen statues or walking on petroglyphs. The volcanic tuff is soft and easily broken off or scuffed. Incredibly, some people have scraped ancient rock carvings with stones to make them easier to photograph! Cruise ships can unload hundreds of people a day, and the large groups often spin out of control, swarming over the quarry at Rano Raraku or standing on the stone house tops at Orongo (several of which have collapsed in recent years). The national park has had to erect stone walls around many sites to keep out rental vehicles and local residents have organized voluntary projects to pick up trash discarded by tourists.

Though it may seem that these places are remote from the world of high-impact consumer tourism, they are in fact endangered by the selfishness of some visitors and those locals who would profit from them. It's strictly prohibited to remove any ancient artifacts (such as spear heads, fishhooks, or basalt chisels) from the island. The warning signs erected in the park are there for a reason, and the human bones occasionally encountered on the *ahu* and in the caves deserve to be left in peace.

Public Holidays and Festivals

Public holidays in Chile include New Year's Day (January 1), Easter Friday (March or April), Labor Day (May 1), Battle of Iquique Day (May 21), Corpus Christi (June), Saints Peter and Paul Day (June 29), Ascension Day (August 15), National Reconciliation Day (first Monday in September), Independence Day (September 18), Army Day (September 19), Columbus Day (October 12), All Saints' Day (November 1), Conception Day (December 8), and Christmas Day (December 25).

In late January or February is the carnival-like

Tapati Rapa Nui festival, with traditional dancing, sporting events, canoe races, a horse race, fishing tournament, handicraft and agricultural exhibitions, statue-carving contest, shell-necklace-stringing competition, body-painting contest, *kai-kai* (string figure) performances, mock battles, feasts, and the election of Queen Tapati Rapa Nui (who is dramatically crowned on a spotlit Ahu Tahai). A unique triathlon at Rano Raraku involves male contestants in body paint who paddle tiny reed craft across the lake, pick up bunches of bananas on poles and run around the crater and up the hill, where they grab big bundles of *nga'ata* reeds to carry down and

around the lake before a final swim across. There's also *haka pei,* which involves young men sliding down a grassy mountainside on banana-trunk sleds at great speed. Colored lights are strung up along the main street. Needless to say, all flights immediately before and after the festival are fully booked far in advance.

The Tokerau Singing Festival is in July. Chilean Independence Day (September 18) is celebrated with parades and a *fonda* (carnival). Everyone takes three days off for this big fiesta. On the day of their patron saint, the main families stage a traditional feast *(curanto),* complete with an earth oven *(umu ta'o).*

Sights of Easter Island

Hanga Roa

The **Catholic church** (1964) in the center of town is notable for its woodcarvings. Buried next to the church entrance is Father Sebastián Englert, author of *Hotu Matu'a's Land* (1948), who served as parish priest from 1935 until his death in 1969 at the age of 80. Adjacent is the grave of Eugène Eyraud (1820–1868), who introduced Christianity and tuberculosis to the island.

The small boat harbor at **Caleta Hanga Roa** is appealing for its three restored statues, the row of local fishing boats, and the numerous surfers bobbing on the waves just offshore. North along the coast is **Hanga Vare Vare,** a public park featuring contemporary statues, petroglyphs, and sheltered places to swim.

Just north of town at **Ahu Tahai** are three *ahu,* one bearing five restored *moai,* and a large statue complete with a red 10-ton topknot reerected by the late Dr. William Mulloy in 1968. The statue's "eyes" are crude copies recently cemented in place for tourists. The Rapanui once launched their canoes down the ramp leading to the water between the *ahu.* This is a great place to be at sunset.

The **Museo Antropológico Sebastián Englert** (tel. 551-020; Tues.–Fri. 0930–1230/1400–1730, Sat.–Sun. 0930–1230; admission US$2, students US$1), near Ahu Tahai, first opened in 1973 but was modernized and rearranged in 1999. The

museum has an excellent collection of old carvings and artifacts, plus a scale model of the island. Ask to borrow the English translation of the Spanish explanations, and don't miss the white coral and red scoria eye of the *moai* found at Anakena in 1978. The William Mulloy Research Library (weekdays 0930–1230/1400–1730) is adjacent to the museum.

North of Hanga Roa

Four km up the dirt road leading north from the museum is Motu Tautara, the first of two long lava islands pointing straight out from the coast. As you head down to the viewpoint over the islands, watch carefully on the left for the tiny entrance to **Ana Kakenga,** the Cave of the Two Windows. It's not far from the coastal road, near a curve in the track, and is easily missed. This remarkable lava tube gets much larger inside, with two openings in the cliffs directly above the sea.

A km north again, near where the rough coastal road turns sharply inland, is unrestored **Ahu Tepeu** and its fallen *moai.* The site is between the stone marker and the coastal cliffs, beyond the foundations of some canoe-shaped and round houses. Go around to the back of the ruined *ahu* to appreciate the megalithic stonework. In ancient times this area belonged to the powerful Miru clan.

Ana Te Pahu, a km southeast of Ahu Tepeu on the road inland, is one of the most spectacular

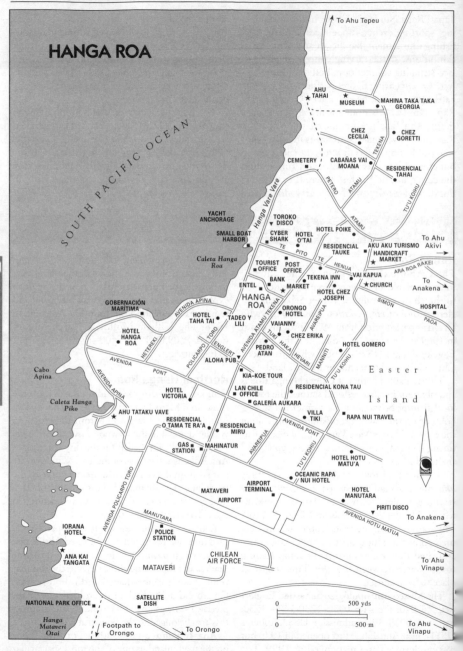

HANGA ROA

To Ahu Tepeu

SOUTH PACIFIC OCEAN

AHU TAHAI ★
MUSEUM ▼
MAHINA TAKA TAKA GEORGIA
CHEZ CECILIA
CHEZ GORETTI
CEMETERY
CABAÑAS VAI MOANA
RESIDENCIAL TAHAI

Hanga Vare Vare

PETERO
ATAMU
ATAMU
TEKENA
TU'U KOIHU

YACHT ANCHORAGE
TOROKO DISCO ▼
HOTEL POIKE
SMALL BOAT HARBOR
CYBER SHARK
HOTEL O'TAI
RESIDENCIAL TAUKE
AKU AKU TURISMO
HANDICRAFT MARKET
To Ahu Akivi

Caleta Hanga Roa

TOURIST OFFICE
POST OFFICE
TE PITO
TE HENUA
VAI KAPUA
ARA ROA RAKEI
To Anakena

ENTEL
BANK
MARKET
TEKENA INN
HOTEL CHEZ JOSEPH
CHURCH ★
SIMON
HOSPITAL
PAOA

GOBERNACIÓN MARITIMA
AVENIDA APINA
ORONGO HOTEL
VAIANNY
AVAREIPUA
MANNITI

HANGA ROA
HOTEL TAHA TAI
TADEO Y LILI
TUKI
HAKAI
HEVARI
CHEZ ERIKA
HOTEL GOMERO

HOTEL HANGA ROA
HETEREKI
POLICARPO TORO
ENGLERT
PEDRO ATAN
TU'U KOIHU

Cabo Apina
AVENIDA PONT
ALOHA PUB

Easter

Island

Caleta Hanga Piko
AVENIDA APINA
AVENIDA
KIA-KOE TOUR
RESIDENCIAL KONA TAU

HOTEL VICTORIA
LAN CHILE OFFICE
GALERÍA AUKARA

AHU TATAKU VAVE ★
RESIDENCIAL O TAMA TE RA'A
RESIDENCIAL MIRU
VILLA TIKI
RAPA NUI TRAVEL

GAS STATION
MAHINATUR
AVAREIPUA
AVENIDA PONT

TU'U KOIHU
HOTEL HOTU MATU'A

OCEANIC RAPA NUI HOTEL

IORANA HOTEL
MANUTARA
MATAVERI AIRPORT
AIRPORT TERMINAL
HOTEL MANUTARA
PIRITI DISCO
To Anakena

ANA KAI TANGATA ★
AVENIDA POLICARPO TORO
POLICE STATION
CHILEAN AIR FORCE
AVENIDA HOTU MATUA
To Ahu Vinapu

MATAVERI

NATIONAL PARK OFFICE ■
SATELLITE DISH

Hanga Mataveri Otai
Footpath to Orongo
To Orongo

0   500 yds
0   500 m

To Ahu Vinapu

lava tubes on the island. There's a stone marker but you'll know the cave from the banana trees and taro growing up through openings in the rock. You could drive a large truck a long distance through this cave (have a flashlight with you).

Inland again via the dirt track is **Ahu Akivi** (Siete Moai), with seven statues restored in 1960 by Dr. Mulloy. The seven much-photographed *moai* once overlooked a village but they now stare silently out to sea. Unfortunately, agricultural development in this area has obliterated many archaeological remains. If you're walking, the dirt track which begins opposite the nearby farm entrance, a bit back toward the coast, runs directly south to Hanga Roa. This 13-km circle hike can be done in a day if you're fit and have food and water with you.

Rano Kau and Orongo

From Hanga Roa, the six-km trip south to Orongo and the vast, circular crater of Rano Kau can be done in a morning, but take along a lunch and make a day of it if you have the time. On the

way, just past the Iorana Hotel, at the foot of the cliff near the water, is **Ana Kai Tangata,** the Cannibal Cave. Since the cave faces west, the paintings of birds gracing the cave's ceiling are best photographed in the afternoon.

The road to Orongo swings left and up the side of 316-meter Rano Kau, but if you're on foot look for the shady footpath on the right which begins immediately after the CONAF office and climbs through the forest. Otherwise, a taxi from Hanga Roa to the summit should cost US$5–6 one way and you can easily walk back. Guavas (an edible round yellow fruit with a pink interior) grow wild along the side of the road to Orongo.

A one-time admission of US$10 (or a bit less if you pay in pesos) is charged at an office up at the entrance to Orongo. The entry fee may seem stiff, but all the other sites on the island are free, and CONAF is desperately short of funds needed to protect and maintain Easter Island's monuments. Save your receipt if you plan a repeat visit up this way.

the colorful crater of Rano Kau adjacent to Orongo

Orongo was the main ceremonial center on the island and many high-relief carvings of frigate bird-headed men are on the rock outcrops. The 47 basalt slab dwellings here (restored by Dr. Mulloy in 1974–1976) were used by island chiefs and participants during the birdman festivals, the last of which occurred in 1866. Every September a race was staged to the farthest offshore island, **Motu Nui,** to find the first egg of the migratory sooty tern *(manutara)*. The winning swimmer was proclaimed birdman *(tangata manu)* and thought to have supernatural powers.

Some of the highest sea cliffs on the island are on Orongo's south side and it's risky to try to hike around the volcano. The island's original vegetation is best preserved inside the crater itself and a good alternative is to hike the 250 meters down to the water's edge. The trail begins at the signposted viewpoint over Rano Kao. On your way back to town, it's possible to cut back toward Ahu Vinapu along the south side of the airstrip.

East of Hanga Roa

Five km from Hanga Roa via the road along the north side of the airstrip are the 11 fallen *moai* and fine Peruvianlike stone walls of the two *ahu* at **Ahu Vinapu.** According to Heyerdahl, the perfectly fitted stonework of one platform dates from the earliest period and is due to contact with South America. Most authorities dispute this claim and suggest it was a later development by the skilled Polynesian stonemasons. This fascinating site is just south of the white oil tanks at the east end of the airport runway.

An easy half day walk is to **Puna Pau,** where the topknots were quarried. The road inland from the north side of the church is the shortest way to go, but you must turn right on the back road to Anakena (ask). About 20 red topknots are in the quarry at Puna Pau, the largest weighing 11 tons. After seeing the topknots, climb to the three crosses atop neighboring Maunga Tangaroa

(270 meters) for a great view of the center of the island. A pilgrimage is held here on Good Friday.

South Coast

Although many of the enigmatic statues *(moai)* are concentrated at moss-covered Rano Raraku (the statue quarry), they are found all around the island. Ninety-two important archaeological sites have been identified along the south coast alone. The stone walls seen at various places date from the English sheep ranch. The tour buses generally stop to visit the eight *moai* laying facedown at **Ahu Vaihu,** eight km east of Hanga Roa. The first king of the island, Hotu Matu'a, is buried at **Ahu Akahanga,** 3.5 km beyond Ahu Vaihu, where over a dozen toppled statues are seen.

> *The top sight on the island is certainly Rano Raraku, an extinct volcano 18 km east of Hanga Roa. The huge sculpture park here contains the island's most finely chiseled* **moai,** *including 70 standing on the inner or outer slopes of the crater and another 30 laying facedown on the ground.*

The top sight on the island is certainly **Rano Raraku,** an extinct volcano 18 km east of Hanga Roa. The huge sculpture park here contains the island's most finely chiseled *moai,* including 70 standing on the inner or outer slopes of the crater and another 30 laying facedown on the ground. A kneeling statue called Tukuturi on the east side of Rano Raraku is unusual. In all, 397 *moai* are still at the quarry in various stages of completion, allowing one to study the process. A few of the unfinished *moai* still attached to the cliffs resemble the reclining Buddhas of Thailand; one unhewn giant measures 21.6 meters long. Work on the statues ended suddenly, and many were abandoned en route to their *ahu.* From the summit of Rano Raraku, you can see clearly several dozen scattered along the ancient Ara O Te Moai, the Way of the Moai to the coast at Ahu Hanga Tetenga. Be aware that the quarry is usually crowded with tour groups around midday—if you arrive early or late you'll have this magical area all to yourself.

After climbing Rano Raraku, continue to nearby **Ahu Tongariki** at Hotu Iti, 20 km from Hanga Roa. This site was ravaged by a huge tsunami in 1960 that tossed the 15 massive statues around like cordwood. In 1994 Chilean archaeologists reconstructed the 200-meter-long *ahu* and reerected the *moai* using an enormous crane donated by the Japanese crane manufacturer Tadano. Some extraordinary petroglyphs of turtles and fish may be seen on the bedrock close to the *ahu* and at a nearby turn in the main road. The cliffs of the Poike Peninsula loom behind Ahu Tongariki.

North Coast

The tallest *moai* ever to stand on Easter Island is at **Ahu Te Pito Kura** on the north coast by La Pérouse Bay. The toppled 10-meter-long statue nicknamed "Paro" lies facedown beside the *ahu*, awaiting restoration. An egg-shaped stone next to the *ahu* is called Te Pito o Te Henua, meaning the Navel of the World. It's alleged that Hotu Matu'a brought the stone with him from Te Hiva, the legendary homeland of the Rapanui. The stone is believed to have magical powers.

The inviting white sands of palm-fringed **Anakena Beach** are 20 km northeast of Hanga Roa via the paved central highway or 30 km via Rano Raraku. The national park has set up picnic tables, barbecue pits, toilets, and a campground here, and many locals come to swim or fish on Sunday. Anakena is the traditional disembarkation point of Hotu Matu'a. The one *moai* at **Ahu Ature Huki** here was reerected by Thor Heyerdahl in 1956, as is indicated on a bronze plaque—the first statue to be restored on the island. **Ahu Nau Nau** at Anakena bears seven *moai*, four with topknots. During the restoration of this *ahu* in 1978, archaeologist Sergio Rapu discovered the famous white coral eyes of the statues.

Hiking

Easter Island offers many outstanding hiking opportunities, but take PABA sunscreen, a wide-brimmed hat, and sturdy boots as the terrain is rough and there's almost no shade. A folding umbrella could also come in handy. Ample food and water are essential as none are available outside Hanga Roa.

One of the most intriguing and practical hikes is along the rocky northwest coast from **Anakena to Hanga Roa.** If you know a bit of Spanish, you should be able to hire a taxi to Anakena for the peso equivalent of US$6–8 one way, then it will take a good six hours to walk back to town along the horse track around the outer edge of Maunga Terevaka. You'll pass several lava tube caves and ruined *ahu* with fallen *moai,* but the real attraction here is the dramatic scenery, which is at its best around Hanga Oteo.

You can also hike up a jeep track up to the summit of **Maunga Terevaka** itself. The route begins near Ahu Akivi (not the road closest to the *ahu* but the other one 20 meters south). From the grassy 507-meter summit there's a rare 360° horizon view and a sweeping panorama of the entire island. Beyond the large eucalyptus forest just southeast of the summit, seven km from Ahu Akivi, is Rapa Nui's shallowest crater lake, Rano Aroi. From the lake one can follow the bed of a usually dry stream down through the fragrant forests another four km to the former English sheep farm at Vaitea.

SPORTS AND RECREATION

The **scuba diving** off Easter Island is not for beginners as one must dive in the open sea and the water is cool (Nov.–April is warmest). On the plus side are the unique caves, walls, corals, and fish.

The **Orca Diving Center** (tel. 550-877 or 550-375, fax 550-448), opposite the small boat harbor at Caleta Hanga Roa, is run by Michel García, a noted underwater photographer who arrived here in 1979. Michel and his brother Henri charge US$50/80 for one/two tanks (US$35 without gear). Certification is mandatory; otherwise take an introductory lesson for US$60. Their two-hour snorkeling trip to Motu Nui is US$30 pp (minimum of two). A three-hour boat trip to the north coast costs US$45. Orca also rents ocean kayaks at US$15/25 a half day for a single/double kayak, surfboards at US$20 a half day, and bodyboards at US$15 a half day.

Mike Rapu Diving (tel. 551-055), right next to Orca Diving on Caleta Hanga Roa, also does scuba diving at US$50 a tank (US$40 a tank after three tanks). It's US$65 for night dives.

The boat trip to the *motu* costs US$30 pp and is offered every Thursday at 0930.

Surfers will find a couple of consistent waves adjacent to town, such as the rights at Caleta Hanga Roa and Ahu Tahai and the left at Hanga Mataveri Otai. On the south side of the island, a powerful right plows into the lava at Hanga Poukura. Some of the highest walls are a couple of kilometers east at Cabo Koe

Koe near Ahu Vaihu. Summer is the best season on the north coast, winter on the south (especially March–September).

Horseback riding is fun, and at about US$25/35 a half/full day, it's reasonable. Anakena is too far to go by horse and return in a day anyway, so look upon riding more as a change of pace than as a way of getting around. The area north of Hanga Roa is ideal to explore by horse.

Practicalities

ACCOMMODATIONS

The median price for guesthouse accommodation in the high season (Nov.–March) is US$35/50/75 single/double/triple. In the low season, subtract US$10 from these rates. The rooms are clean and simple, often facing a garden, and most have private bath. Many of the places called "hotels" are only larger guesthouses and virtually all are single story affairs. The fancy five-star resorts so common in French Polynesia haven't arrived here yet.

All prices include a continental breakfast, but for a full English breakfast you'll have to add US$5–10 pp. Beware if something extra is "offered," as you could end up paying an additional US$40 for one small frozen lobster. If you're asked to choose a meal plan, take only breakfast and dinner as it's a nuisance to have to come back for lunch. You can buy picnic fare at local stores. Unfortunately few places offer cooking facilities.

If you haven't booked a package, accommodations are easily arranged upon arrival as most of the *residenciales* (guesthouses) have booking counters in the baggage collection hall at the airport. Once something is arranged you'll be given a free lift to the place. Don't promise to stay more than one night until you've seen the room and are happy. Many rooms are priced per person, which is a good deal if you're alone.

Room prices fluctuate according to supply and demand, and when things are slow bargaining is possible. During the low season April–October the large hotels stand almost empty and rates are discounted as much as 50 percent. The peak season

with the highest visitor levels is November–February; June is the slackest month. More rooms are available than there are airline seats to fill them, so unless you're very fussy or specific about where you want to stay, reservations are not required, even during the Tapati Rapa Nui festival. You'll just have to pay more when it's busy.

If you want the security of a reservation, the best established travel agency on Easter Island itself is **Mahinatur** (Benito Rapahango, tel./fax 100-220) on Ave. Hotu Matu'a near the airport. Also highly recommended is **Rapa Nui Travel** (Conny Martin, tel. 100-548, fax 100-165, www.rapanuitravel.com). Both can book hotel accommodations, excursions, and rental vehicles in advance, and their services are used by most overseas tour operators. **Chile Hotels** (www.chile-hotels.com/easteris.htm) also handles such bookings. All of the properties listed below (or anyone on the island) can be faxed at fax 56-32/100-105, the Entel telephone office, which will call the hotel and ask it to come and get the fax. (Websites and email addresses are listed in the Easter Island Internet Resources sidebar in this chapter.)

Virtually everyone staying at the large hotels will have been put there by a travel agent or tour operator. Independent travelers invariably choose the smaller hotels and *residenciales,* which are much better value. The rack rates at places such as Hotel Iorana, Hotel Manutara, Hotel Hotu Matu'a, Hotel Hanga Roa, and Hotel Taha Tai are above what their rooms are worth. Especially avoid Hotel Hanga Roa, which has a dilapidated old wing, and Hotel Manutara, which is buffeted by rock music from a nearby disco on Friday and Saturday nights. Hotel Iorana is inconveniently far from everything but has some of the best rooms on the island.

If you're on a very low budget, ask about camping at a *residencial*. Residencial Chez Cecilia listed below provides some of the best camping facilities in Hanga Roa. Camping is also allowed behind the national park attendant's office at Rano Raraku and in the picnic park at Anakena. The park rangers may agree to replenish your water supply, but on very dry years no water is available for campers, so check beforehand. If you camp freelance elsewhere around the island, stay out of sight of motorized transport.

The listings which follow are not exhaustive because almost every family on the island is involved in tourism in some way (and unlike many other South Pacific destinations, tourism here is run almost exclusively by the local people). A few places, including Residencial Ana Rapu and Hostal Martín and Anita, have been deliberately left out. All of the 10 hotels and 40 *residenciales* are in Hanga Roa, arranged here beginning with those closest to the airport. None of the streets have numbers and most *residenciales* don't have signs, so never hesitate to ask directions. Some places are better known by the owner's name.

Under US$50

A friendly young school teacher named Diego Jaime runs **Residencial Kona Tau** (tel./fax 100-321), on a hillside on Avareipua. The eight rooms are US$25, US$35, or US$45 pp high season, US$10, US$15, US$20, or US$25 pp low season, depending on the room. Breakfast is US$5 extra. It operates as a youth hostel and singles are expected to share their room with one or two other people if need be. However, despite the large Hosteling International sign at the entrance, there's no HI discount. Camping is not allowed. A common kitchen and lounge are provided, and it's a good place to meet people.

Cabañas Vaianny (tel. 100-650), on Tuki Haka Hevari, has five rooms in a duplex and triplex at US$20/30 single/double including a good breakfast. It's friendly and central—ask for Teresa Araki at the airport.

Residencial Pedro Atan (tel. 551-027), also known at Hotel Atariki, on Tuki Haka Hevari just off Atamu Tekena, has 14 rooms in a long block at US$30/50 single/double with breakfast (or US$20 pp in the low season). It's run by Juan Atan Paoa, who worked with Thor Heyerdahl on the restoration of Ahu Ature Huki at Anakena in 1956.

A jovial lady named Janet Hei operates **Residencial Miru** (tel. 100-365), behind Gringos Pizza on Atamu Tekena. The three rooms with shared bath are US$10 pp, while the four with private bath go for US$20/30 single/double, breakfast included.

Across Atamu Tekena from Gringos Pizza is **Residencial O Tama Te Ra'a** (tel. 100-635) with three rooms at US$25 pp year-round. Dinner is US$10. This quiet guesthouse features a large garden and a greenhouse. Book through Mahinatur.

Residencial Tekena Inn (Gonzalo Nahoe, tel./fax 100-289), on Atamu Tekena beside Restaurant El Cuerito Regalón in the center of town, has 12 rooms, four inside the house and another eight in a corridor outside. It's US$15 pp without meals (US$17 pp in the high season), and you can use the common kitchen. All day horseback riding tours are US$45 pp including a light lunch, and car rentals are also offered.

Residencial Tauke (Florentino Leiva Neira, tel. 100-253), on Calle Te Pito o Te Henua opposite the Liceo (high school), has four rooms at US$20/15 pp high/low season plus US$5 pp for breakfast.

Up a sidestreet off Te Pito o Te Henu between Restaurant Kopakavana and the church, **Residencial Vai Kapua** (tel. 100-377) offers nine rooms, four in the main house and five facing the lovely garden outside. It's quiet and friendly, and at US$20/15 pp with breakfast high/low season, good value.

On Pasaje Reimiro off Atamu Tekena in the northern part of town, **Residencial Tahai** (María Hey Paoa, tel. 100-395) resembles a rundown Spanish hacienda with a large garden out front. The seven rooms are US$25/40 single/double.

US$50–100

The **Oceanic Rapa Nui Hotel** (tel. 100-356, fax 100-985), on Tu'u Koihu a few minutes walk from the airport, has six attractive, spacious rooms in a quadrangle facing the large dining/sitting area. It's a tad expensive at US$50/100/130 single/double/triple high season, but good value at US$25 pp during the low season.

Residencial Villa Tiki (María Georgina Paoa Hucki, tel./fax 100-327), on Ave. Pont, offers six rooms at US$45/70. There's a great view over Hanga Roa toward Terevaka from the rear garden of this quality establishment. Tiki Tours is based here.

Rapa Nui Travel (Conny Martin, tel. 100-548, fax 100-165), on Tu'u Koihu, has a two-bedroom house for rent next to its office, which is ideal for families of up to five. Cooking facilities are provided and the price varies from US$80 if the children are young to US$100 for a family with teens.

One of the nicer medium-priced places is **Hotel Gomero** (María Icka Araki, tel./fax 100-313), on Tu'u Koihu, with 13 rooms in long blocks at US$49/76/95 single/double/triple. This tasteful, quiet hotel has a swimming pool, and Mani Iti Tours is based here.

Residencial Chez Erika (tel. 100-474), off Tuki Haka Hevari directly behind Cabañas Vaianny, offers 12 rooms at US$35/60 single/double high season, US$25 pp low season, breakfast included. It's quiet and friendly.

The **Hotel Orongo** (Juan Chávez, tel. 100-572, fax 100-294), on Atamu Tekena in the center of town, has 14 rooms at US$35/60/80 single/double/triple, breakfast included. A reduction of US$5 pp is possible in the low season. This hotel has a very good restaurant and a gift shop.

The seven-room **Hotel Victoria** (Jorge Edmunds, tel./fax 100-272), off Ave. Pont, is US$50/70 single/double (or US$40/60 low season). A common kitchen is provided for guests. This comfortable hotel has a breezy hilltop location.

French speakers are catered for at **Residencial Tadeo y Lili** (Liliane Frechet, tel./fax 100-422) at Ave. Apina and Policarpo Toro. Each of the seven rooms accommodates two to five people at US$45/60/81 single/double/triple including breakfast. One three-bedroom house is US$25 pp. Lunch or dinner are US$15 each. The location facing Caleta Hanga Roa is excellent, although some of the rooms are not constructed

in a way which takes full advantage of the site. Island tours and horseback riding are arranged.

Hotel Chez Joseph (José Arimereka Pacomio, tel. 100-373, fax 100-281), on Avareipua just up the street behind Restaurant Kopakavana, charges US$45/85/105 single/double/triple including breakfast for the 15 rooms (US$5 pp less low season). The quiet hilltop location and family atmosphere are its advantages.

The peaceful **Hotel Poike** (Carmen Cardinali, tel. 100-283, fax 100-366), on Petero Atamu a bit north of the church, has 13 rooms at US$40/30 pp high/low season including breakfast.

Cabañas Vai Moana (Edgard Hereveri, tel./fax 100-626), on Atamu Tekena in the northern part of town, has five large duplex units containing a total of 10 rooms and three newer units in a triplex suite. It's US$40/60/90 single/double/triple (or US$5 less low season), plus US$12 for dinner. Many guests book through the website. Vai Moana rents bicycles, scooters, and jeeps.

Residencial Chez Cecilia (Cecilia Cardinali, tel. 100-499), off Atamu Tekena just behind Cabañas Vai Moana and near Ahu Tahai, has 10 rooms at US$40/70/95 single/double/triple high season, US$25/40/60 low season, breakfast included. Camping in a separate area behind the guesthouse is US$10 pp and there's a separate common kitchen and dining area for campers. Dinner is US$15.

Residencial Chez María Goretti (tel./fax 100-459), on Atamu Tekena north of Cabañas Vai Moana, has 15 large rooms at US$50/70/90 single/double/triple, plus US$10 pp for dinner. In the low season you can stay here for US$25 pp with breakfast. It's friendly, and there's a lovely garden and lounge. French is spoken.

Lucía Riroroko de Haoa runs **Mahina Taka Taka Georgia** (tel./fax 100-452), at the north end of town near the museum. The four quiet rooms are US$30 pp (plus US$15 for dinner). You're really made to feel like part of the family.

US$100–150

The **Hotel Iorana** (tel./fax 100-312), on Policarpo Toro south of town, has 52 rooms with minifridge and cable TV. These begin at US$100/134 single/double for the 24 fan-cooled standard rooms on the north side of the complex. The 10 "turista" rooms (US$136/169) in the center are roasted by the afternoon sun and have very weak air-conditioning, so take one of the 18 superior rooms (US$179/200) on the south side of the Iorana if you want real air-conditioning. The bar next to the triangular swimming pool is worth a visit if you're returning from Orongo on foot, and the coastal views are fine.

The **Hotel Hotu Matu'a** (Orlando Paoa, tel. 100-242, fax 100-445) is at the east end of Ave. Pont not far from the airport. The 60 rooms are US$120/140/160 single/double/triple high season, US$60/100/120 low season including breakfast. Some rooms are rather old with worn carpets, so ask to see yours before accepting. There's a 10 percent surcharge if you pay by traveler's check or credit card. Lunch or dinner is US$20. This motel-style complex angles around a half-moon freshwater swimming pool, and there's a bar. The owner's minimuseum off the lobby contains several intriguing artifacts. The LanChile flight crews always stay here.

Hotel Manutara (tel. 100-297, fax 100-768), on Hotu Matu'a east of the airport, has 28 rooms in an L-shaped building facing the pool at US$85/130/146 single/double/triple. The main problem here is the heavy disco beat from nearby PiRiti Disco, which continues all night on Fridays and Saturdays (don't allow your agent to book you here those nights). It's owned by Aku Aku Tourismo.

Hotel O'tai (Nico Haoa, tel. 100-250, fax 100-482) is on Te Pito o Te Henua across from the post office. The 35 rooms are US$72/104 single/double, and there are a nice garden and swimming pool. Unfortunately the O'tai is just around the corner from the island's other disco, the Toroko, so avoid staying here on a weekend.

US$150–250

The **Hotel Hanga Roa** (tel. 100-299, fax 100-426), overlooking the bay at the west end of Ave. Pont, was used by Hollywood moviemakers for six months in 1993 and they really tore the place apart. A year later the Hanga Roa was taken over by the Panamericana hotel chain, which added 10 bungalows, each containing three small air-con-

ditioned rooms at US$270 double. The 60 worn rooms in the prefabricated main building are poor value at US$130/150/175. In the low season the old rooms are reduced to US$72 single or double, the bungalows to US$100. Lunch or dinner is US$30.

Also not recommended is the **Hotel Taha Tai** (tel. 551-192), off Policarpo Toronto and Ave. Apina. Opened in 2001 and owned by Kia-Koe Tour, the Taha Tai has 30 rooms with no view in a main building, plus 10 cabañas in rows behind. It's way overpriced at US$140/165/180 single/double/triple—even the small pool is often dry.

FOOD AND ENTERTAINMENT

Food

A growing number of restaurants and snack bars exist along Atamu Tekena and Te Pito o Te Henua. The seafood is good, although the local lobsters *(langostas)* have become scarce (and expensive) through overharvesting. Avoid *nanue* (rudderfish), an oily fish with a pungent taste much appreciated by the Rapanui but distasteful to the Western palate. Tuna *(kahi)* is a safer fish to order, and be sure to try *ceviche de pescado,* raw tuna marinated with lemon juice (US$6–8). Also watch for tasty local pastries called *empanadas.* A *completo* is a hot dog. Be wary of restaurants with prices quoted only in dollars!

The **Tunu-Ahi Barbecue** (Mon.–Sat. 0800–1500), on Atamu Tekena directly opposite the market (no sign), is a great place for a breakfast of *sopaipillas* (pancakes) at US$.50 each with coffee for under a dollar. For lunch have a skewer of barbecued meat (US$3) or a large *ensalada poroto verde* salad (US$3). You can eat on the terrace.

Restaurant El Cuerito Regalón (tel. 551-232; daily 0900–midnight), just north on Atamu Tekena, features Chilean dishes, including *ceviche,* chicken, or tuna for US$7, red meat at US$9, and lobster for US$32. It's always crowded with tourists in the evening. The peso menu is less expensive than the one priced in dollars.

One of the cheapest places to eat is **Restaurante Tavake** (tel. 100-300), near the park on Atamu Tekena at the north end of the downtown strip. Sandwiches are US$3–4 and pizza

US$4–5, but better value are the *platos económicos* for US$4. Vegetarian dishes cost the same.

A few blocks south on Atamu Tekena at the corner of Sebastián Englert is the **Aloha Pub** (tel. 551-383; Tues.–Sun. 1900–0300) with a coconut tree growing through the porch. It's more of a late-night drinking place (large beer US$2.50) than a restaurant, but the light meals are fair value at US$5–8 (lobster US$39). The *ceviche* here is especially good.

Across Atamu Tekena and just down the hill from the Aloha Pub is **Ariki o te Pana** (Berta Hey, tel. 100-171; Mon.–Sat. 1000–midnight, Sun. 1000–1300) or The Queen of Empanadas. As usual there's no sign, but the *empanadas* made from cheese (US$1.50) or tuna (US$2) are really huge.

Easter Island's most expensive eatery by far is **Restaurant La Taverne Du Pêcheur** (tel. 100-619; Mon.–Sat. 1200–1400/1800–2200), near the small boat harbor at Caleta Hanga Roa. The menu is priced exclusively in dollars: spaghetti US$11–15, fish or steaks US$13–15, lobster US$35–50. The portions are small and there's no view.

Restaurant Playa Pea (tel. 100-382; Tues.–Sun. 1200–1600), a bit south along the waterfront opposite Sernatur, is less expensive than La Taverne Du Pêcheur and the view is good. The menu includes a choice of seven fish dishes at US$8–10. The coffee and beer are reasonable, and you can sometimes get *empanadas* (US$1.50).

Restaurant Avarei Pua (tel. 100-431; Thurs.–Tues. 1200–2300), across the street from La Taverne Du Pêcheur, is much cheaper than its neighbor (most dishes US$8).

Restaurant Caleta O'tai (tel. 100-607; Thurs.–Tues. 1100–2200), on Te Pito o Te Henua opposite Caleta Hanga Roa, is a good place for an afternoon drink with a nice sea view from the terrace. Main plates here are US$8, seafood soup US$6, and sandwiches US$4–6. It's run by the same people as Hotel Chez Joseph.

Despite the unpretentious appearance, **Restaurant La Tinita** (tel. 100-833; Mon.–Sat. 1200–1600/1800–2200), on Te Pito o Te Henua between hotels Manavai and O'tai, is one of the best restaurants in Hanga Roa. At US$8, the fish dishes,

especially the tuna steak, are excellent. There's also fish soup for US$6 and sandwiches at US$3–5. The menu is in English and the portions large.

Finally, **Restaurant Kopakavana** (tel. 100-447; daily 1100–1500/1900–midnight) near the church offers a nice terrace with a view down Te Pito o Te Henua. The local fish dishes are US$8, lobster US$30.

The local tap water piped down from Rano Kao has a high magnesium content and may be a little brown, but it's quite safe to drink. Otherwise beer is available everywhere. Try the Chilean *pisco* (brandy) cocktails made from grapes. Liquor is sold cheaply in the local supermarkets.

Kai Nene Supermarket (tel./fax 100-492; weekdays 0930–1330/1700–2130, Sat. 0930–1400/1700–2130), on Atamu Tekena in the center of town, is the largest grocery store. The **Municipal Market** (Mon.–Sat. 0800–1200) or *feria municipal* on Atamu Tekena sells more handicrafts than food, and the best vegetables are sold out of the back of pickup trucks across the street. The snack bar in the market has coffee and sandwiches for under a dollar.

Entertainment

The discos, **Toroko** on Policarpo Toro and **PiRiTi** on Ave. Hotu Matu'a, crank up on Friday and Saturday nights (admission US$3). During the peak summer season (Dec.–Feb.), they may operate other nights as well. The doors open around 2230, but nothing much happens before midnight, then the action continues until dawn.

The **Kari Kari Ballet Cultural** performs at Hotel Hanga Roa Tuesday or Wednesday and Saturday nights at 2200 (the days vary according to flight schedules). Admission is US$15. It's sometimes possible to buy a package including dinner and the show for US$22, but you must specifically request it at the hotel reception. Kari Kari also performs December–February at Hotel Iorana on Fridays. This skillful traditional troupe formed in 1996 is well worth seeing. A second group, the **Ballet Folklórico Polinesia,** performs September–February at Restaurant Kopakavana (tel. 100-447) twice a week. Other cultural groups staging performances both here and abroad include Topatangi, Nga Poki, and Matato'a.

Sunday at 0900 there's singing in Rapanui in the Catholic church. April–October you can watch the local soccer teams compete in the field opposite Caleta Hanga Roa. Matches start at 2000 on Tuesday and Thursday, at 1400 on Sunday. Expect everything except church to start late.

Tito at **Rapa Nui Tattoo** (tel. 100-727), on Atamu Tekena a bit south of the LanChile office, does traditional tattooing beginning at US$20.

SHOPPING

Aside from shell necklaces and feather ornaments, the main things to buy here are woodcarvings, dance paddles, miniature stone *moai,* small pieces of tapa, and imitation *rongorongo* tablets. The onyx *moai* sold locally are imported from mainland Chile. Don't buy anything at all made from coral as you'll only be encouraging unscrupulous individuals to damage the island's small reefs. Prices vary considerably from shop to shop.

The **Handicraft Market** (Mon.–Sat. 0930–1300/1600–1900, Sun. 1000–1300), opposite the church, sells overpriced woodcarvings, and is one of the only places in Polynesia where bargaining is expected. The vendors at this market are usually willing to trade woodcarvings for jeans, windbreakers, T-shirts, sneakers, toiletries, cosmetics, and rock music cassettes.

Handicrafts are also sold at the *Municipal Market* on Atamu Tekena, and inside a new pavilion in front of the airport terminal. The gift shop inside the **Museo Antropólogico Sebastián Englert** sells books, maps, videos, CDs, postage stamps, jewelry, and T-shirts at rather high prices. Consider the surcharge a donation to the museum.

A commercial art gallery, the **Galería de Arte Aukara** (tel. 100–539), on Ave. Pont off Atamu Tekena not far from the LanChile office, displays museum-quality woodcarvings by internationally known sculptor Bene Tuki. These are priced US$100–700 and each is a unique work of art. Bene Tuki's wife, Ana María Arredondo, prepares numbered prints on tapa at US$15–50 apiece. This gallery doesn't keep regular hours so call ahead for an appointment to be sure someone will be there.

INFORMATION AND SERVICES

Information

There's a Sernatur tourist office (tel. 100-255; weekdays 0730–1300/1400–1800, Sat. 0830–1300) on Tu'u Maheke a few doors west of the bank. In Santiago de Chile, the Servicio Nacional de Turismo (tel. 56-2/731-8300, fax 56-2/251-8469), Ave. Providencia 1550, can supply a brochure and list of hotels on Easter Island.

Overpriced island maps of variable quality are sold locally at the museum and souvenir shops, such as Hotu Matu'a's Favorite Shoppe on Atamu Tekena.

Money

The local currency is the Chilean peso (approximately US$1 = 650 pesos), which comes in notes of 500, 1,000, 2,000, 5,000, 10,000, and 20,000 pesos. Chilean currency is almost worthless outside Chile itself, so only change what you're sure you'll need, and get rid of the remainder before you leave. Duty-free purchases aboard LanChile flights can be paid for in pesos.

The Banco del Estado (tel. 100-221; weekdays 0800–1300), beside the tourist office in Hanga Roa, charges a flat US$10 commission to change any number of traveler's checks. Cash U.S. dollars are changed without commission at the same rate. An ATM inside the bank gives cash advances on MasterCard; cash advances on Visa cards are available at the counter (US$400 daily maximum). All cash advances are paid out in pesos, not dollars.

All tourist-oriented establishments accept dollars as payment, though not always at good rates. If you're coming from Santiago, bring a supply of pesos. Outside banking hours, the Shell gas station on Ave. Hotu Matu'a west of the airport changes U.S. cash at a rate 5 percent lower than the bank (posted in the office). Currencies other than U.S. dollars (including Polynesian CFP) can be difficult to exchange.

Credit cards are rarely usable on Easter Island as those accepting them have to wait a long time to be paid. Some hotels levy a 10 percent service charge for the use of credit cards.

If you want to pay something approaching

EASTER ISLAND INTERNET RESOURCES

Accommodations

Cabañas Vaianny
www.angelfire.com/pop2/vaianny
www5.gratisweb.com/vaiannyy
taraki@entelchile.net

Cabañas Vai Moana
www.vai-moana.cl
consultas@vai-moana.cl

Chile Hotels
www.chile-hotels.com/easteris.htm

Hotel Chez Joseph
chezjoseph@entelchile.net

Hotel Gomero
www.hotelgomero.com
hotelgomero@entelchile.net

Hotel Hanga Roa
reshangaroa@panamericanahoteles.cl

Hotel Hotu Matu'a
tokitour@entelchile.net

Hotel Iorana
www.ioranahotel.cl
ioranaof@entelchile.net

Hotel Manutara
manutarahotel@entelchile.net

Hotel O'tai
otairapanui@entelchile.net

Hotel Poike
ngaeheehe@entelchile.net

Hotel Taha Tai
www.hotel-tahatai.co.cl
hoteltahatai@entelchile.net

Hotel Victoria
jedmunds@entelchile.net

Mahina Taka Taka Georgia
riroroco@entelchile.net

Residencial Chez Cecilia
www.chezcecilia.co.cl
ccardinali@entelchile.net

Residencial Kona Tau
konatau@entelchile.net

Residencial O Tama Te Ra'a
jlagos@mahinatur.cl

Residencial Pedro Atan
ataraki@hotmail.com

Residencial Tadeo y Lili
tadeolili@entelchile.net

Residencial Tahai
mariahey@latinmail.com

local prices, ask how much the item or service costs in pesos. Only tourists pay in U.S. dollars and dollar prices are invariably higher. When prices *are* quoted in dollars, you can usually save a small amount by asking to pay in pesos. Virtually all accommodations are priced (and can be paid) in dollars, but beware of restaurants, taxis, or shops quoting dollar prices. The prices in this book are given only in dollars to compensate for inflation and the depreciating Chilean peso, but almost everything can (and should) be paid for directly in pesos.

Post and Telecommunications

All mail is routed through Chile and Chilean postage stamps are used. The post office (tel. 100-332; weekdays 0900–1300/1430–1800, Sat. 0900–1230), on Te Pito o Te Henua opposite Hotel O'tai, sometimes has special Rapa Nui postage stamps valid only on the island. Occasionally it runs out of stamps altogether. If you bring along your passport, the postmaster may be willing to stamp it too!

The Entel Telephone Center (fax 56-32/100-105; weekdays 0800–1800, Sat. 0800–1930), opposite the bank, sells telephone cards valued at US$1.50, US$4.50, US$8, and US$16, which can be used from all public telephones (the US$16 card will get you about 15 minutes to North America). You can receive faxes here for less than a dollar. The "AT&T Direct" access number from Easter Island is tel. 800-

Residencial Vai Kapua
vaikapua@entelchile.net

Residencial Villa Tiki
tiki@entelchile.net

Sports and Recreation

Mike Rapu Diving
www.mikerapudiving.cl
mikerapudiving@entelchile.net

Orca Diving Center
seemorca@entelchile.net

Transportation and Tours

Aku Aku Turismo
www.akuakuturismo.cl
aku_aku@entelchile.net

Haunani Rent a Car
haunani@aclaris.cl

Kia Koe Tour
www.kiakoetour.co.cl
kiakoe@entelchile.net

LanChile Airlines
www.lanchile.com

Mahinatur
www.mahinatur.cl
mahina@mahinatur.cl

Rapa Nui Travel
www.rapanuitravel.com
rntravel@entelchile.net

Others

Cámara de Turismo
www.turismo.rapanui.cl
camararapanui@entelchile.net

Easter Island Foundation
www.islandheritage.org

Easter Island Home Page
www.netaxs.com/~trance/rapanui.html

Museo Antropólogico Sebastián Englert
www.museorapanui.cl

Rapanui.cl
www.rapanui.cl

Rongorongo of Easter Island
www.rongorongo.org

Servicio Nacional de Turismo
sernatur_rapanui@entelchile.net

EASTER ISLAND/RAPA NUI

800-311. When calling Easter Island from abroad, dial your international access code plus 56 for Chile, 32 for Easter Island, and the six-digit local number (which always begins with 100, 550, or 551).

Interestingly, a phone call from Valparaíso, Chile, to Easter Island is a local call. However, from the island to Valparaíso it's long distance.

Internet Access

Cyber Shark (tel./fax 100-600; Mon.–Sat. 1300–2000), next to Restaurant Caleta O'tai near Caleta Hanga Roa, offers Internet access at US$1.50 per 15 minutes. Several shops and travel agencies along Atamu Tekena offer the same at similar rates.

Visas and Officialdom

Most visitors require only a passport valid six months ahead to stay 90 days in Chile. Visas are not necessary for North Americans, Australians, New Zealanders, and most Europeans. Check this at any LanChile Airlines office. An entry tax or *cobro por reciprocidad* is collected upon arrival in Chile, with the amount varying according to nationality (U.S. passports US$61, Canada US$55, Australia US$30, Mexico US$15, etc.). No vaccinations are required.

Yachting Facilities

Arriving yachts make contact over VHF channel 16. The Gobernación Marítima Hanga Roa (tel. 100-222) on Ave. Apina, the building on the coast with the Chilean flag, handles clearance.

About 30 cruising yachts a year visit Easter Island between Galapagos/South America and Pitcairn/Tahiti. Because of Rapa Nui's remoteness, the boats will have been at sea two to four weeks before landfall. As Easter Island is well outside the South Pacific hurricane zone, they usually call January–March, so as to time their arrival in French Polynesia for the beginning of the prime sailing season there. The southeast tradewinds extend south to Easter Island most reliably December–May, allowing for the easiest entry/exit. The rest of the year, winds are westerly and variable.

Anchorages include Hanga Roa, Vinapu, Hotu Iti, and Anakena/Ovahe, and a watch must be maintained over yachts at anchor at all times as the winds can shift quickly in stormy weather. The anchorages are deep with many rocks to foul the anchor and little sand. Landing can be difficult through the surf. The frequent moves necessitated by changing winds can be quite exhausting, and crews often have only one or two days a week ashore. Luckily the things to see are quite close to these anchorages.

A pilot is required to enter the small boat harbor at Hanga Piko and US$100 is charged. Entry through the breakers and rocks is possible only in calm weather. Mooring to the concrete wharf here is stern to as at Tahiti (no charge), but there's little space and this is supposed to be done only by boats in need of repairs. The harbor has 2.8 meters of water at low tide. Barges used to unload cargo from oceangoing ships are kept here.

Media

No newspapers or magazines are published on Easter Island, so the easiest way to keep in touch is to subscribe to Georgia Lee's *Rapa Nui Journal* (Easter Island Foundation, www.islandheritage.org). The *Journal* comes out twice a year, and contains an interesting mix of scientific studies, announcements, and local gossip—well worth the US$30 annual subscription price (US$40 airmail outside Canada and the United States).

Radio Manukena broadcasts in Rapanui over 88.9 MHz FM weekdays 0800–1100/1400–1700 (in Spanish at other times). The local TV station, channel 13 Mata Ote Rapa Nui, is on the air Friday–Sunday 1900–0100. Both are owned by the municipality. Chilean television programs are on at other times.

Health

The island hospital (tel. 100-215), on Simon Paoa, charges US$16 for medical consultations. It's open 24 hours for emergencies. For nonemergencies, you must make an appointment a few days in advance. There's a pharmacy here. To see the hospital's dentist, come in person around noon to get on the waiting list for that day (US$10 for a basic examination).

The private Consulta Médica (tel. 551-500; weekdays 1000–1400/1800–2200, Sat. 1100–1300), on Atamu Tekena next to Hotel Orongo, charges US$40 for consultations.

Transportation

Getting There

LanChile Airlines flies a Boeing 767 from Tahiti and Santiago to Easter Island twice a week. In the high season December–March, extra Santiago–Easter Island flights are added. From North America and Europe, LanChile has direct flights to Santiago from Los Angeles, Miami, New York, Madrid, and Frankfurt. (See this book's main Introduction for sample fares.) In North America, call LanChile toll-free at tel. 800/735-5526 for information. People in Europe and Australia can have Easter Island included in a cheap round-the-world ticket, something that usually isn't possible in North America.

Book and reconfirm your onward flight well ahead, as the plane is often overbooked between Easter Island and Santiago—a week is enough time to see everything. Between Easter Island and Tahiti, the plane is seldom full. We've heard from several readers who were forced to upgrade to business class when they tried to fly "standby" to Santiago. The local LanChile office (tel. 100-279; weekdays 0900–1300/1500–1730), on Atamu Tekena at Ave. Pont, will tell you there's no need to reconfirm your flight, but you should still visit the office and leave a local contact phone number to make sure your reservation is in the system. Don't be fooled by the nonchalant attitude of the LanChile employees—things go wrong on this route all the time.

The Gobernación Marítima Hanga Roa (tel. 100-222), on Ave. Apina near Hotel Hanga Roa, handles passenger bookings for the naval supply ship *Aquiles* to/from Valparaíso. It calls twice a year, usually in March and September, but you need to know someone with pull in the Chilean navy or administration to get aboard. If you do get on, passage costs around US$250 one way. On the continent, inquire at the Office of Naval Transport, Primera Zona Naval (weekdays 0800–1200), Plaza Sotomayor 594, Valparaíso, Chile.

Package Tours

(Turn to Tours to Easter Island in the Papeete listings for information on package tours from Tahiti to Easter Island. Also see Organized Tours in this book's main introduction.)

Getting Around

There's no public transport but the locals are pretty good about giving lifts. Sunday is an easy time to hitch a ride as many people go fishing or to their gardens. Out on the island, drivers will often stop to offer you a ride even if you aren't hitchhiking.

More than 100 clearly marked taxis patrol the streets of Hanga Roa, charging the locals US$1–2 for a ride around town or US$6–8 one-way to Anakena. Tourists are expected to pay much more and bargaining may be required. You'll get a better price dealing directly with a driver rather than by having your hotel receptionist call a taxi, in which case you'll pay the top tourist price.

For hikers, the taxis are handy to get somewhere in the morning with the intention of walking back to town. Sernatur has a list of official round-trip taxi fares to many points with waiting time built in. To be expected to pay half that amount to be dropped somewhere without any waiting is unreasonable, yet some drivers still try and you may have to ask several of them. Flag a taxi down on the street and tell the driver straight away how many pesos you're willing to pay to be dropped somewhere. One-way, drop-off taxi fares from Hanga Roa start at US$5–6 to Orongo, US$6–8 to Anakena, and US$7–9 to Rano Raraku, paid in pesos. A knowledge of Spanish goes a long way here. The translation of "I only want to be dropped there" is *Solo quiero que me deje allá.*

The hotels and several offices along Atamu Tekena rent vehicles at US$40–60 a day. Most are 4WD jeeps because of the rugged terrain. Ask around, as prices vary (bargaining possible in the off-season), and check to make sure the car has a spare tire *(neumático),* jack *(gata),* and gas tank cap. Insurance is not available but gasoline is relatively cheap at US$2.25 a U.S. gallon and the distances are small. Scooters can be hired at US$30–45 a day, but a motorcycle license is mandatory. The roads to Anakena and Rano Raraku are now fully paved, making bicycling a lot more practical, and you should be able to rent a bike for US$10 a day.

Oceanic Rent a Car (tel. 100-985), on Atamu Tekena opposite Hotel Orongo, rents bicycles/motorcycles/jeeps at US$10/30/40.

Haunani Rent a Car (tel. 100-353), on Atamu Tekena next to Kai Nene Supermarket, rents bicycles/cars at US$8/40 a day. You can also arrange tours here with noted archaeologist Sergio Rapu of Easter Island Ecotours.

Several companies offer half/full day minibus tours of the island at US$25/35 pp. Boat tours to the *motu* off the southwestern tip of the island cost about US$30 pp a half day. The full-day tour to Rano Raraku and Anakena is an excellent introduction to Easter Island, but unfortunately all of the companies seem to do the same thing at the same time, so you're part of a moving crowd.

Aku Aku Turismo (tel. 100-770), Tu'u Koihu just north of the church, has a half-day tour to Orongo and Tahai, and a full-day tour to Rano Raraku and Anakena. Its half-day "adventure tour" to Ana Kakenga and the summit of Maunga Terevaka by 4WD is US$30. Another adventure tour is to Ana o Keke, a cliffside cave on the Poike Peninsula. Horseback riding is also US$30. Lunch on the full-day tour costs US$15 extra, so take your own. Aku Aku is the largest tour company and the most likely to have the tour you want when you it. The narration will be in English and Spanish.

Kia-Koe Tour (tel. 100-852, fax 100-282), Atamu Tekena at Sebastián Englert, does much the same.

Rapa Nui Travel (tel. 100-548, fax 100-165), on Tu'u Koihu, caters to smaller groups and provides more personalized service for the same prices as Aku Aku and Kia Koe. German-speaking guides can be provided. Rapa Nui's departures aren't as frequent as those of the others, so check early on in your stay. For a French-speaking tour, ask at **Residencial Tadeo y Lili** (tel./fax 100-422), Ave. Apina and Policarpo Toro.

Airport

At 3,353 meters long, Mataveri Airport (IPC) has the second-longest runway in the South Pacific, only a little shorter than the one at the former French military base at Hao in the Tuamotu Islands. A rough airstrip was begun here in the early 1950s, and in the 1960s the U.S. Air Force improved it as an "ionospheric observation center." In fact, the Americans used the base to spy on the French nuclear testing. The Americans left after the election of Salvador Allende in 1970, but in 1986 they were back with Pinochet's blessing to extend both ends of the airstrip for use as an emergency landing strip by NASA space shuttles. Recently a plan to erect a new control tower in the form of a giant *moai* was scrapped after local objections.

The hotels and *residenciales* provide free airport transfers, or you can walk to any of them within half an hour. There's no bank, left-luggage office, or duty free shop, but there are many souvenir stands. The departure tax is US$26 to Tahiti or US$7 to Santiago, but it's usually included in the ticket price (ask). To control pests it's prohibited to export fresh fruit or vegetables. *Iorana* means hello and goodbye in Rapanui.

Cook Islands

Introduction

The Cook Islands lie in the center of the Polynesian triangle about 4,500 km south of Hawaii. They range from towering Rarotonga, the country's largest island, to the low oval islands of the south and the solitary atolls of the north. Visitors are rewarded with natural beauty and colorful attractions at every turn. There is motion and excitement on Rarotonga and Aitutaki, peaceful village life on the rest. Since few tourists get beyond the two main islands, a trip to Atiu, Mangaia, or Mauke can be a fascinating experience. After Tahiti, the Cook Islands is inexpensive, and the local tourist industry is efficient and competitive. It's a safe, quiet place to relax and you feel right at home. The local greeting is *kia orana* (may you live on). Other words to know are *meitaki* (thank you), *aere ra* (goodbye), and *kia manuia!* (cheers!).

The Land

These 15 islands and atolls, with a land area of only 240 square km, are scattered over 1.83 million square km of the South Pacific, leaving a lot of empty ocean in between. It's 1,433 km from Penrhyn to Mangaia. The nine islands in the southern group are a continuation of the Austral Islands of French Polynesia, formed as volcanic material escaped from a southeast/northwest fracture in the earth's crust. Five of the northern islands stand on the 3,000-meter-deep

Manihiki Plateau, while Penrhyn rises directly out of seas 5,000 meters deep.

Practically every different type of oceanic island can be found in the Cooks. Rarotonga is the only high volcanic island of the Tahiti type. Aitutaki, like Bora Bora, consists of a middle-aged volcanic island surrounded by an atoll-like barrier reef, with many tiny islets defining its lagoon. Atiu, Mangaia, Mauke, and Mitiaro are raised atolls with a high cave-studded outer coral ring *(makatea)* enclosing volcanic soil at the center. It's believed these islands were uplifted during the past two million years due to the weight of Rarotonga on the earth's crust. There are low rolling hills in the interiors of both Atiu and Mangaia, while Mauke and Mitiaro are flat. The swimming and snorkeling possibilities at Atiu, Mangaia, Mauke, and Mitiaro are limited, as there's only a fringing reef with small tidal pools. Aitutaki and Rarotonga have protected lagoons where snorkeling is relatively safe. The rich, fertile southern islands account for 89 percent of the Cooks' land area and population.

Manihiki, Manuae, Palmerston, Penrhyn, Pukapuka, Rakahanga, and Suwarrow are typical lagoon atolls, while tiny Takutea and Nassau are sand cays without lagoons. All of the northern atolls are so low that waves roll right across them during hurricanes, and you have to be within 20 km to see them. This great variety makes the Cook Islands a geologist's paradise.

Climate

The main Cook Islands are about the same distance from the equator as Hawaii and have a similarly pleasant tropical climate. Rain clouds hang over Rarotonga's interior much of the year, but the coast is often sunny, and the rain often comes in brief, heavy downpours. The other islands are drier and can even experience severe water shortages. Winter evenings June–August can be cool. On both Rarotonga and Aitutaki, the best combination of prolonged hours of sunshine, fresh temperatures, and minimal rainfall runs July–September.

The trade winds blow steadily May–October from the southeast in the southern Cooks and from the east in the more humid northern Cooks; the rest of the year winds are sometimes from the southwest or west (often a sign of bad weather). The summer hurricane season is November–April, with an average of one every other year, coming from the direction of Samoa. In December 2001 Hurricane Trina roared across Mangaia, flooding the taro fields and turning the sea red with eroded soil.

For weather information call the Meteorological Office (tel. 20-603) near Rarotonga Airport.

Flora and Fauna

The lush vegetation of the high islands includes creepers, ferns, and tall trees in the interior, while coconuts, bananas, and grapefruit grow on the coast. Avocados and papayas are so abundant that the locals feed them to their pigs. On the elevated atolls the vegetation in the fertile volcanic center contrasts brusquely with that of the infertile limestone *makatea*. Taro and yams are subsistence crops. The *au* is a native yellow-flowered hibiscus. The flower of this all-purpose plant is used for medicine, the leaves to cover the *umu* (earth oven), the fiber for skirts, reef sandals, and rope, and the branches for

THE ISLANDS OF THE COOKS

Island	Area in Hectares	Population (2001)
Rarotonga	6,718	12,206
Mangaia	5,180	745
Atiu	2,693	622
Mitiaro	2,228	230
Mauke	1,842	468
Aitutaki	1,805	1,937
Penrhyn	984	357
Manuae	617	0
Manihiki	544	516
Pukapuka	506	664
Rakahanga	405	161
Palmerston	202	48
Takutea	122	0
Nassau	121	69
Suwarrow	40	4
COOK ISLANDS	24,007	18,027

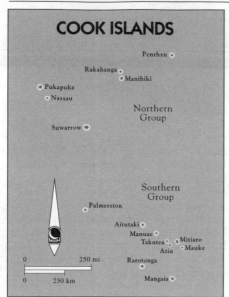

COOK ISLANDS

Penrhyn

Rakahanga
Manihiki

Pukapuka
Nassau

Northern
Group

Suwarrow

Southern
Group

Palmerston

Aitutaki
Manuae
Takutea · Mitiaro
Atiu · Mauke

Rarotonga

Mangaia

0   250 mi
0   250 km

© DAVID STANLEY

walling native cottages on outer islands. The flamboyant trees bloom red November–March.

The only native mammals are bats and rats. The mynah is the bird most often seen, an aggressive introduced species that drives native birds up into the mountains and damages fruit trees. By 1989 only about 29 examples of the Rarotonga flycatcher or *kakerori* remained because of attacks on the birds' nests by ship rats. Fortunately a local landowners' group, the Takitumu Conservation Area, took an interest in the *kakerori*'s survival and began laying rat poison in the nesting areas during the breeding season. By 2001 there were 241 *kakerori*.

The forest birds of the Cook Islands include the Atiu swiftlet (*kopeka*), blue lorikeet (*kuramo'o*), chattering kingfisher (*ngotare*), common mynah (*manu kavamani*), Cook Islands fruit dove (*kukupa*), Cook Islands reed warbler (*kererako*), long-tailed cuckoo (*karavia*), Mangaia kingfisher (*tanga'eo*), Pacific pigeon (*rupe*), Rarotonga flycatcher (*kakerori*), and Rarotonga starling (*'i'oi*).

Shorebirds include the bristle-thighed curlew (*teue*), grey duck (*mokoro rauvai*), Pacific golden plover (*torea*), spotless crake (*mo'omo'o*), and wandering tattler (*kuriri*).

Among the seabirds are the black noddy (*rakia*), blue-grey noddy (*kara'ura'u*), brown booby (*kona*), brown noddy (*ngoio*), great crested tern (*kakavai maui*), great frigatebird (*kota'a nui*), masked booby (*lulu*), red-footed booby (*toroa*), red-tailed tropic bird (*tavake*), sooty tern (*tara*), white-tailed tropic bird (*rokoa*), and white tern (*kakaia*).

Unfortunately the activities of local sharpshooters have made the Cook Islands less attractive as a bird-watching venue, and spearfishing using scuba gear has done much damage to the marinelife. To control this, five lagoon areas around Rarotonga have been closed to fishing and shell collecting since 1998 under a traditional system known as *ra'ui*. In one of the *ra'ui* areas, the number of fish species increased from 14 to 31 in the first two years. Humpback whales can sometimes be seen cruising along the shorelines July–September, having migrated 5,000 km north from Antarctica to bear their young. Pilot whales (up to six meters) are in the Cooks year-round. In 2001 the Cook Islands declared its large exclusive economic zone a whale sanctuary. Sharks are not a problem in the Cook lagoons.

HISTORY AND GOVERNMENT

Discovery

Though peppered across a vast expanse of empty ocean, the Polynesians knew all these islands by heart long before the first Europeans happened on the scene. One of several legends holds that Rarotonga was settled about A.D. 1200 by two great warriors, Karika from Samoa and Tangiia-nui from Tahiti. The story goes that Karika and Tangiia-nui met on the high seas but decided not to fight because there would be no one to proclaim the victor. Instead they carried on to Rarotonga together and divided the island among themselves by sailing their canoes around it in opposite directions, with a line between their starting and meeting points becoming the boundary. Even today, tribes in the Cooks refer to themselves as *vaka* (canoes), and many can trace their ancestry back to these chiefs.

Archaeologists believe Rarotonga was reached

much earlier, probably before A.D. 800 from Raiatea or the Marquesas. The mythical chief Toi who built the Ara Metua on Rarotonga is associated with this earlier migration. Recent excavations of a *marae* on a *motu* in the Muri Lagoon point to an even earlier date, perhaps A.D. 500. Even earlier sites have been found on Mangaia. Atiu was a chiefly island that dominated Mauke, Mitiaro, Takutea, and sometimes Manuae.

The Spanish explorer Mendaña sighted Pukapuka in 1595, and his pilot, Quirós, visited Rakahanga in 1606. Some 500 inhabitants gathered on the beach to gaze at the strange ships. Quirós wrote:

They were the most beautiful white and elegant people that were met during the voyage—especially the women, who, if properly dressed, would have advantages over our Spanish women.

Then the islands were lost again to Europeans until the 1770s when Captain Cook contacted Atiu, Mangaia, Manuae, Palmerston, and Takutea—"detached parts of the earth." *He* named Manuae the Hervey Islands, a name others applied to the whole group; it was not until 1824 that the Russian cartographer, Johann von Krusenstern, labeled the southern group the Cook Islands. Cook never saw Rarotonga, and the Pitcairn-bound *Bounty* is thought to be its first European visitor (in 1789). The mutineers gave the inhabitants the seeds for their first orange trees. Aitutaki was discovered by Captain Bligh just before the famous mutiny. Mauke and Mitiaro were reached in 1823 by John Williams of the London Missionary Society.

European Penetration

Williams stopped at Aitutaki in 1821 and dropped off two Tahitian teachers. Returning two years later, he found that one, Papeiha, had done particularly well. Williams took him to Rarotonga and left him there for four years. When he returned in 1827, Williams was welcomed by Papeiha's many converts. The missionaries taught an austere, puritanical morality and believed the white man's diseases such as dysentery, measles, smallpox, and influenza,

which killed two-thirds of the population, were the punishment of God descending on the sinful islanders. The missionaries became a law unto themselves; today, the ubiquitous churches full to overflowing on Sunday are their legacy. (The missionaries arrived from Australia, and since they weren't aware of the idea of an international date line, they held Sunday service on the wrong day for the first 60 years of their presence!) About 63 percent of the population now belongs to the Cook Islands Christian Church (CICC), founded by the London Missionary Society. Takamoa College, the Bible school they established at Avarua in 1837, still exists.

Reports that the French were about to annex the Cooks led the British to declare a protectorate over the southern group in 1888. The French warship approaching Manihiki to claim the islands turned back when it saw a hastily sewn Union Jack flying, and in 1889 the northern atolls were added to the protectorate at the behest of the missionaries. The local chiefs petitioned the British to have their islands annexed to the British Crown. Thus on June 11, 1901, both the northern and southern groups were included in the boundaries of New Zealand. During World War II, the United States built air bases on Aitutaki and Penrhyn.

A legislative council was established in 1946, followed by an assembly with greater powers in 1957. After decolonizing pressure from the United Nations, a new constitution was granted in 1964, and on August 4, 1965 the Cook Islands was made a self-governing state in free association with New Zealand. Today the Cook Islands manages its own internal and external affairs. The islanders are New Zealand and Cook Islands dual citizens and have the right of free entry to New Zealand and Australia. In fact, over three times more of them live in New Zealand and Australia than on their home islands. New Zealanders and Australians, on the other hand, do not have the reciprocal right to live permanently in the Cook Islands. The Cook Islands belongs to many United Nations agencies but has never applied for full U.N. membership as this might lead to New Zealand's withdrawing citizenship privileges. In recent years the Cook Islands has sought closer economic and cultural ties with French Polynesia to balance its relationship with New Zealand.

Government

The Cook Islands' 25-member Parliament operates on the Westminster system, with a prime minister as the head of government. The cabinet consists of up to eight ministers. While almost all members of parliament are men, most of the chiefly titles are held by women, who are also the main landowners. In theory, the 21-member House of Ariki (chiefs) should be consulted on custom and land issues, but in practice this seldom happens.

On all the outer islands there's an appointed chief administrative officer (CAO), formerly known as the resident agent. Although each island also has an elected Island Council, the CAO runs the local administration on behalf of the local and central governments.

Politics

Party politics, often based on personalities, is vicious. The most dramatic event of the early years of self-government was the removal of Premier Albert Henry and the Cook Islands Party from office in 1978 by the chief justice of the High Court when it was proven that Henry had misused government funds to fly in his voters from New Zealand during the preceding election. Then, Queen Elizabeth II stripped Sir Albert of his knighthood. This was the first time in Commonwealth history that a court ruling had changed a government; the shock waves are still being felt on Rarotonga. Albert Henry died in 1981, it's said of a broken heart.

Albert Henry's successor, Sir Tom Davis of the Democratic Party, served as prime minister from 1978 until 1987. The Cook Islands Party, led by Sir Geoffrey Henry, a cousin of Albert, won the 1989 and 1994 elections. Henry's tenure was marked by financial disasters and a population collapse. In the 1999 elections the vote was split between the Cook Islands Party, the Democratic Alliance Party, and the New Alliance Party, and the post of prime minister has been rotating as politicians switch sides for personal advantage. Office space, vehicles, expense accounts, jobs for relatives, and overseas travel are among the perks

parliamentarians enjoy in addition to their generous salaries. After lengthy public consultations in 1998, a Commission of Inquiry into Political Reform called for a reduction in the number of members of parliament. However, this and the commission's 44 other recommendations have just been ignored by the politicians.

ECONOMY

The Cook Islands has a severe trade imbalance, with imports outweighing exports by 11 times. Food imports alone cost three times the value of all exports. New Zealand benefits greatly from this situation by supplying 70 percent of the Cook Islands' imports. Around NZ$11 million comes back in the form of New Zealand aid to health, education, and special projects. Money remitted by Cook Islanders resident in New Zealand does its part to cover the country's import bill, and quite often durable goods included in the import figures are actually gifts sent home by family members abroad. Tourism plays a vital role in correcting the balance of payments, and licensing fees from South Korean and other foreign fishing companies exploiting the exclusive economic zone bring in additional income. A local tuna fishing industry is also developing.

The largest exports are cultured pearls, fruits and vegetables, clothing, and fish and seafood in that order. Cultured pearls alone account for 90 percent of the country's exports and the percentage continues to grow. Fresh fruit production is hindered by the small volume, uneven quality, inadequate shipping, poor marketing, and the unreliability of island producers. Most food is imported and the local produce markets are usually empty.

The economy's small size is illustrated by the importance of the post office's Philatelic Bureau. A number of small clothing factories in Avarua supply tropical beachware to the local and tourist markets. Subsistence fishing and agriculture are important on the outer islands.

Future wealth may come from the mining of undersea deposits of cobalt, copper, and nickel inside the exclusive economic zone. In 1997 the Cook Islands signed a deal theoretically worth

US$600 million with the American mining giant Bechtel Corporation. After a careful study in 2001, mining experts from Norway found that current world cobalt prices of around US$15 a pound made exploiting these reserves unviable. They did note that if prices were to increase to US$25, a 30 percent profit on investment was possible.

Finance

Since 1984 the Cook Islands has operated as an "international finance center" providing offshore banking facilities to foreign corporations and individuals attempting to avoid taxation and regulation in their home countries. In contrast to local businesses, which are heavily taxed and regulated, more than 3,000 companies, trusts, banks, and insurance companies that don't operate in the Cooks are now registered in the Rarotonga "tax haven," bringing in about NZ$4 million a year in banking and licensing fees. Offshore "banks" can be owned by a single person and it's believed that millions of illicit dollars have been laundered through Rarotonga. The number of Asian companies involved is significant.

Such arrangements allow individuals in other jurisdictions to transfer revenue to "asset protection trusts" in the Cook Islands that are safe from creditors in the event of a subsequent bankruptcy. Thus unscrupulous individuals can plunder their own companies elsewhere in order to build up tax-free nest eggs on Rarotonga. Profits can be routed through the Cook Islands to avoid taxation. Scams such as these helped generate the Asian financial crisis of 1997, and teams of highly paid lawyers and accountants based on Rarotonga and abroad facilitate the process.

In June 2001, the 26-nation Financial Action Task Force of the Organization for Economic Cooperation and Development put the Cook Islands and 10 other countries on a blacklist of "uncooperative jurisdictions" with regulatory systems that make them attractive money laundering locations. Australia and New Zealand have revised their tax laws to restrict the use of tax havens by their citizens (penalties of up to 125 percent of the tax due and five years in prison).

The country has a NZ$119 million national debt, most of it incurred during the administration

an outer island schoolhouse on Palmerston atoll

of Sir Geoffrey Henry in the 1990s for tourism-related developments such as the Sheraton Hotel project, the National Cultural Center, power generation, and telecommunications. Much of the money is owed to the governments of Italy and Nauru, which foolishly guaranteed huge unsecured loans to this tiny country, but NZ$27 million of it came from the Asian Development Bank, which has had to intervene several times to save the Cook Islands from bankruptcy.

In mid-1994 local branches of the ANZ and Westpac banks began to severely restrict private credit after the government proved unable to service its heavy debt load. A few months later the banks stopped clearing checks drawn in the Cook Islands dollars through the New Zealand banking system and announced that these would have to be collected locally. Local businesses began moving money offshore, and in late 1994 the Reserve Bank of New Zealand confirmed that it no longer guaranteed the convertibility of the Cook Islands dollar. The threat of imminent financial collapse forced the government to withdraw the currency from circulation in 1995. New Zealand banknotes are used at present.

Until 1996 the Cook Islands had a bloated public service of 3,600 people or 60 percent of the workforce. Then, after the Westpac Bank bounced official salary checks because of a US$5 million dollar overdraft in the government's current account, civil servants were forced to accept a 15 percent across-the-board pay cut. As interest on unpaid government loans continued to mount, it became clear that harsher measures were required. Thus it was announced that government employee numbers would be reduced to 1,200 and the pay cut increased to 65 percent; 1996–1999, 3,969 Cook Islanders, a quarter of the population, voted with their feet and left for greener pastures in Australia and New Zealand. State assets (including four hotels and the telephone company) were hurriedly sold off and the number of government departments cut in half. The country is still recovering from this disaster.

The Cook Islands runs a discount "flag of convenience" ship registry that allows foreign shipping companies to avoid the more stringent safety and labor regulations of industrialized countries. Because of unexplained sinkings and other costly mishaps, most insurance companies won't touch ships registered in the Cooks. (Despite all the infighting and chicanery described herein, the Cook Islands is completely safe and stable for tourism. The Australian guidebooks conveniently leave out most of this information and are generally uncritical in order to curry favor on Rarotonga.)

Tourism

Since the opening of the international airport in 1973, tourism has been important, and directly or indirectly, it now employs more than a quarter of the workforce and accounts for NZ$75 million of the NZ$158 million gross national product. The Cook Islands has the highest tourist density in the South Pacific with four tourists a year for every local resident, compared to two Fijians, three Samoans, and four Tongans for every tourist visiting those countries. At times Rarotonga (with six tourists a year per Cook Islander) really has the feel of a little Hawaii.

After the civil coup in Fiji in May 2000, many tourists switched their holidays to the Cook Islands and arrivals jumped 50 percent. About a third of the 75,000-odd arriving tourists are New Zealanders who spend all their time at resorts on Rarotonga and Aitutaki on prepaid packaged holidays. The rest are fairly evenly divided between Americans, Australians, Canadians, and Europeans. Few Asian tourists make it this far. Fears have been expressed that Rarotonga's waste disposal, electricity generation, and water supply systems won't be able to keep pace with the rapid expansion of tourism, and tourist demand has led to double-digit inflation in the local housing market.

In 1984 "experts" from the United Nations Development Program advised that the way to make tourism more "profitable" was to allow more large hotels and stop construction of the smaller, family-operated motels. Finding itself unable to attract the required foreign investment, the government itself decided to bankroll construction of a four-star luxury hotel, and in 1987 NZ$52 million was borrowed from an Italian bank. A year later the Democratic Party government collapsed, and in 1989 Sir Geoffrey Henry's Cook Islands Party was voted in after promising to stop the project. Once in office, however, Sir Geoffrey did an about-face and announced that he now backed the hotel. A management contract was signed with the Sheraton chain and in May 1990, despite many objections from local residents, construction began on the south side of Rarotonga using Italian building materials and contractors.

The 204-room Cook Islands Sheraton Resort was conceived as a cluster of two-story buildings, similar to the Fiji Sheraton, with the inevitable 18-hole golf course. The project suffered repeated delays, and then it was announced that the Italian construction company had gone broke after spending NZ$30 million of the government's loan money without getting much done. A second Italian construction company (Stephany SpA) was brought in, and the government borrowed another NZ$20 million so work could resume. In mid-1993 the Italian government began its "clean hands" crackdown on Mafia activities, and several people involved in the Sheraton project were arrested in Italy, causing the Italian insurers to freeze coverage on the loans, and work on the Sheraton stopped again.

In late 1998 the government attempted to restart the project by letting its lease on the property lapse and turning the project over to Hawaiian/Japanese investors who paid the landowner a NZ$300,000 advance on the annual rent. A few months later the Japanese partner was arrested for tax fraud and the deal collapsed. In late 2000, another company announced that it was willing to finish the hotel, which would become a Hilton, provided it got a casino license. This outraged the pious Rarotongans, who held meetings and circulated petitions vehemently opposed to gambling, and the casino idea had to be dropped. The uncertainty continues and demolition of the shell of what is now euphemistically called the 'Vaimaanga Hotel" may be the only solution.

What has gone on behind the scenes in all of this is largely unknown and the Cook Islands Government claims it doesn't have the resources/ability to mount a proper investigation. Most of the records are said to be missing, and between 10 and 20 million New Zealand dollars have simply "disappeared." In 1998 the government's NZ$120 million Italian debt was rescheduled to NZ$55 million to be paid over 27 years. (Sheraton had nothing to do with the construction scandal and would have become involved only had the project been completed.)

Pearls

In 1982 research began into the possibility of creating a cultured-pearl industry similar to that of French Polynesia. The first commercial farms were set up on Manihiki in 1989 and more than two million cultured oysters are now held there. By 1994 the Manihiki lagoon was thought to be approaching its maximum sustainable holding capacity and farms began to be established on Penrhyn. Hundreds of thousands of oysters are held at the various farms, and the Penrhyn hatchery is constantly producing more. Oyster farming has also begun on Rakahanga and the industry may soon spread to Suwarrow.

To establish a farm, an investment of NZ$5,000 is required, and no return will be forthcoming for five years. There are now more than 300 farms with just 20 percent of them accounting for 80 percent of the oysters. The oysters are seeded once or twice a year by Japanese, Chinese, and Cook Islands experts screened by the Ministry of Marine Resources. Fluctuations in water temperature and overstocking can affect the amount of plankton available to the oysters and reduce the quality of the pearls. Rising water temperatures and overcrowding can have an immediate impact, as demonstrated by an algal bloom at Manihiki in 2001 that killed 15 percent of seeded oysters, leading to an estimated loss of NZ$34 million over five years.

Annual production is around 200 kilograms, with Japanese and Chinese dealers the big buyers. Black pearls are the Cook Islands' largest export by far, bringing in NZ$15 million a year and employing 700 people. Fortunately a major hurricane at Manihiki in 1997 did little harm to the underwater oysters although surface facilities were destroyed. Pearl prices are falling as production increases and some producers are worried that the pearl boom may have already peaked.

THE PEOPLE

About 84 percent of the people are Polynesian Cook Island Maoris, most of whom also have some other ancestry. They're related to the Maoris of New Zealand and the Tahitians, although the Pukapukans are unique in that they are closer to the Samoans. Almost everyone on Rarotonga and most people on the outer islands speak flawless English, while their mother tongue will be one of the 11 dialects of Cook Islands Maori. Rarotongan is now spoken throughout the southern group. Penrhyn is closely related to Rarotongan, Rakahanga-Manihiki is more distantly related, and Pukapukan is related to Samoan.

Over half the population lives on Rarotonga; only 13 percent live in the northern group. Cook Islanders live near the seashore, except on Atiu and Mauke, where they are interior dwellers. The old-style thatched *kikau* houses have almost disappeared from the Cook Islands, even though they're cooler, more esthetic, and much cheaper to build than modern housing. A thatched pandanus roof can last 15 years.

While 18,027 (2001) Cook Islanders live in their home islands, some 60,000 live in New Zealand and another 10,000 in Australia. Emigration to New Zealand increased greatly after the airport opened in 1973. During the 1980s the migratory patterns reversed and many ex-islanders returned from New Zealand to set up tourism-related businesses, but because of the economic crisis the steady flow of people to New Zealand and Australia resumed in 1996 and the total population has actually decreased. The loss of many teachers and students forced schools and classes to be amalgamated and led to an increase in the dropout rate among teenagers. Education is compulsory until the age of 15.

There are almost no Chinese in the Cooks because of a deliberate policy of discrimination initiated in 1901 by New Zealand Prime Minister Richard Seddon, although many islanders have some Chinese blood resulting from the presence of Chinese traders in the 19th century. A quarter of the population was born outside the South Pacific and the proportion of Americans, New Zealanders, Australians, and others is increasing rapidly as "lifestyle investors" arrive to run businesses in the Cook Islands while the islanders themselves move in the opposite direction.

Under the British and New Zealand regimes, the right of the Maori people to their land was protected, and no land was sold to outsiders. These policies continue today, although foreigners can lease land for up to 60 years. The fragmentation of inherited landholdings into scattered miniholdings hampers agriculture and many fine late-19th-century stone buildings have fallen into ruins because of ownership disputes.

The powerful *ariki*, or chiefly class, that ruled in pre-European times is still influential today. The *ariki* were the first to adopt Christianity, instructing their subjects to follow suit and filling leadership posts in the church. British and New Zealand colonial rule was established with the approval of the *ariki*. Today materialism, party politics, and emigration to New Zealand are eroding the authority of the *ariki. Ariki* titles are tied to land and cannot be carried overseas (the title passes to another family member if a holder decides to migrate to New Zealand). Until self-government, Cook Islanders were allowed to consume alcohol only if they had a permit; now it's a serious social problem.

Dangers and Annoyances

When stepping out at night or choosing a place to stay, women should keep in mind that sexual assault is not unknown here. There's safety in numbers. Scanty dress outside the resorts will cause offense and maybe trouble. To go to church

> *The people of the Cook Islands are related to the Maoris of New Zealand and the Tahitians, although the Pukapukans are unique in that they are closer to the Samoans. Almost everyone on Rarotonga and most people on the outer islands speak flawless English, while their mother tongue will be one of the 11 dialects of Cook Islands Maori.*

women should wear a dress with long sleeves and a hat, while men need long trousers and a proper shirt. Be aware of petty theft, particularly if you're staying somewhere with young children running loose. Don't leave things unattended on a clothesline or the beach and keep your shoes in your room at night. Try to avoid being bitten by mosquitoes, as dengue fever epidemics have occurred on Rarotonga in recent years (see Health in the main introduction).

Exploring the Islands

HIGHLIGHTS

Everyone will arrive on **Rarotonga** and the short-list of "musts" includes an island night dance show, a bicycle ride around the island, a swim in the Muri Lagoon, and a hike up to the Needle on the Cross-Island Track. The main town Avarua has two museums and various monuments associated with 19th century missionaries. The finest snorkeling is at Titikaveka on the southeast side of the island.

The snorkeling at **Aitutaki** is even better and it's another nice place to hang loose. The lagoon trips by boat to One Foot Island are very popular and traditional dance shows are staged at the resorts almost every night.

However, to get a real feel for the Cook Islands, you must travel beyond this rather touristy pair to an outer island. Most of the people on **Atiu** live in the center of the island. Deep caves penetrate the island's uplifted limestone ring, and Atiu has the added attraction of *tumunus* where bush beer is served. **Mauke** is similar and even less visited. **Mangaia** has some of the most spectacular elevated coral formations in the world. All three islands have regular flights from Rarotonga and a few small lodgings, although other visitor facilities are scanty—they're that unspoiled.

Because of infrequent and expensive transportation, the Northern Group is seldom visited by tourists. In recent years these far-flung atolls have been rediscovered thanks to the cultured pearl industry.

SPORTS AND RECREATION

Several professional scuba diving companies are based on Rarotonga and Aitutaki, and there are many snorkeling possibilities. Both islands offer lagoon tours by boat, with those at Aitutaki by far the better.

Operators based on Rarotonga's Muri Beach rent water-sports equipment, including windsurfers, sailboats, and kayaks, with training in their use available. The surfing possibilities are very limited in the Cook Islands—windsurfing's the thing to do. Horseback riding and deep-sea fishing are other popular activities.

Most of the hiking possibilities are on mountainous Rarotonga, but uplifted islands such as Atiu, Mauke, and Mangaia are also fascinating to wander around. The nine-hole golf courses on Aitutaki and Rarotonga aren't too challenging, but greens fees are low and the atmospheres amicable. Tournaments are held at both in September.

The spectator sports are cricket December–February, with matches every Saturday afternoon from 1300, and rugby May–July. Rugby is the main male team sport played in the Cooks; soccer is a more recent introduction (played year-round). On Rarotonga, ask about rugby matches at Tereora National Stadium, on the inland side of the airport, and in the sports ground opposite the National Cultural Center in Avarua. Netball is the most popular women's sport, especially in March and April.

ENTERTAINMENT AND EVENTS
Music and Dance
Among main genres of Cook Islands music and dance are drum dancing *('ura pa'u)*, choreographed group dancing *(kaparima)* to string band music, dance dramas *(peu tupuna)* based on island legends, religious pageants *(nuku)*, formal chants *(pe'e)*, celebratory song/chants *('ute)*, and polyphonic choral music *('imene tapu)* or hymns.

COOK ISLANDS

Among the drums used are the small *pate* or *to'ere* slit drum used to guide the dancers, the *pa'u*, a double-headed bass drum that provides the beat, and the upright *pa'u mango* that accompanies the *pa'u*. The larger *ka'ara* slit drum and the conch shell accompany chanting. Tahitian drummers have often copied Cook Island rhythms. String band music is based on the ukulele although guitars are also used.

The top traditional dancing is seen during annual events on Rarotonga when the outer islanders arrive to compete. The drum dancing at hotel shows features the sensuous side-to-side hip movements of the women (differing somewhat from the circular movements seen on Tahiti) and the robust knee snapping of the men. In the Cook Islands the dancers keep their feet apart, while in Tahiti the feet are together. In the *hura* (equivalent of the Hawaiian *hula)* the female dancers must keep their feet flat on the ground and shoulders steady as they sway in a stunning display.

Public Holidays and Festivals

Public holidays include New Year's Day (January 1), ANZAC Day (April 25), Good Friday, Easter Monday (March/April), Queen Elizabeth's Birthday (first Monday in June), Constitution Day (August 4), National Gospel Day (October 26), Christmas Day (December 25), and Boxing Day (December 26). On Rarotonga, Gospel Day is celebrated on July 26; elsewhere it's October 26.

The Dancer of the Year Competition is in late April. The 10-day Te Maeva Celebrations is the big event of the year, culminating on Constitution Day (August 4). There are parades, drumming and singing contests, sporting events, and an agricultural fair. The Round Raro Road Race is a 31-km marathon held on the first Saturday of October (the record time is 98 minutes set by Kevin Ryan in 1979). There's the annual *tivaevae* show mid-October–mid-November at the National Museum on Rarotonga. National Gospel Day (October 26) recalls October 26, 1821, when the Reverend John Williams landed on Aitutaki. Ask about Biblical pageants *(nuku)* on that day. On All Souls Day (November 1) Catholics visit the cemeteries to place candles and flowers on the graves of family members. The third or fourth week in November is the Tiare Festival, with flower shows, a parade, and beauty contests.

ACCOMMODATIONS

There's an abundance of accommodations in all price categories on Rarotonga and Aitutaki, and most outer islands also have one or two places to stay. Accommodations accredited by the Cook Islands Tourism Corporation must meet certain standards and those that do can include a distinctive tick mark in their advertising. The accreditation system recognizes three categories: budget, self-catering, and hotels. Essentially you have a "hotel" if you have a restaurant (and a few other minor things). In fact, many of the "self-catering" places are nicer that most of the hotels, so don't go by price alone. The nonaccredited establishments aren't mentioned in the official tourist brochures, though the vast majority of them are also quite okay.

You'll save money and get closer to the people by staying at the smaller, locally owned "self-catering" motels and guesthouses. A "motel" in the Cooks is styled on the New Zealand type of motel, which means a fully equipped kitchen is built into each unit. Some of them are quite attractive, nothing like the dreary roadside motels of North America. The motels generally offer rooms with private bath and hot water, but some guesthouses and hostels do not, although communal cooking facilities are usually available.

The policy set by the Cook Islands Immigration Department is to have at least one night's accommodation booked before you arrive. Although many visitors wait to book their rooms upon arrival, they are taking the risk of being refused entry to the country if they happened to come on a day when everything was full. In practice this rarely happens, but to avoid the possibility, simply write the name of one of the places to stay listed herein on your arrivals card. As you come out of the airport terminal, ask for the representative of that place. If the person is not there or the place happens to be full, ask for something similar.

The backpacker hostels always have empty dorm beds, but accommodation is sometimes tight in the medium-priced range. If you're sure you want to stay at a particular place, you can easily make a booking by emailing the hostel or hotel directly. Most places have a two-night minimum stay and you shouldn't promise to stay longer than that. Then if you end up with something you don't like, you can easily move elsewhere. Hotel rates tend to fluctuate in the Cook Islands and when things are slow some places cut their prices to attract guests, so in some cases you could end up paying less than the amounts quoted herein.

Camping is not allowed in the Cook Islands. There's a shortage of flights into the Cooks and airline seats are often at a premium. The government would rather see those seats being used by regular resort tourists who'll be spending more money and thereby paying more taxes. The main aim of campers is to save money, the exact opposite of what the government wants. And since the government makes the rules, camping has always been banned. The officials would also like to reduce the number of backpacker dormitories on Rarotonga, but the dorms are owned by local people and closing them now would have political repercussions.

Travel with Children

Unlike French Polynesia, where children are welcome at virtually all of the resorts and charged reduced rates at most, many accommodations in the Cook Islands have a "no children" policy that's designed to enhance their appeal to "romantic couples" and honeymooners. The age limit varies and is noted in the listings whenever possible. Among the Rarotonga properties excluding young children are Maiana Guesthouse, Manuia Beach Hotel, Oasis Village, Paradise Inn, Rarotongan Sunset Motel, Reflections on Rarotonga, Shangri-La Beach Cottages, Sokala Villas, Sunhaven Beach Bungalows, Takitumu Romantic Villas, and The Little Polynesian. On Aitutaki, the Are Tamanu Beach Hotel doesn't admit children.

In contrast, the largest properties, including the Aitutaki Pearl Beach Resort, the Edgewater Re-

sort, the Pacific Resort, and the Rarotongan Beach Resort, give discounts to families and have special programs for kids. Other Rarotonga accommodations with special deals for families include Lagoon Lodges, Palm Grove Lodges, and Moana Sands. If you suspect that the sight and sound of children might blemish your holiday, choose an adults-only property.

Booking Agencies

Island Hopper Vacations (tel. 22-576, fax 23-027, www.islandhopper.co.ck), next to the Banana Court in Avarua, offers accommodation deals and outer island flights. **Jetsave Travel** (tel. 27-707, fax 28-807, www.jetsave.co.ck), just west of the Westpac Bank, and **Tipani Tours** (www.tipanitours.com) are similar. These companies also offer transfers, wedding arrangements, and dive packages.

Be aware that these agents charge commissions as high as 35 percent to the owners and you can often get a better rate by checking the hotel's website and emailing directly. On the plus side, the companies just mentioned do book the smaller, budget properties travel agents outside the Cooks won't touch because the commissions are so small.

FOOD

The Rarotonga restaurant scene has improved in recent years and you now have a good choice. A few restaurants are found on Aitutaki, but none exist on the outer islands. When ordering, keep in mind that an "entrée" is actually an appetizer and not a main dish.

By law all bars are required to close at midnight, except on Fridays when they can stay open until 0200 Saturday morning. On Sunday no alcohol may be sold at grocery stores, and that day even restaurants are allowed to serve alcohol only with a meal, although this rule is not always followed. Wine is expensive at restaurants, because of high import duties, and drinking alcoholic beverages on the street is prohibited. You'll

Locals insist that slippery foods such as bananas lead to forgetfulness, while gluey foods such as taro help one to remember.

COOK ISLANDS

save a lot on meals if you stay at one of the many motels and guesthouses offering cooking facilities.

Rukau is Cook Islands *palusami,* made from spinachlike young taro leaves cooked in coconut cream. *Ika mata* is marinated raw fish with coconut sauce. Locals insist that slippery foods such as bananas lead to forgetfulness, while gluey foods like taro help one to remember. Dogs are sometimes eaten by young men on drinking sprees. (Turn to the Atiu section for information on "bush beer"—called "home-brewed" on Rarotonga and Aitutaki).

INFORMATION AND SERVICES

Information

For advance information about the country, write to one of the overseas branches of government-operated **Cook Islands Tourism Corporation** listed in the back of this book, or to its head office at P.O. Box 14, Rarotonga (www .cook-islands.com). Ask for its free magazine, *Jasons What's On in the Cook Islands,* and the color map *Jasons Passport Cook Islands.* Be aware that the Tourism Corporation's publications and website list only "accredited" businesses, and the Jasons publications are slanted toward their advertisers.

Elliot Smith's *Cook Islands Companion* is recommended for those who want more detailed information on the country than can be included here. It's possible to buy a personally autographed copy directly from the author at Shangri-La Beach Cottages on Muri Beach.

Visas and Officialdom

No visa is required for a stay of up to 31 days, but you must show a ticket to leave (the airline can be fined as much as NZ$10,000 if it's caught carrying a passenger without an onward ticket). For NZ$70 you can get extensions up to six months in the Cooks. Apply at the Immigration office (tel. 29-347, fax 21-247) on the top floor of the Government Office Building behind the post office. Actually, one week is plenty of time to see Rarotonga and 31 days is sufficient to visit all of the southern Cook Islands.

If you're thinking of taking a boat trip to the northern group, be sure to get a visa extension before you leave Rarotonga. Otherwise you could have problems with Immigration if your entry permit has expired by the time you get back.

People with business skills or money to invest can obtain work and residence permits through the **Cook Islands Development Investment Board** (tel. 24-296, fax 24-298), a one-stop shop for "lifestyle investors." (For details, consult its website www.cookislands-invest.com.)

Foreigners can obtain permanent residency in the Cook Islands after five years but such status is granted only in exceptional circumstances, such as to those who have made significant financial investments in the country. Cook Islands citizenship has never been extended to Europeans.

Rarotonga, Aitutaki, and Penrhyn are ports of entry for cruising yachts; the only harbors for yachts are at Aitutaki, Penrhyn, Suwarrow, and Rarotonga.

Money

The currency is the New Zealand dollar, which was valued at US$1 = NZ$2 at press time. After the financial crisis of 1995 the Cook Islands dollar, which had circulated at par with the New Zealand dollar since 1987, was withdrawn. Cook Islands coins are still in use, however, although these are worthless outside the Cook Islands. The Cook Islands dollar coin bearing an image of the god Tangaroa makes an offbeat souvenir.

Traveler's checks are worth about 3 percent more than cash at the banks. Changing money on an outer island is difficult or impossible—do it before you leave Rarotonga. The upmarket hotels and restaurants accept the main credit cards, and the banks will give cash advances. Many places won't allow credit cards to be used for petty charges.

A 12.5 percent value-added tax (VAT) is added to all sales, services, activities, and rentals. Most places include it in the price, but some add it on, so ask. Bargaining has never been a part of the local culture and some locals find it offensive when tourists try to beat prices down. The way to do it is to ask for "specials." Thankfully tipping is still not widespread in the Cooks.

COOK ISLANDS INTERNET RESOURCES

General Interest

Cook Islands Tourism Corporation
www.cook-islands.com
tourism@cookislands.gov.ck

Media and Services

Cook Islands Development Investment Board
www.cookislands-invest.com

Cook Islands Herald
www.ciherald.co.ck

Cook Islands News
www.cinews.co.ck

Radio Cook Islands
www.radio.co.ck

Telecom Cook Islands
www.telecom.co.ck

Transportation and Tours

Air Rarotonga
www.airraro.com
bookings@airraro.co.ck
enrhyn@airraro.co.ck

Cook Islands Tours
www.cookislandstours.co.ck
raroinfo@citours.co.ck

Hugh Henry & Associates
tours@hughhenry.co.ck

Island Hopper Vacations
www.islandhoppervacations.com
info@islandhopper.co.ck

Jetsave Travel
www.jetsave.co.ck
jetsave@cooks.co.ck

Matina Travel
trvlsave@matinatravel.co.ck

Raro Tours
coaches@rarotours.co.ck

Tipani Tours
www.tipanitours.com
info@tipani.co.ck

Communications

Telecom Cook Islands (tel. 29-680, fax 26-174) charges a flat rate for international telephone calls with no off-hour discounts. Three-minute operator-assisted calls cost NZ$11.50 to the United States, NZ$12.40 to New Zealand, and NZ$13 to Australia. Person-to-person calls attract an additional two-minute charge.

It's cheaper to use a local telephone card for international calls as there's no three-minute minimum with a card (dial the international access code 00, the country code, the area code, and the number). More important, with a card you can't lose track of the time and end up being presented a tremendous bill. The cards come in denominations of NZ$5, NZ$10, NZ$20, and NZ$50 and are good for all domestic and international calls. Calls to outer islands within the Cook Islands cost NZ$1 a minute with a card.

You'll need a card to make local calls as there aren't any coin telephones here.

Collect calls can be placed to Australia, Canada, Fiji, French Polynesia, Malaysia, Netherlands, New Zealand, Niue, Tonga, United Kingdom, and the United States only. To call collect, dial the international/outer island operator at tel. 015. Directory assistance numbers within the Cook Islands are tel. 010, international tel. 017 (NZ$0.20 fee). The country code of the Cook Islands is 682.

For calls to the United States, the "AT&T Direct" service is more expensive than using a local telephone card, but perhaps useful in emergencies. To be connected to this service dial 09-111 from any phone in the Cook Islands. The Telecom New Zealand Direct number is tel. 0964-09682.

Many local businesses now have email. Visitors can check their email at any of the numerous

Internet outlets around Rarotonga at between NZ$.20 and NZ$.35 a minute. You may also find such a place on Aitutaki, and on the other islands your guesthouse may provide access for the usual fee.

Media

Be sure to pick up a copy of the *Cook Islands News* (tel. 22-999, fax 25-303), published daily except Sunday (NZ$1 weekdays, NZ$1.35 Saturday). Its stories on island affairs really give you a feel for where you are, and local happenings are listed.

The *Cook Islands Herald* (tel. 29-460) is a weekly paper published on Rarotonga. Although published in Auckland, the weekly *Cook Islands Star* is available on Rarotonga and it's worth buying for Jason Brown's investigative reporting. The *Cook Islands Sun* is a free tourist newspaper also published in New Zealand.

On Rarotonga, **Radio KC FM** (tel. 23-203) broadcasts over 103.3 MHz from 0530–2400 with overseas news at 0600 and 0700. The FM station can be difficult to pick up on the south side of Rarotonga, but **Radio Cook Islands** (tel. 29-560) at 630 kHz AM can be heard anywhere on the island (and even on nearby islands such as Mauke in the evening). This station, the *Herald,* and Television Cook Islands are owned by the influential Pitt family.

Measurements and Time

The electric voltage is 240 volts DC, 50 cycles, the same as in New Zealand and Australia. American appliances will require a converter. The type of plug varies, but bring a three-pin adaptor. On outer islands other than Aitutaki electricity is provided only a few hours a day.

The time is the same as in Hawaii and Tahiti, two hours behind California and 22 hours behind Fiji and New Zealand. "Cook Islands time" also runs a bit behind "Western tourist's time," so relax and let things happen. Most banks and government offices are closed on Saturday, although the shops and restaurants in Avarua are usually open until noon. In recent years regulations have been relaxed and many small shops and car rental outlets on Rarotonga are now open on Sunday.

TRANSPORTATION

Getting There

Air New Zealand (tel. 26-300), with an office at Rarotonga Airport, has direct service to Rarotonga from Auckland (daily), Nadi (weekly), Papeete (weekly), and Los Angeles (three a week). In early 2003 Aloha Airlines began flying to Rarotonga from Honolulu, with connections from the North American west coast.

Air services into Rarotonga are heavily booked, so reserve your inward and outward flights as far ahead as possible. If you try to change your outbound flight after arrival you could be put on standby.

Check in for your outgoing international flight at least one hour before the scheduled departure time, as the airlines are short of staff: if everyone is needed to attend to a flight arrival, they may simply close the check-in counter and you'll be out of luck.

Getting Around by Air

Air Rarotonga (tel. 22-888, fax 23-288) carries the distinction of being one of the only South Pacific airlines that is entirely privately owned and profitable to boot. It provides regular air service from Rarotonga to all of the main islands of the southern Cooks and a few of the northern group, although no flights operate on Sunday. It uses a 34-seat SAAB 340 SF3 aircraft to Aitutaki; all other flights are in an 18-seat Embraer Bandeirante.

The flights to Aitutaki (NZ$158 one way) are three times daily except Sunday. A reduced NZ$128 one-way fare to Aitutaki is available northbound on the afternoon flight and southbound on the morning flight. Air Rarotonga runs day trips from Rarotonga to Aitutaki at NZ$389 including round-trip airfare, transfers, a lagoon tour, lunch, and drinks, but these are too rushed. Northbound sit on the left side of the aircraft for the best views.

Air Rarotonga flies from Rarotonga to Atiu (NZ$142) daily except Sunday, to Mauke (NZ$158) every weekday, to Mangaia (NZ$142) four times a week, and to Mitiaro (NZ$158) three times a week.

The interisland connection Atiu–Mitiaro–Mauke works only once a week, and interisland flights Atiu–Mitiaro and Mitiaro–Mauke are NZ$90 each. There's no flight Atiu–Mauke and you must stop over on Mitiaro at least one night en route to make the connection. Once a week you can fly between Atiu–Aitutaki–Atiu (NZ$142 one-way).

Air Rarotonga's "Island Discovery" ticket costs NZ$355 for a trip Rarotonga, Aitutaki, Atiu, Rarotonga. With Mitiaro included it's NZ$429. Add Mauke and it's NZ$505. To include Mangaia in any of the above is another NZ$107. This nonrefundable pass is valid for 45 days maximum and date changes (but not route changes) are allowed. Reservations are required, as space is limited.

Manihiki (NZ$1,085 round-trip) and Penrhyn (NZ$1,203 round-trip) receive Air Rarotonga flights weekly. There's no flight Manihiki–Penrhyn and only charter flights operate to Pukapuka. The plane can't land at all on Rakahanga. Sitting in a Bandierante for four hours from Rarotonga to Manihiki or Penrhyn can be quite an experience!

Children under 12 pay half price. In late 2001 a NZ$4 per flight insurance surcharge was imposed and this will be added to all ticket prices above. Try to reconfirm your return flight, and beware of planes leaving early! Avoid scheduling your flight back to Rarotonga for the same day you're supposed to catch an International flight.

The baggage allowance is 16 kilos, though you can sometimes get by with more. On flights to Manihiki and Penrhyn the limit is 10 kilos. Overweight is not expensive, but if the plane is full and too heavy for the short outer-island runways the airline will refuse excess baggage from all passengers. Thus it pays to stay below the limit.

Getting Around by Ship

Taio Shipping Ltd. (Teremoana Taio, tel. 24-905, fax 24-906), opposite the Ports Authority Building on Rarotonga's Avatiu Harbor, operates the interisland vessels *Manu Nui* and the smaller *Maungaroa*. Taio tries to run a ship around the southern and northern groups

KILOMETERS BETWEEN ISLANDS

	Rarotonga	Aitutaki	Mauke	Mitiaro	Atiu	Mangaia	Palmerston	Pukapuka	Nassau	Manihiki	Rakahanga	Penrhyn
Aitutaki	259											
Mauke	278	296										
Mitiaro	263	241	59									
Atiu	215	209	93	235								
Mangaia	204	385	213	232	215							
Palmerston	500	367	657	611	574	704						
Pukapuka	1,324	1,089	1,361	1,304	1,296	1,470	843					
Nassau	1,246	1,000	1,278	1,217	1,209	1,382	756	89				
Manihiki	1,204	946	1,145	1,102	1,093	1,304	880	530	500			
Rakahanga	1,248	991	1,189	1,146	1,137	1,348	922	535	506	44		
Penrhyn	1,365	1,111	1,241	1,204	1,222	1,433	1,130	889	859	363	354	
Suwarrow	950	713	978	926	917	1,111	533	398	310	385	417	733

monthly. The schedule varies according to the amount of cargo waiting to move and the only way to find out is to ask at the office. Also ask about special trips to Apia in Samoa.

To do a four- to five-day round-trip to the southern group costs NZ$130–150. To sail around the northern group for 12–13 days costs NZ$750. On a one-way basis it's NZ$65 from Rarotonga to any of the islands of the southern group, or NZ$25 deck between Atiu, Mauke, and Mitiaro only. One-way fares to the northern group are around NZ$300. Passengers must bring their own food.

Be forewarned that accommodations on this sort of ship are often next to noisy, hot engine rooms and tend to be cluttered with crates. Passengers sleep may have to under a canvas awning, and although it may be a little crowded, the islanders are friendly and easy to get along with. The *Manu Nui* has two three-bunk cabins, but the *Maungaroa* has only an open dorm. On the outer islands, check with the radio operator in the post office to find out when a ship from Rarotonga might be due in. Delays of a few days are routine. In practice, not many visitors travel this way.

Airport

Rarotonga International Airport (RAR) is 2.4 km west of Avarua. Immigration will stamp a 31-day entry permit onto your passport. Be sure to write the name of a hotel in the relevant space on your arrivals card—to leave blank that space will prompt the Immigration clerk to ask where you plan to stay.

As you come out of customs you'll find representatives from most of the backpacker's hostels waiting to the left, at a counter marked "budget accommodations." State the name of the establishment you think best suits your needs and its representative will inform you whether it has any vacant rooms. Have a second name ready in case your first choice is fully occupied. Being prepared will make it easier for you to deal with the drivers eagerly jostling for your business. Most offer a free transfer to their lodging on the understanding that you'll stay at least two nights with them (the upscale places charge NZ$10 for the transfer). A taxi to Avarua will cost around NZ$5.

All the main travel agencies and rental car companies have offices outside arrivals at the airport. There's a card telephone at the airport;

interisland vessels tied up at Avatiu Harbor, Rarotonga

otherwise you can use the public phone at the RSA Club across the street. If you're stuck here waiting for a flight the RSA Club is a much better place to relax than the dreary airport terminal.

The **Westpac Bank** at the airport charges NZ$2.50 commission per transaction. The ANZ Bank has an ATM at the airport, just to the left as you leave the terminal. There are about a dozen left luggage lockers around the side of the arrivals building near the airport fire de-partment (NZ$5 a day). **Raro Tours** (tel. 25-325) at the airport holds luggage at NZ$6 a day per bag. Several duty-free shops open for inter-national arrivals and departures, and arriving passengers are also allowed to duck into the duty-free liquor shop (tel. 29-297) to the right before clearing customs.

A NZ$25 departure tax is charged for inter-national flights (children aged 2–11 pay NZ$10, and transit passengers staying fewer than 24 hours are exempt).

COOK ISLANDS

Rarotonga

The name Rarotonga means "in the direction of the prevailing wind, south," the place where the chief of Atiu promised early explorers they would find an island. It's fairly small, just 31 km around. Twisting valleys lead up to steep ridges covered with luxuriant green vegetation and towering mountains crowned in clouds. Yet, Te Manga (653 meters) is only a fraction of the height Rarotonga reached before the last volcanic eruption took place, more than two million years ago.

Though Rarotonga is younger than the other Cook islands, continuous erosion has cut into the island, washing away the softer material and leaving the hard volcanic cones naked. The mountains are arrayed in a U-shaped arch, start-ing at the airport and then swinging south around to Club Raro, with Maungatea plopped down in the middle. Together they form the surviving southern half of the great broken volcanic caldera that became Rarotonga.

The reef circling the island defines a lagoon that is broad and sandy to the south, and narrow and rocky on the north and east. The finest beaches are on the southeast side near the Muri Lagoon, with crystal-clear water and a sandy bot-tom, but the best snorkeling is at Titikaveka. Elsewhere the water can be cloudy or shallow, with a lot of coral and shells that make wading difficult. Take care everywhere, as several snorkel-ers have drowned after being sucked out through

the passes where a lot of water moves because of surf and tidal swings. Scuba diving on Rarotonga features coral drop-offs, canyons, caves, walls, sharks, wrecks, and swim-throughs. All beaches on the island are public.

In recent years Rarotonga has become New Zealand's answer to Honolulu with 75,000 visitors to an island of 12,000 inhabitants, the same six-to-one visitor/resident ratio experienced in Hawaii. Lodges and resorts completely encircle Rarotonga, and to find that "last heaven on earth" promised in the brochures you must escape to an outer island. Yet Raro remains one of the most beautiful islands in Polynesia, somewhat reminiscent of Moorea (though only half as large). If you enjoy the excitement of big tourist resorts with plenty of opportunities for shopping and eating out, you'll like Rarotonga.

Sights of Rarotonga

Avarua

This attractive town of around 5,000 inhabitants is strung along the north coast beneath the green, misty slopes of Maungatea. The name means "two harbors." Somehow Avarua retains the air of a 19th-century South Seas trading post, and offshore in Avarua Harbor lies the boiler of the Union Steam Ship SS *Maitai,* wrecked in 1916. Near the bridge over Takuvaine Stream is the **Seven-in-One Coconut Tree** planted in 1906.

Inland and south of the post office is the stone on which in 1823 Papeiha preached the first Christian sermon on Rarotonga. It's set on a pedestal in the middle of the crossing with the Ara Metua, Rarotonga's old interior road. Turn left and follow the Ara Metua 150 meters east to a small bridge and a gate leading into the original missionary compound, now **Takamoa Theological College.** You pass a row of student residences, and at the next crossroad you'll find a monument to the missionaries of the London Missionary Society who have served in the Cook Islands. Across the street is an impressive monument to Polynesian missionaries from the college who carried the Gospel to other Pacific Islands. In 1837 the third LMS missionary, Reverend Aaron Buzacott, erected the two-story **Takamoa Mission House** facing the monuments. The adjacent lecture hall dates from 1890.

Follow the road north between the monuments and you'll reach the **Cook Islands Library and Museum** (tel. 26-468; Mon.–Sat. 0900–1300, Tues. also 1600–2000, NZ$2 admission) with assorted artifacts, many of them on loan from museums in New Zealand. Across the street from the museum is the **Cook Islands Center** (tel. 29-415) of the University of the South Pacific, which is worth entering for the interesting books in the showcase on the right.

The massive white walls and roof of the **Cook Islands Christian Church** (1853) are visible from here. Check out the massive wooden balcony inside. It's worth being here Sunday morning at 1000, if only to see the women arrive in their Sunday best and to stand outside and listen to the wonderful singing (go inside and sit down only if you're prepared to stay for the entire service). Near the front of the church is the tomb of Albert Henry (1907–1981), topped by a lifelike statue of the man. American writer Robert Dean Frisbie (1895–1948), author of *The Book of Pukapuka* and *The Island of Desire,* is buried in the southwest corner of the cemetery.

Across the road, beyond some old graves, is the **Para O Tane Palace** of the Makea Takau Ariki, high chief of the landowning clan of most of the Avarua town area. **Marae Taputaputea** and a basalt investiture pillar are on the palace grounds.

Backtrack to the Cook Islands Center and turn left along a wide road to the massive green and white **Are-Karioi-Nui National Auditorium** with 2,000 seats. The four huge buildings to the left of this road are hostels used to house outer islanders when they visit Rarotonga. The auditorium itself forms part of the **National Cultural Center,** erected for the sixth Festival of Pacific Arts in 1992. The two yellow buildings beyond the auditorium contain the **National Library** (tel. 20-725; weekdays 0900–1600) in the building to the right, and the **National Museum** (tel.

PARLIAMENT

AIRPORT TERMINAL

RAROTONGA AIRPORT

Panama

LIQUOR CENTER

Avatiu Harbor

TANGAROA SHOPPING CENTER

GOLF CLUB

Black Rock

NATIONAL STADIUM

TIARE VILLAGE

Avatiu

ARA METUA

TEACHER'S COLLEGE

Nikao

REEFCOMBER SUNSET MOTEL

OASIS VILLAGE

RAROTONGAN SUNSET MOTEL

ARA TAPU

ATUPA ORCHID

Avarua

Maungapiko (154 m)

HOSPITAL

EDGEWATER RESORT

TUMUNU BAR

AUNTY NOO'S

PRISON

POWER STATION

DIVE RAROTONGA

CROWN BEACH RESORT

COOK ISLAND DIVERS

Te Kaki Motu (344 m)

Avatiu Stream

MANUIA BEACH HOTEL

CULTURAL VILLAGE

Te Reinga O Pora (438 m)

ARE RENGA HOTEL

CICC CHURCH

Arorangi

Maungatea (523 m)

ATI'S BEACH VILLAS

Maungaroa (509 m)

SUNHAVEN

ETU BUNGALOWS

Cross

Island

MARIA'S BACKPACKERS

RAROTONGA BACKPACKERS

HIGHLAND PARADISE

Raemaru (350 m)

Track

ROSE FLATS

Te Rua Manga (Needle) (413 m)

Muriavai Stream

Te (58

PUAIKURA REEF LODGE

Papua Stream

BACKPACKERS INTERNATIONAL

Maungatongaite (222 m)

Aroa

Rutaki Stream

Papua Waterfall

LAGOON LODGES

AROA PONY TREKS

ARA TAPU

RAROTONGAN HOTEL

DAYDREAMER

RUINS OF SHERATON RESORT

WIGMORE'S SUPERSTORE

PALM GROVE LODGES

PIRI'S HOSTEL

VAIMA CAFE AND COCKTAILS

Rutaki Passage

Papua Passage

Avaavaroa Passage

0   1 mi

0   1 km

RAROTONGA

PARADISE INN
Avarua
LOVELY PLANET
DENTAL CLINIC
GAME FISHING CLUB
CLUB RARO
KIIKII MOTEL
Pue
ARA
ARA TAPU
METUA
Pue Stream
ARIANA BUNGALOWS MOTEL
MARAE ARAI-TE-TONGA
Takuvaine Stream

Ikurangi (485 m)
Oroenga (292 m)
Tupapa Stream
Matavera
CICC CHURCH

Matavera Stream

Te Manga (653 m)
Te Vaakauta (450 m)
POKATA MARAE
Turangi Stream

Te Atukura (638 m)

TROPICAL SANDS

SUNRISE BEACH BUNGALOWS
Ngatangiia
CICC CHURCH
AVANA MARINA CONDOS
Avana Stream
VAKA VILLAGE
Ngatangiia Bay
Motutapu
AROKO BUNGALOWS
Arore (198 m)
SOKALA VILLAS
PACIFIC DIVERS
KURA'S KABANAS
MANEA BEACH
FLAME TREE
Oneroa
Muri
PACIFIC RESORT
RAROTONGA SAILING CLUB
Koromiri
VARA'S LODGE
Toroume (329 m)
AREMANGO GUESTHOUSE
AMBALA GARDENS
MURI BEACHCOMBER
VARA'S BUDGET ACCOMMODATIONS
Taakoka
ARA TAPU
SHANGRI-LA
QUEEN'S REPRESENTATIVE
Akapuao Stream
TIANA'S BEACH VILLAS
NA HOUSE
A'S BEACH NGALOWS
CICC CHURCH
Titikaveka
ARA METUA
FRUITS OF RAROTONGA
REFLECTIONS ON RAROTONGA
TAKITUMU VILLAS
RAINA BEACH APARTMENTS
MOANA SANDS RESORT
THE LITTLE POLYNESIAN
MAIRE NUI CAFE

COOK ISLANDS

© DAVID STANLEY

20-725; weekdays 0800–1600) in the one on the left. The museum has a collection of model canoes, old photos, carvings, paddles, drums, woven items, and costumes. This huge complex was one of the grandiose projects of the Honorable Sir Geoffrey Henry, who put his country millions of dollars in debt to finance construction of the island's second museum and library.

The Ara Metua

Two roads circle Rarotonga: the new coastal road (the Ara Tapu) and an old inner road (the Ara Metua). The main sights are arranged below for a counterclockwise tour of the island on the Ara Tapu with the distances from Avarua shown in parentheses. On a scooter you should be able to do it in four hours with stops; by bicycle give yourself a leisurely day.

On your second time around try using the scenic Ara Metua, which goes two-thirds of the way around the island. You'll encounter lush gardens, orchards, and good viewpoints. This inner road is said to be the oldest in Polynesia, the coral-block foundation laid 1,000 years ago by chief Toi. Up until the mid-19th century, when the missionaries concentrated the population in seven coastal villages, most of the people lived on the inland side of this road. During World War II the road was resurfaced and much of it is now paved. There's very little traffic, which makes it perfect for cycling.

Around the Island

Just under a km west of Rarotonga airport is the **Parliament of the Cook Islands** in a building originally used to house workers during construction of the airport in 1973. Parliament meets February–March and July–September, and if you're properly dressed (no shorts or jeans), you can observe the proceedings from the public gallery (Mon., Tues., and Thurs. 1300–1700, Wed. and Fri. 0900–1300). Call 26-500 for information. Notice how all the important positions here are occupied by men.

Across the street from the Golf Club (see Sports and Recreation, in this chapter) west of the airport is a beach park with toilets and outdoor showers. From here it's not far to **Black Rock**

(6 km), standing alone in a coral lagoon (good snorkeling at high tide). This rock marks the spot where the spirits of deceased Rarotongan Polynesians pass on their way back to the legendary homeland, Avaiki. The Tahitian missionary Papeiha is said to have swum ashore here, holding a Bible above his head (in fact, he landed in a small boat).

Arorangi (8.5 km) was established by the Rev. Aaron Buzacott (who served in the Cooks 1828–1857) as a model village, and Papeiha is buried in the historic white cemetery at the old CICC church (1849). It was the LMS missionaries who resettled the people near the coast and built the **Tinomana Palace** beside the church for the last native ruler of this district.

Mount Raemaru (350 meters tall) rising behind Arorangi has a flattened top—a local legend tells how Aitutaki warriors carried off the missing upper part. (To climb Raemaru, take the steep track off the Ara Metua when you see the sign for Maria's Backpackers Accommodation, then via a trail to the right up the fern-covered ridge to Raemaru's western cliffs. When you get close to the forest at the base of the cliffs, take the right fork of the trail up to the cliff itself. The final climb to the mountain's flat summit can be dangerous if the rocks on the cliff are wet and slippery, but once on top, you can see the whole western side of Rarotonga. There's an easier track down the back of Raemaru that you can use to return, but you'd probably get lost if you tried to climb it. Along this route you circle down a taro-filled valley back to the Ara Metua.)

Takitumu

The southeast side of Rarotonga is known as Takitumu. The skeletal **Sheraton Resort** with its ironic monument to the Honorable Sir Geoffrey A. Henry is the most visible physical reminder of the financial calamities that gripped these islands in the 1990s. The building with the flagpole a couple of kilometers east is the residence of the representative of Queen Elizabeth II (his salary comes out of local taxes). East again and on the corner before Kent Hall in **Titikaveka** is Te Pou Toru Marae. Beyond this another fine coral-block CICC church (1841) stands beside

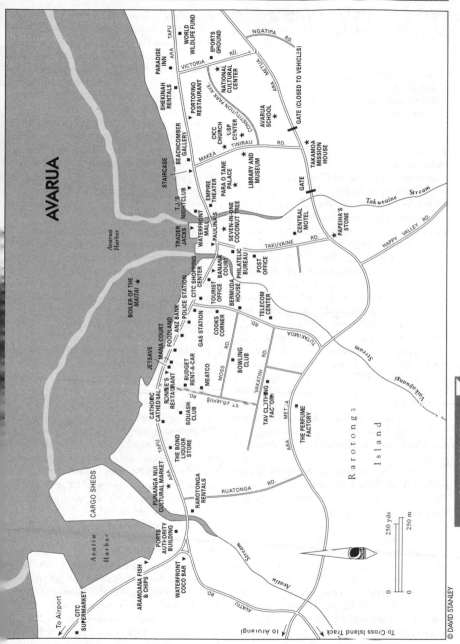

AVARUA

Avarua Harbor

Avatiu Harbor

CARGO SHEDS

To Airport

CITC SUPERMARKET

ARAMOANA FISH & CHIPS

WATERFRONT COCO BAR

PORTS AUTHORITY BUILDING

PUNANGA NUI CULTURAL MARKET ★

RAROTONGA RENTALS

RUATONGA RD.

ATIU RD.

AVATIU RD.

To Cross Island Track

To Arorangi

CATHOLIC CATHEDRAL ✝

THE BOND LIQUOR STORE

RENILE'S RESTAURANT

BUDGET RENT-A-CAR

SQUASH CLUB

MEATCO

ST. JOSEPHS

TAV CLOTHING FACTORY

THE PERFUME FACTORY

JETSAVE

MANA COURT

FOODLAND

ANZ BANK

POLICE STATION

GAS STATION

COOKS CORNER

MOSS RD.

BOWLING CLUB

VAKATINI RD.

META RD.

Rarotonga Island

Avatiu Stream

TUTAKIMOA RD.

BOILER OF THE MAITAI ★

CITC SHOPPING CENTER

TRADER JACKS

WATERFRONT MALL

PAULINA'S

BANANA COURT

TOURIST OFFICE

BERMUDA HOUSE

PHILATELIC BUREAU

POST OFFICE

TELECOM CENTER

TAKUVAINE RD.

SEVEN-IN-ONE COCONUT TREE

CENTRAL MOTEL

PAPEIHA'S STONE

HAPPY VALLEY RD.

Takuvaine Stream

Vakatunoi Stream

T.J.'S NIGHTCLUB

STAIRCASE

EMPIRE THEATER

PARA O TANE PALACE ★

LIBRARY AND MUSEUM

CENTRAL GATE

BEACHCOMBER GALLERY

MAKEA TINIRAU RD.

CICC CHURCH ✝

USP CENTER

PARADISE INN ●

SHEKINAH RENTALS ●

PORTOFINO RESTAURANT ●

VICTORIA

WORLD WILDLIFE FUND ●

SPORTS GROUND

NGATIPA RD.

ARA TAPU

METUA RD.

AVARUA SCHOOL

NATIONAL CULTURAL CENTER ★

CONSTITUTION PARK AVE.

GATE (CLOSED TO VEHICLES)

TAKAMOA MISSION HOUSE ★

ARA TAPU

0 250 yds
0 250 m

RAROTONGA HIGHLIGHTS

National Cultural Center: exhibitions, library, buildings
The Needle: hiking, geology, nature
Muri Beach: swimming, activities, facilities
Titikaveka snorkeling: marinelife
Sheraton ruins: history, island politics

the road, 19 km from Avarua counterclockwise or 14 km clockwise.

Some of the finest **snorkeling** on Rarotonga is off the beach opposite Raina Beach Apartments, behind the cemetery with the radio mast. Fruits of Rarotonga Café, a few hundred meters east, is another great base for snorkeling (the folks in the café will hold bags). There's not a lot of coral but plenty of small fish. Some of the scuba operators bring their clients here for diving.

Turn in at the Rarotonga Sailing Club, four km northeast, to see the lovely **Muri Lagoon,** with the nicest swimming, kayaking, and windsurfing area on the island. The southeast trades blow the mosquitoes away. At low tide you can wade across to uninhabited Koromiri Island, where hermit crabs forage as bathers enjoy the oceanside beach. Full nautical gear is for rent at the club (open daily) and Sails Restaurant serves a good lunch.

The road up the **Avana Valley** begins near the bridge over Avana Stream and runs along the south bank. You can cycle halfway up, then continue on foot.

On the right just beyond the Avana Stream bridge is **Vaka Village** with a monument marking the historic gathering of ocean voyaging and war canoes here during the 1992 Festival of Pacific Arts. Local fishing boats anchor on the spot today. A little beyond is another old white **CICC church** on the left, once the seat of the Reverend Charles Pitman, who translated many works into Maori during his stay here 1827–1854. Across the street from the church is a small park with a good view of the tiny islands or *motu* in the Muri Lagoon and **Ngatangiia Harbor.** Legend claims seven canoes departed from here in A.D. 1350 on a daring voyage to New Zealand, and the names of the canoes are inscribed on a monument. Cruising yachts sometimes anchor here, though it's rather exposed to the southeast trades.

Back near the bridge is a road in to the **Ara Metua.** On the right a short distance along this road is an old burial ground with a Polynesian *marae* among the trees on a hillock behind. Many other similar *marae* are in the vicinity.

Continue along the Ara Metua and turn left up the road alongside Turangi Stream, on the far side of a small bridge. The **Turangi Valley** is larger and more impressive than Avana, and swamp taro is grown in irrigated paddies. Once again, you cycle halfway up and continue on foot.

Toward Ikurangi

At **Matavera** there's yet another lovely CICC church (1865) beside the road. Farther along, just a few km before Avarua, watch for a signboard on Maotangi Road pointing the way in to **Marae Arai-te-tonga,** on the Ara Metua. Marae Arai-te-tonga, the most sacred on the island, was a *koutu,* or place where the *ta'unga* (priest) invested and anointed the high chiefs *(ariki)* of the island. The route of the ancient Ara Metua is quite evident here, and there are other stone constructions 100 meters along it to the east.

Take the road inland between these ruins as far as Tupapa Stream, where two rather difficult climbs begin. Just a km up the trail is a fork in the path: the right fork leads to the top of **Ikurangi** (485 meters), while the one up the stream continues to **Te Manga** (653 meters). Neither climb is easy, so a local guide would be a good idea. From the top of Ikurangi (Tail of the Sky) you can see the whole wave-washed reef, tomato patches, and plantations of grapefruit, orange, tangerine, and lemon trees. This climb is best done in the cool hours of the early morning.

The Cross-Island Track

From Avarua walk three km up the Avatiu Valley. Just beyond the power station you get your first view of Te Rua Manga, **the Needle** (413 meters). In another 10 minutes the road ends at a concrete water intake; you continue up a footpath for 15 minutes until you reach a huge boulder. Pass it and head up the steep forested incline.

This climb is the hardest part of the trip, but when you reach the top, the Needle towers majestically above you (the hike from the end of the road to the top takes less than an hour).

There's a fork at the top of the ridge: the Needle on your right, the trail down to the south coast on the left. After scrambling around the Needle, start down the trail to the south coast, past the giant ferns along the side of Papua Stream. On this part of the trek you really get to see Rarotonga's interior rainforest. The road out begins at **Papua Waterfall**, also known as Wigmore's Waterfall, at the bottom of the hill. The stream above Papua is a drinking water source, and you're also not supposed to swim in the pool below the falls (which will be dry anyway unless there have been rains recently). The hapless Sheraton Resort is to your right just before you reach the main road.

Though sometimes slippery, the cross-island track can be covered in all weather, and even if it has been raining, you can still do the trip the next day. Parts of the track are badly eroded, so it might not be a good idea to go alone. Allow 45 minutes to walk up Avatiu Road, then an hour and a quarter to climb to the Needle. The descent down the Papua Valley takes two hours, and it's easier to do a round-trip to the Needle from the end of the road on the Avatiu side, allowing a return to a parked vehicle. If you'll be hiking right across it's best to go Monday–Saturday as onward bus service on the other side will be very limited on Sunday.

Several companies offer guided cross-island treks Monday–Saturday at 0930 if the weather is okay, but lots of visitors do this hike on their own and you don't really need a guide. Unfortunately, some hikers have inflicted environmental damage here. Don't attempt shortcuts by following the plastic water lines along the way as these lines can be damaged if you use them as handholds and they lead to very dangerous slopes. The trail will remain open only if visitors behave responsibly.

The Cultural Village in Arorangi enthusiastically demonstrates Cook Islands history, medicine, cooking, arts, crafts, dances, and traditions during an informative three-hour program, which includes a lunch of local foods.

Commercial Visitor Attractions

Weekdays at 1000 the **Cultural Village** (tel. 21-314, fax 25-557; admission NZ$54), on the back road in Arorangi, enthusiastically demonstrates Cook Islands history, medicine, cooking, arts, crafts, dances, and traditions during an informative three-hour program, which includes a lunch of local foods. Reservations through a hotel, travel agency, or directly by phone are required. Several readers have written in strongly endorsing the Cultural Village.

Another attraction accessible weekdays at 1000 is **Highland Paradise** (tel. 20-611; admission NZ$30 including lunch), a private botanical garden where old *marae* and other historic sites are scattered among the vegetation. The steep access road begins next to Rose Flats, a km south of the Cultural Village. The Arorangi people lived up here before being moved down to the coast by the missionaries.

SPORTS AND RECREATION

Dive Rarotonga (Barry and Shirley Hill, tel. 21-873, fax 21-878) offers scuba trips every afternoon at 1300 (including Sunday!). A one-tank dive is NZ$60 (NZ$50 if you have your own equipment). Snorkelers can go along for NZ$20 pp including snorkeling gear.

Scuba diving is also offered by Greg Wilson's **Cook Island Divers** (tel. 22-483, fax 22-484), just up the road. If the weather looks at all bad, Dive Rarotonga may cancel that day's diving, whereas Cook Island Divers tries to go out in almost any weather. Greg does two trips a day, at 0800 and 1300 (NZ$60 per dive), and he runs a highly professional show. His four-day NAUI or PADI scuba certification course is NZ$499—what better place to learn? Call for free hotel pickup. A reader's comment: "It was a really enjoyable day."

Pacific Divers (Graham McDonald, tel./fax 22-450), opposite the Flame Tree Restaurant at

Muri Beach, offers dives on the nearby Titikaveka Reef at 0800 and 1300 daily (at 1230 only on Sunday). It's NZ$75/130 for one/two tanks and two people together get a NZ$10 discount. A PADI open water certification course (four days) will run NZ$485. The feedback we've received about Pacific Divers is mixed. All three scuba operators offer discounts for multiple dives.

Monday–Saturday at 1100 **Captain Tama's Aquasportz Center** (Tamaiva Tuavera, tel. 23-350), next to the Rarotonga Sailing Club on Muri Beach, offers lagoon cruises in a glass-bottom boat with a thatched sunroof for around NZ$60 pp including a barbecue lunch. Before signing up, check with the folks in the Beach Hut at the nearby Pacific Resort whose glass-bottom snorkeling cruise is only NZ$20 (or NZ$37 with sandwiches for lunch). Captain Tama's rents double kayaks (NZ$12 an hour), windsurfers (NZ$15 an hour), and snorkeling gear (NZ$5 a half day). Lessons in windsurfing (NZ$35) are given. Equipment rental is possible every day.

The **Reef-Sub** (tel. 25-837) at Avatiu Harbor is a sort of glass-bottom boat with tiny jewelry case windows in an underwater viewing deck (it's not a real submarine). The 90-minute trips Monday–Saturday at 1000 and 1400 cost NZ$45.

Pacific Marine Charters (Wayne Barclay, tel. 21-237, fax 25-237) at Avatiu Harbor offers deep-sea fishing from its two cabin cruisers. Also at Avatiu is the larger 10-meter *Seafari* of **Seafari Charters** (Elgin Tetachuk, tel. 20-328). Over four hours of fishing costs about NZ$100 pp (NZ$50 pp for nonfishing passengers), a light lunch included. Both boats depart weekdays around 0800 (weather permitting) and the fishing takes place right off Rarotonga, so you get very good views of the island and don't waste time commuting. Brent Fisher's **Fisher's Fishing Tours** (tel. 23-356, fax 23-354) is based at Ngatangiia Harbor, and his catamaran, the *Corey-Anne,* goes out at 0800 or 1330 (NZ$70 pp).

Another catamaran, the *Tangaroa III* based next to Trader Jack's at Avarua Harbor, is similar. Most of these operators will allow you to keep a few smaller fish for personal use, though larger fish belong to the boat. Ask about this before booking, if it matters. From August to October you might see whales from your boat!

For horseback riding it's **Aroa Pony Trek** (Georgina and Tiki Daniel, tel. 21-415), up the road from Kaena Restaurant near the Rarotongan Beach Resort. Weekdays at 1000 and 1500 it offers two-hour rides to Papua Waterfall, returning along the beach (NZ$40/25 adult/child). Book ahead as participants are limited.

Try your swing at the nine-hole **Rarotonga Golf Club** (tel. 20-621; closed Sun.), under the radio towers near the end of the airstrip. Greens fees and club rentals are NZ$15 each. If you hit a mast, wire, or stay during your round, there's a compulsory replay; balls have been known to bounce back at players. Getting a tee time during the week is easy but on Saturday it's usually busy. There's an annual tournament here in late September and the club has a very pleasant colonial-style bar perfect for a cold beer (visitors are always welcome).

The bar at the **Rarotonga Bowling Club** (tel. 26-277) on Moss Road, Avarua, opens at 1600 weekdays, at 1000 on Saturday. If you've never tried lawn bowling before, do so—it's only NZ$1 greens fees plus NZ$1 bowls hire (a white outfit is required on Saturday).

The **Rarotonga Squash Club** (tel. 21-056; daily 0900–2230), directly behind the Catholic cathedral in Avarua, charges NZ$5 a session.

Both the Edgewater Resort and Rarotongan Beach Resort have **tennis court** open to the public, and the Edgewater also has squash courts.

Monday at 1730 you can jog with the **Hash House Harriers.** For the venue, call David Lobb at tel. 27-002 or scrutinize the back page of the Monday edition of the *Cook Islands News*. It's good fun and a nice way of meeting people.

Practicalities

ACCOMMODATIONS

There's such a glut of accommodations on Rarotonga that you'd have to be very unlucky to arrive on a day when everything was full. Bargaining for rooms isn't done but it's okay to ask if they have any "specials" on. The arrival of email has made booking ahead from overseas much easier and you can sometimes get specially reduced rates through the hotel's own website.

If saving money is a concern, get a place with cooking facilities as restaurant meals can add up. All of the budget and medium-priced hotels are self-catering, but many of the upmarket resorts are not. When choosing, keep in mind that the west coast is drier and gets beautiful sunsets, while the finest snorkeling is at windy Titikaveka in the south and the top beach faces the gorgeous Muri Lagoon in the east. The places near Avarua are best for those more into shopping, sight-seeing, and entertainment than beachlife.

Most places include the 12.5 percent VAT in the quoted rate but some charge it extra. Check out time at the motels is 1000. Most of the budget hotels provide free transfers from the airport to their properties (from international flights only) but charge NZ$10 for the ride back to the airport. The more upscale places charge NZ$10 each way. The listings below are arranged counterclockwise around the island in each price category.

Under US$25

The first budget place to the west of town is **Atupa Orchid Units** (tel. 28-543, fax 28-546), run by a German woman named Ingrid Caffery who has been in the Cooks since 1970. There are nine rooms in four screened houses in a garden setting, each house with its own cooking facilities and hot water. Prices vary from NZ$30/44 single/double in a budget room to NZ$65/75 for a one/two-bedroom bungalow. It's excellent value and discounts are available when things are slow. Quiet and comfortable, and central Avarua is just a 10-minute walk away.

A 20-minute walk west of town are the A-frame chalets and guesthouse of the **Tiare Village Hostel** (Adrienne and Lucky Matapuku, tel. 23-466, fax 21-874). This 23-bed establishment has three fan-cooled, self-contained chalets, each with two singles and one double, at NZ$25/44 single/double, and three triples in the main house at NZ$18 pp to share. In addition, there are six self-catering duplex units facing a circular swimming pool at NZ$28 pp. Guests staying in the dorms share the communal cooking facilities, lounge, and hot water showers, and the tropical garden is bursting with fruit there for the picking. Don't expect to get a lot of sleep as this is a bit of a party hostel. Free luggage storage facilities are available.

Aunty Noo's Beach Lodge (tel. 21-253), halfway down to the beach behind Snowbird Laundry in Arorangi, offers the cheapest accommodations on Rarotonga and is thus the choice of backpackers on the barest of budgets. Beds in the crowded dorm are NZ$10 pp, the two four-bed "double" rooms are NZ$12 each, or you can camp in the back yard for NZ$8 pp. Rudimentary cooking facilities are provided and many guests sit and play cards at the picnic tables in the lounge all day. A party ensues whenever a duty-free bottle appears. Aunty Noo is rather eccentric (and she has quite a reputation on Rarotonga!) but it's unlikely you'll see much of her. This place isn't "accredited" so you won't find it in the official tourism brochures.

The **Are Renga Motel** (tel. 20-050, fax 29-223) at Arorangi has 20 simple thin-walled units with well-equipped kitchens at NZ$30/50 single/double. The quality varies, so ask to see another room if the first one you're shown isn't to your liking. Beware of rooms with open ventilation spaces near the ceiling, as these let in every sound from adjacent rooms. The Are Renga offers a reduced "backpacker's rate" of NZ$20 per bed in six shared double rooms. The location is good with a store and other facilities nearby, and a lending library is available in the office. Use of the washing machine costs NZ$7, but there's no dryer. In season you may harvest fruit from the large orchard behind the property. Airport transfers are free when you arrive, NZ$5 when you leave.

Maria's Backpackers Accommodations (Exham and Maria Wichman, tel. 21-180) is just off the Ara Metua in Arorangi, up near the trailhead of the Raemaru trek. From the main road in Arorangi turn inland opposite Bunny's Diner. There are two self-catering rooms at NZ$20/36 single/double. Extra beds in the main house are NZ$15 pp. This is a place for people who like peace and quiet; those interested in meeting other travelers should head elsewhere.

In late 2002 **Rarotonga Backpackers** (Paul and Rebecca, tel./fax 21-590) opened on a hillside off the Ara Metua in Arorangi, inland from Sunhaven Beach Bungalows. It's near the start of the invigorating hiking trail to the summit of Raemaru. There are two six-bed dorms at NZ$20 pp and four poolside rooms with shared bath at NZ$30/48 single/double in this multilevel complex. Common cooking and laundry facilities are available, and the large common area on the upper deck offers splendid sunset views. Rentals of bicycles/motorbikes (NZ$6/15) and surfboards (NZ$10) are possible. The Friday night barbecue and pub crawl (NZ$20) is a very popular event! Free airport pickups are provided for those who have booked ahead through the website (NZ$5 pp for the departure transfer).

Backpackers International Hostel (Mal and Tua Bates-Tuisila, tel./fax 21-847) is in the southwest corner of the island, only 100 meters from a grocery store, the Island Bus, an Internet outlet, and six km of white sandy beach. It offers six rooms with double beds and another 12 rooms with twin beds at NZ$32 double. In addition, there are six singles at NZ$26 and 21 dorm beds in rooms of three to eight at NZ$15 pp. A common TV lounge and cooking area are provided. It's convivial, and on Monday night the family prepares a special buffet dinner at NZ$20 pp (NZ$30 for nonguests).

Piri's Coconut Beach Hostel (tel. 20-309), on the beach just west of the Sheraton site, offers 16 mattresses in an open dorm at NZ$15 or a basic room at NZ$25. There are communal cooking facilities, but it's all really scruffy and to be avoided. Be aware, we've received many complaints about this place. The manager, Piri Puruto III, puts on tacky coconut tree climbing shows for tourists here and at other locations around the island.

A new place to stay is **Maiana Guesthouse** (Ina and Mano Pokia, tel./fax 20-438), just west of the residence of the Queen's Representative on the south coast. It has five double rooms at NZ$40, three triple rooms at NZ$54, and one seven-bed dorm at NZ$18 pp (no children under 12 please). A common kitchen and fridge are provided. Maiana is cleaner and quieter than some of the Muri Beach places such as Vara's. Turoa Bakery and the Saltwater Cafe are next door and a white sandy beach is across the road.

One of the best established backpacker places is the **Aremango Guesthouse** (tel. 24-362, fax 24-363), just 50 meters from Muri Beach, south of Vara's Budget Accommodation. The 10 spacious fan-cooled rooms with shared bath are NZ$22 pp. Singles must be prepared to share or pay for both beds. Reductions are offered if you stay three or more nights. Communal cooking facilities are available, and lockable cupboards for groceries are provided. Cleanliness could be an issue here, and peace and quiet will be up to your fellow guests.

Vara's Budget Accommodation (Vara Hunter, tel. 23-156, fax 22-619), on the south side of the Muri Beachcomber, consists of two distinct sections. The beach complex includes several wooden buildings and a newer two-story block containing a mix of double rooms, upscale studios, and squashy dorms. Four hundred meters up the hillside are a "villa," "cottage," "apartment," and "lodge" with lots more rooms and dorms. At NZ$20 pp in a multibed dorm, NZ$48 double with shared bath, NZ$70 double with private bath, or NZ$80/100 single/double in a studio, both sections cost the same with a surcharge payable by those staying fewer than three nights. The hillside accommodations are quieter, but Vara's is definitely for the backpacker who doesn't mind living in close quarters with lots of other backpackers. The fabulous beach draws people here, and all guests have access to laundry facilities (NZ$4), communal cooking facilities (a grocery store is adjacent), and cold showers.

Vara's office is up in the hillside section. If you want a double room, you should definitely reserve (no credit card number is required and it overbook to compensate for no-shows, so a reservation doesn't always guarantee a room).

Ariana Bungalows (Bob Healey, tel./fax 20-521), a couple of km east of Avarua, offers quite a range of accommodations. The seven self-catering bungalows with bath are NZ$60 for up to three people, whereas the six shared doubles are NZ$20/30 single/double. Three newer duplex studio rooms are NZ$65 for up to three. The nine-bed dorm is NZ$18 pp. On a weekly basis it's 25 percent off. Ariana is 400 meters off the main road and quite a distance from town or the beach. It's slightly rundown but almost never full—a good choice is you want to escape the crowds at Muri Beach. Airport pickups are free but departure transfers are NZ6 pp.

Lovely Planet Budget Accommodation (tel./fax 25-100) is opposite the Medical Clinic at Tupapa, a km east of central Avarua. The five four-bunk rooms start at NZ$20 pp. A shared kitchen, refrigerator, and laundry room are provided, and bicycles are for rent. Despite the name, this colonial-style home hostel with a spacious porch is run by Papa Ross Grant and has no connection with a certain mass-market Australian guidebook company.

A few travelers have managed to rent rooms in the large outer island hostels on Constitution Park Ave. opposite the Are-Karioi-Nui National Auditorium in Avarua. For example, the **Manihiki Hostel** charges about NZ$16 per person with communal cooking facilities. It's quite noisy because of the thin walls but clean and convenient.

US$25–50

Etu Bungalows (tel./fax 25-588) in Arorangi has four self-catering bungalows at NZ$70 single or double.

Tiana's Beach Villas (tel. 24-452), at the south end of Muri Beach opposite Taakoka Island, is down the lane next to the Baha'i Center just south of Shangri-La Beach Cottages. The one duplex and one separate bungalow with full cooking and laundry facilities begin at NZ$100/325 a night/week. There's no on-site manager, so carefully lock up before you go out. Book through Jetsave Travel.

The **Sunrise Beach Bungalows** (Caryn Kenny, tel. 20-417, fax 24-417) at Ngatangiia has four oceanfront and two garden bungalows at NZ$105 double, while the two duplex garden units are NZ$95. The rates are reduced when things are slow. All have cooking facilities, color TV, and laundry access—good value. The beach here is poor but there's a large swimming pool. It's peaceful and a store is close by. Some lovely nature hikes are available in the nearby valleys and it's an easy walk to Muri Beach.

The clean, pleasant **KiiKii Motel** (Pauline and Harry Napa, tel. 21-937, fax 22-937), a 30-minute walk west of Avarua, has an attractive swimming pool overlooking a rocky beach. The four older "budget rooms" in this solid two-story motel are NZ$70/90 single/double. The eight standard rooms in the west wing go for NZ$95/120/155 single/double/triple, while the 12 deluxe rooms are NZ$120/150 single/double (NZ$130/160 overlooking the sea). All 24 rooms have good cooking facilities, and the efficient staff is helpful in assisting with any special arrangements. KiiKii is probably the closest you'll come to a U.S.-style motel, although much nicer. Airport transfers are NZ$9 each way.

A good bet very near Avarua's shopping, entertainment, and sight-seeing possibilities is the **Paradise Inn** (Dianne Haworth, tel. 20-544, fax 22-544), just east of Portofino Restaurant. In a former existence "the Paradise" was the Maruaiai Dancehall, but it has been completely refurbished into a cozy little 16-room motel. The fan-cooled split-level rooms are NZ$70/88/102 single/double/triple, and there are two smaller budget singles that are NZ$52. Cooking facilities are provided, and there's a large lounge and a nice terrace overlooking the ocean where you can sit and have a drink. Children under 12 are not accommodated.

The only hotel right in Avarua itself is the **Central Motel** (tel. 25-735, fax 25-740), up the road from the post office. The 16 units in this two-story concrete block edifice are NZ$76 single or double. No real cooking facilities are provided although a fridge, toaster, kettle, cups, and plates have been placed in the units as an afterthought. It's clean and convenient and might be okay if you were there on business.

US$50–100

The **Reefcomber Sunset Motel** (tel. 25-673, fax 26-432), opposite the road to the hospital a bit south of Black Rock, has 12 units from NZ$150. Cooking facilities are not provided.

The **Oasis Village** (Don and Pat Hawke, tel. 28-213, fax 28-214), near the beach in Arorangi, has four air-conditioned units starting at NZ$120 single or double. Children under 12 are not accepted. Cooking facilities are not provided but there's a convenience store adjacent to the property.

The **Rarotongan Sunset Motel** (tel. 28-028, fax 28-026), next door to the Oasis Village, has 19 self-catering units in long blocks of four or five units at NZ$153 double in the garden or from NZ$226 beachfront. These prices may be discounted 10 percent if you prepay direct. There's a swimming pool. It's good value and often full. Children under 12 are not accepted.

Seashells Deluxe Serviced Apartments (tel. 24-317, fax 24-318), adjacent to the Manuia Beach Hotel in Arorangi, offers four two-bedroom duplex apartments at NZ$185 double, plus NZ$35 per additional person up to four maximum (children under 12 free). Full cooking facilities are provided.

Ati's Castaway Beach Villas (Dorothy and Cameron Robertson, tel. 21-546, fax 25-546), on the beach a little south of the church in Arorangi, offers 11 units with cooking facilities and hot-water showers. It's NZ$190 double for one of the two pool units, NZ$120/160 double/triple for one of the five garden bungalows, or NZ$190/230 for one of the four duplex beach bungalows. There are a communal TV lounge and a restaurant/bar beside the pool. A pole outside bears the flags of all the countries currently represented there, and the new owners from Scotland do their utmost to make guests feel at home. Airport transfers are NZ$15 pp return.

Sunhaven Beach Bungalows (Dennis and Patti Hogan, tel. 28-465, fax 28-464), south of Ati's Castaway and just north of Etu Bungalows, offers six new self-catering units at NZ$180–240 double (NZ$55 per extra person). Five are right on the beach and the other is in the garden. There's an attractive swimming pool. Children under 12 are not accepted.

backroad in sleepy Avarua

Puaikura Reef Lodge (tel. 23-537, fax 21-537), on the southwest side of the island, offers 12 self-catering rooms in three single-story motel wings arranged around a cloudy swimming pool at NZ$135 single or double. A grocery store is adjacent, and the beach is just across the road with no houses blocking access to the sea. A paperback library is available for guests. The motel office is open only weekdays 0900–1600, Saturday 0900–1200, and the no-nonsense manager would rather you booked ahead rather than just showing up unannounced on his doorstep.

Lagoon Lodges Motel (tel. 22-020), on spacious grounds near the Rarotongan Beach Resort, has 19 attractive self-catering units of varying descriptions beginning at NZ$140/155 single/double including breakfast. There are a swimming pool, terrace café, and NZ$25 Sunday night barbecue for in-house guests only. It's a good choice for families with small children, though it's not right on the beach. Lagoon Lodges is run by Des Eggelton, who arrived on Raro to help build the airport in 1973 and just couldn't bring himself to leave.

Daydreamer Moemoea Apartments (Bruce and Nga Young, tel. 25-965, fax 25-964), offers five attractive self-catering units in one long block just west of the Sheraton site and across the street from Piri's Hostel. It's NZ$120 single or double. The beach along here is great, but when snorkeling beware of dangerous currents in passes draining the lagoon.

Palm Grove Lodges (Tom and Shirley Wills, tel. 20-002, fax 21-998), on the south side of the island, has 16 self-catering units beginning at NZ$190 single or double garden, NZ$290 beachfront, breakfast included. In the new beachfront units, you don't need to cross the road to swim.

Bella's Beach Bungalows (Eugene Bella, tel. 26-004), east of the Queen's representative in Titikaveka, offers four quiet self-catering units on a white sandy beach at NZ$135. Kayaks and canoes are lent free. Book through Shekinah Homes.

Raina Beach Apartments (tel. 23-601, fax 23-602) in Titikaveka has four self-catering units in a three-story main building at NZ$150 single or double. Its main advantages are proximity to a good snorkeling area and the view from the roof.

The same company also has six self-catering bungalows on the south side of the Manuia Beach Hotel in Arorangi, which go for NZ$390 double.

Kura's Kabanas (Kura Bullen, tel./fax 27-010), beside Sokala Villas on the Muri Lagoon, has four comfortable, self-catering units with large terraces facing the lagoon at NZ$150 double. Laundry facilities are available. Airport transfers are NZ$10 pp each way.

Daniel Roro's **Aroko Bungalows** (tel. 21-625 or 23-625, fax 24-625), at Ngatangiia, is one of the few medium-priced places facing Muri Beach. The 11 small bungalows with basic cooking facilities are NZ$110 single or double roadside or NZ$120 beachside. They're very tightly packed together, making the beachside units preferable.

The **Tropical Sands Bungalows** (tel. 23-564), at Ngatangiia a km north of Avana Marina Condominiums, has two self-catering units at NZ$120 double.

Club Raro (tel. 22-415, fax 24-415), two km east of Avarua, has 17 garden rooms at NZ$115 single or double, 20 poolside rooms at NZ$135, and 15 "beachfront" rooms at NZ$235 (a misnomer since there's no beach here). A swimming pool is provided but cooking facilities are not. It's walking distance from town.

US$100–150

If your flight is delayed, Air New Zealand may accommodate you at the **Edgewater Resort Hotel** (tel. 25-435, fax 25-475), a tight cluster of two/three-story blocks and service buildings facing a mediocre beach. This is Raro's largest hotel, with 208 smallish air-conditioned rooms beginning at NZ$210 single or double for those in the most unfavorable locations and rising to NZ$550 for the VIP suite. A third person is NZ$75 extra. No cooking facilities are provided but many restaurants are nearby (avoid the hotel restaurant, which has received mixed reviews). Traditional dancing is presented at the Edgewater twice a week. Frankly, this hotel is overpriced unless you're on a "cheap" package tour.

The **Manuia Beach Hotel** (tel. 22-461, fax 22-464) at Arorangi has 20 Polynesian bungalows starting at NZ$295 double (children under 12 not admitted). Cooking facilities are not provided but there's a restaurant which has an island night on Saturdays. You can swim off its beach or use the swimming pool.

At Titikaveka is the **Moana Sands Beachfront Hotel** (tel. 26-189, fax 22-189) with 17 units packed together in a two-story building at NZ$225 for up to three people including breakfast and the use of snorkeling gear and kayaks. A reduced rate may be available if you book ahead by email. The 12 standard units have limited cooking facilities but the five suites with better cooking facilities are NZ$2,800 a week for up to six people. The beach is good and some water sports are offered.

The Little Polynesian (Dorice Reid and Jeannine Peyroux, tel. 24-280, fax 21-585), also at Titikaveka, has eight well-spaced self-catering duplex units at NZ$250 single or double, plus a lagoonside cottage at NZ$290. Children under 12 are not accepted. This property faces one of the finest snorkeling beaches on the island (a swimming pool is also provided). Inquiries are possible only during office hours (weekdays 0800–1600, Sat. 0900–1200).

Travel writer Elliot Smith operates **Shangri-La Beach Cottages** (tel. 22-779, fax 22-775) on the beach south of the Muri Beachcomber Motel. The six air-conditioned cottages are NZ$250 single or double with whirlpool bath, microwave, fridge, and lounge (no children under 18 years). An "early bird/self-servicing special" rate of only NZ$165 may be available through the website. There's a large pool and kayaks are lent free. After serving as a California judge for many years, Elliot dropped out of the legal profession and became a South Sea islander, sort of. His *Cook Islands Companion* is a best-seller on Rarotonga and he'll be able to tell you anything you want to know about the Cook Islands.

Near the south end of Muri Beach is the **Muri Beachcomber** (Phil and Juliet Wells, tel. 21-022, fax 21-323) with 16 self-catering "seaview" units in eight older duplex blocks at NZ$195/215/275 single/double/triple. Children under 12 are accepted only in two larger air-conditioned garden units facing the pool, which cost NZ$280 for four. Three "watergarden" units back near the road cost NZ$300/320/400.

The popular **Pacific Resort** (tel. 20-427, fax 21-427) at Muri offers 64 self-catering rooms beginning at NZ$299 single or double, NZ$344 triple (children under 12 free). Breakfast and airport transfers are included. Only 15 rooms face right onto the beach. A swimming pool, watersports facility, Barefoot Bar, and evening entertainment are part of this well-rounded resort that fits nicely into its surroundings. The resort's restaurants are mediocre, however. The sandy beach is good for swimming but not for snorkeling.

Manea Beach (tel. 23-487, fax 25-320), between the Flame Tree Restaurant and Sokala Villas on Muri Beach, has five air-conditioned units with cooking, fridge, and terrace at NZ$250 single or double. A large three-bedroom beachfront villa is NZ$400. Opened in 2001, this place has a beachside swimming pool and free kayaks.

Avana Marina Condominiums (tel. 20-836, fax 22-991), on a rocky shore facing the north side of Ngatangiia Bay, has five two- and three-bedroom townhouses starting at NZ$325 double. These two-story self-catering units accommodate up to five people. Also available are four studios with microwaves at NZ$280. The minimum stay is three nights. There's a swimming pool and free rowboats are provided to reach nearby secluded beaches.

US$150–250

Crown Beach Resort (tel. 23-953, fax 23-951), south of the Edgewater Resort in Arorangi, opened in 1998. The 22 air-conditioned units start at NZ$495 single or double, continental breakfast included. All have small kitchenettes, and a swimming pool and watersports are available. The water off its beach is rather shallow for swimming. The Windjammer Restaurant (closed Tuesday) is on the premises. The whole operation is overpriced.

The **Rarotongan Beach Resort** (tel. 25-800, fax 25-799), in the southwest corner of Rarotonga, has been the island's premier hotel since its opening in 1977. In 1997 the complex was fully renovated and made wheelchair-accessible, one of the few South Pacific resorts where this is so. The 156 air-conditioned rooms in nine one- and two-story blocks begin at NZ$360 single or double (no cooking facilities). Children under 13 eat and sleep free, and other deals are available for families. Some water sports are also included. The beach and swimming pool are fine, and island nights with traditional dancing are held twice a week. Airport transfers are NZ$30 pp round-trip. **Takitumu Romantic Villas** (tel. 24-682, fax 24-683), near Kent Hall on the south side of the island, has 10 deluxe one-bedroom thatched villas between a swimming pool and the white sand beach (good snorkeling). It's self-catering and rates start at NZ$375. Children under 12 are not admitted.

Tucked away amid luxuriant vegetation next to the Flame Tree Restaurant is **Sokala Villas** (tel. 29-200, fax 21-222) with seven self-catering bungalows. The one garden villa without its own swimming pool is NZ$320 for up to three people; the other six villas with pools or on the beach go as high as NZ$690. Children under 12 are not admitted. Office hours are weekdays 0900–1600, Saturday 0900–1300 only.

US$250 and up

The most luxurious accommodations in the Cook Islands may be **Reflections on Rarotonga** (tel. 23-703, fax 23-702), southwest of Muri Beach and a few hundred meters east of Fruits of Rarotonga. Opened in 2002, this pair of two-story duplex units faces a white beach with excellent snorkeling. Each sleeps up to five people at NZ$750 double in the master bedroom, then NZ$70 pp for the extra beds upstairs (no children please). Full kitchens and private swimming pools are provided. Plopped in behind these units is a self-catering "waterfall villa" at NZ$350 double. Airport transfers are included. Unfortunately the whole complex is squeezed together on a tiny lot with little space even to park.

House Rentals

Renting an entire house by the week or month can be excellent value, and due to the outflow of Cook Islanders to New Zealand in the late 1990s, there are lots of places available. Advertisements for furnished houses are often published in the classified section of the *Cook Islands News;* otherwise watch for signs around the island or ask at Cook Islands Tourism Corporation. Be aware of

security when choosing a place as break-ins (usually by teenagers) are not unknown here.

Shekinah Homes (tel. 26-004, fax 26-005), between the Paradise Inn and the Portofino Restaurant, handles rentals at 30 properties (NZ$450–1,000 a week).

Cook Islands Tours (tel. 28-270, fax 27-270) at the airport has a variety of furnished houses for rent, including the Beach Lodge next to the Queen's Representative on the south side of the island. Check its website for listings.

KiiKii Motel (tel. 21-937, fax 22-937) rents four fully equipped two-bedroom cottages near the Rarotongan Beach Resort in Arorangi. These cost NZ$435 a week plus NZ$35 for electricity for up to four people.

Jetsave Travel (tel. 27-707) books the Studio at Muri Beach Cottages for NZ$175 per week.

FOOD

Some upmarket restaurants don't include the value-added tax in their menu prices. If in doubt, ask beforehand rather than get a 12.5 percent surprise on the bill. Most of the budget eateries popular among local residents are in Avarua, but you'll find fancy tourist restaurants all around the island with a cluster near the Edgewater Hotel.

Budget Eateries

Mama's Cafe (tel. 23-379; weekdays 0730–1530, Sat. 0730–1200), beside Foodland in Avarua, offers an interesting combination of healthy sandwiches and fattening desserts. The ice-cream cones are great!

The outdoor lunch counter at the **Cooks Corner Cafe** (tel. 22-345; weekdays 0700–1430, Sat. 0700–1230), beside the Island Bus stop, is also popular with the locals. Specials are posted on blackboards.

Paulina's Polynesia Restaurant (tel. 28-889; Mon.–Sat. 0800 until late), near the traffic circle at Avarua Harbor, serves local foods, such as raw fish (NZ$8.50), sausage, eggs, and chips (NZ$8.50), and steaks (NZ$14.50). Breakfast is NZ$6.50–10. Seated at a picnic table between the Banana Court and Trader Jacks, you can wash it all down with beer.

At Avatiu Harbor there's **Aramoana Fish N' Chips** (tel. 21-250; weekdays 1000–2200, Sat. 1200–2200, Sun. 1200–2000) with a large fish and chips at NZ$7, parrot fish or flounder for NZ$5.50 a piece, plus oysters, mussels, calamari, and scallops. It's surprisingly pleasant with a nice terrace overlooking the harbor.

In Arorangi **Flamboyant Place Takeaway** (tel. 23-958; daily 0800–0100), opposite Dive Rarotonga, serves inexpensive meals at its picnic tables. The ice-cream cones here are good.

Avarua

Ronnie's Bar and Restaurant (Ronnie Siulepa, tel. 20-823; Mon.–Sat. 1130–1430/1800–2130), on the Avarua waterfront, serves seafood, steak, and enchiladas in the NZ$12.50–18.50 range. The *ika mata* (marinated raw fish) is excellent at NZ$10, or try the curried octopus for NZ$15.50. It's okay to bring your own bottle of wine to dinner. Beside the restaurant bar is a pleasant, shady patio for cool drinks and conversation. The Friday night karaoke here is great fun.

Much celebrated **Trader Jacks** (tel. 26-464; Mon.–Sat. 0900–2400, Sun. 1700–2200), on the waterfront at Avarua Harbor, serves full meals (NZ$16.50–24.40), but many people come only to consume *kati kati* bar snacks (NZ$9.50–12.50) and drink. It's one of the few places away from the resorts where you can get a beer on Sunday night, and weekdays at happy hour you may meet some very senior, very drunken members of the local administration. It's lots of fun when the crew off one of the longliners working out of Avatiu Harbor rolls in. A 10-drink card that can be used on different days by different people is NZ$36. A live band plays here Friday nights from 2100.

The **Staircase Restaurant and Bar** (tel. 21-254; nightly from 1830), upstairs in a building beside the Beachcomber Gallery, has good value dinner specials advertised on blackboards outside (large portions). There's live music some nights, including Polynesian dancing Thursdays at 2030 (NZ$5 cover charge). After the show you too can dance the night away.

The **Portofino Restaurant** (tel. 26-480; Mon.–Sat. 1830–2100), on the east side of town, specializes in Italian dishes such as pizza (NZ$12–20), pasta (NZ$16–20), steaks (NZ$28–33), and seafood (NZ$27–35). It gets good reviews from readers ("good food, lots of it, and well prepared") and could be crowded, so try to reserve. The take-out pizzas are NZ$12/18 regular/large.

Arorangi

Alberto's Steakhouse (tel. 23-597; Mon.–Sat. 1800–2100), near the Rarotongan Sunset Motel, offers steaks NZ$23.50–34.50 or pastas in the NZ$15–19 range. The cook is Swiss.

Hopsing's Chinese Restaurant (tel. 20-367), near the Edgewater Resort, serves some pretty decent Asian food. The Mongolian beef arrives steaming at your table. Friday nights there's a buffet.

The much-advertised **Spaghetti House** (tel. 25-441; daily from 1700), at the entrance to the Edgewater Resort, offers pizzas, pastas, and meats.

Seafood, steaks, and chicken are available nightly 1800–2130 at the **Tumunu Tropical Garden Bar and Restaurant** (tel. 20-501), also near the Edgewater. This spacious bar opened in 1979 and the bartender, Eric, offers sight-seers a popular guided tour of his picturesque establishment for a NZ$1 tip. Ask the waitress if you can see Eric's scrapbooks of life on Raro in the early 1970s.

Titikaveka to Muri

The **Vaima Restaurant and Bar** (tel. 26-123; Thurs.–Tues. 1830–2200), on the south coast just east of the Sheraton site, has a reputation for good food (mains NZ$17.50–18.50). Friday–Monday nights there's live music. Call to ask about its NZ$4 hotel transfers.

Sails Restaurant (tel. 27-349; daily 1100–2300), at the Rarotonga Sailing Club, serves a classic baguette sandwich (NZ$9.50) at lunch. Dinner mains are NZ$17–24. The full á la carte menu is supplemented with a good selection of fresh seafood, fruits, and vegetables.

The **Flame Tree Restaurant** (tel. 25-123; nightly from 1830), on Muri Beach, has been the island's top restaurant since it opened in 1988. Every day it offers a different set three-course menu for NZ$28.50. À la carte starters are in the NZ$9–14 range and main plates run NZ$19–34. It opens at 1830 daily and reservations are recommended.

That's Pasta Italian Pasta Shop (tel. 22-232; Wed.–Sun. 1700–2100), next to The Internet Cafe at Muri, serves homemade pasta freshly prepared by Roberta and Stefano.

Cafés

The **Blue Note Café** (tel. 23-236; weekdays 0800–1730, weekends 0800–1400), on the Banana Court verandah, has the best coffee in town (NZ$3.50). It's a good choice for lunch and there's a stack of New Zealand newspapers on the counter for free reading. Check out the adjacent art gallery.

The Café (tel. 21-283; weekdays 0730–1500, Sat. 0630–1300), between Avarua Harbor and T. J.'s Nightclub, is a spacious locale serving lunches at NZ$11–17 (Saturday brunch NZ$11–13), plus coffee and cakes all day.

Mairenui Botanical Garden and Café (tel. 22-796; weekdays 0900–1600, Sat. 1200–1600), opposite The Little Polynesian at Titikaveka, is a tropical garden you may visit for NZ$3 admission. The café serves breakfast for under NZ$10, lunch for NZ$12.50. Tea or coffee is NZ$4, spaghetti on toast NZ$6.

Fruits of Rarotonga (tel. 21-509; weekdays 0800–1700, Sat. 0900–1700), by the road in the southeast corner of the island, sells a variety of jams, chutneys, pickles, sauces, and dried fruits made on the premises. It's a fine place to stop for coffee and muffins on your way around the island, and you can snorkel right off the beach.

The **Ambala Garden and Café** (tel. 26-486), inland from just south of Shangri-La Beach Cottages, is run by Sue Carruthers, former owner of the Flame Tree Restaurant and author of two cookbooks. This appealing café, plant nursery, and art gallery can be visited Thursday–Saturday 0900–1500 only (organic meals).

Sunday Barbecues

Several of the hotels prepare a special Sunday barbecue dinner or "roast" open to everyone. The favorite of those in the know takes place at 1900 at Ati's Castaway Beach Villas (tel. 21-546), a bit south of the church in Arorangi (NZ$20 pp, reservations required). Return minibus transfers from anywhere on the island can be arranged at NZ$10 pp.

At the main hotels, there's a barbecue at the Rarotongan Sunset Motel (tel. 28-028) at 1730 (NZ$25 pp) and an Indian buffet at the Edgewater Resort (tel. 25-435) at 1830 (NZ$30). Call ahead to check times, prices, transportation arrangements, and bookings. Other possibilities may be advertised in the local paper.

Groceries

Every budget hostel or motel provides kitchen facilities, so Rarotonga is perfect for those who enjoy preparing their own food. At the supermarkets newcomers to the South Pacific will be surprised to find the milk and juice in boxes on the shelves and long loaves of unwrapped bread in barrels near the check-out. Unfortunately it's almost impossible to buy fresh fish because the lagoons have been fished out and anything that does get caught goes straight to the hotel kitchens.

CITC Supermarket (tel. 22-777; Mon.–Wed. 0800–1700, Thurs. and Fri. 0800–1800, Sat. 0800–1600), west of Avatiu Harbor, is generally cheaper than Foodland Supermarket in town. **Meatco** (tel. 27-652), just down from Budget Rent-a-Car in Avarua, usually has the least expensive vegetables and the best meat (except pork).

For beer or liquor, go to the **CITC Liquor Center** (tel. 28-380; Mon.–Thurs. 0900–1700, Fri. and Sat. 0900–1900) next to CITC Supermarket on the way to the airport.

Fresh milk and fruit juices are sold at **Frangi Dairy** (tel. 22-152), beside Parliament. You can also buy imported frozen meat and vegetables here, large containers of water, and super ice-cream cones.

On the south side of the island you can usually get everything you need at **Wigmore's Super Store** (tel. 20-206; Mon.–Sat. 0600–2100, Sun. 0600–0900/1400–2100) between the Sheraton site and Palm Grove Lodges. The food bar next to Wigmore's opens Tuesday–Saturday 1130–2030, Sunday 1130–1800.

The water on Rarotonga is safe to drink.

ENTERTAINMENT AND EVENTS

The **Empire Theater** (tel. 23-189) in Avarua projects feature films in two separate halls nightly except Sunday at 1930 and 2130 (NZ$5). On

M

COOK ISLANDS

Tuesday you get two movies for NZ$5 and on Saturday there's a matinee at 1000. It's almost worth going just to experience the enthusiasm of the local audience!

The most famous watering hole on the island is the historic **Banana Court** (tel. 23-397) in central Avarua, in what was once a hostel for expatriate workers. This place just isn't what it used to be, but it still opens Monday–Saturday after 1700.

T. J.'s Nightclub (tel. 24-722), next to BECO Hardware Store just east of The Waterfront Mall, opens Wednesday–Saturday around 2000. There's karaoke singing and a disco. It's popular with the local teenagers, and dress regulations are in force to maintain standards.

The **Arorangi Clubhouse,** at the Raemaru Park Sports Ground near the CICC church in Arorangi, has a good bar open on Friday and Saturday nights only. There's often live music. A predominately local crowd comes here and it can get rough, but it's a good place to mix.

For a cheap thrill, find out when one of Air New Zealand's Boeing 767s will be arriving and position yourself on the sea wall at the west end of the runway a bit before. It's quite an experience to have a big jet pass only 15 meters above your head!

Bars

The only bars likely to be open on Sunday are those at Trader Jacks, the Edgewater Hotel, the Rarotongan Beach Resort, Sails Restaurant, and Club Raro.

Waterfront Coco Bar (tel. 20-340; Mon.–Sat. 1100–midnight, Fri. until 0200), across the street from Avarua Harbor, is a breezy hangout with mugs of cold beer and occasional live music. It's the sort of place where you might expect to meet a former prime minister and other colorful local characters. Special events are posted on the blackboard outside (NZ$5 cover charge Wed.–Sat. after 2000 if there's live music).

Another good drinking place is the **Cook Islands Game Fishing Club** (tel. 21-419; Mon.–Sat. 1200–midnight) near Club Raro east of town. There's a terrace out back with picnic tables overlooking the beach and a large paperback library inside. This is a private club, but a little tact and charm will see you through. Other agreeable bars

include those at the **Rarotonga Bowling Club** (tel. 26-277; opens at 1600 weekdays) in Avarua and at the **Rarotonga Golf Club** (tel. 20-621) west of the airport. Both are closed on Sunday.

The **Returned Services Association Club** or "RSA" (tel. 20-590; weekdays 1200–2400, Sat. 1100–2400, public holidays 1300–2400, closed Sun.), directly across the street from the airport terminal, is a good place for a beer while you're waiting for a flight. It also has two pool tables, but food service is erratic. Tom Neale, who wrote a well-known book about his experiences living alone on Suwarrow atoll in the northern Cooks, is buried in the cemetery next to the club.

Cultural Shows for Visitors

Cook Islands dancers are renowned and "island night" performances are staged regularly at the hotels and restaurants. A buffet of traditional Cook Island food *(umukai)* is laid out, and those ordering the meal can watch the show for free; otherwise there's usually a cover charge (NZ$5–20). Things change, so call the hotels to check. Best of all, try to attend a show related to some special local event when the islanders themselves participate (look in the newspaper for listings).

The **Edgewater Resort** (tel. 25-435) has island nights Tuesday and Saturday at 2030, costing NZ$49 for the buffet or NZ$15 cover if you don't take dinner. The Taakoka Troupe often performs at the Edgewater on Tuesday with Orama on Saturday (ask). The **Rarotongan Beach Resort** (tel. 25-800) usually has shows Wednesday and Saturday at 2030 (NZ$45 buffet or NZ$20 cover). On Thursday there's an island night at the **Staircase Restaurant** (tel. 21-254) in Avarua (NZ$25 for dinner or NZ$5 show only). The **Pacific Resort** (tel. 20-427) at Muri has an island night with children dancing Friday at 1900 (dinner NZ$40). The **Manuia Beach Hotel** (tel. 22-461) in Arorangi has an island night on Saturday and to attend you must buy the buffet (NZ$42).

SHOPPING

Shopping hours in Avarua are weekdays 0800–1600, Saturday 0800–1200 only. Supermarkets in Avarua stay open about an hour longer, and small general stores around the island are open as late as 2000 weekdays and also on weekends. The **Dive Shop** (tel. 26-675), in Mana Court in Avarua, sells quality snorkeling gear.

Raro Records (tel. 25-927), next to Empire Theater, sells Tahitian compact discs and cassettes a third cheaper than what you'd pay in Tahiti! **CITC Shopping Center** (tel. 22-000) nearby has more recordings of Cook Islands music.

The **Philatelic Bureau** (tel. 29-336, fax 22-428) next to the post office has colorful stamps, first-day covers, and mint sets of local coins, which make good souvenirs. In addition to the Cook Islands issues, it also sells stamps of Aitutaki and Penrhyn (valid only for postage on those islands). A crisp, new Cook Islands $3 bill costs NZ$7 here.

Crafts

Check out the **Punanga Nui Cultural Market** near Avatiu Harbor, where you'll find grass skirts,

> *Check out the Punanga Nui Cultural Market near Avatiu Harbor, where you'll find grass skirts, baskets, dancing shakers, pandanus* rito *hats, and hat bands. Woods used by the carvers include beach hibiscus* (aue) *for tropical fish, ironwood* (toa) *for tangaroa figures, and mahogany* (tamano) *for slit drums.*

baskets, dancing shakers, pandanus *rito* hats, and hat bands. *Tivaevae* quilts are available on request (NZ$250 and up for a medium-sized one).

Woods used by the carvers include beach hibiscus *(aue)* for tropical fish, ironwood *(toa)* for tangaroa figures, and mahogany *(tamano)* for slit drums. Friday nights 1600–2000 a large flea market occurs here with lots of local food (NZ$5 a plate) and live music. Saturday mornings are also lively. The large open area at Punanga Nui is used for cultural festivals.

More expensive but well worth a look is **Island Craft** (tel. 22-009), beside the Westpac Bank, selling teak or mahogany carvings of Tangaroa, the fisherman's god (a fertility symbol), white woven hats from Penrhyn, mother-of-pearl jewelry, and good, strong bags. Other popular items include handbags, fans, tapa cloth, replicas of staff gods, wooden bowls, food pounders,

breadfruit leaf–shaped bowls carved from *miro* wood on Mauke

pearl jewelry, seats *(no'oanga)*, headrests, slit gongs *(tokere)*, and fishhooks. It's also got a branch at the airport that opens for international departures, but the selection in town is much better.

A branch of **Bergman and Sons** (tel. 21-901), between the Cook Islands Visitor Center and the Banana Court, also has a reasonable selection of woodcarvings. Also check **Tarani Crafts and Pearls** (tel. 21-124), next to Empire Theater, which has pandanus hats and black pearls.

Pearls and Souvenirs

The black pearls of Manihiki and Penrhyn may be inspected at the main **Bergman and Sons** store (tel. 21-902, fax 21-903) at Cooks Corner. Unfortunately, prices are not marked.

The **Beachcomber Gallery** (tel. 21-939; weekdays 0930–1600, Sat. 0930–1200), at the corner of the Ara Tapu and Makea Tinirau Road, is housed in a former London Missionary Society school building (1843). It's worth entering this museumlike gallery to peruse the lovely black pearl jewelry and other artworks on sale.

The **Perfume Factory** (tel. 22-690), on the Ara Metua behind town, sells a variety of coconut oil–based lotions and soaps produced on the premises. It also has the distinctive Tangaroa coconut coffee liqueur sold in souvenir ceramic Tangaroa bottles at NZ$60 for a 350-ml bottle or NZ$25 for a 150-ml bottle. A regular 750-ml glass bottle of the same is NZ$35.

Clothing

Visit **Tav's Clothing Factory** (Ellena Tavioni, tel. 23-202), on Vakatini Road, for the attractive lightweight tropical clothing and swimsuits screen-printed and sewn on the premises. Special-sized items can be made to measure. Tav's designer garments are in fashion in Australia.

Get into style with some bright tropical apparel from **Joyce Peyroux Garments** (tel. 20-201), opposite the Are Renga Motel in Arorangi. Joyce Peyroux and other retailers carry beautiful selections of hand-printed dresses, pareus, tie-dyed T-shirts, bikinis, etc.—all locally made.

INFORMATION AND SERVICES

Information

The government-run Cook Islands Tourism Corporation Visitor Center (tel. 29-435, fax 21-435; weekdays 0800–1600), has official brochures and information sheets giving current times and prices. Ask for a free copy of *Jasons What's On in the Cook Islands,* which contains a wealth of useful information about their advertisers. This office does not make hotel or tour bookings.

The Statistics Office (tel. 29-511, fax 21-511), on the second floor of the Government Office Building behind the post office, sells the informative *Annual Statistic Bulletin* (NZ$10).

The World Wide Fund for Nature (tel. 25-091, fax 25-093) is a bit beyond the Paradise Inn east of town.

The Bounty Bookshop (tel. 27-770, fax 24-555), next to the post office in Avarua, carries books on the Cook Islands, the latest regional news magazines, and the *Cook Islands News.*

The University of the South Pacific Center (tel. 29-415), opposite the Cook Islands Library and Museum, has for sale an excellent selection of text books on the region.

The harbormaster (tel. 28-814; weekdays 0800–1200/1300–1600), at Avatiu Harbor, sells nautical charts of the Cook Islands, Tonga, and New Zealand at NZ$30 apiece.

Visitors can become temporary members of the Cook Islands Library and Museum (tel. 26-468; Mon.–Sat. 0900–1300, Tues. also 1600–2000) for an annual fee of NZ$25, of which NZ$10 is refunded upon departure. The library also sells good cultural books.

Island Hopper Vacations (tel. 22-576, fax 23-027), next to the Banana Court, Jetsave Travel (tel. 27-707, fax 28-807), just west of the Westpac Bank, Matina Travel (tel. 21-780, fax 24-780), and Tipani Tours (tel. 25-266) arrange package tours to the outer islands with flights and accommodations included.

Money

Two banks serve Rarotonga, the Westpac Bank (tel. 22-014; weekdays 0900–1500, Sat. 0900–1200), next to Island Craft on the main street and the ANZ Bank (tel. 21-750; Mon.–Thurs. 0900–1500, Fri. 0900–1600), next to the Visitor Information Center. Both change traveler's checks and give cash advances on Visa and MasterCard. The Westpac branch at the airport charges NZ$2.50 commission on traveler's checks, while the branch of the same bank in Avarua charges no commission. The ANZ Bank charges NZ$2 commission on traveler's checks but gives a slightly better rate. If you're changing hundreds of dollars, check both banks and compare. The ANZ Bank has ATMs outside its downtown branch and at the airport. The Westpac Bank represents American Express.

Post and Telecommunications
The post office (tel. 29-940) in Avarua holds general delivery mail 28 days and there's no charge to pick up letters.

Telecom Cook Islands (tel. 29-680, fax 26-174) at the Earth Station Complex on Tutakimoa Road, Avarua, is open 24 hours a day for overseas telephone calls and telegrams. If you want to receive a fax here, the public fax number for Rarotonga is fax 682/26-174 and it costs NZ$2.20 to receive the first page, plus NZ$.55 each additional page.

TelePost (tel. 29-940; weekdays 0800–1600, Sat. 0830–1200), in CITC Shopping Center next to the ANZ Bank, will receive faxes sent to fax 682/29-873 at the same rate. To send a fax is NZ$5.50 a page, plus long distance charges (NZ$1.45 per minute to New Zealand, NZ$1.60 to Australia, NZ$3 to the United States, and NZ$4 to Canada or the United Kingdom). TelePost has telephone cards which can be used in the public phones outside and around town. Postage stamps are sold.

Internet Access
Both Telecom Cook Islands and TelePost at the locations just mentioned offer Internet access from their "cyberbooths" at NZ$1.75 per five minutes. If you have a computer and are staying while, you can get connected to the Internet at Telecom Cook Islands for NZ$25 registration plus NZ$7 an hour. Of course, you'll need access to a phone line.

Slightly cheaper Internet access is available at

Pacific Gifts and Souvenirs (tel. 23-458; weekdays 0900–1600, Sat. 0900–1200), behind Cooks Corner, at NZ$.30 a minute.

The Internet Shop (tel. 20-727; weekdays 0900–1700, Sat. 0900–1330), run by Pacific Computers in The Waterfront Mall opposite Empire Theater, charges NZ$.20 a minute.

The Internet Cafe (tel. 27-242; Mon.–Sat. 1000–1800, Sun. 1200–1800), between the Pacific Resort and Flame Tree Restaurant at Muri Beach, provides access at US$.25 a minute. It also rents bicycles at NZ$7/35 day/week. Blue Rock (weekdays 0930–1700, weekends 1030–1700) nearby at the entrance to Sokala Villas is slightly cheaper at US$.20 a minute or NZ$10/18 per one/two hours.

In Arorangi, the Moko Café (tel. 27-632; weekdays 0800–1600, Sat. 1100–1500), next to Island Car and Bike Hire a bit north of the Are Renga Motel, provides Internet access, food, and coffee.

Visas and Officialdom
For an extension of stay go to the Immigration office (tel. 29-347) on the top floor of the Government Office Building behind the post office. Visa extensions cost NZ$70 to extend your initial 31 days to three months. Otherwise you can pay NZ$120 and get a five-month extension on the spot. The maximum stay is six months. You must show a plane ticket valid for your scheduled departure date and proof of funds. If you lose your passport, report to the Ministry of Foreign Affairs in the same building.

The Honorary Consul of Germany is Dr. Wolfgang Losacker (tel. 23-306) near the tourist office in Avarua. The New Zealand High Commission (tel. 22-201; weekdays 1030–1430) is next to the Philatelic Bureau.

Other Services
Snowbird Laundry (tel. 20-952), next to the Tumunu Restaurant in Arorangi, will do your wash for NZ$9.50 a load including washing and drying.

There are public toilets at Cooks Corner and at the Punanga Nui Cultural Market.

Yachting Facilities
Yachts pay a fee to anchor Mediterranean-style at Avatiu Harbor and are subject to the NZ$25 pp

RAROTONGA INTERNET RESOURCES

Accommodations

Are Renga Motel
arerenga@oyster.net.ck

Aremango Guesthouse
www.ck/aremango
aremango@oyster.net.ck

Ariana Bungalows
bobh@ariana.co.ck

Aroko Bungalows
aroko@bungalows.co.ck

Ati's Castaway Beach Villas
www.atiscastaway.co.ck
bungalows@atisbeach.co.ck

Atupa Orchid Units
www.atupaorchids.co.ck
ingrid@atupaorchids.co.ck

Avana Marina Condominiums
www.avanacondos.co.ck
avanaco@oyster.net.ck

Backpackers International Hostel
annabill@backpackers.co.ck

Central Motel
www.cookpages.com/CentralMotel

Club Raro
www.clubraro.co.ck
holiday@clubraro.co.ck

Crown Beach Resort
www.crownbeach.com
info@crownbeach.com

Daydreamer Moemoea Apartments
byoung@daydreamer.co.ck

Edgewater Resort Hotel
www.edgewater.co.ck
stay@edgewater.co.ck

Etu Bungalows
anietu@oyster.net.ck

Kiikii Motel
www.kiikiimotel.co.ck
relax@kiikiimotel.co.ck

Kura's Kabanas
www.kkabanas.co.ck
kkabanas@oyster.net.ck

Lagoon Lodges Motel
www.lagoonlodges.com
info@lagoonlodges.com

Maiana Guesthouse
www.maianaguesthouse.co.ck
maiana@oyster.net.ck

Manea Beach
stay@manea.co.ck

Manuia Beach Hotel
www.manuia.co.ck
rooms@manuia.co.ck

Moana Sands Beachfront Hotel
www.moanasandshotel.co.ck
beach@moanasands.co.ck

Muri Beach Cottages
www.ck/muribeachcottages

Muri Beachcomber
www.beachcomber.co.ck
muri@beachcomber.co.ck

Oasis Village
www.ck/oasisvillage

Pacific Resort
www.pacificresort.com

Palm Grove Lodges
www.palmgrove.net
beach@palmgrove.co.ck

Paradise Inn
www.cookpages.com/ParadiseInn
paradise@oyster.net.ck

Puaikura Reef Lodges
www.puaikura.co.ck
accommodation@puaikura.co.ck

COOK ISLANDS

Raina Beach Apartments
www.raina.com
raina@oyster.net.ck

Rarotonga Backpackers
www.rarotongabackpackers.com
rarotongabackpackers@hotmail.com

Rarotongan Beach Resort
www.rarotongan.co.ck
info@rarotongan.co.ck

Rarotongan Sunset Motel
www.rarotongansunset.co.ck
welcome@rarosunset.co.ck

Reefcomber Sunset Motel
www.soltel.co.ck
solomon@oyster.net.ck

Reflections on Rarotonga
www.reflections-rarotonga.com
reflect@reflections-rarotonga.co.ck

Shangri-La Beach Cottages
www.shangri-la.co.ck
relax@shangri-la.co.ck

Shekinah Homes
helenura@shekinah.co.ck

Sokala Villas
www.sokala.com
villas@sokala.co.ck

Sunhaven Beach Bungalows
www.ck/sunhaven
sunhaven@beachbungalows.co.ck

Sunrise Beach Bungalows
www.sunrise.co.ck
motel@sunrise.co.ck

Takitumu Romantic Villas
www.takitumuvillas.co.ck
comfort@takitumuvillas.co.ck

The Little Polynesian
littlepoly@beach.co.ck

Tiare Village Hostel
http://cookpages.com/TiareVillage
kiaorana@tiarevillage.co.ck

Tropical Sands Bungalows
holiday@tropicalsands.co.ck

Vara's Budget Accommodation
www.varas.co.ck
backpac@varas.co.ck

Shopping

Bergman and Sons
www.blackpearl.co.ck

Island Craft
www.islandcraft.com

Pacific Gifts and Souvenirs
www.gifts.co.ck

Raro Records
www.rarorecords.musicpage.com

Sports and Recreation

Aroa Pony Trek
tikigina@oyster.net.ck

Captain Tama's Aquasportz Center
wedding@cookislands.co.ck

Cook Island Divers
http://cookpages.com/CookIslandDivers
gwilson@ci-divers.co.ck

Dive Rarotonga
www.diveraro.com
diveraro@oyster.net.ck

Dive Shop
www.palm.co.ck
hallink@palm.co.ck

Fisher's Fishing Tours
www.ck/fisher
bafisher@oyster.net.ck

Pacific Divers
www.pacificdivers.co.ck
dive@pacificdivers.co.ck

Pacific Marine Charters
pacmarine@cookislands.co.ck

continued on next page

RAROTONGA INTERNET RESOURCES (cont'd)

Raro Lagoon Scuba
www.rarolagoonscuba.co.ck

Seafari Charters
elgin@seafari.co.ck

Transportation and Tours

Avis
www.avis.co.ck
rentacar@avis.co.ck

Budget/Polynesian
www.budgct.co.ck
rentals@budget.co.ck

Island Car and Bike Hire
www.islandcarhire.co.ck

Raro Mountain Safari Tours
www.rarosafaritours.co.ck
sambo@rarosafaritours.co.ck

Rarotonga Rentals
www.rarotongarentals.co.ck

departure tax. The harbor is overcrowded and it's wise to do exactly what the harbormaster (tel. 28-814; office hours weekdays 0800–1200/ 1300–1600) asks as he's been around for a while. If you're trying to hitch a ride on a yacht to Aitutaki, Suwarrow, or points west, the harbormaster would be a good person to ask. There's a freshwater tap on the wharf, plus cold showers on the ground floor of the Ports Authority building. During occasional northerly winds November–March, this harbor becomes dangerous, and it would be a death trap for a small boat during a hurricane.

Health

Rarotonga's main hospital (tel. 22-664), on a hill between the airport and Arorangi, attends to emergencies 24 hours a day. To call an ambulance dial 998.

The Tupapa Community Clinic (tel. 20-066) at Tupapa, a km east of town, is open weekdays 0800–1800, Saturday 0800–1100. Consultations are NZ$35. In the same building is Dental Services (tel. 29-312; weekdays 0900–1200/ 1300–1600). The registration fee here is NZ$12 and a full examination costs NZ$112.

It's usually more convenient to see a private practitioner, such as Dr. Tereapii Uka (tel. 23-680; weekdays 0800–1200/1330–1500, Sat. 0900–1200), upstairs in Ingram House opposite Avatiu Harbor. A private dentist, Dr. K. Henry (tel. 29-605; weekdays 0900–1500, Sat. 0900–1100), has an office adjacent to Dr. Uka.

You could also turn to Dr. Teariki Noovao

(tel. 20-835), between the Teachers College and the Golf Club opposite Avatea School on the Ara Metua. His medical clinic is open weekdays 1630–2030, Saturday 0900–1200. A private Dental Surgery (tel. 20-169; weekdays 0800–1600) is a few hundred meters east along the same road back toward town.

Dr. Wolfgang Losacker (tel. 23-306; weekdays 1000–1300), operates a medical clinic and photo gallery between the Banana Court and the tourist office in Avarua. He's a specialist in internal and tropical medicine, cardiology, and parasitology, and at his office he sells his own Cook Islands photo books and postcards.

The CITC Pharmacy (tel. 29-292; weekdays 0800–1630, Sat. 0800–1200) is in central Avarua at CITC Shopping Center.

TRANSPORTATION

(For information on air and sea services from Rarotonga to other Cook islands turn to the Cook Islands Introduction.)

By Road

The **Cook's Island Bus Passenger Transport Ltd.** (tel. 25-512, fax 25-513) operates a daily round-the-island bus service. These yellow, 32-seat buses alternate in traveling clockwise and counterclockwise. The clockwise buses leave Cooks Corner in Avarua on the hour Monday–Saturday 0700–1400, Sunday 0800–1200/ 1400–1600. The counterclockwise buses leave

25 minutes after the hour weekdays 0825–1630, Saturday 0825–1230.

The clockwise night bus leaves town Monday–Saturday at 1800, 2100, and 2200, plus midnight and 0130 on Friday. The counterclockwise night bus leaves Monday–Saturday at 1900 with some additional services (ask).

Current timetables are usually available at the Visitor Center and are reproduced in *What's On in the Cook Islands*. Fares are NZ$2.50 one-way, NZ$4 round-trip. A 10-ride ticket which can be shared is NZ$17, a day pass NZ$9/16 adult/family. Tourists are the main users of this excellent, privately run service and the drivers make a point of being helpful.

Taxi rates are negotiable, but the service is slightly erratic. Ask the fare before getting in and clarify whether it's per person or for the whole car. Some drivers will drive you the long way around the island to your destination. Beware of prebooking taxis to the airport over the phone, as they often don't turn up, especially at odd hours. Service is generally 0600–2200 only. Hitchhiking is not really accepted here.

Rentals

A Cook Islands Driver's License (NZ$10) is required to operate a motorized rental vehicle. This can be obtained in a few minutes at the police station (tel. 22-499) in the center of Avarua weekdays 0930–1430, Saturday 0830–1030, upon presentation of your home driver's license (minimum age 16 years). This whole exercise is purely a moneymaking operation and the International Driver's License is not accepted.

If you wish to operate a scooter they'll require you to show something that states explicitly that you're licensed to drive a motorcycle, otherwise you'll have to pass a test (NZ$5 extra fee) that involves riding one up and down the street without falling off. Bring your own scooter, and don't worry, nobody fails the test. (The person giving the driving tests knocks off for lunch 1200–1300, so don't come then if you need a test.) Without a license the insurance on the vehicle won't be valid and you'll be liable for a stiff fine if caught. No license is required to ride a bicycle.

You're supposed to wear a helmet while operating a motorbike. Although it's unlikely you'll ever see anybody with one on, an antitourist cop could always bring it up. Take care when getting on or off the motorbike as many people receive burns on their lower right legs from the hot exhaust pipe.

Drive slowly, as local children tend to run onto the road unexpectedly, and beware of free-roaming dogs, which often cause accidents by suddenly giving chase at night. Take special care on Friday and Saturday nights, when there are often more drunks on the road than sober drivers. The radar-enforced speed limit is 40 km per hour in Avarua, 50 km per hour on the open road, and driving is on the left. Motorcycle accidents involving tourists are common.

The prices listed below are for the cheapest car. Rates include unlimited km, and the seventh consecutive day is usually free. Some places quote prices including the 12.5 percent government tax, others without the tax. Check all the agencies for special deals—most are also open on Sunday. Most cars and scooters rent for 24 hours, so you can use them for a sober evening on the town.

Budget/Polynesian (tel. 20-895, fax 20-838), in Avarua and at the Edgewater Resort and Rarotongan Beach Resort, has the best quality cars and bicycles. Its cars are NZ$62 a day, scooters NZ$25 a day, bicycles NZ$8 a day, tax included. You can also get a 12-passenger van at NZ$96 daily, great if you want to organize your own group tour. Discounts are offered on rentals of three days or more. Insurance is included but you're still responsible for the first NZ$300 "insurance excess" on the scooters and NZ$1,000 on the cars.

Avis (tel. 22-833, fax 21-702), next to the Cook Islands Trading Company in Avarua, charges NZ$56 for cars. Avis also has scooters at NZ$23/108 a day/week. At Avis the 12.5 percent tax is charged extra and you're responsible for the first NZ$2,000 in "excess" damages.

Rarotonga Rentals (tel. 22-326; weekdays 0800–1600, Sat. 0800–1200), next to Odds 'n Ends opposite the Punanga Nui Cultural Market, has cars from NZ$55 a day (reduction after for three days) and scooters at NZ$18 a day (or NZ$91 a week). Jeeps are also available.

Raymond Pirangi at **T.P.A. Rental Cars** (tel. 20-611), opposite the Rarotongan Sunset Motel in Arorangi, offers some of the cheapest car rentals on the island, so don't expect to receive a new car from him. Also try **Tipani Rentals** (tel. 22-328, fax 25-611), opposite the Edgewater Resort in Arorangi.

Many smaller companies rent motor scooters and bicycles—ask your hotel for the nearest. **Island Car and Bike Hire** (tel. 22-632), also known as Hogan Rentals, 250 meters north of the Are Renga Motel in Arorangi, rents cars/bicycles from NZ$40/8 a day. Island's 12-speed mountain bikes have baskets on the front and are fairly sturdy, but there are no lamps for night riding. **BT Bike Hire** (tel. 23-586), right next to the Are Renga Motel, also has bicycles and scooters.

There aren't enough women's bicycles to go around, but men's cycles are easy to rent. The main advantage to renting a bicycle for the week is that you have it when you want it. Rarotonga is small enough to be easily seen by bicycle, which makes renting a car or scooter an unnecessary expense—you also avoid the compulsory local driver's license rip-off. Bicycles are also quiet, easy on the environment, healthy, safe, and great fun. One of the nicest things to do on a sleepy Rarotonga Sunday is to slowly circle the island by bicycle.

Tours

The **Takitumu Conservation Area project** (tel. 29-906) operates four-hour guided nature hikes into the bush on the south side of the island. You'll be shown the colorful flora and if you're lucky you'll catch a glimpse of the endangered *kakerori* or Rarotonga flycatcher that the group is working to save. It's a gentle walk through lush forest suitable for all ages. Hikes start at 0930 Tuesday, Thursday, and Friday, costing NZ$45 pp including light refreshments and transfers.

Pa's Nature Walk (tel. 21-079) is another good way to get acquainted with the natural history of Rarotonga. The four-hour hike through the bush behind Matavera includes a light lunch; both it and Pa's guided cross-island hike are NZ$60 pp with hotel transfers included. Pa's hikes are recommended for bird-watchers. With his blond Rastafarian good looks, Pa is quite a character and it's worth signing up just to hear his spiel.

Air Rarotonga (tel. 22-888) offers 20-minute scenic flights (NZ$65 pp) around Rarotonga out of its hangar, 500 meters west of the main terminal. The traditional time is 1400, but you can usually arrange this on the spur of the moment if there are two of you and a pilot and plane are available.

Hugh Henry (tel. 25-320, fax 25-420) and **Raro Tours** (tel. 25-324) offer 3.5-hour, NZ$25 circle-island tours weekday mornings. Call ahead and they'll pick you up at your hotel. Ask how much time will be spent on "shopping sprees" as some tours waste half the allotted time in souvenir shops. Sunday mornings at 0930 a church service is included in this tour (NZ$30).

Monday, Wednesday, and Friday at 1000 the **Cultural Village** (tel. 21-314) offers a full-day combined circle-island tour and cultural show for NZ$85 including lunch.

More adventurous tours in 4WD vehicles are offered by **Raro Mountain Safari Tours** (tel. 23-629), opposite the Rarotongan Beach Resort. The 3.5-hour tours (NZ$60/30 adult/child) begin weekdays at 0900 and 1330, Sunday at noon. It's the best way to see the island's interior without walking.

The **Bond Liquor Store** (tel. 21-007), opposite the Punanga Nui Cultural Market, offers a free guided tour of its on-site brewery Monday–Thursday at 1400.

Southern Group

Aitutaki

Aitutaki, 259 km north of Rarotonga, is the second-most-visited Cook Island and the scenery of this "dream island" is actually quite lovely. The low rolling hills are flanked by banana plantations, taro fields, and coconut groves. Atiu-type coffee is grown here. A triangular barrier reef 45 km around catches Aitutaki's turquoise lagoon like a fishhook. The maximum depth of this lagoon is 10.5 meters but most of it is less than five meters deep. The 15 picture-postcard *motu* (islets) and numerous sandbars on the eastern barrier reef all feature the soft white sands and aquamarine waters of your usual South Seas paradise.

The main island is volcanic: its highest hill, Maungapu (124 meters), is said to be the top of Rarotonga's Raemaru, chopped off and brought back by victorious Aitutaki warriors. All of the *motu* are coralline except for Rapota and Moturakau, which contain some volcanic rock. Legend holds that just as the warriors were arriving back with their stolen mountain they clashed with pursuing Rarotongans and pieces of Maungapu fell off, creating Moturakau and Rapota. Moturakau served as a leper colony from the 1930s to 1967. Motikitiu at the south end of the lagoon is the nesting area of many of

AITUTAKI ATOLL

GOLF CLUB

AIRSTRIP

Maungapu
(124 m)

Amuri   Ootu
Ureia   Vaipeka   Akitua

Arutanga   Angarei
Reureu   Niura
Nikaupara   Vaipae
        Tautu   Mangere

TAUTU
JETTY

Te Koutu   Papau

        Tavaerua-iti

    Tavaerua-nui

Lagoon   Akaiami

Maina   Muritapua

        Moturakau
    Rapota   Tekapua

            Tapuaetai

        Motukitiu

0   3 mi

0   3 km

© DAVID STANLEY

Aitutaki is the only Cook island other than Rarotonga where there's a good choice of places to stay, entertainment, and organized activities. One way to go is to catch a Thursday or Friday flight up from Rarotonga so as to be on hand for "island night" that evening. Book a lagoon trip for Saturday and you'll still have Sunday to scooter around the island or laze on the beach. Fly back on Monday or Tuesday, having sidestepped Rarotonga's dull Sunday. This is probably too short a stay, however, and a week on the island would be better.

Aitutaki is north of Rarotonga and therefore warmer. During the hot season December–March, sand flies and mosquitoes are at their worst. They're more of a nuisance on the north side of the main island, far less so on the *motu*. Around Arutanga beware of theft from the beach and back yards of the guesthouses by small children.

History

A Polynesian myth explains how Aitutaki is a giant fish tethered to the seabed by a vine. After a perilous journey from Tubuai in the canoe *Little Flowers,* the legendary hero Ru landed here with four wives, four younger brothers, and 20 virgins to colonize the island. Ru named the atoll Utataki-enua-o-Ru-ki-te-moana, meaning "a land sought and found in the sea by Ru," which

Aitutaki's native birds, as mynahs have taken over the main island. Be on the lookout for the blue lorikeet *(kuramo'o)* with its white bib and orange beak and legs.

The 2,000 people live in eight villages strung along the roads on both sides of the main island. The roads are red-brown in the center of the island, coral white around the edge, and the locals generally get around on motor scooters. The administration and most local businesses are clustered near the wharf at Arutanga. All of the villages have huge community halls built mostly with money sent from New Zealand. There's tremendous rivalry among the villages to have the biggest and best one, although they're unused most of the time. The *motu* are uninhabited, and there aren't any dogs at all on Aitutaki.

SOUTHERN GROUP HIGHLIGHTS

island night, Aitutaki: dancing, culture, food, fun
Tapuaetai, Aitutaki: swimming at One Foot Island, lagoon trips
Takitaki Cave, Atiu: birdlife, hiking, nature
CICC Church, Mauke: history, architecture
***makatea* of Mangaia:** geology, hiking, nature

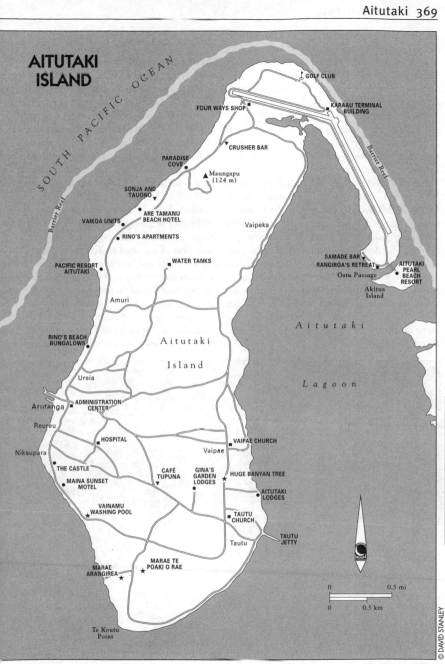

AITUTAKI ISLAND

SOUTH PACIFIC OCEAN

Barrier Reef

GOLF CLUB

FOUR WAYS SHOP

KARAAU TERMINAL BUILDING

CRUSHER BAR

PARADISE COVE

Maungapu (124 m)

SONJA AND TAUONO

Barrier Reef

ARE TAMANU BEACH HOTEL

Vaipeka

VAIKOA UNITS

RINO'S APARTMENTS

WATER TANKS

PACIFIC RESORT AITUTAKI

SAMADE BAR
RANGIROA'S RETREAT

AITUTAKI PEARL BEACH RESORT

Ootu Passage

Amuri

Akitua Island

Aitutaki

RINO'S BEACH BUNGALOWS

Aitutaki Island

Lagoon

Ureia

ADMINISTRATION CENTER

Arutanga

Reureu

HOSPITAL

VAIPAE CHURCH

Vaipae

Nikaupara

THE CASTLE

CAFÉ TUPUNA

GINA'S GARDEN LODGES

HUGE BANYAN TREE

MAINA SUNSET MOTEL

AITUTAKI LODGES

VAINAMU WASHING POOL

TAUTU CHURCH

MARAE TE POAKI O RAE

TAUTU JETTY

Tautu

MARAE ARANGIREA

N

MOON

0   0.5 mi
0   0.5 km

Te Koutu Point

COOK ISLANDS

the first Europeans corrupted to Aitutaki. Ru named various parts of the island for the head, stomach, and tail of the fish, but more places he named for himself. His brothers became angry when most of the land was divided among the 20 virgins, and they left for New Zealand where they won great honor. Ru himself suffered the consequences of his arrogance as higher chiefs eventually arrived and relegated him to the subordinate position held by his descendants today.

Captain William Bligh "discovered" Aitutaki in 1789, only 17 days before the notorious mutiny. In 1821, this became the first of the Cook islands to receive Christian missionaries when the Tahitian pastors Papeiha and Vahapata were put ashore. The Americans built the island's huge airfield during World War II. Tasman Empire Airways (now Air New Zealand) used Akaiami Island as a refueling stop for its four-engined Solent flying boats during the 1950s. The Coral Route, from Auckland to Tahiti via Suva and Apia, became obsolete when Faa'a Airport opened near Papeete in 1961.

SIGHTS OF AITUTAKI
Arutanga and the South
Opposite the Administration Center at Arutanga is the colonial-style residence of the government representative set amid lovely gardens. The limestone **CICC church** just south was begun in 1828, only a few years after Papeiha converted the islanders. It's usually solidly locked but you can still peek in the windows of this oldest church in the Cook Islands and admire the monument to missionaries John Williams and Papeiha out front.

South of Arutanga beyond Nikaupara, the road turns inland at a dry stream where the old **Vainamu Washing Pool** has been rebuilt. Continue east along this road, turning right at the junction of the road to Te Koutu Point. About 700 meters south is **Marae Te Poaki O Rae,** down a short trail to the left. A signpost visible east of the road marks this double row of stones beneath a huge *puka* tree. A more overgrown road running west toward the beach from the Te Poaki O Rae junction leads to **Marae Arangirea.** Look for another line of stones about 150 meters down

Graves crowd the churchyard at the CICC in Arutanga.

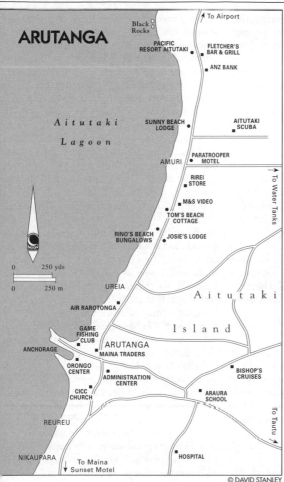

ARUTANGA

Black Rocks

To Airport

PACIFIC RESORT AITUTAKI

FLETCHER'S BAR & GRILL

ANZ BANK

Aitutaki Lagoon

SUNNY BEACH LODGE

AITUTAKI SCUBA

AMURI

PARATROOPER MOTEL

To Water Tanks

RIREI STORE

M&S VIDEO

TOM'S BEACH COTTAGE

RINO'S BEACH BUNGALOWS

JOSIE'S LODGE

0   250 yds
0   250 m

UREIA

Aitutaki

Island

AIR RAROTONGA

GAME FISHING CLUB

ANCHORAGE

ARUTANGA

MAINA TRADERS

ORONGO CENTER

ADMINISTRATION CENTER

BISHOP'S CRUISES

CICC CHURCH

ARAURA SCHOOL

REUREU

To Tautu

NIKAUPARA

To Maina Sunset Motel

HOSPITAL

© DAVID STANLEY

a leisurely half-hour jaunt up an obvious track and from the top you get a sweeping view of Aitutaki's entire barrier reef.

The Lagoon

At low tide you can walk and wade along a sandbar from the Pacific Resort Aitutaki right out to the reef, but wear something on your feet to protect yourself from the coral, sea urchins, eels, stonefish, algae, etc. Stonefish are not common, but they're almost impossible to spot until it's too late. At high tide snorkel out from the black rocks on the beach just north of the resort. Snorkelers and paddlers must keep at least 200 meters inside the main reef entrance at Arutanga because of the strong outgoing current.

The finest snorkeling off the main island is at the far west end of the airstrip and to the south. Beware of dangerous currents in the passes near the edge of the reef here. Elsewhere on the main island the snorkeling is poor.

The top beach on the main island is at the southeast end of the airstrip near the bridge to the Aitutaki Pearl Beach Resort. It's fine to swim here, but snorkelers won't see many fish or corals.

on the left, in high grass just before you enter the eerie chestnut forest along the coast.

The Interior

An easy afternoon or sunset hike from the guesthouses at Arutanga is up to the **water tanks** on a hill in the middle of the island. Go up the road marked Pirake/Vaipeka on the south side of the Paratrooper Motel.

The trail to the radio towers on the summit of **Maungapu** starts from opposite Paradise Cove on the main road up the west side of the island. It's

SPORTS AND RECREATION

Neil Mitchell's **Aitutaki Scuba** (tel. 31-103, fax 31-310) offers diving at the drop-off once or twice a day (except Sunday). If you have your own equipment, diving is NZ$75 per dive (NZ$10 extra if you need gear). Snorkelers are welcome to go along at NZ$35 pp when space is available. No reservations are required, but bring your own mask; wetsuits are handy June–December. The diving here is better March–November. Aitutaki is good place to learn to dive and Neil does four-day PADI certification courses for NZ$550 (minimum of two people). You'll find Neil about a hundred meters down the side road that branches off the main road at Sunny Beach Lodge. Aitutaki is not an easy dive destination. The lagoon may be great for snorkeling, but it's too shallow for serious diving and the drop-off outside the reef is very steep (not for beginners).

Aitutaki Sea Charters (tel. 31-281) offers deep-sea fishing off the 10-meter cruiser *Foxy Lady*. Captain Jason and his father, Don Watts, live near the Crusher Bar toward the airport. Skipjack tuna, giant trevally, mahimahi, and barracuda are caught year-round off Aitutaki. The billfish (marlin) season is November–March, while in August and September wahoo are frequently caught.

The **Aitutaki Golf Club** (no phone) beside the airport welcomes visitors. Greens fees and club rentals are NZ$10 each. If your ball falls on the airstrip, it's considered out of bounds. The Aitutaki Open Golf Tournament is in mid-October.

ACCOMMODATIONS

There are lots of places to stay on Aitutaki in every price category and the rooms are almost never fully booked. Air Rarotonga or any travel agent on Rarotonga can reserve the places mentioned below and discounts are possible if you stay a week or more. Most of the cheaper places offer rooms with shared bath only.

Under US$25

Josie's Lodge (Josie Sadaraka, tel. 31-341, fax 31-518), an older island home in Arutanga, has five rooms with shared bath (cold showers) at NZ$20/40/51 single/double/triple. The rooms are screened to keep out insects, and communal cooking facilities are provided.

Tom's Beach Cottage (Taraota Tom, tel. 31-051, fax 31-409) is a large island-style house on the beach a bit north of Josie's. The seven rooms with old-fashioned brass beds and mosquito nets are NZ$32/48/58 single/double/triple, but the two facing the street get considerable traffic noise. A "honeymoon" bungalow a bit closer to the beach is NZ$86/94 single/double. When things

are slow these rates are reduced. A communal kitchen is available (beware of mice), plus a lounge with a pool table and a sitting room with photos of the family. Local calls on the house phone are NZ$.50 each. Tom rents scooters (NZ$15) and bicycles (NZ$5) to guests.

Matriki Adventure (tel. 31-564), on a great beach next door to the fancy Are Tamanu Beach Hotel north of town, has three simple beach cabins at NZ$35/45 single/double (or NZ$280 a week). Each has cooking facilities and a private outdoor shower but the shared toilet is beside the main house. Owners Matias and Riki rent scooters to guests at NZ$100 a week.

Junior Maoate's **Paradise Cove Lodge** (tel. 31-218, fax 31-456) is at Anaunga, between the airstrip and the Pacific Resort Aitutaki. Spacious grounds lead down to a white sand beach with excellent snorkeling just offshore. The four rooms in the main house are NZ$25/35 single/double, while the six thatched Polynesian beach huts with shared bath are NZ$35/50. Six newer beach bungalows with balconies and private bath (hot water!) are NZ$150 single or double. Junior provides good communal cooking facilities and special reduced rates are sometimes offered.

Josie's Beach Lodge (tel. 31-659), at Ootu Beach to the right as you approach the bridge over to the Aitutaki Pearl Beach Resort, has six double rooms with shared bath and cooking facilities in an older building at NZ$25 pp. The lodge will prepare an excellent breakfast for you at NZ$10. It's good value. Information is available from Greta at Four Square Store (tel. 31-188) near the Administrative Center in Arutanga.

US$25–50

The Castle (Teetu and Tschan Tatira, tel. 31-012), a 10-minute walk south of the post office in Arutanga, has one- and two-bedroom self-catering apartments in a two-story concrete building starting at NZ$60.

The **Paratrooper Motel** (tel. 31-563 or 31-523) in Amuri consists of four wooden buildings in a crowded compound a block back from the beach. It's run by an ex-New Zealand paratrooper named Geoffrey Roi and his wife, Maine. Geoffrey's rates are NZ$75/250 single or double a night/week for their two one-bedroom apartments with full cooking facilities. The three two-bedroom family units are NZ$120/350. The minimum stay is three nights.

Sunny Beach Lodge (tel./fax 31-446), on the beach toward the north end of the tourist strip, has a row of five self-catering units in a single-story block at NZ$75/85/100/115 single/double/triple/quad. The rooms face the wrong way and the beach is out of sight. If it's closed when you arrive, the owners live behind the Seventh-Day Adventist church across the street.

Vaikoa Units (tel. 31-145), a km north of the Pacific Resort Aitutaki, offers seven self-catering units in parallel wooden blocks at NZ$40/80 single/double (no hot water). The nearest grocery store is a 15-minute walk away. It's right on one of the best snorkeling beaches on the main island. The managers are friendly but guests tend to keep to themselves.

US$50–100

On the beach almost opposite Josie's Lodge in Arutanga is **Rino's Beach Bungalows** (Rino and Ngatere George, tel. 31-197, fax 31-559) with four hotplate-equipped units in a two-story road-side block at NZ$70/111/137 single/double/triple. Four new beachfront duplex apartments are NZ$169–221 single or double complete with fridge, stove, and terrace. Rino's also has an older three-bedroom house across the street that is rented out at NZ$450 a week (up to six people). Three large apartments in a building on the hillside near Vaikoa Units are NZ$130.

Ranginui's Retreat (Steve Schofield, tel. 31-157, fax 31-658), on Ootu Beach near the Samade Bar, has four self-catering duplex rooms at NZ$110/120/140 single/double/triple (no hot water). Children under 12 are free. It rents mini-cars at NZ$80 a day, scooters at NZ$15/20 half/full day, and an outboard dingy at NZ$80. Return airport transfers are NZ$16. The location right next to the Aitutaki Pearl Beach Resort is great and several other budget resorts are planned or under construction in this vicinity.

In late 2002 **Popoara Ocean Breeze Villas** (Allen and Maria Mills, tel./fax 31-739) opened between Ranginui's Retreat and the Aitutaki Pearl

Beach Resort. The 10 self-catering units are NZ$180 double. There's a restaurant and bar.

Gina's Garden Lodges (tel./fax 31-058), between Arutanga and Tautu (just before Kingdom Hall), has four self-catering bungalows with lofts in a quiet garden setting at NZ$75/120/150 single/double/triple. An extra child is NZ$20. Two radio antennas are available for amateur ham operators. The inland location near Tautu is inconvenient to both Arutanga and the beach. Gina's is run by Queen Manarangi Tutai, one of the *ariki* of the island. She owns a beach house on lovely Akaiami Island that is accessible to guests.

In 1995 the **Maina Sunset Motel** (tel. 31-511, fax 31-611) opened in Nikaupara district, a 20-minute walk south of Arutanga. The 12 units are arranged in a U-shape around a freshwater swimming pool that faces an ugly boat passage dug out of the shallow lagoon (no beach). The eight rooms without cooking are NZ$165 double, while the four with cooking are NZ$195. It's peaceful as you don't get a lot of traffic noise down here. Scooter hire is NZ$25 a day and airport transfers are NZ$16 pp round-trip.

One Foot Hideaway (McBirney Enterprises, tel. 31-418, fax 31-486), on One Foot Island in the southeast corner of the lagoon, gives you the opportunity to spend a night on an otherwise uninhabited *motu*. It's NZ$180 double to sleep in this two-story bungalow a bit east of the One Foot Post Office (take insect repellent). The lighting is by kerosene lamp. Book through Kit Cat Lagoon Cruises at Mango Trading next to Fletcher's Bar and Grill in Amuri or Jetsave Travel. Transfers to the island are NZ$50 pp round-trip.

US$100–150

Aitutaki Lodges (tel. 31-334, fax 31-333), near Tautu Jetty on the opposite side of the main island from Arutanga, offers six self-catering bungalows on stilts facing the lagoon at NZ$230 single or double, with reductions for three or more nights. You'll need to hire a scooter if you want to stay here as it's far from everything. Although the lagoon view from your porch will be lovely, the beach below the units is too muddy for swimming and the water

SOUTHERN GROUP INTERNET RESOURCES

Accommodations

Aitutaki Lodges
www.ck/aitutakilodges
aitlodge@aitutaki.net.ck

Aitutaki Pearl Beach Resort
www.aitutakipearlbeach.com
akitua@aitutaki.net.ck

Ara Moana Bungalows, Mangaia
www.aramoana.com
holiday@aramoana.com

Are Manuiri Guest House, Atiu
www.adc.co.ck
adc@adc.co.ck

Are Tamanu Beach Hotel, Aitutaki
www.aretamanu.com
aretamanu@aitutaki.net.ck

Gina's Garden Lodges, Aitutaki
www.pacific-resorts.com/ginaslodge
queen@aitutaki.net.ck

Kopeka Lodge, Atiu
stay@kopekalodge-atiu.co.ck

Maina Sunset Motel, Aitutaki
solomon@oyster.net.ck

Pacific Resort Aitutaki
www.pacificresort-aitutaki.com
presort@aitutaki.net.ck

Paradise Cove Lodge, Aitutaki
mtl@aitutaki.net.ck

Popoara Ocean Breeze Villas, Aitutaki
fishing@aitutaki.net.ck

Rino's Beach Bungalows, Aitutaki
rinos@aitutaki.net.ck

Sunny Beach Lodge, Aitutaki
sunnybeach@aitutaki.net.ck

Other Resources

Aitutaki Scuba
scuba@aitutaki.net.ck

Atiu Tours, Atiu
atiutours.ck@ihug.co.nz

Cook Islands Aitutaki
www.aitutaki.com

Bishop's Lagoon Cruises, Aitutaki
bishopcruz@aitutaki.net.ck

Kit Cat Lagoon Cruises, Aitutaki
mango@aitutaki.net.ck

M&S Video and Internet, Aitutaki
marste@aitutaki.net.ck

Paradise Islands Cruises, Aitutaki
lagoon@aitutaki.net.ck

too murky for snorkeling. We've received several bitter complaints about the service here.

US$150–250

The **Are Tamanu Beach Hotel** (tel. 31-810, fax 31-816), on a white sandy beach between Arutanga and the airport, offers 12 thatched bungalows with full cooking facilities and fridge at NZ$400/485 double/triple (no children under 12). Only one unit actually faces the lagoon, the others face each other. There's no restaurant but a free tropical breakfast is served at the bar next to the swimming pool and you can buy sandwiches all day. There's a barbecue Sunday at 1930

(NZ$25) and it's okay to bring your own booze to the bar or beach. This compact resort is run by local politician Mike Henry and all of the employees are his relatives. The Are Tamanu is off limits to outsiders, so don't bother trying to drop in for a drink. Bicycles and canoes are lent free to guests. It's often fully booked.

US$250 and up

In October 2002 the **Pacific Resort Aitutaki** (tel. 31-720, fax 31-719) opened on the site of the former Rapae Motel just north of Arutanga. A branch of the Pacific Resort on Rarotonga, this property includes 19 bungalows at NZ$710/785 double/triple six suites at NZ$930/1,005, and three villas at NZ$1,150/1,225, including breakfast, tax, and transfers. A pool and restaurant are provided. Ongoing construction is intended to increase the number of rooms to 75. The snorkeling here is good.

The **Aitutaki Pearl Beach Resort** (tel. 31-203, fax 31-202), on Akitua Island near Ootu Beach at the east end of the airstrip, is connected to the main island by a small wooden bridge. The 16 air-conditioned garden bungalows with private bath and fridge are NZ$440 single or double, the nine lagoon bungalows NZ$660, the five beachfront bungalows NZ$920, and the seven so-called overwater bungalows NZ$1,120, tax included. Three garden rooms close to the main complex are NZ$320. A third person in all cases is NZ$100 (children under 12 free). Only the front deck of the "overwater" bungalows is partially overwater—the rear entrance is firmly anchored to the shore. Cooking facilities are not provided and half/full board is NZ$89/114 pp extra. The resort's Wednesday night seafood buffet is NZ$90, the Saturday barbecue NZ$75, both with traditional dancing. There's a swimming pool and the beach is lovely, but the water offshore is murky and there's nothing much to see through your mask. A NZ$5 surcharge is added to any tours or cruises booked through this resort.

FOOD AND ENTERTAINMENT

Food

The **Blue Nun Cafe** (tel. 31-604; Mon.–Thurs. 0800–2200, Wed., Fri., and Sat. 0800–midnight), in the Orongo Center, serves substantial portions of inexpensive food to be consumed at tables overlooking the lagoon. The name refers to the small *kuramoo* bird depicted on its sign, not religious nuns. The menu on the wall lists fish and chips (NZ$7), mussels and chips (NZ$9.50), curried chicken rice (NZ$8.50), and hamburgers (NZ$4–5). Wednesday and Saturday nights there's island dancing at 2030 (NZ$25 for the buffet dinner or you can watch for the price of a beer).

Fletcher's Bar and Grill (tel. 31-950; daily 1130–1500/1830–2100), across the street from the Pacific Resort Aitutaki, is owned by Steve Christian, a direct descendant of Fletcher Christian. For lunch you can have a fishburger (NZ$12.50) or fish and chips (NZ$12.50) at the picnic tables outside. (No lunch is available on Sunday.) Dinner is served á la carte in an air-conditioned room. The Friday night buffet (NZ$25.50) includes a Polynesian show, which you can also watch while standing at the bar nursing a drink.

Tauono's Garden Café (tel. 31-562), between Paradise Cove and Vaikoa Units, is easily the best place on the island for a home-cooked lunch (NZ$13.50) served in the garden. It's available daily 1200–1400, but on Sundays you must book ahead.

The **Crusher Bar and Restaurant** (tel. 31-283), near Paradise Cove on the way to the airport, is a funky open-air bar with picnic tables under a tin roof. The Monday dinner and cultural show by Tamanu is only NZ$15. Thursday night is island night with a Polynesian buffet (NZ$25.50 pp) followed by an excellent show by the dance group Tiare Aitutaki. The Friday special grilled fish or steak dinner with live entertainment is NZ$15.50. Saturday night is "backpackers nite" with main course and dessert at NZ$12.50, plus reduced drink prices and disco music after 2000. Sunday nights it's a roast or fish of the day. The á la carte menu (NZ$12.50–26.50) is available nightly from 1800. Animation is provided by the infamous lady killer Riki de Von (also an excellent cook). Call ahead for reservations and NZ$5 hotel pickups.

The **Samade Bar** (tel. 31-526), run by Sam and Adrienne at Ootu Beach, is a great escape for those staying at the nearby Aitutaki Pearl Beach Resort. For others it makes an excellent base for a day at the beach. You can order drinks on their white sand terrace all day, and weekdays they serve lunch (1100–1500) and dinner (from 1900). Choices include fish burgers (NZ$6.50) and steak burgers (NZ$8.50). There's an island night with traditional dancing Tuesday at 1930 (NZ$25 including dinner). The Friday night beach party and barbecue (NZ$25) and the generous Sunday *umukai* (earth oven) with string band music at 1330 (NZ$18) are also recommended. It's best to reserve the evening meals, and Poo Bishop (tel. 31-109) does transfers at NZ$5 pp round-trip.

Café Tupuna (tel. 31-678; daily 1730–2130), near Gina's Garden Lodges between Arutanga and Tautu, is good for a nicely presented, semi-upscale dinner (mains NZ$22–25). Tupuna Slattery is an ingenious cook, specializing in curries, steaks, and fish. Try the *sashimi* (NZ$12). A selection of wines is offered and the floor is pleasingly sandy. Book ahead as seating is limited (transfers available at NZ$5 round-trip).

Maina Traders Ltd. (tel. 31-055; Mon.–Sat. 0700–2000), near the wharf, offers a good selection of groceries, fresh vegetables, and drinks.

Rirei Store (Mon.–Sat. 0700–2000), the place with the Heiniken sign a few hundred meters north of Rino's Beach Bungalows, scoops out ice-cream cones as well as selling fresh vegetables.

Ask the people where you're staying if the water is safe to drink. Rainwater is okay but the well water is sometimes slightly brackish and boiling won't help much in that case.

Entertainment

Polynesian dance shows take place almost nightly: Monday at the Crusher Bar (tel. 31-283), Tuesday at the Samade Bar (tel. 31-526), Wednesday at the Blue Nun (tel. 31-604) and the Aitutaki Pearl Beach Resort (tel. 31-200), Thursday at the Crusher Bar (tel. 31-283), Friday at Fletcher's Bar (tel. 31-950), and Saturday at the Blue Nun (tel. 31-604) and Aitutaki Pearl Beach Resort (tel. 31-203). Call ahead to confirm this schedule. Most of these venues provide round-trip transfers at NZ$5 pp.

The **Aitutaki Game Fishing Club** (no phone, VHF channel 16; open Wed.–Sat. from 1600), in a container behind the Ports Authority on the way to the harbor, has cheap beer and is a good place to meet people at happy hour.

PRACTICALITIES

Shopping

Several handicraft stalls with bright pareus and beachware are in the **Orongo Center** (closed Sunday), in the former banana packing house near Arutanga wharf.

Services

Traveler's checks can be cashed at the Westpac Bank agency (tel. 31-714; Mon. and Thurs. from 0930–1500), in the Administration Center opposite Arutanga wharf, and the ANZ Bank agency (tel. 31-486; weekdays 0900–1500), next to Fletcher's Bar and Grill. It's smarter to change your money on Rarotonga beforehand as the rates here are poor.

The post office (tel. 31-680; weekdays 0800–1600), in the Administration Center, sells local telephone cards (NZ$10, NZ$20, and NZ$50), which can be used for international calls at the public telephone outside (dial 00 for international access). If you need to receive a fax, the number is fax 682/31-683. The Aitutaki postage stamps sold here can be used only to post letters on Aitutaki itself (not accepted on Rarotonga).

M&S Video (tel. 31-712), just north of Tom's Beach Cottage, offers Internet access.

Public toilets are behind the Blue Nun Cafe at the Orongo Center.

Outpatients are accepted at the hospital (tel. 31-002) Monday–Friday 0830–1200/1300–1600, Saturday 0830–1200, emergencies anytime.

TRANSPORTATION

Because Aitutaki's small population doesn't justify a regular ferry service from Rarotonga, getting here is more expensive than visiting similar outer islands in French Polynesia, Tonga, and Fiji, almost always involving a stiff plane ticket. (For flight and boat information see the Cook Islands Introduction.) **Air Rarotonga** (tel. 31-888, fax 31-414; weekdays 0800–1600, Sat. 0800–1200) has an office at Ureia.

The shipping companies have no local agent, but the people at the Ports Authority (tel. 31-050) near the wharf will know when a ship is due in. Dangerous coral heads and currents make passage through Aitutaki's barrier reef hazardous, so passengers and cargo on the interisland ships must be transferred to the wharf by lighters. The Americans built Arutanga Wharf during World War II. They had planned to dredge the anchorage and widen the pass, but the war ended before they got around to it. Blasting by the New Zealand military in 1986 improved Arutanga Passage somewhat, but it's still narrow, with a six-knot current draining water blown into the lagoon from the

south. The depth in the pass is limited to two meters at high tide, but reader C. Webb reports that:

> *the bottom of the pass is sand, so it's a good place to be somewhat aggressive.*

Once inside, the anchorage off Arutanga is safe and commodious for yachts. This is an official port of entry to the Cooks and the local customs officials readily approve visa extensions for yacht crews. "Having fun" is sufficient reason.

No taxis or buses operate on Aitutaki but there's considerable scooter and pickup traffic along the west coast. Mike Henry (tel. 31-379 or 31-810) does airport transfers at NZ$8 pp.

Rentals

Temporary Cook Islands driver's licenses can be obtained at the Police Department Center (tel. 31-015) in the Orongo Center for NZ$2.50. No photo is required and they're also valid on Rarotonga.

The T&M Ltd. gasoline station (tel. 31-900), next to the Ports Authority at the wharf, opens weekdays 0700–2000, Saturday 0700–1230/1600–2030.

Rino's Rentals (tel. 31-197, fax 31-559), near Tom's Beach Cottage, has Suzuki jeeps (NZ$70 for 24 hours), cars (from NZ$85 daily), motor scooters (from NZ$25 the first day, NZ$20 subsequent days), and pushbikes (from NZ$5 daily). Rino's has a NZ$120 weekly rate for Honda 100s.

Some of the guesthouses and hotels also rent bicycles— all you really need.

The **Samade Bar** (tel. 31-526) at Ootu Beach rents two-person kayaks at NZ$10/15/20 hour/half/day. Call ahead if you want a kayak. From Ootu you can paddle a kayak to Angarei in 15 minutes, Papua in an hour, and Akaiami in 2.5 hours. Hobie cat sailing with a captain is NZ$35 for the first hour, NZ$20 additional hours (four-hour maximum). Two can go for this price.

Lagoon Tours

Several companies offer boat trips to uninhabited *motu* around the Aitutaki Lagoon, such as Akaiami or Tapuaetai (One Foot Island). The swimming in the clear deep-green water at these islands is great but the snorkeling is mediocre. Thus the

boats take passengers to much better snorkeling spots on the reef. Unfortunately the very popularity of these trips has become their undoing as "desert islands" such as Tapuaetai can get rather overcrowded when all of the tourist boats arrive!

Some trips also go to Maina, or "Bird Island," at the southwest corner of the lagoon. Only a few tropic birds still nest on a sandbar called "Honeymoon Island" next to Maina as most have been scared off by marauding tourists and their guides. There's good snorkeling at Honeymoon Island as the fish are fed here. But when the wind whips up the sea it gets hard to snorkel and you miss out on half the fun.

Different tour operators concentrate on varying aspects and the smaller independent operators tend to serve you a bigger and better lunch for a lower price. If snorkeling is your main interest you should find out if they plan to spend all afternoon eating and drinking at Tapuaetai (also great fun). Bishop's Cruises is the most reliable company and it tries to run on a schedule. This may be what you want if you have only one chance to get it right, but it's inevitably touristy and the amateur operators you learn about by word of mouth or from notices taped on the walls of the backpackers hostels are more personal (and less dependable). It's also possible to arrange to be dropped off for the day on Akaiami or Maina.

Bishop's Lagoon Cruises (Teina Bishop, tel. 31-009, fax 31-493), inland from Arutanga Wharf, and **Kit Cat Lagoon Cruises** (tel. 31-418), at Mango Trading next to Fletcher's Bar and Grill, offer lagoon trips daily except Sunday. One trip goes to Maina, another to Akaiami, and both continue to Moturakau and Tapuaetai. The Maina trip is the better and to get it you must specifically request a visit to Maina when booking, otherwise they'll only take you to Akaiami and Tapuaetai. Either way, the price is NZ$55 including lunch. **Paradise Islands Cruises** (Tai Herman, tel. 31-248, fax 31-398) operates the Aitutaki day tour cruises (NZ$65 cruise only) for Air Rarotonga using a large catamaran, and both it and Bishop's are rather commercialized and jaded. Often the cooks can be rather miserly rationing out the fried fish in order to have an ample supply left over for themselves and the boat crews. You'll probably be whisked back to the main island earlier than you would have liked so the day-trippers from Rarotonga can catch their flight.

Teariki George of **Teking Water Taxi Service** (tel. 31-582) at Tautu shuttles snorkelers over to Maina Island at NZ$35 pp including gear but no lunch.

If you're on a low budget you can get comparable snorkeling off the west end of the airstrip for free. Whatever you decide, take sunscreen and insect repellent.

Reef Tours

Sonja and Tauono Raela (tel. 31-562), who live between Paradise Cove and Vaikoa Units, offer unique reef tours in a traditional outrigger sailing canoe. The NZ$35 pp fee (NZ$45 if you go out alone) includes a light lunch, and they'll prepare any of the fish you catch for an additional fee of NZ$10–15, depending on what you want. You may also take your fish back to your guesthouse and cook it yourself. If you'd like to do any reef walking or fishing with a bamboo rod you must go at low tide; the swimming and snorkeling are better at high tide. Tauono is a sensitive guide more than willing to explain Aitutaki's delicate reef ecology during the four hours the trips usually last. Call the night before to arrange a time. Tauono and Sonja keep the only organic garden on Aitutaki and it's always worth stopping by to buy some vegetables, herbs, cakes, or fresh fish. Sonja will happily spend time with you providing cooking suggestions and general information on their produce and the cuisine of the islands.

Atiu

The original name of Atiu, third largest of the Cook Islands, was Enuamanu, meaning "land of birds." These days native birds are found mostly around the coast as the interior has been taken over by an influx of mynahs. In 2001 the 10 endangered Rarotonga flycatchers (*kakerori*) were introduced on Atiu in an effort to save the birds from extinction. Unlike neighboring Mauke and Mitiaro, which are flat, Atiu has a high central plateau (71 meters) surrounded by low swamps and an old raised coral reef known as a *makatea*. This is 20 meters high and covered with dense tropical jungle.

The red soil on Atiu's central plateau is formed from volcanic basalt rock and it's rather poor. The slopes up to the central plateau have been reforested to check erosion. Taro is the main crop and taro patches occupy the swamps along the inner edge of the *makatea*. Arabica coffee is grown, processed, roasted, packaged, and marketed as "Kaope Atiu."

Atiu is one of the only islands in Polynesia where the people prefer the center to the shore, and cooling ocean breezes blow across Atiu's plain. Once fierce warriors who made cannibal raids on Mauke and Mitiaro, the islanders became Christians after missionary John Williams converted high chief Rongomatane in 1823. Today the 650 Atiuans live peacefully in five villages on the high central plain. The villages radiate from an administrative center where the main churches, hospital, PWD workshops, stores, and government offices are all found. Only 11 people on Atiu have full-time jobs, and 1996–2001 a third of the island's people left for New Zealand. Pigs outnumber people four to one.

The good beaches, varied scenery, and geological curiosities combine with satisfactory accommodations and enjoyable activities to make a visit well worthwhile. Atiu beckons the active traveler keen to experience a real slice of outer island life. It will appeal to hikers who want to explore the island's lonely roads, to adventurers who enjoy looking for caves and archaeological remains hidden in the bush, or to anyone in search of a restful holiday and a chance to spend some time on an unspoiled island without sacrificing creature comforts. Atiu has little to offer those interested in scuba diving, fancy resorts, or lagoon trips.

SIGHTS OF ATIU

The massive white walls of the **CICC church** dominate Teenui village in the exact center of the island. Just south, a road leads east toward Tengatangi village from almost opposite the Atiu Administra-

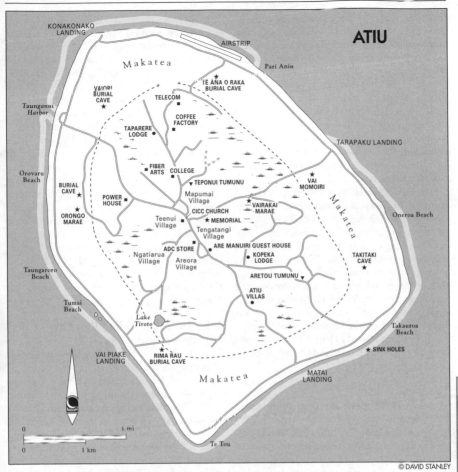

ATIU

KONAKONAKO LANDING

AIRSTRIP

Makatea

Pari Aniu

Taunganui Harbor

TARAPAKU LANDING

TE ANA O RAKA BURIAL CAVE

VAIORI BURIAL CAVE ★

TELECOM

COFFEE FACTORY

TAPARERE LODGE ●

Orovaru Beach

FIBER ARTS

COLLEGE

TEPONUI TUMUNU ▼

VAI MOMOIRI ★

Makatea

BURIAL CAVE ★

POWER HOUSE ■

Mapumai Village

CICC CHURCH

VAIRAKAI MARAE ★

Oneroa Beach

ORONGO MARAE ★

Teenui Village

▼ MEMORIAL

Tengatangi Village

ADC STORE

ARE MANUIRI GUEST HOUSE ●

TAKITAKI CAVE ★

Taungaroro Beach

Ngatiarua Village

Areora Village

KOPEKA LODGE ●

ARETOU TUMUNU ▼

Tumai Beach

ATIU VILLAS ●

Takauroa Beach

Lake Tiroto

VAI PIAKE LANDING

RIMA RAU BURIAL CAVE ★

★ SINK HOLES

Makatea

MATAI LANDING

0 _____ 1 mi

0 _____ 1 km

Te Tou

© DAVID STANLEY

tion Building. On the right just beyond the house behind the tennis court is a stalagmite with twin inscribed stones in front. This marks the spot where John Williams preached in 1823. Next to the monument is a row of huge stalagmites or stalactites indicating the rectangular site of **Teapiripiri Marae.** Farther south on the main road south into Areora village is the picturesque **Catholic mission.**

Andrea Eimke's **Atiu Fiber Arts Studio** (tel. 33-031; weekdays 09100–1500, Sat. 0900–1300), at the north end of Teenui village, makes wall hangings and bedspreads in the *tivaevae* quilt style, plus women's jackets, dresses, and vests.

The East Coast

The 20-km road around Atiu is best covered in stages. From Atiu Villas it's a 15-minute walk down to **Matai Landing** and its white-sand beach. You can swim here only if the sea is fairly calm, but it's a nice picnic spot anytime. About 800 meters east of Matai Landing you'll come into a partly cleared area where pigs have been kept. Here search for a small trail out to the coast, where two **sinkholes** drain the reef. The lagoon along the south coast is a meter above sea level, and when no waves are crashing over the reef sending water into the lagoon, the whole lagoon drains through these sinkholes. With nowhere else to go, all of the lagoon fish congregate in the sinkholes, which become natural aquariums accessible to snorkelers. Because of the currents, it's safe to swim here only when the sea is very calm, and even then it's wise to remain on guard for changing or unexpected conditions. About 200 meters farther east along the coast is a road down from the interior and a cut through the cliffs to **Takauroa Beach.** In calm weather at low tide you can also walk to the sinkholes along the reef from this beach.

A stretch of reefless shoreline on the northeast coast lets breakers roll right in to the cliffs. Look for the high white sands of **Oneroa Beach** and continue to **Tarapaku Landing** where the islanders keep their dugout canoes. There's a ladder down to the water here. From the landing take the Tengatangi road inland through the *makatea* watching for **Vai Momoiri,** a large water-filled cave that tunnels under the track then opens up on both sides. The route crosses a taro swamp passing **Vairakaia Marae,** a wall of upright stones right beside the road, and **Vai Inano** pool where the legendary chief Rongomatane's 12 wives used to bathe. (Rongomatane later adopted Christianity and forsook all of his wives except the youngest.)

The West Coast

The coastal road up the west shore of the island runs through a beautiful shady forest. A few really huge *puka* trees sport low bird's-nest ferns to create a dense green cover. These leaves are used to wrap fish for cooking in the *umu.* **Taungaroro** is the nicest beach on Atiu, and one of the finest in the Cooks, with white sands descending far into the quiet blue-green lagoon, protected from ocean breakers by the surrounding reef. The cliffs of the *makatea* frame this scenic masterpiece.

Orovaru Beach, where Captain Cook arrived on April 3, 1777, is easily identified by a large coral rock that sits 15 meters out in the lagoon. On the island side of the road opposite Orovaru is a stone trail once used by Cook's crew to reach the main settlement of that time around **Orongo Marae,** the most important *marae* on Atiu. Once you're on the trail it's fairly easy to follow, bending right toward the end and terminating at a pig

farm on an interior road. This interesting hike offers a chance to view the vegetation on the *makatea* up close. Beyond the pigs, turn right and go about 100 meters south on the road to a track on the right toward a huge Barringtonia or *utu* tree. Orongo Marae is just behind the tree—one of the best-preserved archaeological sites in the Cook Islands. Cut coral slabs and giant stalagmites form the walls of several rectangular structures here.

Farther north is **Taunganui Harbor** with a striking zigzag configuration, constructed in 1975. Barges can dock here in all weather but large ships must stand offshore. The swimming and snorkeling in the deep, clear harbor water is good, and if you're here at 1500 you may be able to buy fresh fish from returning fishermen. Below the cliffs just south of the harbor is the wreckage of the SV *Edna,* a two-masted Dutch sailing vessel built in 1916. One stormy night in 1990 this magnificent metal vessel was wrecked here while carrying cargo to the island from Rarotonga. Fortunately no lives were lost.

Lake Tiroto and Rima Rau Cave

According to legend, the eel Rauou dug Lake Tiroto and, when he was finished, traveled to Mitiaro to dig the lakes there. Eels still inhabit all these lakes! A tunnel runs under the *makatea* from Lake Tiroto right through to the seashore.

The Rima Rau burial cave near Lake Tiroto is said to contain the bones of those who died in a battle involving 1,000 Atiu warriors. Ask someone to tell you the legend of this cave's dead. Kiikii Tatuava (tel. 33-063) of Areora village can guide you to the cave, with side trips to the lake, taro fields, Katara Marae, and Vaitapoto Sinkhole.

Takitaki Cave

This cave is one of the few in the Cooks inhabited by birds: little *kopekas,* a type of swiftlet, nest in the roof. Their huge saucerlike eyes help them catch insects on the wing. They never land nor make a sound while outside the cave; inside, they make a cackling, clicking sound, the echoes of which help them find their way through the dank dark. Fewer than 200 pairs of this bird remain and their nesting success is poor. Visitors to the cave should keep at least two meters away from bird nests and discourage their guide from catching the tiny creatures.

Takitaki is in the middle of the *makatea*, east of Atiu Villas, a taxing 40-minute hike in from the road. A guide (NZ$15) is required. The main part of the cave is large and dry, and you can walk in for quite a distance. Many stalactites, broken off by previous visitors, lie scattered about the floor. The story goes that Ake, wife of the hero Rangi, lived many years alone in this cave before being found by her husband, led to the spot by a *ngotare* (kingfisher) bird.

Keep an eye out for *unga* (coconut crabs) while exploring the *makatea*, and wear boots or sturdy shoes as the coral is razor-sharp. Go slowly and take care, as a fall could lead to a very nasty wound.

PRACTICALITIES
Accommodations
Atiu Villas (Roger and Kura Malcolm, tel. 33-777, fax 33-775), eight km south of the airstrip, offers four comfortable self-catering chalets, each capable of accommodating four people, at NZ$90/100/110 single/double/triple. There's also a six-bed family unit at NZ$110 single, plus NZ$10 per additional guest. These A-frame units are constructed of native materials with beams of coconut-palm trunks and cupboard fronts of hibiscus. In your room's pantry and fridge you'll find almost everything you might wish to consume —except vegetables and bread. You mark what you've used on a stock list and settle up when you leave (normal prices). Otherwise Kura will prepare your dinner at NZ$25 pp and up complete with her famous pavlova (order by 1500). An entertainment evening is staged some Saturday nights in the bar overlooking the grass tennis court.

A less-expensive place to stay is the **Are Manuiri Guest House** (tel. 33-031, fax 33-032) opposite the bakery in Areora village, 200 meters south of ADC/ANZ Store and on the left. This three-room family house with communal cooking and bathing facilities is NZ$30 pp in a shared room, NZ$60 single or double in a private room, or NZ$75 for a larger family room. There's a lounge and verandah. It's run by Juergen Manske-Eimke, who arrived on Atiu in 1986 and runs the

local coffee factory (tours NZ$10 pp). Juergen often provides free coffee for his guests.

Kopeka Lodge (Tou Unuia, tel. 33-283), west of Areora village, has two spacious two-bedroom wooden units with large porches at NZ$85/95 single/double, then NZ$20 for each additional person. Backpackers pay NZ$30 pp if they're willing to share. You can cook here.

Taparere Lodge (tel./fax 33-034), in a new concrete building on the north side of Teenui village, has two self-catering units at NZ$60/75/80 single/double/triple. It's run by local historian Paiere Mokoroa, who has many stories to tell about Atiu.

Food
There are three main shops on Atiu, and two bakers make bread weekdays and Sunday. **ADC/ANZ Store** (tel. 33-028; weekdays 0700–1900, Sat. 0700–0900/1700–1900), in Areora village, may have some fresh produce (cabbage, lettuce, tomatoes, potatoes, papaya).

Kura Malcolm runs the **Center Store** (tel. 33-773; Mon.–Thur. 0700–1830, Fri. 0700–1930, Sat. 0700–1200/1700–1930), just beyond the CICC church, which dispenses liquor and cold drinks, as well as basic foodstuffs.

Purutu's Bakery is between ADC/ANZ shop and the tennis court in Areora village. **Akai Bakery** is a bit beyond Atiu College. Both sell bread around 1500 daily except Saturday.

Marshall Humphreys (tel./fax 33-041) sells fresh fruit and vegetables.

Entertainment
Tennis and volleyball are popular on Atiu and village rivalry has produced no fewer than nine tennis courts (for under 650 people). As each village constructed its tennis court it was made a little bigger than the last. The first village had a single netball court; the fourth built two tennis courts, two netball courts, and erected floodlights. The fifth village said it was "all too hard" and gave up.

Atiu won the Constitution Day dancing competitions on Rarotonga in 1982, 1983, 1984, 1985, 1988, 1992, 1993, and 1998, so ask where you can see them practicing. Special performances are held on Gospel Day and Christmas Day.

Bush Beer

Venerable institutions of note are the bush beer schools, of which there are seven on Atiu. Bush beer is a local moonshine made from imported yeast, malt, hops, and sugar. The concoction is fermented in a *tumunu*, a hollowed-out coconut tree stump about a meter high. Orange-flavored "jungle juice" is also made. The mixing usually begins on Wednesday, and the resulting brew ferments for two days and is ready to drink on the weekend. A single batch will last three or four nights; the longer it's kept, the stronger it gets.

Gatherings at a school resemble the kava ceremonies of Fiji and the practice clearly dates back to the days before early missionaries banned kava drinking. Only the barman is permitted to ladle bush beer out of the *tumunu* in a half-coconut-shell cup and the potent contents of the cup must be swallowed in one hearty gulp. Those who've developed a taste for the stuff usually refer to regular beer as "lemonade." The village men come together at dusk, and after a few rounds, the barman calls them to order by tapping a cup on the side of the *tumunu*. A prayer is said. Announcements are made by various members, and work details assigned to earn money to buy the ingredients for the next brew. After the announcements, guitars and ukuleles appear, and the group resumes drinking, dancing, and singing for as long as they can. The barman, responsible for maintaining order, controls how much brew each participant gets.

Nonmembers visiting a school are expected to bring along a kilo of sugar, or to put NZ$5 pp on the table, as their contribution (enough for the whole week). The two best-established bush beer establishments are the **Aretou Tumunu** ("Sam and the boys"), down in the bush east of Areora, and the more commercial **Teponui Tumunu** in Mapumai.

Post and Telecommunications

You can make telephone calls using phone cards and buy postage stamps at Telecom Cook Islands (tel. 33-680; weekdays 0730–1600), north of Mapumai village.

Transportation

The Air Rarotonga office (tel. 33-888) is a block back from the CICC church in the center of the island. There are six flights a week from Rarotonga (NZ$142), plus weekly services from Aitutaki (NZ$142) and Mitiaro (NZ$90). Most of the guesthouse owners provide airport transfers at NZ$8 pp each way.

Atiu Villas and some of the other places to stay rent bicycles/scooters/jeeps at NZ$10/25/60 a day.

The Humphreys family of **Atiu Tours** (tel./fax 33-041) leads kopeka bird cave tours at NZ$15 pp and half-day island tours at NZ$35 pp. George Mateariki (tel. 33-047) does a bird-watching and bush walk for NZ$20 pp. These tours are worthwhile as nothing is signposted on Atiu and finding your own way is hard.

Mitiaro

Mitiaro, formerly known as Nukuroa, is a low island with two lakes and vast areas of swampland. Of the lakes, Rotonui is much longer and broader than Rotoiti. This surprisingly large lake is surrounded by an unlikely combination of pine trees and coconut palms. The lake bed is covered by a thick layer of black and brown peat, and the eastern shore is firmer than the western. On one side of the lake is the small, coconut-studded island of Motu. Banana and taro plantations grow in the interior of Mitiaro and a stand of rare Mitiaro fan palms *(iniao)* remains in the south of the island. The main export is *maire*

eis (leis) to Hawaii and paths have been cut into the makatea to facilitate collection of the maire leaves. Like its neighboring islands, Mitiaro has a chronic water shortage.

The People

Before the arrival of Europeans, the people occupied the center of the island near their gardens. Today they all live in one long village on the west coast. The village is neat and clean, with white sandy roads between the Norfolk pines and houses. Four different sections of the village maintain the names of the four original villages,

© DAVID STANLEY

and each has a garden area inland bearing the same name. Because the *makatea* cannot support crops, it's used for keeping pigs or growing coconuts. There are no mynah birds on Mitiaro, so you'll see abundant Pacific pigeons *(rupe)*, warblers, and reef herons.

The fine outrigger canoes of Mitiaro are made of hollowed-out *puka* logs, held together with coconut-husk rope. These are used for longline tuna and *paara* fishing outside the reef. Even from shore you'll see lots of fish on the reef at Mitiaro. From July to December flying fish swarm off Mitiaro for three days during the first quarter of the moon each month and local fishermen in outriggers scoop them up using handnets, returning to shore to unload again and again until every freezer on the island is full. Tradition dictates that it's not allowed to use outboard motors in this fishery or for the anglers to sell their catch, but neither rule is followed these days.

Sights of Mitiaro

The small church in the center of the village is quite exquisitely decorated. From the church a lane leads past a row of dugout canoes to a landing blasted out of the reef that serves as a saltwa-

ter swimming pool for the local kids. At low tide many people fish from the edge of the reef with long bamboo poles.

South of the village cut over to the beach when you reach the graveyard and football field. This long stretch of white sand is the best beach nearby and has many shallow pools in the reef where you can lounge while the tide is out. Walking along the reef at low tide all around Mitiaro is fascinating, and the restless rhythm and flow of the waves beating against the reef at low tide is almost hypnotic. If you're looking for secluded coves, you'll find many around the island.

Around the Island

It's 20 km around Mitiaro but the road across the center of the island offers more variety than the coastal road (no shade on either road, so be prepared). **Vai Marere,** to the left of the road from Takaue, is an easy 10-minute walk inland from the village. The locals enjoy swimming in the green, sulfur-laden waters of this cave *(vai)*. Continue across the picturesque center of Mitiaro toward Teunu. Five minutes before you reach the coast you pass on your left **Te Pito o Kare,** a deep cave containing a pool that was once a source of drinking water for people living in the area.

Turn right at Teunu and follow the coastal road about 600 meters on your right. A trail on the right through this forest leads into the *makatea* to an old **Polynesian fort** *(tepare)* that the people of Mitiaro once used to defend themselves against raids from Atiu. Back at the Teunu junction you'll note the upright coral slabs of a small *marae* among the trees and 100 meters east on the coastal road to Parava is another larger *marae* just to the left of the road. Several more are on either side of the road to the east.

It's easy to find **Vai Tamaroa** on the east side of the island as there's a headstone commemorating the Boys Brigade Camp on Mitiaro in April 1985 at the trailhead. It's a rough 15-minute scramble over the *makatea* to this deep water-filled crevice but you probably won't be able to swim beecause of Vai Tamaroa's steep sides.

Less than a km north of the headstone is Parava with a small golden beach down by the seashore and a road in toward the east side of **Lake Rotonui.** Small, edible black tilapia are abundant, each with a red streak along its back fins. They grow to about 15 cm long and provide sustenance for the lake's black eels (*'itiki*). The much larger milk fish also found in the lakes are caught by humans for food. The lake water is fresh and clear, although the bottom is muddy. The low-lying surroundings are peaceful and serene, but the mud will make you forget about swimming.

About 600 meters north of the Lake Rotonui road is the access road to **Vai Nauri,** a cool, crystal-clear freshwater cave pool. A stairway leads down to the water's edge, and on a hot afternoon a swim here is almost divine. From this pool it's about an hour's walk back to the village.

Practicalities

Mitiaro receives fewer than 50 tourists a year and there are no motels or tourist cottages. **Seabreeze Lodge** (Joe and Mikara Herman, tel. 36-153, fax 36-165), at the north end of the village, has one room with shared bath at NZ$60 single or double (meals extra). **Nane Pokoati** (tel. 36-107), next to the *ariki's* house south of the church, accepts guests at NZ$50 pp including three good meals. She's also the Air Rarotonga agent. Because of flight connections, anyone flying from Atiu to Mauke will have to spend one night (not enough) or five nights (far too long) on Mitiaro.

Two small stores on Mitiaro sell canned foods and bread is at the bakery opposite the CICC church.

Mauke

Mauke, the easternmost of the Cooks, is a flat raised atoll. It and neighboring Mitiaro and Atiu are collectively known as Ngaputoru, "The Three Roots." As on its neighbors, the crops grow in the center of Mauke; the *makatea* ringing the island is infertile and rocky. Both the *makatea* and the central area are low, and you barely notice the transition as you walk along the road inland from the coast to the taro swamps and manioc plantations. Mauke exports bags of *maire* leaves to Hawaii, to be used in floral decorations, and taro is sent to Rarotonga. Pigs and chickens run wild across the island, and many goats can be seen. Thankfully dogs are banned from Mauke.

The men fish for tuna just offshore in small outrigger canoes and the women weave fine pandanus mats with brilliant borders of blue, red, yellow, and orange. There are also wide-rimmed pandanus hats and *kete* baskets of sturdy pandanus with colorful geometric designs. The men carve the attractive white-and-black *tou* or red-and-brown *miro* wood into large bowls shaped like breadfruit leaves. They also carve large spoons and forks, miniature models of chiefs' seats, and small replicas of the canoe of Uke, legendary founder of Mauke, who gave the island its name.

Mauke has the best beaches of the three neighboring islands, but it's too shallow for snorkeling. Coral overhangs provide shade at many of the beaches and in August and September whales are often seen off Mauke. It's a very friendly island to poke around for a few days and a good choice for a prolonged stay.

Sights of Mauke

The harbor, market, Catholic mission, government residency, and administration building are all at **Taunganui Landing.** The area behind the administration building is known as **Te Marae O Rongo** with a stone circle and a large boulder once used as a seat by the chief. Inland at Makatea village, opposite a store with massive masonry walls, is the two-story concrete palace of the last queen of Mauke, who died in 1982. Unfortunately the building is falling into ruins because of squabbles among her descendants. At one end of the taro swamp in the valley behind the palace is **Koenga Well,** a source of fresh drinking water in years gone by.

The **CICC church** (1882) at the hub of the island has an almost Islamic flavor, with its long rectangular courtyard, tall gateways, perpendicular alignment, and interior decoration of crescents and interlocking arches. Because of an old

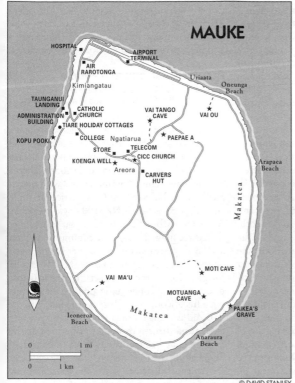

MAUKE

© DAVID STANLEY

ing stalactites. The locals swim and bathe here. There are large rooms farther back in the cave but you'd need scuba gear and lamps to reach them.

A *marae* called **Paepae A,** 50 meters beyond the Vai Tango turnoff, was reconstructed from scratch in 1997. The stalagmites standing on the *marae* platform are two pieces of a single pillar once carried by the legendary chief Kai Moko (Eater of Lizards). On the ground behind Paepae A are four huge stones remaining from Marae Terongo. The origin of these volcanic rocks, unique on this coral island, is lost in time.

Back in Areora village, visit the woodcarvers who work in the house next to the Catholic church. One of their fine breadfruit leaf-shaped bowls would make a unique souvenir.

If you're still keen, you might wish to try to find **Moti Cave,** a large, open cave in the *makatea.* From the irrigation dam in the center of the island, follow the road south and take the left turn at a point where three roads separate. The cave is beyond the end of this road and you'll probably spend some time searching unless you have a guide. A guide is definitely required to find the freshwater pools of **Motuanga Cave,** the "Cave of 100 Rooms," which is deeper into the *makatea* from here. Limestone growth has made all but the first three rooms inaccessible.

Around the Island

It's only 18 km around Mauke, and no one lives on the south or east sides of the island, so the secluded beaches there are ideal for those who want to be completely alone. There's good reef walking at low tide on the west side of Mauke, but ocean swimming is difficult everywhere. A coral trail just south of Tiare Cottages gives access to a small beach, and south around the point from this beach is a sea cave known as **Kopu**

dispute between Areora and Ngatiarua villages, the church was divided across the center and each side was decorated differently. The dividing partition has been removed, but dual gateways lead to dual doors, one for each village. The soft pastels (green, pink, yellow, and blue) harmonize the contrasting designs, and the pulpit in the middle unifies the two. Inset into the railing in front of the pulpit are nine old Chilean pesos. Look carefully at the different aspects of this building; it's one of the most fascinating in the Cook Islands.

Vai Tango Cave is fairly easy to find. From the Telecom office, go 500 meters northeast through Ngatiarua village and turn left after the last house. The cave is 500 meters northwest of the main road, at the end of a trail along a row of hibiscus trees. A large circular depression with Barringtonia trees growing inside, Vai Tango has a clear freshwater pool under the overhang-

Pooki (Stomach Rock). It's about two meters deep and small fish congregate there.

About 450 meters southeast of Tukune junction, just past the second rock quarry, a trail leads 150 meters inland between the Barringtonia or *utu* trees to **Vai Ma'u,** a deep water-filled crack in the *makatea* with a tall coconut tree growing out. The water is very clear but the opening narrow and steep.

The finest beaches on Mauke are on the south side of the island and the white sands of **Ieoneroa** are just 500 meters southeast of Vai Ma'u. Also most inviting is the beach at **Anaraura,** where a long stretch of clean white sand borders a green lagoon. This piece of paradise is flanked by rugged limestone cliffs and backed by palm, pine, and pandanus. A short track leads down to the beach.

Two upright stone slabs to the right of the road about a km beyond Anaraura mark the site of **Paikea's grave.** A secluded white beach is just behind. Yet another good beach is found at **Arapaea,** three km north of Paikea's Grave.

At Oneunga, just under two km northwest of Arapaea, two huge stones thrown up between the shore and the road have trees growing out of them. Directly opposite these two rocks is a trail leading across the *makatea* to **Vai Ou,** a series of three caves. You can swim in the first cave's pool, about 800 meters in from the coastal road. A

five-minute scramble beyond Vai Ou is **Vai Moraro,** and beyond that **Vai Tunamea.** The coastal road meets the road to the interior villages and the airstrip less than a km west of Oneunga.

Accommodations and Food

Tiare Holiday Cottages (Tautara and Kura Purea, tel./fax 35-077), a few hundred meters south of Taunganui Landing, offers a duplex unit with two single rooms, two larger cottages with double beds, and one deluxe cottage with double beds. All units have their own fridge, but only the deluxe unit has a private bathroom and shower. There's no hot water. The accommodations with shared facilities are NZ$25/45/60 single/double/triple while the deluxe unit is NZ$100 single or double. A NZ$5 discount is offered if you stay longer than three nights. A separate communal kitchen and dining area sits in the center of the compound. If you don't wish to cook (NZ$10 charge for gas), filling meals are served at reasonable prices, and tea, coffee, and tropical fruit are supplied free. Scooters and bicycles are for rent.

Bread is made on the island, and you can buy fresh tuna directly from the fishermen at the landing. The brown insides of sea urchins, collected along the reef, are eaten raw (the egg cases are the most delicious part—the texture of raw liver and a strong taste of the sea).

Mangaia

Mangaia is pronounced "mahng-AH-ee-ah," not "man-gaia," as there's no "g" sound in the Polynesian languages. It's 204 km southeast of Rarotonga and just north of the tropic of Capricorn, a position that makes it the southernmost and coolest of the Cook Islands. South of here you don't strike land again until Antarctica. At 52 square km it's also the country's second-largest island, just slightly smaller than Rarotonga. Without soaring peaks or an azure lagoon, Mangaia doesn't fit the tropical island stereotype and it remains an undiscovered tourist destination.

One of the major geological curiosities of the South Pacific, Mangaia is similar to Atiu and Mauke but much more dramatic. A *makatea* or

raised coral reef forms a 60-meter-high ring around the island with sheer cliffs towering as high as 80 meters on the inland side. Lifted from the sea in stages over the past 18 million years, this outer limestone rim has eroded into quite remarkable rock formations with numerous caves hundreds of meters in length, some of them below sea level.

The volcanic earth inside the *makatea* is the only fertile soil on the island; this rises in rolling hills to slopes once planted with pineapples. At 169 meters elevation, Rangimotia is the island's highest point. Forested ridges radiate from this hill with the valleys between them used for farming. Near the inner edge of the *makatea,* where

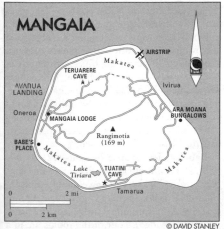

MANGAIA

AIRSTRIP

Makatea

TERUARERE
CAVE

AVARUA
LANDING

Ivirua

Oneroa

MANGAIA LODGE

ARA MOANA
BUNGALOWS

BABE'S
PLACE

Makatea

Rangimotia
(169 m)

Makatea

Lake
Tiriara

TUATINI
CAVE

Tamarua

0   2 mi

0   2 km

© DAVID STANLEY

water is caught between the coral cliffs and the hills, low taro swamps are flanked by banana fields and miscellaneous crops. Nothing but bush and pandanus grow on the *makatea* itself, and pigs are kept there in makeshift pens. However, some areas of *makatea* are covered by lush green indigenous forest excellent for hiking.

Legend tells how Rongo rose from the deep with his three sons to colonize the island. Captain Cook "discovered" Mangaia in 1777 and Polynesian missionaries followed in 1826. Mangaia was the last Cook Island to accept Christianity, and traditionally the 750 Mangaians have a rep utation for being a cautious lot, but you'll probably find them quite friendly when you get to know them. They live in three scattered coastal villages, Oneroa, Tamarua, and Ivirua. The population is continuing to drop as people depart for New Zealand and Australia, with 33 percent of the inhabitants leaving 1996–2001. The Mangaians speak a language similar to that of Rarotonga, part of the great Austronesian family.

Crafts

Mangaia is represented in museum collections around the world by large ceremonial adzes, which were used to decapitate prisoners taken in battles. The head, right arm, and right leg were regarded as prized possessions because of the mana they possessed. Later the missionaries

had the adzes changed to incorporate "steeple stands," reproducing church steeples. This was used to symbolize church authority over the *ariki.* A local carver named Uria makes ceremonial adzes, which sell at NZ$150. Glen Tuara carves pendants and other items from stone.

The yellow *pupu* shell necklaces *(ei)* of Mangaia are also unique. The tiny gray *pupu* shells are found on the *makatea* only after rainfall. The yellow color comes from boiling them in caustic soda, though they can also be bleached white or dyed other colors. The shells are pierced one by one with a needle and threaded to make the *ei.*

Sights of Mangaia

A 25-km road along the coastal strip rings most of the island. It's seven km from the airstrip to **Oneroa,** the main village, where a monument in front of the church recalls Mangaian church ministers and missionaries (such as the Reverend William Wyatt Gill, who served in the Cooks 1852–1883). If the church is open, enter to see the sennit rope bindings in the roof. On a large stone near Avarua landing are the footprints of the legendary giant, Mokea, and his son; both jumped across the island in a race to this spot. The huge stones on the reef to the north were thrown there by Mokea to prevent a hostile canoe from landing. The queen of Mangaia still has a large flag given to her grandfather by Queen Victoria.

Tuara George (tel. 34-314) will guide you through **Teruarere Cave** for NZ$25 pp. Used as a burial ground in past, the cave has old skeletons that add a skin-crawling touch of reality. The opening is small and you have to crawl in, but the cave goes on for a great distance. A lamp is necessary. Below Teruarere on the cliff is **Touri Cave.** There are two streams in this cave: one freshwater, the other salty.

An impressive cut leads up through the *makatea* from Oneroa. Follow a jeep track up to the flat summit of Rangimotia for varied views. From the plateau you can follow a footpath back down to Ivirua and return to Oneroa via **Tamarua,** a rather longish day hike. The church at Tamarua has a sennit-bound roof.

A water-filled cave at **Lake Tiriara** was the hiding place of the warlord Panako in the 1600s.

Water from the lake runs through the cave under the *makatea* to the sea, and rises and falls slightly with the tide.

Beaches

There are several beautiful sandy beaches around the island. A spectacular one is **Araoa** about 700 meters southwest of the airport terminal. As always around Mangaia, the lagoon is shallow, but at low tide you can wade out toward the north to a deep natural pool on the reef isolated from the ocean. Another beach is near Ara Moana Bungalows, although the water is quite shallow. Four hundred meters southeast of this beach is an opening where freshwater from the interior comes out, resulting in a large natural pool on the reef called **Vai-Nga-Tara** where you can snorkel at low tide. You can also explore the watery tunnel in to about 50 meters, but you need a light.

Accommodations

Ara Moana Bungalows (tel. 34-278, fax 34-279), on the coast just southeast of Ivirua village, about three km from the airport, is run by a Swede named Jan Kristensson and his wife, Tu. There are four small thatched bungalows at NZ$60/80 single/double and two larger units at NZ$115/135/145 single/double/triple, all with private shower/toilet. Two tiny backpacker cabins without facilities are sometimes available at NZ$35/55 single/double. Airport transfers are included, but add NZ$35 pp a day for breakfast and a memorable dinner. Island nights with Polynesian dancing and singing are organized according to the number of guests present. Kawasaki 100 cc motor bikes are rented at NZ$30 a day. From Ara Moana, Teremanuia Tauakume (tel. 34-223) leads fascinating three-hour *makatea* hikes along the old village trail visiting four caves at NZ$35 pp. Island tours by 4WD vehicle or fishing trips that circumnavigate the island are NZ$50 each.

Babe's Guest House (tel. 34-092, fax 34-078), just south of Oneroa, has six rooms with bath at NZ$75/120/150 single/double/triple including all meals. There's a large common room with TV and a communal fridge (cooking facilities not provided). Four of the rooms are in a long block, the other two in a family house. The nearby bar gets lively during the Friday night dances. Clark's Tours does island tours from Babe's at NZ$50 pp. Clark occasionally takes guests on an inflatable boat ride across Lake Tiriara and to Tuatini Cave (NZ$30) near the lake. Bicycles and scooters can be arranged.

Mangaia Lodge (Torotoro Piiti, tel. 34-324, fax 34-239), near the hospital above Oneroa, charges NZ$25 pp including breakfast. A filling dinner is NZ$10 extra. It's basic but has the advantage of providing cooking facilities for guests staying in the three rooms with shared bath in this large colonial-style house. Airport transfers are NZ$5 each way.

Other Southern Islands

Manuae

This small island consists of two islets, Manuae and Te Au O Tu, inside a barrier reef. The unspoiled wealth of marinelife in this lagoon has prompted the government to offer the atoll as an international marine park. It's said you can still catch large parrot fish in the lagoon by hand. There's no permanent habitation. Copra-cutting parties from Aitutaki once used an abandoned airstrip to come and go, though they haven't done so for years. In 1990 the 1,600 traditional Aitutaki-origin owners of Manuae rejected a government proposal to lease the island to an Australian company for tourism development. Captain Cook gave Manuae its other, fortunately rarely used, name, Hervey Island.

Takutea

Clearly visible 16 km off the northwest side of Atiu, to whose people it belongs, Takutea is in no place over six meters high. The island's other name, Enuaiti, means "Small Island." Until 1959 the people of Atiu called here to collect copra, but Takutea gets few visitors now. There are a few abandoned shelters and a freshwater collection tank. The waters along the reef abound with fish; many red-tailed tropic birds and red-footed boobies nest on the land. Permission of the Atiu Island Council is required for visits.

Palmerston

Palmerston, 367 km northwest of Aitutaki, is an atoll 11 km across at its widest point. About 35 tiny islands dot its pear-shaped barrier reef, which encloses the coral head-studded lagoon completely at low tide. Although Polynesians had once lived on what they called Ava Rau ("200 channels"), Palmerston was uninhabited when Captain Cook arrived in 1774.

William Marsters, legendary prolific settler, arrived here in 1863 to manage a coconut plantation. He brought with him from Penrhyn his Polynesian wife and her cousin, who were soon joined by another cousin. Marsters married all three, and by the time he died in 1899 at the ripe age of 78 he had begotten 21 children. Thousands of his descendants are now scattered around the Cook Islands, throughout New Zealand, and beyond, but the three Marsters branches on Palmerston are down to about 50. The grave of William Marsters the Patriarch may be seen beside the church. The current island patriarch, Reverend Bill Marsters (born 1923), has a mere 12 children.

The three Marsters families, the Tepou, Akakaingaro, and Mataiva, live on tiny Home or Palmerston Island on the west side of the atoll, where they grow taro and sugarcane in pits. All 35 islands are divided into sections between these three families, members of which cannot intermarry within their own group. Many of the older residents suffer from asthma. Like lonely Pitcairn Island where the inhabitants are also of mixed British descent, on Palmerston the first language is English, the only island in the Cooks where this is so. And as in any small, isolated community, there's some tension between the families. In 1995 officials from Rarotonga arrived on Palmerston and by playing one group off against another, succeeded in undermining the authority of the island council and imposing centralized rule on independence-minded Palmerston.

The central government wants to build an airport on Toms Island, two islands away from Home Island, by 2005. Meanwhile the launch *Marsters Dream* runs monthly from Rarotonga to Palmerston bringing ordered supplies and taking away parrot fish. The vessel carries 13 passengers who must batten down inside for the 24-hour journey from Rarotonga (NZ$150/300 one-way/round-trip). Contact **Marsters Marine** (tel. 24-005) on Rarotonga. It'll also be able to arrange accommodations with families on the island at NZ$30 pp including meals.

About a dozen yachts call at Palmerston each year, and since boats drawing over 1.5 meters cannot enter the lagoon, they must anchor outside the reef. Yachties can hail "Palmerston Island" over VHF channel 16 when they're within 15 km of the atoll. The Republic of Palmsterston Yacht Club near the church in the center of the village provides cooking facilities, a washing machine, toilets, and hot showers (rain water) to yachties who pay NZ$20 for five years' membership. Cold beer is sold daily except Sunday. Reader Sidsel Wold aboard *Northern Quest* send us this:

As soon as a sailboat is sighted there's a competition among the islanders to see who can get out first in a small boat to meet the yacht. That person's family then becomes the hosts of the visitors on Palmerston. The Marsters people told us that as long as we were on Palmerston we were regarded as Marsters too, and we certainly felt like part of the family. Every day we shared meals with them, joined them on fishing trips, etc. After crossing the Pacific, Palmerston became the highlight of our trip. We certainly didn't regret checking for their mail at the post office before leaving Rarotonga, or bringing magazines, books, coffee, tea, sugar, and fresh fruit. Such goods are always needed. We'd also been in touch with some Marsters people on Raro who gave us bananas and presents to take along. This atoll is certainly worth a stop, although the anchorage can be difficult.

COOK ISLANDS

Northern Group

The northern Cooks are far more traditional than the southern Cooks. Their location closer to the equator makes them much hotter than Rarotonga or Aitutaki. All of the northern atolls except Penrhyn sit on the 3,000-meter-deep Manihiki Plateau; the sea around Penrhyn is 5,000 meters deep. These low-lying coral rings are the very image of the romantic South Seas, but life for the inhabitants can be hard and large numbers have left for New Zealand in recent years. Reef fish and coconuts are abundant, but fresh water and everything else is limited. Now a commercial cultured pearl industry is bringing prosperity to several of the atolls.

All of the scattered atolls of the northern Cooks except Nassau have central lagoons. Only the Penrhyn lagoon is easily accessible to shipping, although yachts can anchor in the pass at Suwarrow. Until recently these isolated islands were served only by infrequent ships from Rarotonga, and tourist visits were limited to the ship's brief stop, as to disembark would have meant a stay of several weeks or even months. Air Rarotonga has flights to Manihiki and Penrhyn, taking 4.5 hours each way.

Anyone desiring a fuller picture of life of the northern atolls should read Robert Dean Frisbie's *The Book of Pukapuka,* serialized in the *Atlantic Monthly* in 1928. Though interesting, Frisbie's book may seem distorted to some contemporary eyes, catering to European stereotypes.

BOB RACE

NORTHERN GROUP HIGHLIGHTS

Suwarrow Lagoon: sharks, yacht anchorage
Tom Neale's house, Suwarrow: history, beach-
comber tales
Manihiki pearls: shopping, story
Pukapuka people: a Samoan-speaking people
Penrhyn Lagoon: largest lagoon, sharks, pearls

Suwarrow

In 1814 the Russian explorer Mikhail Lazarev discovered an uninhabited atoll, which he named for his ship, the *Suvarov*. A mysterious box containing US$15,000 was dug up in 1855, probably left by the crew of a wrecked Spanish galleon in 1742. Later an additional US$2,400 was found. Early in the 20th century, Lever Brothers unsuccessfully attempted to introduce to the lagoon gold-lipped pearl oysters from Australia's Torres Straits. In the 1920s and 1930s A. B. Donald Ltd. ran Suwarrow as a copra estate, until the island became infested with termites and the export of copra was prohibited. During World War II New Zealand coastwatchers were stationed here—the few decrepit buildings on Anchorage Island date from that time.

At various times from 1952 onward, New Zealander Tom Neale lived alone on Suwarrow and wrote a book about his experiences titled, not surprisingly, *An Island to Oneself.* Tom never found the buried treasure he was searching for on Suwarrow, and in 1977 he died of cancer on Rarotonga. Today coconut-watchers serve on Suwarrow to ensure that none of the termite-infested nuts are removed. The numerous rats are not afraid of humans. Officially Suwarrow is a Marine Park, and the caretakers live in Tom Neale's house. A government meteorologist may also be present, and pearl divers from Manihiki and Penrhyn visit occasionally.

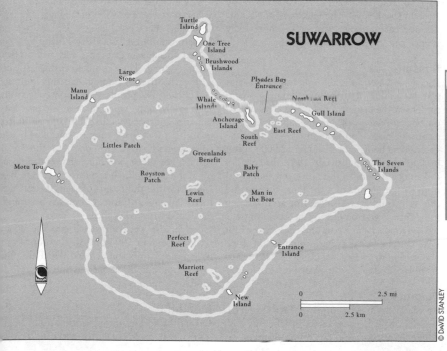

COOK ISLANDS

Yachts often call on their way from Rarotonga or Bora Bora to Samoa. The wide, easy lagoon entrance is just east of Anchorage Island on the northeast side of the atoll and a 40-meter-long coral rock jetty points to the deep anchorage. There's good holding, but in stormy weather the lagoon waters can become very rough. Though Suwarrow is not an official port of entry, yachts often stop without clearing in at Rarotonga or Aitutaki. Passports must be taken to the caretakers in Tom's house, who also accept outgoing mail (yachties often volunteer to carry mail to/from Rarotonga). The table and chairs outside the caretaker family's home provide welcome neutral ground for whiling away the time.

Of the 25 *motu*, only five are sizable. The snorkeling in the lagoon is fantastic, with lots of shark action—they won't usually bother you unless you're spearfishing. Scuba diving is not allowed. In the past, hurricanes have washed four-meter waves across the atoll and during one storm in 1942 those present survived by tying themselves to a large tamanu tree (see *The Island of Desire*, by Robert Dean Frisbie). Thousands of seabirds, turtles, and coconut crabs nest on this historically strange and still mysterious island.

Nassau

Egg-shaped Nassau is the only northern island without an inner lagoon; instead, taro grows in gardens at the center of the island. The American whaler *Nassau* called in 1835. Europeans ran a coconut plantation here until 1945, when the government bought the island for £2,000 to get it back for the Pukapukans. In 1951, the chiefs of Pukapuka, 89 km to the northwest, bought it from the government for the same amount and they've owned it ever since. Korean fishermen from Pago Pago stop illegally at Nassau to trade canned foods, fishing gear, and cheap jewelry for love. The children of these encounters add an exotic element to the local population. There's no safe anchorage and many ships have been lost here.

Pukapuka

An island sits at each corner of this unusual triangular atoll. Because of its treacherous reef, where no anchorage is possible, Pukapuka was

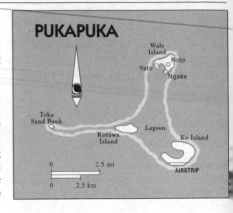

formerly known as "Danger Island." The only landing place for small boats or canoes is on the west side of Wale. Discovered by Mendaña in 1595 and rediscovered by Byron in 1765, Pukapuka was outrageously victimized during a Peruvian slave raid in 1863. Captain Gibson of HMS *Curacao* annexed the island in 1892.

Pukapuka is closer to Samoa than to Rarotonga, so the people differ in language and custom from other Cook Islanders. Three villages on Wale (pronounced "WAH-lay") island have coexisted since precontact times, each with its own island council. They compete enthusiastically with each other in singing, dancing, contests, and cricket. The people make copra collectively, each receiving an equal share in the proceeds. Bananas and papaya also grow here in limited quantities; their harvesting is controlled by the councils. Each village owns one of the three main islands. The nicest swimming and snorkeling are off Kotawa Island, also known as Frigate Bird Island for the thousands of seabirds that nest there. Pukapuka's Catholic church is beautifully decorated with cowry shells.

An airstrip was constructed over the lagoon on Pukapuka in 1994 but Air Rarotonga call only if there's sufficient demand. The Rarotonga office should know about this and any accommodation options.

Manihiki

One of the Pacific's most beautiful atolls, Manihiki's reef bears 39 coral islets enclosing a close-

COCONUT CRABS

The coconut crab *Birgus latro* is a nocturnal creature that lives under logs, in holes, or at the base of pandanus or coconut trees. The females lay their eggs in the sea and the tiny crabs float around a few months, then crawl into a seashell and climb up the beach. When a crab is big enough, it abandons the shell and relies on its own hard shell for protection. Its food is ripe pandanus or coconut. The crab will appear dark blue if it's a coconut eater, rich orange if it feeds on pandanus. First it will husk a coconut using its two front claws, then break the nut open on a rock. It might take a crab two nights to get at the meat. Coconut crabs can grow up to three feet across. Although tasty, they are endangered in much of the South Pacific and should not be eaten.

lagoon four km wide that's thick with sharks. The dark green, coconut-covered *motu* are clearly visible across the blue waters. Until 1852, Manihiki was owned by the people of Rakahanga, who commuted the 44 km between the two islands in outrigger canoes, with great loss of life. In that year the missionaries convinced the islanders to divide themselves between the two islands and give up the hazardous voyages. In 1889 some disenchanted Manihiki islanders invited the French to annex their island. When a French warship arrived to consummate the act, anxious missionaries speedily hoisted the Union Jack, so the French sailed off. The same August Britain officially declared a protectorate over the island.

Mother-of-pearl shell was once taken from the lagoon by island divers who plunged effortlessly to depths of 25–30 meters. Today more than 100 farms on Manihiki produce cultured pearls from the 1.5 million oysters hanging on racks below the surface of the lagoon. In 2001 a bacterial pearl shell disease caused by a combi-

nation of overfarming and high water temperatures wiped out almost half the juvenile oyster population, proving what some had been saying all along: that the rapid growth in pearl farming during the past decade has pushed some sections of the Manihiki lagoon well beyond their maximum carrying capacity of oysters. In November 1997, Hurricane Martin passed near Manihiki leaving 20 people dead, Tauhunu village in a shambles, and pearl industry installations above water blown away. Fortunately, most of the oysters survived.

Manihiki is famous for its handsome people. The administrative center is Tauhunu on the west side of the atoll, and there's a second village at Tukao next to the airstrip. Permission of the chief of Tauhunu is required to dive in the lagoon. The anchorage off Tauhunu is not entirely safe. With the pearl boom in full swing, Air Rarotonga now flies here weekly from Rarotonga (1,204 km) and the airline can arrange accommodations in a local home at around NZ$50/75 single/double including meals.

A reader from New York sent us this:

We spent nine days on Manihiki and were told by the locals that we were the first tourists ever to stay overnight. Could that be true in this day and age? The difficulty in getting there was considerable. It cost about US$500 each from Rarotonga, and we had to provide Air Rarotonga with the name of the family we would be staying with, otherwise no plane reservations would be given.

We have been to all of the southern Cooks, Samoa, Fiji, and Tahiti, but here we encountered a warmth and happiness the source of which remains a mystery to us here in New York. In extremely tight clusters of homes they live, inescapably sharing each other's noises, emotions, and actions with a tolerance perhaps only possible in a homogeneous society

> *One of the Pacific's most beautiful atolls, Manihiki's reef bears 39 coral islets enclosing a closed lagoon four km wide that's thick with sharks. The dark green, coconut-covered* motu *are clearly visible across the blue waters.*

COOK ISLANDS

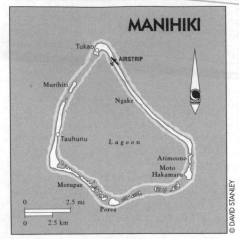

MANIHIKI

Tukao
AIRSTRIP
Murihiti
Ngake
Tauhunu
Lagoon
Atimoono
Moto
Hakamaru
Motupae
Porea

0   2.5 mi
0   2.5 km

© DAVID STANLEY

shrivel, was on the horizon as we waited for the next boat shipment of petrol. And, in typical island fashion, I received so much misinformation about the flight that was or was not to be that I became numb until the day of our scheduled departure. Then that day, it took us away, that bird of salvation, right on schedule.

in which so much is tacitly understood and accepted, to the point of resembling a genetic disposition. And the laughter, the giggling—it never ceased!

Our host was gracious and tender beyond justification. Of course, not only did we provide some monetary relief for putting us up, we took along pounds of meat, vegetables, and gifts for each member of the family. But I was convinced that none of this was the impetus for our most tender treatment.

Now for the downside. As soon as the aspiring snorkeler descends below the Manihiki lagoon, sharks come at you with the utmost curiosity. I saw at least three species, not to mention the black ones that attack you between the motu *(the* motu *themselves were absolutely gorgeous). Another problem was the drinking water situation. Clearly visible in a random glass of water from the cement tanks were little tadpolelike creatures swimming merrily about. This stuff shot through our systems like lightening.*

Then, as if matters could not get any worse, there came the news that there may not be enough fuel on the island for our plane to make the return trip. The prospect of staying on Manihiki, dehydrating to a

Rakahanga

Two opposing horseshoe-shaped islands almost completely encircle the lagoon of this rectangular atoll. The pearl industry is still in its infancy here and this is a much quieter island than Manihiki. There are several small *motu* that can be reached on foot at low tide. Breadfruit and *puraka* (a tarolike vegetable) are the staples here, and copra is made for export. So that not too many coconuts are taken at one time, the island councils regulate visits to the *motu*. These usually take place only two or three times a year, so as to give nature a chance to regenerate. Coconut crabs, a delicacy on Rakahanga, are mostly caught on the small uninhabited *motu*. Nivano village is at the southwest corner of the atoll. Although unable to enter the lagoon, ships can anchor offshore. An airstrip in the middle of the west side of the atoll was destroyed by Hurricane Wasa in December 1991 and has not been repaired.

An old Polynesian legend explains the origin of Rakahanga and Manihiki. The mythological fisherman Huku caught an island he considered too small to take, so he tied it up to give it time to grow. After Huku left, the demigod Maui happened along and, with the help of a mermaid, finished Huku's work by fishing the island from the sea. When Huku returned, a great struggle ensued, and Maui leapt straight into the sky to escape, leaving his footprint embedded in the reef. His fishhook became the stars, and such was the force of his jump that the island was split in two, forming these neighboring atolls, which were later colonized by Huku's sister and her husband Toa, a warrior banished from Rarotonga.

Rakahanga has a place in the annals of Pa

cific exploration since it was on this island's reef that the raft *Tahiti Nui* met its end after sailing from Tahiti to Chile and back between 1956 and 1958. The expedition's leader, Éric de Bisschop, died in the mishap after having proved that the ancient Polynesians could have sailed to South America and returned.

Penrhyn

Penrhyn's turquoise 280-square-km lagoon is so wide that you can just see the roof of the church at Tautua from Omoka, the administrative center. The *motu* at the far end of the lagoon are too far away to be seen. The lagoon is thick with sharks, mostly innocuous black-tips; only the black shark is dangerous. The islanders ignore them as they dive for oysters. Now pearl farming is developing with 150,000 cultured oysters already hanging on racks in the lagoon and an oyster hatchery near Omoka is adding to their numbers every day.

Penrhyn was named for the British ship *Lady Penrhyn,* which arrived in 1788, although one of the Polynesian names is Tongareva. The legendary hero Vatea fished Penrhyn up from the sea using a hook baited with a piece of flesh

> *Aluminum from the wreck of a four-engined WWII Liberator bomber named* **Go-Gettin' Gal** *was used by the islanders to make combs. Not much is left other than three engines near Warwick Latham's house and a fourth engine in the village.*

from his own thigh. In 1863 four native missionaries on Penrhyn were tricked into recruiting their congregation for Peruvian slavers at $5 a head and sailed with them to Callao as overseers for $100 a month in the hope of obtaining enough money to build a new church! The blackbirders dubbed Penrhyn the "Island of the Four Evangelists" in gratitude. This tragedy wiped out the chiefly line and Penrhyn is today the only Cook Island without an *ariki.* Remnants of old graves and villages abandoned after the raid can still be seen on the *motu,* and the ruins of an unfinished church crumble away at Akasusu.

The island has a good natural harbor, one of the few in the Cook Islands, and vessels can enter the lagoon through Taruia Passage, just above Omoka, to tie up at Omoka wharf. In 1995 a fuel depot opened here for ships patrolling the fisheries zones of the Cook Islands and Kiribati (Penrhyn is closer to Christmas Island than it is to Rarotonga). Development plans by the Rarotonga government have been resisted as various local factions vie for influence. Fine pandanus *rito* hats and mother of pearl shell jewelry are made on Penrhyn and visiting yachties can trade kitchen- and tableware, dry cell batteries, rope, and small anchors for crafts and pearls.

American forces occupied Penrhyn during 1942–1946 and built a giant airfield at the south end of Omoka about five km from the present village. Aluminum from the wreck of a four-engined WWII Liberator bomber named *Go-Gettin' Gal* was used by the islanders to make combs and not much is left other than three engines near Warwick Latham's house and a fourth engine in the village. Concrete building foundations from the war and from a base camp that supported British and American atmospheric nuclear tests on Christmas Island in the early 1960s can be seen. The waters around the atoll are a rich fishing ground, and

PENRHYN

Siki Rangi Passage
Takuua Passage
Ruahara
Matunga
Tautua
Taruia Passage
Omoka
Lagoon
Patanga
AIRSTRIP
Maketau
Aka Susunui
Ahumiria
Vaiere
Atutahi

0   5 mi
0   5 km

© DAVID STANLEY

Penrhyn is used as a base for patrol boats and planes monitoring the activities of foreign fishing fleets.

Air Rarotonga flies once a week from Rarotonga (1,365 km) to this most northerly Cook island. The airfare (NZ$1,203 return from Rarotonga) is high partly because of an exorbitant landing fee levied by the island council. **Tarakore Guest House** (Doreen and Purua Heria, fax 42-683) in the center of Omoka village and a few other families accept guests. As well, the local Air Rarotonga agent Warwick Latham (tel. 42-888, fax 42-023) can arrange a house rental with schoolteacher Rara Taia (tel. 42-132).

Resources

Glossary

afa: a *demi* or person of mixed Polynesian/European blood

ahimaa: an underground, earthen oven. After A.D. 500, the Polynesians had lost the art of making pottery, so they were compelled to bake their food, rather than boil it.

ahu: a Polynesian stone temple platform

aito: ironwood

anse: cove (French)

aparima: a Tahitian dance which tells a story with the hands

archipelago: a group of islands

ariki: a Cook Islands high chief; the traditional head of a clan or tribe; in Tahitian, *ari'i*

Arioi: a pre-European religious society, which traveled among the Society Islands presenting ceremonies and entertainments

atoll: a low-lying, ring-shaped coral reef enclosing a lagoon

bareboat charter: chartering a yacht without crew or provisions

bark cloth: see *tapa*

barrier reef: a coral reef separated from the adjacent shore by a lagoon

bêche-de-mer: sea cucumber; an edible sea slug; in Tahitian, *rori;* in French, *trépang*

B.P.: *boîte postale*

breadfruit: a large, round fruit with starchy flesh grown on an *uru* tree *(Artocarpus altilis)*

BYO: Bring Your Own (an Australian term used to refer to restaurants that allow you to bring your own alcoholic beverages)

C: Centigrade

C$: Canadian dollar

caldera: a wide crater formed through the collapse or explosion of a volcano

cassava: manioc; the starchy edible root of the tapioca plant

casse-croûte: a large sandwich made with a baguette

CEP: Centre d'Expérimentation du Pacifique; the former French nuclear-testing establishment in French Polynesia

CETAD: Centre d'études de Techniques Adaptés au Développement; a vocational training unit at the larger high schools

CFP: *cour de franc Pacifique;* the currency in French Polynesia

chain: an archaic unit of length equivalent to 20 meters

ciguatera: a form of fish poisoning caused by microscopic algae

CMAS: Confédération Mondiale des Activités Subaquatiques; the French counterpart of PADI

code share: a system whereby two or more airlines own seats on a single flight

coir: coconut husk sennit used to make rope, etc.

copra: dried coconut meat used in the manufacture of coconut oil, cosmetics, soap, and margarine

coral: a hard, calcareous substance of various shapes, composed of the skeletons of tiny marine animals called polyps

coral bank: a coral formation over 150 meters long

coral bleaching: the expulsion of symbiotic algae by corals

coral head: a coral formation a few meters across

coral patch: a coral formation up to 150 meters long

cyclone: Also known as a hurricane (in the Caribbean) or typhoon (in Japan). A tropical storm that rotates around a center of low atmospheric pressure; it becomes a cyclone when its winds reach force 12 or 64 knots. At sea the air will be filled with foam and driving spray, the water surface completely white with 14-meter-high waves. In the Northern Hemisphere, cyclones spin counterclockwise, while south of the equator they move clockwise. The winds of cyclonic storms are deflected toward a low-pressure area at the center, although the "eye" of the cyclone may be calm.

demi-pension: a breakfast and dinner meal plan, also called the modified American plan (MAP); *pension complète* means three meals, the American plan (AP)

desiccated coconut: the shredded meat of dehydrated fresh coconut

DOM-TOM: Départements et Territoires d'Outre-Mer; the French colonial bureaucratic structure

EEZ: Exclusive Economic Zone; a 200-nautical-mile offshore belt of an island nation or seacoast state that controls the mineral exploitation and fishing rights

endemic: native to a particular area and existing only there

ESCAP: Economic and Social Commission for Asia and the Pacific

expatriate: a person residing in a country other than his/her own; in the South Pacific such people are also called "Europeans" if their skin is white, or simply "expats."

FAD: fish aggregation device

fafa: a "spinach" of cooked taro leaves

farani: French; *français*

fare: Tahitian house

filaria: parasitic worms transmitted by biting insects to the blood or tissues of mammals. The obstruction of the lymphatic glands by the worms can cause an enlargement of the legs or other parts, a disease known as elephantiasis.

fissure: a narrow crack or chasm of some length and depth

FIT: foreign independent travel; a custom-designed, prepaid tour composed of many individualized arrangements

fringing reef: a reef along the shore of an island

gendarme: a French policeman on duty only in rural areas in France and French overseas territories

GPS: Global Positioning System, the space age successor of the sextant

guano: manure of seabirds, used as a fertilizer

guyot: a submerged atoll, the coral of which couldn't keep up with rising water levels

Havai'i: legendary homeland of the Polynesians

Hiro: the Polynesian god of thieves

hoa: a shallow channel between *motu*

hurricane: *see* cyclone

kaina: country; *kaina* music is Tahitian country music, usually a string band

knot: about three kilometers per hour

lagoon: an expanse of water bounded by a reef

lapita **pottery:** pottery made by the ancient Polynesians from 1600 to 500 B.C.

lava tube: a conduit formed as molten rock continues to flow below a cooled surface during the growth of a lava field. When the eruption ends, a tunnel is left with a flat floor where the last lava hardened.

LDS: Latter-day Saints; the Mormons

leeward: downwind; the shore (or side) sheltered from the wind; as opposed to windward

lei: a garland, often of fresh flowers, but sometimes of paper, shells, etc., hung about the neck of a person being welcomed or feted

le truck: a truck with seats in back, used for public transportation on Tahiti

live-aboard: a tour boat with cabin accommodation for scuba divers

LMS: London Missionary Society; a Protestant group that spread Christianity from Tahiti (1797) across the Pacific

maa tahiti: Tahitian food

maa tinito: Chinese food

mahimahi: dorado, Pacific dolphinfish (no relation to the mammal)

mahu: a male Tahitian transvestite, sometimes also homosexual

mairie: town hall

makatea: an uplifted reef around the coast of an elevated atoll

mama ruau: actually "grandmother," but also used for the Mother Hubbard long dress introduced to Tahiti by missionaries

mana: authority, prestige, virtue, "face," psychic power, a positive force

manahune: a commoner or member of the lower class in pre-Christian Tahitian society

mangrove: a tropical shrub with branches that send down roots forming dense thickets along tidal shores

manioc: cassava, tapioca, a starchy root crop

maohi: a native of French Polynesia

Maori: the Polynesians of New Zealand and the Cook Islands

mape: Tahitian chestnut tree

maraamu: southeast tradewinds or *alizés*

marae: a Tahitian temple or open-air cult place, called *me'ae* in the Marquesas

marara: flying fish

matrilineal: a system of tracing descent through the mother's familial line

Melanesia: the high island groups of the western Pacific (Fiji, New Caledonia, Vanuatu, Solomon Islands, Papua New Guinea); from *melas* (black)

Micronesia: chains of high and low islands mostly north of the Equator (Carolines, Gilberts, Marianas, Marshalls); from *micro* (small)

moai: an Easter Island statue

monoï: perfumed coconut oil

motu: a flat reef islet

mynah: an Indian starlinglike bird

NAUI: National Association of Underwater Instructors

NGO: nongovernment organization

NFIP: Nuclear-Free and Independent Pacific movement

noanoa: perfume

noni: the knobby green tree fruit of the *noni* or *nono* tree *(Morinda citrifolia)*

no-nos: sand flies

NZ$: New Zealand dollar

Oro: the Polynesian god of war

ORSTOM: Office de la Recherche Scientifique et Technique d'Outre-Mer

ote'a: a Tahitian ceremonial dance performed by men and women in two lines

pa: ancient Polynesian stone fortress

Pacific rim: the continental landmasses and large countries around the fringe of the Pacific

PADI: Professional Association of Dive Instructors

pandanus: screw pine with slender stem and prop roots. The sword-shaped leaves are used for plaiting mats and hats. In Tahitian, *fara*.

papa'a: a Tahitian word used to refer to Europeans

parasailing: a sport in which participants are carried aloft by a parachute pulled behind a speedboat

pareu: a Tahitian saronglike wraparound skirt or loincloth

pass: a channel through a barrier reef, usually with an outward flow of water

passage: an inside passage between an island and a barrier reef

patrilineal: a system of tracing descent through the fathers familial line

pawpaw: papaya

pelagic: relating to the open sea, away from land

peretane: Britain, British in Tahitian

pétanque: French lawn bowling in which small metal balls are thrown

pirogue: outrigger canoe (French), in Tahitian *vaa*

PK: *pointe kilométrique,* a system of marking kilometers along highways in French Polynesia

poe: a sticky pudding made from bananas, papaya, pumpkin, or taro mixed with starch, baked in an oven, and served with coconut milk; in Rapanui *po'i*

poisson cru: (French) raw fish marinated in lime; in Tahitian *ia ota*, in Japanese *sashimi*

Polynesia: divided into Western Polynesia (Tonga and Samoa) and Eastern Polynesia (French Polynesia, Cook Islands, Hawaii, Easter Island, and New Zealand); from *poly* (many)

pp: per person

pukao: the red stone topknot on an Easter Island *moai*

punt: a flat-bottomed boat

pupu: traditional Tahitian dance group

raatira: Tahitian chief, dance leader

rain shadow: the dry side of a mountain, sheltered from the windward side

reef: a coral ridge near the ocean surface

rongorongo: an ancient Easter Island script

roulotte: a mobile food van or truck

Glossary

scuba: self-contained underwater breathing apparatus

SDA: Seventh-Day Adventist

self-catering: *see* self-contained

self-contained: a room with private facilities (a toilet and shower not shared with other guests); the brochure term "en-suite" means the same thing; as opposed to a "self-catering" unit with cooking facilities

sennit: braided coconut-fiber rope

shareboat charter: a yacht tour for individuals or couples who join a small group on a fixed itinerary

shifting cultivation: a method of farming involving the rotation of fields instead of crops

shoal: a shallow sandbar or mud bank

shoulder season: a travel period between high/peak and low/off-peak seasons

SPREP: South Pacific Regional Environment Program

subduction: the action of one tectonic plate wedging under another

subsidence: geological sinking or settling

symbiosis: a mutually advantageous relationship between unlike organisms

tahua: in the old days a skilled Tahitian artisan or priest; today a sorcerer or healer

tamaaraa: a Tahitian feast

tamure: a new name for Ori Tahiti, a very fast erotic dance

tapa: a cloth made from the pounded bark of the paper mulberry tree *(Broussonetia papyrifera)*. It's soaked and beaten with a mallet to flatten and intertwine the fibers, then painted with geometric designs.

tapu: taboo, sacred, set apart, forbidden, a negative force

taro: a starchy elephant-eared tuber *(Colocasia esculenta),* a staple food of the Pacific islanders

tatau: the Tahitian original of the adopted English word tattoo

tavana: the elected mayor of a Tahitian commune (from the English "governor")

tifaifai: a Tahitian patchwork quilt based on either European or Polynesian motifs; in the Cook Islands *tivaevae*

tiki: a humanlike sculpture representing an anonymous ancestor used for protection in the days of religious rites and sorcery

timeshare: part ownership of a residential unit with the right to occupy the premises for a certain period each year in exchange for payment of an annual maintenance fee

tinito: Tahitian for Chinese

TNC: transnational corporation (also referred to as a multinational corporation)

to'ere: a hollow wooden drum hit with a stick

trade wind: a steady wind blowing toward the equator from either northeast or southeast

trench: the section at the bottom of the ocean where one tectonic plate wedges under another

tridacna clam: eaten everywhere in the Pacific, its size varies between 10 centimeters and one meter

tropical storm: a cyclonic storm with winds of 35 to 64 knots

tsunami: a fast-moving wave caused by an undersea earthquake; sometimes erroneously called a tidal wave

tu'i (Polynesian): king, ruler

umara: sweet potato *(Ipomoea batatas)*

US$: U.S. dollar

vigia: a mark on a nautical chart indicating a dangerous rock or shoal

VTT: vélo à tout terrain; mountain bike

windward: the point or side from which the wind blows, as opposed to leeward

zoreille: a recent arrival from France; from *les oreilles* (the ears); also called a *métro*

zories: rubber shower sandals, thongs, flip-flops

Alternative Place Names

Bass Islands: Marotiri Islands
Bellingshausen: Motu One
Danger: Pukapuka
Easter Island: Isla de Pascua
Easter Island: Rapa Nui
Hatutaa: Hatutu
Hatutu: Hatutaa
Hervey: Manuae
Hull: Maria
Isla de Pascua: Easter Island
Maiao: Tapuaemanu
Manuae: Hervey
Maria: Hull
Marotiri Islands: Bass Islands
Maupihaa: Mopelia
Maupiti: Maurau
Maurau: Maupiti
Mohotani: Motane
Mopelia: Maupihaa
Moruroa: Mururoa
Motane: Mohotani
Motu Iti: Tupai
Motu One: Bellingshausen
Mururoa: Moruroa
Penrhyn: Tongareva
Puamotu: Tuamotu
Pukapuka: Danger
Rapa Nui: Easter Island
Scilly: Manuae
Suvarov: Suwarrow
Suwarrow: Suvarov
Taha'a: Uporu
Tapuaemanu: Maiao
Temoe: Timoe
Timoe: Temoe
Tongareva: Penrhyn
Tuamotu: Puamotu
Tupai: Motu Iti
Uporu: Taha'a

Basic Tahitian

ahiahi: evening
ahimaa: earth oven
aita: no
aita e peapea: no problem
aita maitai: no good
aito: ironwood
amu: eat
ananahi: tomorrow
arearea: fun, to have fun
atea: far away
atua: god
avae: moon, month
avatea: midday (1000–1500)

e: yes, also *oia*
eaha te huru?: how are you?
e haere oe ihea?: where are you going?
e hia?: how much?

faraoa: bread
fare: house
fare iti: toilet
fare moni: bank
fare niau: thatched house
fare punu: tin-roofed house
fare pure: church
fare rata: post office
fare toa: shop
fenua: land
fetii: parent, family
fiu: fed up, bored

haari: coconut
haere: goodbye (to a person leaving)
haere mai io nei: come here
haere maru: go easy, take it easy
hauti: play, make love
hei: flower garland, lei
here hoe: number-one sweetheart
himene: song, from the English "hymn"
hoa: friend

ia orana: good day, may you live, prosper
i nanahi: yesterday
ino: bad
inu: drink

ioa: name
ite: know

ma'a: food
maeva: welcome
mahana: sun, light, day
mahanahana: warm
maitai: good, I'm fine; also a cocktail
maitai roa: very good
manava: welcome
manu: bird
manuia: to your health!
manureva: airplane
mao: shark
mauruuru: thank you
mauruuru roa: thank you very much
meka: swordfish
miti: salt water
moana: deep ocean
moemoea: dream
moni: money

nana: goodbye
naonao: mosquito
nehenehe: beautiful
niau: coconut-palm frond

'a oa: happy
ohipa: work
ora: life, health
ori: dance
oromatua: the spirits of the dead
otaa: bundle, luggage
oti: finished

pahi: boat, ship
painapo: pineapple
pape: water, juice
parahi: goodbye (to a person staying)
pareu: sarong
pia: beer
pohe: death
poipoi: morning
popaa: foreigner, European
poti'i: teenage girl, young woman
raerae: effeminate
roto: lake

taapapu: understand
taata: human being, man
tabu: forbidden
tahatai: beach
tama'a: lunch
tama'a maitai: bon appetit
tamaaraa: Tahitian feast
tamarii: child
tane: man, husband
taofe: coffee
taote: doctor
taravana: crazy
tiare: flower
to'e to'e: cold
tupapau: ghost

ua: rain
uaina: wine
uteute: red

vahine: woman, wife
vai: fresh water
veavea: hot

Numbers
hoe: 1
piti: 2
toru: 3
maha: 4
pae: 5
ono: 6
hitu: 7
vau: 8
iva: 9
ahuru: 10
ahuru ma hoe: 11
ahuru ma piti: 12
ahuru ma toru: 13
ahuru ma maha: 14
ahuru ma pae: 15
ahuru ma ono: 16
ahuru ma hitu: 17
ahuru ma vau: 18
ahuru ma iva: 19
piti ahuru: 20
piti ahuru ma hoe: 21
piti ahuru ma piti: 22
piti ahuru ma toru: 23
toru ahuru: 30

maha ahuru: 40
pae ahuru: 50
ono ahuru: 60
hitu ahuru: 70
vau ahuru: 80
iva ahuru: 90
hanere: 100
tauatini: 1,000
ahuru tauatini: 10,000
mirioni: 1,000,000

Basic French

bonjour: hello
bonsoir: good evening
salut: hi
Je vais à . . . : I am going to . . .
Où allez-vous?: Where are you going?
Jusqu'où allez-vous?: How far are you going?
Où se trouve . . . ?: Where is . . . ?
C'est loin d'ici?: Is it far from here?
À quelle heure?: At what time?
un horaire: timetable
hier: yesterday
aujourd'hui: today
demain: tomorrow
Je désire, je voudrais . . . : I want . . .
J'aime . . . : I like . . .
Je ne comprends pas.: I don't understand.
une chambre: a room
Vous êtes très gentil.: You are very kind.
Où habitez-vous?: Where do you live?
Il fait mauvais temps.: It's bad weather.
le gendarmerie: police station
Quel travail faites-vous?: What work do you do?
la chômage, les chômeurs: unemployment, the unemployed
Je t'aime.: I love you.
une boutique, un magasin: a store
le pain: bread
le lait: milk
le vin: wine
le casse-croûte: snack
les conserves: canned foods
les fruits de mer: seafood
un café très chaud: hot coffee
l'eau: water

le plat du jour: set meal
Combien ça fait?, Combien ça coûte?, Combien? Quel prix?: How much does it cost?
la clef: the key
la route, la piste: the road
la plage: the beach
la falaise: the cliff
la cascade: waterfall
les grottes: caves
Est-ce que je peux camper ici?: May I camp here?
Je voudrais camper.: I would like to camp.
le terrain de camping: campsite
Devrais-je demander la permission?: Should I ask permission?
s'il vous plaît: please
oui: yes
merci: thank you
cher: expensive
bon marché: cheap

Numbers
un: 1
deux: 2
trois: 3
quatre: 4
cinq: 5
six: 6
sept: 7
huit: 8
neuf: 9
dix: 10
onze: 11
douze: 12
treize: 13
quatorze: 14
quinze: 15
seize: 16
dix-sept: 17
dix-huit: 18
dix-neuf: 19
vingt: 20
vingt-et-un: 21
vingt-deux: 22
vingt-trois: 23
trente: 30
quarante: 40
cinquante: 50
soixante: 60
soixante-dix: 70

quatre-vingts: 80
quatre-vingt-dix: 90
cent: 100

mille: 1,000
dix mille: 10,000
million: 1,000,000

Suggested Reading

Guidebooks

Amsler, Kurt. *The French Polynesia Dive Guide.* New York: Abbeville Press, 2001. Describes and maps the territory's 27 top dive sites.

Bier, James A. *Reference Map of Oceania.* Honolulu: University of Hawaii Press, 1995. A fully indexed map of the Pacific Islands with 51 detailed inset maps of individual islands. Useful details such as time zones are included.

Chester, Sharon, et al. *Mave Mai, The Marquesas Islands.* San Mateo, CA: Wandering Albatross, 1998. A useful 137-page guide by a team of authors, several of whom have worked aboard the freighter *Aranui.* Each island is described in detail and the natural history sections are complete and well illustrated. Practical listings of accommodations, restaurants, and transport are not included.

Cruising Guide to the Leeward Islands of Tahiti in French Polynesia. The Moorings. Especially designed for yacht charter clients, this guide covers the islands between Huahine and Bora Bora.

Davock, Marcia. *Cruising Guide to Tahiti and the French Society Islands.* Stamford, CT: Wescott Cove Publishing, 1985. Though researched nearly three decades ago, this large-format, spiral-bound guide is still a must for anyone intending to sail around Tahiti and Moorea. The coverage of islands other these two is sketchy.

Lee, Georgia. *An Uncommon Guide to Easter Island.* Arroyo Grande, CA: International Resources, 1990. Though over a decade old, this is still the only real travel guide to Rapa Nui.

Ryan, Paddy. *The Snorkeler's Guide to the Coral Reef.* Honolulu: University of Hawaii Press,

1994. An introduction to the wonders of the Indo-Pacific reefs. The author spent 10 years in the region and knows it well.

Saquet, Jean-Louis. *The Tahiti Handbook.* Tahiti: Editions Avant et Après, 2000. A nicely illustrated introduction to the history, culture, and natural environment of French Polynesia. Most Papeete bookstores and souvenir shops sell copies.

Description and Travel

Danielsson, Bengt. *From Raft to Raft.* New York: Doubleday and Co., 1960. The story of one of the greatest sea adventures of modern times: Éric de Bisschop's raft voyage from Tahiti to South America and back, as told by one of the survivors.

Ellis, William. *Polynesian Researches.* Rutland, VT: Charles E. Tuttle Co., 1969. An early missionary's detailed observations of Tahiti during the years 1817–25.

Finney, Ben. *Voyage of Discovery: A Cultural Odyssey through Polynesia.* University of California Press, 1994. A complete account of the 1985 journey of the traditional sailing canoe *Hokule'a* through Polynesia.

Frisbie, Robert Dean. *The Book of Pukapuka, A Lone Trader On A South Sea Atoll.* Honolulu: Mutual Publishing. Frisbie's charming account of his first years on a remote northern atoll in the Cook Islands in the interwar period. A 1944 sequel *The Island of Desire* deals with his time on Suwarrow.

Grey, Zane. *Tales of Tahitian Waters.* Lanham, MD: Derrydale Press. The famous American author of cowboy tales tries his hand at deep-sea fishing off Tahiti.

Heyerdahl, Thor. *Fatu Hiva: Back to Nature.* New York: Doubleday, 1974. In 1936 Heyerdahl and his wife, Liv, went to live on Fatu Hiva. This book describes their year there.

Heyerdahl, Thor. *Kon Tiki.* Convinced that the mysterious origin of the Polynesians lies in the equally mysterious disappearance of the pre-Incan Indians of Peru, the author finds that only by sailing some 6,500 km across the Pacific in a balsa raft can he substantiate his theory.

Lee, Georgia. *Te Moana Nui.* Los Osos, CA: Easter Island Foundation, 2001. Georgia Lee lectured aboard the cruise ship *World Discoverer* between Tahiti and Chile. This book is a summary of her impressions.

Lewis, David. *We, the Navigators.* Honolulu: University of Hawaii Press, 1994. A second edition of the 1972 classic on the ancient art of land-finding in the Pacific. Lewis' 1964 journey from Tahiti to New Zealand was the first in modern times on which only traditional navigational means were used.

McCall, Grant. *Rapanui: Tradition and Survival on Easter Island.* Honolulu: University of Hawaii Press, 1994. A comprehensive summary of what is known about the island and its current inhabitants.

Neale, Tom. *An Island to Myself.* New York: Holt, Rinehart, and Winston, 1966. Tom's tale of six years spent alone on Suwarrow atoll in the Cooks in the 1950s and early 1960s.

Patterson, Rosemary I. *Mission Moruroa: An Adventure Novel Set in Tahiti.* Philadelphia, PA: Xlibris Corporation, 2001. A thriller about activists who decide to hijack a research vessel to the French testing site to focus attention on nuclear materials leaking into the South Pacific.

Silk, Don. *From Kauri Trees to Sunlit Seas: Shoestring Shipping in the South Pacific.* Auckland: Godwit, 1994. Don Silk and Bob Boyd created an inter-island shipping company which carried passengers and cargo around the Cook Islands for decades. Silk's dry humor and understatement is a delight, and his account of the farcical seizure of the *Marthalina* by inept Sri Lankan officials for alleged gun running is a classic.

Stevenson, Robert Louis. *In the South Seas.* New York: Scribner's, 1901. The author's memoir of his travels through the Marquesas, Tuamotus, and Gilberts by yacht in the years 1888–1890.

Sylvain, Adolphe. *Sylvain's Tahiti.* Los Angeles, CA: TASCHEN America, 2001. Timeless black-and-white images of Tahiti by a romantic photographer who spent 45 years in the islands.

Theroux, Paul. *The Happy Isles of Oceania.* London, Hamish Hamilton, 1992. The master of railway travelogues sets out with kayak and tent to tour the Pacific.

Natural Science

Allen, Gerald R, and Roger Steene. *Indo-Pacific Coral Reef Field Guide.* El Cajon, CA: Odyssey Publishing, 1998. Essential for identifying the creatures of the reefs.

Bahn, Paul, and John Flenley. *Easter Island, Earth Island.* London: Thames and Hudson, 1992. A well-illustrated study of man's impact on an isolated island environment, and how that led to a people's degradation. A message from our past for the future of our planet.

Harrison, Peter. *Seabirds of the World.* Princeton, NJ: Princeton University Press, 1996. An ideal field guide to carry aboard a yacht or ship.

MacLeod, Roy M., and Philip F. Rehbock. *Darwin's Laboratory.* Honolulu: University of Hawaii Press, 1994. Evolutionary theory and natural history in the Pacific.

Pratt, Douglas. *A Field Guide to the Birds of Hawaii and the Tropical Pacific.* Princeton, N.J.: Princeton University Press, 1986. The best in a poorly covered field.

Randall, John E., Gerald Robert Allen, and Roger C. Steene. *Fishes of the Great Barrier Reef and Coral Sea.* Honolulu: University of Hawaii Press, 1997. An identification guide for amateur diver and specialist alike.

Safina, Carl. *Song for the Blue Ocean.* New York: Owl Books, 1999. Safina chronicles the decline of the world's marine resources due to human activities—an enthralling and alarming read.

Veron, J. E. N. *Corals of Australia and the Indo-Pacific.* Honolulu: University of Hawaii Press, 1993. An authoritative, illustrated work.

Whistler, W. Arthur. *Wayside Plants of the Islands.* Honolulu: University of Hawaii Press, 1995. A guide to the lowland flora of the Pacific islands.

History

Aldrich, Robert. *France and the South Pacific since 1940.* Honolulu: University of Hawaii Press, 1993. A lively view of the French presence in the islands.

Bahn, Paul, Catherine Orliac, and Michel Orliac. *Easter Island: Mystery of the Stone Giants.* New York: Harry N Abrams, 1995. A factual, balanced account of the island's history.

Buzacott, Aaron. *Mission Life in the Islands of the Pacific.* Suva: Institute of Pacific Studies. A reprint of the 1866 classic in which a long-standing LMS missionary on Rarotonga tells piously of the trials and triumphs of his mission.

Danielsson, Bengt, and Marie-Thérèse Danielsson. *Poisoned Reign: French Nuclear Colonialism in the Pacific.* Penguin Books, 1986. An updated version of *Moruroa Mon Amour,* first published in 1977. A wealth of background on the former French nuclear testing program in Polynesia.

Denoon, Donald, et al. *The Cambridge History of the Pacific Islanders.* Australia: Cambridge University Press, 1997. A team of scholars examines the history of the inhabitants of Oceania from first colonization to the nuclear era. While acknowledging the great diversity of Pacific peoples, cultures, and experiences, the book looks for common patterns and related themes, presenting them in an insightful and innovative way.

Gill, William Wyatt. *From Darkness to Light in Polynesia.* Suva: Institute of Pacific Studies. Originally published in 1884, it's a tale of treachery, war, cannibals, exiles, murder, forgiveness, and the calming effect of Christianity by an ethnographer and LMS missionary who worked on Mangaia for two decades. If the moralizing doesn't put you off, you'll find it fascinating.

Henningham, Stephen. *France and the South Pacific: A Contemporary History.* Honolulu: University of Hawaii Press, 1991. This lucid book brings French policy in the South Pacific into clear focus.

Hough, Richard. *Captain James Cook.* New York: W.W. Norton and Company, 1997: W.W. Norton, 1997. A readable new biography of Captain Cook that asserts that Cook's abrupt manner on his third journey may have been due to an intestinal infection that affected his judgment and indirectly led to his death at the hands of Hawaiian islanders.

Howarth, David. *Tahiti: A Paradise Lost.* New York: Penguin Books, 1985. A readable history of European exploration in the Society Islands until the French takeover in 1842.

Howe, K. R. *Nature, Culture, and History.* Honolulu: University of Hawaii Press, 2000. A wide range of contemporary Pacific issues are examined in this timely book.

Irwin, Geoffrey. *The Prehistoric Exploration and Colonization of the Pacific.* Cambridge, UK: Cambridge University Press, 1992. Geoffrey Irwin uses an innovative model to establish a detailed theory of prehistoric navigation.

Kirch, Patrick Vinton. *On the Road of the Winds.* Berkeley, CA: University of California Press, 2000. This archaeological history of the Pacific islands before European contact is easily the most important of its kind in two decades.

Lamont, E. H. *Wild Life Among the Pacific Islanders.* Suva: Institute of Pacific Studies, 1994. The account first published in 1867 of the first foreigner to live on Penrhyn in the Northern Cooks.

Langdon, Robert. *Tahiti: Island of Love.* Australia: Pacific Publications, 1979. A popular history of Tahiti since the European discovery in 1767.

Maclellan, Nic, and Jean Chesneaux. *After Moruroa: France in the South Pacific.* Melbourne, Australia: Ocean Press, 1998. This timely examination of French colonialism from the French Revolution to the Matignon Accords speculates on France's future in the region in light of the end of nuclear testing and the political changes in Europe.

Maretu. *Cannibals and Converts: Radical Change in the Cook Islands.* Suva: Institute of Pacific Studies, 1983. Translated and edited by Marjorie Tuainekore Crocombe. The reminiscences of an elderly Cook Islander who personally witnessed the switch from paganism to Christianity, including the destruction of *marae,* breakup of polygamous families, epidemics, and struggles for power.

McEvedy, Colin. The Penguin Historical Atlas of the Pacific. New York: Penguin USA, 1998.

Through stories and maps, McEvedy brings Pacific history into sharp focus—a truly unique book.

Suggs, Robert C. *The Hidden World of Polynesia.* New York: Harcourt Brace, 1962. The Chronicle of an archaeological expedition to Nuku Hiva in the Marquesas Islands in 1956.

Stevenson, Christopher, ed. *Easter Island in Pacific Context.* Los Osos, California: Easter Island Foundation, 1998. A collection of 64 papers by 92 authors at the South Seas Symposium held at Albuquerque, New Mexico, in August 1997.

Van Tilburg, Jo Anne. *Easter Island: Archaeology, Ecology, and Culture.* Washington: Smithsonian Institution Press, 1995. Through numerous photographs, drawings, and references, Van Tilburg examines the island's prehistory, legends, and environment to explain the construction and transportation of the famous statues.

Social Science

Danielsson, Bengt. *Work and Life on Raroia.* Danielsson spent 18 months on this atoll observing Tuamotu life and this book published in 1956 is still the only detailed history of the Tuamotu Islands.

Levy, Robert. *Tahitians: Mind and Experience in the Society Islands.* Chicago: University of Chicago Press, 1973. Levy's study, based on several years of field work on Tahiti and Huahine in the 1960s, includes an intriguing examination of the *mahu* (transvestite) phenomenon.

Marshall, Don. *Raivavae.* New York: Doubleday and Co., 1961. The author, who is a professional anthropologist, did field work on this high island in the Austral group in 1957–1958, to find out what was left of the old orgiastic pagan religion and sexual rites.

Metraux, Alfred. *Ethnology of Easter Island.* Honolulu: Bishop Museum Press, 1971. Originally published in 1941, this is almost an encyclopedia of Easter Island with everything from the language, culture, art, flora and fauna, geography, religion, and many mysteries of the island.

Oliver, Douglas L. *Oceania: The Native Cultures of Australia and the Pacific Islands.* Honolulu: University of Hawaii Press, 1988. A massive, two-volume, 1,275-page anthropological survey of the precontact anthropology, history, economy, and politics of the entire region.

Literature

Briand, Jr., Paul L. *In Search of Paradise.* Honolulu: Mutual Publishing. A joint biography of Charles Nordhoff and James Norman Hall.

Brooks, Peter. *World Elsewhere.* New York: Simon and Schuster, 1999. An historical novel about an impoverished aristocrat aboard the first French ship to visit Tahiti.

Davis, Tom. *Vaka: Saga of a Polynesian Canoe.* Suva: Institute of Pacific Studies, 1992. This historical novel's protagonist is a legendary voyaging canoe that sails between the diverse isles of Oceania for 12 generations. The lore of three centuries of Polynesian migration, including legends, customs, navigational and sailing techniques, genealogies, tribal hierarchies, and titles, is encapsulated in this simple chronicle. Prosaic elements such as female offspring, commoners, the passage of time, illness, and failure receive scant attention from Davis.

Day, A. Grove, and Carl Stroven, eds. *Best South Sea Stories.* Honolulu: Mutual Publishing. Fifteen extracts from the writings of famous European authors.

Day, A. Grove. *The Lure of Tahiti.* Honolulu: Mutual Publishing, 1986. Fifteen choice extracts from the rich literature of "the most romantic island in the world."

Hall, James Norman. *The Forgotten One and Other True Tales of the South Seas.* Honolulu: Mutual Publishing. A book about expatriate writers and intellectuals who sought refuge on the out-of-the-world islands of the Pacific.

Hall, James Norman, and Charles Bernard Nordhoff. *The Bounty Trilogy.* Retells in fictional form the famous mutiny, Bligh's escape to Timor, and the mutineers' fate on Pitcairn.

London, Jack. *South Sea Tales.* Honolulu: Mutual Publishing. Stories based on London's visit to Tahiti, Samoa, Fiji, and the Solomons in the early 20th century.

Loti, Pierre. *The Marriage of Loti.* This tale of Loti's visits to Tahiti in 1872 helped foster the romantic myth of Polynesia in Europe.

Maugham, W. Somerset. *The Moon and Sixpence.* Story of a London stockbroker who leaves his job for Tahiti and ends up leading an artist's primitive life that isn't as romantic as he had hoped.

Maugham, W. Somerset. *The Trembling of a Leaf.* Honolulu: Mutual Publishing. The responses of a varied mix of white males—colonial administrator, trader, sea captain, bank manager, and missionary—to the peoples and environment of the South Pacific. Maugham is a masterful storyteller, and his journey to Samoa and Tahiti 1916-1917 supplied him with poignant material.

Melville, Herman. *Typee, A Peep at Polynesian Life.* In 1842 Melville deserted from an American whaler at Nuku Hiva, Marquesas Islands. This semifictional account of Melville's four months among the Typee people was followed by *Omoo* in which Melville gives his impressions of Tahiti at the time of the French takeover.

Michener, James A. *Tales of the South Pacific.* Greenwich, CT: Fawcett Books. Short stories based on Michener's wartime experiences in the islands.

The Arts

Cachin, Francoise. *The Quest for Paradise.* New York: Harry N. Abrams, 1992. An illustrated biography of Gauguin.

Charola, A. Elena. *Death of a Moai. Easter Island Statues: Their Nature, Deterioration, and Conservation.* Los Osos, CA: Easter Island Foundation, 1997. Explores the problems involved in preserving the statues and rock art of Easter Island.

Danielsson, Bengt. *Gauguin in the South Seas.* New York: Doubleday, 1966. Danielsson's fascinating account of Gauguin's 10 years in Polynesia.

Kaeppler, Adrienne, C. Kaufmann, and Douglas Newton. *Oceanic Art.* New York: Abrams, 1997. The first major survey of the arts of Polynesia, Melanesia, and Micronesia in over three decades, this admirable volume brings the reader up to date on recent scholarship in the field. Of the 900 illustrations, over a third are new.

Lee, Georgia. *The Rock Art of Easter Island: Symbols of Power, Prayers to the Gods.* Monumenta Arqueologica 17. A readable 1992 examination of a fascinating subject. Also recommended are Alan Drake's *The Ceremonial Center of Orongo* and Dr. William Liller's *The Ancient Solar Observatories of Rapa Nui.*

Rongokea, Lynnsay. *The Art of Tivaevae.* Honolulu: University of Hawaii Press, 2001. A well-illustrated study of the patchwork quilts introduced to the Cook Islands by missionaries a century ago.

Weaver Kurze, Joan T. *Ingrained Images: Carvings in Wood from Easter Island.* Los Osos, CA: Easter Island Foundation, 1997. A lavishly illustrated study of contemporary Rapanui wood carvings with comparisons to historic pieces.

Thomas, Nicholas. *Oceanic Art.* London: Thames and Hudson, 1995. Almost 200 illustrations grace the pages of this readable survey.

Language

Anisson du Perron, Jacques, and Mai-Arii Cadousteau. *Dictionaire Moderne, Tahitien-Français et Français-Tahitien.* Papeete: Stepolde, 1973.

Buse, Jasper, et al. *Cook Islands Maori Dictionary.* Suva: Institute of Pacific Studies, 1995. Incorporates a wealth of knowledge on Cook islands language, culture, and society.

Carpentier, Tai, and Clive Beaumont. *Kai Korero.* Honolulu: University of Hawaii Press, 1996. This Cook Islands Maori coursebook comes with a cassette tape.

Haoa Rapahango, Ana Betty, and William Liller. *Speak Rapanui! Hable Rapanui!* Los Osos, CA: Easter Island Foundation, 1996. A most useful trilingual language-phrase booklet.

Lynch, John. *Pacific Languages: An Introduction.* Honolulu: University of Hawaii Press, 1998. The grammatical features of the Oceanic, Papuan, and Australian languages.

Tryon, Darrell T. *Say It In Tahitian.* Sydney: Pacific Publications, 1977. For lovers of Polynesia, an instant introduction to spoken Tahitian.

Reference Books

Atlas de la Polynésie française. France: Editions de l'ORSTOM, 1993. A major thematic atlas summarizing the geography, population, and history of the territory.

Craig, Robert D. *Dictionary of Polynesian Mythology.* Westport, CT: Greenwood Press, 1989. Aside from hundreds of alphabetical entries listing the legends, stories, gods, goddesses, and heroes of the Polynesians, this book charts the evolution of 30 Polynesian languages.

Crocombe, Ron. *The South Pacific.* Suva: Institute of Pacific Studies, 2000. A new edition of the classic text on the economies, social life, culture, politics, and history of Oceania by one of the region's leading academics.

Douglas, Ngaire and Norman Douglas, eds. *Pacific Islands Yearbook.* Suva: Fiji Times Ltd, 1994. First published in 1932, this is the 17th edition of the original sourcebook on the islands. Although the realities of modern publishing have led to the demise of both the *Yearbook* and its cousin *Pacific Islands Monthly,* this final edition remains an indispensable reference work for students of the region.

Jackson, Miles M., ed. *Pacific Island Studies: A Survey of the Literature.* Westport, CT: Greenwood Press, 1986. In addition to comprehensive listings, there are extensive essays that put the most important works in perspective.

Lal, Brig V., and Kate Fortune, eds. *The Pacific Islands: An Encyclopedia.* Honolulu: University of Hawaii Press, 2000. This important book combines the writings of 200 acknowledged experts on the physical environment, peoples, history, politics, economics, society, and culture of the South Pacific. The accompanying CD-ROM provides a wealth of maps, graphs, photos, biographies, and more.

Booksellers and Publishers

Some of the titles listed above are out of print and not available in bookstores. Major research libraries should have a few, otherwise try the specialized antiquarian booksellers or regional publishers which follow. Most of these titles can be ordered online through www.southpacific.org/books.html.

Bibliophile, 24A Glenmore Rd., Paddington, Sydney, NSW 2021, Australia (tel. 61-2/9331-1411, fax 61-2/9361-3371, www.bibliophile.com.au). An antiquarian bookstore specializing in books about Oceania. View its extensive catalog on line.

Bluewater Books and Charts, 1481 S.E. 17th St., Fort Lauderdale, FL 33316, U.S.A., tel. 954/763-6533 or 800/942-2583, fax 954/522-2278, www.bluewaterweb.com). An outstanding source of navigational charts and cruising guides to the Pacific.

Book Bin, 228 S.W. Third St., Corvallis, OR 97333, U.S.A. (tel. 541/752-0045, fax 541/754-4115, www.bookbin.com). Its searchable catalog of books on the Pacific Islands lists hundreds of rare books, including some from the Institute of Pacific Studies.

Books of Yesteryear, P.O. Box 257, Newport, NSW 2106, Australia (tel./fax 61-2/9918-0545, www.abebooks.com/home/booksofyesteryear). Another source of old, fine, and rare books on the Pacific.

Books Pasifika, P.O. Box 68-446, Newtown, Auckland 1, New Zealand (tel. 64-9/303-2349, fax 64-9/377-9528, www.ak.planet.gen.nz/pasifika/Pasifika.html). Besides being a major publisher, Pasifika Press is one of New Zealand's best sources of mail order books on Oceania, including those of the Institute of Pacific Studies.

Institute of Pacific Studies, University of the South Pacific, P.O. Box 1168, Suva, Fiji Islands (www.usp.ac.fj/ips). Its catalog, *Book from the Pacific Islands,* lists numerous books about the islands written by the Pacific islanders themselves. Some are rather dry aca demic publications of interest only to specialists, so order carefully. The University of the South Pacific Center on Rarotonga sells many of these books over the counter. For Internet access to the catalog, see the University Book Centre listing below.

Jean-Louis Boglio, P.O. Box 72, Currumbin, Queensland 4223, Australia (tel. 61-7/5534-9349, fax 61-7/5534-9949, www.maritimebooks.com.au). An excellent source of new and used books on the French territories in the Pacific.

Mutual Publishing Company, 1215 Center St., Suite 210, Honolulu, HI 96816, U.S.A. (tel. 808/732-1709, fax 808/734-4094, www.mutualpublishing.com). The classics of expatriate Pacific literature, available in cheap paperback editions.

Pacific Island Books, 2802 East 132nd Circle, Thornton, CA 80241, U.S.A. (tel. 303/920-8338, www.pacificislandbooks.com). One of the best U.S. sources of books about the Cook Islands. It stocks many titles published by the Institute of Pacific Studies.

Serendipity Books, P.O. Box 340, Nedlands, WA 6009, Australia (tel. 61-8/9382-2246, fax 61-8/9388-2728, http://members.iinet.net.au/~serendip). The largest stocks of antiquarian, secondhand, and out-of-print books on the Pacific in Western Australia.

University Book Centre, University of the South Pacific, P.O. Box 1168, Suva, Fiji Islands (fax 679/330-3265, www.uspbookcentre.com). An excellent source of books written and produced in the South Pacific itself.

University of Hawaii Press, 2840 Kolowalu St., Honolulu, HI 96822-1888, U.S.A. (tel. 808/956-8255, www.uhpress.hawaii.edu). Its *Hawaii and the Pacific* catalog is well worth requesting if you're trying to build a Pacific library.

Periodicals

Commodores' Bulletin. Seven Seas Cruising Assn., 1525 South Andrews Ave., Suite 217, Fort Lauderdale, FL 33316, U.S.A. (tel. 954/463-2431, fax 954/463-7183, www.ssca.org; US$57 a year worldwide by airmail). This monthly bulletin is chock-full of useful information for anyone wishing to tour the Pacific by sailing boat. All Pacific yachties and friends should be Seven Seas members!

The Contemporary Pacific. University of Hawaii Press, 2840 Kolowalu St., Honolulu, HI 96822, U.S.A. (www.uhpress.hawaii.edu, published twice a year, US$35 a year). Publishes a good mix of articles of interest to both scholars and general readers; the country-by-country "Political Review" in each number is a concise summary of events during the preceding year. The "Dialogue" section offers informed comment on the more controversial issues in the region, while recent publications on the islands are examined through book reviews. Those interested in current topics in Pacific island affairs should check recent volumes for background information.

Europe-Pacific Solidarity Bulletin. Published quarterly by the European Center for Studies Information and Education on Pacific Issues, P.O. Box 151, 3700 AD Zeist, the Netherlands (www.antenna.nl/ecsiep). It's a useful source of information on the compensation claims of those affected by French nuclear testing in the South Pacific.

Islands Business. P.O. Box 12718, Suva, Fiji Islands (tel. 679/330-3108, fax 679/330-1423, email: subs@ibi.com.fj; annual airmailed subscription A$35 to Australia, NZ$55 to New Zealand, US$45 to North America, US$55 to Europe). A monthly newsmagazine with in-depth coverage of political and economic trends around the Pacific. It even has a "Whispers" gossip section that is an essential weather vane for anyone doing business in the region. Travel and aviation news gets some prominence.

Pacific Magazine. P.O. Box 913, Honolulu, HI 96808, U.S.A. (www.pacificislands.cc; US$30 a year). This monthly newsmagazine, published in Hawaii since 1976, will keep you up to date on what's happening in the South Pacific and Micronesia.

Pacific News Bulletin. Pacific Concerns Resource Center, 83 Amy St., Toorak, Private Mail Bag, Suva, Fiji Islands (fax 679/330-4755, email: pcrc@is.com.fj: US$$15 a year in the South Pacific, US$20 in North America and Asia, US$30 elsewhere). A 16-page monthly newsletter with up-to-date information on nuclear, independence, environmental, and political questions.

Rapa Nui Journal. P.O. Box 6774, Los Osos, CA 93412-6774, U.S.A. (www.islandheritage.org; quarterly, US$30 a year in North America, US$40 elsewhere). An interesting mix of scholarly reports and local news of interest to Rapanuiphiles.

Surfer Travel Reports. P.O. Box 1028, Dana Point, CA 92629, U.S.A. (www.surfermag.com/travel/pacific). These reports provide a detailed analysis of surfing conditions at different destinations. Back issues on specific countries are available at US$7 each (the last issue on Tahiti was 6.4, on Tubuai 15.5, on Easter Island 9.10, and on Rarotonga 6.1). This is your best source of surfing information by far.

Tahiti Pacifique. Alex W. du Prel, B.P. 368, 98728 Moorea (tel. 689/56-28-94, fax 689/56-30-07, www.tahiti-pacifique.com, annual subscription US$85). For those who read French, this monthly magazine offers a style of informed and critical commentary quite unlike that seen in the daily press of the French territories.

Tahiti Beach Press. Jan Prince, B.P. 887, 98713 Papeete, Tahiti, French Polynesia (tel. 689/42-68-50, fax 689/42-33-56, monthly subscription US$37 a year to North America). Established in 1980, this is Tahiti's only English-language newspaper.

Tok Blong Pasifik. Pacific Peoples Partnership, Suite 407, 620 View St., Victoria, BC V8W 1J6, Canada (www.sppf.org, C$25 a year in Canada, US$25 elsewhere). This lively quarterly of news and views focuses on regional development, social justice, environmental, and other issues of importance to Pacific islanders.

Undercurrent. 125 East Sir Francis Drake Blvd., Suite 200, Larkspur, CA 94939-9809, U.S.A. (tel. 800/326-1896 or 415/461-5906, www.undercurrent.org, US$78 a year). A monthly consumer protection-oriented newsletter for serious scuba divers. Unlike virtually every other diving publication, *Undercurrent* accepts no advertising or free trips, which allows its writers to tell it as it is.

Discography

Music lovers will be pleased to know that authentic Pacific music is readily available on compact disc. In compiling this selection we've tried to list noncommercial recordings that are faithful to the traditional music of the islands as it exists today. Island music based on Western pop has been avoided. You can buy many of these CDs at music shops in Papeete and Avarua, or order them online through www.southpacific.org/music.html.

Air Mail Music: South Pacific Songs and Rhythms Manuiti/Playasound. A collection of music largely from Tahiti, with a few pieces from Tuvalu Solomon Islands, and Samoa also included.

A Journey to Tahiti. Manuiti/Playasound. A collection of songs by Bimbo, Emma, Tahiti ma Poline, Heikura, and Charley Manu.

Bastille Celebrations in Polynesia. Arion Records Music from the Heiva i Tahiti recorded live on Tahiti and Bora Bora.

Coco's Temaeva. Manuiti/Playasound. Founded by Coco Hotahota in 1962, Temaeva has won more prizes at the annual Heiva i Tahiti festivals than any other professional dance troupe. These recordings are from 1966-1972.

Echo des Iles Tuamotu et Bora Bora. Manuiti/Playasound. Classic songs recorded 1954-1969 by the late Marie Mariteragi, queen of Tuamotu kaina music.

Fanshawe, David, ed. *Exotic Voices and Rhythms of the South Seas.* Arc Records. Cook Island drum dancing, a Fijian tralala meke, a Samoan fiafia, a Vanuatu string band, and Solomon Islands panpipes selected from 1,200 hours of tapes in the Fanshawe Pacific Collection.

Fanshawe, David, ed. *Heiva i Tahiti: Festival of Life.* Arc Records. Fanshawe has captured the excitement of Tahiti's biggest festival in these pieces recorded live in Papeete in 1982 and 1986. Famous groups led by Coco Hotahota, Yves Roche, Irma Prince, and others are represented.

Fanshawe, David, ed. *Spirit of Polynesia.* Saydisc Records. An anthology of the music of 12 Pacific countries recorded between 1978 and 1988. More than half the pieces are from French Polynesia and the Cook Islands.

Heart of Tahiti. GNP Crescendo Records. Twenty top Tahitian tunes by stars like Charley Manu, Yves Roche, and Eddie Lund.

Linkels, Ad, and Lucia Linkels, eds. *Hula, Haka, Hoko!* Pan Records. A selection of traditional Polynesian dance music recorded on Easter Island, Cook Islands, Tuvalu, Rotuma, Tonga, and Samoa between 1982 and 1996.

Linkels, Ad, and Lucia Linkels, eds. *Te Pito O Te Henua.* Pan Records. Thirty-two tracks of songs and dances of Easter Island recorded in 1995.

Melodies des Atolls, Manuiti/Playasound. Twenty outstanding Tahitian songs from the 1950s in the Tahiti Belle Epoque series.

Nuutania: Songs from Tahitian Jails. Last Call Records. An unusual collection of prison singing from paradise.

Quinn's Tahitian Hut. Manuiti/Playasound. A retrospective of the orchestras which played at the famous Papeete nightclub established in 1933 by Robert E. Quinn.

Rapa Iti, Vol. II. Shanachie Records. Choral singing and chanting from the Austral Group.

Royal Folkloric Troupe. Manuiti/Playasound. Volume 2 of Coco's Temaeva featuring Coco Hotahota's Royal Folkloric Troupe of Tahiti, renowned for its original choreography.

South Pacific Aparima. Manuiti/Playasound. Music of the legendary Tahitian aparima dance in which the hands tell a story.

South Pacific Drums. Manuiti/Playasound. A compilation of 39 of the best percussion recordings in Manuiti's archives—an excellent introduction to the traditional music of Polynesia.

Tahiti Belle Epoque, Vol. 7. Manuiti/Playasound. Classics from the years 1971-1977 by the great vocalist Emma Terangi (1938-2000) from Hikueru atoll in the Tuamotus.

Tahiti Kaina 2000, Vol. 1. Manuiti/Playasound. Rod Dannys sings Tamarii Punaruu-style kaina songs made famous at the Heiva.

Internet Resources

Top 20 Polynesia Websites

Air Rarotonga
www.airraro.com
Captain Ewan Smith's aerial photography and the convincing descriptions of each island make this site worth visiting. Information on Air Rarotonga's flights and tours are provided and you can book online.

Cook Islands
www.cook-islands.com
The official Cook Islands Tourism Corporation site provides a business directory of its accredited partners. Details of accommodations and activities can be downloaded in PDF format and there's a page on each island.

Cook Islands News Online
www.cinews.co.ck
Come here for the weekly news from Rarotonga's daily paper, including local news, features, events, letters, notice boards, and sports. It's an easy way of keeping up on political developments.

Dream Islands Travel Guide
www.dream-islands.com
For specific tourism listings with exact prices quoted, this online guide to French Polynesia is hard to beat. You can access the information by island name or via the maps. It's a rich resource—colorful and easy to navigate.

Easter Island Foundation
www.islandheritage.org
This well-organized website provides an online guide, history, legends, photos, publications, and a discussion of tourism's impact.

Easter Island Home Page
www.netaxs.com/~trance/rapanui.html
Beside the useful historical and cultural introductions, this site offers about the best collection of Easter Island links you'll find. There's also a sample of Rapa Nui music.

Haere Mai
www.haere-mai.pf
The home page of the federation of guesthouses and family accommodations in French Polynesia provides listings in all five archipelagoes. Photos, descriptions, and prices are supplied.

Hémisphère Sub
www.diveraiatea.com
Follow the arrows to experience a virtual dive at Raiatea. Though the text is in French only, you can't help but admire the designer's imagination and sense of humor.

Jetsave Travel
www.jetsave.co.ck
Comprehensive listings of most Cook Islands travel arrangements are available here. The New Zealand dollar rates quoted are similar to what you'd pay locally and you can book by email.

Maui Pearls
www.mauipearls.com
A buyers' guide with general information on Cook Islands black pearls. The exact prices quoted in U.S. dollars give you an idea of how much you'll need to budget.

Philatelic Center of French Polynesia
www.tahiti-postoffice.com
The Philatelic Bureau's site is appealing for the varied background information provided on local stamp issues and telephone cards. If you're curious about the arrival of the gospel in Polynesia, Tahitian music, seashells of Polynesia, the return of the Pacific Battalion, etc., look here. The site is bright and orderly—a pleasure to use.

Présidence du Gouvernement
www.presidence.pf
This official site explains the system of government and takes you on a virtual tour of the new presidential palace in Papeete. The writeups on the history, culture, geography, and economy of French Polynesia are precise, and it's an excellent source of information on the outer islands.

Rongorongo of Easter Island
www.rongorongo.org
Something different, this site presents the ancient culture of Easter Island, especially the mysterious *rongorongo* hieroglyphic script. There's even a Rapanui-English dictionary.

Tahiti1.Com
www.tahiti1.com
A news and information portal with the finest selection of links. You can sample Tahitian cooking and cocktails, view the flowers, visit surfing spots off Tahiti and Moorea, check boat timetables to the outer islands, read the legends of old Polynesia, learn about tattooing, and much more.

Tahiti Black Pearls
www.perlesdetahiti.net
The site of GIE Perles de Tahiti is about the best you'll find on the subject—a must for anyone in the market for a black pearl. The background information on the industry is excellent and it's not just a sales pitch.

Tahiti Diving Guide
www.diving-tahiti.com
Ten diving destinations are briefly described and mapped on this attractive site. The underwater photography is unsurpassed.

Tahiti Explorer
www.tahiti-explorer.com
Here you can learn about black pearls, cruises, diving, flights, hotels, the weather, people and geography, etc. The photo albums and trip reports are a huge resource, and there's a travel forum.

Tahiti Nui Travel
www.tahitinuitravel.com
Travel agents should check here for facts about upmarket facilities of the area. If you want to book a cruise, flight, or tour through a Papeete-based travel agency, come here. The site also features island information, photos, diving spots, a message board, and tourism news.

Tahiti Tourisme
www.tahiti-tourisme.com
This official tourism site provides another useful introduction to French Polynesia. The many outside links allow you to access additional information, and there's an events calendar and address listings. Many of Tahiti Tourisme's overseas offices have sites of their own.

Travelmaxia
www.travelmaxia.com
This Internet portal provides a vast amount of information on accommodations in French Polynesia and the Cook Islands. You're able to email the properties directly using the online forms—this is not a tour company.

Information Offices

Regional

South Pacific Tourism Organization, P.O. Box 13119, Suva, Fiji Islands (tel. 679/330-4177, fax 679/330-1995, info@spto.org, www.spto.org)

South Pacific Tourism Organization, 48 Glentham Road, Barnes, London SW13 9JJ, United Kingdom (tel. 44-20/8741-6082, fax 44-20/8741-6107, uk@spto.org, www.interfaceinternational.co.uk)

South Pacific Tourism Organization, Petersburg Strasse 94, D-10247 Berlin, Germany (tel. 49-304/225-6026, fax 49-304/225-6287, germany@spto.org)

French Polynesia

Tahiti Tourisme, B.P. 65, Papeete, 98713 Tahiti, Polynésie Française (tel. 689/50-57-00, fax 689/43-66-19, tahiti-tourisme@mail.pf, www .tahiti-tourisme.com)

Tahiti Tourisme, 300 North Continental Blvd., Suite 160, El Segundo, CA 90245, U.S.A. (tel. 310/414-8484, fax 310/414-8490, tahitilax@earthlink.net, www.gototahiti.com)

Tahiti Tourisme, Level 1, 26 Ponsonby Rd., Ponsonby, Auckland, New Zealand (tel. 64-9/360-8880, fax 64-9/360-8891, www.tahiti-tourisme.co.nz)

Tahiti Tourisme, 12 Ann St., Surry Hills, NSW 2010, Australia (tel. 61-2/9281-6020, fax 61-2/9211-6589, www.traveltotahiti.com.au)

Pacific Leisure Group, 8th floor, Maneeya Center Building, 518/5 Ploenchit Rd., Bangkok 10330, Thailand (tel. 66-2/255-9966, fax 66-2/652-2850)

Tahiti Tourisme, Sankyo Building (No. 20) Room 802, 3-11-5 Ildabashi, Chiyoda-Ku, Tokyo 102, Japan (tel. 81-3/3265-0468, fax 81-3/3265-0581)

Oficina de Turismo de Tahiti, Casilla 16057, Santiago 9, Chile (tel. 56-2/251-2826, fax 56-2/233-1787, tahiti@cmet.net)

Tahiti Tourism, c/o CIB Group, 1 Battersea Church Rd., London, SW11 3LY, United Kingdom (tel. 44-20/7771-7023, fax 44-20/7771-7059)

Office du Tourisme de Tahiti, 28 Boulevard Saint-Germain, 75005 Paris, France (tel. 33-1/5542-6121, fax 33-1/5542-6120, www.voyageatahiti.com)

Fremdenverkehrsamt von Tahiti, Bockenheimer Landstrasse 45, D-60325 Frankfurt/Main, Germany (tel. 49-69/971-484, fax 49-69/729-275, www.tahititourisme.de)

Tahiti Tourisme, Piazza Caiazzo 3, 20124 Milano, Italy (tel. 39-2/6698-0317, fax 39-2/669-2648, www.tahiti-turismo.com)

Easter Island

Cámara de Turismo Isla de Pascua, Atamu Tekena s/n, Hanga Roa, Rapa Nui, Chile (tel./fax 56-32/550-055, camararapanui@entelchile.net, www.turismo.rapanui.cl)

Cook Islands

Cook Islands Tourism Corporation, P.O. Box 14, Rarotonga, Cook Islands (tel. 682/29-435, fax 682/21-435, tourism@cookislands.gov.ck, www.cook-islands.com)

Cook Islands Tourism Corporation, 2250 E. Imperial Highway, Suite 2000, El Segundo, CA 90245, U.S.A. (tel. 888/994-2665, fax 877/468-6643)

Cook Islands Tourism Corporation, 280 Nelson Street, Suite 202, Vancouver, BC V6B 2E2, Canada (tel. 604/301-1190, fax 604/687-3454, cookislands@earthlink.net)

Cook Islands Tourism Corporation, 1/127 Symonds St., P.O. Box 37391, Auckland, New Zealand (tel. 64-9/366-1106, fax 64-9/309-1876)

Cook Islands Tourism Corporation, P.O. Box H95, Hurlstone Park, NSW 2193, Australia (tel. 61-2/9955-0446, fax 61-2/9955-0447)

Information Offices

The Islands at a Glance

Island Group	Land Area (sq km)	Highest Point (m)	Population	Latitude	Longitude
Society Islands					
Bora Bora	29.3	727	7,295	16.45°S	151.87°W
Huahine	74.8	669	5,757	16.72°S	151.10°W
Maiao	8.3	180	283	17.67°S	150.63°W
Manuae	4.0	4	24	16.52°S	154.72°W
Maupihaa	3.6	4	30	16.87°S	154.00°W
Maupiti	11.4	380	1,191	16.45°S	152.25°W
Moorea	125.2	1,207	14,226	17.57°S	150.00°W
Motu One	2.8	4	12	15.80°S	154.55°W
Raiatea	171.4	1,017	11,133	16.82°S	151.43°W
Tahaa	90.2	590	4,845	16.62°S	151.49°W
Tahiti	1,045.1	2,241	169,674	17.32°S	149.35°W
Tetiaroa	4.9	3	14	17.00°S	149.57°W
Austral Islands					
Raivavae	17.9	437	1,049	23.92°S	147.80°W
Rapa	40.5	650	521	26.60°S	144.37°W
Rimatara	8.6	84	929	22.67°S	153.42°W
Rurutu	32.3	389	2,104	22.48°S	151.33°W
Tubuai	45.0	422	1,979	23.35°S	149.58°W
Tuamotu Islands					
Ahe	12.2	4	377	14.50°S	146.33°W
Amanu	25.0	4	209	17.72°S	140.65°W
Anaa	37.7	4	411	17.50°S	145.50°W
Apataki	20.0	4	387	15.50°S	146.33°W
Aratika	8.3	4	260	15.55°S	146.65°W
Arutua	15.0	4	520	15.17°S	146.67°W
Faaite	8.8	4	246	16.75°S	145.17°W
Fakahina	8.3	4	104	16.00°S	140.08°W
Fakarava	13.8	4	467	16.17°S	145.58°W
Fangatau	5.9	4	150	15.75°S	140.83°W
Hao	18.5	4	1,412	18.25°S	140.92°W
Hereheretue	3.4	4	45	19.87°S	144.97°W
Hikueru	2.8	4	134	17.53°S	142.53°W
Katiu	10.0	4	208	16.52°S	144.20°W
Kauehi	15.0	4	699	15.98°S	145.15°W
Kaukura	11.0	4	379	15.72°S	146.83°W
Makatea	29.5	111	84	16.17°S	148.23°W
Makemo	13.1	4	588	16.43°S	143.93°W
Manihi	13.0	4	789	14.50°S	145.92°W
Marokau	4.5	4	65	18.00°S	142.25°W
Marutea South	4.0	4	214	21.09°S	135.06°W
Mataiva	15.0	4	227	14.88°S	148.72°W
Moruroa	10.5	6	1,062	21.82°S	138.80°W
Napuka	8.1	4	319	14.17°S	141.20°W
Nengonengo	0.7	4	56	18.70°S	141.77°W
Niau	21.6	5	160	16.18°S	146.37°W
Nihiru	2.0	4	30	16.68°S	142.88°W

Island Group	Land Area (sq km)	Highest Point (m)	Population	Latitude	Longitude
Tuamotu Islands (continued)					
Nukutavake	3.6	4	190	19.18°S	138.70°W
Nukutipipi	0.8	4	1	20.67°S	142.50°W
Pukapuka	5.4	4	175	14.80°S	138.82°W
Pukarua	6.5	4	205	18.27°S	137.00°W
Rangiroa	79.2	4	2,334	15.80°S	147.97°W
Raraka	7.0	4	130	16.13°S	145.00°W
Raroia	7.5	2	184	15.93°S	142.37°W
Reao	9.4	4	313	18.47°S	136.47°W
Taenga	4.9	4	81	16.30°S	143.80°W
Taiaro	3.3	5	7	15.77°S	144.62°W
Takapoto	15.0	4	612	14.53°S	145.23°W
Takaroa	16.5	4	488	14.37°S	144.97°W
Takume	4.5	4	84	15.65°S	142.10°W
Tatakoto	7.3	4	247	17.28°S	138.33°W
Tematangi	5.5	4	54	21.64°S	140.62°W
Tepoto North	1.8	4	65	14.00°S	141.33°W
Tikehau	20.0	4	400	14.87°S	148.25°W
Toau	12.0	4	25	15.97°S	145.82°W
Tureia	8.3	4	205	20.78°S	138.50°W
Vahitahi	2.5	4	68	18.58°S	138.83°W
Vairaatea	3.0	4	70	19.23°S	139.32°W
Gambier Islands					
Aukena	1.3	198	21	23.13°S	134.90°W
Mangareva	15.4	482	1,072	23.13°S	134.92°W
Taravai	5.7	255	4	23.13°S	135.03°W
Marquesas Islands					
Fatu Hiva	83.8	960	631	10.40°S	138.67°W
Hiva Oa	315.5	1,276	2,015	9.78°S	138.78°W
Nuku Hiva	339.5	1,224	2,652	8.95°S	140.25°W
Tahuata	69.3	1,040	637	9.93°S	139.10°W
Ua Huka	83.4	884	571	8.92°S	139.56°W
Ua Pou	105.3	1,203	2,013	9.40°S	140.08°W
Cook Islands					
Aitutaki	16.5	124	1,937	18.88°S	159.74°W
Atiu	29.1	71	622	19.99°S	158.10°W
Mangaia	34.5	169	745	21.94°S	157.90°W
Manihiki	5.2	4	516	10.40°S	161.20°W
Mauke	19.7	30	468	20.15°S	157.35°W
Mitiaro	22.8	15	230	19.86°S	157.70°W
Nassau	1.2	4	69	11.55°S	165.42°W
Palmerston	2.6	7	48	18.07°S	163.17°W
Penrhyn	9.8	4	357	9.00°S	158.00°W
Pukapuka	7.0	4	664	10.88°S	165.82°W
Rakahanga	4.0	4	161	10.50°S	161.10°W
Rarotonga	67.6	653	12,206	21.23°S	159.78°W
Suwarrow	1.7	3	4	13.25°S	163.08°W

This chart covers only the permanently inhabited islands of French Polynesia and the Cook Islands.

Index

Index

Index

Index

WWW.SOUTHPACIFIC.ORG

Southpacific.org takes you beyond Tahiti and the Cook Islands to Fiji, Niue, Samoa, Solomon Islands, Tonga, Tuvalu, Vanuatu, and everything in between. Author David Stanley's personal website provides mini-guides to South Pacific destinations, island maps, listings of films, music, and books, FAQs, and links to numerous other travel sites.

Acknowledgments

The nationalities of those listed below are identified by the following signs which follow their names: au (Australia), ca (Canada), ch (Switzerland), ck (Cook Islands), cl (Chile), de (Germany), fr (France), gb (Great Britain), nl (Netherlands), no (Norway), pf (French Polynesia), and us (United States).

Most of the antique engravings by M. G. L. Domeny de Rienzi are from the classic three-volume work *Oceanie ou Cinquième Partie du Monde* (Paris: Firmin Didot Frères, 1836).

I'm most grateful to Rob Kay for agreeing to write a foreword to this book. Rob is the original author of Lonely Planet's guide to Tahiti and the author of *Hidden Tahiti*. He also pioneered Internet publishing in the South Pacific and his Fijiguide.com is one of the best travel websites on the region.

Special thanks to Madame Jacques Brel for kind permission to reproduce *Les Marquises*, to Philippe Hujoel (us) and Jean Ageron (fr) for correcting the translation of *Les Marquises*, to Paul Atallah (us) to Robert Suggs (us) for help with dating Polynesian prehistory, Paul Atallah (us) for doing a complete update of the Huahine section, to Jibralta Merrill (us) for her impressions of Moorea and the Tuamotus, to Laura W. Simpkins (us) for a report on Huahine, to Georgia Lee (us), Conny Martin (cl), and Grant McCall (au) for correcting sections of the Easter Island text, to Wouter Adamse (nl) for information on Easter Island, to Garry Hawkins (gb) for detailed reports on the Cook Islands and Easter Island, to Elliot Smith (us) and Ron Crocombe (ck) for help with the Cook Islands, to Andrea Eimke (ck) for information on Atiu, to Jan Kristensson (ck) for updating Mangaia, to Francis Mortimer (nz) and Lucy Powell (us) for updating airfares, and to my wife, Ria de Vos, for her continuing assistance, suggestions, and support.

Thanks too to the following readers who took the trouble to write us letters about their trips: Linnea Berg (us), Inger Best (us), Stephanie Boisson (pf), Rochard Bondurant (us), Claude and Martine Bordier (pf), Jimmy Cornell (gb), Marjorie Crocombe (ck), Nari Crocombe (ck), Nick Deahl (gb), Feng Ding (us), Richard Gebert (ca), Fred George (us), Brenda-Ger (nl), Jerome Guedj (pf), Cindy and Mark Gibbs (us), Chris Godfrey (ca), John Goese (us), Heinz Hermann (ch), Arthur Hoyle (us), Gordon Hull (us), Rob Jenneve (us), Karen and Paulo Kaiser (us), Swan Krejcarek (ca), Dr. Siegrun Krauss (au), Jorgen Langballe (no), Pat Marsh (us), Elmah McBirney (ck), Terry Meanwell (au), Natalie Minnis (gb), Emily Mulloy (us), Marcus Myers (us), Cheryl Olson (us), Thanos Papadimitinou (gr), Don Parker (us), Jean Parker (us), Jon Peverley (gb), Torotoro Piiti (ck), Steve Rasmussen (us), Julia Ratzmann (de), Andrew Rayner (us), Larry Richards (us), Arnold Siegel (us), F. J. D. Swabey (gb), Wendy Traver (us), Dieter Walden (de), Rob Weltman (us), Brandon Wilson (us), Philip James Worthington (ca), and Pauline Youssef (pf).

All their comments have been incorporated into the volume you're now holding. To have your own name included here next edition, write: David Stanley, *Moon Handbooks Tahiti,* Avalon Travel Publishing, 1400 65th St., Suite 250, Emeryville, CA 94608, U.S.A., atpfeedback@avalonpub.com.

From the Author

While out researching my books I find it cheaper to pay my own way, and you can rest assured that nothing in this book is designed to repay freebies from hotels, restaurants, tour operators, or airlines. I prefer to arrive unexpected and uninvited, and to experience things as they really are. On the road I seldom identify myself to anyone. Unlike many other travel writers I don't allow myself to be chaperoned by local tourist offices or leave out justified criticism that might have an impact on book sales. The essential difference between this handbook and the myriad travel brochures free for the taking in airports and tourist offices all across the region is that this book represents you, the traveler, while the brochures represent the travel industry. The companies and organizations included herein are here for information purposes only, and a mention in no way implies an endorsement.

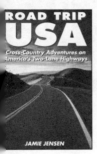

U.S. ~ Metric Conversion

1 inch	=	2.54 centimeters (cm)
1 foot	=	.304 meters (m)
1 yard	=	0.914 meters
1 mile	=	1.6093 kilometers (km)
1 km	=	.6214 miles
1 fathom	=	1.8288 m
1 chain	=	20.1168 m
1 furlong	=	201.168 m
1 acre	=	.4047 hectares
1 sq km	=	100 hectares
1 sq mile	=	2.59 square km
1 ounce	=	28.35 grams
1 pound	=	.4536 kilograms
1 short ton	=	.90718 metric ton
1 short ton	=	2000 pounds
1 long ton	=	1.016 metric tons
1 long ton	=	2240 pounds
1 metric ton	=	1000 kilograms
1 quart	=	.94635 liters
1 US gallon	=	3.7854 liters
1 Imperial gallon	=	4.5459 liters
1 nautical mile	=	1.852 km

To compute Celsius temperatures, subtract 32 from Fahrenheit and divide by 1.8. To go the other way, multiply Celsius by 1.8 and add 32.

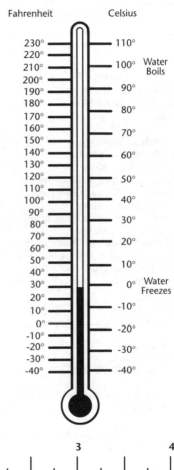

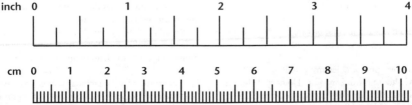

Keeping Current

Although we strive to produce the most up-to-date guidebook humanly possible, change is unavoidable. Between the time this book goes to print and the moment you read it, a handful of the businesses noted in these pages will undoubtedly change prices, move, or even close their doors forever. Other worthy attractions will open for the first time. If you have a favorite gem you'd like to see included in the next edition, or see anything that needs updating, clarification, or correction, please drop us a line. Send your comments via email to atpfeedback@avalonpub.com, or use the address below.

Moon Handbooks Tahiti
Avalon Travel Publishing
1400 65th Street, Suite 250
Emeryville, CA 94608, USA
www.moon.com

Editor: Rebecca Browning
Series Manager: Kevin McLain
Copy Editor: Karen Bleske
Graphics Coordinator: Melissa Sherowski
Production Coordinator: Amber Pirker
Cover Designer: Kari Gim
Interior Designers: Amber Pirker, Alvaro Villanueva, Kelly Pendragon
Map Editor: Naomi Adler Dancis
Cartographers: Sheryle Veverka, Mike Morgenfeld
Proofreader: Marisa Solís
Indexer: Judy Hunt

ISBN: 1-56691-412-4
ISSN: 1544-0842

Printing History
1st edition—1989
5th edition—September 2003

Text and maps © 2003 by David Stanley.
All rights reserved.

Avalon Travel Publishing is a division of Avalon Publishing Group, Inc.

Some photos and illustrations are used by permission and are the property of the original copyright owners.

Front cover photo: © Jeremy Woodhouse 2002
TOC photos: Intro: © M.G.L. Domeny de Rienzi; Tahiti: © M.E. De Vos; Moorea: © David Stanley; Huahine: © David Stanley; Raiatea and Taha'a:
© M.E. De Vos; Bora Bora: © David Stanley; Maupiti: © M.G.L. Domeny de Rienzi; Austral Islands: © David Stanley; Tuamotu Islands: © M.G.L. Domeny de Rienzi; Gambier Islands: © M.G.L. Domeny de Rienzi; Marquesas Islands: © M.G.L. Domeny de Rienzi; Easter Island: © David Stanley; Rarotonga: © M.E. De Vos; Southern Group: Bob Race; Northern Group: Bob Race

Printed in China through Colorcraft Ltd., Hong Kong.